CULTURAL ANTHROPOLOGY

THIRD EDITION

CULTURAL ANTHROPOLOGY

BARBARA D. MILLER
George Washington University

PEARSON

Boston   New York   San Francisco
Mexico City   Montreal   Toronto   London   Madrid   Munich   Paris
Hong Kong   Singapore   Tokyo   Cape Town   Sydney

Series Editor: Jennifer Jacobson
Development Editor: Ohlinger Publishing Services
Editorial Assistant: Emma Christensen
Editorial-Production Administrator: Susan Brown
Editorial-Production Service: Kathleen Deselle
Photo Researcher: Sarah Evertson, Image Quest
Composition and Prepress Buyer: Linda Cox
Manufacturing Buyer: Megan Cochran
Cover Administrator: Linda Knowles
Interior Design: Anne Flanagan
Illustrations: LMY Studios
Electronic Composition: Publishers' Design and Production Services, Inc.

Internet: www.ablongman.com

Photo credit pg. ii: © Jim Erikson/CORBIS

Between the time Website information is gathered and then published, it is not unusual
for some sites to have closed. Also, the transcription of URLs can result in unintended
typographical errors. The publisher would appreciate notification where these occur so
that they may be corrected in subsequent editions.

Library of Congress Cataloging-in-Publication Data
Miller, Barbara D.
    Cultural anthropology / Barbara D. Miller—3rd ed.
      p.   cm.
    Includes bibliographical references and index.
    ISBN 0-205-40139-2 (pbk.)
      1. Ethnology.   I. Title.
    GN316.M49 2004
    306—dc22   2004046155

Printed in the United States of America

10 9 8 7 6 5 4 3 2 1   RRDW   08 07 06 05 04

BRIEF CONTENTS

CONTENTS

PART I
INTRODUCTION TO CULTURAL ANTHROPOLOGY

1
Anthropology and the Study of Culture   1

2
Methods in Cultural Anthropology   27

PART II
ECONOMIC AND DEMOGRAPHIC FOUNDATIONS

3
Economies and Their Modes of Production   51

4
Consumption and Exchange   79

5

Birth and Death 105

6

Personality, Identity, and Human Development 129

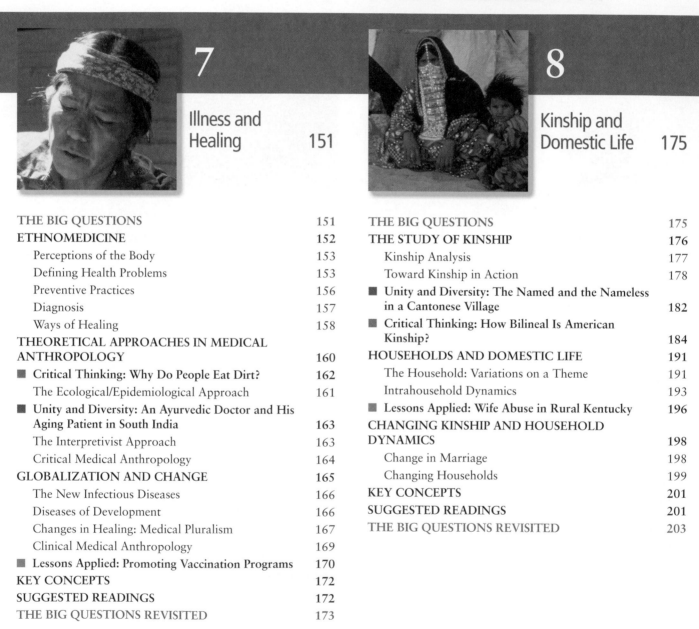

PART III
SOCIAL ORGANIZATION

7
Illness and Healing 151

8
Kinship and Domestic Life 175

9

Social Groups and Social Stratification 205

10

Politics and Leadership 231

PART IV
SYMBOLIC SYSTEMS

11

Social Order and
Social Conflict 251

12

Communication 273

13

Religion   297

14

Expressive Culture   323

PART V
CONTEMPORARY CULTURAL CHANGE

15
People on the Move 345

16
Development Anthropology 367

Lessons Applied

Unity and Diversity

Critical Thinking

PREFACE

Why would anybody write an introductory cultural anthropology textbook? Such a project requires years of research, writing, and rewriting, and is a humbling task as one continually faces how much material there is yet to read and how much more rethinking of categories and questions must be done. One catalyst for my undertaking the writing of this book was that over the three years of my teaching large classes in introductory cultural anthropology each spring semester at the University of Pittsburgh, my enrollments went from 100 in 1991 to 200 in 1992 to 300 in 1993. I figured that I must have been doing something right.

On top of that experience, throughout the many years of my teaching introductory cultural anthropology—from my first course in 1979 to now—it became clear to me what I find dissatisfying in other cultural anthropology textbooks: They mainly treat the topic of social inequality and diversity in just one chapter (usually on "social stratification"), rather than considering it as woven into every topic in cultural anthropology. Thus, their treatment of material about economies, kinship, politics, religion, and language involves little attention to how these topics relate to social inequality and diversity. While I appreciate cultural similarities worldwide, I find differences important, too, since they often divide people in ways that are dangerous, hurtful, and yet also changeable.

I am also aware of how "dead" many of the long-standing subjects in cultural anthropology have become. I have found it difficult to teach many of cultural anthropology's core topics, such as kinship and language. The material seemed irrelevant to cultural anthropology's goal of understanding why people do what they do and think the way they do.

Last, I found that my strong interest in culture change was poorly presented in the available books. I live and teach in Washington, D.C., a highly politicized and policy-focused environment. This niche impresses on me every day the need for cultural anthropology to be relevant to the contemporary world of power, policy, and change. My academic appointment at the George Washington University is located within the Elliott School of International Affairs and the Department of Anthropology. This double focus is important in terms of helping me to integrate cultural anthropology into international affairs and promoting concerns with international policy debates within anthropology. Many of my students, both undergraduates and graduates, find paid or unpaid work at various governmental and nongovernmental institutions at some point during their training. I hope that *Cultural Anthropology* conveys a sense, either directly or indirectly, of the importance of anthropological research and learning for the understanding and potential amelioration of world problems such as poverty, hunger, violence, and illness. The threads of these issues, and a sense of policy relevance in cultural anthropology, run throughout the book.

I set out to write a textbook that would reshape and enliven the teaching and learning of cultural anthropology along all of these lines. Whether you are interested in environmental studies, peace studies, international business, or health studies, knowing about the world's cultures is a crucial foundation for shaping a vision of what is both possible and appropriate in terms of goals and actions. *Cultural Anthropology,* to this end, presents interesting and informative material about "exotic" and distant cultures as well as paying substantial attention to contemporary "Western" cultures (primarily European and European-American). Readers coming from diverse cultural perspectives will be able to "make the strange familiar and the familiar strange," to use the powerful words of Melford Spiro (1990).

HOW THIS BOOK IS ORGANIZED

Cultural Anthropology pursues its goal of promoting learning about the world's cultures in two ways, one that will be more familiar (the delivery of information) and another that may be unsettling and disturbing (asking questions about the information at hand that will make readers unsure of what they thought they knew).

In the first place, readers will encounter abundant, up-to-date *information* about what is known about cross-cultural lifeways: How do people in different parts of the world obtain food, conceive of their place in the universe, and deal with rapid cultural change? This substantive material of cultural anthropology begins with two chapters that establish a foundation for understanding what the discipline of anthropology in general is about, how cultural anthropology fits with it, and what the concept of *culture* means.

In the book's first section, Chapter 1 ("Anthropology and the Study of Culture") establishes the importance of the themes of social diversity and inequality that will accompany us throughout the book, especially class, race, ethnicity, gender, and age. Chapter 2 ("Methods in Cultural Anthropology") takes us to the question of how one does research in cultural anthropology and how findings are analyzed and presented. Students will be able to link what they already know about general research concepts (for example, inductive versus deductive approaches, qualitative versus quantitative data) with what they learn here about how cultural anthropologists have used such concepts in their research and also come up with distinct approaches to data collection, analysis, and presentation.

The book then moves into a consideration of cross-cultural ways of behaving and thinking in many domains from economics to religion. All aspects of life are interrelated, and it is often difficult, in "real life" as well as in scholarly analysis, to separate them. I use the theoretical framework of cultural materialism to organize knowledge in cultural anthropology in a way that will help readers to handle all the rich and interesting information on cultures that they will meet. This theoretical framework moves from infrastructure to structure and then superstructure.

Chapter 3 ("Economies and Their Modes of Production") and Chapter 4 ("Consumption and Exchange") appear at the beginning of the topical chapters as the foundation of culture. The book proceeds to the subject of the human life cycle in cross-cultural perspective (Chapter 6, "Personality, Identity, and Human Development"), presenting material from the exciting subfield of psychological anthropology. This chapter connects with introductory psychology courses that many students will take. The next chapter in this cluster about "making people" is Chapter 7 on "Illness and Healing." A rare chapter in introductory cultural anthropology textbooks, this one will be particularly interesting to the many students who are considering careers in health-related fields.

Next is the third major section of the book, which includes chapters dealing with various aspects of "people in groups," the social "structure," or second floor, beginning with Chapter 8 on "Kinship and Domestic Life." This chapter incorporates up-to-date research that enlivens the traditional core of cultural anthropology. Although many of the classic categories and definitions are presented, the emphasis is on "kinship in action" and on bringing kinship into a more relevant place in cultural anthropology. Chapter 9 ("Social Groups and Social Stratification") widens the lens to examine social groups beyond the domestic situation, including clubs and cooperatives. It also addresses how, in different societies, groups may be arranged hierarchically in relation to one another, for example, in India's caste system. Chapter 10 ("Politics and Leadership") presents some standard material on the various forms of political organization cross-culturally but includes more than the usual amount of material on contemporary state-level societies. Chapter 11, "Social Order and Social Conflict," enters the subfield of legal anthropology, an area of interest to pre-professional students considering careers in law and law enforcement.

The next chapters take the reader to the fourth section, the top floor of the house, where belief systems and values reside. All the previous chapters have related to belief systems and values in one way or another. But here the focus becomes explicit, addressing three areas of "mental culture": Chapter 12 on "Communication," including verbal language, nonverbal language, and mass media; Chapter 13 on "Religion," and Chapter 14 on "Expressive Culture," which includes the arts, the representation of culture in museums, play, and leisure.

The last two chapters shift to contemporary cultural change. Chapter 15, "People on the Move," discusses the politics of migration in a globalizing world and highlights the "new immigrants" to the United States and Canada. Chapter 16, the final chapter, brings together many of the topics addressed in earlier chapters in its examination of an important aspect of contemporary change: international development. Chapter 16 shows how cultural anthropologists have contributed to making international development projects and processes more culturally appropriate and less harmful to local people, especially marginalized indigenous peoples and minorities. Chapter 16 highlights the "action" aspect of cultural anthropology and underlines how it can be relevant to policy issues in the contemporary world.

DISTINCTIVE FEATURES OF THE THIRD EDITION

During the six years since the appearance of the first edition of *Cultural Anthropology,* I have noticed important changes in the world and the way anthropologists study and write about it. Features of this edition take into account these changes while maintaining thorough attention to classic and enduring contributions of cultural anthropology.

Several features make it unique. First, much attention is given to **globalization** as a force of change worldwide and how **localization** of global forces can be seen in various domains of cultural change including making a living, marriage and family, and religion. Each chapter contains material on such change discussing, for example, transnationalism, migration, cyberspace communities, and cultural pluralism.

Second, I emphasize the importance of studying **social inequality and social diversity** (including class, race, ethnicity, gender, and age), and I present material on these topics throughout the book with more in-depth attention in particular places. For example, the major social categories of class, race, ethnicity, age, and gender are introduced in Chapter 1 as analytical categories, examined in Chapter 2 in terms of how they affect research methods and strategies, and discussed in greater depth in Chapter 9 ("Social Groups and Social Stratification").

Third, extensive coverage of **cultures of the contemporary United States** (and the "West") is integrated into the text. Examples include theft and looting during the LA riots as a form of exchange (Chapter 4), Western biomedicine examined (Chapter 7), fraternities and body modification groups (Chapter 9), neighborhood conflicts over dogs (Chapter 11), Protestantism in Appalachia (Chapter 13), and the role of Western-modeled development institutions such as the World Bank (Chapter 16).

Fourth, an up-to-date and lively **chapter on language and communication** (Chapter 12) is innovative in that it de-emphasizes more "formal" aspects of linguistic anthropology such as phonetics and phonemics and gives more material on everyday language in use: children's disputes, adolescent girls' "fat talk," and dress and looks as forms of communication. I also include current research on mass media and how it is culturally shaped, for example, an in-depth study of international news reporting and another on Japanese television. This enhanced treatment will make teaching about language more interesting for instructors and more exciting and engaging for students. It also offers more relevance to students who are interested in careers in the many areas of communication.

Fifth, a unique **chapter on medical anthropology** (Chapter 7) is included. Students in general and especially the large numbers of pre-med students or students interested in some sort of health career will find much of interest in this chapter.

Sixth, a chapter on migration, called "People on the Move" (Chapter 15), provides updated material on this important subject. Students will learn about risks and opportunities facing various categories of migrants and gain insight from detailed cases of "new immigrant" groups in North America.

Finally, the pedagogy of this book is unique in the many ways that it promotes a **critical thinking approach** to the information provided. Instead of simply accepting what we hear or read, a critical thinking approach prompts us to ask questions. It establishes a dynamic relationship between the material and the reader rather than merely allowing for a passive form of information transferal. By providing a sense of engagement with the material, this approach promises to advance student thinking more effectively than traditional forms of learning. While many textbooks provide "thought questions" at the end of their chapters, none integrates substantial material focused around questions through the use of boxes. This edition also provides "discovery" questions within the captions of the photographs, more effectively using these illustrations as learning tools.

BOXED FEATURES

The pedagogical goals of this book are advanced through the use of three distinctive and original boxes. These features show the interconnection of anthropology to other disciplines and to career opportunities.

New to this edition, **Lessons Applied** boxes provide in-depth examples of how research in cultural anthropology can be applied to real-world problems. They highlight different anthropological roles in applied work, for example, in conducting social impact assessments, in advocacy anthropology working with indigenous peoples, or as a cultural broker. For example:

- "Multiple Methods in a Needs Assessment Study in Canada"
- "Promoting Vaccination Programs"
- "Anthropology and Community Activism in Papua New Guinea"

Unity and Diversity boxes present cultural examples from the perspectives of both difference and similarity. While most writings of cultural anthropologists docu-

ment variation and diversity, it is important to remember that humans everywhere share certain features of life in common.

For example:

- "Tejano Women and Tamales"
- "The Rules of Hospitality in Oman"
- "The Named and the Nameless in a Cantonese Village"
- "An Ayurvedic Doctor and His Aging Patient in South India"

The book's commitment to giving students practice in how to think critically is carried out in each chapter through a **Critical Thinking** box. In most of these boxes, students will read about an issue and how it has been interpreted from two different, conflicting perspectives. The students are then asked to consider how the researchers approached the issue, what kind of data they used, and how their conclusions are influenced by their approach. Many of the boxes carry through on the three theoretical major debates within cultural anthropology presented in Chapter 1 as characterizing contemporary cultural anthropology (biological determinism versus cultural constructionism, interpretivism versus cultural materialism, and individual agency versus structurism). For example:

- "Adolescent Stress: Biologically Determined or Culturally Constructed?"

In other boxes, students are asked to reflect on "received wisdom" from a new angle:

- "Was the Invention of Agriculture a Terrible Mistake?"

Or, new categories of analysis are introduced and old ones are reassessed:

- "Probing the Categories of Art"

IN-TEXT PEDAGOGY

I have included many pedagogical tools in the book to help students learn and to help teachers teach. Each chapter opens with a chapter outline that shows the boxed features as well as the main topics to be covered.

Chapter introductions include a "preview" paragraph that outlines the broad strokes of each chapter so students see how topics are connected and can navigate through the material more easily.

"The Big Questions" is a feature located at the beginning of each chapter that identifies the three key questions students should keep in mind as they read the chapter. Each chapter concludes with "The Big Questions Revisited," a section that reviews concepts and provides answers to "The Big Questions" in a summary format. This feature makes key concepts clearer and more accessible to students.

A new feature of the third edition is the increased number of "locator" maps. In each chapter, locator maps within the text, integrated with the discussions of indigenous peoples and ethnographic material, enable students to easily locate the cultures discussed within their geographical contexts.

To further reinforce a major goal of the text to improve critical thinking skills, photo captions include

discovery questions for student consideration or topics for research and class discussion.

A list of Key Concepts can be found at the end of each chapter. Each boldface key concept in the text is listed along with the page number on which it appears; key concepts are also included in the glossary at the end of the book.

Each chapter ends with a list of suggested readings. These readings come with a brief annotation to guide students who may be looking for books to read for a class project or report.

SUPPLEMENTS

Along with this textbook come an array of supplements that will assist instructors in using the book and enriching the students' learning experience.

Instructor's Manual and Test Bank

An unusual feature of the Instructor's Manual and Test Bank is that it is written by the textbook author herself. In this manual, I include teaching tips and classroom exercises that I have used in many years of teaching cultural anthropology.

Computerized Test Bank

This computerized version of the test bank is available with Tamarack's easy-to-use TestGen software, which lets you prepare tests for printing as well as for network and online testing. Full editing capability for Windows and Macintosh.

Allyn & Bacon Interactive Video and User's Guide

This custom video covers a variety of topics, both national and global. The up-to-the-minute video segments are great to launch lectures, spark classroom discussion, and encourage critical thinking. The user's guide provides detailed descriptions of each video segment, specific tie-ins to the text, and suggested discussion questions and projects.

Allyn & Bacon Video Library

Qualified adopters may select from a wide variety of high-quality videos from such sources as Films for the Humanities and Sciences and Annenberg/CPB.

PowerPoint Presentation

This PowerPoint presentation for *Cultural Anthropology*, substantially revised for the new edition, combines dozens of graphic and text images into teaching modules. Using either Macintosh or DOS/Windows, a professor can create customized graphic presentations for lectures. PowerPoint software is not required to use this program; a PowerPoint viewer is included to access the images.

Study Guide

This author-written student Study Guide offers students a traditional format in which they can test their understanding of key material presented in the text through practice questions, key concept review, and other tools. Available as a printed supplement that can be packaged free with the textbook or online at *www.ablongman .com/miller3e*.

The Anthropology Experience

A valuable multimedia resource for teaching and learning cultural anthropology that includes a National Geographic video, an audio glossary, PowerPoint presentations, an illustrated supplementary cultural anthropology booklet, world-class anthropological photos in an accessible image bank, online activities, and more. Please visit *www.ablongman.com/miller3e* for more information on how to make use of these exciting media resources and how to make them available to your students.

Research Navigator for Anthropology

Research Navigator for Anthropology is a handy booklet designed to teach students how to conduct high-quality online research and to document it properly. Complete with extensive help on the research process and an access code to four exclusive databases of reliable source material including the EBSCO Academic Journal and Abstract Database, New York Times Search by Subject Archive, "Best of the Web" Link Library, and Financial Times Article Archive and Company Financials, Research Navigator helps students quickly and efficiently make the most of their research time. Available free when packaged with any Anthropology textbook.

Careers in Anthropology

This resource by W. Richard Stephens contains biographies of anthropology professionals that help students and professors answer the often-asked question, "What can I do with a degree in anthropology?" The booklet provides information about career options targeted to typical students who are taking their first anthropology course. The biographies are organized by various fields and include discussions of what can be done with a B.A., M.A., Ph.D., or a combination of degrees.

The Blockbuster Approach: A Guide to Teaching Anthropology with Film

This supplement effectively guides the instructor on how to integrate feature films into the introductory course successfully and offers hundreds of film suggestions for the general topics covered in this course. *Includes the latest Hollywood films!*

IN THANKS

This book has evolved out of my long relationship with cultural anthropology, which began with the first anthropology course I took as an undergraduate at Syracuse University in 1967. Agehananda Bharati was an important figure in my undergraduate training as was Michael Freedman and cultural geographer David Sopher. Beginning with the writing of my dissertation, my theoretical perspectives were most deeply influenced by the work of anthropologists Marvin Harris, Jack Goody, G. William Skinner, and economist Ester Boserup. My research in India was enriched especially by the work of Pauline Kolenda, Stanley Tambiah, Gerry Berreman, and Sylvia Vatuk. The list of my favorite writers within and beyond anthropology today is too long to include here, but much of their work is woven into the book.

Four anthropologists carefully reviewed drafts of the first edition of the book, and I will always be grateful to them for their contribution: Elliot Fratkin (Pennsylvania State University), Maxine Margolis (University of Florida), Russell Reid (University of Louisville), and Robert Trotter II (University of Arizona). Their words of praise were just as welcome. By pointing out positive features of the book, they helped a sometimes discouraged author regain strength and continue writing and revising. Several other anthropologists offered comments about how I should revise the second and third editions: Ann E. Kingsolver, University of South Carolina; Charles R. de Burlo, The University of Vermont; Corey Pressman, Mt. Hood Community College; Diane Baxter, University of Oregon; Ed Robbins, University of Wisconsin; Elizabeth de la Portilla, University of Texas at San Antonio; G. Richard Scott, University of Nevada, Reno; Jason Antrosio, Albion College; Katrina Worley, Sierra College; Leslie Lischka, Linfield College; Peter Brown, University of Wisconsin, Oshkosh; Howard Campbell, University of Texas, El Paso; Wesley Shumar, Drexel University; William M. Loker, California State University, Chico; and William W. Donner, Kutztown University. I have tried my best to incorporate their advice without sacrificing the original spirit of the book.

During my years of research and writing, many anthropologists have provided invaluable comments, encouragement, and photographs for this book, including Lila Abu-Lughod, Vincanne Adams, Catherine Allen, Joseph Alter, Donald Attwood, Christopher Baker, Nancy Benco, Marc Bermann, Alexia Bloch, Lynne Bolles, John Bowen, Don Brenneis, Alison Brooks, Judith K. Brown, D. Glynn Cochrane, Jeffery Cohen, Carole Counihan,

Liza Dalby, Loring Danforth, Patricia Delaney, Timothy Earle, Elliot Fratkin, Martin Fusi, David Gow, Curt Grimm, Richard Grinker, Daniel Gross, Marvin Harris, Michael Herzfeld, Barry Hewlett, Danny Hoffman, Michael Horowitz, Robert Humphrey, Anstice Justin, Laurel Kendall, David Kideckel, Stuart Kirsch, Dorinne Kondo, Conrad Kottak, Ruth Krulfeld, Joel Kuipers, Takie Lebra, David Lempert, Lamont Lindstrom, Samuel Martinez, Catherine McCoid, Leroy McDermott, Jerry Milanich, Kirin Narayan, Sarah Nelson, Gananath Obeyesekere, Ellen Oxfeld, Hanna Papanek, Deborah Pellow, Gregory Possehl, David Price, Joanne Rappaport, Jennifer Robertson, Nicole Sault, Joel Savishinsky, Nancy Scheper-Hughes, Richard Shweder, Chunghee Soh, Martha Ward, James (Woody) Watson, Rubie Watson, Van Yasek, and Kevin Yelvington.

Several others, who are not anthropologists, also made important contributions to this book: Elson Boles, Nathan Brown, Cornelia Mayer Herzfeld, Edward Keller III, Qaiser Khan, and Roshani Kothari. These people, and no doubt many more whom I have failed to name, were helpful in a variety of ways, including providing critiques of sections and sending material and photographs. Harry Harding, Dean of the Elliott School of International Affairs at the George Washington University, has helped my involvement with this book from its beginning by counting it as a valid research activity for a faculty member in his School. Over the years since the first edition, several assistants have tracked down library material and done reference checking: Joseph Mineiro, Han Quyen Thi Tran, Hena Khan, Omar McDoom, and Carolyn Walkley.

My students are always a major source of inspiration. Many students in my introductory cultural anthropology classes have offered corrections and additions. They enjoy and benefit from looking at cultural anthropology from a "critical thinking" perspective, thus giving me hope that this approach does indeed work. I thank them for their support and interest.

Sylvia Shepard, my development editor for the first edition, was a crucial factor in making this book happen. I can say with surety that, without Sylvia, this book would not exist. For this edition, I was fortunate in being able to work with truly excellent people in conceptualizing and implementing the revision plan. Series editor Jennifer Jacobson is everything an author could hope for—smart, strong, and also lots of fun. Her assistant, Amy Holborow, was always there at the right time with the right ideas. My development editor for this edition is Monica Ohlinger, who heads Ohlinger Publishing Company in Columbus, Ohio. She led the process with great skill, care, and enthusiasm. Her attention to detail helped tremendously. Joanne Vickers, another member of the Ohlinger development team, provided many helpful insights throughout the process. Kathleen Deselle, in New Hampshire, took over when we got to the copyediting and proofreading stage. Kathleen also managed additions and revisions to the artwork. She and her team added yet another extremely pleasant stage to the work. Back at Allyn & Bacon headquarters in Boston, Susan Brown coordinated the research for new photographs. In Washington, I was ably assisted in reviewing the Instructor's Manual and student Study Guide by Jessica Gibson, my program assistant in the CIGA (Culture in Global Affairs) Research and Policy Program, in the Elliott School of International Affairs. This team, dispersed as we were, nonetheless shared a single vision of making this edition even more current, compelling, and coherent. Please let me know if we succeeded and how we might do better.

Bernard Wood is a source of perspective, with his wry sense of humor, on my writing and on life in general. I also thank "the Millers"—my parents, siblings, aunts and uncles, and nieces and nephews—for their interest and support throughout the years of the writing and revising. The same applies to "the Heatons"—my former in-laws, including parents-in-law, brothers- and sisters-in-law, and nieces and nephews. I thank my son, Jack Heaton, for being an inspiration to my writing, a superb traveling companion on our trip around the world with the Semester at Sea Program in 1996, and a delicately effective critic of my (occasional) excesses in thinking. This book is dedicated to him.

Barbara D. Miller
Washington, D.C.

AFGH. = Afghanistan
ALB. = Albania
ARM. = Armenia
AUS. = Austria
AZER. = Azerbaijan
BANG. = Bangladesh
BEL. = Belgium
BELA. = Belarus
B & H. = Bosnia and Herzegovina
BUL. = Bulgaria
BURK. FASO = Burkina Faso
C. AFR. REP. = Central African Republic
CAM. = Cameroon
CAMB. = Cambodia
CRO. = Croatia
C. V. = Cape Verde
CYP. = Cyprus
CZE. = Czech Republic
DEN. = Denmark
EQ. GUINEA = Equatorial Guinea
EST. = Estonia
GAM. = Gambia
G.-B. = Guinea-Bissau
GER. = Germany
GUI. = Guinea
HOND. = Honduras
HUN. = Hungary
ISR. = Israel
KRYG. = Kyrgyzstan
LAT. = Latvia
LEB. = Lebanon
LITH. = Lithuania
LUX. = Luxembourg
MAC. = Macedonia
MOL. = Moldova
MYAN. = Myanmar
NETH. = Netherlands
POL. = Poland
REP. OF THE CONGO = Republic of
   the Congo
ROM. = Romania
RUS. = Russia
SER. & MON. = Serbia & Montenegro
SLO. = Slovakia
SLOV. = Slovenia
SWITZ. = Switzerland
SYR. = Syria
TAJIK. = Tajikistan
THAI. = Thailand
TURK. = Turkmenistan
UZBEK. = Uzbekistan
U.A.E. = United Arab Emirates

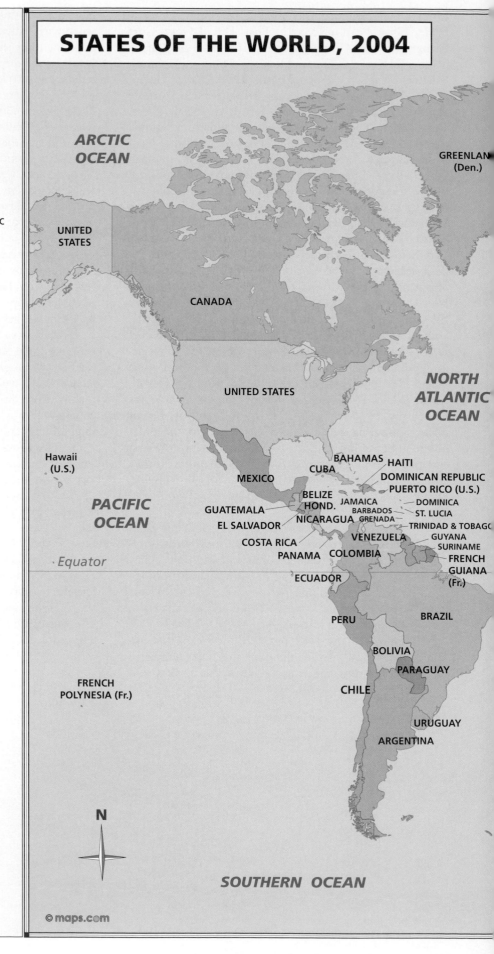

STATES OF THE WORLD, 2004

ARCTIC OCEAN

GREENLAN
(Den.)

UNITED
STATES

CANADA

NORTH
ATLANTIC
OCEAN

UNITED STATES

Hawaii
(U.S.)

BAHAMAS
CUBA
HAITI
MEXICO
DOMINICAN REPUBLIC
PUERTO RICO (U.S.)
BELIZE
HOND.
JAMAICA
DOMINICA
GUATEMALA
BARBADOS
ST. LUCIA
NICARAGUA
GRENADA
EL SALVADOR
TRINIDAD & TOBAGO
VENEZUELA
GUYANA
COSTA RICA
SURINAME
PANAMA
COLOMBIA
FRENCH
GUIANA
(Fr.)
ECUADOR

PACIFIC
OCEAN

Equator

PERU
BRAZIL

BOLIVIA

PARAGUAY

FRENCH
POLYNESIA (Fr.)

CHILE

URUGUAY

ARGENTINA

N

SOUTHERN OCEAN

© maps.com

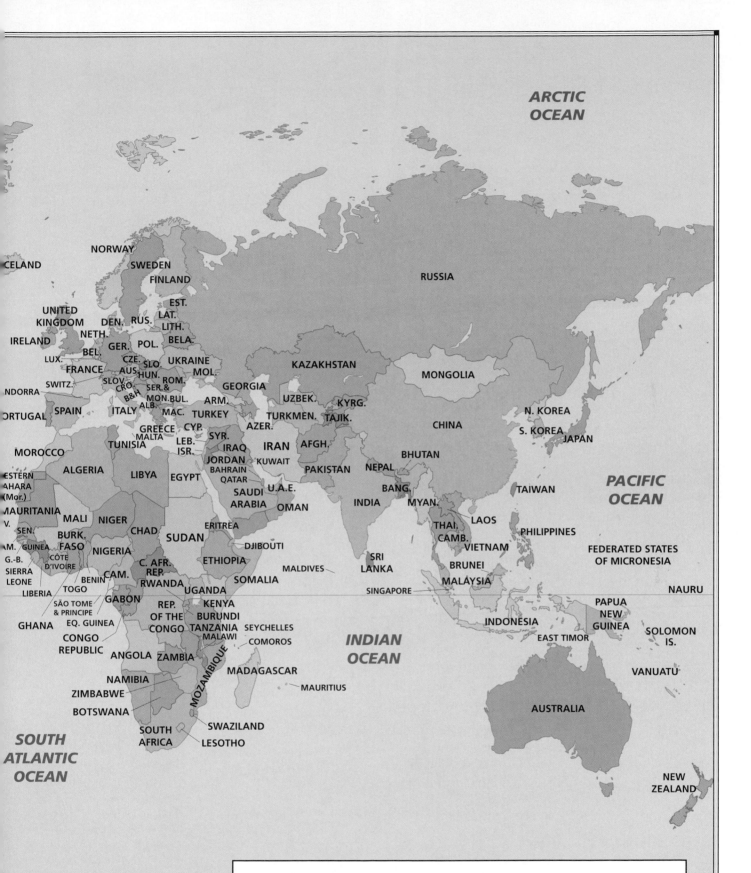

ARCTIC OCEAN

NORWAY

ICELAND

SWEDEN

FINLAND

RUSSIA

UNITED KINGDOM

IRELAND

EST.
LAT.
LITH.
DEN. RUS.
NETH.
BELA.
LUX.
BEL. GER. POL.
FRANCE CZE. SLO. UKRAINE
AUS. HUN. MOL.
SWITZ. SLOV. ROM.
NDORRA CRO. SER.&
B&H MON. BUL.
ALB. MAC.
SPAIN ITALY
GREECE CYP.
MALTA LEB.
ISR.

KAZAKHSTAN

MONGOLIA

GEORGIA

ARM.
TURKEY
AZER.

UZBEK.
KYRG.
TURKMEN. TAJIK.

N. KOREA

S. KOREA

JAPAN

CHINA

ORTUGAL

MOROCCO

TUNISIA

SYR.
IRAQ IRAN AFGH.

PACIFIC OCEAN

ESTERN AHARA (Mor.)

ALGERIA

LIBYA

EGYPT

JORDAN KUWAIT
BAHRAIN
QATAR

SAUDI ARABIA

U.A.E.

OMAN

PAKISTAN

NEPAL

BHUTAN

BANG.

INDIA

MYAN.

TAIWAN

MAURITANIA

V.

SEN.

AM. GUINEA

G.-B.

SIERRA LEONE

LIBERIA

MALI

BURK. FASO

CÔTE D'IVOIRE

NIGER

NIGERIA

CHAD

SUDAN

ERITREA

DJIBOUTI

ETHIOPIA

SOMALIA

MALDIVES

SRI LANKA

THAI.
CAMB.

LAOS

VIETNAM

PHILIPPINES

BRUNEI

MALAYSIA

FEDERATED STATES OF MICRONESIA

NAURU

GHANA

TOGO

BENIN

C. AFR. REP.

CAM.

RWANDA

UGANDA

KENYA

SINGAPORE

SÃO TOME & PRINCIPE

EQ. GUINEA

GABON

REP. OF THE CONGO

BURUNDI

TANZANIA

SEYCHELLES

INDONESIA

EAST TIMOR

PAPUA NEW GUINEA

SOLOMON IS.

CONGO REPUBLIC

MALAWI

COMOROS

INDIAN OCEAN

VANUATU

ANGOLA

ZAMBIA

MOZAMBIQUE

MADAGASCAR

MAURITIUS

NAMIBIA

ZIMBABWE

BOTSWANA

SOUTH ATLANTIC OCEAN

SOUTH AFRICA

SWAZILAND

LESOTHO

AUSTRALIA

NEW ZEALAND

Barbara Miller's *Cultural Anthropology*, Third Edition, helps you navigate the world!

THE BIG QUESTIONS

- **WHAT** is anthropology?
- **WHAT** is cultural anthropology?
- **WHAT** are the major theoretical debates in cultural anthropology?

1

ANTHROPOLOGY AND THE STUDY OF CULTURE

A Tswana woman. About 800,000 Tswana live in Botswana, which means the "homeland of the Tswana." Many Tswana are leaving their villages and taking up work in cities. Instant communication via cell phones is contributing to cultural change in unforseen ways. (Source: © Strauss/Curtis/CORBIS)

The Maasai, a people of East Africa, make their living mainly by tending cattle. Although many Maasai interact increasingly with international tourists, their knowledge of the outside world is limited. Some villages lack electricity, so there are no televisions. Recently, in one community located in a remote area of Kenya, most people hadn't heard about the attacks on the United States on September 11, 2001; others had gained a vague idea of what had happened from radio announcements aired soon after the attacks occurred (Lacey 2002). Thus, when Kimeli Naiyomeh returned to his village from his medical studies at Stanford University, he told them stories that stunned them. He told of huge fires in buildings that stretched high into the clouds and of men with special equipment who entered the buildings to save people's lives. The villagers couldn't believe that a building could be so tall that people jumping from it would die.

These stories saddened the villagers, and they decided they should do something to help the victims. Cows are the most precious objects among the Maasai. As Kimeli Naiyomeh comments, "The cow is almost the center of life for us . . . . It's sacred. It's more than property. You give it a name. You talk to it. You perform rituals with it" (p. A7). In June 2002, in a solemn ceremony, the villagers gave 14 cows to the United States. After the cows were blessed, they were transferred to the deputy chief of the U.S. embassy in Kenya. He expressed his country's gratitude and explained that transporting the cows to the United States would be difficult, so he would sell them and buy Maasai jewelry to take instead.

Old bones, *Jurassic Park,* cannibalism, hidden treasure, *Indiana Jones and The Temple of Doom.* In America, the popular impression of anthropology is based mainly on movies and television shows that depict anthropologists as adventurers and heroes. Many anthropologists do have adventures, and some discover treasures such as ancient pottery, medicinal plants, and jade carvings. But most of their research is less than glorious, involving repetitive and tedious activities. What do anthropologists do, and why do people study anthropology?

This chapter offers an overview of general anthropology, an academic discipline devoted to the study of human life throughout history and in all its variations. General anthropology encompasses several subareas, or fields. After a brief overview of each field, we turn to the field that is the focus of this book: cultural anthropology, the study of **culture**, learned and shared patterns of behavior and beliefs. We review issues related to cultural differences and ways to understand such differences. We discuss various characteristics of culture, including how culture is related to nature but is not the same as nature. Class, race, gender, and other bases of cultural identity are introduced as important factors that will receive attention throughout this book. Last, we introduce three major theoretical debates.

THE FOUR FIELDS OF GENERAL ANTHROPOLOGY

Most anthropologists agree that the discipline of anthropology, or general anthropology, is divided into four fields:

- archaeology (or prehistory),
- biological anthropology (or physical anthropology),
- linguistic anthropology,
- cultural anthropology (or social anthropology).

Most anthropologists in North America say that training in anthropology should include all four fields. In Europe and in much of the world, where anthropology has a more European heritage, the word *anthropology* refers only to cultural anthropology, and there is no insistence on four-field knowledge. In recent decades, anthropology has developed in universities around the world and is acquiring local characteristics. For instance, in much of Latin America and Africa, anthropology is more explicitly political. Anthropologists in postcolonial settings raise questions such as "Anthropology for what, for whom and by whom?" Increasingly, anthropologists trained and working in the West are entering into creative dialogue with anthropologists in postcolonial contexts. For example, American anthropologists' writings on Mayan people's activist movements have been criticized, by the emerging new generation of Mayan anthropologists who are themselves Mayan, for perpetuating outsiders' views of Mayan cultures (Warren 1998, Fischer 2001). This kind of global interchange is helping to move the discipline in new directions away from its Western roots and perspectives.

Archaeology

This field is devoted to studying the lifeways of past cultures by examining material remains. Data include stone and bone tools, skeletal material, remains of buildings, and refuse such as potsherds (broken pieces of pottery) and coprolites (fossilized fecal matter). Since its beginnings in the mid-eighteenth century, archaeology has contributed knowledge about the emergence of the great early states of Egypt, Phoenicia, the Indus Valley, and Mexico. New research challenges previous conclusions about "kingdoms." For example, excavations at a royal burial site of the Old Silla Kingdom of Korea, which extended from 57 BCE to AD 668, reveal that queens were often the rulers (Nelson 1993). This finding alters the earlier generalization that centralized state systems always involved male political dominance.

The traditional focus of archaeological research on discovering grand sites and artifacts of gold and jade created a "capital-centric" bias in understanding forms of states (Bermann 1994). The quest for spectacular finds meant that small towns and villages were overlooked, as well as aspects of everyday life such as the household. Now, some archaeologists are "going local" in their attempt to learn about the daily lives of ordinary people. In order to avoid a too-narrow view of everyday life, these researchers also look at center–local interactions as a way of learning about how cultural change occurs at both levels.

The archaeology of the recent past is an important new research direction. An example is the "Garbage Project" conducted by archaeologists at the University of Arizona at Tucson (Rathje and Murphy 1992). The "Garbage Archaeologists" are excavating the Fresh Kills landfill on Staten Island, near New York City. Its mass is estimated at 100 million tons and its volume at 2.9 billion cubic feet. Thus, it is one of the largest human-made structures in North America. Through excavation of artifacts such as poptop can tabs, disposable diapers, cosmetics containers, and telephone books, the Garbage Archaeologists learn about recent consumption patterns. These findings provide lessons for the future because they reveal how long it takes for contemporary goods to decompose. One surprising finding is that the kinds of garbage people often blame for filling up landfills, such as fast-food packaging and disposable diapers, cause less serious problems than paper. Newspaper, especially, is a major culprit because of sheer quantity. This kind of information can help improve recycling efforts throughout the world.

Biological or Physical Anthropology

In seeking to understand human variation, adaptation, and change, biological anthropologists study many forms of life, human and nonhuman, past and present. This field deals with topics ranging from evolutionary theory to the human fossil record and the identification of human skeletal remains from crime scenes and accidents. Genetics, anatomy, animal and human behavior, ecology, nutrition, and forensics are subject areas included in this field. Many biological anthropologists do research on animals other than humans in order to understand human origins or to use them as models for understanding contemporary human behavior. (See the Lessons Applied box on pages 4–5.)

Within biological anthropology, the subfield of primatology focuses on studies of nonhuman primates and how their behavior compares with that of human primates. Primatologists are well known for their pioneering work in studying nonhuman primates in their natural habitats. Jane Goodall's (1971, 1986) research on Tanzanian chimpanzees revealed rich details about their social relationships.

Biological anthropologists share many research interests with archaeologists, given their study of evidence from the past. One shared area is *paleopathology*, the study of diseases in prehistory. Analysis of trace elements in bones, such as strontium, provides surprisingly detailed information about the diets, activities, and health of prehistoric people, including whether they were primarily

Primatologist Dian Fossey interacts with a gorilla during fieldwork in Rwanda. ■ *Why might women researchers be more prominent in primatology than other areas of biological anthropology?* (Source: © Richard Wrangham/AnthroPhoto)

Lessons Applied

ORANGUTAN RESEARCH LEADS TO ORANGUTAN ADVOCACY

Biruté Galdikas in Indonesia. She has been studying the orangutans for over three decades and is an active supporter of conservation of their habitat. ■ *What can you learn about her work, or the status of wild orangutans, by searching on the Web?* (Source: © Spooner/Redmond-Callow/Gamma Press)

PRIMATOLOGIST BIRUTÉ GALDIKAS (pronounced Beer-oo-TAY GAL-dee-kas) first went to Indonesia to study orangutans in 1971 (Galdikas 1995). She soon became aware of the threat to the orangutans from local people who, as a way of making a lot of money, capture them for sale to zoos around the world. These poachers separate the young from their mothers, often killing the mothers in the process. Sometimes local police locate and reclaim the captured orphans. They try to return them to the rain forest, but the transition into an unknown niche is extremely difficult, and many do not survive.

Orangutan juveniles are highly dependent on their mothers, maintaining close bodily contact with them for at least two years and nursing until they are eight. Because of this long period of orangutans' need for maternal contact, Galdikas set up her camp to serve as a way station for orphans, and she became the maternal figure. Her first "infant" was an orphaned orang, Sugito, who clung to her like its own mother for years.

Now, the survival of orangutans on Borneo and Sumatra (their only habitats worldwide) is seriously endangered by massive commercial logging and illegal logging, population resettlement programs, cultivation, and other pressures on the forests where the orangutans live. Biruté Galdikas is focusing her efforts on preventing this from happening. She says, "I feel like I'm viewing an animal holocaust and holocaust is not a word I use lightly . . . . The destruction of the tropical rain-forest is accelerating daily." (Dreifus 2000:D3).

Galdikas is world-renowned as the leading expert on orangutans and their environment. She has studied orangutans longer than anyone else and in as close contact as these solitary creatures allow. She links her knowledge of and love for the orangutans with applied anthropology and advocacy on their behalf. She is working at many levels—local, national and international—in a variety of ways to help prevent orangutan extinction.

Since the beginning of her fieldwork in Borneo, she has maintained and expanded the Camp Leakey field site and research center (named after her men-

meat eaters or vegetarians and how their diets affected their health. Stress marks on bones provide information on work patterns—for example, who threw spears, who carried heavy loads, and how these activities affected health.

Another area of research in biological anthropology is contemporary human biological variation. Topics of research include human growth and development, nutrition, health, and changes in all of these as a result of factors such as urbanization. Another topic of study is genetic distributions across populations and how genetic change occurs over time. Biological anthropologists have suggested that there is no biological validity to the Western concept of "race," because each major so-called race includes within it greater genetic variation than exists between the so-called races. In the 1970s, there emerged a new approach known as *sociobiology*, which links Dar-

winian principles of natural selection and group fitness with the study of culture and society. Thus sociobiologists view culture and society as determined by the rules of natural selection. They interpret practices such as female infanticide as contributing to group fitness and survival. Sociobiology has also affected primatology by promoting selective fitness as the explanation for certain forms of nonhuman primate behavior, such as food sharing and fighting.

Linguistic Anthropology

Linguistic anthropology emerged in the United States in the later nineteenth century when researchers began to document disappearing Native American languages. Early cultural anthropologists studied linguistic anthro-

tor, Lewis Leakey, who inspired her research on orangutans). In 1986 she cofounded the Orangutan Foundation International (OFI), which now has several chapters worldwide. She has published scholarly articles and given public talks around the world on her research. Educating the public about the imminent danger to the orangutans is an important part of her activism. She believes that public awareness will help promote programs to protect and regenerate the forests that are the life support of the orangutans.

The parks employ many local people in diverse roles, including anti-poaching guards. OFI sponsors study tours for international students and opportunities for them to contribute to conservation efforts by working on infrastructure around the orangutan parks and reserves. At the global policy level, she and other orangutan experts are lobbying international institutions such as the World Bank to promote forest conservation as part of their loan agreements.

The success of Galdikas's activism depends on her deep knowledge of orangutans. Over the decades, she has filled thousands of notebooks with her observations of orangutan behavior, along with such details about their habitat as the fruiting times of different species of trees. She hasn't yet had time to analyze these rich data. A kind donor recently gave software and funding for staff to analyze the raw data (Hawn 2002). The findings will indicate, for example, how much territory is needed to support a viable orangutan population. In turn, these findings will facilitate conservation policy and planning. Here, as often happens, research and advocacy go hand in hand.

FOOD FOR THOUGHT

Some people claim that science should not be linked with advocacy and activism because that will create biases in research. Others say that scientists have an obligation to use their knowledge for the human good. Where do you stand in this debate and why?

pology to learn how to document unwritten languages because they often researched cultures with no writing system. Both purposes have declined in importance, however, because most "disappearing" languages have been either recorded or lost, and most previously unwritten languages have been transferred into written form. Thus, some anthropologists say that linguistic anthropology is no longer needed as a separate field and should be merged with the field of cultural anthropology or the discipline of linguistics.

Others offer strong reasons for maintaining it as a separate field. First, languages change all the time, and anthropologists should document and analyze what kinds of changes are occurring and why. Many changes in language use are related to politics and conflict worldwide. For example, in Moldova, a former Soviet republic, speakers of Russian and Ukrainian in eastern Moldova have been in conflict since 1992 over the official language policy of Moldova. Second, instead of having a shrinking area of study, linguistic anthropology is broadening its scope to include many aspects of communication such as the media, electronic mail, popular music, and advertising. These new research directions connect linguistic anthropology with psychology, journalism, television and radio, education, and marketing. Because linguistic anthropology is so closely related to cultural anthropology, this book includes an entire chapter on it (Chapter 13).

Cultural Anthropology

Cultural anthropology is devoted to studying how cultures differ from or resemble one another, and why, and how different cultures influence each other. Ultimately, cultural anthropology decenters us from our own cultures, teaching us to look at ourselves from the "outside" as somewhat "strange." Melford Spiro (1990) aptly asserts that the work of cultural anthropology is to "make the strange familiar and the familiar strange." A good example of "making the familiar strange" is the case of the Nacirema, who were first described in 1956:

> They are a North American group living in the territory between the Canadian Cree, the Yaqui and the Tarahumare of Mexico, and the Carib and the Arawak of the Antilles. Little is known of their origin, though tradition states that they came from the east. According to Nacirema mythology, their nation was originated by a culture hero, Notgnihsaw, who is otherwise known for two great feats of strength—the throwing of a piece of wampum across the river Pa-To-Mac and the chopping down of a cherry tree in which the Spirit of Truth resided. (Miner 1965 [1956]: 415)

The anthropologist goes on to describe the Nacirema's unusually intense focus on the human body and its beauty and their wide variety of private and personal rituals. He gives a detailed account of one ritual that is performed daily within the home at a specially constructed shrine area:

> The focal point of the shrine is a box or chest which is built into the wall. In this chest are kept the many charms and magical potions without which no native believes he could live. These preparations are secured from a variety of specialized practitioners. The most powerful of these are the medicine men, whose assistance must be rewarded with substantial gifts. . . . Beneath the charm box is a small font. Each day every member of the family, in succession, enters the shrine room, bows his head before the charm-box, mingles different sorts of holy water in the font, and proceeds with a brief rite of ablution. (415–416)

If you don't know this tribe, try spelling its name backwards! (One note: Please forgive Miner for his use of the masculine pronoun in describing Nacirema society in general; his writings are now a half-century old.)

Cultural anthropology encompasses all aspects of human behavior and beliefs: making a living and distributing goods and services, reproduction and group formation, political patterns, religious systems, forms of communication, and expressive aspects of culture such as art, dance, and music. In addition, cultural anthropologists consider how change occurs in all of these areas.

Applied Anthropology: Separate Field or Cross-Cutting Focus?

Applied anthropology involves the use or application of anthropological knowledge to help solve social problems.

In the United States, applied anthropology emerged during and after World War II. Its first concern was with living peoples and their needs, which initially placed applied anthropology within the field of cultural anthropology. The number of anthropologists working in applied anthropology grew substantially in the later twentieth century. One reason for this growth was the decline in college and university teaching positions in anthropology since the late 1970s. This prompted anthropologists to explore jobs outside academia and led to positive change in the discipline by promoting the use of anthropological knowledge to deal with current issues. Given this expanded role of applied anthropology, many anthropologists feel that applied anthropology should be considered a fifth field.

An alternative position is that the application of knowledge to solve problems is, and should be, part of all four fields (see Figure 1.1). Just like theory, application should be a valued aspect of every branch of the discipline. Many archaeologists in the United States are employed, for example, in cultural resource management (CRM), assessing possible archaeological remains before construction projects such as roads and buildings can proceed. Biological anthropology has many applied aspects. For example, forensic anthropologists participate in criminal investigations through labwork identifying bodily remains. Others work in the area of primate conservation. Applied linguistic anthropologists consult with educational institutions about how to improve stan-

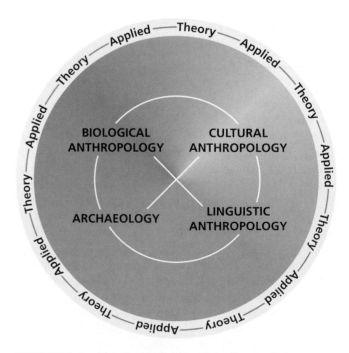

FIGURE 1.1 The Four Fields of Anthropology

dardized tests for bilingual populations and conduct policy research for governments. Development anthropology (Chapter 16) is concerned with how people's lifeways in so-called developing countries change and how knowledge in anthropology can play a role in formulating and implementing more positive kinds of change.

Many current anthropologists are concerned that applied anthropology address more directly and with greater force the effects of capitalist globalization, particularly some of its negative consequences, such as the increasing wealth gap between powerful industrialized countries and less powerful, less industrialized countries (Hackenberg 2000). This need takes anthropologists in a new and challenging direction because it involves the study of global–local interactions and change over time, neither of which were part of cultural anthropology's original focus. Moreover, it asks that cultural anthropologists abandon an attitude of noninvolvement in change. One anthropologist goes so far as to state, "Can anthropology in the 21st century be anything *except* applied anthropology?" (Cleveland 2000:373).

INTRODUCING CULTURAL ANTHROPOLOGY

This section provides a brief history of the field of cultural anthropology in order to examine its theoretical and methodological roots. We then turn to a discussion of the central concept of *culture*. Last, we consider several distinctive features of cultural anthropology that will appear repeatedly throughout this book.

A Brief History of the Field

One can trace aspects of cultural anthropology all the way back to writers such as Herodotus, Marco Polo, and Ibn Khaldun, who traveled extensively and wrote reports about "other" cultures that they encountered. More recent conceptual roots can be found in writers of the French Enlightenment, such as philosopher Charles Montesquieu (1689–1755). His book *The Spirit of the Laws*, published in 1748 [1949], discussed the temperament, appearance, and government of people around the world and explained the differences among them in terms of the differing climates in which people lived (Barnard 2000:22ff). European colonial expansion increasingly exposed Western thinkers to cultural differences and prompted them to question the biblical narrative of human prehistory. The Bible, for example, does not mention the existence of people in the New World, and Enlightenment thinkers were forced to ponder how such people came to be.

In the latter half of the nineteenth century, the discovery of principles of biological evolution by Charles Darwin and others had a strong impact on anthropology and resulted in the overturn of Western biblical explanations for the human condition and human variation. Biological evolution says that early forms evolve into later forms through the process of natural selection, whereby the most biologically fit organisms survive to reproduce while those that are less fit die out. Darwin's model is thus one of continuous progress of increasing fitness. It also promotes the idea that change occurs through struggle among competing organisms.

Several founding fathers of cultural anthropology, such as Lewis Henry Morgan in the United States and Sir Edward Tylor (1832–1917) and Sir James Frazer (1854–1941) in England, invoked the concept of evolution to explain apparent cultural differences, mainly the differences between Euro-American culture (considered as "civilization") and non-Western peoples (considered as "primitive"). They assumed that Western culture was the most evolved form and that other cultures would eventually catch up or die out. Their models of kinship evolution, for example, said that early forms of kinship centered on women, with inheritance passing through the female line, whereas more evolved forms centered on men, with inheritance passing through the male line. Regarding belief systems, they said that magic comes before religion and that religion is then replaced by science. In all these models, there is a sense that the later forms are better, more advanced.

In terms of research methods, most thinkers of the nineteenth century were "armchair anthropologists." They read reports by travelers, missionaries, and explorers and then wrote a summary of these materials. Thus they wrote about culture without the benefit of close-up study. Lewis Henry Morgan (1818–1881), a lawyer in Rochester, New York, diverged from armchair anthropology by conducting field research over many years with the Iroquois of central New York (Patterson 2001:26). Morgan was interested in the main question of the day: Were all contemporary people descended from one line or from several lines? He undertook a comparative study of Native American kinship terms and Asian kinship terms. He concluded that Native American and Asian kinship systems were essentially similar and proved that Native Americans were related to people in Asia. Morgan was thus a strong supporter of the unity of humankind. He explained apparent differences across cultures in terms of their economic systems. He viewed agriculture and private property as the most highly evolved system. Through borrowing by one group from another, cultural evolution to a higher stage would occur.

Polish-born Bronislaw Malinowski (1884–1942) is considered one of the main founding figures of contemporary anthropology. He established a major theoretical approach called **functionalism:** the view that a culture is similar to a biological organism, wherein various parts work to support the operation and maintenance of the whole. Thus, a culture's kinship system or religious system contributes to the functioning of the whole culture of which it was a part. Functionalism is linked to the concept of **holism,** the view that one must study all aspects of a culture in order to understand the whole culture. Malinowski is also considered the father of cultural anthropology's cornerstone method of fieldwork (discussed in Chapter 2).

Another major figure of the early twentieth century is Franz Boas (1858–1942). Born in Germany and educated in physics and geography, Boas came to the United States in 1887 (Patterson 2001:46ff). He brought with him a skepticism toward Western science gained from a year's study with the Inuit of Baffin Island (west of Greenland) where he learned that a physical substance such as "water" can be very differently perceived in different cultures. Boas recognized the plural validity of different cultures and introduced the concept of **cultural relativism,** or the position that each culture must be understood in terms of the values and ideas of that culture and should not be judged by the standards of another. In his view, no culture is more advanced than another—a position that was a radical rejection of evolutionism.

Boas promoted the detailed study of individual cultures within their own historical contexts as the only way to understand them. This approach is called **historical particularism,** or the view that individual cultures must be studied and described on their own terms and that cross-cultural comparisons and generalizations ignore the realities of individual cultures and are thus invalid. Boas made an enormous contribution in the United States to building the discipline of anthropology through his role as a professor at Columbia University. He trained many students who became prominent anthropologists. He founded several professional organizations in cultural anthropology and archaeology, and he supported the development of anthropology museums. He was also involved in policy research, and his socially progressive philosophy embroiled him in controversy.

One of his most renowned studies, commissioned by President Theodore Roosevelt, was on the effects of the environment (in the sense of where one lives) on immigrants and their children. He and his research team measured 17,821 people and found substantial differences in measurements between the older and younger generations. He concluded that head size changes quickly in response to environmental change, thus being culturally shaped rather than biologically ("racially") determined. The U.S. Immigration Commission dismissed his findings, and Congress passed the Immigration Restriction Act in 1924. Boas referred to the act as "Nordic nonsense" (Patterson 2001: 49). Boas's legacy to anthropol-

Franz Boas is an important figure in the history of anthropology for many reasons including his emphasis on a four-field approach and the principle of cultural relativism. ■ *Conduct research on Boas to learn about his life and contributions to anthropology.* (Source: © Bettmann/CORBIS)

ogy includes a strong critique of racism and the view that culture, not biology, determines behavior. The biology–culture (or nature–nurture) debate is still vigorous in anthropology; it is discussed in greater detail at the end of this chapter.

Following World War II, cultural anthropology in the United States expanded substantially in terms of number of professionals and university departments. Along with the increased number of trained anthropologists came increased theoretical diversity. Several anthropologists developed theories of culture that were based in environmental factors. Such thinkers postulated that similar environments (for example, deserts or tropical rainforests or mountains) would predictably lead to the emergence of similar cultures. In contrast to Boasian particularism, this approach supported the attempt to formulate cross-cultural predictions and generalizations. American anthropologist Julian Steward (1902–1072) was a major supporter of *environmental determinism*. This approach left a theoretical legacy in cultural anthropology, discussed below, in a modified form. At the same time another trend, led by French anthropologist Claude Lévi-Strauss (born 1908), began to emerge in Europe. Lévi-Strauss was more concerned with so-called tribal people's thoughts, myths, and symbols. He believed that underlying all myths is a binary opposition (two clearly different themes, such as male or female, raw or cooked). He maintained that we can best learn about a culture by analyzing its myths and stories to discover the themes that are the underlying structure of the culture. Lévi-Strauss established *symbolic anthropology* as a foundation for much future research in cultural anthropology.

Based more or less on the previous two approaches, two theoretical perspectives that developed following the 1960s continue to dominate cultural anthropology. The first of these, related to environmentalism, is **cultural materialism.** This approach reflects the conviction that understanding of a culture should be pursued first by examining the material aspects of life: the natural environment and how people make a living within particular environments. Only then should attention be devoted to other aspects of culture, including social organization and ideology (people's way of thinking). The second major theoretical position, descended in many ways from Lévi-Strauss's symbolic anthropology, is now called **intepretivism** or **interpretive anthropology.** This perspective focuses on understanding culture by studying what people think about, their ideas, and the meanings that are important to them. These perspectives will also be discussed in more depth in the last section of the chapter.

Since the 1990s, two other theoretical approaches have gained prominence. Both have been influenced by **postmodernism,** which questions such aspects of modernism as the scientific method, urbanization, technological change, mass communication, and the idea that human progress is based on scientific knowledge. The first theoretical approach influenced by postmodernism can be termed **structurism,** which says that powerful structures such as the political economy and media shape cultures and create entrenched systems of inequality and oppression rather than social progress. The second theoretical trend emphasizes human **agency,** or free will, and the power of individuals to create and change culture by acting against structures. The debate between structurists and the human agency approach is also examined in more detail at the end of the chapter.

Throughout its brief history, cultural anthropology has been a dynamic field characterized by lively debate. Its many different theoretical approaches have often been influenced by thinkers outside the field, such as Charles Darwin and Karl Marx. Its changing interests and approaches are also tied to the contexts within which it exists. In other words, as the world changes, cultural anthropology changes in response. Global colonialism, beginning in the 1500s, set anthropology in motion. The global economic and political integration of our own times is prompting major changes in cultural anthropology's theories and methods. The present shape of cultural anthropology is thus complex, and its future is impossible to predict.

The Concept of Culture

The question of how to define culture has intrigued anthropologists for over a century. Even now, spirited discussions take place between animal scientists and cultural anthropologists about whether nonhuman animals have culture and, if so, how it resembles or differs from human cultures (McGrew 1998). This section surveys approaches to defining culture in cultural anthropology, the characteristics of culture, and several bases for cultural identity formation.

Definitions of Culture

Culture is the core concept in cultural anthropology, so it seems likely that cultural anthropologists would agree about what it is. This may have been the case in the early days of the discipline when there were far fewer anthropologists. In the 1950s, though, an effort to collect definitions of culture produced 164 different ones (Kroeber and Kluckhohn 1952).

The first definition was proposed by British anthropologist Edward Tylor in 1871. He said that "Culture, or civilization . . . is that complex whole which includes knowledge, belief, art, law, morals, custom, and any other capabilities and habits acquired by man as a member of society" (Kroeber and Kluckhohn 1952:81). The phrase "that complex whole" has been the most durable feature of this proposition. Note that two other features of Tylor's definition have not stood the test of time. First, most anthropologists now avoid using *man* to refer to all humans and instead use generic words such as *humans* and *people.* One might argue that the word *man* can be used generically according to its linguistic roots, but many studies indicate that this usage can be confusing. Second, most anthropologists no longer equate culture with civilization. The term *civilization* implies a sense of "highness" versus noncivilized "lowness" and sets up an invidious distinction placing "us" (the so-called civilized nations of Europe and North America) in a superior position to "them"—the other societies.

In contemporary cultural anthropology, the theoretical positions of the interpretists and the cultural materialists correspond to two different definitions of culture. Clifford Geertz, speaking for the interpretivists, states that culture consists of symbols, motivations, moods, and thoughts. This definition focuses on people's perceptions, thoughts, and ideas and does not include behavior as a part of culture. Cultural materialist Marvin Harris states that "A culture is the total socially acquired life-way or life-style of a group of people. It consists of the patterned repetitive ways of thinking, feeling, and acting that are characteristic of the members of a particular society or segment of society" (1975:144). The definition of culture used in this book follows this more comprehensive definition of behavior and beliefs.

Culture, as all learned and shared behavior and ideas, is found universally among human beings. Thus it exists in a general way as something everyone has. Some anthropologists have referred to this universal concept of culture as Culture with a capital "C." Culture also exists in a more specific way because all cultures are not the same. The term **microculture,** or local culture, refers to distinct patterns of learned and shared behavior and ideas found in localized regions and among particular groups. Microcultures include ethnic groups, racial groups, genders, and age categories. **Macroculture** refers to learned and shared ways of behaving and thinking that cross local boundaries, such as a sense of national culture that some governments seek to promote to enhance unity, or the global consumer culture that pervades upper-middle-class and upper-class groups transnationally.

Characteristics of Culture

This section outlines a few characteristics of the elusive concept of culture. We will examine culture as related to nature but not the same as nature, as based on symbols, as something that is learned, as integrated, and as something that changes.

Culture Is Not the Same as Nature The relationship between nature and culture is of great interest to cultural anthropologists in their quest to understand people's behavior and thinking. This book emphasizes the importance of culture over nature, while recognizing that in some instances, nature shapes and interacts with culture. For example, the biological traits that affect people's behavior and lifestyles include certain diseases, such as sickle-cell anemia and hemophilia. But even in these cases, it is not easy to predict how a person possessing them in Culture A will resemble or differ from a person possessing them in Culture B.

Another way of seeing how culture diverges from nature, even though related to it, is to see how basic "natural" demands of human life are met in different ways because of culturally defined variations. The universal human functions that everyone must perform to stay alive are eating, drinking, sleeping, and eliminating. (Requirements for shelter and clothing vary, depending on the climate. Procreation is not necessary for individual survival, although it is for group survival, so it is not

included here.) But we cannot predict how, when, or where these functions will be fulfilled because culture plays a major role in defining them. Nor can we say much about the meanings that they all have in various cultures without in-depth study.

Eating Culture shapes what one eats, how one eats, and when one eats, and it affects ideas about eating. The human body requires certain nutrients for survival, but they can be provided in many ways. For example, eating meat is not a necessity for survival. Many vegetarian cultures have avoided meat eating of any sort for centuries.

Preferences about what tastes good vary markedly, and many examples exist of foods that are acceptable in one culture and not in another. In China, most people think that cheese is disgusting, but in France, most people love cheese. One distinction exists between eating animals that are alive and animals that are dead. In a few cultures, consumption of live, or nearly live, creatures is considered a gourmet specialty; for example, one Philippine dish includes ready-to-be-born chicks. In many cultures where hunting and fishing are dominant ways of procuring food, people believe that the freshness of the catch is important. They consider canned meat or fish highly undesirable. Although some scientists and anthropologists have attempted to delineate universal taste categories into four basic types (sweet, sour, bitter, and salty), cross-cultural research disproves these as universals. Among the Weyéwa people of the highlands of

Two Ethiopian women dining at an Ethiopian restaurant. The main meal consists of several meat and vegetable dishes, cooked with special spices and laid out on *injera* bread, a soft, flat bread which is torn into small pieces and used to wrap bite-sized bits of meat and vegetables. The entire meal can be eaten without utensils. ■ *How does this dining scene resemble or differ from a recent meal that you have had in a restaurant?* (Source: © Michael Newman/PhotoEdit)

Sumba, an island in Eastern Indonesia, the categories of flavors are sour, sweet, salty, bitter, tart, bland, and pungent (Kuipers 1991).

How to eat is also an important aspect of food behavior. Rules about eating are one of the first things one confronts when entering another culture. Proper dining manners in India require that a person eat using only the right hand because the left hand is reserved for assisting in elimination. A clean right hand is believed to be the cleanest dining implement, because silverware, plates, and glassware that have been touched by others, even though they have been washed, are never truly pure.

Drinking   The cultural elaboration of drinking is as complex as for eating. Every culture defines the appropriate substances to drink, when to drink, and with whom. French culture allows for consumption of relatively large amounts of table wine with meals. In the United States, water is commonly consumed during meals, but in India one takes water only after the meal is finished. Different categories of people drink different beverages. In cultures where alcoholic beverages are consumed, males tend to consume more than women. The meaning of particular drinks and the style of drinking and serving them are heavily influenced by culture. If you were a guest and the host offered you water, you might think it odd. If your host explained that it was "sparkling water from France," you might be more impressed.

Social drinking, whether the beverage is coffee, beer, or vodka, creates and reinforces bonds. Beer-drinking "rituals" of American college fraternities are a dramatic example. In a brief ethnographic film entitled "Salamanders," made at a university in the northeastern United States, the brothers run to various "stations" in the fraternity house, downing a beer at each (Hornbein and Hornbein 1992). One brother chugs a beer, turns with a stagger toward the next station, and then falls flat on his face and passes out (most viewers laugh when he falls). The movie also documents a drinking ritual in which both young men and women at fraternity parties swallowed live salamanders, sometimes two or three at a time, with large gulps of beer.

Sleeping   Going without sleep for an extended period would eventually lead to insanity and even death. Common sense might say that sleep is the one natural function that is not shaped by culture, because people tend to do it every twenty-four hours, everyone shuts their eyes to do it, everyone lies down to do it, and almost everyone sleeps at night. But there are many cultural aspects to sleep, including the question of who sleeps with whom. Cross-cultural research reveals varying rules about where infants and children should sleep: with the mother, with both parents, or by themselves in a separate room. Among indigenous cultures of the Amazon, mothers and babies share the same hammock for many months, and breastfeeding occurs whenever the baby is hungry, not on a schedule. Culture shapes the amount of time a person sleeps. In rural India, women sleep fewer hours than men because they have to get up earlier to start the fire for the morning meal. In fast-track, corporate North America, "A-type" males sleep relatively few hours and are proud of that fact—to sleep too much is to be a wimp.

Elimination   This subject takes the discussion into more private territory. How does culture affect the elimination process? Anyone who has traveled internationally knows that there is much to learn about elimination when you leave familiar territory. The first question is where to eliminate. Differences emerge in the degree to which elimination is a private act or can be done in more or less public areas. Public options include street urinals for males but not for females, as in Paris. In most villages in India, houses do not have interior bathrooms. Instead, early in the morning, groups of women and girls leave the house and head for a certain field where they squat and chat. Men go to a different area. Everyone carries in the left hand a small brass pot full of water with which they splash themselves clean. This practice has ecological advantages because it adds fertilizer to the fields and leaves no paper litter. Westerners may consider the village practice unclean, but village Indians would think that the Western system is unsanitary because paper does not clean one as well as water.

In many cultures, the products of elimination (urine and feces) are considered dirty, polluting, and disgusting. People do not try to keep such things, nor do they in any way revere them. Among some groups in Papua New Guinea, in the South Pacific, people take great care to bury or otherwise hide their fecal matter. They fear that someone will find it and use it for magic against them. A negative assessment of the products of elimination is not universal, however. In some cultures, these substances are believed to have positive effects. Among Native American cultures of the Pacific Northwest, urine, especially women's urine, was believed to have medicinal and cleansing properties and was considered the "water of life" (Furst 1989). In certain death rituals, it was sprinkled over the corpse in the hope that it might rejuvenate the deceased. People stored urine in special wooden boxes for ritual use, including the first bath that a baby was given (the urine was mixed with water for this purpose).

Culture Is Based on Symbols   Making money, creating art, and practicing religion are all based on symbols. A **symbol** represents something else. Symbols are arbitrary (bearing no necessary relationship to that which is symbolized), unpredictable, and diverse. Because symbols are arbitrary, we cannot predict how a particular

In India, a white sari (women's garment) symbolizes widowhood. ■ *What might these women think about the Western custom of a bride wearing white?* (Source: Barbara Miller)

culture will symbolize any particular thing. Although we might predict that people who are hungry would have an expression for hunger involving their stomach, no one could predict that in Hindi, the language of much of northern India, a colloquial expression for being hungry says that "rats are jumping in my stomach." The linguistic history of Barbara—the name of the author of this book—reveals that originally, in the Greek, it referred to people who were outsiders, "barbarians," and, by extension, uncivilized and savage. On top of that, it referred to such people as "bearded." The symbolic content of the American name Barbara does not immediately convey a sense of beardedness in its current context because symbolic content can change. Through symbols, culture is shared, stored, and transmitted over time.

Culture Is Learned   Because culture is based on arbitrary symbols, it cannot be predicted or intuited but must, rather, be learned. Cultural learning begins from the moment of birth, if not before (some people think that an unborn baby takes in and stores information through sounds heard from the outside world). This learning can be unconscious or conscious. A large but unknown amount of people's cultural learning is unconscious, occurring as a normal part of life through observation. Schools, in contrast, are a formal way to learn culture. Not all cultures throughout history have had formal schooling. Instead, children learned appropriate cultural

patterns through guidance from elders and by observation and practice. Hearing stories and seeing performances of rituals and dramas are other longstanding forms of cultural learning.

Cultures Are Integrated   To state that cultures are internally integrated is to assert the principle of holism. Thus, studying only one or two aspects of culture provides understanding so limited that it is more likely to be misleading or wrong than more comprehensively grounded approaches. Consider what would happen if a researcher were to study intertribal warfare in Papua New Guinea and focused only on the actual practice of warfare without examining other aspects of culture. A key feature of highland New Guinea culture is the exchange of pigs at political feasts. To become a political leader, a man must acquire many pigs. Pigs eat yams, which men grow, but pigs are cared for by women. This division of labor means that a man with more than one wife will be able to produce more pigs and rise politically by giving more feasts. Such feasting enhances an aspiring leader's status and makes his guests indebted to him. With more followers attracted through feasting, a leader can gather forces and wage war on neighboring villages. Success in war brings gains in territory. So far, this example pays attention mainly to economics, politics, and marriage systems. But other aspects of culture are involved, too. Supernatural powers affect the success of warfare. Painting spears and shields with particular designs helps increase their power. At feasts and marriages, body decoration (including paint, shell ornaments, and elaborate feather headdresses) is an important expression of identity and status. It should be obvious that looking at just warfare itself will yield a severely limited view of its wider cultural dimensions.

The fact of cultural integration is relevant to applied anthropologists who are involved in suggesting certain kinds of cultural change. Attempting to introduce change in one aspect of culture without considering what its effects will be in other areas is irresponsible and may even be detrimental to the survival of a culture. For example, Western missionaries and colonialists in parts of Southeast Asia banned the practice of head-hunting. This practice was embedded in many other aspects of culture, including politics, religion, and psychology (a man's sense of identity as a man sometimes depended on the taking of a head). Although stopping head-hunting might seem like a good thing to readers of this book, it had disastrous consequences for the cultures in which it had been a practice.

Cultures Interact and Change   Cultures interact with and affect each other in many ways, through trade networks, telecommunications, education, migration, and tourism. Change through cultural contact and interaction is nothing new. But since the 1980s, the increased connectedness of regions of the world via electronic communication and high-speed transportation is something that many feel is new. **Globalization** is a process of intensified global interconnectedness and movement of goods, information, and people. But globalization is not an even flow of goods, information, and people from all points to all other points. Power issues influence these flows, and critics of globalization insist that the all-powerful nations of the West, especially the United States, dominate global flows to the detriment of less powerful nations and groups. Many cultural anthropologists are also concerned that globalization will accelerate and obliterate local cultures.

At the same time, cultural anthropologists' research often documents strong movements toward **localization,** or the modification and transformation of global forces by local cultures into new forms that are clearly different from the global—a kind of cultural remaking of the global by the local. For example, the popularity of reggae involves aspects of both globalization and localization. When Jamaican reggae singer Bob Marley started singing in Jamaica, he was first popular locally, in Kingston, and then on the entire island. Subsequently, his popularity expanded to the regional (Caribbean) level, and finally he gained international fame. From the international level, reggae has filtered down into localities where it has been reinterpreted into new forms.

The culture of dominant groups often serves as the "index culture" for other groups. Index cultures are found at all levels: a village elite, a city compared to a rural area, and global capitals, which influence cultures in the periphery. In Bolivia, many indigenous Aymara women migrate from the rural highlands to the capital city of La Paz, where they work as domestic servants for the wealthy (Gill 1993). In the city, they stop wearing their traditional dress and adopt the urban styles of skirts, hats, and haircuts. In Kathmandu, Nepal, the index culture for hairstyles among some upper-class women is Parisian (Thompson 1998).

Global cultural dominance is influenced by the material and political interests of the powerful nations and international corporations. The spread of American merchandise, including items such as Coca-Cola, Marlboro cigarettes, and pharmaceuticals, is part of conscious marketing. Many cultural anthropologists question the value of much of this marketing because it often does more to enhance the profits of Western businesses than to improve human health and welfare. The promotion of American cigarettes in developing countries, as a compensation for the declining market in America, is an alarming example. Defenders of the practice, who emphasize human agency, argue that global marketing simply increases people's choices and stress that it's up to individuals to decide whether to purchase a particular item.

Multiple Cultural Worlds

As mentioned earlier, numerous microcultures exist within larger cultural clusters. Much of this internal cultural differentiation is shaped by the factors of class, race, ethnicity, gender, age, and institutions. A particular individual is likely to be a member of several microcultures and may identify more or less strongly with a particular microculture. Microcultures are not necessarily positioned next to each other. They may overlap or they may be related to each other hierarchically. The contrast between difference and hierarchy is important. People and groups can be considered different from each other on a particular criterion, but not unequal. For example, people with blue or brown eyes might be recognized as different, but this difference does not entail unequal treatment or status. In other instances, such differences *do* become the basis for inequality.

Class

Class is a category based on people's economic position in society, usually measured in terms of income or wealth and exhibited in terms of lifestyle. Class societies may be divided into upper, middle, and lower classes. An earlier definition of class that is associated with Karl Marx and Frederick Engels says that class membership is determined by people's relationship to production, or how people make a living. Separate classes are, for example,

A view into the yard of a house of a low-income neighborhood of Kingston, Jamaica. ■ *Why do you think people in these neighborhoods prefer the term low-income to poor?* (Source: Barbara Miller)

the working class (people who trade their labor for wages) and the landowning class (people who own land on which they or others labor). Classes are related in a hierarchical system, with certain classes dominating others. Class struggle, in the classic Marxist view, is inevitable as those at the top seek to maintain their position while those at the bottom seek to improve theirs. People at the bottom of the class structure may attempt to improve their class position by gaining access to resources and by adopting aspects of upper-class symbolic behavior, such as speech, dress, and leisure and recreation.

Class is a relatively recent social development in human history. For example, in precontact tribal groups in the Amazonian region, all members had roughly equal wealth. Some scholars say that global systems of social integration mean that indigenous tribal groups are now part of a global class structure, occupying a position at the bottom.

Race

Race is a pervasive, though not universal, basis for social differentiation. The term refers to bounded groups of people distinguished by selected biological traits. In South Africa, race is mainly defined on the basis of skin color, as it is in the United States. In pre-twentieth-century China, however, the basis of racial classification was body hair (Dikötter 1998). Greater amounts of body hair were associated with "barbarian" races and the lack of "civilization." Chinese writers typified male missionaries from Europe, with their beards, as "hairy barbarians." Even in the twentieth century, some Chinese anthropologists and sociologists divided humans into evolutionary stages on the basis of their body hair. One survey of humankind provided a detailed classification on the basis of types of beards, whiskers, and moustaches.

Physical features do not explain or account for culture, as Boas proved a century ago. Instead, the fact of being placed in a particular racial category and the status of that category in society explain "racial" behaviors and ideas. Rather than being a biological category, race is a cultural or social construct. Racial differentiation has been the basis for some of the most invidious oppression and cruelty throughout history. A warped notion of racial purity inspired Hitler to pursue his program of exterminating Jews and others who were not of the Aryan "race." Racial apartheid in South Africa denied citizenship, security, and a decent life to all those labeled "Black." Political scientist Andrew Hacker states that race is the most important criterion of social difference in the United States. In his book, *Two Nations: Black and White, Separate, Hostile, Unequal* (1992), he writes that no one who is White in America can truly understand what it is like to be Black. Hacker discusses the racial income gap, inequities in schooling, and crime. In all these areas, the Black population of America in general participates in a different cultural world than the better-off White population.

Ethnic Groups and Indigenous Peoples

Ethnicity refers to a sense of group affiliation based on a distinct heritage or worldview as a "people"—for example, African Americans or Italian Americans of the United States, the Croats of Eastern Europe, and the Han peoples of China. This sense of identity can be vigorously expressed through political movements or more quietly stated. It can be a basis for social ranking, claimed enti-

Native American dancers perform at the annual Gateway Pow Wow in Brooklyn, New York. ■ *Are there examples in any of your microcultural experiences of attempts to revitalize aspects of the culture?* (Source: © CRDPHOTO/CORBIS)

Unity and Diversity

TEJANO WOMEN AND TAMALES

AMONG TEJANO MIGRANT farm workers in the United States, preparing tamales is a symbol of women's commitment to their families and thus of the "good wife" (Williams 1984). The Tejanos are people of Mexican descent who live in Texas. Some of them move to Illinois in the summer, where they are employed as migrant workers.

Among Tejanos, tamales are the most important cultural identity marker. Wrapped in corn husks that contain a soft outer paste of flour and a rich inner mash of pig's head meat, tamales demand extremely time-consuming preparation. Only women make tamales. Many women cooperate over several days in the required tasks: buying the pigs' heads, stripping the meat, cooking the mash, preparing the paste, and stuffing, wrapping, and baking or boiling the tamale itself. Tamales symbolize and emphasize women's nurturance of men. Such immersion in domestic tasks might be considered oppressive by middle-class people in the United States, but most Tejano women value their role in food preparation. One elderly migrant woman, at home in Texas for Christmas, made 200 tamales with her daughters-in-law, nieces, and goddaughter. They were distributed to friends, relatives, and local taverns. The effort and expense involved were enormous, but it was worth it as a way for her to commemorate the holiday, obligate people she may need to call on later, and befriend the tavern owners so that they will watch over her male kin who drink there.

Tamales may also become statements of rebellion on the part of women. One way for a woman to express dissatisfaction with her marriage is to refuse to make tamales. Because the link between being a good wife and making tamales is so strong, such refusal could be taken by a husband as grounds for divorce. In fact, one young migrant male sued his wife for divorce in Illinois on the grounds that she refused to cook tamales for him (in addition to dancing with other men at fiestas). The judge refused to grant a divorce on such grounds. The Tejano community was outraged and insisted that a proper wife should cook tamales for her husband.

FOOD FOR THOUGHT

Can you provide an example from your own microcultural experience about food being used as a way to express social solidarity or social rebellion?

---

tlements to resources such as land or artifacts, and a perceived basis for defending or retrieving those resources.

Compared to the term *race, ethnicity* is often used as a more neutral or even positive term. But ethnicity, too, has often been a basis for discrimination, segregation, and oppression. The "ethnic cleansing" campaigns conducted in the early 1990s by the Serbs against Muslims in the former Yugoslavia are an extreme case of ethnic discrimination. Expression of ethnic identity has been politically suppressed in many cultures, such as the Tibetans in China. Tibetan refugees living outside Tibet are struggling to keep their ethnic heritage alive. Among many Native American groups in South and North America, a shared ethnicity is an important basis of tribal revival. Among many recent immigrant groups throughout the world, ethnic culture is being "tested" in terms of its resilience in the face of larger cultural patterns. (See the Unity and Diversity box above)

Another important but hard-to-define category is that of **indigenous peoples**. Indigenous peoples, following guidelines laid down by the United Nations, are defined as people who have a longstanding connection with their home territory that predates colonial or outside societies that prevail in the territory (Sanders 1999). They are typically a numerical minority and often have lost the rights to their original territory. The United Nations distinguishes between indigenous peoples and minority ethnic groups such as the Rom of various European countries, the Tamils of Sri Lanka, and African-Americans. While this distinction may be useful in some ways, it should not be taken as a hard-and-fast difference (Maybury-Lewis 1997b). It is more useful to think of all minority groups who exist as groups that were relocated from an original homeland.

Gender

Gender refers to patterns of culturally constructed and learned behaviors and ideas attributed to males, females, or sometimes a blended or "third" gender. Gender can be contrasted to *sex*, which uses biological markers to define categories of male and female. Sex determination relies on genital, chromosomal, and hormonal distributions and depends on Western science to determine who

---

is male or female. Cultural anthropology shows that a person's biological makeup does not necessarily correspond to gender. Only a few tasks, such as nursing infants, are tied to biology. Cross-culturally, gender differences vary from societies in which male and female roles and worlds are similar or overlapping to those in which genders are sharply differentiated. In much of rural Thailand, males and females are about the same size, their clothing is quite similar, and their agricultural tasks are complementary and often interchangeable (Potter 1977). Among the Hua of the New Guinea Highlands, extreme gender segregation exists in nearly all aspects of life (Meigs 1984). The men's house physically and symbolically separates the worlds of men and women. The men live in strict separation from the women, and they engage in rituals seeking to purge themselves of female influences and substances: nose or penis bleeding, vomiting, tongue scraping, sweating, and eye washing. Men possess the sacred flutes, which they parade though the village from time to time. If women dare to look at the flutes, men have the right to kill them for that transgression. Strict rules govern the kinds of food that men and women may eat.

In many cultures, the lives of gay and lesbian people are adversely affected by discrimination based on gender identity and sexual preferences. Other cultures are less repressive, notably cultures of Southeast Asia and native North America.

Age

The human life cycle, from birth to old age, takes people through cultural stages for which appropriate behavior and thinking must be learned anew. In many African herding societies, elaborate age categories for males define their roles and status as they move from being boys with few responsibilities and little status, to young men who are warriors and live apart from the rest of the group, to adult men who are allowed to marry, have children, and become respected elders. "The Hill," or the collective members of the United States Senate and the House of Representatives, is a highly age-graded microculture (Weatherford 1981). The Hill can be considered a gerontocracy (a group ruled by senior members) in which the older politicians dominate younger politicians in terms of amount of time for speaking and how much attention a person's words receive. It may take a junior member between 10 and 20 years to become as effective and powerful as a senior member, by which time, of course, she or he *is* a senior member.

In many cultures, adolescents are in a particularly powerless category because they are neither children, who have certain well-defined rights, nor adults. Given this threshold position, many adolescents behave in ways that the larger society disapproves of and defines as deviance,

crime, or even psychopathology (Fabrega and Miller 1995). Concerning women, cross-cultural research shows that in many nonindustrial societies, middle-aged women have the highest status in their life cycle if they are married and have children (Brown 1982).

Institutions

Institutions, or enduring group settings formed for a particular purpose, have their own characteristic microcultures. Institutions include hospitals, boarding schools and universities, and prisons. Anyone who has entered such an institution has experienced a feeling of strangeness. Until you gain familiarity with the often unwritten cultural rules, you are likely to make mistakes that offend or perplex people, that fail to get you what you want, and that make you feel marginal.

Consider the microculture of a large urban hospital in the United States. Melvin Konner, an anthropologist who studied among a hunting–gathering group of southern Africa, decided to go to medical school. In his book *Becoming a Doctor* (1987), he reports on his experience in medical school, providing an anthropologist's insights into the hospital as a cultural institution. One of his most striking conclusions is that medical students undergo training that functions to dehumanize them, numbing them to the pain and suffering that they will confront each day. Medical training involves, for example, the need to memorize massive amounts of material, sleep deprivation, and the learning of a special form of humor and vocabulary that seems crude and even cruel. Some special vocabulary items are: *boogie*—a verb meaning to move patients along quickly in a clinic or emergency room (as in "Let's boogie!"); a *dud*—a patient with no interesting findings; and a *gomer*—an acronym for Get Out of My Emergency Room, referring to an old, decrepit, hopeless patient whose care is guaranteed to be a thankless task, and who is usually admitted from a nursing home.

Relationships of power and inequality exist within institutions and between different institutions. These relationships cut across those of other microcultures, such as gender. In the United States, women prisoners' recent claims of rape and abuse by prison guards are an example of intrainstitutional inequality linked with gender inequality. Schools have their own institutional cultures. Within the classroom, studies show that many teachers are not egalitarian in the way they call on and respond to students, depending on their gender, race, or "looks." In the Kilimanjaro region of Tanzania, a lesson about proper sexual behavior directed to secondary school students advised boys to "preserve your bullets" and girls to "lock your boxes" (Stambach 2000:127–130). The surface message is that boys should learn to control their mental processes and girls should look after their possessions which they keep in a metal trunk beneath their bed. The underlying message is that boys should learn to control their sexual desire and that girls should protect their bodies. The separate metaphors, bullets and boxes, for the boys and the girls, reflect and reinforce gender differences in moral codes and expected behavior.

Distinctive Features of Cultural Anthropology

Several features of cultural anthropology have traditionally distinguished it from other disciplines. Scholars in other disciplines, however, have adopted some aspects of anthropological approaches, so some of cultural anthropology's characteristic features are no longer unique to the field but are still part of its identity.

Ethnography and Ethnology

Cultural anthropologists approach the study of contemporary human life in two basic ways. The first is in-depth study of one culture. This approach, **ethnography**, meaning "culture writing," provides a firsthand, detailed description based on personal observation of a living culture. Ethnography is usually presented in the form of a full-length book. It is based on experiences gained by going to the place of study and living there for an extended period.

In the early twentieth century, ethnographers wrote about "exotic" cultures located far from their homes in Europe and North America. Classics of this phase include A. R. Radcliffe-Brown's *The Andaman Islanders* (1964 [1922]), a study of people living on a group of small islands off the coast of Burma; Bronislaw Malinowski's *Argonauts of the Western Pacific* (1961 [1922]), concerning a complex trade network linking several islands in the South Pacific; and Reo Fortune's *Sorcerers of Dobu* (1959 [1932]), which describes a culture in the Western Pacific islands, with a focus on its social and religious characteristics.

For several decades, ethnographers tended to treat a particular tribal group or village as a bounded unit. The era of "village studies" in ethnography extended from the 1950s through the 1960s. Anthropologists typically studied in one village and then wrote an ethnography describing that village, inspired by the perspective of holism.

From the 1980s onward, ethnographers have changed in several ways. First, they are more likely to treat local cultures as embedded within regional and global forces. Carolyn Sargent studied medical care and childbirth among the Bariba people of Benin, West Africa (1989). She gathered interview data on people's traditional medical beliefs and practices and on their experiences with an urban hospital's obstetrics facility that employed more Westernized medical care. In her book, *Maternity, Medicine, and Power*, she interweaves attention to the clinical setting, women's beliefs about how to be a proper Bariba woman—they must not express pain during delivery—and power struggles between practitioners of Westernized medicine and traditional Bariba medicine. Second, many contemporary ethnographies are focused on one topic of interest and avoid a more holistic approach. Edward Fischer's book *Cultural Logics and Global Economics: Maya Identity in Thought and Practice* (2001) takes the topic of Mayan political activism in Guatemala as its focus but also sets it within the context of changing economic structures, family life, and individual action. A third trend is expanded interest in history. Gillian Feeley-Harnick's book *A Green Estate: Restoring Independence in Madagascar* (1991) traces the effects of French colonial domination on this island located off the coast of East Africa and the emergence of Madagascar as an independent country after 1960. Her research required a combination of archival data and fieldwork data. A fourth trend is for ethnographic studies to be situated in Western, industrialized cultures. Philippe Bourgois's research in East Harlem in New York City for his book *In Search of Respect: Selling Crack in El Barrio* (1995) explores how people in one neighborhood cope with poverty and dangerous living conditions. This topic may seem to resemble something that a sociologist might study, but the cultural anthropologist provides the everyday perspective of the people gained through intensive, long-term research.

In contrast to ethnography, **ethnology** is cross-cultural analysis, or the study of a particular topic in more than one culture using ethnographic material. Ethnologists have compared such topics as marriage forms, economic practices, religious beliefs, and childrearing practices in order to discover patterns of similarity and variation and possible causes for them. For example, some anthropologists have studied the length of time that parents co-sleep with their babies and how that variation might be related to different types of personality formation—does a longer co-sleeping period lead to less individualistic personalities? Although the Boasian influence on cultural anthropology, especially in North America, raised serious questions about the validity and value of ethnology, a strong case continues to be made for careful, contextualized comparison as the important counterpoint to excessive particularism. A new trend in cultural anthropology is revitalizing the comparative approach, especially in terms of making our findings relevant to public issues and formulation of public policy (Fox and Gingrich 2002).

It is most fruitful to think of ethnography and ethnology as mutually illuminating. Ethnography provides rich, culturally specific insights. Ethnology, by looking beyond individual cases to wider patterns, provides new insights and raises new questions that prompt future ethnographic research.

Cultural Relativism

Most people grow up thinking that their culture is *the* way of life and that other ways of life are strange and inferior. Other cultures may be considered less than human. Cultural anthropologists have labeled this attitude **ethnocentrism**: judging other cultures by the standards of one's own culture rather than by the standards of those other cultures. Ethnocentric views have fueled centuries of efforts at changing "other" people in the world, sometimes in the guise of religious missionizing and sometimes in the form of colonial domination. European colonial expansion beginning in the fifteenth century was intended to extract wealth from the colonies. But in addition to plundering their colonies, the Europeans imposed their culture on indigenous groups. The British poet Rudyard Kipling reflected the dominant view when he said that it was "the white man's burden" to spread British culture throughout the world. Christian missionaries played a major role in transforming non-Christian cultures. Many contemporary Western powers hold similar attitudes, making foreign policy decisions that encourage the adoption of Western economic, political, and social systems.

The opposite of ethnocentrism is **cultural relativism,** the idea that each culture must be understood in terms of its own values and beliefs and not by the standards of another culture. Cultural relativism assumes that no culture is better than any other. How does a person gain a sense of cultural relativism? Besides living with other people, ways to develop a sense of cultural relativism include traveling, especially extended periods of study abroad, taking a course in cultural anthropology, eating differ-

ent foods, listening to music from Appalachia or Brazil, reading novels by authors from other cultures, making friends who are "different" from you, and exploring the multicultural world on your campus. In sum, exposure to "other" ways, with a sympathetic eye and ear to understanding and appreciating differences, is the key.

Can a person ever completely avoid being ethnocentric? The answer is probably no, because we start learning about other cultures from the position of the one we know first. Even the most sensitive person who has spent a long time living within another culture still carries an original imprint of her or his native culture. As much as we might say that we think we are viewing Culture B from the inside (as though we were natives of Culture B), that is a logical impossibility because everything about Culture B—the language, dress, food habits, social organization, work habits, leadership patterns, and religion—was learned in relation to or in comparison with what we already knew about Culture A.

One way that some anthropologists have interpreted cultural relativism is what I call **absolute cultural relativism,** which says that whatever goes on in a particular culture must not be questioned or changed because no one has the right to question any behavior or idea anywhere—it would be ethnocentric to do so. The position of absolute cultural relativism can lead, however, in dangerous directions. Consider the example of the Holocaust during World War II in which millions of Jews and other minorities in much of Eastern and Western Europe were killed as part of the German Nazis' Aryan supremacy campaign. The absolute cultural relativist position becomes boxed in, logically, to saying that since the Holocaust was undertaken according to the values of the culture, outsiders have no business questioning it. Can anyone feel truly comfortable with such a position?

Richard Lee (left) asks several Ju/wasi men about food plants of the Kalahari desert in Botswana. This photograph was taken in 1968. ■ *Locate Botswana and do research to learn about its population and other social characteristics.* (Source: © Stan Washburn/AnthroPhoto)

Critical cultural relativism offers an alternative view that poses questions about cultural practices and ideas in terms of who accepts them and why, and who they might be harming or helping. In terms of the Nazi Holocaust, a critical cultural relativist would ask, "Whose culture supported the values that killed millions of people on the grounds of racial purity?" Not the cultures of the Jews, Gypsies, and other victims. It was the culture of Aryan supremacists, who were one subgroup among many. The situation was far more complex than a simple absolute cultural relativist statement takes into account, because there was not "one" culture and its values involved. Rather, it was a case of **cultural imperialism,** in which one dominant group claims supremacy over minority cultures and proceeds to change the situation in its own interests and at the expense of the other cultures. Critical cultural relativism avoids the trap of adopting a homogenized view of complexity. It recognizes internal cultural differences and winners/losers, oppressors/victims. It pays attention to different interests of various power groups. Beyond the clear case of the German Holocaust, critical cultural relativism can be applied to illuminate many recent and contemporary conflict situations, such as those in the former Yugoslavia, Rwanda, and Iraq.

A growing number of cultural anthropologists seek to critique (which means to probe underlying power interests, not just to come up with negative comments as in the general usage of the term *criticism*) the behavior and values of groups from the standpoint of some set of generally agreed-upon human rights. But even they recognize how difficult it is to generate a universally agreed-upon list of what different cultures view as good and right. Clearly, no single culture has the answer and can dictate to others. As prominent French anthropologist Claude Lévi-Strauss commented, "No society is perfect" (1968:385). While considering the "imperfections" of any and all cultures, cultural anthropologists should examine and discuss their own biases and then try to view all cultures equally. This means looking equally critically at all cultures—their own and those of "others."

Valuing and Sustaining Diversity

Most anthropologists value and are committed to cultural diversity just as environmentalists value and are committed to biological diversity. Thus, cultural anthropologists regret the decline and extinction of different cultures. Anthropologists contribute to the preservation of cultural diversity by describing cultures as they have existed, as they now exist, and as they change. Many cultural anthropologists have become activists in the area of cultural survival. An organization called Cultural Survival has been helping indigenous people and ethnic minorities deal as equals in their interactions with out-

siders. Cultural Survival's guiding principle is printed on the inside cover of its publication, *Cultural Survival Quarterly* (1998),

> We insist that cultural differences are inherent in humanity; protecting this human diversity enriches our common earth. Yet in the name of development and progress, native peoples lose their land, their natural resources, and control over their lives. The consequences often are disease, destitution, and despair—and war and environmental damage for us all. The destruction is not inevitable.

Cultural Survival sponsors programs to help indigenous peoples and ethnic minorities help themselves in protecting and managing natural resources, claiming land rights, and diversifying their means of livelihood.

THREE THEORETICAL DEBATES

Within anthropology, enduring theoretical debates both divide the discipline and give it coherence. Three important contemporary debates, discussed here, will resurface throughout the book. Each is concerned with cultural anthropology's basic questions of how people behave and think and why they behave and think the way they do.

Biological Determinism versus Cultural Constructionism

Biological determinism seeks to explain why people do and think what they do by considering biological factors such as people's genes and hormones. Thus biological determinists search for the gene or hormone that might lead to behavior such as homicide, alcoholism, or adolescent stress. (See the Critical Thinking box on page 20.) They examine cultural practices in terms of how these contribute to the "reproductive success of the species," or how they contribute to the gene pool of subsequent generations by boosting the numbers of surviving offspring produced in a particular population. Behaviors and ideas that have reproductive advantages are more likely than others to be passed on to future generations. Biological determinists, for example, have provided an explanation for why human males apparently have "better" spatial skills than females. They say that these differences are the result of evolutionary selection because males with "better" spatial skills would have an advantage in securing both food and mates. Males with "better" spatial skills impregnate more females and have more offspring with "better" spatial skills.

ADOLESCENT STRESS: BIOLOGICALLY DETERMINED OR CULTURALLY CONSTRUCTED?

MARGARET MEAD, one of the first trained anthropologists of North America, went to eastern Samoa in 1925 to spend nine months studying child-rearing patterns and adolescent behavior. She sought to answer these questions: "Are the disturbances which vex our adolescents due to the nature of adolescence itself or to the civilisation? Under different conditions does adolescence present a different picture?" (1961:24). She observed and interviewed 50 adolescent girls of three different villages. Her conclusion, published in the famous book *Coming of Age in Samoa* (1961 [1928]), was that, unlike the typical experience in the United States, children in Samoa grew up in a relaxed and happy atmosphere. As young adolescents, they made a sexually free and unrepressed transition to adulthood. These findings had a major impact on thinking about child rearing in North America, prompting attempts at more relaxed forms of child rearing in the hope of raising less stressed adolescents.

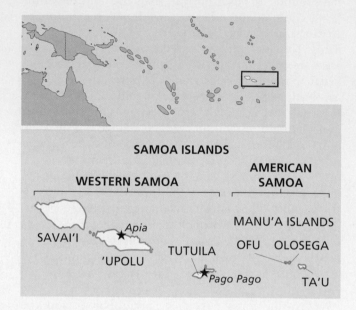

In 1983, five years after Mead's death, the Australian anthropologist Derek Freeman published a strong critique of Mead's work on Samoa. Freeman said that Mead's findings on adolescence were wrong. Freeman, a biological determinist, believes that universally, adolescents are driven by hormonal changes that cause social and psychological upheavals. He claims that Mead's work was flawed in two major ways. First, he says her fieldwork was inadequate because she spent a relatively short time in the field and had insufficient knowledge of the Samoan language. Second, he says that her theoretical bias against biological determinism led her to overlook or underreport evidence that was contrary to her interests. In addition, he marshalls statistical evidence against Mead's position. He compares rates of adolescent delinquency in Samoa and England and finds that they are similar. On the basis of this result, he argues that sexual puritanism and social repression also characterized Samoan adolescence. In other words, Samoa is not so very different from the West with its supposedly pervasive adolescent problems.

Freeman's critique prompted a vigorous response from scholars, mostly in defense of Mead. One response in defense of Mead came from Eleanor Leacock, an expert on how colonialism affects indigenous cultures. Leacock claims that Freeman's position fails to take history into account: Mead's findings apply to Samoa of the 1920s, whereas Freeman's analysis is based on data from the 1960s. By the 1960s, Samoan society had gone through radical cultural change because of the influence of World War II and intensive exposure to Western influences, including Christian missionaries. Freeman's data, in her view, do not contradict Mead's because they are from a different period.

CRITICAL THINKING QUESTIONS

Mead felt that finding one "negative case" (no adolescent stress in Samoa) was sufficient to disprove the view that adolescent stress is a cultural universal. Do you agree that one negative case is sufficient?

If an anthropologist found that a practice or pattern of behavior was universal to all cultures, does that necessarily mean that it is biologically driven?

Cultural constructionism, in contrast, maintains that human behavior and ideas are best explained as products of culturally shaped learning. In terms of the example of "better" male spatial skills, cultural constructionists would provide evidence that such skills are passed on culturally through learning, not genes. They would say that parents and teachers socialize boys and girls differently in spatial skills and are more likely to promote learning of spatial skills among boys. Anthropologists who favor cultural construction and learning as an explanation for behaviors such as homicide and alcoholism point to childhood experiences and family roles as being more important than genes or hormones. Most cultural anthropologists are opposed to biological determinism and support cultural constructivism. They feel that cultural anthropology makes an important contribution to the understanding of human nature by showing how important human culture is!

Interpretivism versus Cultural Materialism

Interpretivism is a perspective that focuses on understanding culture by studying what people think about, their explanations of their lives, and the meanings that are important to them. For example, in understanding why Hindus do not eat beef, interpretivists ask Hindus why

Top: Traffic in the city of Varanasi (Banaras), in northern India. Foreign visitors to India have often commented that the presence of wandering cows is a sign of wastefulness and inefficiency. Bottom: SUVs, trucks, and buses share the road in Los Angeles. SUVs are increasingly popular in the United States even as they are criticized by environmentalists for their poor gas mileage. ■ *If you were an energy policy-maker, what lessons would you draw from the photographs on this page?* (Sources: © Jack Fields/CORBIS, top; AP/Wide World Photos, bottom)

they don't eat beef. They learn from Hindus that the cow is sacred in the Hindu religion and therefore cannot be killed for its products. Interpretivists say that such beliefs are the explanation for cultural behavior.

Cultural materialism, in contrast, attempts to learn about culture by first examining the material aspects of life: the natural environment and how people make a living within particular environments. Cultural materialists believe that these basic facts of life shape culture, even though people may not realize it. They use a simple hierarchical, three-level model to explain culture. Since that is the model that this book follows in organizing its chapters, it is worth spending a little time exploring it. The bottom level is **infrastructure,** a term that refers to basic material factors such as natural resources, the economy, and population. According to this model, infrastructure tends to shape the other two domains of culture: **structure** (social organization, kinship, and political organization) and **superstructure** (ideas, values, and beliefs). Cultural materialists seek explanations for behavior and ideas by looking first and primarily at infrastructural factors. A materialist explanation for the taboo restricting the eating of beef considers the possibility that cattle play a more important role alive than they do dead—as meat (Harris 1974). For example, cattle wandering the streets look useless to Westerners, but they are performing an important social and environmental role by eating trash as they amble along. In addition, their excrement is "brown gold," useful as fertilizer or, when mixed with straw and formed into dried patties, as cooking fuel. Most important, cattle are used to plow fields. Cultural materialists argue that the sacred value of cattle in Hinduism helps to protect the lives of these extremely useful animals, which, if killed for burgers, would have far less importance in the long run.

The debate between interpretivism and cultural materialism has a long history in cultural anthropology, and its philosophical roots can be traced back to Plato (who emphasized that the only reality is ideas) and Aristotle (who emphasized that there is some sort of reality that can be learned about through observation). These days, although some cultural anthropologists are strong interpretivists or strong cultural materialists, most take an approach that combines the best of both views.

Individual Agency versus Structurism

This debate concerns the question of how much individual will, or agency, affects the way people behave and think, compared with the power of forces, or "structures," that are beyond individual control. Western philosophical thought gives much emphasis to the role of agency, the ability of individuals to make choices and exercise free will. In contrast, structurism emphasizes that free choice is an illusion because choices are structured by larger forces such as the economy, social and political organization, and ideological systems. Explaining why people are poor, unemployed, or on welfare in the United States has been approached from both positions by cultural anthropologists and others. Those who emphasize agency in explaining behavior and ideas say, for example, that people are poor, unemployed, or on welfare because of their own choices. If they wished, they could choose to be otherwise. Structurists would say that the poor and unemployed are trapped by larger forces and cannot escape these traps. They would argue that the people at the bottom of the economic ladder have, in reality, little opportunity to exercise choice to be elsewhere than at the bottom.

Beyond the Debates: Holists at Heart

Anthropologists often take different theoretical positions. Some apply their work while others stick to academic pursuits. But I think it is fair to say that we all care deeply about humanity—its past, present, and future.

KEY CONCEPTS

SUGGESTED READINGS

Thomas J. Barfield, ed. *The Dictionary of Anthropology.* Malden, MA: Blackwell Publishing, 1997. This reference work contains hundreds of brief essays on a wide variety of concepts in anthropology, including evolution, myth, functionalism, and applied anthropology, and on important figures such as Tylor, Morgan, Boas, and Lévi-Strauss.

Stanley R. Barrett, *Anthropology: A Student's Guide to Theory and Method.* Toronto: University of Toronto Press, 2000. This book organizes the theoretical history of cultural anthropology into three phases and summarizes trends in each. The author provides insights about how to design and conduct research in cultural anthropology.

Douglas Cole, *Franz Boas: The Early Years, 1858–1906.* Seattle: University of Washington Press, 1999. This biography of Boas reveals how his vision for a four-field discipline emerged.

Merryl Wyn Davies and Piero, *Introducing Anthropology.* Cambridge: Icon Books, 2002. This book offers snappy insights on key thinkers, developments, and arguments in anthropology. Each page is illustrated with cartoon-like drawings that make for lively reading.

Marvin Harris. *Our Kind: Who We Are, Where We Came From and Where We Are Going.* New York: Harper-Collins, 1989. This book contains 100 thought-provoking essays on topics in general anthropology's four fields, including early human evolution, tool making, Neanderthals, food preferences, sex, sexism, politics, animal sacrifice, and thoughts on the survival of humanity.

Thomas C. Patterson, *A Social History of Anthropology in the United States.* New York: Berg, 2001. This history of anthropology in the United States emphasizes the social and political context of the discipline and how that context shaped theories and methods.

Richard J. Perry, *Five Key Concepts in Anthropological Thinking.* Upper Saddle River, NJ: Prentice-Hall, 2003. This concise book introduces anthropological theory by considering the concepts of evolution, culture, structure, function, and relativism. The author raises thought-provoking questions about anthropology as Eurocentric, about the appropriation of the culture concept beyond anthropology, and about "unsettled issues."

Pearl T. Robinson and Elliott P. Skinner, eds. *Transformation and Resiliency in Africa: As Seen by Afro-American Scholars.* Washington, DC: Howard University Press, 1983. Framed by an introductory essay on Black scholarship on Africa and a conclusion that looks toward the future, nine chapters explore different areas of African culture, including labor migration in Kenya, politics and government in Nigeria, religion in the Ivory Coast, religion and popular art in urban Africa, and the transformation of African music.

Pat Shipman, *The Evolution of Racism: Human Differences and the Use and Abuse of Science.* Cambridge, MA: Harvard University Press, 1994. This book offers a readable history of the "race" concept in Western thought from Darwin to contemporary DNA studies. The author addresses thorny issues such as racism in the United States and Nazi Germany's use of Darwinism.

George W. Stocking, Jr. *The Ethnographer's Magic and Other Essays in the History of Anthropology.* Madison: University of Wisconsin Press, 1992. This book provides a detailed examination of the emergence of cultural anthropology from Tylor through Boas and Mead, with a summary chapter on major paradigms in the history of general anthropology.

Eric R. Wolf. *Europe and the People Without History.* Berkeley: University of California Press, 1982. This book examines the impact since 1492 of European colonial expansion on the indigenous cultures with which they came into contact. It also traces various phases of trade relationships, including the slave trade and goods such as fur and tobacco, and the emergence of capitalism and its effects on the movement of people and goods between cultures.

WHAT is anthropology?

Anthropology is an academic discipline, like history or economics. It comprises four interrelated fields in its attempt to explore all facets of human life from its very beginnings until the present: archaeology, biological or physical anthropology, linguistic anthropology, and cultural anthropology. Each field contributes a unique but related perspective. Each is capable of making both theoretical and applied contributions. Cultural anthropology is mainly concerned with describing and analyzing contemporary people's learned and shared behaviors and beliefs.

WHAT is cultural anthropology?

Cultural anthropology is the field within general anthropology that focuses on the study of contemporary human culture—that is, on patterned, learned, and shared ways of behaving and thinking. It has several distinctive features that set it apart from the other fields of general anthropology and from other academic disciplines. It uses ethnographical and ethnological approaches, supports the view of cultural relativism, and values cultural diversity.

Culture is the key concept of cultural anthropology. Some anthropologists define culture as both shared behavior and ideas, whereas others equate culture with ideas alone and exclude behavior as a part of culture. Culture is related to nature but not the same as nature, is based on symbols, and is learned. Cultures are integrated within themselves. They also interact with other cultures and thereby change. People participate in cultures of different levels, including global and macrocultures and local microcultures shaped by such factors as class, race, ethnicity, gender, age, and institutions.

WHAT are the major theoretical debates in cultural anthropology?

Over the history of anthropology, many theoretical approaches have risen and fallen, while others have endured through time with important transformations. Three of the most important and enduring theoretical debates are biological determinism versus cultural constructivism, interpretivism versus cultural materialism, and individual agency versus structurism. Each, in its own way, attempts to explain why people behave and think the way they do—that is, to account for differences and similarities across cultures.

THE BIG QUESTIONS

- **HOW** do cultural anthropologists conduct research on culture?
- **WHAT** does fieldwork involve?
- **WHAT** are some special issues in cultural anthropology research?

2

METHODS IN CULTURAL ANTHROPOLOGY

During the course of winter travels with the Hare Indians in Canada, anthropologist Joel Savishinsky holds a 25-pound lake trout. His dog team is resting behind him. (*Source: © Joel Savishinsky*)

Tau, Manu'a

March 24, 1926

At dawn on March 8th, a boat arrived from Ofu and lured by thoughts of ethnological gain I decided to go back with the boat—a 15-foot rowboat . . . I decided it would be expensive but pleasant. So we set out in the broiling sun with a crew of some nine Samoans. The girls were desperately seasick but I rested my head on a burlap bag of canned goods, and . . . enjoyed the three-hour pull in the open sea. The swell is impressive when viewed from such a cockleshell of a boat. The Samoans chanted and shouted. . . .

The whole conduct of the *malaga* [ceremonial visiting party] was charming. My two companions were my talking chiefs, functionally speaking. They made all the speeches, accepted and dispersed gifts, prepared my meals, etc. . . . And these were merry companions. Even when they went to wash my clothes, one carried the clothes but the other carried the ukelele. . . . There were some slight difficulties. Once I killed 35 mosquitoes *inside* my net *in the morning,* and all had dined liberally. (Mead 1977:55–57)

There are important differences between being a tourist and doing research in cultural anthropology, as this excerpt from one of Margaret Mead's letters from Samoa demonstrates. Most cultural anthropologists gather data by doing **fieldwork**—that is, going to "the field," which includes any place where people and culture are found (Robson 1993). The cornerstone method of fieldwork in cultural anthropology is **participant observation**, in which an anthropologist simultaneously lives in and studies a culture for a long period of time.

Compared to the other three fields of general anthropology, cultural anthropology is most associated with participant observation as its primary technique for gathering data. Because archaeologists work mainly with artifacts from bygone cultures, they cannot truly participate in the cultures they study. Primatologists live in natural habitats for long periods of time, but the limited degree to which humans and nonhuman primates can communicate with each other constrains true participation. Linguistic anthropologists who work with contemporary populations most resemble cultural anthropologists in their use of fieldwork among living humans. They are able both to observe and to participate in the same ways that cultural anthropologists do.

In this chapter we explore how cultural anthropologists learn about culture through fieldwork and participant observation. The entire process of fieldwork is considered, from coming up with an idea for research to leaving the field, analyzing the data, and writing up one's findings. Later in the chapter, we consider some special topics, such as the importance of ethics and doing fieldwork in dangerous situations. Throughout this chapter, you might consider the similarities and differences between research in cultural anthropology and research in other areas of study such as psychology, economics, and history.

CHANGING METHODS IN CULTURAL ANTHROPOLOGY

Methods in cultural anthropology have changed dramatically since the nineteenth century. This section presents a brief historical overview of research approaches and then introduces the key method of participant observation.

From the Armchair to the Field

Research in the early years of cultural anthropology was not based on fieldwork and participant observation. Referred to as "armchair anthropology," it involved reading reports from travelers, missionaries, and explorers and then providing an analysis. Edward Tylor (1871), who proposed the first definition of culture, was an armchair anthropologist. So was James Frazer, another famous founding figure of anthropology, who wrote *The Golden Bough* (1978 [1890]), a multivolume collection of myths, rituals, and symbols from around the world compiled from reading other people's reports. In the late nineteenth and early twentieth centuries, some anthropologists left their homes and libraries and traveled to foreign countries, where they spent time living near, but not with, the people they were studying. This pattern is nicknamed "verandah anthropology" because typically the anthropologist would send out for "native" informants to come to the verandah for interviewing. Verandah anthropology was practiced by many anthropologists who worked for colonial governments. They lived within colonial settlements, not with the indigenous people. The current approach of fieldwork and participant observation replaced verandah anthropology in the early twentieth century.

The field can be anywhere: a school, a rural community, a corporation, a clinic, an urban neighborhood, in any part of the world. In some ways, the field is equivalent to a scientist's lab. A cultural anthropologist, however, does not perform experiments with people.

Participant Observation: An Evolving Method

An early lesson about the values of participant observation as a fieldwork method came from Lewis Henry Morgan, a nineteenth-century lawyer who lived in upstate New York near the Iroquois. Morgan did not do participant observation in the sense of living for a long time, say a year or two, with the people, but he did make several two-week field trips to Iroquois settlements (Tooker 1992). This experience, though brief, provided him with important insights into the lives of the Iroquois and formed the basis for his book, *The League of the Iroquois* (1851). This book helped dismantle the prevailing Euro-American perception of the Iroquois as "dangerous savages."

Bronislaw Malinowski is considered the "father" of participant observation because he first used it while studying the people of the Trobriand Islands in the South Pacific during World War I. "For two years, he set his tent in their midst, learned their language, participated as much as he could in their daily life, expeditions, and festivals, and took everything down in his notebooks" (Sperber 1985:4). Malinowski made the crucial step of learning the local language, and therefore he was able to dispense with interpreters. Direct communication brings the researcher much closer to the lived reality of the people being studied, as is evident in his ethnography about the Trobrianders, *Argonauts of the Western Pacific* (1961 [1922]).

In the early days of cultural anthropology (the late 1800s and early 1900s), a primary goal was to record as much as possible of a people's language, songs, rituals, and social life because many cultures were disappearing. Given the belief that small, localized cultures could be studied in their totality, early cultural anthropologists focused on gaining a holistic view of a single group (Chapter 1). Today, few isolated cultures remain to be studied. The integration of most cultures into wider economic and political spheres generates new research topics and revised methods of study that can take in both local and global factors.

A methodological innovation that helps cultural anthropologists take globalization, complexity, and change into account is **multi-sited research**, or fieldwork in more than one location (Marcus 1995). Cultural anthropologists are adopting this approach, particularly in studies of migrant populations (Chapter 15). Studying migration challenges traditional cultural anthropology's focus on one village or neighborhood and creates the need to take into account national and global economic, political, and social forces (Lamphere 1992; Basch, Glick Schiller, and Szanton Blanc 1994). Anthropologists study

Bronislaw Malinowski during his fieldwork in the Trobriand Islands, 1915–1918. ■ *What are some of the differences between what his field research revealed about men's lives in the Trobriand Islands and what a "verandah anthropologist" would have learned?* (Source: Pearson Education)

A food vendor at the Brazilian Independence Day street festival celebrated on West 46th Street in Manhattan, an area known as "Little Brazil." ■ *Locate a Web site of a migrant community to see what issues are prominent.* (Source: J. T. Milanvich)

why people move and analyze their adjustments to living in a new place, especially the challenges and opportunities of maintaining their culture or constructing a new cultural identity. Fieldwork in rural Brazil, for example, is a first step, followed by research among Brazilian immigrants in New York City (Margolis 1994). This approach enables the anthropologist to compare Brazilian culture in these locations and to understand Brazilian New Yorkers' attempts to retain and recreate Brazilian culture in the new context.

Lanita Jacobs-Huey has been conducting multi-sited fieldwork for many years in order to learn about the culture of hair styles among English-speaking African American women (2002). She chose a range of sites in order to explore the many facets of this far-from-simple topic. She has conducted participant observation in beauty salons, regional and international hair expos, training seminars for lay and licensed stylists, Bible study meetings of a not-for-profit group of Christian cosmetologists, a computer-mediated discussion about the politics of black hair, and a cosmetology school in Charleston, South Carolina. Bronislaw Malinowski would be amazed at how methods have changed since the early part of the twentieth century!

DOING RESEARCH IN CULTURAL ANTHROPOLOGY

Conducting research in cultural anthropology is challenging, exciting, sometimes frustrating, and full of surprises. No doubt all cultural anthropologists would agree that their fieldwork experiences have altered their own lives immeasurably. Here we explore all the stages of a fieldwork research project, from the initial planning to the concluding analysis and writing up of the findings.

Beginning the Fieldwork Process

Two important activities characterize the first stage of cultural anthropology research: project selection and preparing for the field.

Project Selection

Cultural anthropologists often find a topic to research by reviewing reports on what has been done already. Through library research, also called secondary research, they may find a gap that needs to be filled. For example, in the 1970s, many cultural anthropologists began to focus on women because they realized that little previous research had addressed women's lives (Miller 1993). Other topics emerge because of historical events. The discovery of the HIV/AIDS virus and its social dimensions stimulated interest from cultural anthropologists, many working within the subfield of medical anthropology. The recent rise in the numbers of immigrants and refugees in the United States prompted studies of the adaptation of these groups of people. The fall of state socialism in Russia and Eastern Europe shifted attention to that region. Conflicts in Ireland, Rwanda, the former Yugoslavia, and other places have spurred cultural anthropologists to ask what keeps states together and what makes them fall apart (Harris 1992). Even luck can lead to a research topic. Spanish anthropologist María Cátedra (1992) stumbled on an important issue during exploratory fieldwork in rural northern Spain. A suicide occurred in a hamlet in the mountains near where she was staying. She learned that the local people did not consider suicide strange. In fact, the area was characterized by a high rate of suicide. Later she went back and did long-term research on the social dynamics of suicide in this area.

"Restudies" are another way to design a research project. Decades of previous anthropological field studies provide a base of information. It makes sense for contemporary anthropologists to go back to a place that was studied earlier to examine changes that have occurred or to look at the culture from a new angle. For her dissertation research, Annette Weiner (1976) decided to go to the Trobriand Islands, following in the footsteps of Malinowski. She was surprised at what she discovered about Trobriand women's lives. (See the Critical Thinking box.)

Preparing for the Field

Once the project is defined and funding secured, it is time to prepare for going to the field. Visas, or formal research

Critical Thinking

SHELLS AND SKIRTS IN THE TROBRIAND ISLANDS

A LASTING contribution of Malinowski's ethnography, *Argonauts of the Western Pacific* (1961 [1922]), is its detailed examination of the *kula*, a trading network linking many islands in the region in which men have longstanding partnerships for the exchange of both goods such as food and highly valued necklaces and armlets.

More than half a century later, Annette Weiner (1976) traveled to the Trobriand Islands to study wood carving. She settled in a village less than a mile from where Malinowski had done much of his research and began making startling observations: "On my first day in the village, I saw women performing a mortuary [death] ceremony in which they distributed thousands of bundles of strips of dried banana leaves and hundreds of beautifully decorated fibrous skirts. Bundles of banana leaves and skirts are objects of female wealth with explicit economic value" (xvii).

She decided to investigate women's activities and exchange patterns. Weiner discovered a cultural world of production, exchange, social networks, and influence that existed among women but that Malinowski had overlooked. Men, as Malinowski described, exchange shells, yams, and pigs. Women, as Weiner discovered, exchange bundles of leaves and intricately made skirts. Power and prestige derive from both. Reading Malinowski alone informs us about the dramatic and exciting world of men's status systems. But that is only half the picture. Weiner's *Women of Value, Men of Renown* (1976) provides an account of the linkages between

domains of male and female power and value. She shows how understanding one domain requires knowledge of the other.

CRITICAL THINKING QUESTIONS

How is it possible that Malinowski missed the importance of women's exchange patterns?

Do the findings of Annette Weiner simply provide another one-sided view?

---

permission from the host government, may be required and may take a long time to obtain. The government of India, for example, is highly restrictive about research by foreigners, and "sensitive" topics such as "tribal people" and family planning are off limits. Some nations have been completely closed to anthropological research for decades and are only now relaxing their restrictions. China's restrictions against American anthropologists doing research there have been lifted only in the past fifteen years or so, and Russia's restrictive policies have changed even more recently. Recent rulings in the United States, largely inspired by concerns in the medical research community, require investigators who plan to

do research with "human subjects" to get approval for their project from their university or funding agency before starting the research. Approval is contingent on satisfactory provisions safeguarding "human subjects" from any kind of harm related to the research.

Preparation for the field may involve buying equipment, such as a tent or special clothing. For example, fieldwork in Siberia may necessitate a special sleeping bag to keep one warm at nighttime where temperatures are below −20° Fahrenheit. Health preparations may involve having a series of shots for immunization against contagious diseases such as yellow fever. For research in malaria-endemic areas, individuals are advised to start

Jennifer Robertson (far left) celebrates the publication of her book *Native and Newcomer* (1991) with several administrators from Kodaira city hall. This informal gathering at a local restaurant followed a formal ceremony at the city hall, where Robertson presented her book to the mayor of Kodaira, an event covered by city and regional newspapers. ■ *What cultural features are noteworthy about this gathering?* (Source: Jennifer Robertson)

Site Selection

The researcher often has a basic idea of the area where the fieldwork will occur—for example, a *favela* (shanty town) in Rio de Janeiro or a village in Scotland—but it is difficult to know exactly where the project will be located until after one arrives. Selecting a research site depends on many factors. It may be necessary to find a large village if the project involves looking at social class differences in work patterns and food consumption or to find a clinic if the study concerns health care behavior. Locating a place where the people welcome the researcher and the project, which offers adequate housing, and which fits the requirements of the project may not be easy.

Jennifer Robertson's (1991) selection of Kodaira as a research site in Japan for research on urban population change and interactions between long-time urban residents and immigrants was based on a combination of factors: good advice from a Japanese colleague, available housing, a match with her research interests, and the happy coincidence that she already knew the area:

> I spent my childhood and early teens in Kodaira [but] my personal past did not directly influence my selection of Kodaira as a fieldsite and home. . . . That I wound up living in my old neighborhood in Kodaira was determined more by the availability of a suitable apartment than by a nostalgic curiosity about my childhood haunts. As it turned out, I could not have landed at a better place at a better time. (6)

Gaining Rapport

Rapport is the relationship between the researcher and the study population. In the early stages of research, the primary goal is to establish rapport—probably first with key leaders or decision makers in the community who may serve as gatekeepers (people who formally or informally control access to the group or community). Gaining rapport involves trust on the part of the study population, and their trust depends on how the researcher presents herself or himself. In many cultures, people have difficulty understanding why a person would come to study them, because they do not know about universities and research and cultural anthropology. They may provide their own (often inaccurate) explanations based on previous experience with outsiders whose goals differed from those of cultural anthropologists, such as tax collectors, family planning promoters, and law enforcement officials.

Much has been written about the problem of how the anthropologist presents herself or himself in the field and how the local people interpret who the anthropologist is and why the anthropologist is there at all. Stories about such role assignments can be humorous. Richard Kurin (1980) reports that in the earliest stage of his research

taking anti-malaria pills weeks before arrival to build up immunity. If the project is to take place in a remote area far from adequate medical care, a well-stocked medical kit is essential. Research equipment and supplies are another important aspect of preparation. Cameras, video recorders, tape recorders, and laptop computers are becoming basic field equipment.

If a researcher is unfamiliar with the local language, intensive language training before going to the field is a necessity. Even with language training in advance, cultural anthropologists often find that they need to learn the local version of the more standardized language they studied in a classroom. Many researchers rely on help from a local interpreter.

Working in the Field

Fieldwork in cultural anthropology is a difficult and lengthy social process that involves the researcher's coming to terms with an unfamiliar culture. The anthropologist attempts to learn the language of the people, live as they do, understand their lives, and be a friend.

among the Karan in the Punjab region of northwest Pakistan, the villagers thought he was a spy—from America, Russia, India, or China. After he convinced them that he was not a spy, the villagers came up with several other acceptable roles for him—first as a teacher of English because he was tutoring one of the village boys, then as a doctor because he was known to dispense aspirin, then as a lawyer who could help villagers in negotiating local disputes because he could read court orders, and finally as a descendant of a local clan through the similarity between his last name and that of an ancestral king! He gained acceptance in the village in all these roles, but the crowning touch, for him, was being considered a true "Karan."

Gift Giving and Exchange

Giving gifts to local people can help the project proceed, but gifts should be culturally and ethically appropriate. Many cultural anthropologists working in developing countries have provided basic medical care, such as treating wounds. Some have taught in a local school part time. Others have helped support individuals in obtaining a degree in higher education outside their homelands.

Learning the local rules of exchange is important, including what constitutes an appropriate or an inappropriate gift, how to deliver the gift (timing, in private or public, wrapped or unwrapped), and how to behave as a gift giver (for example, should one be modest and emphasize the smallness of the gift?). Matthews Hamabata (1990) learned about the complex forms of gift giving in Japan during his study of Japanese business families. He had developed a close relationship with one family, the Itoos, and had helped their daughter apply for admission to universities in the United States. When the applications were completed, Mrs. Itoo, the girl's mother, invited him to an expensive restaurant to celebrate. After the dinner, she handed him a small, carefully wrapped package, expressing her embarrassment at the inadequacy of her gift in relation to all that he had done for her daughter. When he returned home, he opened the gift. It was a box of chocolates. Upon opening the box to share the chocolates with some friends, he discovered 50,000 yen (about US $250). At first he was shocked and insulted: "Who do the Itoos think they are? They can't buy me or my services!" (21–22). Once his anger had cooled, he consulted some Japanese friends about what to do. They told him that returning the money to the Itoos would be an insult to them because the gift implied a wish to have a longstanding relationship. They advised him to give a return gift, at a later time, in order to maintain the relationship. They advised a gift that would leave him ahead by about 25,000 yen, given his status as an academic researcher in relation to the Itoos' status as a rich business family.

Microcultures and Fieldwork

An anthropologist's class, race, gender, and age all affect how he or she will be interpreted by local people. An anthropologist who is a young, unmarried female studying child-rearing practices may not be taken seriously because she is not herself a mother. Bearded males who look like "hippies" may alienate local people whose experiences with true hippies have not been positive. In the rest of this section, we offer some examples of how class, race/ethnicity, gender, age, and other factors can influence the rapport an anthropologist is able to achieve with the population.

Class In most fieldwork situations, the anthropologist is more wealthy and powerful than the people studied. This difference is obvious to the people. They know that the anthropologist must have spent hundreds or thousands of dollars to travel to the research site. They see the expensive equipment (camera, tape recorder, video recorder, even a vehicle) and valuable trade items (stainless steel knives, cigarettes, flashlights, canned food, medicines). The pattern of the anthropologist having more wealth and status than the people being studied has typified cultural anthropology throughout its history. Laura Nader (1972) urged a departure from this pattern. She says that some anthropologists should "study up" by doing research among powerful people such as members of the business elite, political leaders, and government officials. As one example, research on the high-fashion industry of Japan placed an anthropologist in touch with many members of the Japanese elite, influential people capable of taking her to court if they felt she wrote something defamatory about them (Kondo 1997). "Studying up" has contributed to awareness of the need, in all fieldwork situations, for recognition of the anthropologist's accountability to the people being studied. Some anthropologists deal with this need through collaborative forms of research, which helps ensure that the research "subjects" are part of the research process themselves.

Race For most of its history, cultural anthropology has been dominated by Euro-American White researchers who have studied "other" cultures, most often non-White and non-Euro-American. The effects of "Whiteness" on role assignments range from the anthropologist being labeled as a god or ancestor spirit to his or her being reviled as a representative of a colonialist past. While doing research in Jamaica, Tony Whitehead (1986) learned how race and status interact. For Whitehead, an African American, being essentially the same "race"—of African descent—did not automatically create solidarity between him and the African-descent residents of Haversham. The people of Haversham have a complex status system that relegated Whitehead to a position that he did not predict:

> I am a black American who grew up in the rural South to impoverished sharecropper parents. Regardless of the upward mobility I experienced when I went to Jamaica, I still perceived of myself as one of the little people. . . . (i.e., lower status) because of my experience as an ethnic minority in the United States. . . . With such a self-image in tow, I was shocked when the people of Haversham began talking to me and referring to me as a "big," "brown," "pretty-talking" man. "Big" was not a reference to my weight but to my higher social status as they perceived it, and "brown" referred not only to my skin color but also to my higher social status. . . . More embarrassing than bothersome were the references to how "pretty" I talked, a comment on my Standard English speech pattern. . . . Frequently mothers told me that their children were going to school so that they could learn to talk as pretty as I did. (214–215)

Liza Dalby in full geisha formal dress. ■ *Besides learning to dress correctly, what other cultural skills did Liza Dalby probably have to learn?* (Source: Liza Dalby)

Whitehead's fieldwork was not impeded by the Jamaicans' assignment of him to a higher-status role than he expected, but it did prompt him to rethink the complexities of race and status cross-culturally. For Lanita Jacobs-Huey, in her research on African American women's hair culture, being an African American herself did not automatically gain her acceptance (2002). Hair style is a sensitive subject, and her Internet informants wanted her to tell them how her hair was styled.

Gender   Gender is another important factor in fieldwork. If a female researcher is young and unmarried, she is likely to face more difficulties than a young unmarried male or an older female, married or single, because people in most cultures will consider a young, unmarried female who is on her own as extremely unusual (Warren 1988). Rules of gender segregation may dictate that a young unmarried woman should not move about freely without a male escort, and her status may prevent her from attending certain events or being in some places. Gender boundaries exist cross-culturally to varying degrees, and a researcher probably can never fully overcome them. A woman researcher who studied a male gay community in the United States comments that:

> I was able to do fieldwork in those parts of the setting dedicated to sociability and leisure—bars, parties, family gatherings. I was not, however, able to observe in those parts of the setting dedicated to sexuality—even quasi-public settings such as homosexual bath houses. . . . Thus my portrait of the gay community is only a partial one, bounded by the social roles assigned to females within the male homosexual world. (Warren 1988:18)

Gender segregation may also prevent male researchers from gaining access to a full range of activities. Californian Liza Dalby (1998) lived with the geishas of Kyoto, Japan, and trained to be a geisha. Through this, she learned more about the inner workings of this microculture than a man ever could.

Age   Typically, adult anthropologists are responsible for studying people in all age categories. Although some children and adolescents readily welcome the participation of a friendly adult in their daily lives and respond to questions openly, others are more reserved. Margaret Mead (1986) commented that "Ideally, a three-generation family, including children highly trained to understand what they experience, would be the best way to study a culture" (321). She recognized that this ideal would not be possible or practical, and that the best a fieldworker could do was to be imaginative and flexible in order to gain rapport with members of special age categories. This may involve learning and using age-specific language. A team of anthropologists studying sexuality among American adolescents discovered that using age-appropriate language made it easier to establish rapport.

In our experience, when asking an adolescent, especially a younger adolescent, a sensitive question such as "Have you ever had sexual intercourse?" the child spends far too much time in awe of the word "intercourse," investigating its meaning, and giggling at this clinical term. It is better for the researcher to ask simply, "Have you ever had sex?" (Weber, Miracle, and Skehan 1994:44)

Other Factors The fieldworker's role is affected by many more factors than the characteristics listed above, including religion, dress, and personality. Being the same religion as the elderly Jewish people at the Aliyah Center in California helped a Jewish anthropologist (Myerhoff 1978) establish rapport. This is evident in a conversation she had with one old woman named Basha:

"So, what brings you here?"
"I'm from the University of Southern California. I'm looking for a place to study how older Jews live in the city."
At the word *university,* she moved closer and nodded approvingly. "Are you Jewish?" she asked.
"Yes, I am."
"Are you married?" she persisted.
"Yes."
"You got children?"
"Yes, two boys, four and eight," I answered.
"Are you teaching them to be Jews?" (14)

She was warmly accepted into the lives of people at the Center, and her plan for one year of research grew into a longstanding relationship. In contrast, being Jewish posed a potential problem for another Jewish woman anthropologist (Freedman 1986). She conducted research in Romania, a country where anti-semitism is strong. She was hesitant about telling the villagers that she was Jewish, but she was also reluctant to lie. Early in her stay, she attended the village church. The priest asked what her religion was. Upon revealing that she was Jewish, she found to her relief that this did not result in her being alienated from the community.

Culture Shock

Culture shock consists of persistent feelings of uneasiness, loneliness, and anxiety that often occur when a person has shifted from one culture to a different one. The more "different" the two cultures are, the more severe the shock is likely to be. Culture shock happens to many cultural anthropologists, no matter how much they have tried to prepare themselves for fieldwork. It also happens to students who study abroad, Peace Corps volunteers, and anyone who spends a significant amount of time living and participating in another culture.

Culture shock can range from problems with food to the language barrier. Food differences were a major problem in adjustment for a Chinese anthropologist who came to the United States (Shu-Min 1993). American food never gave him a "full" feeling. An American anthropologist (Ward 1989), who went to an island in the Pacific named Pohnpei, found that language caused the most serious adjustment problems. She spent much time in the early stages of her research learning basic phrases and vocabulary, and she reports on the frustration she felt:

[E]ven dogs understood more than I did. . . . [I will never] forget the agony of stepping on a woman's toes. Instead of asking for forgiveness, I blurted out, "His canoe is blue." (14)

A psychological aspect of culture shock is the feeling of reduced competence as a cultural actor. At home, the anthropologist is highly competent. Everyday tasks like shopping, talking with people, mailing a letter, or sending a fax can be done without thinking. In a new culture, the most simple task becomes difficult and one's sense of self-efficacy is undermined. In extreme cases, an anthropologist may have to abandon a project because of an inability to adapt to the fieldwork situation. For most, however, culture shock is a temporary affliction that subsides as the person becomes more familiar with the new culture.

"Reverse culture shock" can occur on returning home. An American anthropologist (Beals 1980) describes his feelings on returning to San Francisco after a year of fieldwork in a village in India:

We could not understand why people were so distant and hard to reach, or why they talked and moved so quickly. We were a little frightened at the sight of so many white faces and we could not understand why no one stared at us, brushed against us, or admired our baby. (119)

Fieldwork Techniques

Fieldwork is devoted to collecting data for subsequent analysis. The main approaches to data collection, **quantitative research** and **qualitative research**, provide different kinds of data and follow different analytical routes (Bernard 1995; Hammersley 1992). Quantitative data and analysis include numeric information, counting, and the use of tables and charts in presenting results. Qualitative methods are aimed at generating descriptions, and they avoid counting or quantifying. Some researchers concentrate on quantitative data, some rely on qualitative data, and others use a combination. But in all cases, participant observation is the basic research method through which the data are collected.

Varieties of Participant Observation

Once in the field, cultural anthropologists use particular methods to learn about culture. Within the overall approach of participant observation, several different methods are available. The choice of methods for data gathering and the subsequent interpretation and analysis of the data depend on the anthropologist's theoretical perspective. For example, cultural materialists and interpretivists approach the study of culture differently. According to the former, the goal of cultural anthropology is to describe the cultures of all human societies and explain why they differ in some respects and are similar in others (Harris 1975:144). Cultural materialists are likely to use a **deductive research** method, which involves posing a research question or hypothesis, gathering data related to the question, and then assessing the findings in relation to the original hypothesis. Thus, fieldwork should be devoted to the collection of detailed observational and interview data in order to learn what people do as well as how people explain what they do and why they do it. Deeper causes for certain forms of behavior and ideas are sought through cross-cultural comparison.

In contrast, for interpretivists, the goal of anthropological research lies in the pursuit of detailed information on insiders' views (Geertz 1983:5). The primary source of information is **discourse**—people's talk, stories, and myths. People's discourse reveals their perceptions of important themes and concepts. In this view, cross-cultural comparison is a waste of time, because each system of local knowledge makes sense only in itself. Attempts to find causal connections between, say, a people's economic system and its religious beliefs are also rejected as too deterministic and generalizing. Thus interpretivists favor a more **inductive research** approach that avoids hypothesis formation in advance of the research and instead takes its cues from the culture being studied.

Cultural anthropologists use two terms that are related to deductive research and inductive research, respectively. **Etic** (pronounced like the last two syllables of *phonetic*) refers to data gathering and analysis by outsiders that will yield answers to particular questions about the culture posed by the outsider. In contrast, **emic** (pronounced like the last two syllables of *phonemic*) refers to descriptive reports about what insiders say and understand about their culture. Cultural materialists favor an etic approach to explaining cultural patterns. Interpretivists say that we need an emic approach because cultures can be understood only in their own terms, not through the imposition of outside analysis.

Being a participant means that the researcher tries to adopt the lifestyle of the people being studied, living in the same kind of housing, eating similar food, wearing similar clothing, learning the language, and participating in the daily round of activities and in special events. Participation over a long period improves the quality of the data. The more time the researcher spends living a "normal" life in the field area, the more likely it is that the people being studied will also live "normal" lives.

In this way, the researcher is able to overcome the **Hawthorne effect**, a phenomenon first discovered in the 1930s during a study of an industrial plant in the United States, in which informants altered their behavior in ways that they thought would please the researcher.

No matter how well accepted into everyday life the anthropologist becomes, however, the very nature of anthropological research and the presence of the anthropologist will have an effect on the people involved. Since the 1980s, anthropologists have increasingly considered how their presence affects their fieldwork and their findings, an approach called **reflexive anthropology** or **reflexivity**. An emphasis on reflexivity involves "constant awareness, assessment, and reassessment by the researcher of the researcher's own contribution [to and] influence [on] intersubjective research and the consequent research findings" (Salzman 2002:806). This approach is certainly a good corrective to the assumption that an anthropologist can go to the field and conduct research just as a scientist can in a lab. Working closely with real people in their everyday lives is a highly interactive and mutually influencing process: Everyone is changed in some way through the anthropological enterprise because it is a social process itself.

While participating in everyday life, the researcher carefully and thoroughly observes everything that is going on: who lives with whom, who interacts with whom in public, who are leaders and who are followers, what work people do, how people organize themselves for different activities, and far more. Obviously, not everything can be covered. Unstructured observations form the basis for a daily fieldnote diary in which the researcher attempts to record as much detail as possible about what has been observed. This process generates masses of qualitative data.

More formal methods of gathering quantitative data involve planned observations of a particular activity. One type of quantitative observational research is time allocation study, which can be an important tool for understanding people's behavior: work and leisure patterns, social interactions and group boundaries, and religious activities. This method relies on using Western time units as the basic matrix and then labeling or coding the activities that occur within certain time segments (Gross 1984). Each coding system corresponds to its particular context. For example, activity codes for types of "garden labor" designed for a horticultural society—burning, cutting, fencing, planting, soil preparation, weeding, and harvesting—would not be useful in a time allocation study in a retirement home. Observation may be continual, at fixed intervals (for instance, every forty-eight hours), or on a random basis. Continuous observation limits the number of people that can be observed because it is so time-consuming. Spot observations may inadvertently miss important activities. In order to increase coverage, time allocation data can be collected by asking people to keep daily logs or diaries. Of course, self-reporting may include intentional or unintentional biases, but observations by the researcher can help correct some of these.

Interviews and Questionnaires

In contrast to observing and recording events as they happen, an **interview**, or the gathering of verbal data through questions or guided conversation, is a more purposeful approach. An interview involves at least two people, the interviewer and the interviewee, and more during group interviews. Cultural anthropologists use varying interview styles and formats, depending on the kinds of information they seek, the amount of time they have, and their language skills. The least structured type of interview is called open-ended. In an open-ended interview, the respondent (interviewee) takes the lead in setting the direction of the conversation, the topics to be covered, and the amount of time to be spent on a particular topic. The interviewer does not interrupt or provide prompting questions. In this way, the researcher discovers what themes are important to the respondent.

Surveys and questionnaires administered during an interview session are more formal because they involve structured questions. Structured questions limit the range of possible responses—for example, by asking informants to rate their positions on a particular issue as very positive, positive, negative, very negative, or "no opinion." Ideally, the researcher should have enough familiarity with the study population to be able to design a formal questionnaire or survey that makes cultural sense (Fitchen 1990). Researchers who take ready-made questionnaires to the field with them should, at the minimum, ask another researcher who knows the field area to review the instrument to see whether it makes cultural sense. Additional revisions of the questionnaire will no doubt be required in the field to make it fit local conditions. Conducting a pilot survey before proceeding with a formal survey will reveal areas that need to be changed before the final version is used. Such a trial run should be considered an essential step.

Combining Watching and Asking

Many cultural anthropologists agree that formal interviews and questionnaires must be complemented by observational data on what people actually do (Sanjek 2000). For example, people in a particular culture may tell the anthropologist that sons and daughters share equally in the family property when their parents die. Research into the actual patterns of inheritance, however, may reveal more varied and complex patterns such as the daughters giving their shares to their brothers in exchange for their continuing care and support. It is

Marjorie Shostak (right) during fieldwork among the Ju/wasi of Botswana in 1975. Shostak focused her research on women's lives and wrote *Nisa*, a life history of a Ju/wasi woman. ■ *What would an anthropologist study about your everyday life?* (Source: © Mel Konner/AnthroPhoto)

important for the anthropologist to know both what the parents say and what happens—both are "true" aspects of cultural discourse and practice. Similarly, if an anthropologist studied the laws of a particular culture and found that discrimination on the basis of skin color was illegal, that's one part of the story of that culture's race relations. But this anthropologist should also study whether and how discrimination occurs.

Other Data-Gathering Techniques

Besides participating, observing, and asking questions of various types, cultural anthropologists use many other methods to gather data to fit their project goals. This section describes some of these methods.

Life History A **life history** is a qualitative, in-depth portrait of a single life experience as narrated by that person to the researcher. A life history provides the most "micro" perspective on culture possible. In the early days of life history research, the anthropologist tried to choose someone who was somehow typical, average, or representative. Anthropologists differ in their views about the value of the life history as a method in cultural anthropology, however. Early in the twentieth century, Franz Boas rejected this method as unscientific, because informants might lie or exaggerate (Peacock and Holland 1993). Others disagree, saying that a life history reveals rich information on individuals and how they think.

One of the Sri Lankan women whose life story Gananath Obeyesekere analyzed, a priestess to the deity Kataragama, stands in the shrine room of her house holding her long matted hair. ■ *Think of how hair styles in a culture that you know express a person's religion or marital status.* (Source: Gananath Obeyesekere)

fering and provides them with a special status as holy and thus outside the bounds of normal married life and sexual relations.

Life histories of several people within one social category can provide a picture of both shared experiences and individual differences. James Freeman's book *Hearts of Sorrow* (1989) is an example of this approach. It presents "cuts" from several life stories of Vietnamese refugees living in southern California. Together, the story cuts portray both the shared sadness of the refugees about the loss of their homeland and a range of adaptive experiences of the different individuals.

The ability of informants to present a story of their lives varies, depending on the cultural context. An attempt to gather life histories from women on Goodenough Island of Papua New Guinea was difficult because telling one's life story is a masculine style of presentation, and the women were reluctant to adopt it (Young 1983). Marjorie Shostak (1981), in contrast, found a willing and extremely expressive informant for a life story in Nisa, an indigenous woman of the Ju/wasi of the Kalahari Desert in southern Africa. Nisa's book-length story, presented in her voice, includes rich details about her childhood and several marriages.

Texts   Many cultural anthropologists collect and analyze texts. The category of "text" includes written or oral stories, myths, plays, sayings, speeches, jokes, and transcriptions of people's everyday conversations. In the early twentieth century, Franz Boas collected thousands of pages of texts from Native American groups of the Northwest Coast of Canada, including myths, songs, speeches, and accounts of how to perform rituals. These texts are useful records of cultures that have changed since the time of his fieldwork. Surviving tribal members have even referred to the texts to recover forgotten aspects of their culture. Texts also provide data with which linguistic and symbolic analyses can be undertaken.

Historical Sources   History is culture of the past, and it therefore has much relevance to understanding contemporary cultures. Ann Stoler (1985, 1989) is a pioneer in the anthropological use of archival resources in her study of Dutch colonialism in Java. Her research exposed details about colonial strategies, the culture of the colonizers themselves, and their impact on indigenous Javanese culture. Most countries have libraries and historical archives in which written records of the past are maintained. Local official archives are rich sources of information about land ownership, agricultural production, religious practices, and political activities. National archives in London, Paris, and Amsterdam contain records of colonial contact and relations. Parish churches throughout Europe have detailed family histories. Land-

It is not possible to find any one person who is representative of an entire culture. Thus some anthropologists seek informants who occupy a particularly interesting social niche. For example, Gananath Obeyesekere's book *Medusa's Hair: An Essay on Personal Symbols and Religious Experience* presents the life histories of four Sri Lankan people, three women and one man (1981). Each one became a religious devotee and ascetic, physically distinguished by thickly matted hair that became mysteriously twisted in a snake-like fashion. These four people cannot comb out their hair: It is permanently matted. The devotees explain that the god's presence is in their hair. Using material in the life histories of these people, Obeyesekere provides an interpretation suggesting that they all suffered deep psychological afflictions, including sexual anxieties. Their matted hair symbolizes this suf-

holding records and family registers are a source of cultural data in Japan and China.

Fieldwork among living people can also yield rich historical information. The "anthropology of memory" is a current research topic. Anthropologists study patterns of what people remember and what they don't, how culture shapes their memories and how their memories shape their culture. Jennifer Robertson's (1991) study of neighborhood people's memories of life in Kodaira, Japan, before the influx of immigrants is an example of this kind of research. She relied on interview data, in addition to archival data, to reconstruct people's remembered past.

Whereas Robertson looked at how people adjusted to what can be seen as a relatively normal process of population change, Emma Tarlo (2003) gathered personal narratives from people who had experienced a traumatic event—the Indian "Emergency" of 1975–1977. During this period, Prime Minister Indira Gandhi declared martial law and denied human rights to a large segment of the population, mainly the poorest people. Tarlo's research site was a low-income area of New Delhi where people had been forcibly relocated during the Emergency. She focused on people's memories of this traumatic period, in which harsh state intervention

New Delhi citizens read a newspaper billboard reporting the electoral defeat of Indira Gandhi in 1977. This event marked the end of the Emergency and martial law. ■ *Consider why and how Emma Tarlo's research on the Emergency differed from standard anthropological fieldwork based on participant observation.* (Source: © Bettman/CORBIS)

affected their entire lives. In order to "clean up" the city, the government bulldozed the settlements of thousands of poor people, forcing them into resettlement areas on the outskirts of Delhi. Thousands were also forcibly sterilized (vasectomy for men, tubectomy for women) as part of the population control program. The many narratives that people shared with Tarlo reveal both their experience of oppression and the many facets of human agency in response to state actions. For example, people were told that unless they were sterilized, they would lose their job. Some men who were at the end of their fertile years signed up to be sterilized. Doctors were often complicit in such ruses, allowing these men to be sterilized.

Multiple Research Methods and Team Projects

Most cultural anthropologists use several different methods for their research, because just one would not provide all the kinds of data necessary to understand a given problem. For example, a small survey of forty households provides some breadth of coverage, but adding some life histories (of five men and five women, perhaps) provides depth. **Triangulation** is a technique that involves obtaining information on a particular topic from more than one angle or perspective (Robson 1993:290). Asking only one person something provides information from only that person's viewpoint. Asking two people about the same thing doubles the information and often reveals that perspectives differ. The researcher may then want to check other sources, such as written records or newspaper reports, for additional perspectives (see the Lessons Applied box on page 40).

Team projects that involve cultural anthropologists and researchers from other disciplines provide additional skills. A research project designed to assess the effects of constructing a dam on the agricultural and fishing practices of people in the Senegal River Valley, West Africa, included cultural anthropologists, hydrologists, and agronomists (Horowitz and Salem-Murdock 1993). In another project, a cultural anthropologist and a nutritionist worked together to study the effects of adopting new agricultural practices in the Amazon (Gross and Underwood 1971).

Recording Culture

How does the anthropologist keep track of all this information and record it for future analysis? As with everything else about fieldwork, things have changed since the early times when a typewriter, index cards, and pencils were the major recording tools. Yet there is continuity: Taking copious notes is still the trademark method of recording data for a cultural anthropologist. This section begins with a discussion of note taking, a process that

Lessons Applied

MULTIPLE METHODS IN A NEEDS ASSESSMENT STUDY IN CANADA

THE UNITED WAY of Canada, a philanthropic agency, wanted to find out what the highest priorities were for their funding operations in Saskatoon, a relatively poor city located in Canada's southwestern prairie (Ervin et al. 1991, van Willigen 1993:204–205). Anthropologist Alexander Ervin led a team of researchers from the University of Saskatchewan's Department of Anthropology and Archaeology to respond to the United Way's request. At the time of the study in 1990, the city's population was about 200,000. The economy includes agriculture, mining, forestry, and some manufacturing. The unemployment rate was 10 percent, and food banks and soup kitchens were being increasingly used.

The team designed its research to provide baseline data on perceived social needs to assist the United Way in decision making. The assessment included six data collection activities: reviewing available written reports relevant to Saskatoon's needs, analyzing economic and social indicators, organizing 3 public forums, conducting 135 interviews with key informants from community agencies, holding 6 focus groups, and interviewing 28 United Way agency executive directors. These activities provided breadth and depth about community opinion and agency priorities and interests.

The research team produced a report that included a list of over 200 needs identified. The list was organized into 17 sectors, among them general health, mental health, the senior population, Native American issues, racism, and discrimination, and immigrant and refugee resettlement. The report also included a set of recommendations for the United Way.

FOOD FOR THOUGHT

Conducting a community needs assessment entails a research approach quite different from traditional fieldwork in cultural anthropology. What are some of the pros and cons of anthropologists conducting such applied research?

---

you may think is simple and needs no elaboration. But when you are in the field for a year—or even for a month—you will find that "just" taking notes is quite complicated. After discussing note taking, we turn to such other forms of recording data as tape recording, photography, and video.

Field Notes

The classic impression of anthropological research is that of the cultural anthropologist observing a ritual, with notebook and pen in hand. From the beginning of cultural anthropology, field notes have been the basic way to record observations. Field notes include daily logs, personal journals, descriptions of events, and notes about those notes. Ideally, researchers should write up their field notes each day. Otherwise, a backlog accumulates of daily "scratch notes," or rough jottings made on a small pad or note card carried in the pocket (Sanjek 1990a:95–99). Trying to capture, in the fullest way possible, the events of a single day is a monumental task and can result in dozens of pages of handwritten or typed field notes each day. The bulk of an anthropologist's time in the field is probably spent taking scratch notes by hand. The laptop computer now enables anthropologists to enter many of these notes directly into the computer.

Tape Recording, Photography, and Videos

Tape recorders are an obvious aid to fieldwork because they make possible the accurate recording of much more information. However, tape recording may raise problems such as informants' suspicions about a machine that can capture their voices, and the ethical issue of maintaining anonymity of informants whose actual voices are preserved on tape. María Cátedra (1992) reports on her use of tape recording during research in rural Spain in the 1970s:

> At first the existence of the "apparatus," as they called it, was part wonder and part suspect. Many had never seen one before and were fascinated to hear their own voice, but all were worried about what I would do with the tapes. . . . I tried to solve the problem by explaining what I would do with the tapes: I would use them to record correctly what people told me, since my memory was not good enough and I could not take notes quickly enough. . . . One event helped people to accept my integrity in regard to the "apparatus." In the second *braña* [small settlement] I visited, people asked me to play back what the people of the first *braña* had told me, especially some songs sung by a group of men. At first I was going to do it, but then I instinctively refused because I did not have the first people's permission. . . . My stand was quickly known in the first *braña* and commented on with approval. (21–22)

A multidisciplinary team comprising anthropologists, engineers, and agricultural experts from the United States and Sudan meet to discuss a resettlement project. ■ *Have you ever carried out research as part of a team? If so, what are the pros and cons?* (Source: Michael Horowitz)

A problem with tape recordings is that they have to be transcribed (typed up), either partially or completely. Each hour of recorded talk takes between five and eight hours to transcribe. Even more time is needed if the recording is garbled, many voices are heard at once, or complications in translation arise.

Like tape recordings, photographs or videos capture more detail than scratch notes. Any researcher who has watched people performing a ritual, taken scratch notes, and then tried to reconstruct the details of the ritual later on in field notes will know how much of the sequencing and related activity is lost to memory within just a few hours. Reviewing photographs or a video recording of the ritual provides a surprising amount of forgotten, or missed, material. But there is a trade-off. Using a camera or video recorder precludes taking notes simultaneously. Since field notes are invaluable, even if the video is also available, it is best to use a team approach.

Kirsten Hastrup (1992) provides an insightful description of her use of photography—and its limitations—in recording the annual ram exhibition in Iceland that celebrates the successful herding in of the sheep from mountain pastures. This event is exclusively for males, but she was allowed to attend.

> The smell was intense, the light somewhat dim and the room full of indiscernible sounds from some 120 rams and about 40 men. A committee went from one ram to the next noting their impressions of the animal, in terms of its general beauty, the size of the horns and so forth. Measurements were made all over but the decisive measure (made by hand) was the size and weight of the ram's testicles. The air was loaded with sex and I realized that the exhibition was literally and metaphorically a competition of sexual potence. . . . I heard endless sexual jokes and very private remarks. The bursts of laughter followed

by side-glances at me conveyed an implicit question of whether I understood what was going on. I did. (9)

Hastrup took many photographs. After they were developed, she was struck by how little of the totality of the event they conveyed.

Photographs and videos, just like field notes and other forms of recorded culture, provide only partial images of a cultural event. Furthermore, photographs and videos are no more objective than any other form of recorded culture because it is the researcher who selects what the camera will capture. Visual records are best regarded as important complements to other forms of cultural data.

Data Analysis

During the research process, a vast amount of data is collected in many forms. The question is how to put these data into some presentable form. In data analysis, as with research, two basic varieties exist: qualitative (prose-based description) and quantitative (numeric) data. Often, researchers analyze qualitative data in qualitative terms, as described below. Similarly, quantitative data lend themselves to quantitative analysis. But matters are never this straightforward. Qualitative data are often rendered in quantitative terms, and reporting on quantitative results necessarily requires descriptive prose to accompany graphs, charts, and computations.

Analyzing Qualitative Data

Qualitative data include descriptive field notes, informants' narratives, myths and stories, and songs and sagas. Relatively few set guidelines exist for undertaking a qualitative analysis of qualitative data. One general procedure of qualitative analysis is to search for themes, or regularities, in the data. This approach involves exploring the data, or "playing" with the data, either "by hand" or with the use of a computer. Jennifer Robertson's analysis of her Kodaira data was inspired by writer Gertrude Stein's approach to writing "portraits" of individuals, such as Picasso (1948). Robertson says that Stein was a superb ethnographer who was able to illuminate the "bottom nature" of her subjects and their worlds through a process that Stein referred to as "condensation." To do this, "she scrutinized her subjects until, over time, there emerged for her a repeating pattern of their words and actions. Her literary portraits . . . were condensations of her subjects' repeatings" (Robertson 1991:1). Like Stein, Robertson reflected on all that she had experienced and learned in Kodaira, beginning with the years when she lived there as a child. Emerging from all this was the dominant theme, *furusato,* which literally means "old village." References to *furusato* appear frequently in people's accounts of the past, conveying a sense of nostalgia for a more "real" past. Many qualitative anthropologists use computers to help sort for tropes (key themes). Computer scanning of data offers the ability to search vast quantities of data more quickly and perhaps accurately than with the human eye. The range of software available for such data management—for example ETHNO and The Ethnograph—is expanding. Of course, the quality of the results depends on, first, careful and complete inputting of the data and, second, an intelligent coding scheme that will tell the computer what it should be scanning for in the data.

The ethnographic presentation of qualitative data relies on the use of quotations of informants—their stories, explanations, and conversations. Although most ethnographies also include analytical commentary, some provide just the informants' words. Lila Abu-Lughod followed this approach in her book *Writing Women's Worlds* (1993). She presents Bedouin women's stories and conversations within a light authorial framework that organizes the stories into thematic clusters such as marriage, production, and honor. Although she provides a traditional, scholarly introduction to the narratives, she offers no conclusion, because a conclusion would give a false sense of authorial control over the narratives. She prefers to prompt readers to think for themselves about the meanings of the stories and what they say about Bedouin life.

Some anthropologists question the value of interpretive analyses on the ground that they lack verifiability: Too much depends on the individual selection process of the anthropologist, and too much is built around too few cases. Qualitative anthropologists would respond that verifiability in the scientific sense is not their goal and is not a worthwhile goal for cultural anthropology in general. Instead, they seek to provide a plausibly attractive interpretation, an evocation, or new understanding that

has detail and richness as its strengths rather than representativeness or replicability. They criticize purely quantitative research for its lack of richness and depth of understanding, even though it has the appearance of validity.

Analyzing Quantitative Data

Analysis of quantitative, or numeric, data can proceed in several directions. Some of the more sophisticated methods require knowledge of statistics, and many require the use of a computer and a software package that can perform statistical computations. In my research on low-income household budgeting patterns in Jamaica, I used computer analysis first to divide the sample households into three income groups (lower, medium, higher). I then used the computer to calculate percentages of expenditures in the three categories on individual goods and groups of goods such as food, housing, and transportation (see Table 2.1). Because the number of households I was working with was relatively small (120), the analysis could have been done "by hand." However, using the computer made the analysis proceed more quickly and more accurately.

Writing About Culture

Ethnography, or descriptive writing about culture, is one of the main projects of cultural anthropology. Ethnographies have been categorized into several different types; two of the most distinct categories can be called realist ethnography and reflexive ethnography (Van Maanen 1988). Both types provide insights about culture.

In *realist ethnography,* authors include little material about themselves directly in the text. The author typically reports the findings in a dispassionate, third-person voice. The ethnography includes attention to the behavior of members of the culture, theoretical coverage of certain features of the culture, and usually a brief account of why the work was undertaken. The result is a description and explanation of cultural practices. Realist ethnographies attempt to present findings that any skilled and objective person would be able to discover about another culture. Most classic works by such anthropologists as Malinowski, Mead, and Radcliffe-Brown fall in the category of realist ethnography. Realist ethnography is still the predominant form of ethnography. For example, Katherine Verdery's study of economic and political change in Romania, *What Was Socialism, and What Comes Next?* (1996), is a realist ethnography. She writes about how Romanian socialism operated politically and economically and how its effects are being felt in terms of Romanian nationalism and nationalist sentiments in the postsocialist era.

In contrast, the main goal of *reflexive ethnography* is to explore the research experience itself. Reflexive ethno-

TABLE 2.1 Mean Weekly Expenditure Shares (Percentage) in Eleven Categories by Urban and Rural Expenditure Groups, Jamaica, 1983–1984

Item	Urban Group 1	Urban Group 2	Urban Group 3	Urban Total	Rural Group 1	Rural Group 2	Rural Group 3	Rural Total
Number of Households	26	25	16	67	32	30	16	78
Food	60.5	51.6	50.1	54.7	74.1	62.3	55.7	65.8
Alcohol	0.2	0.4	1.5	0.6	0.5	1.1	1.0	0.8
Tobacco	0.8	0.9	0.9	0.9	1.1	1.7	1.2	1.4
Dry Goods	9.7	8.1	8.3	8.7	8.8	10.2	14.3	10.5
Housing	7.3	11.7	10.3	9.7	3.4	5.7	3.9	4.4
Fuel	5.4	6.0	5.0	5.6	3.7	3.9	4.1	3.9
Transportation	7.4	8.2	12.4	8.9	3.0	5.3	7.6	4.9
Health	0.3	0.6	0.7	0.5	1.5	1.4	1.7	1.5
Education	3.5	2.8	3.1	3.2	1.2	2.1	3.0	1.9
Entertainment	0.1	0.9	1.1	0.6	0.0	0.1	0.3	0.2
Other	5.2	8.3	6.9	6.8	2.1	6.0	6.9	4.6
Total*	100.4	99.5	100.3	100.2	99.4	99.8	99.7	99.9

*Totals may not add up to 100 due to rounding.

Source: From "Social Patterns of Food Expenditure Among Low-Income Jamaicans" by Barbara D. Miller in *Papers and Recommendations of the Workshop on Food and Nutrition Security in Jamaica in the 1980s and Beyond*, ed. by Kenneth A. Leslie and Lloyd B. Rankine, 1987.

graphies are distinguished by the degree to which the authors include their fieldwork experience as an important part of the ethnography. They are characterized by highly personalized styles and findings. Reflexive ethnographers frequently use the word *I* in their writings and offer more poetically insightful perspectives than are found in a realist ethnography. An example is Vincent Crapanzano's (1980) book *Tuhami,* which explores the life history of a Moroccan man who believed he was possessed by spirits. Crapanzano interweaves the effects of his own presence and perspectives, illustrating how this type of ethnography is an interactive, intersubjective process. Crapanzano explains, "As Tuhami's interlocutor, I became an active participant in his life history. . . . Not only did my presence, and my questions, prepare him for the text he was to produce, but they produced what I read as a change of consciousness in him. They produced a change of consciousness in me, too" (11).

SPECIAL ISSUES IN FIELDWORK

This section considers some enduring and emerging issues in anthropological fieldwork. The first topic is the important matter of fieldwork ethics. No one should undertake any kind of research without training in ethical principles and careful consideration of how to protect people involved in the project from harm. The second topic is that of danger to the researcher while conducting fieldwork. Last is a topic of emerging importance: account-

ability in cultural anthropology. Our discussion of this topic includes questions of who benefits from the research and how, and in what way the research can be relevant to the people studied.

Fieldwork Ethics

Anthropology was one of the first disciplines to devise and adopt a code of ethics. Two major events in the 1950s and 1960s led cultural anthropologists to reconsider their role in research in relation to both the sponsors (or funders) of their research and the people whom they were studying. The first was the infamous "Project Camelot" of the 1950s. Project Camelot was a plan of the United States government to influence political leadership and stability in South America (Horowitz 1967). To further this goal, the United States government employed several anthropologists, who were to gather detailed information on political events and leaders in particular countries, without revealing their purpose, and then report to their sponsor (the United States government) about their findings. It is still unclear whether the anthropologists involved were completely informed about the purposes to which their data would be put.

The second major event was the Vietnam War (or the American War, as it is called in Vietnam). This brought to the forefront conflicts about government interests in ethnographic information, the role of the anthropologist, and the protection of the people studied. Two bitterly opposed positions emerged within anthropology. On one side was the view that all Americans as citizens should support the American military effort in Vietnam and that

Unity and Diversity

SEX IS A SENSITIVE TOPIC

RICHARD PARKER went to Brazil to study the historical and political aspects of *carnaval* (1991). As he explored the festival and got to know participants, he began to realize how closely linked it is to sexual symbolism and sexuality, both heterosexual and homosexual. Simultaneously, he realized how important an understanding of these topics was to a better understanding of Brazilian culture in general. As his research continued, he began to be trusted by both heterosexuals and gay men and lesbians and therefore gained access to their multiple cultural worlds. The quality of his personal relationships with his some thirty participants was the key factor in the success of the study. Parker mentions passing "a set of initial barriers," though he does not elaborate on these (177).

Parker's focus on sexual culture, in fact, supported a shared sense of breaking the rules of social decorum, something that would not arise out of a study of a less sensitive topic such as work roles or family life. Parker found that once he had gained people's trust, "informants often seemed to take a certain pleasure in being part of a project which seemed to break the rules of proper decorum . . . that while they often resisted, understandably, speaking too directly about their own sexual lives, they seemed to enjoy (and, at times, to take a positive delight in) the opportunity to speak freely about the question of sex more generally" (177).

Parker's personal skills and rapport with his informants are evident in the rich data that he collected on such taboo topics as masturbation, oral sex, and anal sex. Thus the sheer sensitivity of a topic does not always prevent its study—as long as the researcher is sensitive, too.

A participant in Carnaval in Rio de Janeiro, Brazil. Throughout the world, the celebration of Carnaval is a time of heightened merriment and display of sexuality. ■ *Think of a special event, or events, in your microcultural experience in which fun and sexuality are expressed in an "out of bounds" way. What are the characteristics of this special event?* (Source: © AFP/CORBIS)

FOOD FOR THOUGHT

Do you think that sexual behavior is a sensitive topic in all cultures? Is it in your microculture(s)?

In what ways might the Internet be changing how some people talk about sexuality?

Do you think Parker could do research on Brazilian people's sexuality through the Internet as effectively as in person—or perhaps even more effectively?

any anthropologists who had information that could help subvert communism should provide that information to the United States government. The conflicting position stated that the anthropologist's responsibility is first and always to protect the people being studied and that this responsibility takes priority over politics. Anthropologists in this position tended to oppose the United States's participation in the war and to see the people of South Vietnam as victims of Western imperialist interests. They revealed cases in which anthropological research about local leadership patterns and political affiliations had been turned over to the United States government and had resulted in military actions against those people. This

period was the most divisive in the history of American anthropology.

In 1971 the American Anthropological Association (AAA) adopted a code of ethics. It stated that the anthropologist's primary responsibility is to ensure the safety of the people being studied. By implication, individuals wishing to help their government during wartime by providing sensitive information on people that could result in the people's deaths should not do so in the role of an anthropologist. A related principle is that cultural anthropology does not condone covert or "undercover" research. The people being studied should be informed that they are being studied and should be told the purposes for which they are being studied. The principle of **informed consent** requires that the researcher fully inform the research participants of the intent, scope, and possible effects of the study and seek their consent to be in the study. Many anthropologists say that the nature of anthropological research often makes it difficult to apply the strict standards of informed consent that are used in medical settings (Fluehr-Lobban 1994). For example, people in nonliterate societies may be frightened by being asked to sign a typed document of consent that they cannot read. Given that the intent of informed consent is a good one—people should be aware of the purpose and scope and possible effects of a study involving them—each anthropologist should consider some way to achieve this goal. Holding a "town meeting" with all community members present and explaining the research project is one approach.

In presenting one's research results, whether in a book or in a film, one should make every effort to protect the anonymity of the people in the study unless they give permission for their identities to be revealed. The usual practice in writing ethnographies has been to change the name of the specific group, area, or village, blur the location, and use made-up names for individuals mentioned.

Some research topics are more sensitive than others, and some topics are sensitive to some groups and not to others (Lee and Renzetti 1993). Governments may decree that certain subjects are simply off limits for research by foreigners. Strictly speaking, an American anthropologist should abide by the AAA code of ethics guideline stating that rulings of host governments are to be respected.

Sexual behavior is a potentially sensitive research issue, more from the point of view of informants than from that of host governments. In most cultures, homosexuality is even more difficult to research than heterosexuality, because it is more likely to be taboo in terms of mainstream norms or even laws. (See the Unity and Diversity box.)

Danger in the Field

Fieldwork can involve serious physical and psychological risks to the researcher and to members of his or her family if they are also in the field. The image of "the anthropologist as hero" has muffled, to a large degree, both the physical dangers and the psychological risks of fieldwork. Dangers from the physical environment can be fatal. The slippery paths of the highlands of the Philippines caused the death in the early 1980s of Michelle Zimbalist Rosaldo, a major figure in cultural anthropology of the later twentieth century. Disease is another important risk factor.

Violence figures prominently in some recent research experiences. During the five years that Philippe Bourgois

(1995) lived in East Harlem in order to research crack culture, he witnessed a shooting outside his window, a bombing and machine-gunning of a numbers joint, a shoot-out and police car chase in front of the pizza parlor where he was eating, the aftermath of a fire-bombing of a heroin house, a dozen serious fights, and "almost daily exposure to broken-down human beings, some of them in fits of crack-induced paranoia, some suffering from delirium tremens, and others in unidentifiable pathological fits of screaming and shouting insults to all around them" (1995:32). He was rough-handled by the police several times because they could not believe that he was "just a professor" doing research, and he was mugged for the sum of $8. Bourgois's research placed him in physical danger and at psychological risk. Nevertheless, it also enabled him to gain an understanding of oppression from the inside.

Research within combat zones is another area where danger is clearly present, and the anthropologist must be especially prepared (Hoffman 2003). **Frontline anthropology,** or research conducted within zones of violent conflict, can provide important insights into topics such as the militarization of civilian lives, civilian protection, the cultural dynamics of military personnel, and the prospects for postconflict reconstruction. Frontline anthropologists require special training and experience in how to behave and survive in a conflict zone, and the most effective frontline anthropologists have, in addition to anthropology coursework, previous experience in conflict zones as workers in international aid organizations or the military.

What do we know about danger in fieldwork in supposedly normal situations? After more than twenty years of fieldwork in Southern Africa, Nancy Howell suddenly had to confront the issue of danger in the field:

> [I]t came horribly into focus for me in June 1985 when my 14-year-old son, Alex Lee, was suddenly killed and my other son, David, was injured, in a truck accident in Botswana. In the months that followed that accident, many anthropological friends and acquaintances offered information on similar and different fieldwork accidents. (1990:ix)

She pointed out to the American Anthropological Association the lack of attention to fieldwork safety. The AAA responded with financial support for her to undertake a detailed inquiry into regional variations, and types of hazards within anthropology. She devised a way to draw a sample of 311 anthropologists listed as employed in the AAA's Guide to Departments. She sent them a questionnaire asking about their gender, age, work status, health status, and work habits in the field, and she asked them to give reports of health and other hazards they had experienced in the field. Of the 311 people in the sample,

The food ration queue at an emergency clinic near Buedu, Sierra Leone. While conducting his dissertation research in war-torn Sierra Leone in 2001, Danny Hoffman combined traditional fieldwork techniques such as participant observation and interviews. But he also had to be alert to sudden danger and other risks specific to research during war. He believes anthropologists must be willing to take such risks in order to provide essential knowledge about the complex causes and consequences of war that are overlooked by war correspondents writing for the media. ■ *Do you agree or disagree with this position?* (Source: © Danny Hoffman)

236 completed the questionnaire. Regional variations appeared, Africa being the area of highest hazard rates, followed by India, Asia and the Pacific, and Latin America. Howell ends her study with recommendations about how fieldworkers can prepare themselves more effectively for risks they may face.

Accountability and Collaborative Research

The freedom of a cultural anthropologist to represent a culture as she or he perceives it is a power issue that is increasingly being brought into question, especially by indigenous peoples who read about themselves in Western ethnographies. The people whom anthropologists have traditionally studied—the nonelites of rural India, Ireland, and Papua New Guinea—are now able to read English, French, and German. They can therefore critique what has been written about their culture. Annette Weiner (1976) learned from people in the Trobriand Islands that some Trobrianders who had read sections of *Argonauts of the Western Pacific* thought that Malinowski had not gotten things right (xvi).

One of the newest directions in cultural anthropology fieldwork is the attempt to involve the study population in actively shaping the data collection and presentation. This change reflects a commitment on the part of anthropologists not to treat people as "subjects" and to consider them more as collaborators in writing culture. Anthropologists also are taking more responsibility for the effects that their work may have on the cultures they study.

KEY CONCEPTS

culture shock, p. 35
deductive research, p. 36
discourse, p. 36
emic, p. 36
etic, p. 36
fieldwork, p. 28
frontline anthropology, p. 45
Hawthorne effect, p. 36
inductive research, p. 36
informed consent, p. 45

interview, p. 37
life history, p. 37
multi-sited research, p. 29
participant observation, p. 28
qualitative research, p. 35
quantitative research, p. 35
rapport, p. 32
reflexive anthropology, or reflexivity, p. 36
triangulation, p. 39

SUGGESTED READINGS

Nigel Barley. *The Innocent Anthropologist: Notes from a Mud Hut.* New York: Henry Holt and Company, 1983. This first-person account of the author's experiences doing fieldwork among the Dowayos in Cameroon, West Africa, provides details on research permission, site selection, and adjustment challenges.

H. Russell Bernard. *Research Methods in Cultural Anthropology: Qualitative and Quantitative Approaches.* 2nd edition. Newbury Park, CA: Sage Publications, 1995. This is a sourcebook of anthropological research methods—from how to design a research project to data analysis and presentation.

Sidney C. H. Cheung. *On the South China Track: Perspectives on Anthropological Research and Teaching.* Hong Kong: Hong Kong Institute of Asia-Pacific Studies, 1998. Thirteen chapters explore aspects of anthropological research and teaching in Chinese cultures including Hong Kong, China, Taiwan, and Singapore.

Kathleen M. DeWalt and Billie R. DeWalt. *Participant Observation: A Guide for Fieldworkers.* New York: AltaMira Press, 2002. This book is a comprehensive guide to doing participant observation. It covers research design, taking field notes, data analysis, and theoretical issues.

Peggy Golde, ed. *Women in the Field: Anthropological Experiences.* 2nd edition. Berkeley: University of California Press, 1986. This text provides fifteen chapters on fieldwork by women anthropologists, including Margaret Mead's fieldwork in the Pacific, Laura Nader's fieldwork in Mexico and Lebanon, Ernestine Friedl's fieldwork in Greece, and Jean Briggs's fieldwork among the Inuit of the Canadian Arctic.

Bruce Grindal and Frank Salamone, eds. *Bridges to Humanity: Narratives on Anthropology and Friendship.* Prospect Heights, IL: Waveland Press, 1995. The fourteen chapters of this text explore the "humanistic" dimension of fieldwork, in which the anthropologist reflects on the friendships established in the field, how they contributed to the fieldwork, and how or whether they can be continued once the anthropologist leaves the field.

Joy Hendry. *An Anthropologist in Japan: Glimpses of Life in the Field*. London: Routledge, 1999. This book is a first-person account of a research project in Japan. It includes information on her original research design, how the focus changed, and how she reached unanticipated conclusions.

Choong Soon Kim, *One Anthropologist, Two Worlds: Three Decades of Reflexive Fieldwork in North America and Asia*. Knoxville: University of Tennessee Press, 2002. The author reflects on his fieldwork, conducted over thirty years, on Japanese industry in the American South and, in Korea, on families displaced by the war and partition. Korean-born and educated in the United States, Kim is of multiple cultural worlds himself.

Carolyn Nordstrom and Antonius C. G. M. Robben, eds. *Fieldwork Under Fire: Contemporary Studies of Violence and Survival*. Berkeley: University of California Press, 1995. After an introductory chapter discussing general themes, examples are provided of fieldwork experiences in dangerous situations, including Palestine, China, Sri Lanka, the United States, Croatia, Guatemala, and Ireland.

Sarah Pink, *Doing Visual Ethnography: Images, Media and Representation in Research*. Thousand Oaks, CA: Sage Publications, 2001. The author considers a wide variety of topics in visual ethnography, including the role of reflexivity and subjectivity, the usefulness of visual methods, ethics, photography, video, and electronic texts.

Roger Sanjek, ed. *Fieldnotes: The Makings of Anthropology*. Ithaca, NY: Cornell University Press, 1990. This book includes sixteen chapters by cultural anthropologists on taking and using field notes in ethnographic research in diverse settings.

Lyn Shumaker. *Africanizing Anthropology: Fieldwork, Networks, and the Making of Cultural Knowledge in Central Africa*. Durham, NC: Duke University Press, 2001. This social history concerns the anthropological presence in the mid-twentieth century at the Rhodes-Livingston Institute in Northern Rhodesia (now Zambia). The author discusses major figures in British anthropology, their African research assistants, and local people's response to fieldwork within the context of expanding Western capitalism and Christian missionary work in the region.

HOW do cultural anthropologists conduct research on culture?

Cultural anthropologists conduct research by doing fieldwork and using participant observation. Fieldwork and participant observation became the cornerstones of cultural anthropology research after Malinowski's fieldwork in the Trobriand Islands during World War I. These methods emphasize the importance of living for an extended period of time with the people being studied and learning the local language.

WHAT does fieldwork involve?

The first steps in doing fieldwork include site selection, gaining rapport, and dealing with culture shock. Depending on one's theoretical perspective, specific research techniques may emphasize gathering quantitative or qualitative data. Cultural materialists tend to focus on quantitative data, whereas interpretivists gather qualitative data. Taking notes by hand has always been the hallmark of data recording, but now it is complemented by other methods, including laptop computers, photography, and audio and video recording. Data analysis and presentation, like data collection, are guided by the anthropologist's theoretical orientation and goals. Emphasis on quantitative or qualitative techniques of data collection shape the way the data are organized and presented— for example, whether statistics and tables are used or avoided. Interpretivist anthropologists attempt to present accounts that are as emic as possible, with little analysis by an outsider.

WHAT are some special issues in cultural anthropology research?

Questions of ethics have been paramount to anthropologists since the 1950s. In 1971 American anthropologists adopted a set of ethical guidelines for research to address their concern about what role, if any, anthropologists should play in research that might harm the people being studied. The first rule listed in the AAA code of ethics states that the anthropologist's primary responsibility is to maintain the safety of the people involved. Thus anthropologists should never engage in covert research and should always endeavor to explain their purpose to the people in the study and to preserve the anonymity of the location and of individuals. Special issues include the safety of anthropologists who are conducting research in dangerous conditions.

THE BIG QUESTIONS

- **WHAT** is the scope of economic anthropology?
- **WHAT** are the characteristics of the five major modes of production?
- **WHAT** are some directions of change in the five modes of production?

3

ECONOMIES AND THEIR MODES OF PRODUCTION

In August 2003, residents of Baghdad had no running water, but many new businesses with international connections sprang up, including this Internet café. *(Source: Maxim Marmur/AFP/Gety Images)*

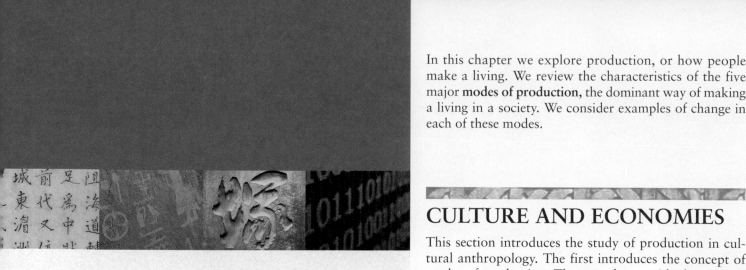

For thousands of years of human life, people made their living by gathering food and other basic necessities from nature. Everyone had equal access to life-sustaining resources. We now live in a rather different cultural world. A woman in Florida recently established the name of the Yanomami, an Amazonian tribe who live in the rain forest in Venezuela, for a web site address. She was auctioning *http://www.yanomami.com* for $25,000.

When leaders of the Yanomami people heard about this, they were not happy. In order to use their own tribal name for their site, they would have to buy it. Private property has moved into the virtual realm. Economic anthropology, which is the cross-cultural study of economic systems. Economic systems include three major areas: production, or making goods or money; consumption, or using up goods or money; and exchange, or the transfer of goods or money between people or institutions.

Cultural anthropologists have long studied economic systems cross-culturally. In this globalizing world, they have to study much more: the new global economy, e-commerce, and how these changes affect economic systems that have existed for thousands of years.

In this chapter we explore production, or how people make a living. We review the characteristics of the five major **modes of production,** the dominant way of making a living in a society. We consider examples of change in each of these modes.

CULTURE AND ECONOMIES

This section introduces the study of production in cultural anthropology. The first introduces the concept of modes of production. These modes provide the conceptual foundation for all the material that appears in subsequent chapters of this book, so you must know them well. Second, this section initiates a discussion of how global economic change in recent years, especially the spread of capitalism, is affecting local forms of production and how cultural anthropologists study such changes.

Typologies: Modes of Production

In their study of production cross-culturally, cultural anthropologists have gathered rich data that are then placed into analytical categories called modes of production. Categorizing a certain society as having a particular mode of production implies an emphasis on that type of production and does not mean that it is the only kind of production undertaken. In a given society, not everyone will necessarily be involved in the dominant mode of production. Also, a particular individual may be involved in more than one; for example, a person could be both a farmer and a herder. In most cultures, however, a dominant mode of production exists that analysts use as a basis for classification. These categories blend with and overlap each other, but they are nonetheless useful as broad generalizations.

The modes of production are discussed in order of their historical appearance in the human record (see Figure 3.1). This continuum does not mean that a particular mode of production evolves into the one following it—for example, foragers do not necessarily transform into horticulturalists—and so on, across the continuum. Nor does this ordering imply any kind of judgment about level of sophistication or superiority of the more recent modes of production. Even the oldest system involves complex and detailed knowledge about the environment that a contemporary city dweller, if transported to a rain forest, would find difficult to learn as a basis for survival. None of these systems of production is frozen in time, for they have all undergone change and indeed are still changing.

FIGURE 3.1 **Modes of Production**

FORAGING	HORTICULTURE	PASTORALISM	AGRICULTURE	INDUSTRIALISM (CAPITALIST)
Reason for Production Production for use Consumption level: low Exchange: sharing-based				**Reason for Production** Production for profit Consumption level: high Exchange: market-based
Division of Labor Family-based Overlapping gender roles				**Division of Labor** Class-based High degree of occupational specialization
Property Relations Egalitarian and collective				**Property Relations** Stratified and private
Resource Use Extensive and temporary				**Resource Use** Intensive and expanding
Sustainability High degree				**Sustainability** Low degree

Links: Globalization and the World Economy

The spread of Western capitalism in recent centuries has had far-reaching effects on modes of production that it meets. The intensification of global trade created a global division of labor, or world economy, in which countries compete unequally for a share of the wealth (Wallerstein 1979). The modern world-system is stratified into three major areas: core, peripheral, and semiperipheral. Core areas monopolize the most profitable activities of the division of labor, such as the high-tech service, manufacturing, and financial activities, and they have the strongest governments, which play a dominating role in the affairs of other countries. Peripheral areas are stuck with the least profitable activities, including the production of raw materials, foodstuffs, and labor-intensive goods and import high-tech goods and services from other areas. They tend to have weak governments and are dominated, either directly or indirectly, by core country governments and policies. Semiperipheral areas stand in the middle with a mixture of wealth and power.

According to this analysis, all areas are equally interdependent in the division of labor, but the benefits that accrue from their specialized roles are highly unequal. Core states, with about 20 percent of the system's population, control 80 percent of the system's wealth and put out 80 percent of world pollution. In the political sphere, the core states have increased their economic power and influence through international organizations such as the World Trade Organization (WTO), which forces "free trade" policies on peripheral countries and appears to be yet another mechanism that intensifies the unequal division of labor and wealth.

This chapter examines several modes of production that, over many centuries, have been variously but increasingly affected by the capitalist logic of commodity production for markets for ceaseless capital accumulation.

MODES OF PRODUCTION

While reading this section, bear in mind that most anthropologists are uneasy about typologies because they often don't reflect the rich reality that ethnographic research presents. This scheme is presented as a way to help you organize the vast amount of ethnographic information this book will present to you.

Foraging

Foraging is based on using food that is available in nature, provided by gathering, fishing, or hunting. It is the oldest economic system, having existed since the appearance of *Homo sapiens* around 100,000 years ago, perhaps earlier. Foraging has thus survived as the predominant mode of production for 90 percent (or more) of human existence. Foraging is now in danger of extinction as a "pure" form. Very few people—roughly a quarter of a million people—support themselves predominantly from foraging. European colonialism and contemporary economic globalization have drastically changed their lifeways. Foragers now are mostly located in what are considered marginal areas, such as deserts, the circumpolar region, and dense tropical forest regions.

Successful foraging requires sophisticated knowledge of the natural environment: how to find particular roots buried deep in the ground, how to follow animal tracks and other signs, and how to judge the weather and water supply. It also relies on a diverse set of tools to aid in the processing of wild foods, including nutcrackers, seed-grinders, and cooking containers. Depending on the environment, the main activities of foraging include gathering such food as nuts, berries, roots, honey, insects, and eggs; trapping or hunting birds and animals; and fishing. Tools include digging sticks for removing roots from the ground and for penetrating the holes dug by animals in order to get the animals out, bows and arrows, spears, nets, and knives. Baskets are important for carrying foodstuffs. For processing raw materials into edible food, foragers use stones to mash, grind, and pound. Meat can be dried in the sun or over fire, and fire is used for cooking either by boiling or by roasting. Obtaining and processing food requires few nonrenewable fuel sources beyond wood or other combustible substances for cooking.

Foraging is an **extensive strategy,** a mode of production involving temporary use of large areas of land and much spatial mobility. Before being contained in reservations and settled into agricultural contexts, the Ju/wasi of southern Africa moved several times during a year, depending on the seasonal availability of water sources. Each cluster of families would return to "their" territory, reconstructing or completely rebuilding their shelters with sticks for frames and leaf or thatch coverings. Sometimes the shelters were attached to two or three small trees or bushes for support. Among the Ju/wasi, the amount of investment of time, labor, and material in constructing shelters is modest.

In contrast to foragers of temperate climates, such as the Ju/wasi, those of the circumpolar regions of North America, Europe, and Asia have to devote more time and energy to obtaining food and providing shelter. The specialized technology of circumpolar peoples includes spears, nets, and knives, as well as sleds and the use of domesticated animals to pull them. Dogs or other animals that are used to pull sleds are an important aspect of circumpolar peoples' economic technology. (See the

During a time of food shortage in 1999, a Sudanese mother and her daughter collect leaves to eat. ■ *What knowledge and skills would people require to obtain "famine foods" in such circumstances? How capable would* you *be of foraging for food in a similar situation?* (Source: © Reuters/George Mulala/Archive Photos)

Unity and Diversity box on page 56.) Considerable amounts of labor are needed to construct durable igloos or permanent log houses, which are necessary adaptations to the cold temperatures. Protective clothing, including warm coats and boots, is another feature of circumpolar economic adaptation.

Division of Labor

Among foraging peoples, occupational specialization (assigning particular tasks to particular individuals) exists to varying degrees and depends mainly on gender and age. Among temperate foraging cultures, a minimal gender-based division of labor exists. People get the majority of their food by gathering roots, berries, grubs, small birds and animals, and fish. One difference is that when hunting is done, men are more likely to be involved in long-range expeditions to hunt large animals. However, hunting large animals provides only a small portion of the diets of temperate-climate foragers. In contrast, hunting large animals (including seals, whales, and bears) and capturing large fish is important in circumpolar groups, and gender-based specialization is therefore more marked.

Many anthropologists have emphasized a "Man the Hunter" model for prehistoric humans and contemporary foragers in general (for example, Lee 1979). This view takes men's hunting roles in some foraging groups and uses them as the model for all foraging groups. Early cultural anthropologists used these roles as the basis for theories about patterns of male dominance in the past and the present. Comparative studies of foragers around the world, however, indicate that greater male involvement in hunting is found in more depleted and resource-limited environments (Hiatt 1970). The implication is that men's hunting of large game is an adaptation to increasing resource scarcity in recent times and thus was not necessarily common throughout the long history of foraging.

In contrast to the "Man the Hunter" model, some cultural anthropologists have proposed a "Woman the Gatherer" model (Slocum 1975). This model makes more sense, because the bulk of everyday food in most foraging systems came from gathering, the primary work of women. Among the Ju/wasi, women's gathering provided 75 to 80 percent of the diet, and large game provided by men accounted for the rest. In some cultures, women have roles in hunting game similar to those of men, as among the Agta of the Philippines (Estioko-Griffin 1986; Estioko-Griffin, Goodman, and Griffin 1985). Among the Agta, some women go hunting while other women stay at the camp caring for the small children—thus disproving the proposition that women's maternal roles universally prevent them from hunting. Most cultural anthropologists now agree that the "Man the Hunter" model is an example of male bias in interpretation. Yet "Man the Hunter" lives on in much popular thinking and is perpetuated through textbook images and museum displays (Gifford-Gonzalez 1993).

Age is a basis for task allocation in all societies because children and the aged generally spend less time in food provision. In foraging societies, both boys and girls perform various tasks that North Americans would label as "work," particularly gathering food. Among the Ju/wasi, young boys begin practicing hunting skills through the games they play with small bows and arrows. They gradually take on more adult skills as they mature. Among the Agta of the Philippines, both girls and boys learn to hunt along with their mothers.

Property Relations

The concept of private property, in the sense of owning something that can be sold to someone else, does not exist in foraging societies. Instead, the term **use right** is more appropriate. It means that a person or group has socially recognized priority in access to particular resources such as gathering areas, hunting and fishing areas, and water holes. This access is willingly shared with others by permission. Among the Ju/wasi, family groups are known to control access to particular water holes and the territory surrounding them (Lee 1979: 58–60). Visiting groups are welcome and will be given food and water. In turn, the host group, at another time, will visit other camps and be offered hospitality there. In India's Andaman Islands, each family group controls a known offshore area for fishing, and sharing is a common practice if permission has been given. Encroaching on someone else's area without permission is a serious misdemeanor that could result in violence. In foraging groups, use rights are generally invested in the collective group and passed down equally to all children who are members of the group.

Foraging as a Sustainable System

When untouched by outside influences and with abundant land available, foraging systems are sustainable, which means that crucial resources are regenerated over time in balance with the demand that the population makes on them. One island in India's Andaman Islands provides a clear case because its inhabitants have lived in a "closed" system. The few hundred Andamanese on Sentinel Island, which has never been entered by outsiders, have maintained their lifestyle within a fairly limited area since earliest observations of them in the late nineteenth century.

One reason for the sustainability of foraging is that foragers' needs are modest. Some anthropologists have typified the foraging lifestyle as the "original affluent

HARE INDIANS OF NORTHWEST CANADA AND THE IMPORTANCE OF DOGS

SEVENTY-FIVE Hare Indians live in the community of Colville Lake in Canada's Northwest Territories (Savishinsky 1974). They survive by hunting, trapping, and fishing in one of the harshest environments in the world. Joel Savishinsky's major research interest was to analyze the experience of stress, tension, and anxiety among this isolated group and observe how they cope with it. Ecological stress factors include "extreme temperatures, long and severe winters, prolonged periods of isolation, hazardous weather and travel conditions, an often precarious food supply, and the constant need for mobility during the harshest seasons of the year" (xiv). Social and psychological stress factors also exist, including contact with White fur traders and missionaries.

Savishinsky discovered the importance of dogs in relation to the economy and the people's psychological well-being:

> [L]ater in the year when I obtained my own dogteam, I enjoyed much greater freedom of movement, and was able to camp with many people whom I had previously not been able to keep up with. Altogether I travelled close to 600 miles by dogsled between mid-October and early June. This constant contact with dogs, and the necessity of learning how to drive, train and handle them, led to my recognition of the social and psychological, as well as the ecological, significance of these animals in the lives of the people. (xx)

Among the 14 households, there are a total of 224 dogs. Some households have as many as 4 teams, with an average of 6 dogs per team, corresponding to people's estimation that 6 dogs are required for travel. More than being only economically useful, dogs play a significant role in people's emotional lives. They are a frequent topic of conversation: "Members of the community constantly compare and comment on the care, condition, and growth of one another's animals, noting special qualities of size, strength, color, speed, and alertness" (169). Emotional displays, uncommon among the Hare, are significant between people and their dogs:

> The affectionate and concerned treatment of young animals is participated in by people of all ages, and

Hare Indian children use their family's sled to haul drinking water to their village. ■ *What tasks are children responsible for in a microculture that you know?* (Source: Joel Savishinsky)

the nature of the relationship bears a striking resemblance to the way in which people treat young children. Pups and infants are, in essence, the only recipients of unreserved positive affect in the band's social life, all other relationships being tinged with varying degrees of restraint and/or negativism. (169–170)

FOOD FOR THOUGHT

Think of another culture in which animals are a focus of intense human interest. Which animals are important in what ways and to whom in that culture?

Do you know of a culture in which people have no interest in animals?

society" because needs are satisfied with minimal labor efforts. This term is used metaphorically to indicate that foraging economies should not be dismissed as poor and inadequate attempts at making a living. That is an ethnocentric judgment made from the perspective of a consumer culture with different economic and social values. In the 1960s, when the Ju/wasi of the Kalahari desert were still a foraging system, their major food source was the mongongo nut, which was so abundant that there was never a shortage (Howell 1986). In addition, hundreds of species of plants and animals were considered edible. Yet the people were thin and often complained of hunger, year round. Their thinness may be an adaptation to seasonal fluctuations in food supply. Rather than maximizing food intake during times of plenty, they minimize it. Mealtime is not an occasion for stuffing oneself with treats until there is no room for anything more. Ju/wasi culture taught that one should have a hungry stomach, even in the midst of plentiful food.

Because foragers' needs for goods are not great, minimal labor efforts are required to satisfy them. Foragers typically work fewer hours a week than the average employed North American. In traditional (undisturbed) foraging societies, people spend as few as five hours a week collecting food or making and repairing tools, so they have more leisure time for activities such as storytelling, playing games, and resting. Foraging people also traditionally enjoyed good health records. During the 1960s, the age structure and health status of the Ju/wasi compared well with those of the United States of around 1900—without any modern medical facilities (Lee 1979:47–48). They were a "healthy and vigorous population with a low incidence of infections and degenerative diseases."

Horticulture

Both horticulture and pastoralism emerged only within the last several thousand years of human existence. Each mode of production involves a dependence on the **domestication** of plants and animals, or their control by humans in terms of both their location and their reproduction. No one is sure when and where domestication first occurred or whether the domestication of plants and animals occurred at the same time or sequentially. Some evidence indicates that plant domestication came first.

Horticulture is a mode of production based on the cultivation of domesticated crops in gardens using hand tools. It emerged around 12,000 BCE in the Middle East, China, and Africa. A horticultural economy is based mainly on food crops that people plant and harvest. The food grown in gardens is often supplemented by foraging

for wild foods and trading with pastoralists for animal products. Horticulture is still practiced by many thousands of people mainly in sub-Saharan Africa; South and Southeast Asia, including the Pacific island of Papua New Guinea; Central and South America; and some parts of the Caribbean islands. Prominent horticultural crops include yams, corn, beans, grains such as millet and sorghum, and several types of roots, all of which are rich in protein, minerals, and vitamins.

Horticulture involves the use of hand-held tools, such as digging sticks, hoes, and carrying baskets. Rain is the sole source of moisture. Horticulture requires rotation of garden plots in order to allow used areas to regenerate and thus is also termed "shifting cultivation." Average plot sizes are less than 1 acre, and 2.5 acres can support a family of five to eight members for a year. Yields are sufficient to support semipermanent village settlements of 200 to 250 people. Overall population density per square mile is low because horticulture, like foraging, is a land-extensive strategy. But horticulture is more labor-intensive than foraging because of the energy required for plot preparation and food processing. Horticulturalists supplement their diets by fishing or hunting, or both, and they may trade with nearby foragers.

Anthropologists distinguish five phases in the horticultural cycle:

- *Clearing:* A section of the forest is cleared, partially or completely, by cutting down trees and brush and then setting the area on fire to burn off other growth. This burning creates a layer of ash that is rich fertilizer. The term "slash and burn cultivation" refers to the two stages of cutting and burning.

- *Planting:* This is accomplished with a digging stick to loosen the soil, into which seeds or slips of plants are placed, or through the broadcasting method of scattering the seeds by hand over the ground.

- *Weeding:* Weeds are a minor problem because of the ash cover and shady growing conditions.

- *Harvesting:* This phase requires substantial labor to cut or dig crops and carry them to the residential area.

- *Fallowing:* After cultivating the same garden plot for a certain number of years (which varies depending on the environment and the type of crop grown), the land must be left unused for a period of time so that it regains its fertility.

Surpluses in food supply are possible in horticulture. These surpluses enable trade relationships to increase and cause greater affluence for some people. In some cases, horticulture was the foundation for complex civilizations—for example, in Central Africa and in the Mayan civilization of Central America.

Division of Labor

As with foraging, no class differences exist in horticultural societies. A family of husband, wife, and children forms the core work group for cultivation, but groups of men form for hunting and fishing expeditions, and women often work in collective groups for food processing. Gender is the key factor structuring the organization of labor, with male and female work roles often being clearly differentiated. Most commonly, men do the clearing, and men and women plant and tend the staple crops that are the basis of the people's everyday diets. This pattern exists in Papua New Guinea, much of Southeast Asia, and parts of West and East Africa.

Diet is often supplemented through hunting, primarily by men. In rural Malawi, in southern Africa, for example, hunting is strictly associated with men, whereas food crops are women's responsibility (Morris 1998). In some horticultural societies, women grow the staple crops and men grow the "prestige foods" used in ritual feasts. In these contexts, men tend to have higher public status than women. Two unusual horticultural cases involve extremes in terms of gender roles and status. The first involves the pre-contact Iroquois Indians of central New York State (Brown 1975). Iroquois women cultivated maize, the most important food crop, and they controlled its distribution. This control meant that they were able to decide whether the men would go to war, because a war effort depended on the supply of maize to support it. A contrasting example is that of the Yanomami Indians of the Venezuelan Amazon (Chagnon 1992). Yanomami men clear the fields and tend and harvest the crops. They also do much of the cooking for ritual feasts. Yanomami women, though, are not idle. They play an important role in providing the staple food that comes from manioc, a starchy root crop that requires substantial processing work—it has to be soaked for a long time to remove toxins and then scraped into a mealy consistency. Among the Yanomami, women's status is very low.

We have no simple explanation why different divisions of labor in horticulture emerge, but their differences have clear implications for gender status (Sanday 1973). Cross-cultural, comparative analysis of many horticultural societies shows that women's contribution to food production is a necessary but not sufficient basis for status. In other words, if women do not contribute to producing food, their status will be low. If they do contribute, their status may be high—but it may not be. The critical factor appears to be control over the distribution of what is produced, perhaps especially its public distribution beyond the family. Slavery is a prime illustration of a contribution to production that does not bring high status because a slave has no control over the product.

Children do much productive work in horticultural societies, perhaps more than in any other type of econ-

Cassava, also called manioc, is a root crop grown extensively in western Africa. Here, a man displays his crop in Niger. Cassava and millet, a grain, are the staple foods for many West Africans. ■ *Do research to learn about growing cassava and millet, how they are prepared for eating, and what they contribute to nutrition.* (Source: © Charles O. Cecil)

omy. A comparative research project, the "Children of Six Cultures" study (Whiting and Whiting 1975), examined children's roles in different modes of production. Children among the Gusii of Kenya, horticulturalists, performed more tasks at younger ages than children in the other cultures. Both boys and girls were responsible for caring for siblings, fetching fuel, and hauling water. The reason why horticultural societies involve children in "responsible" tasks more than other societies is that in most horticultural societies, adult women's time allocation to work is very high and children's labor serves as a replacement in the domestic domain.

Property Relations

As in foraging societies, the concept of private property as something that an individual can own and sell is not found in horticultural societies. Use rights are important and more clearly defined than in foraging societies. By clearing and planting an area of land, an individual puts a claim on it and its produce. With the production of surplus goods, the possibility of social inequality in access to goods and resources emerges. Rules about group sharing may decline or even disappear as some people gain access to higher status.

Horticulture as a Sustainable System

Crop rotation and fallowing are crucial factors in the sustainability of horticulture. Crop rotation varies the demands made on the soil. Fallowing allows the plot to rest completely and recover its nutrients. It also promotes soil quality and helps prevent compaction by allowing the growth of weeds, whose root systems help keep the soil loose. Once the fallow period is over, the weeds are burned off, providing a layer of ash that serves as a rich source of natural fertilizer. The benefits of a well-managed system of shifting cultivation are clear.

A major constraint in horticulture is the time required for fallowing in situations of pressure on the land. In general, seven years or more of fallow time are required for a year of cultivation. Reducing fallowing time quickly brings negative consequences, including depletion of soil nutrients and soil erosion. Several factors contribute to overuse of plots that should be left fallow (Blaikie 1985):

- Reduced access to land as a consequence of incursions from ranchers, miners, farmers, tourists
- Government pressure on horticulturalists to intensify production for cash in order to pay taxes and other fees
- Interest of horticulturalists in boosting production for cash in order to buy manufactured commodities.
- Pressure from population growth when outmigration is not an option

The last factor, population growth, is often blamed as the sole culprit, but often it is not involved at all. For example, in one case in eastern India, the major causes of land degradation were heavy government taxes and growing indebtedness to merchants in the plains:

> Up to thirty years ago, the hill area occupied by the Sora was covered by dense jungle, while today the hillsides are near-deserts of raw red soil. Shifting agriculture is practised with only three to four year fallow periods, as opposed to over ten years some generations ago. The population has grown only slowly, and certainly at a much slower rate than the rapidly increased destruction of the environment might suggest. (Blaikie 1985:128)

Pastoralism

Pastoralism is a mode of production based on the domestication of animal herds and the use of their products, such as meat and milk, for 50 percent or more of the diet. Pastoralism has long existed in the "old world"—Europe, Africa, and Asia, notably in regions where rainfall is limited and unpredictable. In the Western hemisphere, before the arrival of the Spanish in the fifteenth century, the only indigenous herding system existed in the Andean region and involved llamas. Sheep, goats, horses, and cattle became prominent after the Spanish conquest (Barfield 2001). Some Native American groups, especially in the southwestern United States, still rely on herding animals. Pastoralists raise a limited variety of animals. The six most popular species are sheep, goats, cattle, horses, donkeys, and camels. Three others have more restricted distribution: yaks at high altitudes in Asia, reindeer in northern sub-Arctic regions, and llamas in highland South America. Many pastoralists keep dogs for protection and for help with herding. Pastoralism can succeed in a variety of environments, depending on the animal involved. For example, reindeer herding is done in the circumpolar regions of Europe and Asia, and cattle and goat herding is common in India and Africa.

Pastoralism is geared to providing daily food, primarily milk and milk products. Thus, this mode of production is limited in what it can provide, so pastoralist groups forge trade links with settled groups. In this way, they secure food and other goods that they cannot produce themselves, particularly grains and manufactured items such as cooking pots, in return for their animals, hides, and other animal products. Pastoralism may seem to resemble contemporary large-scale ranching operations, but in fact, ranches resemble modern industry more than traditional pastoralism (Fratkin, Galvin, and Roth 1994; Loker 1993). The primary purpose of ranching is to provide meat for sale, whereas pastoralism provides many animal products. Also, pastoralism involves the movement of animals to pasture, whereas ranching moves the fodder to the animals.

A common problem for all pastoralists is the continued need for fresh pasture for their animals. This need makes pastoralism, like foraging and horticulture, an extensive form of economic adaptation. Herds must move or else the pasture area will become depleted. A useful distinction between pastoralists is whether they move their herds for short or long distances (Fratkin, Galvin, and Roth 1994). The Nuer are an example of short-distance herders. E. E. Evans-Pritchard's (1965 [1947]) classic study describes the Nuer, cattle herders of Sudan in the late 1930s. Depending on the availability of water, the Nuer spent part of the year in settled villages and part in temporary camps. Cows provided food for the Nuer from their milk, meat, and blood (the Nuer, and other pastoralists, extract blood from the cow's neck, which they then drink). Cows also furnished hides, horn, and other materials for everyday use and were the medium of exchange for marriage and payment of fines. The importance of cattle is reflected in the Nuer's detailed vocabulary for cattle on the basis of their colors and markings.

Pastoralist systems vary greatly in their level of wealth and in the degree of political organization among groups. Environmental setting seems to explain much of this variation. The Qashqa'i of Iran are long-distance sheep herders and camel drivers (Beck 1986). Iran is lush, with a rich and varied natural resource base that supports agriculture and urban centers, including the city of Shiraz. The nomadic pastoralism of the Qashqa'i involves seasonal migration to remote pastures separated by about three hundred miles. Long-distance herding makes the Qashqa'i vulnerable to raids and requires negotiation with settlements along the way for permission to cross their land. This vulnerability prompted them to develop a confederacy of tribes into a centralized political organization for protection. In areas with fewer resources and sparser settlements, such as Mongolia in Central Asia and the circumpolar region, pastoralist groups are less politically organized and less wealthy than the Qashqa'i.

Labor

Families and clusters of related families are the basic unit of production. Gender is an important factor in the allocation of work. In many pastoralist cultures, little overlap exists between male and female tasks. Men are in charge of the herding activities—moving the animals from place to place. Women are responsible for processing the herd's products, especially the milk. A cultural emphasis on masculinity characterizes many herding populations. Traditional reindeer herding among the Sami of Finland was connected to male identity (Pelto 1973). The definition of being a man was to be a reindeer herder. As traditional herding declined and men no longer made their living from herding, they had to redefine their sense of identity.

Among the Ariaal, herders of Kenya, men are in charge of herding camels. ■ *Why do you think an adult man is in charge of these baby camels?* (Source: Elliott Fratkin)

In contrast, women are the predominant herders among the Navajo of the American Southwest. Navajo men traditionally had little to do with herding the sheep. Instead, their major role is crafting silver jewelry.

The size of the animal involved appears to be a factor in the gender division of labor. Women are often herders of smaller animals, perhaps because smaller animals need to graze less widely and can be kept penned near the house. Men tend the animals that are pastured farther away. This distinction between men's wider spatial range than women's is further accentuated in many agricultural systems.

Children play important roles in tending herds. Among the cattle-herding Maasai of Kenya and Tanzania, parents prefer to have many children so that they can help with the herds. Before boys in these pastoralist societies advance to the "warrior" stage, beginning around adolescence, their main task is herding.

Property Relations

The most important forms of property among pastoralists are animals, housing (such as tents or yerts), and domestic goods (rugs, cooking ware). Use rights regulate pasture land and migratory routes. Some sense of private property exists with animals, because they may be traded by the family head for other goods. A family's tent or yert is also their own. However, no private rights in land or travel routes exist; instead, these are generally accepted informal agreements. Many pastoral societies emphasize male ownership of the herds, and sons inherit herds from their fathers. In other societies, such as the sheepherding

Girls are in charge of herding water buffaloes to the Ganges River, at Varanasi, India, for watering. ■ *What knowledge might these girls have to possess in order to do their job?* (Source: Barbara Miller)

Navajo of the southwestern United States, women are the primary herders and the herds pass from mother to daughter.

Pastoralism as a Sustainable System

Pastoralism is a highly extensive system, requiring that groups be able to range widely with their herds in search of grass and water. Pastoralists have been able to develop sustainable cultures in extremely limited environments; an example is the Mongolian herders, who created a vast and powerful empire. Thus pastoralism can be a highly successful and sustainable economic adaptation that functions complementarily with other economic systems. As with horticulture, however, when outside forces begin to squeeze the space available for migration, overexploitation of the environment results, and pastoralism is then accused of depleting the environment. Outside pressure, including national interests bent on sedentarizing (settling down) pastoralists so that they will be easier to tax, and commercial interests that covet pastoralists' land, threaten the sustainability of pastoralism.

Agriculture

Compared to horticulture, agriculture is an **intensive strategy** of production. Intensification involves new techniques that allow the same land to be used repeatedly without losing its fertility. Key inputs include more labor power for weeding, use of natural and chemical fertilizers, and control of water supply. The earliest agricultural systems are documented from the time of the Neolithic period, beginning around 10,000 BCE in the Tigris-Euphrates valley, India, and China. Agricultural systems now exist on all continents except Antarctica.

Agriculture involves the use of domesticated animals for plowing, transportation, and organic fertilizer—manure or composted materials. It also relies on irrigation as a source of water and on the construction of elaborate terraces and other ways of increasing the amount of land available for cultivation. Like the modes of production we have already considered, agriculture involves complex local forms of knowledge about the environment, including plant varieties, pest management, precipitation patterns, and soil types. Anthropologists refer to this knowledge as **indigenous knowledge** (IK) to distinguish it from Western, scientific knowledge. As long-standing agricultural traditions are increasingly displaced by methods introduced from the outside, indigenous knowledge is threatened. It is in danger of becoming extinct, along with the cultures and languages associated with it. Many anthropologists are now actively involved in recording indigenous knowledge as a resource for the future (see the Lessons Applied box on page 63).

Permanent homes, investment in private property, and increased yields all promote larger family size as a way of further increasing production through the use of household labor. Population density increases substantially in agricultural societies, and urban centers of thousands of people develop. Occupational specialization increases. Instead of people repairing their own tools and weapons, some people take on this work as a full-time job and no longer grow their own food but become dependent on trading their skills for food with farmers. Other specializations that emerge as full-time occupations are political leaders, religious leaders or priests, healers, artisans, potters, musicians, and traders. Three major types of agriculture are described here (see Figure 3.2 on page 62).

Family Farming

Over a billion people, or about one-sixth of the world's population, belong to households involved in family farming (formerly termed "peasant agriculture"). In family farming, farmers "produce much of their own subsistence as well as some food or fiber to sell, supplying labor largely from their own households, and possessing continuing, heritable rights to their own resources" (Netting 1989:221). Family farming is always part of a larger market economic system (Wolf 1966a:8). It is found throughout the world but is more prevalent in primarily agrarian countries such as Mexico, India, Poland, and Italy than in more industrialized countries. Family farmers exhibit much cross-cultural variety. They may be full-time or part-time farmers; they may be more or less closely linked to urban markets; and they may or may not grow cash crops such as coffee or sugar cane. Major tasks include plowing, planting seeds and cuttings, weeding, caring for terraces and irrigation systems, harvesting, and processing.

Division of Labor   The family is the basic unit of production. Gender and age are important factors around which productive roles are organized. A marked gender-based division of labor characterizes most family farm economies. Cross-cultural analysis of gender roles in forty-six cultures revealed that men perform the "bulk" of the labor in more than three-fourths of the sample (Michaelson and Goldschmidt 1971). The few societies in which females were found to predominate in agriculture were located in Southeast Asia. Men work more hours in agricultural production than in the previous systems considered, and women's work tends to be more devoted to activities near the home, such as processing food and child care (Ember 1983). This division of labor is the basis of the **public/private dichotomy** in family farm societies, in which men are more involved with the public world and women are increasingly involved in activities in or near the home.

Analysis of time allocation data for men and women in horticultural and agricultural societies reveals that both men's and women's work hours are substantially higher in agricultural economies, but in differing proportions for inside and outside work (Ember 1983). Women's contribution to production is not less in agriculture. Instead, the shares of time devoted to particular activities shift. Women's inside work hours increase absolutely and relatively (compared to men's), and their outside work hours increase absolutely but decline relative to those of men.

Why do many family farm agricultural systems increase men's workloads and increase women's involvement in the domestic domain? One hypothesis is based on the importance of plowing fields in preparation for planting and the fact that plowing is almost exclusively a male task (Goody 1976). Some anthropologists argue that men plow because they are stronger than women or have the advantage of greater "aerobic capacity" (the ability of the circulatory system to nourish the blood through processing air). In south-central India, weather patterns require that plowing be accomplished in a very narrow time band (Maclachlan 1983). Assigning the task to the physically stronger gender ensures that the work can be done more quickly. This is thus an adaptive strategy because it optimizes chances for a good crop. Another hypothesis is that women are not involved with plowing and other fieldwork because such tasks are incompatible with child care (J. K. Brown 1970).

Yet another view emphasizes that agriculture increases the demand for labor within and near the house (Ember 1983). Winnowing, husking, grinding, and cooking of agricultural products such as rice are extremely labor-intensive. The high demand for family labor in agriculture prompts people to want many children, so child care becomes a more demanding task that is relegated to women. As women become isolated within their households, they are less able to depend on labor contributions from other women than in modes of production where women live and work collectively.

FIGURE 3.2   Characteristics of Three Forms of Agriculture

	Family Farming	Industrial Capital Agriculture	Industrial Collectivized Agriculture
Labor Inputs	Kin-based	Hired, impersonal	Communal
Capital Inputs	Low-moderate	High	Moderate-High
Sustainability	High	Low	Low-Moderate

Lessons Applied

THE GLOBAL NETWORK OF INDIGENOUS KNOWLEDGE RESOURCE CENTERS

IN 1992 the United Nations Conference on Environment and Development, held in Rio de Janeiro, first promoted global awareness of the complementary relationships between indigenous knowledge about the environment and biodiversity (Warren 2001). Scholars had long recognized the links (Scott 1998), but its official recognition in 1992 led to action directed at preserving and promoting IK in order to prevent loss of biodiversity. Cultural anthropologists have documented IK about agriculture in matters such as emic classification of soil types, what kinds of foods grow best in what contexts, how to mix crop plantings effectively, and how to prevent pests from destroying crops. Studies also reveal that IK is microculturally variable: Men know some things, women know other things, and the young and old have different kinds of IK, as do members of different economic niches within the same cultural area. All these varying "knowledges" need to be documented as part of indigenous cultural/agricultural heritage, because they have local specificity and validity that outside systems often lack.

An effort is now under way to link universities and agricultural research laboratories worldwide in order to support IK data collection and documentation. Over thirty IK resource centers exist, housing computerized databases of case studies and ethnographic reports. Coordination among the centers is leading to improved guidelines and recommendations about data recording, archiving, and sharing. All of these practices are aimed at both preserving the knowledge for the future and providing wider access to it. Although the primary goal of the project is to support biodiversity, it will have the effect of supporting cultural diversity as well.

FOOD FOR THOUGHT

This global information network will clearly help inform agricultural policy makers, but how will it benefit the people whose knowledge is being recorded and preserved in the databanks?

In family farms in the United States, husbands are primarily responsible for daily farm operations, while wives' participation ranges from equal to that of husbands to minimal (Barlett 1989:271–273). Women do run farms in the United States, but generally only when they are divorced or widowed. Wives are usually responsible for managing the domestic domain. On average, women's daily work hours are 25 percent more than those of men. A new trend is for family farm women to take salaried jobs off the farm to help support the farm. Children in the United States are not formally employed in farm work, but many family farms rely on children's contributions on weekends and during summer vacations. Amish farm families rely to a significant extent on contributions from all family members (Hostetler and Huntington 1992).

In other family farming systems, females play an equal role or even a more important role than males in agricultural production and distribution. Such "female farming systems" are numerically fewer than male farming systems. Most are found in Southeast Asia, a region where wet rice agriculture is practiced. This is a highly labor-intensive way of growing rice that involves start-

ing the seedlings in nurseries and transplanting them to flooded fields. Males play a role in the initial plowing of the fields, but this work is less arduous than in dry-field agriculture, because the earth is wet. Women's labor and decision making are the backbone of the operations. Why women predominate in wet rice agriculture is an intriguing question (Bardhan 1974; Goody 1976; Winzeler 1974). Its consequences are clearer than its causes: Where female farming systems exist, women are more likely to own land, to play a greater role in household decision making, and to have more autonomy and higher status in general (Dyson and Moore 1983; Stivens et al. 1994).

A third variation in the gender division of labor in family farming involves complementary and balanced task allocations between males and females, with males involved in agricultural work and females involved in food processing and marketing. This form of gender division of labor is common among highland communities of Central and South America. For example, among the Zapotec Indians of southern Mexico's state of Oaxaca (pronounced Wah-haka), men grow maize, the staple crop, and cash crops—bananas, mangoes, coconuts, and

---

sesame (Chiñas 1992). Zapotec women sell produce in the town markets and make tortillas and sell them from their houses. The farming household thus derives its income from the labor of both genders working interdependently on different aspects of the production process. Male status and female status are balanced.

Children's roles in agricultural societies range from prominent to minor, depending on the context (Whiting and Whiting 1975). The Children of Six Cultures study found lower rates of child work in the North Indian and Mexican agricultural villages, compared to the horticultural village in Kenya. But in some agricultural societies, children's work rates are high, as shown through detailed observations of children's activities in two Asian villages, one in Java and the other in Nepal. In these villages, an important task of children, even as young as six to eight years old, is tending the farm animals (Nag, White, and Peet 1978), and children spend more time caring for animals than adults do. Girls aged six to eight spend more time than adults in child care. Some Javanese children in the six- to eight-year-old group work for wages. In general, girls work more hours each day than boys.

Property Relations Family farmers make substantial investments in land, such as the clearing, terracing, and fencing that are linked to the development of firmly delineated and protected property rights. Rights to land can be acquired and sold. Clear guidelines exist about inheritance and transfer of rights to land through marriage. Social institutions such as law and police emerge to protect private rights to resources. The more marked gender division of labor in many family farming systems means that men tend to have access to the more highly valued tasks and to goods that have value in the outside world. The women are more involved with food processing, childbearing and child rearing, and family maintenance—tasks that generate no income and have no exchange value.

In family farming systems where male labor and decision making predominate, women and girls tend to be excluded from land rights and other forms of property control. Conversely, in female farming systems, inheritance rules regulate the transmission of property rights more often through females. Class distinctions are more rigid, and there are greater gaps between those who have access to resources and those who do not.

Industrial Agriculture

Industrial capital agriculture produces crops through means that are capital-intensive, using machinery and inputs such as processed fertilizers instead of human and animal labor (Barlett 1989:253). It is most practiced in the United States, Canada, Germany, Russia, and Japan and is increasingly being adopted in developing nations such as India and Brazil as well as in socialist countries such as China.

Corporate Farming in the United States Industrial agriculture has brought the advent of a new subcategory of **corporate farms,** huge enterprises that produce goods solely for sale and that are owned and operated by companies that rely entirely on hired labor. Studies reveal four aspects of the evolution of industrial agriculture over the past 150 years:

- The increased use of complex technology, including machinery, chemicals, and genetic research on new plant and animal varieties. This new technology has social impacts. Replacing mules and horses with tractors for plowing in the South during the 1930s led to the eviction of small-scale sharecroppers from the land, because the landowners were able to cultivate larger units. The invention of mechanical cotton pickers prompted research on varieties of cotton that were more easily picked by machine. These innovations combined to displace field laborers.

- Increased use of **capital**—that is, wealth used in the production of more wealth, in the form of either money or property. Industrial agriculture uses the most capital per unit of production of all farming systems (Barlett 1989:260). The high ratio of capital to labor has enabled farmers to increase production, but it reduces flexibility. If a farmer invests in an expensive machine to harvest soybeans and then the price of soy-

This farmer works near a highly urbanized area of Kyoto, in Japan, where farming combines elements of industrial mechanization with intensive labor. ■ *Which features fit with industrialized agriculture? Which do not?* (Source: Barbara Miller)

Family farming in highland Ecuador. A man plows while women in the family follow, planting seed potatoes. ■ *What are some differences between this kind of farming and corporate agriculture?* (Source: © Jeremy Horner/ CORBIS)

beans drops, the farmer cannot simply switch from soybeans to a more profitable crop.

■ Increased use of energy—primarily gasoline to run the machinery and nitrates for fertilizer—to grow crops which often exceeds the calories of food energy yielded in the harvest. Calculations of how many calories of energy are used to produce a calorie of food in industrial agricultural systems reveal a high ratio of perhaps 2.5 calories of fossil fuel to harvest 1 calorie of food, and more than 6 calories are invested when processing, packaging, and transport are counted (Barlett 1989:261). Industrial agriculture is thus a less efficient mode of production than foraging, horticulture, and pastoralism.

■ Decline of the family farm. In the United States, family farms were the predominant pattern until a few decades ago. Now, experts speak of "the death of the family farm." Many family farms have fallen into debt, unable to compete with industrial farms. In Canada, foreclosure notices to family farms tripled between 1984 and 1990 (Young and Van Beers 1991).

A key difference exists between corporate farms and family farms in terms of labor force. Corporate farms depend completely on hired labor rather than on family members. Much of the labor demand in industrial agriculture is seasonal, creating an ebb and flow of workers, depending on the task and time of year. Large ranches hire seasonal cowboys for round-ups and fence mending. Crop harvesting is another high-demand point. Leo Chavez (1992) studied the lives of undocumented ("illegal") migrant laborers from Central America who work in the huge tomato, strawberry, and avocado fields owned by corporate farms in southern California. Many of the migrants are Indians from Oaxaca, Mexico. They sneak across the border to work in the United States as a way of making ends meet. In the San Diego area, they live temporarily in shantytowns, or camps. Here is what a camp, where all male workers live, is like on Sunday when the men do not go to work in the fields:

> On Sundays, the campsites take on a community-like appearance. Men bathe, and wash their clothes, hanging them on trees and bushes, or on lines strung between the trees. Some men play soccer and basketball, using a hoop someone has rigged up. Others sit on old crates or treestumps as they relax, talk, and drink beer. Sometimes the men talk about fights from the night before. With little else to do, nowhere to go, and few outsiders to talk to, the men often drink beer to pass the time on Saturday nights and Sundays. Loneliness and boredom plague them during nonworking hours. (65)

Industrial Collectivized Agriculture   Industrial collectivized agriculture is a form of industrialized agriculture that involves nonprivate control of land, technology, and goods produced. In China, Mao Tse-tung undertook a massive effort to establish collective production in China. Collectivism's basic goal was to provide for greater economic equality and a greater sense of group welfare than is possible under competitive capitalism. A variety of collective agriculture arrangements have been used, with varying degrees of success, in places such as Russia and Eastern Europe, China, Tanzania, Ethiopia, and Nicaragua. Cultural anthropology studies of collectivized agriculture are rare. This section presents some findings from a study conducted in Romania,

Migrant workers picking broccoli in Salinas, California.

■ *Compare how corporate agriculture labor is organized to that on a collective farm under Romanian socialism.* (Source: © Morton Beebe/ CORBIS)

specifically its Olt Land region, which comprises about sixty-five villages and a high degree of social homogeneity (Kideckel 1993). David Kideckel conducted fieldwork in two periods: first in 1974, during a period of optimism for socialism, and later in 1990, after the revolution that brought socialism's end.

Romanian socialism, brought in through Soviet support, was Stalinist and involved highly centralized state planning. Romania had the most comprehensive and centralized system of Eastern Europe. The state oversaw nearly every aspect of society, from university enrollments to the production of steel and tractors. Romanian agriculture was organized into state farms and collective farms. With the completion of collectivization in the early 1960s, about 30 percent of the land was in state farms, 60 percent in collectives, and 10 percent privately held. Workers on state farms were paid wages and received a small garden for their own use. Organized like a rural factory, the state farm provided services such as child care facilities and shopping centers. Collective farms, in contrast, were "ostensibly" owned and controlled by their members, who pooled land, labor, and resources. Their earnings were determined by total farm production, and their wages tended to be lower than state farm workers' wages. Collective farm workers were entitled to a "use plot" of the collective land.

Labor was separated into tasks according to whether it was manual or mental labor. Although manual laborers were elevated in state rhetoric and were more highly paid than intellectuals, intellectual work was more highly valued than manual work. In spite of the socialist rhetoric proclaiming equality among all workers, economic distinctions remained between males and females. Women were relegated to agricultural and reproductive labor, whereas rural men moved into industry. Although women were the mainstay of collective farm labor, they were underrepresented among the leadership. Nevertheless, women's increased involvement in wage earning and their roles in cultivating household use plots strengthened their influence in the household and the community. Overall, the gender division of labor involved substantial overlap between male and female roles in the rural sector.

The 1980s brought dramatic economic decline to Romania. In December 1989, the Romanian revolution began. Conflict continued through 1990, when the opposition party won the national election. By 1991, about 80 percent of the farm land had reverted to private ownership. The revolution had mixed results throughout Romania and Olt Land: "At first it improved people's daily lives and brightened their outlook. . . . Ultimately, however, the persistent uncertainties intensified the competitive and divisive forces that had so long been at work in Olt Land society" (216). The transition to private land was not easy. State farms gave up land reluctantly, and many collective farmers had second thoughts about private agriculture:

> One couple in their early forties . . . were horrified when they heard a rumor that people were to be required to take back the land. . . . They had no desire to work in agriculture, and to them the half hectare to which they were entitled was a burden. Many people who were close to retirement or recently pensioned and some younger unmarried people also saw private agriculture as not worth the effort. They had grown accustomed to the shared risk and shorter workdays of collective farming. . . . Some young people liked the idea of private agri-

culture but doubted that they knew enough to be successful at it. (221–222)

The Sustainability of Agriculture

Agriculture requires more in the way of labor inputs, technology, and the use of nonrenewable natural resources than the systems discussed earlier. The ever-increasing spread of corporate agriculture is displacing other longstanding economic systems, resulting in the destruction of important habitats, notably rainforests, in its search for agricultural land (along with commercial ranching and other aspects of industrialism, discussed next) and for water and other energy sources to support its enterprises. Intensive agriculture itself is nonsustainable. It is also undermining the sustainability of other systems. Anthropologists have pointed to some of the costs of agriculture. (See the Critical Thinking box on page 68.)

Industrialism and Post-Industrialism

Industrialism is the production of goods through mass employment in business and commercial operations. In industrial capitalism, the form of capitalism found in most industrialized nations, the bulk of goods are produced not to meet basic needs but to satisfy consumer demands for nonessential goods. Employment in agriculture decreases while jobs in manufacturing and the service sector increase. In some industrialized countries, the number of manufacturing jobs is declining, with more people being employed in service occupations and in the growing area of "information processing" (such as computer programming, data processing, communications, and teaching). Some experts feel that the United States, for example, has moved out of the industrial age and into the "information age." As the growth of cybersystems and virtual economies continues worldwide, cultural anthropologists are beginning to conduct research on these new developments.

Within industrial capitalism an important distinction exists between the **formal sector,** which is salaried or wage-based work registered in official statistics, and the **informal sector,** which includes work that is outside the formal sector, not officially registered, and sometimes illegal. If you have done babysitting and were paid cash that was not formally recorded by your employer (for tax deduction purposes) or by you (for income tax purposes), then you have participated in the informal sector. Informal sector activities that are illegal are referred to as being part of the "underground economy."

The Formal Sector

The formal sector comprises a wide array of occupations, ranging from stable and lucrative jobs in the "primary labor market" to unstable or part-time and less lucrative jobs in the "secondary labor market" (Calhoun, Light, and Keller 1994). Cultural anthropologists conduct research in any number of domains, ranging from huge multinational corporations to neighborhood beauty parlors, but the tendency has been to focus on small-scale organizations, especially factories. Fieldwork techniques in factory studies include conducting interviews with workers and managers in the plant and in their homes and observing plant operations. Findings shed light on how people adapt to this environment and on the stresses that arise.

In one factory study, a team of cultural anthropologists and graduate students focused on the role of ethnicity in social relationships in a Miami clothing factory (Grenier et al. 1992). The clothing plant, a subsidiary of the largest U.S. clothing manufacturer, employs about 250 operators, mainly women. The majority of employees are Cuban women who, fleeing from the Castro regime, immigrated to Miami many years ago. As these employees are aging and beginning to retire, they are being replaced by new immigrants from Central America, some Haitians, and some African Americans. The workers are organized into a union, but members of the different ethnic groups have more solidarity with each other than with the union. Interethnic rivalry exists around the issue of management's treatment of members of different groups. Many non-Cuban workers claim there is favoritism toward Cuban employees. Some supervisors and managers expressed ethnic stereotypes, but not always consistent ones: "Depending on whom one listens to, Haitians are either too slow or too fast; Cubans

Members of this Romanian collective farm work team are sorting potatoes. Teams were composed of close friends, relations, and neighbors. ■ *How might this form of organization contribute to productivity?* (Source: David Kideckel)

Critical Thinking

WAS THE INVENTION OF AGRICULTURE A TERRIBLE MISTAKE?

MOST EURO-AMERICANS have a "progressivist" view that agriculture is a major advance in cultural evolution because it brought with it so many things that Westerners admire: cities, centers of learning and art, powerful state governments, and monumental architecture:

> Just count our advantages. We enjoy the most abundant and varied foods, the best tools, and material goods, some of the longest and healthiest lives, in history. . . . From the progressivist perspective on which I was brought up, to ask "Why did almost all our hunter–gatherer ancestors adopt agriculture?" is silly. Of course they adopted it because agriculture is an efficient way to get more food for less work. (Diamond 1994[1987]:106)

Another claim about the advantage of agriculture is that it allows more leisure time, so art could flourish. Why would one rather be a forager, struggling every day to make ends meet?

On the other hand, many scholars raise serious questions about the advantages of agriculture. These "revisionists" argue that agriculture may be "the worst mistake in the history of the human race," "a catastrophe from which we have never recovered" (Diamond 1994[1987]:105–106). Some of the "costs" of agriculture include social inequality; disease; despotism; and destruction of the environment from soil exhaustion and chemical poisoning, water pollution, dams and river diversions, and air pollution from tractors, transportation, and processing plants. With agriculture, life did improve for many people, but not for all. Elites emerged with distinct advantages, but the gap between the haves and the have-nots increased. Health improved for the elites, but not for the landless poor and laboring classes. With the vast surpluses of food created by agricultural production, elaborate state systems developed with new forms of power exercised over the common people.

CRITICAL THINKING QUESTIONS

What is your definition of "the good life"?

What are the benefits and costs of achieving the good life among, say, the Ju/wasi compared to your vision of the good life in your microculture?

Who gets to live the good life in each type of economy?

---

may talk too much or be extraordinarily dedicated workers" (75). Managers see ethnic-based competition and lack of cooperation as a key problem that they attempt to deal with in various ways. For example, management banned workers from playing personal radios and installed a system of piped-in music by a radio station that supposedly alternates between "American" and "Latin" songs.

The Informal Sector

Studying the informal sector presents several challenges. People who work in the informal sector are unlikely to be clustered in one location such as a factory. Often, workers in the informal sector are involved in illegal activities, which means they are even less willing than other people to be studied. In general, it is easier to do research on aspects of people's lives of which they are proud. Work in the informal economy may yield a sense of pride less often than work in the formal economy. On the other hand, some research advantages exist. Compared to a CEO of a multinational corporation, people involved in the informal economy may have more time to share with an anthropologist. This is not always the case, however, since many informal sector workers are involved in more than one enterprise in an attempt to make ends meet, as well as being responsible for child care.

The illegal drug industry is an important part of the globalized informal economy. Neither international drug dealers nor street sellers pay income tax on their profits, and their earnings are not part of the official GNP of any nation. In the United States, many young males are drawn into the drug economy as sellers. Their lives are fractured with danger and violence (Bourgois 1995).

In many parts of the world, sex work is illegal but exists as part of the informal sector, both locally and globally. In the United States, sex work is legal only in the state of Nevada, where income from sex work is taxable just like any other occupation. In other states, it is illegal and part of the informal economy.

In Thailand, the sex industry is the leading sector of the economy, accounting for about 10 percent of Thailand's GNP. Much of the income derives from Thailand's international popularity as a place for "sex tourism." Thai

Child labor is prominent in many modes of production. In this photograph, a girl picks coffee beans in Guatemala. ■ *Should a child have the right to work, or should more international pressure be brought to bear against child labor?* (Source: © Sean Sprague/Stock Boston, LLC)

sex workers are also part of the international export sex industry. Over 200,000 Thai sex workers live in Europe, and many others live in Japan, Hong Kong, Taiwan, Singapore, the United States, Saudi Arabia, and Kuwait.

Child sex work in Thailand is an increasingly important part of this informal economy. The number of child sex workers under sixteen years old is estimated to be about 800,000, or 40 percent of the total prostitute labor force. Recent changes, especially the increased fear of AIDS, have stepped up the demand for ever younger sex workers, because people associate child sex with safe sex. In the 1990s, recruitment of children as young as 6 years old began (Petras and Wongchaisuwan 1993). Declining rural incomes in the northern areas of Thailand prompt more parents to sell their children into sex work; the price of a child ranges between $280 and $1200, depending on the child's looks. AIDS is increasing rapidly among child sex workers.

An anthropological study of child prostitutes in a tourist community in Thailand sought to elicit the voices and views of the children themselves (Montgomery 2001). The study found that the children themselves do not feel that they fit the uniform view of child prostitutes that international organizations have. Their stories are varied, complicated, and full of internal contradictions, questions, and struggles. They believe that the work they do is moral because it is carried out mainly in support of their family. The child sex workers and their pimps, also children, exercise some choice in deciding which clients to accept and which to reject. This more complex view of child prostitution does not deny that the child sex work-

ers are exploited and often seriously harmed, but it does show that the simple model of "victim" does not easily apply either.

This study and other research on various kinds of child labor raises universal questions about what childhood is, what a good childhood is, and what child rights are (Panter-Brick and Smith 2000). Surely, the voices and views of the children must be heard. But scholars and activists alike must look beyond the children's microeconomy to the global, macroeconomic structures that generate and support the people who pay for sex with children and the poverty in the communities that send children into sex work.

CHANGING MODES OF PRODUCTION

This section draws attention to the changes that have occurred in recent times in each of the modes of production. Contemporary economic globalization is only the latest force of outside change to be exerted on local economies. European colonialism had major effects on indigenous economies, mainly by introducing cash cropping in place of production for household use.

In the later part of the twentieth century, major economic growth in Asia, the demise of socialism in the former Soviet Union, and the increasing economic power of the United States throughout the world combined to create the current "global economy" or economic globalization. The term *global economy* refers to the interconnectedness of all aspects of international, transnational, national, and local economies: raw materials, labor supply, transportation, finance, and marketing (Robins 1996). This interconnectedness is also characterized by its instantaneity-electronic forms of communication mean, more than ever, that when a world economic power center sneezes, the rest of the world will catch a cold. Social scientists vigorously debate the effects of economic globalization on poverty and inequality (Ravaillon 2003). Economists, who tend to rely on national figures about changing income levels and distribution, have often espoused the view that economic globalization is beneficial overall, because it increases economic activity. Cultural anthropologists, who work with localized data and a more "on the ground" view, tend to emphasize the negative effects of capitalist expansion into noncapitalist settings (Blim 2000). They point to three major transformations:

■ Increases in commercial production in local and periphery regions in response to the demands of a global market

- Recruitment of former foragers, horticulturalists, pastoralists, and family farmers to work in the industrialized sector and their exploitation in that setting

- Dispossession of local people of their land and other resource bases and substantial growth in the numbers of unemployed, displaced people

Although there are instances in which local cultural groups have selectively taken advantage of outside economic influences and remade them to fit their own interests, in many other cases, local economies have been almost completely transformed and local knowledge abandoned.

Foragers: The Tiwi of Northern Australia

The Tiwi live on two islands off the north coast of Australia (Hart, Pilling, and Goodale 1988). As foragers, the Tiwi gathered food, especially vegetables (such as yams) and nuts, grubs, small lizards, and fish. Women provided the bulk of the daily diet with their gathered vegetables and nuts that were ground and cooked into a porridge. Occasionally men hunted kangaroos, wildfowl, and other game such as *goanna*, larger lizards. Vegetables, nuts, and fish were abundant the year around. The Tiwi lived a more comfortable life than Aboriginal groups of the mainland, where the environment was less hospitable.

The Tiwi have long been in contact with different foreign influences, beginning in the 1600s with the arrival of the Portuguese, who were attracted to the islands as a source of iron. Later, in 1897, an Australian buffalo hunter named Joe Cooper came to the islands and kidnapped two native women to train as mainland guides in the Tiwi language. Cooper and his group greatly changed the Tiwi by introducing a desire for Western goods, especially tobacco. Later, Japanese traders arrived, offering Tiwi men manufactured goods in return for Tiwi women. In the early 1900s, the French established a Catholic mission on one island. The mission disapproved of the traditional Tiwi marriage pattern of polygamy (multiple spouses, in this case a man having more than one wife) and promoted monogamy instead. The year 1942 brought World War II to the Tiwi as the Japanese bombed and strafed an American airstrip. Military bases were prominent on the islands. Tiwi dependency on Western manufactured goods increased.

Tiwi residence patterns have changed substantially. The Tiwi have become settled villagers living in houses built of corrugated iron sheets. Tiwi men now play football (soccer) and water polo and engage in competitive javelin throwing. Tiwi art, especially carving and painting, is widely recognized in Australia and, increasingly, internationally. Tiwi are active in public affairs and politics, including the aboriginal rights movement. Another major factor of change is international tourism, a force that the Tiwi are managing with dignity and awareness. One Tiwi commented that tourism may mean "that white people too will learn to live with and survive in the country" (Hart, Pilling, and Goodale 1988:144–145).

Horticulturalists: The Mundurucu of the Brazilian Amazon

Outside economic and political factors have major effects on horticultural societies. The rubber industry's impact on indigenous peoples of the Amazon ranges from maintenance of many aspects of traditional life to the complete loss of traditional lifeways. Like the Tiwi, the Mundurucu illustrate the complexities of change that are neither complete cultural retention nor complete loss (Murphy and Murphy 1985). After the arrival of Brazilians who were commercial rubber producers in the Amazon in the late nineteenth century, many Indians began to work for the Brazilians as latex tappers. For over a century, Mundurucu men combined their traditional horticultural life with seasonal work in the rubber area collecting latex. Marked cultural change occurred when many Mundurucu opted to leave their traditional villages, migrating to live in the rubber area year-round.

In the traditional villages, men still live in a separate house at one side of the village, with husbands visiting

Aboriginal artist Eymard Tungatalum retouches a traditional Tiwi carving in an art gallery in Australia's northern territory. Tungatalum's carvings, along with songs and poems, are an important part of the Aboriginal people's efforts to revive their culture. ■ *Have you ever seen any Australian Aboriginal art in person? Or on a web site? Was it placed within its cultural context so that you could learn about the people who made it?* (Source: © Reuters/Megan Lewis/Archive Photos)

wives and children in their group houses. In the rubber settlement, husbands and wives live in their own houses and there is no separate men's house. In the traditional villages, women's communal work groups shared water-carrying tasks. Such groups do not exist in the rubber settlement villages. The husbands have taken over the task of carrying the water, so men work harder than in the traditional village. Although women in the settlement area work more hours per day than men, they believe that life is better because they like living in the same house with their husbands.

Pastoralists: Herders of Mongolia

In the early 1990s, cultural anthropologist Melvyn Goldstein and physical anthropologist Cynthia Beall (1994) were allowed to do fieldwork among herders in Mongolia, a landlocked and mountainous country located between Russia and China. The Mongolian rural economy has long been, and still is, heavily dependent on animal herds. The "big five" animals are sheep, goats, cattle (mostly yak), horses, and camels. As one herder said, "The animals are our food and money. They give us our dairy products and meat to eat, dung to warm our *ger* [tent], and wool and skins to make our felt and clothes . . ." (p. 38). Sheep and goats provide meat and clothing and some milk, yaks are most important for dairy products because they give milk all year, and horses and camels provide transportation. Goldstein and Beall wanted to study how the transformation from a socialist, collectivized, pastoral economy to a capitalist, market system was affecting the people.

Since the 1950s, the then USSR ruled Mongolia and sought to transform it into an agricultural and industrial state. As urban centers were established, the urban population began to grow and the rural population declined. The state provided all social services such as health and education. There was no homelessness or unemployment.

The official policy regarding pastoralism was to ban private ownership and collectivize the herds. The transition was not smooth or easy. Collectivization resulted in a 30 percent reduction of livestock, as owners chose to slaughter animals rather than collectivize them (Barfield 1993). Subsequently, policy was altered and the people were allowed to control some of their own animals.

Starting in the late 1980s, the transition away from socialist economic policies spread to Mongolia. By the early 1990s, privatization, a process of transferring the collective ownership and provision of goods and services to a system of private ownership, was the government's policy guideline. Collective ownership of herds was abandoned, and family-organized production was reinstated.

Goldstein and Beall (1994) selected a more traditional region for their research: the Moost district in the Altai Mountain area in the southeastern part of the country. The district includes over 10,000 square miles of mountain and valley land, of which 99.9 percent is pasture. The area contains about 4000 people and about 115,000 head of livestock. Goldstein and Beall set up their *ger* and were immediately welcomed by an invitation to have milk-tea, a hot drink made of tea, water, milk, butter, and salt. During their stay, they spoke with many of the nomads, participated in their festivals, and learned about perceptions of economic change.

Changes in the wider Mongolian economy during privatization created serious problems for the herders. Their standard of living declined markedly in the early 1990s. Goods such as flour, sugar, candy, and cooking oil were no longer available. Prices for meat fluctuated widely, and the herders, who had become accustomed to the security of state-controlled prices, had to adjust to market fluctuations. Lower meat prices meant fewer herd animals were slaughtered. Larger herd sizes exceeded the carrying capacity of the grasslands.

External political and economic policies and events have had major effects on Mongolian herders' lifestyle. They have had to adjust to dramatic restructuring of their economy, from private family herding to collectivized herding and then back to private herding, in the space of a few decades. Along with these changes, social services such as health care and schools, which were relatively easy to access during the collective period, became less readily available with privatization. We can only wonder how individual agency and choice have played a part within these massive structural changes. One scholar of central Asian pastoralists comments in an upbeat way that the cultural identity and pride of the descendants of Genghis Khan will endure (Barfield 1993:176) even though their numbers have dwindled, their standard of living has declined, and their herding practices are now part of the global economy.

In parts of Mongolia and Siberia, many pastoralists continue to herd reindeer as a major part of their economy. ■ *Do some research to learn about the worldwide distribution of reindeer in the wild and the people who herd them.* (Source: © Xinhua-Chine Nou/Gamma Liaison)

Family Farmers: The Maya of Chiapas, Mexico

Some applied anthropologists and other development specialists have said that family farmers in closed communities are "risk averse" because they avoid adopting innovations such as new techniques for cultivation, new seed varieties, and new forms of fertilizer. Economic anthropologists have shown, in contrast, that such conservatism may be adaptive. Family farmers have intimate knowledge of the systems within which they work, and they are capable of assessing costs and benefits of innovations. These two perspectives both emphasize the farmers' agency as decision makers, determining whether they should change in certain directions. In contrast, development projects such as the construction of roads, global patterns in demand for certain products, and labor opportunities shape the options that farmers have to consider.

Economic anthropologist Frank Cancian first studied production among the Mayan Indians of Zinacantán, located in the Chiapas region of Mexico's far south, in 1960. He returned in 1983 to conduct a restudy and thus gained insight into changes that had taken place in the intervening twenty years (1989). At the time of his first research, most Zinacantecos earned their livelihood by growing corn and selling some of their crops in a

nearby city. They were largely independent of outside forces in terms of their own food supply. The community was closely knit, its social boundaries defined by people's commitment to community roles and ceremonies. Twenty years later, both the local economy and the social system had changed, reflecting the much greater effects of the world system economy on the region. Zinacantán's economy had become much more connected with forces beyond its borders.

The major direct cause of change was the massive increase in public spending by the government in the 1970s. This spending supported the construction of roads, dams, schools, and housing throughout the Chiapas region. The government also sponsored outreach programs to promote agricultural change, mainly crop diversification and ways to increase production. Another important factor was the oil boom in northern Chiapas and nearby Tabasco province, which brought huge amounts of cash into the local economy.

By 1983, 40 percent of the households had no land at all and planted no corn. The majority of the population had become involved in wage work, and unemployment, rather than a bad farming season, was the major threat to food security. Wage work included the new opportunities in road construction, government jobs, transportation (of people, food goods, and flowers), and full-time trading in urban markets reachable by the new roads.

This story, in its general outlines, is similar to that of many family farmers throughout the world, especially in developing countries. It involves transformation from production for own-use to production for sale within a monetized system of trade for profit. Having sold the family farm, self-employed farmers enter the wage economy and become dependent on it for their livelihood. Many Zinacantecos raised their income level substantially during this period, and a clear income gap emerged among different categories of people. Being able to buy one or more trucks and take advantage of the new opportunities for urban trade created by the new roads was the most reliable way to become richer. In contrast, households with the least access to cash were left behind; these households were characteristically headed by a woman on her own.

Overall, the area became more prosperous, more monetized, and more dependent on the outside economy. Internally, social differentiation increased, and social solidarity within the community declined.

Industrialists: Taiwanese in South Africa

In South Africa during the 1990s, after the dismantling of apartheid, political leaders adopted a neoliberal economic policy (Hart 2002). Links with Taiwanese industry were forged, and several Taiwanese industries were established outside major urban areas. There is no simple explanation for the Asian economic "miracle," but one component was the family model of production in which age and gender hierarchies ensure compliance. Inclusion of women in production was another key factor.

Taiwanese managers tried to use such a family system in South Africa as a way of ensuring a smoothly functioning labor force. An anthropologist who studied Taiwanese knitwear factories in two locations in KwaZulu-Natal province, South Africa, learned of substantial worker resentment against management. Women workers were especially vocal. Taiwanese patterns of negotiating with women workers by using an idiom of kinship and family did not work at all. The South African women frequently commented that they felt as though they were being treated like animals. The Taiwanese industrialists were separated by a wide racial, economic, and social divide from the factory workers. They lived far from the townships, which they considered dangerous. Imposing hierarchical kinship metaphors in such a context failed to create a viable workforce, and ultimately, many of the Taiwanese industrialists found themselves a focal point of local political conflict. In one town, a Chinese welcome monument was removed.

Industrial Workers: Barberton

Increased mechanization is another major aspect of change in industry worldwide, and it has marked impacts on labor. Unemployment and manufacturing declines in America's Rust Belt are well-known trends in industrial lifeways. Gregory Pappas (1989) studied unemployment in Barberton, a working-class Ohio town. A tire company that had been the town's major employer closed in 1980, eliminating 1200 jobs. Pappas lived in Barberton for a year, interviewing many people and sending a questionnaire to over 600 displaced workers for further information. His work sheds light on how unemployed workers cope either by migrating or by finding new ways to spend their time in Barberton. These people are faced with having to construct a new identity for themselves: "For factory workers the place of employment is crucial; their identities are bound up in a particular place, and plant shutdowns compromise their ability to understand themselves" (83). As one unemployed man commented, "I don't know who I am anymore." In this context of decline, levels of stress and mental disorder have increased for many people.

Anthropologists and other experts question the current and future sustainability of a mode of production that relies so heavily on the use of nonrenewable resources and creates high levels of pollution. Others suggest that new forms of energy will be discovered and planets besides earth will be able to provide resources and places of human habitation. Given the global interconnections of industrialism—its demand for raw materials, markets, and labor, and its social and environmental effects—cultural anthropologists are being challenged to devise new theories and methods to study such complexity and contribute to policies that will have positive social effects.

Capitalism Goes Global

Although Karl Marx predicted that capitalism would wither away, it hasn't done so yet. In its latest aspect, global incorporation, its effects are ever more powerfully felt in localities worldwide. Marx would be interested to observe how the Tiwi are developing international tourism, how Mayans in Chiapas took up road construction for cash and their abandoned corn farming declined, and how Taiwanese knitwear manufacturers in KwaZulu-Natal encountered problems in cross-cultural labor management. He would perhaps be amused to see how, at the same time, cultural anthropologists are trying to understand and document all these changes.

KEY CONCEPTS

SUGGESTED READINGS

Anne Allison. *Nightwork: Sexuality, Pleasure and Corporate Masculinity in a Tokyo Hostess Club*. Chicago: University of Chicago Press, 1994. Based on the author's participant observation, this book explores what it is like to work as a hostess in a club that caters to corporate male employees and discusses how that microculture is linked to men's corporate work culture.

Jans Dahl. *Saqqaq: An Inuit Hunting Community in the Modern World*. Toronto: University of Toronto Press, 2000. This ethnography of Saqqaq, a hunting community located on Disko Bay, eastern Greenland, is based on fieldwork carried out at several times since 1980 in order to provide a diachronic perspective. Hunting beluga is a central community activity and still forms the basis of community identity, even though commercial fishing and other economic activities have gained importance in recent times.

Frances Dahlberg, ed. *Woman the Gatherer*. New Haven, CT: Yale University Press, 1981. These path-breaking essays examine the role of women in four different foraging societies, provide insights on human evolution from studies of female chimpanzees, and give an overview of women's role in human cultural adaptation.

Elliot Fratkin. *Ariaal Pastoralists of Kenya: Surviving Drought and Development in Africa's Arid Lands*. Boston: Allyn and Bacon, 1998. Based on several phases of ethnographical research among the Ariaal beginning in the 1970s, this book provides insights about pastoralism in general and the particular cultural strategies of the Ariaal. It focuses on social organization and family life.

David Uru Iyam. *The Broken Hoe: Cultural Reconfiguration in Biase Southeast Nigeria*. Chicago: The University of Chicago Press, 1995. Based on fieldwork among the Biase people by an anthropologist who is a member of a Biase group, this book examines changes since the 1970s in the traditional forms of subsistence—agriculture, fishing, and trade—and the related issues of environmental deterioration and population growth.

Anna M. Kertula. *Antler on the Sea: The Yup'ik and Chukchi of the Russian Far East*. Ithaca, NY: Cornell University Press, 2000. Economic and social changes among two groups—sea mammal hunters and reindeer herders—in a Siberian village on the Bering Seas are the focus of this ethnography. The author explores adjustments in intergroup relations, conflict, identity, and cooperation that have taken place since the breakup of the former Soviet Union and the subsequent collapse of the local economy in the study region.

Heather Montgomery. *Modern Babylon? Prostituting Children in Thailand*. New York: Bergahn Books, 2001. The author conducted fieldwork in a tourist community in Thailand where parents frequently commit their children to prostitution. She sought to gain a view of this system from the perspective of the children and the parents. She found that these insiders' views are far more complex than the monolithic "victim" picture painted by international agencies.

Brian Morris. *The Power of Animals: An Ethnography*. New York: Berg, 1998. This book is an ethnography of Malawi, southern Africa. It is based on in-depth fieldwork in one region, supplemented by travel and study throughout the country. It focuses on men's roles in animal hunting and women's roles in agriculture as crucial to under-standing wider aspects of Malawian culture, including diet and food preparation, marriage and kinship, gender relations, and attitudes about nature.

Katherine S. Newman. *Falling from Grace: The Experience of Downward Mobility in the American Middle Class*. New York: The Free Press, 1988. This book provides ethnographic research on downwardly mobile people of New Jersey as a "special tribe," with attention to loss of employment by corporate managers and blue-collar workers and the effects of downward mobility on middle-class family life.

Richard H. Robbins. *Global Problems and the Culture of Capitalism*. Boston: Longman, 1999. Robbins takes a critical look at the role of capitalism and global economic growth in creating and sustaining many world problems, such as poverty, disease, hunger, violence, and environmental destruction. The last section includes case studies.

Deborah Sick. *Farmers of the Golden Bean: Costa Rican Households and the Global Coffee Economy*. Dekalb: Northern Illinois University Press, 1999. This book is an ethnography of coffee-producing households in Costa Rica that describes the difficulties that coffee farmers face as a consequence of unpredictable global forces and examines the uncertain role of the state as a mediator between the global and the local.

WHAT is the scope of economic anthropology?

Economic anthropology encompasses the study of production, consumption, and exchange. Economic anthropology approaches these processes from a cross-cultural perspective and does not assume that Western economic patterns and values are universal. Economic anthropologists study a wide range of modes of production, or ways of making a living through goods or money. The five modes of production anthropologists address are foraging, horticulture, pastoralism, agriculture, and industrialism.

WHAT are the characteristics of the five major modes of production?

The five modes of production involve the factors of labor, property relations, and sustainability. In foraging societies, the division of labor is based on gender and age, with temperate foragers having more gender overlap in tasks than circumpolar foragers. Property is shared, and all people have equal rights to resources such as land and water holes. These resources are managed by family groups and shared with others as needed. With its strategy of limited exploitation of local resources in combination with seasonal migration, foraging has long-term sustainability when not affected by pressure from the outside world.

Horticulture and pastoralism are also extensive strategies, requiring the sequential fallowing of plots in horticulture and migration of animals to fresh pastures in pastoralism. We cannot easily generalize about the division of labor in these modes of production. They include those in which men do most of the work, those in which women do most of the work, and those in which work loads are shared more evenly. As with foraging peoples, use rights are the prominent form of property relations, but increased levels of production through the domestication of plants and animals yield more food and goods, as well as heightened interest in protecting group rights to land. Given the mobile strategies of shifting use of plots in horticulture and shifting use of pasture land in pastoralism, these modes of production have long-term sustainability when not affected by encroachments from other economic systems.

Early agriculture, like many agricultural contexts now, was family-based in terms of labor. Most family farming systems involve more male labor in the fields and more female labor in the domestic domain, although some examples of dominant female roles in field labor exist. Socialist states created another form of labor organization for farming through the collective, which organized workers into teams regardless of family affiliation or gender. In collectivized agriculture, men and women were supposed to have equal roles, but women tended to have lower-status positions than men. With settled agriculture came the emergence of private property and of social control and laws to protect private interests. Social inequality in access to the primary means of production—land—emerged, along with gaps between the rich landed people and the poor landless people. Agriculture's sustainability is limited by the need to replenish the land, which is used continuously for crops and animals.

In industrialism, labor is highly differentiated by class in addition to gender and age. Widespread unemployment is found in many industrial economies. In capitalist industrial societies, private property is the dominant pattern, with high rates of imprisonment for people who violate the rules. Socialist industrial societies have attempted to distribute property among all people, but most such attempts have not been successful. Given its intensive and ever-expanding exploitation of nonrenewable resources, industrialism lacks long-term sustainability.

WHAT are some directions of change in the five modes of production?

Foragers are being incorporated into more settled economies as their access to large amounts of land is decreased by outside economic forces. Many former foraging people now work, for example, as farm laborers, jobs typically of low status in the mainstream cash economy. Others are participating in the revitalization of their culture in the new global economy, producing art for sale on the world market or developing cultural tourism opportunities for outsiders. Horticulture and pastoralism exist on a larger scale than foraging, but these land-extensive systems are also under great pressure from the competing economic forms of agriculture and industrialism. Many former horticulturalists have migrated to plantations or urban areas and become part of the cash economy. States have pressured pastoralists to settle down or (in communist systems) to become collectivized and then (with the decline of communism) de-collectivized. In many parts of the world, family farms are declining in number as corporate farms increase. The labor supply has changed from being family-based to including a high proportion of migrant laborers who are often transnationals.

A possible sixth mode of production is emerging with the information age and economic processes being carried out via the Internet. E-commerce is creating new ways of making a living, new labor patterns, new forms of property, and new questions about sustainability. Cultural anthropologists are beginning to address this latest stage in economic change with more complex and varied research methods than in the early days of the discipline.

THE BIG QUESTIONS

- **HOW** are modes of production related to consumption?

- **HOW** are modes of production related to exchange?

- **WHAT** are some examples of how contemporary economic change affects consumption and exchange?

4

CONSUMPTION AND EXCHANGE

A member of the Kayapó tribe of Brazil eats a popsicle during a break in a meeting of indigenous peoples to protest a dam-building project. The incidence of tooth decay, diabetes, and obesity is rising among indigenous peoples worldwide as a result of changing consumption patterns. (*Source: © Wilson Melo/CORBIS*)

This sketch demonstrates how closely linked production, consumption, and exchange are. Potlatches are related to levels of production; they are opportunities for consumption; and they involve exchange of goods among groups. This chapter considers the areas of economic anthropology that deal with **modes of consumption,** or the predominant patterns within a culture of using up goods and services, and **modes of exchange,** or the predominant patterns within a culture of transferring goods, services, and other items between and among people and groups. (See Figure 4.1.)

Imagine that it is the late eighteenth century and you are a member of the Kwakwaka'wakw tribe of British Columbia in Canada's Pacific Northwest region. Along with the rest of your local tribal group, you have been invited to a **potlatch,** a grand feast in which guests are feasted and receive gifts from the hosts (Suttles 1991).

Be prepared to eat a lot because potlatch guests are given abundant helpings of the most honorable foods: eulachon oil (oil from the eulachon fish), high-bush cranberries, and seal meat, all served in ceremonial wooden bowls. The chief will present the guests with many gifts: hand-embroidered blankets, canoes, carefully crafted household articles such as carved wooden boxes and woven mats, and food to be taken back home.

The more the chief gives, the higher his status will rise, and the more his guests will be indebted to him. Later, when it is the guests' turn to hold a potlatch, they will try to give away as much as—or more than—their host did, thus shaming him into giving the next potlatch.

Before the arrival of the Europeans, tribes throughout the Pacific Northwest were linked with each other through a network of potlatching relationships. The Europeans tried to stop potlatching because they thought it was "wasteful" and because it contained elements that offended Christian principles they were trying to promote. In spite of the fact that the colonialists even made potlatching illegal, it survived to the present among some groups and is being revived by others.

A granary in West Africa allows for saving food crops for several months. The fact that it is raised above ground protects the food from being eaten by animals and from moisture damage. ■ *How do people in your microculture store food and why do they choose such storage systems?* (Source: Roshani Kothari)

FIGURE 4.1 Modes of Production, Consumption, and Exchange

FORAGING	HORTICULTURE	PASTORALISM	AGRICULTURE	INDUSTRIALISM (CAPITALIST)
Mode of Consumption				**Mode of Consumption**
Minimalism				Consumerism
Finite needs				Infinite needs
Social Organization of Consumption				**Social Organization of Consumption**
Equality/sharing				Class-based inequality
Personalized products are consumed				Depersonalized products are consumed
Primary Budgetary Fund				**Primary Budgetary Fund**
Basic needs				Rent/taxes, luxuries
Mode of Exchange				**Mode of Exchange**
Balanced exchange				Market exchange
Social Organization of Exchange				**Social Organization of Exchange**
Small groups, face-to-face				Anonymous market transactions
Primary Category of Exchange				**Primary Category of Exchange**
The gift				The sale

CULTURE AND CONSUMPTION

What Is Consumption?

In this section, we examine the concept of consumption and review various modes of consumption in relation to modes of production (Chapter 3). We look at several consumption funds, or areas to which people devote resources.

Consumption has two senses: First, it is a person's "intake" in terms of eating or other ways of using things; second, it is a person's "output" in terms of spending or using resources. Thus, consumption includes eating habits and household budgeting practices. People consume many things: Food, drink, clothing, and shelter are the most basic consumption needs. Beyond that, they may acquire and use tools, weapons, means of transportation, computers, books and other items of communication, art and other luxury goods, and energy for heating and cooling their residence.

In order to consume, one must have something to consume or to trade for something consumable. In a market economy, most consumption depends on having cash, and a person's ability to consume is measured in terms of cash income. However, cultural anthropologists are interested in all economic systems, not just market economies, so we broaden our analysis to include noncash forms of income or expenditure. In nonmarket economies, instead of spending cash, people "spend" time, labor, or trade goods in order to provide for their needs.

The relationship between the processes of consumption and exchange differs in nonmarket and market systems. In nonmarket economies, many consumption needs are satisfied without any exchange at all, or only to a limited degree. In market economies, most consumption items are not self-produced and must be purchased. When a horticulturalist grows food for home consumption using seeds saved from the previous year, no exchange is involved in providing for consumption. If a farmer purchases seeds and fertilizer to grow food, then exchange is an essential part of providing for consumption needs. In nonmarket economies, few goods are obtained through exchange, whereas in market economies, most goods are obtained this way.

Modes of Consumption

Modes of consumption, or the dominant pattern of using things up or spending resources to satisfy demand, correspond generally with the modes-of-production continuum (see Figure 4.1 on page 81). At the opposite ends of the continuum, two contrasting modes of consumption exist, defined in terms of the relationship between demand (what people want) and supply (the resources available to satisfy demand). **Minimalism** is a mode of consumption that emphasizes simplicity and is characterized by few and finite (limited) consumer demands and an adequate and sustainable means to achieve them. At the other end of the continuum is **consumerism,** in which people's demands are many and infinite, and the means of satisfying them are therefore insufficient and become depleted in the effort to meet demands. Minimalism is most clearly exemplified in (free-ranging) foraging societies; consumerism is the distinguishing feature of industrial cultures (of the capitalist variety). In between these two extremes are blended patterns, with a decreasing trend toward minimalism and an increasing trend toward consumerism as one moves from left to right. Changes in the mode of production influence the transformation in consumption. Notably, the increase of surpluses and the ability to store wealth for long periods of time allow for a more consumerist lifestyle to emerge.

The social organization of consumption also changes as one moves across the continuum. As we noted in Chapter 3, social inequality in access to resources increases as one moves from foraging to agricultural and industrial (especially capitalist) societies. In foraging societies, everyone has equal access to all resources. Food, land, water, and materials for shelter are communally shared, as among the traditional Ju/wasi:

> Food is never consumed alone by a family; it is always (actually or potentially) shared out with members of a living group or band of up to 30 (or more) members. Even though only a fraction of the able-bodied foragers go out each day, the day's return of meat and gathered foods are divided in such a way that every member of the camp receives an equitable share. The hunting band or camp is a unit of sharing, and if sharing breaks down it ceases to be a camp. (Lee 1979:118)

The distribution of personal goods such as clothing, or "leisure" items such as musical instruments or smoking pipes, is also equal. In horticultural and pastoral societies, group sharing is still a prevalent ethic, and it is the duty of leaders to make sure that everyone has food and shelter.

At the other end of the continuum, we find the United States to be the major consumerist culture of the world

A view of Seoul, the capital of the Republic of Korea. The demand for electricity in urban centers worldwide has prompted construction of many high dams to generate power. Food must be shipped to urban markets. In general, cities have high energy costs compared to rural areas. ■ *How would you assess the energy costs of an average day in your life—what are your major energy requirements? Are they high or low compared to those of other students in the class?* (Source: © Kim Newton/ Woodfin Camp & Associates)

(Durning 1993). Consumption levels in the United States, since the 1970s, have been the highest of any society in human history. Consumerism is widely promoted as a good thing, a path to happiness. Increasing one's consumption level and quality of life is a primary personal goal of most people—and of the government, too. Many other nations have growing economies that allow some of the population to demand consumer goods and have the energy capabilities to support a Westernized lifestyle (cars, air conditioning, and other appliances). These countries include the rapidly developing nations of Asia, such as China, the Republic of Korea, and Vietnam, and many countries in Africa and Latin America. For example, Ghana's economy grew at about 5 percent a year in the 1990s. At the same time, electricity consumption increased almost 11 percent a year in the nation; in Accra, the capital, it grew at over 13 percent a year. The increase is the result of both industrial growth and increased consumer demand for electrical appliances, including fans, refrigerators, televisions, stereos, air conditioners, VCRs, computers, and fax machines.

In all, the amount of goods that the world's population consumed in the past fifty years equals what was consumed by all previous generations in human history. Minimalism was sustainable over hundreds of thousands of years.

Some industrialized nations, such as Sweden, have taken steps to control consumerism and its negative environmental effects, especially through reducing the use of cars (Durning 1993).

In small-scale societies, such as those made up of foragers, horticulturalists, and pastoralists, consumption items are typically produced by the consumers themselves. If not, they are likely to be produced by people with whom the consumer has a personal, face-to-face relationship. We can refer to this kind of consumption as personalized. Everyone knows where products came from and who produced them. This pattern contrasts markedly with consumption in our contemporary globalized world, which we might call radically depersonalized consumption. Multinational corporations manage the production of most of the goods that people in industrialized countries consume. Many of these products are multi-sourced, with parts assembled in diverse parts of the world by hundreds of unknown workers. Some anthropologists believe that depersonalized consumption is harmful to the workers who actually produce goods (see the Critical Thinking box on page 84).

Depersonalized consumption is linked with mass production, which ensures a high level of production—the production of infinite goods to satisfy infinite needs. Even in the most industrialized contexts, though, depersonalized consumption has not completely replaced personalized consumption. The popularity of farmers' markets in urban centers is one example of personalized consumption in which the consumer buys apples from the person who grew them and with whom the consumer is likely to have a friendly conversation, perhaps while eating one of the apples.

Consumption Funds

A **consumption fund** is a category of a person's or household's budget used to provide for their demands. Cross-cultural analysis of expenditures (including both time or labor and cash) reveals the existence of a set of categories that are universal, although the amount of the budget allocated to each category varies according to the mode of production and the amount of surplus goods available in the society. In looking at a typical set of consumption funds, it is important to remember that people in non-monetized contexts "spend" time or labor, not cash.

In a forager's budget, the largest share of expenditures goes into the **basic needs fund,** which includes food, beverages, shelter, fuel, clothing, and the tools needed to obtain these items. In other words, foragers "spend" the largest proportion of their budget on providing basic needs. The next most important category for foragers is the **recurrent costs fund,** which supports repair and maintenance of tools and baskets, weapons, and shelter. Smaller amounts of expenditure are made to the **entertainment fund,** for personal leisure, and the **ceremonial fund,** for public events beyond the immediate group such as a potlatch. No funds go to the **tax fund,** which are payments to a government or landowner for civic responsibilities or use of land or housing.

Consumption budgets in consumerist cultures differ in the overall size of the budget and in the proportions allocated to particular funds. First, the budget size is larger. People in agricultural and industrial societies work longer hours (unless they are unemployed); thus they "spend" more time and labor than foragers. They also have cash budgets that may be substantial, depending on class position. In terms of budget shares, the basic needs fund shrinks to being the smallest fund, in line with the economic principle that budgetary shares for food and housing decline as income rises. The word *shares* is important. People with higher incomes may spend more on food and housing in an absolute sense than people with lower incomes, but the proportion of their total budget devoted to food and housing is less. For example, someone who earns a total of $1000 a month and spends $800 on food and housing expends 80 percent of his budget in that category. Someone who makes $10,000 a month and spends $2000 a month on food and housing expends only 20 percent of her budget in this category, even though she spends more than twice as much as the first person, in an absolute sense. Another difference is that people living in agricultural and industrial cultures devote the largest proportion of their budget to the tax fund. In some agricultural contexts, tenant farmers and sharecroppers provide one-third or one-half of their crops to the landlord as rent. Income taxes claim over 50 percent of income in countries such as Japan, Sweden, the Netherlands, and Italy (Pechman 1987). Another difference is the increased importance of the entertainment fund, which is used for recreation such as movies, sports events, travel, and buying home entertainment appliances.

Consumption Inequalities

Amartya Sen (1981), an economist and a philosopher, proposed the theory of **entitlements,** which are socially defined rights to life-sustaining resources, in order to explain why some groups suffer more than others during a famine. We can extend the use of the concept of entitlements to nonfamine situations as a way of looking at consumption inequalities in everyday life. Also, Sen's original use of the entitlement concept was in terms of intrasocietal patterns, but we will use it at three levels: global, national, and household. The concept of entitlements helps us understand how social inequality works and can change.

According to Sen, a person possesses a set or "bundle" of entitlements. A person may own land, earn cash from a job, be on welfare, or live off an inheritance, for

CAN THE INTERNET CREATE RESPONSIBLE CONSUMERS?

ONE IMPORTANT feature of increasingly globalized production is that the role of the producer is hidden from the consumer. In other words, commodities are no longer linked with particular producers. Furthermore, many products are assembled with parts from all over the world, created by many invisible workers. Daniel Miller (no relation to the author!) says that such labor invisibility and product depersonalization make it all too easy for consumers to be irresponsible and to support practices that are harmful to the distant, unseen laborers (2003). Most people are happy enough to blame the higher profits of multinational corporations for the poor treatment of producers, but Miller points out that the major responsibility should lie with us, the consumers. It is our search for the cheapest possible goods that drives the commercial competition that results in further exploitation of workers. It is consumers who must be persuaded to pay more in a way that directly facilitates better conditions for producers.

If consumers were educated about the actual dynamics of production and the role of the laborers, they would be more likely to make wiser and more responsible choices about which products to buy. For example, they would avoid products made by the more exploitive companies or by less ecologically responsible companies. And they might be willing to pay higher prices to discourage abuse of workers and of the environment.

Miller sees a major gap in the school curriculum in his home country, the United Kingdom. It is extraordinary, he says, that we call people "educated" who know more about ancient Rome or physics than about the products they consume every day. Most students will never use the higher math or physics that they study in school, but they will be consumers for the rest of their lives. So why not, he asks, provide consumer education for students?

To that end, Miller devised an Internet education project for school children that would teach them about the role of workers in relation to the products they consume and would put the human faces of producers behind commodities. Having discovered the importance of "interactivity" from his earlier fieldwork on people's use of the Internet in Trinidad, he created a plan for an interactive narrative about a product. The Internet could enable students to talk in real time with actual producers going about their work. To avoid a power differential between workers and viewers, the producers should be able to question the students (the consumers) about *their* lives as well. This interactive personalization would include, in the case of a relatively simple product like a banana, not just the plantation worker but also the wider system and process of banana production: plantation managers, packers, and transporters. The students would choose a banana company, web cams would be supplied to the workers, and both students and workers would be connected online once a week. In order to push the reality of production all the way, Miller hopes that the students would actually end up eating the same bananas that they saw being produced.

This is a big project, even for just a single commodity. Miller is well aware that we cannot, within reason, learn everything about the production of everything we consume. He suggests that three exemplary products be chosen for the education project, starting with the banana. The second product should be more complex to illustrate the multiple sourcing of most goods. The third product might be locally produced by a small-scale firm.

Miller sought government funding for his project, but was denied. Undaunted, he published an article in a journal in order to share his idea and inspire others to develop similar consumer education projects elsewhere. This Critical Thinking box asks you, as students of cultural anthropology, to consider his project.

CRITICAL THINKING QUESTIONS

Is Miller's idea of enhancing the school curriculum in this way important?

Is it feasible?

What suggestions do you have for two products in addition to bananas?

example. Through these entitlements, people provide for their consumption. Some kinds of entitlements, however, are more secure and more lucrative than others, and thus they provide more secure and luxurious levels of consumption. **Direct entitlements** are the most secure form of entitlement; in an agricultural society, for example, owning land that produces food is a direct entitlement. **Indirect entitlements** are ways of gaining subsistence that depend on exchanging something in order to obtain consumer needs—for example, labor, animal hides, welfare checks, or food stamps. Indirect entitlements entail dependency on other people and institutions and are thus riskier bases of support than direct entitlements. For example, labor or animal hides may drop in value or no longer be wanted, and food stamps may cease to be awarded. People who have no direct entitlements and only one or two forms of indirect entitlements in their bundle are the most vulnerable during times of economic decline, scarcity, or disaster.

In foraging societies, everyone has the same entitlement bundles and, except for infants and the very aged, the bundles are direct (infants and the aged are dependent on sharing from members of the group for their food and shelter and so could be said to have indirect entitlements). In industrial capitalist societies, entitlement bundles, in terms of access to food and resources, are preponderantly indirect. The few people who still grow their own food are a small proportion of the total population, and even they are dependent on indirect entitlements for electricity and other aspects of maintaining their lifestyle. In the highly monetized economies of industrialized societies, the most powerful entitlements are those that provide a high and steady cash income, such as a good job, savings, and a retirement fund.

Entitlements at Three Levels

Applied globally, entitlement theory enables us to differentiate nations that have secure and direct access to life-supporting resources from those that do not. Countries with high rates of food production have a more secure entitlement to food than nations that are dependent on imports, for example. Growing cash crops rather than food crops puts a nation in a situation of indirect entitlement to food. The same applies to access to energy sources that may be important for transportation to work or for heating homes. Direct access to energy resources is preferable to indirect access. The current structure of the global economy places some countries in far more secure positions than others.

In a parallel way, the entitlement concept can be applied at the micro level of the household to examine within-household entitlement structures. In contemporary industrial societies, having a job, owning a business or farm land, owning a home, or having savings and investments puts a person in a more secure position. This means that adults, and often males more than females, have more secure entitlements than other household members. Depending on the cultural context, inheritance practices may ensure that certain children receive entitlements to certain assets (the family business, for example) and others are left out.

Famine offers us a way of examining how entitlement theory works out in practice. Famine is massive death resulting from food deprivation in a geographically widespread area. It tends to reach a crisis point and then subside. Famines have been recorded throughout history for all parts of the world, including Europe (Dando 1980: 113). Between AD 10 and 1850, 187 famines were recorded in what is now the United Kingdom. India, Russia, and China experienced major famines in the twentieth century. Most recently, famines have occurred mainly in Africa: the Sahelian famine of 1969–1971, the Ethiopian famine of 1982–1984, the Sudan and Somalian famines of 1988–1992. The North Korean famine (or near-famine) of the late 1990s is one of the few cases that have occurred outside Africa in recent times.

Most people think that famines are caused by "too many people to feed" or by natural disasters such as droughts and floods. Neither overpopulation nor natural disasters, however, are sufficient explanations for famine (Sen 1981). First, calculations of world food supply in relation to population indicate that there is enough food produced every year to feed the world's population. Second, natural factors are often catalysts of famines, but natural disasters happen in many parts of the world and are not necessarily followed by famine. For example, Florida's devastating Hurricane Andrew did not cause a statewide famine. The answer to what causes famine lies in entitlement failures at three levels: global, national, and household.

The Global Level Throughout history, many countries that were colonized by external powers are now more resource-depleted than before and more dependent on food imports. Colonization changed local production from food crops for the people themselves to cash crops for sale. Thus, massive replacement of direct entitlements to food by indirect entitlements occurred. International relations in contemporary times often involve the "politics of food." As a journalist reported on the Sudan in 1988: "There is, cruelly, food to be had. The land is fertile, the rains were good, and this year's harvest will be the best in a decade. But 4 million people are starving because of a civil war. . . . On both sides the terrible weapon is increasingly food, not bullets" (Wilde 1988: 43). The northern army blocked the delivery of food aid to the south, and the food that did get through was often diverted by the southern rebel troops. Norway donated substantial amounts of maize, but the United States was slow to get involved because it did not want to upset its diplomatic relationship with the Sudanese government.

Global politics were also a key causal factor in the Bengal famine of 1943–1944. This massive famine was related to British efforts during World War II to stop the Japanese forces from advancing into India from Burma. The region of Bengal at that time included what is now a state of India (named West Bengal) and the nation of Bangladesh (called East Bengal when it was part of British India). Bengal was a lush food-producing region located, unfortunately, adjacent to Burma. As the Japanese moved closer to India, the British devised and implemented a plan to destroy food supplies in Bengal that could be used by the advancing enemy. The British burned standing crops and seeds that were being stored, and they destroyed fishing boats as well (Greenough 1982; Sen 1981). This policy succeeded in stopping the Japanese, but at a terrible cost of thousands of Bengalis' lives.

The National Level   Within countries, entitlement inequalities lead to particular patterns of suffering. In no famine, ever, has everyone in the affected area starved. Instead, many people grow wealthy by hoarding food and selling it at inflated prices. During the Bengal famine, the people most affected were those who lacked direct entitlements to food: the landless poor who normally worked as laborers for the landowners and were paid in cash food shares, and fishing people who could not fish without boats (Sen 1981). In the meantime, rich landowners and merchants bought up the rice that existed and secretly stored it. As food prices rose astronomically during the famine, they grew even richer by selling hoarded rice.

The Household Level   Within households, famine conditions force decisions about how to allocate scarce resources or deal with the absence of any resources at all. No cultural anthropologist was on the scene during the Bengal famine, studying intrahousehold decision making. However, historical evidence of how decisions were made is found in records about people who came to relief centers for food, medicine, and clothing (Greenough 1982). One finding is that the famine caused the breakup of households. In Bengali culture, males are valued over females and adults are valued over children. In the household, the senior male is the head of household and has the highest authority and responsibility.

Spouses frequently separated, with the husband either leaving the wife behind or sending her away. Women said that "their husbands were unable to maintain them at the present moment and asked them to go elsewhere to search for food" (quoted in Greenough 1982:220). Many abandoned women migrated to cities, such as Calcutta, where their options for survival were limited to relief hand-outs, begging, and prostitution. Some women and girls were sold by their families into prostitution.

Consumption Microcultures

This section provides examples of consumption microcultures, in the basic categories of class, gender, race, and age. People's consumption patterns are rarely the consequences of just one microculture but, rather, are shaped by affiliation with multiple and intersecting microcul-

Homeless children rest by a storefront grate in Ho Chi Minh City, Vietnam. ■ *Consider how the entitlement system affected children under pure socialism, compared to the current transition to a more capitalist system. (Hint: These children and their families depend on begging to survive.)* (Source: Edward Keller)

tures that determine entitlement bundles and ways of consuming resources.

Class   Class differences, defined in terms of levels of income and wealth, are reflected in class-specific consumption patterns. In cultures with class structures, upper-class people spend more on consumption than the poor. The poor, however, spend a higher percentage of their total income on consumption, especially on basic needs such as food, clothing, and shelter.

Class differences in consumption in contemporary industrial societies may seem so obvious that they are scarcely worth studying. A team of French researchers, however, undertook a national sample survey with over 1000 responses to study class differences in consumer preferences and tastes (Bourdieu 1984). The results revealed strong class patterns in, for example, choice of favorite painters or pieces of music, most closely associated with people's level of education and their father's occupation. An overall pattern of "distance from necessity" in tastes and preferences characterized members of the educated upper classes, who were more likely to prefer abstract art. Their goal was to keep "necessity" at a distance. In comparison, the working classes were closer to "necessity," and their preference was for realist art. Bourdieu provides the concept of the "game of distinction," in which people of various classes take on the preferences of others in order to enhance their own standing. Education, according to Bourdieu, provides the means for lower-class people to learn how to play the game of distinction according to upper-class rules.

Gender

Consumption patterns are often gender-marked. Specific foods may be thought to be "male foods" or "female foods." In cultures where alcoholic beverages are consumed, the general pattern is that males drink more than females. Following is a vivid example of differences in food consumption in highland Papua New Guinea, where males have higher status than females. This story begins with the eruption of a mysterious disease, with the local name of *kuru,* among the Fore (pronounced FOR-AY), a highland horticultural group (Lindenbaum 1979). Between 1957 and 1977, about 2500 people died of *kuru.* The victims were mostly women. A victim of the disease would first have shivering tremors, followed by a progressive loss of motor ability along with pain in the head and limbs. People afflicted with *kuru* could walk unsteadily at first but would later be unable to get up. Death occurred about a year after the first symptoms appeared.

The Fore believed that *kuru* was caused by sorcery, but a team of medical researchers and a cultural anthropologist (Lindenbaum) showed that *kuru* was a neurological disease caused by consumption of the flesh of deceased people who were themselves *kuru* victims. Who was eating human flesh, and why? Among the Fore, it was considered acceptable to cook and eat the meat of a deceased person, although it was not a preferred food. Some Fore women turned to eating human flesh because of rising scarcity of the usual sources of animal protein in the region. Population density had increased, areas under cultivation had increased, forest areas had decreased, and wild animals as a protein source were scarce in the Fore region. This scarcity acted in combination with the Fore's male-biased system of consumption in which preferred protein sources go to men. Women, therefore, turned to consumption of less-preferred food, contracted *kuru,* and died.

Race/Ethnicity

Racial apartheid was a matter of national policy in South Africa until 1994 and is a clear example of explicit racial inequalities in consumption. Whites owned property, had wealth, and lived prosperous lives that included good food, housing, and educational opportunities for their children. Blacks were denied all of these things. The current government in South Africa is still attempting to redress decades of deprivation linked to racial categories and now has to face the additional burden of widespread HIV/AIDS.

In the United States, racial differences in consumption and welfare continue to exist in spite of anti-discrimination legislation (Hacker 1992). One area in which racial discrimination affects consumption is access to housing. Access by Blacks to housing in integrated neighborhoods is limited by the tendency of Whites to move out as more Black families move in.

Overconsumption is a relative term that introduces an emerging and controversial social issue in the United States and the United Kingdom: obesity. In both countries, the rate of obesity (as medically defined) is high and increasing. Theories to account for this "epidemic" abound. One point is clear: Within the general population, certain people are more likely to be obese than others. Ethnicity often appears relevant, and it interacts with other factors such as gender and age. Among Puerto Ricans in Philadelphia, the overall incidence of obesity is 20 percent higher for women than for men (Massara 1997). Women between forty and eighty years of age are 67 percent more likely to be obese than Puerto Rican women under the age of twenty-five. The culture of food in many American Puerto Rican families emphasizes strong links between being a good wife and mother and her role as food preparer and server. A woman may eat dinner with her children and then, once again, join her husband when he comes home later for his dinner. Some of the heavier women explained that their size made them appear asexual and allowed them to lead a more active social life outside the home without provoking their husbands' anger. Many women in the study thought that a certain amount of overweight, in medical terms, is acceptable. A deeper analysis, though, hinted that for many adult Puerto Rican women, overeating is a response to stress or to feelings of neglect in the family.

Age

Age categories often have characteristic consumption patterns that are culturally shaped. Certain foods may be believed appropriate for infants, young children, adolescents, adults, or the aged. Consider the category of "the aged." Biologically, the elderly have "more critical and unique nutritional needs" than other age groups (Shifflett and McIntosh 1986–1987). In spite of these special needs, in many cultures the very old fall into a category with declining entitlements and declining quality of consumption. In the United States, the elderly tend to omit important food groups, especially fruits and vegetables. Among elderly Virginians, several factors related to dietary change were discovered, including lack of social support and loneliness. One respondent reported that she had been widowed for ten years and that she had undergone a negative change in her food habits soon after her husband died. For several years she felt she "had nothing to live for." She ate only junk foods and meals she could prepare with the least effort. She experienced a rapid weight gain up to 200 pounds, but "One day I realized what I was doing to my health and I went on a diet. I tried to eat a balanced diet and am still trying to eat better now" (10).

Aging affects everyone, regardless of class level, but wealth can protect the elderly from certain kinds of marginalization and deprivation. Money can often buy better health care, and studies show that income level is positively related to longevity (lifespan) around the world. Wealthier people can afford home care when they become infirm and unable to care for themselves. In the United States, middle-class people may spend their last years in a nursing home, but the poor fare even worse. Park benches and shelters provided by local governments and volunteer organizations may be their only option (Vesperi 1985).

Forbidden Consumption: Food Taboos

Cultural anthropologists have a longstanding interest in trying to explain culturally specific food taboos, or rules of prohibition. This interest has generated conflicting theories, and those of the cultural materialists and the symbolic anthropologists differ widely.

Cultural Materialism and Food Taboos

Marvin Harris (1974), cultural materialist, asks why there are Jewish and Muslim taboos on eating pig when pig meat is so enthusiastically consumed in many other parts of the world. He says, "Why should gods so exalted as Jahweh and Allah have bothered to condemn a harm-

Preparations for a feast in the highlands in Papua New Guinea where people place much value on consuming roasted pig meat. ■ *What are the high-status foods in your cultural world(s)? Propose a materialist or meaning-centered theory about one such food.* (Source: © David Austen/Stock Boston, LLC)

less and even laughable beast whose flesh is relished by the greater part of mankind?" (36). Harris proposes that we consider the role of environmental factors during early Hebrew times and the function of this prohibition in terms of its fit to the local ecology:

> Within the overall pattern of this mixed farming and pastoral complex, the divine prohibition of pork constituted a sound ecological strategy. The pig is thermodynamically ill-adapted to the hot, dry climate of the Negev, the Jordan Valley, and the other lands of the Bible and the Koran. Compared to cattle, goats, and sheep, the pig has an inefficient system for regulating its body temperature. Despite the expression "To sweat like a pig," it has recently been proved that pigs can't sweat at all. (41–42)

Raising pigs in this context would be a luxury. On the other hand, in "pig-loving" cultures of Southeast Asia and the Pacific, climatic factors including temperature, humidity, and the presence of forest cover (good for pigs) promote pig raising. There, pigs offer an important protein source that complements yams, sweet potatoes, and taro. In conclusion, Harris acknowledges that not all religiously sanctioned food practices can be explained ecologically, and he allows that food practices do have a social function in promoting social identity. But first and foremost, analysis of food consumption should consider ecological and material factors of production.

Food Taboos as Systems of Meaning

Interpretive anthropologist Mary Douglas (1966) claims that what people eat has less to do with the material conditions of life (notably hunger) than with the value of food as a way of communicating meaning about the world. For Douglas, people's emic categories provide a psychological ordering of the world. Anomalies, or things that don't fit into the categories, become reminders to people of moral problems or things to avoid.

She uses this approach in her analysis of food prohibitions in the Old Testament book of Leviticus. One rule is that people may eat animals with cloven hoofs and that chew a cud. Several tabooed animals are said to be unclean, such as the camel, the pig, the hare, and the rock badger. Among a pastoral people, she says, it is logical that the model food animal would be a ruminant (a cloven-hoofed, cud-chewing, four-footed animal such as cattle, bison, goats, and sheep). In contrast, a pig is a four-footed animal with cloven hoofs, but it does not chew a cud; thus the pig is an anomaly and taboo as food. In this way, Leviticus sets up a system that contrasts sacred completeness and purity (the animals one can eat) with impurity and sinfulness (the animals one cannot eat) to remind people of God's holiness and perfectness and people's responsibility toward God.

Scholars who favor either a cultural materialist or interpretive approach to food taboos all acknowledge that there is more to food than just eating. Douglas emphasizes the importance of food rules as ways of communicating meaning, downplaying the "practical" aspects of food, which she says distract analysts from studying the meaning of food. Harris would concur that food rules serve such purposes but insists that focusing only on meaning gives a partial view because it overlooks the material aspects of food practices and rules.

CULTURE AND EXCHANGE

Cultural anthropologists have done much research on gifts and other forms of exchange, starting with the early-twentieth-century studies by Malinowski of the *kula* of the Trobriand Islands and Boas's research on the potlatch of the Pacific Northwest. In all economic systems, individuals and groups exchange goods and services with others, so exchange is a cultural universal. But variation arises in several areas: what is exchanged, how are goods exchanged, when exchange takes place, and how exchange varies from culture to culture.

What Is Exchanged?

Exchange is the transfer of something that may be material or immaterial between at least two persons, groups, or institutions. The items exchanged may be purely utilitarian or they may carry meanings and have a history, or "social life," of their own (Appadurai 1986).

In contemporary industrial societies, money is a key item of exchange. No dollar bill has more meaning or significance than any other. In nonmarket economies, money plays a less important role, and time, labor, and goods are prominent exchange items.

But nonmonetary exchange exists in contemporary industrial societies, too. Hosting dinner parties, exchanging gifts at holiday times, and sharing a bag of potato chips with a friend are examples of common forms of nonmonetary exchange. Some scholars would even include giving caresses, kisses, loyalty, and glances (Blau 1964).

Material Goods

Food is one of the most common exchange goods in everyday life and on ritual occasions. Marriage arrangements often involve many stages of food gifts and countergifts exchanged between the groom's family and the bride's family. Wedding exchanges among the Nias of northern Sumatra, Indonesia, provide a good illustration. From the betrothal to the actual marriage, there unfolds a scheduled sequence of events at which food and other gifts are exchanged between the families of the bride and groom (Beatty 1992). At the first meeting, when the prospective groom expresses his interest in a betrothal, he and his party visit the bride's house and are fed: "The guests are given the pig's lower jaw (the portion of honour) and take away with them raw and cooked portions for the suitor's father" (121). Within the next week or two, the groom brings a gift of three to twelve pigs to confirm the engagement. He also returns the container used for the pig meat given to him on the previous visit, filled with a certain kind of nut. The groom gives pigs and gold as the major gift that seals the marriage. Gifts are exchanged between the two families over many years.

Exchanges of food are important in signaling and reaffirming friendships. Among friends, food exchanges involve their own, largely unconscious rules of etiquette. (See the Unity and Diversity box on page 90.)

Exchanging alcoholic beverages is an important feature of many communal, ritual events in Latin America. In an Ecuadorian village called Agato, the San Juan fiesta is the high point of the year (Barlett 1980). The fiesta consists of four or five days during which small groups of celebrants move from house to house, dancing and drinking. The anthropologist reports on the event:

> I joined the groups consisting of the president of the community and the elected *alcaldes* (councilmen and police), who were accompanied by their wives, a few friends, and some children. We met each morning for a hearty breakfast at one house, began drinking there, and then continued eating and drinking in other homes throughout the day and into the evening. . . . Some people drink for only one or two days, others prefer to make visits mainly at night, while some people drink day and night for four days. . . . (118–119)

Guests who drink at someone's house will later serve their former hosts alcohol in return. Functional theorists would view this system of exchange as contributing to social cohesion (review Chapter 1).

Symbolic Goods

Intangible valuables such as myths (sacred stories) and rituals (sacred practices) are sometimes exchanged in ways similar to material goods. In lowland areas of Papua New Guinea, men trade myths, rituals, dances, flutes, costumes, and styles of body decoration for the pigs of highland men (Harrison 1993). Certain secret spells were some of the most prestigious trade items. In the Balgo Hills region of Australia, longstanding exchange networks transfer myths and rituals among groups of women (Poirier 1992). Throughout the region, the women may keep important narratives and rituals only for a certain time and then must pass them on to other groups. One such ritual is the *Tjarada*, a love-magic ritual with an accompanying narrative. The Tjarada came to the women of Balgo Hills from the north. They kept

Unity and Diversity

THE RULES OF HOSPITALITY IN OMAN

IN MUCH of the Middle East, where women spend little time in the public domain, social visits among women are much anticipated and carefully planned events with complex rules about what should be served (Wikan 1982). In Oman, when women do venture outside, they wear head veils, face masks, and full-length gowns. Their main social activity outside the home consists of visits to other women in their homes. A typical visit involves sitting, chatting, and eating snacks. Social etiquette dictates what should be served and how:

> Dates and coffee compose the traditional food of entertainment between close neighbors. Nowadays, biscuits, inexpensive caramels, and popcorn tend to be favored substitutes. Between neighbors who interact on a daily basis, or nearly so, a single dish will do. But all other visitors, even solitary ones, should be offered at least two plates, with different contents, or the hostess is thought stingy. If the guests are more numerous, the amounts or variety must be increased, up to a minimum of four plates. Three or four plates may also be offered to one or two guests when the hostess wishes to honor them.
>
> The rules of etiquette require that approximately half of the food served be left for the hostess' household. (130–132)

Cooked food, such as meat and sweets, is served when one entertains more important guests, or for weddings, seasonal feasts, and burials. With cooked food, though, the hosts may never eat with their guests: "Even if the consequence is that the guest must eat all alone,

in a separate room, it would be disrespectful to arrange it otherwise." (133)

FOOD FOR THOUGHT

How does this Omani pattern of hospitality resemble or differ from forms of hospitality you know?

---

it for about fifteen years and then passed it on to another group in a ceremony that lasted for three days. During the time that the Balgo Hills women were custodians of the Tjarada, they incorporated some new elements into it. These elements are retained even after its transfer to the next group. Thus, the Tjarada contains bits of local identity of each group that has had it. A sense of linked community and mutual responsibility thereby develops and is sustained among the different groups that have held the Tjarada.

Labor

In labor-sharing groups, people contribute labor to other people on a regular basis (for seasonal agricultural work such as harvesting) or on an irregular basis (in the event of a crisis such as the need to rebuild a barn damaged by fire). Labor-sharing groups are part of what has been called a "moral economy" because no one keeps formal records on how much any family puts in or takes out. Instead, accounting is socially regulated. The group has a sense of moral community based on years of trust and sharing. In Amish communities of North America, labor sharing is a major economic factor of social cohesion. When a family needs a new barn or faces repair work that requires group labor, a barn-raising party is called. Many families show up to help. Adult men provide manual labor, and adult women provide food for the event. Later, when another family needs help, they call on the same people.

Money

The term **money** refers to things that can be exchanged for many different kinds of items (Godelier 1971:53). Besides being a medium of exchange, money can be a standard of value and a store of value or wealth (Neale 1976). Money can be found in such diverse forms as shells, salt, cattle, furs, cocoa beans, and iron hoes. Compared to other exchange items, money is a recent innovation. Although no one knows when money first appeared, one of the earliest forms of coined money was used by the Greeks in Asia Minor (Turkey) in the seventh century BCE. Pre-coin money undoubtedly existed well before that time.

Items that can be exchanged for only a few other items are called **limited-purpose money**. Raffia cloth serves as limited-purpose money among the Lele of central Africa (Douglas 1962). Raffia cloth, made from the fibers of a kind of palm, is used to pay for certain ritual and ceremonial events, such as a marriage, and as compensation for wrongdoing. It is not used for commercial transactions such as buying food, houses, or land.

Modern money is **multi-purpose money**, or a medium of exchange that can be used for all goods and services available. In addition to its substitutability (money can be exchanged for goods and for other money), modern money is distinguished by its portability, divisibility, uniformity, and recognizability (Shipton 2001). On the other hand, modern money is vulnerable to economic changes such as inflation, which reduce its value. Early anthropologists who proposed evolutionary models of culture (Chapter 1) thought that modern money is more rational than limited-purpose money and that it would replace other forms of money as well as nonmonetized exchanges such as barter. Modern money is indeed spreading throughout the world. Nonmonetary cultures often adopt modern money in limited ways, prohibiting its use in religious exchanges, for example, or in life-cycle rituals such as marriages. Even the most monetized cultures place limits on what may be bought and sold for money.

All kinds of money are symbolic—they have meaning to the user, and they are associated with the user's identity and sense of self. Credit cards may be a positive sign of modernity or may be associated with overspending and wastefulness. They have "class" levels signified by cards of different colors. As e-money becomes increasingly used, we shall see what kinds of meaning are attached to it.

People

Throughout history, some people have been able to gain control of other people and treat them as objects of exchange, as in systems of institutionalized slavery and in underground, criminal activities. The topic of women as "items" of exchange in marriage is a puzzling one in anthropology and has occasioned much debate. Lévi-Strauss proposed many years ago that the exchange of women between men is one of the most basic forms of exchange in human culture. His argument about exchange is based on the universality of some sort of incest taboo, which he defines as a rule preventing a man from marrying or cohabiting with his mother or sister (1969 [1949]). Such a rule, he says, is a logical motivation for equal exchange: "the fact that I can obtain a wife is, in the final analysis, the consequence of the fact that a brother or father has given her up" (62). According to this theory, men are thus impelled to develop exchange networks with other men. This process leads to the emergence of social solidarity between groups. For Lévi-Strauss, the incest taboo is the basis of the original form of exchange and the emergence of an important aspect of culture.

Other anthropologists say that this theory overlooks much ethnographic evidence to the contrary. It disregards the many foraging societies in which men do not have rights in women and in which women choose their own male partners (Rubin 1975). Evidence from horticultural and agricultural societies of Southeast Asia further refutes Lévi-Strauss's universal model of men exchanging women (Peletz 1987). In these systems, the focus of marriage arrangements is on women's exchange of men and control of their labor power. Adult women arrange their daughters' marriages, selecting the groom themselves.

Modes of Exchange

Parallel to the two contrasting modes of consumption described earlier (minimalism and consumerism) two distinct modes of exchange can be delineated (see Figure 4.2 on page 92). They are **balanced exchange,** or a system of transfers in which the goal is either immediate or eventual balance in value, and **unbalanced exchange,** a system of transfers in which one party attempts to make a profit.

Balanced Exchange

The category of balanced exchange contains two subcategories based on the social relationship of the two parties involved in the exchange and the degree to which a "return" is expected. **Generalized reciprocity** is a transaction that involves the least conscious sense of interest in material gain or thought of what might be received in return. When, or if, a possible return might be made is not calculated. Such exchanges often involve goods and services of an everyday nature, such as a cup of coffee. Generalized reciprocity is the predominant form of exchange between people who know each other well and trust each other. It is the predominant form of exchange

FIGURE 4.2 Keeping Track of Exchange

	Balanced Exchange		Unbalanced Exchange	
	Generalized Reciprocity	Expected Reciprocity	Market Exchange	Theft, Exploitation
Actors	Kin, friends	Trading partners	Buyers/sellers	Non-kin, non-friends, unknown
Return	Not calculated or expected	Expected at some time	Immediate payment	No return
Example	Buying coffee for a friend	*Kula*	Internet shopping	Shoplifting

in foraging societies, and it is also found among close kin and friends cross-culturally.

The Pure Gift   A **pure gift** is something given with no expectation or thought of a return. The pure gift is an extreme form of generalized reciprocity. Examples of a pure gift include donating money for a food drive, or making donations to famine relief, blood banks, and religious organizations.

Some people say that a truly pure gift does not exist because one always gains something, no matter how difficult to measure, in giving—even if it is just the good feeling of generosity. Parental care of children is said to be a pure gift by some, but others do not agree. Those who say that parental care is a pure gift argue that most parents do not consciously calculate how "much" they have spent on their children with the intention of "getting

it back" later on. Those who do not consider parental care a pure gift say that even if the "costs" are not consciously calculated, parents have unconscious expectations about what their children will "return" to them, whether the return is material (care in old age) or immaterial (making the parent feel proud).

Expected reciprocity is the exchange of approximately equally valued goods or services, usually between people of roughly equal social status. The exchange may occur simultaneously from both parties, or an agreement or understanding may exist that stipulates the time period within which the exchange will be completed. This aspect of the timing contrasts with generalized reciprocity, in which there is no fixed time limit for the return. In expected reciprocity, if the second party fails to complete the exchange, the relationship will break down. The difference is that balanced reciprocity is less personal than

Shell ornaments are important items worn at ceremonial events, as shown on this man of the Sepik River area of Papua New Guinea. ■ *What are the key items of exchange in your microculture?* (Source: © Chuck Fishman/Woodfin Camp & Associates)

generalized reciprocity and, according to Western definitions, more "economic."

The *kula* is an example of a system of expected reciprocity (recall Chapter 2's discussion of Malinowski's fieldwork in the Trobriand Islands). Men of different Trobriand groups exchange necklaces and armlets, giving them to their exchange partners after keeping them for a while. Partners include neighbors as well as people on faraway islands who are visited via long canoe voyages on high seas. Trobriand men are distinguished by the particular armlets and necklaces that they exchange, and certain armlets and necklaces are more prestigious than others. One cannot keep one's trade items for long because the *kula* code dictates that "to possess is great, but to possess is to give." Generosity is the essence of goodness, and stinginess is the most despised vice. *Kula* exchanges should involve items of equivalent value. If a man trades a very valuable necklace with his partner, he expects to receive in return a very valuable armlet as a *yotile* (equivalent gift). At the time, if one's partner does not possess an equivalent item, he may have to give a *basi* (intermediary gift). The *basi* stands as a token of good faith until a proper return gift can be given. The *kudu* ("clinching gift") will come later and balance the original gift. The equality of exchange ensures a tight social bond between the trading partners and is a statement of trust. When a man sails to an area in which there may be danger because of previous raids or warfare, he can count on having a friend to receive him and give him hospitality.

Redistribution

Redistribution is a form of exchange that involves one person collecting goods or money from many members of a group. Then, at a public event later on, he "returns" the pooled goods to everyone who contributed in the form of a generous feast. In comparison to the two-way pattern of exchange involved in reciprocity, redistribution involves some "centricity." It contains the possibility of institutionalized inequality because what is returned may not always equal what was contributed by each individual. The pooling group may continue to exist in spite of inequality because of the leadership skills of the person who mobilizes contributions.

Highland New Guinea political leadership involves redistribution in a system of contributions and ritual feasts called *moka* that may take several years to organize (discussed in Chapter 10). Formal taxation systems of industrial societies can be considered a form of redistribution. People pay taxes to a central institution, and they receive services from the government in return. Depending on the context, the return may or may not appear to be satisfactory to the contributors. The degree of personal contact in different redistributive systems varies, just as with forms of reciprocity. Similarly, the contexts in which greater personal interaction is involved tend to be more egalitarian and less exploitive than the impersonal forms.

Unbalanced Exchange

Market exchange is the buying and selling of commodities under competitive conditions in which the forces of supply and demand determine value (Dannhaeuser 1989:222). In market transactions, the people involved may not be related to or know each other at all. They may not be social equals, and their exchange is not likely to generate social bonding. Many market transactions take place in a marketplace, a physical location in which buying and selling occur. Markets evolved from other, less formal contexts of **trade**, formalized exchange of one thing for another according to set standards of value. In order for trade to develop, someone must have something that someone else wants.

Specialization in producing a particular good promotes trade between regions. Particular products are often identified with a town or region. In Oaxaca, Mexico, different villages are known for blankets, pottery, stone grinders, rope, and chili peppers (Plattner 1989: 180–181). In Morocco, the city of Fez is famous for its blue-glazed pottery, whereas the Berber people of the mountain region are known for their fine blankets, rugs, and other woven goods. Specialization develops with illegal commodities, too. For example, Jamaican marijuana is well known for its high quality, and many tourists travel to Jamaica, especially the Negril beach area, in order to buy this product.

The periodic market, a site for market transactions that is not permanently set up but occurs regularly, emerged with the development of agriculture and urban settlements. A periodic market, however, is more than just a place for buying and selling, it is also a place of social activity: Government officials drop in on the market, religious organizations hold services, long-term acquaintances catch up with each other, and young people may meet and fall in love.

Worldwide, permanent markets situated in fixed locations have long served the everyday needs of villages and neighborhoods. Permanent markets throughout China, for example, have long provided for the everyday needs of local people (Skinner 1964). The persistence of the role of such localized markets can be seen in the number of neighborhood shops in the city of Shanghai (Lu 1995). Shanghai is the most Westernized city in China, but in the back streets and neighborhoods, small-scale and personalized marketing still prevails, with shops selling sesame cakes, hot water, wine, traditional Chinese medicine, coal, tobacco paper, soy sauce, and locally produced groceries.

More contemporary, less personalized forms of permanent marketplaces include shopping malls and stock exchanges. Shopping on the Internet poses some analytical challenges for anthropologists. Although one might say that it is a highly depersonalized form of shopping, it can provide opportunities for virtual—and even real—social interaction. The author's experience in buying antique pottery on eBay has put her in contact with many sellers in the United States, Canada, and the United Kingdom. In one instance, a miscalculation of postal costs from England resulted in my owing the seller about five dollars. She cheerily told me not to worry about it but that I could buy her a cup of coffee the next time she "crosses the pond"—hardly a depersonalized interaction.

Other Forms of Unbalanced Exchange

Several forms of unbalanced exchange other than market transactions exist. In extreme instances, no social relationship is involved; in others, sustained unequal relationships are maintained over time between people. These forms include taking something with no expectation of giving any return. They can occur in any mode of production but are most likely to be found in large-scale societies where more options for other than face-to-face, balanced exchange exist.

Gambling Gambling, or gaming, is the attempt to make a profit by playing a game of chance in which a certain item of value is staked in hopes of acquiring the much larger return that one receives if one wins the game. If one loses, that which was staked is lost. Gambling is an ancient practice and is common cross-culturally. Ancient forms of gambling involved games such as dice throwing and card playing. Investing in the stock market can

be considered a form of gambling, as can gambling of many sorts through the Internet. Although gambling may seem an odd category within unbalanced exchange, its goals of making a profit seem to justify its placement here. The fact that gambling within "high" capitalism is on the rise justifies anthropological attention to it. In fact, some scholars have referred to the present stage of Western capitalism as "casino capitalism," given the propensity of investors to play very risky games on the stock market.

Native American gambling establishments in the United States have mushroomed in recent years. The state of Michigan alone has nearly twenty Native American casinos. Throughout the country, Native American casinos are so financially successful that they are perceived as an economic threat to many state lotteries. The Pequot Indians of Connecticut, a small tribe of around 200 people, now operate the most lucrative gaming establishment in the world, Foxwoods Resort and Casino, established in 1992 (Eisler 2001). The story of this success hangs on the creativity of one man: Richard "Skip" Hayward. An unemployed shipbuilder in the 1970s, he granted his grandmother's wish that he revive the declining tribe. Hayward used the legal system governing Native Americans to his advantage, forged links with powerful people such as Malaysian industrialist Lim Goh Tong and Bill Clinton (to whose campaign the Pequot donated half a million dollars), made powerful enemies such as Donald Trump, and became the chief of his now-rich tribe.

The Pequots, and many other Native American groups, have become highly successful capitalists. Anthropologists and other social scientists are asking what impact these casinos will have on their Native American owners and the surrounding area and what such newly rich groups will do with their wealth (see the Lessons

In China, many marketers are women. These two women display their wares in a permanent neighborhood food market in a city about an hour from Shanghai.
■ *Assume you are at this market and would like to cook a chicken for dinner. What steps do you take to make that happen?* (Source: Barbara Miller)

Lessons Applied

ASSESSING THE SOCIAL IMPACT OF NATIVE AMERICAN CASINOS

A FEW scattered "impact studies" on Native American casinos were carried out in the 1990s, but they were not based on a large number of casinos, nor did they include in-depth study of particular establishments. Thus their results were not solid enough to provide a foundation for policy makers. One study found that, in terms of effects on the surrounding community, the presence of a Native American casino is much like having a new, large enterprise of any sort: Local employment and income rise, business opportunities are created, and local services such as law enforcement are strained (Lake and Deller 1996). Another study that examined the impact of several casinos over a 4-year period found the following positive effects: young adults moving back to the reservation, increased adult employment, and a decline in the mortality rate (Evans and Topoleski 2002). Negative changes included a 10 percent increase in auto thefts, larceny, violent crime, and bankruptcy in the surrounding counties. The authors caution that their findings cannot be applied to policy formation without further study, because the issues are so complex. For example, many of the people employed in the casinos are not Native Americans.

Given the lack of comprehensive studies of the effects of Native American gaming, USET sought to provide high-quality, policy-relevant information as a tool for tribal leaders. The study is being led by anthropologist Kate Spilde, who works with the Harvard Project on American Indian Economic Development (HPAIED). It is being conducted in collaboration with tribal officials and casino managers. The study seeks to assess impacts on both the Native American gaming tribes and the surrounding communities. Initiated in 2003, it will take two and a half years and will involve on-site research with 100 gaming tribes throughout the United States. The study will also include eight in-depth case studies of individual tribes, chosen to represent the diversity of tribal gaming in terms of market size, tribal population, scope of gaming, profitability, and other factors. The research findings will be presented in a final report to be used by tribal policy makers and United States gaming policy makers.

A report on the pilot project for the national study, carried out in Oklahoma, can be downloaded at *www.ksg.harvard.edu/hpaied/publ.htm.*

FOOD FOR THOUGHT

Consider the development of Native American casinos from the theoretical perspective of structure versus agency. (Recall the discussion of these perspectives in Chapter 1.)

Applied box). In 1992, twenty-four Native American tribes formed an intertribal organization called USET (United South and Eastern Tribes), which is supporting a nationwide study of the social and economic impacts of Native American gaming.

Theft Theft is taking something with no expectation or thought of returning anything to the original owner for it. It is the logical opposite of a pure gift. The study of theft has been neglected by anthropologists, perhaps because it might involve danger. One insightful analysis considers food stealing by children in Africa (Bledsoe 1983). During fieldwork among the Mende of Sierra Leone, Caroline Bledsoe discovered a "clandestine economy" of food stealing practiced by children. Children in town frequently stole fruits such as mangoes, guavas, and oranges. Bledsoe at first dismissed cases of food stealing as rare exceptions, "But I began to realize that I rarely walked through town without hearing shouts of anger from an adult and cries of pain from a child being whipped for stealing food" (2). She decided to look into children's food stealing more closely.

Bledsoe had the children participate in simulations of meal preparation and meal serving. In both situations, children revealed to her subtle methods of tiefing. She also asked them to keep diaries, and these reports were dominated by themes of tiefing. From an analysis of reports from many children, she found that fostered children, children temporarily placed in the care of friends or relatives, do more food stealing than children living with their natal families. Food stealing can be seen as children's attempts to compensate for their less-than-adequate food shares at home. They do this by claiming food that is not part of their rightful entitlement, by "tiefing."

Stealing as a conscious attempt to alter an unfair entitlement system underlies an analysis of the "looting" that occurred in Los Angeles in 1992 following announcement of the Rodney King verdict (Fiske 1994). This looting was an outcome of the economic inequities faced by the African American community of South Central Los Angeles.

> Between 1982 and 1989, 131 factories closed in LA with the loss of 124,000 jobs. . . . The jobs that were lost were ones that disproportionately employed African Americans . . . in the four years before 1982, South Central, the traditional industrial core of LA, lost 70,000 blue-collar jobs. In Black eyes, this pattern is produced not by a raceless free market, but by racism encoded into economics: To them the 50 percent Black male unemployment in South Central does not look like the result of neutral, let alone natural, economic laws. (469–470)

How is all of this related to exchange? The looting during the Los Angeles uprising can be seen as an expression of deep-seated resentment about economic discrimination and as political protest, just as consumer boycotts are protests of a different sort. The media's use of the word *looting* linked the uprising to the domain of crime, leaving prison as the only solution. Framing the uprising as a law-and-order issue only diverted the public's attention from its roots in severe economic discrimination.

Obviously, much theft that occurs in the world is motivated by greed, not economic deprivation or oppression. The world of theft in expensive commodities such as gems and art has not been researched by cultural anthropologists, nor has corporate financial malpractice yet been examined as a form of theft.

Exploitation   Exploitation, or getting something of greater value for less in return, is a form of extreme and persistent unbalanced exchange. Slavery is a form of exploitation in which people's labor power is appropriated without their consent and with no recompense for its value. Slavery is rare among foraging, horticultural, and pastoral societies. Social relationships that involve sustained unequal exchange do exist between members of different social groups that, unlike pure slavery, involve no overt coercion and entail a certain degree of return by the dominant member to the subdominant member. Some degree of covert compulsion or dependence is likely to be present, however, in order for relationships of unequal exchange to endure.

Relationships between the Efe, who are "pygmy" foragers, and the Lese, who are farmers, in Congo (formerly Zaire) exemplify sustained unequal exchange (Grinker 1994). The Lese live in small villages. The Efe are semi-nomadic, and they live in temporary camps near Lese villages. Men of each group maintain long-term, hereditary exchange partnerships with each other. The Lese give cultivated foods and iron to the Efe, and the Efe give meat, honey, and other forest goods to the Lese.

Each Efe partner is considered a member of the "house" of his Lese partner, although he lives separately. Their main link is the exchange of food items, a system conceptualized by the Lese not as trade, per se, but as sharing of co-produced goods, as though the two partners were a single unit with a division of labor and a subsequent division or co-sharing of the goods produced. Yet there is evidence of inequality in these trading relationships, with the Lese having the advantage. The Efe provide much-wanted meat to the Lese, but this role gives them no status, for it is the giving of cultivated foods by the Lese to the Efe that conveys status. Another area of inequality is marital and sexual relationships. Lese men may marry Efe women, and sometimes do, and the children are considered Lese. Efe men cannot marry Lese women.

Theories of Exchange

Here we look at two theories that seek to explain why people participate in patterned processes of exchange. The first is a functional view that sees exchange as creating social and economic safety nets for people, along the lines of the potlatch explanation provided at the beginning of the chapter. The second is a critical theory that points to how patterns of exchange create and sustain social inequality.

Exchange and Risk Aversion

At the beginning of this chapter, the potlatch system was presented as an exchange network with an economic security function. Linking with other groups smooths out, to a certain extent, the unevenness of a particular local economy. Many more such examples can be found cross-culturally.

Carol Stack (1974) was perhaps the first cultural anthropologist to study how exchange patterns among kin and friends in urban America serve as a social safety net. She did research in "The Flats," the poorest section of a Black community in a midwestern city that she calls Jackson Harbor. Jackson Harbor is marked by racial inequality with, for example, a much higher proportion of Blacks than Whites living in deteriorating or severely dilapidated housing. Stack's approach differed from earlier studies of the Black family in America by avoiding negative comparisons with middle-class White lifestyles. She instead looked at the Black family members' strategies for dealing with poverty and uncertainty.

> I found extensive networks of kin and friends supporting, reinforcing each other—devising schemes for self-help, strategies for survival in a community of severe economic deprivation. . . . Their social and economic lives were so entwined that not to repay an exchange meant that someone else's child would not eat. People would tell me, "You have to have help from everybody and anybody," and

Cases of locally produced beer, "333," are unloaded near the port of Ho Chi Minh City, Vietnam, where logos of many Western products are familiar sights in the growing capitalist economy.
■ *What are the five most common logos of products in your cultural world?* (Source: Edward Keller)

"The poorer you are, the more likely you are to pay back." (28)

Stack spent nearly three years in The Flats, studying the complex exchange system. She also became involved in the system: "If someone asked a favor of me, later I asked a favor of him. If I gave a scarf, a skirt, or a cooking utensil to a woman who admired it, later on when she had something I liked she would usually give it to me. Little by little as I learned the rules of giving and reciprocity, I tried them out" (28). Timing is important in the "swapping system." The purpose is to obligate the receiver over a period of time; thus, swapping rarely involves simultaneous exchange. The swapping system of The Flats lies between the categories of generalized and expected reciprocity, both of which are related to the maintenance of social bonds.

Exchange and Social Inequality

In addition to contributing to social ties, exchange may also support and perpetuate social inequality. Paul Bohannan (1955), an economic anthropologist, studied the economy of the Tiv, horticulturalists of Nigeria, before European monetary systems entered their economy. He learned that, besides gift exchange, three spheres of market exchange existed in which items of equivalent value are traded for each other. Each of the three spheres carried different levels of prestige. The lowest-ranking sphere is the arena of women's trade. It includes chickens, hoes, baskets, pots, and grain. "For a woman to sell yams to buy a pot, for her to make a pot and sell to buy yams—these are considered to be normal buying and selling (*yamen a yam*)." This domestic sphere has the most frequent activity, but no prestige.

The second-ranking category included brass rods, special white cloth, guns, cattle, and slaves. Slavery had been abolished at the time of Bohannan's research, and the brass rods were increasingly rare, but the Tiv still talked about the relative value of these items. For example, one brass rod was equivalent to one large piece of white cloth, five rods or pieces of cloth were equal to a bull, and ten equaled a cow. Young men seeking marriage would accumulate such goods in order to enhance their prestige and to impress elder males.

The top-ranking exchange sphere contains only one item: rights in women. This category ranks highest in the Tiv moral sphere because a male's highest goal is to gain and maintain family dependents (wife and children). As Bohannan says, "The drive toward success leads most Tiv, to the greatest possible extent, to convert food into prestige items; to convert prestige items into dependents—wives and children," a process of up-trading he terms *conversion*. Other analyses also show that the Tiv spheres of exchange, like those of many other African cultures, support the power structure of elder males (Douglas and Isherwood 1979). They maintain dominance over the entire social system by keeping control over marriageable women. This forces younger males into competition for marriage and for eventual entry into the ranks of the elders.

Bohannan's analysis dealt with how exchange relationships within one culture strengthen the power position of certain social groups and keep others in subordinate positions because they cannot participate in the highest form of exchange. At the global level, many examples of exchange between powerful and nonpowerful groups show how the powerful groups use exchange to maintain their position and how difficult it is for the nonpowerful groups to escape their position of subordination. Anyone who has grown up in North America has probably heard the tales of European colonialists trading a string of glass beads for the island of Manhattan, and of the colonialists' plying Native Americans with "fire water" (alcoholic drinks) and thus creating their dependency and acquiescence. Similarly, the British introduced opium to China to create a dependency among the Chinese to counterbalance trade deficits created by the heavy British imports of Chinese goods, especially tea.

Cultural anthropologists were not on the scene to bear witness to these reprehensible tactics. They are, however, on the scene within contemporary contexts that strongly resemble what went on during the colonization of North America. The current heavy alcohol consumption among many indigenous peoples worldwide is testimony to the continuing power of alcohol as part of the mode of exchange of colonialism and its modern forms. The introduction of alcohol to the indigenous people of Australia, for example, has created a culture—especially among men—of binge drinking and depletion of cash earnings to buy alcohol (Saggers and Gray 1998). Before the coming of outsiders to Australia, the Aborigines had nothing like alcohol. It arrived with the British. Despite much effort in recent decades to reduce alcohol consumption among Aboriginal peoples, no decline is apparent. One interpretation of this situation is that economic marginalization and social discrimination support continued high levels of alcohol consumption, along with the assurance of a continued supply of alcohol from the global market.

CHANGING PATTERNS OF CONSUMPTION AND EXCHANGE

Several trends are notable in the transformation of consumption and exchange. The powerful market forces of the first world are the predominant shapers of global change. At the same time, local cultures variously adopt and adapt to global patterns of consumption and exchange, and sometimes resist them outright.

Cash Cropping and Declining Nutrition

Increasing numbers of horticultural and agricultural groups have been persuaded to change over from growing crops for their own use to cash crop production. Intuition might tell you that cash cropping should lead to a rising standard of living. Some studies show, to the contrary, that often people's nutritional status declines with the introduction of cash cropping. A carefully documented analysis of how people's nutritional status was affected by introducing *sisal* (a plant that has leaves used for making rope) as a cash crop in Brazil is one such case (Gross and Underwood 1971). Around 1950, sisal was widely adopted in arid parts of northeastern Brazil. The traditional economy was based on some cattle raising and subsistence farming. Many poor farmers gave up farming and took up work in the sisal-processing plants. They thought that steady work would be preferable to being dependent on the unpredictable rains in this dry region.

Processing sisal leaves for rope is an extremely labor-intensive process. One of the most demanding jobs is being a "residue man," whose tasks include shoveling soggy masses of fiber, bundling fiber, and lifting bundles for weighing. In families that contained a "residue man," the amount of money required for food was as much as what the sisal worker earned. In one household studied, the weekly budget was completely spent on food. The greatest share of the food goes to the sisal worker himself because of his increased energy needs for sisal work. Analysis of data on the nutritional status of several hundred children in sisal-processing areas showed that "Some *sisal* workers in northeastern Brazil appear to be forced systematically to deprive their dependents of an adequate diet . . . if they did not they could not function as wage earners. In those cases where the workers' dependents are growing children, the deprivation manifests itself in attenuated growth rates" (736).

The Lure of Western Goods

There is now scarcely any human group that does not engage in exchanges beyond its boundaries to acquire new consumer goods (Gross et al. 1979). Katherine Milton, a biological anthropologist who has studied recently contacted foraging groups in the Brazilian Amazon, comments: "Despite the way their culture traditionally eschews possessions, forest-living people embrace manufactured goods with amazing enthusiasm. They seem to appreciate instantly the efficacy of a steel machete, ax, or cooking pot. It is love at first sight. . . . There are accounts of Indian groups or individuals who have turned their backs on manufactured goods, but such people are the exception" (1992:40). Their love for these goods has brought significant economic, political, and social changes to their lives.

In the early decades of the twentieth century, when the Brazilian government sought to "pacify" Amazonian groups, they placed pots, machetes, axes, and steel knives along Indian trails or hung them from trees. These tech-

An upscale car dealer in Moscow uses a cell phone to communicate with customers. His car lot stands on what was a sports ground during the Soviet era. ■ *Conduct research on the social distribution of wealth in several post-Soviet countries.* (Source: © Caroline Penn/CORBIS)

niques proved so successful that they are still used. Milton describes the process:

> Once a group has been drawn into the pacification area, all its members are presented with various trade goods—standard gifts include metal cooking pots, salt, matches, machetes, knives, axes, cloth hammocks, T-shirts, and shorts. . . . Once the Indians have grown accustomed to these new items, the next step is to teach them that these gifts will not be repeated. The Indians are now told that they must work to earn money or must manufacture goods for trade so that they can purchase new items.
>
> Unable to contemplate returning to life without steel axes, the Indians begin to produce extra arrows or blow-guns or hunt additional game or weave baskets beyond what they normally need so that this new surplus can be traded. Time that might, in the past, have been used for other tasks—subsistence activities, ceremonial events, or whatever—is now devoted to production of barter goods. (40)

Adoption of Western foods has negatively affected the nutrition and health of indigenous Amazonian peoples. "The moment manufactured foods begin to intrude on the indigenous diet, health takes a downward turn" (Milton 1992:41). The Indians have begun to use table salt, which they have been given by outsiders, and refined sugar. Previously, they consumed small quantities of salt made by burning certain leaves and collecting the ash. The sugar they consumed came from wild fruits, in the form of fructose. Sucrose tastes "exceptionally sweet" in comparison, and the Indians get hooked on it. As a result, tooth decay, obesity, and diabetes become new health risks.

The White Bread Takeover

A cross-cultural analysis of food cultures, with attention to contemporary change, reveals an enduring distinction between bread and porridge worldwide (Goody 1977). Bread is associated with dominant, global culture, and porridge is associated with dominated cultures.

An illustration of this dichotomy comes from rural Ecuador (Weismantel 1989). In the village of Zumbagua, white bread has been a high-status, special-occasion food for many years. Recently, children have begun pressuring parents to serve bread regularly to replace the usual barley gruel for breakfast. Children prefer bread. The anthropologist reports, "Many of the early morning quarrels I witnessed in Zumbagua homes erupted over the question of bread. This conflict arises between young children and their parents. Pre-school children, especially, demand bread as their right" (93). But "Zumbagua adults do not feel that bread is appropriate for everyday meals because it is a part of a class of food defined as *wanlla*. Wanlla is anything that is not part of a meal . . . bread is the wanlla par excellence. It is the universally appropriate gift" (95). Importantly, bread consumption requires cash income. The husband (more frequently than the wife) works for wages in the city. He often returns with a gift of bread for the family, while the wife provides the traditional boiled grain soups or gruels.

Children's demands for bread increase the role of purchased foods. This in turn leads to increased dependence on the cash economy and on male wages, rather than on traditional female provisioning.

Privatization's Effects in Russia and Eastern Europe

As the countries of the former Soviet Union have entered the market economy, income inequality has risen. The new rich are enjoying unprecedented levels of comfortable living, including ownership of mansions and Mer-

In China, a market vendor weighs her produce and calculates the price using a laptop. ■ *How might the use of the laptop change her marketing practices?* (Source: © Bill Bachmann/PhotoEdit)

cedes-Benz cars. The influx of Western goods, including sugared soft drinks and junk food, nicknamed "pepsi-stroika" by an anthropologist who did fieldwork in Moscow (Lempert 1996), encourages people to change their traditional diets in ways that nutritional guidelines in the United States would advise against.

At the same time, consumption levels have fallen among the newly created poor. Historically, average reported levels of food intake in what are now Russia and Eastern Europe have exceeded those of most middle-income countries (Cornia 1994). Between 1961 and 1988, consumption of calories, proteins, and fats rose and were generally above the level recommended by the World Health Organization. These countries were also characterized by full employment and low income inequality, so the high consumption levels were shared by everyone. This is not to say that diets were perfect. Characteristic weaknesses, especially in urban areas and among low-income groups, were low consumption of good-quality meat, fruits, vegetables, and vegetable oils, whereas people tended to overconsume cholesterol-heavy products (eggs and animal fats), sugar, salt, bread, and alcohol.

Now, there are two categories of poor people: "the ultra-poor" (those whose incomes are below the subsistence minimum, or between 25 and 35 percent of the average wage) and "the poor" (those whose incomes are above the subsistence minimum but below the social minimum, or between 35 and 50 percent of the average wage). The largest increases in the number of ultra-poor occurred in Bulgaria, Poland, Romania, and Russia, where between 20 and 30 percent of the population could be classified as ultra-poor and another 20 to 40 percent as poor. Overall calorie and protein intake have dimin-

ished significantly. People in the ultra-poor category substitute less expensive sources of nutrients, so now they consume more animal fats and starch, and less milk, animal proteins, vegetable oils, minerals, and vitamins. Rates of low-birthweight babies have risen in Bulgaria and Romania, reflecting the deterioration in maternal diets. The rate of childhood anemia has risen dramatically in Russia.

Credit Card Debt

Throughout the world, certain markets have long allowed buyers to purchase goods on credit. Such informal credit purchasing is usually based on personal trust and face-to-face interaction. It is only recently, however, that the credit card has made credit purchasing a massive, impersonal phenomenon in the United States and many other countries: "New electronic technology in the 1970s and deregulation in the 1980s offered retail bankers exciting opportunities to experiment with credit as a commodity, and they did experiment, wildly, at 'penetrating the debt capacity' of varied groups of Americans" (B. Williams 1994:351). Among middle-class people in the United States, the use of credit cards is related to attempts to maintain a middle-class lifestyle.

In the United States, the primary users of credit cards are between twenty-five and forty-four years old with stagnant or falling incomes. Many use credit cards to support what they see as the appropriate life cycle stages, especially to acquire a college education or to set up a household and buy appliances. Maintaining (and paying monthly interest on) a running debt to credit card companies becomes an expected part of life and a habit that is not easily changed.

A dance during a potlatch in the memory of a Tshimshian elder. The potlatch was held on the island of Metlakatla, southeast Alaska. ■ *What kinds of social gatherings and exchange, if any, take place at death ceremonies of people in your microculture? Are there variations on the basis of the status of the deceased person?* (Source: © Lawrence Migdale)

People's attitudes about their credit card debts vary. Some people express feelings of guilt similar to having a drug dependency. One woman reported, "Last year I had a charge-free Christmas. It was like coming away from drug abuse" (354). Others who are in debt feel grateful: "I wouldn't be able to go to college without my credit card" (355). No matter what people's attitudes are, credit cards are sinking many Americans deeply into debt. The cards buy a lifestyle that is not actually affordable, and therefore they "mask" actual economic decline in America. The culture of electronic credit is a subject that cultural anthropologists will no doubt be devoting more attention to in the future.

Continuities and Resistance: The Enduring Potlatch

Potlatching among native peoples of the northwest coast of the United States and Canada was subjected to decades of opposition from Europeans and Euro-Americans (Cole 1991). The missionaries opposed potlatching and other "un-Christian" activities. The government thought it was wasteful and excessive, out of line with their goals for the "economic progress" of the Indians. In 1885 the Canadian government outlawed the potlatch. Among all the northwest coastal tribes, the Kwakwaka'wakw resisted this prohibition most strongly and for the longest time. Potlatching among the Haida and Tlingit, in contrast, disappeared with relatively little resistance. Potlatches are no longer illegal, but a long battle was required to remove restrictions.

Contemporary reasons for giving a potlatch are similar to those in traditional times: naming children, mourning the dead, transferring rights and privileges, celebrating marriages, and raising totem poles (Webster 1991). However, the length of time devoted to planning a potlatch has changed. In the past, several years were involved in planning a proper potlatch. Now, about a year is enough. Still, much property must be accumulated to make sure that no guest goes away empty-handed, and the guest list may include between 500 and 1000 people. The kinds of goods exchanged are different today. Typical potlatch goods now include crocheted items (such as cushion covers, afghan blankets, and potholders), glassware, plastic goods, manufactured blankets, pillows, towels, articles of clothing, and sacks of flour and sugar.

KEY CONCEPTS

balanced exchange, p. 91
basic needs fund, p. 84
ceremonial fund, p. 84
consumerism, p. 82
consumption fund, p. 84
direct entitlements, p. 84
entertainment fund, p. 84
entitlements, p. 84
expected reciprocity, p. 92

generalized reciprocity, p. 91
indirect entitlements, p. 84
limited-purpose money, p. 91
market exchange, p. 93
minimalism, p. 82
modes of consumption, p. 80
modes of exchange, p. 80
money, p. 91
multi-purpose money, p. 91

potlatch, p. 80
pure gift, p. 92
recurrent costs fund, p. 84
redistribution, p. 93
tax fund, p. 84
trade, p. 93
unbalanced exchange, p. 91

SUGGESTED READINGS

Karl Benediktsson. *Harvesting Development: The Construction of Fresh Food Markets in Papua New Guinea*. Ann Arbor: University of Michigan Press, 2002. This ethnography of new markets in Papua New Guinea takes a theoretical position between structurism and agency to avoid the rigidities of each position. The social networks of food markets (including producers, truck drivers, and marketers) is the central focus.

Jane I. Guyer, ed. *Money Matters: Instability, Values and Social Payments in the Modern History of West African Communities*. Portsmouth, NH: Heinemann/James Currey, 1995. A collection of chapters by historians and cultural anthropologists examines topics such as why people in rural Gambia do not save money in banks, money as a symbol among the Yoruba, and the impact of colonial monetization in Nigeria and elsewhere.

Betsy Hartmann and James Boyce. *Needless Hunger: Voices from a Bangladesh Village*. San Francisco: Institute for Food and Development Policy, 1982. Evidence from fieldwork in rural Bangladesh shows that poverty and hunger in Bangladesh are primarily caused by severe class inequalities in economic entitlements. The text includes a critique of the role of foreign aid in perpetuating inequalities, as well as suggestions for change.

Dwight B. Heath. *Drinking Occasions: Comparative Perspectives on Alcohol and Culture*. New York: Taylor & Francis, 2000. This book provides an ethnological review of drinking. The author focuses on several questions: When do people drink alcohol? Where do people drink? Who drinks and who doesn't? How do people drink? What do people drink? And why do people drink? He asks, in conclusion, where do we go from here with this topic?

Daniel Miller. *The Dialectics of Shopping*. Chicago: University of Chicago Press, 2001. First delivered as the Lewis Henry Morgan lecture series at the University of Rochester, the chapters in this book reflect the author's interest in studying shopping as a clue to social relations. He discusses how shopping is related to kinship, community, ethics and identity, and the political economy. He draws on his own ethnographic research in several locations.

Sidney W. Mintz. *Sweetness and Power: The Place of Sugar in Modern History*. New York: Penguin Books, 1985. Combining historical and anthropological techniques, this book traces an important part of the story of world capitalism—the transformation of sugar from a luxury item to an omnipresent item of consumption worldwide.

Lidia D. Sciama and Joanne B. Eicher, eds. *Beads and Bead Makers: Gender, Material Culture and Meaning*. New York: Berg, 1998. This book includes over a dozen articles on beads, including early international trade in Venetian beads, the relationship between beads and ethnicity in Malaysia, beads and power at the New Orleans Mardi Gras, and rosaries in the Andes. All provide insights about gender roles and meanings.

James L. Watson, ed. *Golden Arches East: McDonald's in East Asia*. Stanford, CA: Stanford University Press, 1997. This book contains five case studies, an introduction written by the editor, and an afterword by Sidney Mintz, noted cultural anthropologist of food and foodways. Case studies are located in China, Taiwan, Korea, and Japan and address topics such as how McDonald's culture becomes localized, dietary effects on children, eating etiquette, and how food choices are related to national identity.

HOW are modes of production related to consumption?

Anthropologists contrast modes of consumption in non-market versus market-based systems of production. In the former, minimalism is the dominant mode of consumption, with finite needs. In the latter, consumerism is the dominant mode of consumption, with infinite needs. Foraging societies typify the minimalist mode of consumption. Industrial capitalist societies typify the consumerist mode of consumption. The modes of production that emerged between foraging and industrialism exhibit varying degrees of minimalism and consumerism. In nonmarket economies, most consumers either produce the goods they use themselves or know who produced them. This is called personalized consumption. In market economies, consumption is largely depersonalized through globalized mass production. Consumers are alienated from producers, and the latter are thus more likely to be exploited by corporate management in terms of low wages and poor working conditions.

HOW are modes of production related to exchange?

The mode of exchange corresponds to the modes of production and consumption. In foraging societies, the mode of exchange is balanced exchange, with the goal of keeping the value of the items exchanged roughly equal over time. The balanced mode of exchange involves people who have a social relationship with each other. The relationship is reinforced through continued exchange. In market exchange, the predominant form of unbalanced exchange, the goal of making a profit overrides social relationships. In market exchange, the people involved in the transaction are less likely to know each other or to have a social relationship.

WHAT are some examples of how contemporary economic change affects consumption and exchange?

Globalizing capitalism is shaping many changes in consumption and exchange around the world. Cultural anthropologists critique this process as being better for capitalism than it is for the people of nonmarket cultures who are swept into the global economy. Western goods, such as steel axes and white bread, are in high demand by people in non-Western, nonindustrialized contexts. Such goods must be purchased, a fact that impels people to work for cash so that they can buy things. The nutritional status of many nonindustrial groups has fallen with the adoption of Western-style foods, especially large amounts of sugar and salt in food. The demand for cash has prompted many people to switch from growing food for their own use to growing crops for sale. This transition means that farmers have relinquished a direct entitlement for an indirect entitlement, thus putting themselves at risk when the market price drops for the crop they grow. Throughout the post-Soviet world, average health and nutrition levels fell after perestroika. Credit card shopping, in combination with middle-class values, is creating high levels of indebtedness in the United States.

THE BIG QUESTIONS

- **HOW** are modes of reproduction related to modes of production?
- **HOW** does culture shape fertility in different contexts?
- **HOW** does culture shape mortality in different contexts?

5

BIRTH AND DEATH

A mother and her infant son, South Africa. *(Source: Roshani Kothari)*

- A common belief among Hindus in India is that men are weakened by sexual intercourse because semen is a source of strength, and it takes a long time to replace even a drop. Yet India has a high rate of population growth.
- The Chinese government policy of urging couples to have only one child significantly decreased the population growth rate. It also increased the death rate of female infants to the extent that there is now a shortage of brides.
- The highest birth rates in the world are found among the Mennonites and Hutterites in the United States and Canada. In these Christian groups, women on average bear nine children.

Such "population puzzles" can be understood using anthropological theories and methods. Population dynamics, along with many other examples of human variation in births and deaths, are an important area of life that is culturally shaped and that changes over time in response to changing conditions. This chapter provides a glimpse into some aspects of **demography,** or the study of population dynamics, and how it is culturally regulated.

Whereas demographers compile statistical reports, cultural anthropologists contribute understanding of what goes on behind the numbers and provide insights about the causes of demographic trends. For example, demographers may find that fertility rates are falling more rapidly in one nation than in another. They may be able to correlate falling fertility rates with certain factors such as changing literacy rates or economic growth. Cultural anthropologists involved in studying these issues would take a closer look at the causes and processes involved in the declining birth rates, including some that might not be included in official censuses or other statistical sources. They would gather information on household-level and individual-level behavior and attitudes.

Demography includes three areas: **fertility,** births, or rate of population increase from reproduction; **mortality,** deaths, or rate of population decline in general or from particular causes; and **migration,** or movement of people from one place to another. When cultural anthropologists examine these processes, they focus on small populations and examine the relationships between population dynamics and other aspects of culture such as gender roles, sexual beliefs and behavior, marriage, household structure, child care, and health and illness.

This chapter starts by discussing how the modes of production (Chapter 3) relate to modes of reproduction. It then examines how and to what extent culture shapes the important natural processes of birth and death in different cultures.

CULTURE AND REPRODUCTION

Every human population, at all times, has had culturally constructed ways to either promote or limit population growth. Archaeologists and cultural anthropologists have enough data to support the construction of general **modes of reproduction** (the predominant pattern of fertility in a culture) corresponding roughly with modes of production (see Figure 5.1). Three general modes of reproduction are proposed. The foraging mode of reproduction, which existed for most of human prehistory, had low rates of population growth because of a combination of moderate birth rates and moderate death rates. The agricultural mode of reproduction emerged with sedentarization (permanent settlements). As increased food surpluses became available to support more people, birth rates increased over death rates, and high population densities were reached in agricultural societies such as India and China. In the industrialized mode of reproduction, exemplified in Europe, Japan, and the United States, population growth rates declined because of falling birth rates and declining death rates. Horticulturalists and pastoralists exhibit some features of the foraging mode of reproduction and the agricultural mode of reproduction, depending on specific conditions. Thus far, anthropologists have done much less research on reproduction than on production, so it is impossible to provide as much detail for modes of reproduction as for modes of production.

FIGURE 5.1 Modes of Production and Reproduction

FORAGING	AGRICULTURE	INDUSTRIAL
Population Growth	**Population Growth**	**Population Growth**
Moderate birth rates	High birth rates	Industrialized nations—negative
Moderate death rates	Declining death rates	population growth
		Developing nations—high
Value of Children	**Value of Children**	**Value of Children**
Moderate	High	Mixed
Fertility Control	**Fertility Control**	**Fertility Control**
Indirect means	Increased reliance on direct means	Direct methods grounded in
Low-fat diet of women	Pronatalist techniques	science and medicine
Women's work and exercise	Herbs	Chemical forms of contraception
Prolonged breastfeeding	Direct means	*In vitro* fertilization
Spontaneous abortion	Induced abortion	Abortion
Direct means	Infanticide	
Induced abortion		
Infanticide		
Social Aspects	**Social Aspects**	**Social Aspects**
Homogeneous fertility	Emerging class differences	Stratified fertility
Few specialists	Increasing specialization	Globally, nationally, and locally
	Midwifery	Highly developed specialization
	Herbalists	

The Foraging Mode of Reproduction

Archaeological evidence about prehistoric populations, from about six million years ago to the Neolithic era of agricultural development around 12,000 years ago, indicates that population growth rates among foragers remained low over millions of years (Harris and Ross 1987). Foraging societies' high level of seasonal spatial mobility calls for a relatively small number of children to facilitate movement. It's impossible for adults to carry several babies. The low population growth rates over thousands of years probably resulted from several factors: high rates of spontaneous abortion because of heavy workloads of women, seasonality of diets that created reproductive stress on women, long breastfeeding of infants (which suppresses ovulation), induced abortion, and **infanticide,** the deliberate killing of offspring. Low birth rates appear to be more important than mortality in leading to population stability, or *homeostasis.*

Nancy Howell (1979), in the first major study in anthropological demography, conducted research on the Ju/wasi that sheds light on how population homeostasis is achieved. Her data show that birth intervals (the time between one birth and a subsequent birth) among the Ju/wasi are often several years in duration. What accounts for the long birth intervals? Two factors emerge as most important: breastfeeding and women's low level of body fat. Frequent and long periods of breastfeeding inhibit progesterone production and suppress ovulation. Also, a certain level of body fat is required for ovulation (Frisch 1978), and Ju/wasi women's diets contain little fat. Their body fat level is also kept low through the physical exercise their foraging work entails.

Thus ecological factors (food supply and diet) and economic factors (women's workloads) are basic determinants of Ju/wasi demography (Howell 1979). This mode of reproduction can be interpreted as highly adaptive to the Ju/wasi environment and sustainable over time. Among the Ju/wasi who have given up foraging and become sedentarized farmers or laborers, fertility levels have increased, because of higher consumption levels of grains and dairy products and less physical mobility.

Members of an Amish household sit around their kitchen table in Indiana. ■ *How many children are in your sibling set? How many, if any, children do you want to have? How does that goal fit with your microculture and mode of production?* (Source: © David & Peter Turnley/CORBIS)

The Agricultural Mode of Reproduction

Settled agriculture promotes and supports the highest fertility rates of any mode of production. Pronatalism, an ideology promoting many children, emerges as a key value of farm families. It is prompted by the need for a large labor force to work the land, care for animals, process food, and do marketing. In this context, having many children is a rational reproductive strategy related to the mode of production. Thus people who live in family farming systems cross-culturally have their own "family planning"—which is to have many children. Examples include the Mennonites and Hutterites of the United States and Canada.

In rural North India, sons are especially important, given the gender division of labor. Men perform the crucial work of plowing the fields and protecting the family in the case of village quarrels over land rights and other matters. When Western family planning agents first visited a village in North India in the late 1950s to promote small families, the villagers did not see the value of their ideas (Mamdani 1972). They equated a large family with wealth and success, not poverty and failure. Western family planning agents made the mistake of thinking that rural Indians had no thoughts of their own about what constitutes the desired family size and that they could simply provide modern contraceptive techniques to an interested market. Having many children in a family farming system "makes sense." When mechanization is introduced, cheap hired labor becomes widely available, or socialized agriculture is established, then farm families change their mode of reproduction and opt for smaller numbers of children because it makes less sense to have many children.

The Industrial Mode of Reproduction

In industrial societies, either capitalist or socialist, reproduction tends to decline to the point of **replacement-level fertility,** when the number of births equals the number of deaths, leading to maintenance of current population size, or **below-replacement-level fertility,** when the number of births is less than the number of deaths, leading to population decline. (See Table 5.1.) Children in these contexts are less useful in production because of the changing labor demands of industrialism. Furthermore, children must attend school and cannot work for their families as much. Parents respond to these changes by having fewer children and by "investing" more resources in the fewer children they have.

Changes during the industrial mode of reproduction correspond to what demographers call the **demographic transition,** a model of change from the high fertility and high mortality of the agricultural mode of reproduction to the low fertility and low mortality of industrialized societies. This model proposes two phases. First, mortality declines as a consequence of improved nutrition and health, leading to high rates of population growth. The second phase is reached when fertility also declines, resulting in low rates of population growth. Cultural anthropologists have critiqued the demographic transition model as being too narrowly focused on the role of industrialism and not allowing for alternative models (Ginsberg and Rapp 1991). They claim that industrialism, with its reduced need for labor, is not the only factor that reduces pronatalism. China, for example, began to reduce its population growth rate before widespread industrialism (Xizhe 1991). Instead, strong government policies and a massive family planning program were key

TABLE 5.1 Some Nations with Below-Replacement-Level Fertility (Fertility Rates Below Two Births per Woman), Late 1990s

Country	Fertility Rate	Country	Fertility Rate	Country	Fertility Rate
Armenia	1.4	Dominica	1.9	Norway	1.8
Australia	1.7	Finland	1.7	Poland	1.4
Austria	1.3	France	1.8	Portugal	1.5
Azerbaijan	1.9	Germany	1.3	Romania	1.3
Barbados	1.8	Greece	1.3	Russia	1.2
Belarus	1.3	Hungary	1.3	Singapore	1.5
Belgium	1.6	Italy	1.2	Slovakia	1.4
Bosnia-Herzegovina	1.6	Ireland	1.9	Slovenia	1.2
Bulgaria	1.1	Japan	1.3	Spain	1.2
Canada	1.5	Kazakhstan	1.7	Sweden	1.5
China	1.8	Korea, South	1.5	Switzerland	1.5
Croatia	1.5	Lithuania	1.3	Taiwan	1.5
Cuba	1.6	Luxembourg	1.7	Thailand	1.9
Cyprus	1.9	Macedonia	1.9	Trinidad & Tobago	1.7
Czech Republic	1.1	Martinique	1.8	Ukraine	1.3
Denmark	1.7	Netherlands	1.6	United Kingdom	1.7

Source: From 2000 *World Population Data Sheet.* Washington, DC: Population Reference Bureau. Copyright © 2000. Reprinted by permission of Population Reference Bureau.

factors: "China's transition has been, by and large, not a natural process, but rather an induced one" (281) because its motivation came mainly from the government rather than from couples themselves.

One prominent characteristic of capitalist industrial states is their socially stratified demographies. Middle- and upper-class people tend to have few children, with high survival rates. Among the poor, both fertility and mortality rates are high. Brazil, a newly industrializing state with the most extreme inequality of income distribution in the world, also has extreme differences in demographic patterns between the rich and the poor.

Another characteristic of industrial countries is population aging. In Japan, for example, the total fertility rate declined to replacement level in the 1950s and subsequently reached the below-replacement level (Hodge and Ogawa 1991). Japan is currently experiencing a decline in population growth of about 15 percent per generation. At the same time, Japan is experiencing a rapid aging of the population. Many people are moving into the senior category, creating a population bulge not matched by population increases in younger age groups.

A third distinguishing feature of industrial demographies is the high level of involvement of scientific (especially medical) technology in all aspects of pregnancy: preventing it, achieving it, and even terminating it (Browner and Press 1995, 1996). The growing importance of the "new reproductive technologies" (NRTs), such as *in vitro* fertilization, is a major part of an expanding market in scientific reproduction. This technologization of reproduction is accompanied by increasing levels of specialization in providing the new services.

SEXUAL INTERCOURSE AND FERTILITY

Cultures shape human reproduction from its very beginning, if that beginning can be said to be sexual intercourse itself. Cultural practices and beliefs about pregnancy and birth affect the viability of the fetus during its gestation as well as the infant's fate after birth.

Sexual Intercourse

Anthropological research on sexuality and sexual practices is particularly difficult to undertake. Sexuality involves private, sometimes secret, beliefs and behaviors. The ethics of participant observation disallow intimate observation or participation, so data can be obtained only indirectly. Biases in people's reports to an anthropologist about their sexual beliefs and behavior are likely for several reasons. They may be too shy to talk about sex, too boastful to give accurate information, or simply unable to remember the answers to questions such as "How many times did you have intercourse last year?" If people do provide detailed information, it might be inappropriate for an anthropologist to publish it because of the need to protect confidentiality. Malinowski (1929) wrote the first anthropological study of sexuality, based on his fieldwork in the Trobriands. He discusses the sexual lives of children; sexual techniques; love magic; erotic dreams; husband–wife jealousy; and a range of topics related to kinship, marriage, exchange, and morals. Since the late 1980s, cultural anthropologists have paid a lot of attention to the study of sexuality, given the increase in cases of sexually transmitted diseases (STDs), including HIV/AIDS.

When to Begin Having Intercourse?

Biologically speaking, sexual intercourse between a fertile female and a fertile male is normally required for human reproduction, although artificial insemination is an option in some contexts. Biology also defines the time span within which a female is fertile: from menarche (the onset of menstruation) to menopause (the cessation of menstruation). The term *menarche* (pronounced MEN-ar-key) refers to the age at which menstruation begins. Globally, it varies from twelve to fourteen years of age, with the average of fourteen years in industrial countries and sixteen years in developing countries. This difference may be due to variations in diet and activity patterns. Average age at menopause varies more widely, from the forties to the fifties, with later ages in industrialized societies. The higher fat content of diets in industrialized nations may be related to this difference.

A bride wearing traditional wedding clothing in the city of Meknès, Morocco. ■ *On the Web, find a detailed map of Morocco. Then locate the city of Meknès and the smaller town of Zawiya.* (Source: © Stephanie Dinkins/Photo Researchers, Inc.)

Cultures socialize children about the appropriate time to begin sexual intercourse. Guidelines for initiating sexual intercourse differ by gender, class, race, and ethnicity. In many cultures, menarche marks the beginning of adulthood for a girl. She should marry soon after menarche and become pregnant as soon as possible in order to demonstrate her fertility.

Cross-culturally, rules more strictly forbid premarital sexual activity of girls than of boys. In Zawiya, a traditional Muslim town of northern Morocco, the virginity of the bride—but not of the groom—is highly valued (Davis and Davis 1987). The majority of brides conform to the ideal. Some unmarried young women do engage in premarital sex, however, and if they choose to have a traditional wedding, then they must somehow deal with the requirement of producing blood-stained wedding sheets. How do they do this? If the bride and the groom have been having premarital sexual relations, the groom may assist in the deception by nicking a finger with a knife and bloodying the sheets himself. Another option is to buy fake blood in the drugstore.

In many cultures, a high value is placed on a woman becoming pregnant soon after she reaches menarche, making "teenage pregnancy" a desired condition instead of a social problem, as perceived by many experts in the United States (Ginsberg and Rapp 1991). In contrast, the concept of a thirty-year-old first-time mother would seem odd to villagers in Bangladesh, who would question both its physical possibility and its social advisability. Commonly in South Asia, Africa, and elsewhere, a married woman's status depends on her having children. The longer she delays, the more her spouse and in-laws might suspect her of being infertile. In that case, they might send her back to her parents or bring in a second wife.

How Often Should One Have Intercourse?

Cross-cultural studies indicate a wide range in frequency of sexual intercourse, confirming the role of culture in shaping sexual desire. However, the relationship between fertility and the frequency of sexual intercourse, the subject of this section, is not simple. A common assumption is that people in cultures with high rates of population growth must have sexual intercourse frequently. Without modern birth control, such as condoms, the birth control pill, and the IUD, intercourse frequency would seem to lead to high rates of fertility.

A classic study of reported intercourse frequency for Euro-Americans in the United States and Hindus in India revealed that Indians had intercourse far less frequently (less than twice a week) than the Euro-Americans did (two to three times a week) in all age groups (Nag 1972). Several features of Indian culture limit sexual intercourse. The Hindu religion teaches the value of sexual abstinence, thus providing ideological support for limiting sexual intercourse. Hinduism also suggests that one should abstain from intercourse on many sacred days: the first night of the new moon, the first night of the full moon, and the eighth day of each half of the month (the light half and the dark half), and sometimes on Fridays. As many as one hundred days each year could be observed as non-sex days. Another factor is Hindu men's belief in what anthropologists term the *lost semen complex*. An American anthropologist learned about this complex during fieldwork in North India: "Everyone knew that semen was not easily formed; it takes forty days and forty drops of blood to make one drop of semen. . . . Semen of good quality is rich and viscous, like the cream of unadulterated milk. A man who possesses a store of such good semen becomes a super-man. . . . Celibacy was the first requirement of true fitness, because every sexual orgasm meant the loss of a quantity of semen, laboriously formed" (Carstairs 1967, 83–86, quoted in Nag 1972: 235).

The fact remains, however, that fertility is higher in India than in many other parts of the world where such religiously based restrictions on sexual intercourse do not exist. Obviously, sheer frequency of intercourse is not the explanation. It takes only one act of sexual intercourse at the right time of the month to create a pregnancy. The point of this discussion is to show that "reverse reasoning" (assuming that high fertility means people have nothing better to do than have sex) is wrong. The cultural dynamics of sexuality in India function to restrain sexual activities and thus keep fertility lower than it otherwise would be.

Fertility Decision Making

This section explores decision making about fertility at three levels: the family level, the national level, and the global level. Within the context of the family unit, decision makers weigh factors influencing why and when to have a child. At the national level, governments seek to plan their overall population goals on the basis of particular goals that are sometimes *pronatalist* (favoring many births) and sometimes *antinatalist* (opposed to many births). At the global level, we can see that powerful economic and political interests are at work influencing the reproductive policies of individual nations and, in turn, of families and individuals within them.

Family-Level Decision Making

At the family level, parental and other family members' perceptions about the value and costs of children influence reproductive decision making (Nag 1983). Assessing the value and costs of children is a complex matter involving many factors. Four variables are most important in affecting the "demand" for children in different cultural contexts: children's labor value, children's value as old-age support for parents, infant and child mortality rates, and the economic costs of children.

In the first three, the relationship is positive: When children's value is high in terms of labor or old-age support, fertility is likely to be higher. When infant and child mortality rates are high, fertility rates also tend to be high in order to "replace" offspring who do not survive. In the case of costs—including direct costs (for food, education, clothing) and indirect costs (employment opportunities that the mother gives up) the relationship is negative. Higher costs promote the desire for fewer children. Industrial society alters the value of children in several ways: "Industrialization, improvement in income, urbanization, and schooling are likely to reduce the labour value of children" (Nag 1983:58) and greatly increase their costs. Provision of old-age security and pension plans by the state may reduce that fertility incentive, although few developing countries have instituted such policies thus far.

In a highland village in the Oaxacan region of southern Mexico, men and women have different preferences about the number of children (Browner 1986). Men are more pronatalist than women. Among women with only one child, 80 percent were content with their present family size. Most men (60 percent) who were satisfied with their present family size had four or more children. One woman said, "My husband sleeps peacefully through the night, but I have to get up when the children need

Girls participating in the Guelaguetza festival, Oaxaca. Oaxaca is a distinctive cultural region and the scene of a vigorous movement for indigenous people's rights. ■ *Find a current events item about Oaxaca from a newspaper or the Internet.* (Source: © Rose Hartman/CORBIS)

something. I'm the one the baby urinates on; sometimes I have to get out of bed in the cold and change both our clothes. They wake me when they're sick or thirsty, my husband sleeps through it all" (714).

Depending on the gender division of labor and other social features related to gender, sons or daughters may be more valued. Son preference is widespread, especially in Asia and the Middle East, but it is not a cultural universal (Williamson 1976). In some cultures, people prefer a balanced sex ratio in their offspring, and in others, daughters are preferred. Daughter preference is found in some Caribbean populations, in Venezuela, and in some parts of Africa south of the Sahara. Longitudinal research conducted from 1956 to 1991 among the Tonga of Gwembe District, Congo, documents a female-biased population system that has persisted since at least the second half of the twentieth century (Clark et al. 1995). At most ages, men's death rates are higher than those of women. Differences in mortality are especially great for the very young and the elderly, among whom males die at twice the rate of females the same age. The kinship system of the Tonga shapes this system of female survival advantage. Among the Tonga, property is passed down from mother to daughter. Also, at the time of marriage, the groom makes valuable payments to the bride's father. Thus daughters, not sons, are the repositories and channels of wealth and property, and their preferential care and enhanced survival reflect their value.

In Tokugawa, Japan, during the eighteenth and nineteenth centuries, husbands and wives had different fertility preferences based on the different value to them of sons versus daughters (Skinner 1993). Tokugawa wives, as is still common in Japan, preferred to have "first a girl, then a boy." This preference is related to the benefit in

having a girl to help the mother in her work and to care for subsequent children, especially the boy it was hoped would come next. Husbands prefer a son-first strategy because a son helps them with *their* work. Thus husbands and wives both tried to achieve their goals with the one method available: **sex-selective infanticide,** or the killing of offspring on the basis of sex. Depending on their relative power, either the husband or the wife would be able

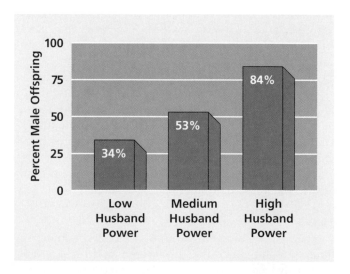

FIGURE 5.2   Gender of First-Born Child According to Spouse Power in the Household, Tokugawa, Japan   Note: Under normal conditions, one would expect roughly equal percentages of male and female births.

Source: From "Conjugal Power in Tokugawa Japanese Families: A Matter of Life or Death" by William G. Skinner, in *Sex and Gender Hierarchies*, ed. by Barbara D. Miller. Copyright © 1993. Reprinted by permission of Cambridge University Press.

to dominate the decision making about whether a child born would be kept. But how to assess the relative power of spouses? Age differences in Japan are a key status index: Seniority commands deference, respect, and obedience. Three categories of marital power can be defined, based on age differences at the time of marriage: low husband power (when the wife is older than the husband), intermediate husband power (when ages are about equal), and high husband power (when the husband is older than the wife). Over one-third of the marriages involved men who were at least ten years older than their wives, about 60 percent were in the intermediate category, and less than 6 percent were in the low-husband-power category. Was the gender of children related to marital power relations? Results in Figure 5.2 clearly show that parental preferences about having a girl or boy did exist and were acted on, depending on whose values won out.

At the National Level

National governments play major roles in decreasing or increasing rates of population growth within their boundaries. Governments are concerned about providing employment and public services, maintaining the tax base, filling the ranks of the military, maintaining ethnic and regional proportions, and dealing with population aging. The former Soviet Union faced significant planning challenges created by the contrasts between the below-replacement fertility of the "European" areas and high fertility rates in the Central Asian and Muslim regions such as Tajikistan and Kyrghizstan. Many countries, including Japan and France, are concerned about declining population growth rates. Their leaders have urged women to have more babies. Israel is openly pronatalist, given its interest in boosting its national population level as a political statement of strength.

At the Global Level

The most far-reaching layer that affects fertility decision making occurs at the international level, where global power structures such as the World Bank, pharmaceutical companies, and religious leaders influence national and individual priorities about fertility. In the 1950s there was an initial wave of enthusiasm among Western nations for promoting family planning programs of many types. Recently, the United States has adopted a more restricted policy of limited advocacy for family planning and has withdrawn support for certain features such as abortion. (See the Critical Thinking box on page 114.)

Fertility Control

All cultures throughout history have had ways of influencing fertility, including ways to increase it, reduce it, and regulate its spacing. Some ways are direct, such as using herbs or medicines that induce abortion. Others are indirect, such as long periods of breastfeeding, which reduce the chances of conception.

Hundreds of direct indigenous fertility control methods are available cross-culturally, and many of them were in existence long before modern science came on the scene (Newman 1972, 1985). One study conducted in Afghanistan in the 1980s found over five hundred fertil-

Afghan women waiting for their turn at the clinic in Bazarak. Throughout Afghanistan, patriarchal norms prevent women from going to clinics, or the geographical terrain and distance make it impossible to get to a clinic in cases of emergency. Rates of maternal mortality in remote areas of Afghanistan are perhaps the highest in the world. ■ *Consult the United Nation's Human Development Report for national statistics on maternal mortality worldwide.* (Source: © Reza; Webistan/CORBIS)

Critical Thinking

FAMILY PLANNING PROGRAMS IN BANGLADESH

BEGINNING IN the 1980s, criticism of Western family planning programs in relation to reproductive rights emerged in the United States. Conservative politicians and some religious groups opposed support of abortion services and other forms of population control at home and abroad. At the same time, critics on the left claimed that the Western-supported and Western-styled family planning programs in the so-called developing countries were a form of neocolonialism. They are concerned about sterilization of women and the use of incentives such as cash payments, radios, and clothing to attract people to being sterilized. This box compares the perspectives of two anthropologists on family planning programs in terms of whether such programs are coercive, and thus limiting of human agency, or whether they provide more choices for people and thus enhance human agency.

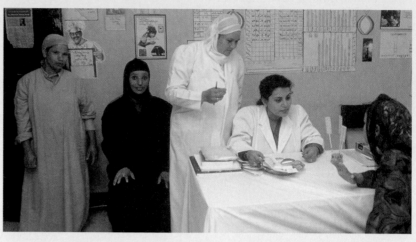

A family planning clinic in Egypt. Throughout much of the world, provision of Western-style family planning advice is controversial because it may conflict with local religious and other beliefs about the value of having many children and women's duty to be child bearers. ■ *In your cultural experience, what is the prevalent attitude about family planning, specifically birth control and women's access to means of fertility management?* (Source: © Barry Iverson/Woodfin Camp & Associates)

Betsy Hartmann takes a negative stand on the promotion of Western family planning programs in developing countries (1987). Her fieldwork in Bangladesh revealed two trends. First, in some areas, women were satisfied with the number of children they had. These women wanted to adopt some form of modern family planning, but none was available. In other areas, population control programs were vigorously promoting various methods—including the pill, the injectible Depo-Provera, and IUDs—without adequate medical screening, supervision, and follow-up. Many women experienced problems and became disillusioned with family planning. The government's response was not to improve existing programs

ity-regulating techniques in just one region of the country (Hunte 1985). In Afghanistan, as in most nonindustrial cultures, it is women who possess this information. Specialists, such as midwives or herbalists, provide further guidance and expertise. Of the total number of methods in the Afghanistan study, 72 percent were aimed at increasing fertility, 22 percent were contraceptives (preventing fertilization of the ovum by the sperm), and 6 percent were used to induce abortion. These methods involve plant and animal substances prepared in different ways. Herbs are made into tea and taken orally. Some substances are formed into pills, some steamed and inhaled as vapors, some vaginally inserted, and others rubbed on the woman's stomach.

Contemporary medical research reveals the efficacy of many indigenous fertility-regulating methods. For example, experiments on animals show that some 450 plant species worldwide contain natural substances that prevent ovulation, block fertilization, stop implantation, or reduce fertility in some other way. In the history of Tibet, the population was stable for long periods of time. The Tibetans subsisted mainly on barley and peas. When mice were fed a diet of 20 percent peas, litter sizes dropped by half. At 30 percent peas, the mice failed to reproduce at all.

The following section considers two areas of family planning, the one that may be the old form of family planning—induced abortion—and the "new reproduc-

but to intensify its population control efforts through promoting female sterilization. In both contexts, Hartmann argues, women were denied control over their reproduction. She does not dispute the value of family planning programs if they are well designed and well run. Her criticism is based on the dearth of good services.

In addition, Hartmann became involved in exposing the United States's involvement in sterilization abuse in Bangladesh, arguing that sterilization was targeted at the poorest women and involved coercive incentives. The incentive given to a man or woman for sterilization was Taka 175, equivalent to several weeks' wages. Women also received an item of clothing worth about Taka 100, and men received an item of clothing worth about Taka 50. In some cases, food incentives were given. The number of sterilizations increased during the autumn months when food was scarcest.

Barbara Pillsbury defends the family planning program in Bangladesh (1990). She was hired to survey the situation there and write a report in response to criticisms from Hartmann and others. Her assessment is based on a review of documents and studies conducted on female sterilization in Bangladesh, rather than on first-hand fieldwork, although she has much experience in the field elsewhere, mainly in Africa. She states that the government of Bangladesh, international aid agencies, and nongovernmental organizations have invested millions of dollars and substantial effort in sterilization-related monitoring and program evaluations, with a focus on the question of female voluntarism. The methods developed to assess women's degree of voluntarism, she says, were sound and reveal that the critics' charges are unfounded.

Specifically, the compensation payment is not an important influence on the decision of whether or not to be sterilized. In most cases, the women gained nothing economically. Pillsbury explains that free choice, not incentives, prompt Bangladeshis to seek sterilization:

> Why do so many Bangladeshis voluntarily choose sterilization? The basic reason is the same as in other countries—they do not want any more children. Why? Mostly to avoid the economic burden of a child that they can ill afford. Many Bangladeshi women also say that they choose sterilization because another pregnancy would be hard on their health, which in many cases is poor already. *No one,* of all the people who were interviewed in all of the studies cited above, said that he or she was compelled or deceived into getting sterilized. (183)

CRITICAL THINKING QUESTIONS

How do you think Betsy Hartmann would respond to Barbara Pillsbury's findings?

If you were hired as an anthropological consultant to follow up on this debate, what further research would you propose to do?

Does the United States government currently support any kind of family planning programs worldwide? What is the rationale for its position, and how is that rationale related to culture?

tive technologies" developed mainly in the West and now being increasingly exported to other contexts.

Induced Abortion

Direct intervention in a pregnancy may be resorted to in order to lead to abortion (expulsion of the fetus from the womb). Induced abortion, in its many forms, is probably a cultural universal. A review of about four hundred societies indicates that it was practiced in virtually all societies (Devereaux 1976). It is usually done either by the woman herself or with assistance from another woman, perhaps a midwife. Attitudes toward abortion range from absolute acceptability to conditional approval (abortion is acceptable under specified conditions), tolerance (abortion is regarded with neither approval nor disapproval), and opposition and punishment for offenders.

Methods of inducing abortion include hitting the abdomen, starving oneself, taking drugs, jumping from high places, jumping up and down, lifting heavy objects, and doing hard work. In Afghanistan, the midwife inserts into the pregnant woman an object such as a wooden spoon or stick treated with copper sulphate that causes bleeding and abortion (Hunte 1985).

Economic and social factors largely explain why people induce abortion (Devereaux 1976:13–21). Nomadic women, for example, work hard and have to carry heavy loads, sometimes for long distances. This lifestyle does

People regularly visit and decorate statues in memory of their "returned" fetuses in Japan. ■ *In your cultural world, how do people define the fetus and how do they treat it?* (Source: © Oliver Pichetti/Gamma Press)

not allow women to care for many small children at one time. Poverty is another motivating factor: When a woman is faced with another birth in the context of limited resources, abortion may appear to be the best option. Culturally defined "legitimacy" of a pregnancy, along with possible social penalties for bearing an illegitimate child, has been a prominent reason for abortion in Western societies.

Some governments have intervened in family decisions to regulate access to abortion, sometimes promoting it and other times forbidding it. Since the late 1980s, China has pursued one of the most rigorous campaigns to limit population growth (Greenhalgh 2003). Its One-Child-per-Couple Policy, announced in 1978, allowed most families to have only one child. It involved strict surveillance of pregnancies, strong group disapproval directed toward women pregnant for the second time or more, and forced abortions and sterilizations. Inadvertently, this policy simultaneously led to an increase in female infanticide, as parents, in their desire for a son, opted to kill or abandon any daughters born to them.

Religion and abortion are often related, but there is no simple relationship between what a particular religion teaches about abortion and what people actually do. Catholicism forbids abortion, but thousands of Catholic women have sought abortions throughout the world. Islamic teachings forbid abortion and female infanticide, yet sex-selective abortion of female fetuses is practiced covertly in Pakistan and by Muslims in India. Hinduism teaches *ahimsa*, or nonviolence toward other living beings, including a fetus whose movements have been felt by the mother. Yet thousands of Hindus seek abortions every year.

In contrast, Buddhism provides no overt rulings against abortion. In fact, Japanese Buddhism teaches that all life is fluid and that an aborted fetus is simply "returned" to a watery world of unshaped life and may later come back (LaFleur 1992). This belief fits well with the fact that abortion has, in recent years, been the most commonly used form of birth control in Japan.

The New Reproductive Technologies

Women's reproductive rights are an important contemporary issue in all cultures. These rights may involve the choice of seeking abortion in some cultures, and in another (such as China), the right to bear a child. They include the issue of the right to decide the gender or other characteristics of an unborn child. Since the early 1980s, new forms of reproductive technology have been developed and have been made available in many places around the world.

One development is the ability to gain genetic information about the fetus, which can be used by parents in decision making about whether to continue or stop the pregnancy. In the United States and some European countries, amniocentesis is a legal test used to reveal certain genetic problems in the fetus, such as Down syndrome and spina bifida. Anthropologists have begun to question the social equity involved in this testing and the ethical issues related to the growing role of technology in birth and reproduction.

Rayna Rapp (1993) did research on the cultural context of genetic testing among poor women in New York City. Nationally, amniocentesis has become a "ritual of pregnancy," mainly among the more educated, urbanized sectors of the White middle classes. In New York City, where Rapp did participant observation in the Prenatal Diagnosis Laboratory (PDL), the situation is different. The PDL of the City of New York was established in 1978 to offer amniocentesis to low-income women who are mainly African American or Hispanic. About 50 percent of the poor clients don't keep their initial appointment for genetic counseling. Upon having an amniocentesis procedure recommended by a counselor, many refuse to follow through with having the test done.

Rapp witnessed many counseling sessions. She interviewed several "refusers" in their homes about their attitudes toward the testing. She found that many people reject the counselor's advice.

> One Haitian father, firmly rejecting prenatal testing on his wife's behalf, said, "The counselor says the baby could be born retarded. They always say Haitian children are retarded. What is this retarded? Many Haitian children are said to be retarded in the public schools. If we send them to the Haitian Academy (a community-based private school) they learn just fine." (392)

Although medical innovations such as amniocentesis are promoted as "advances for women," Rapp finds that poor women who are advised to seek genetic testing during their pregnancy are not fully aware of all that is involved. She argues that the new technology and the increased "choice" it offers does not empower them. Instead, it overpowers them.

In vitro fertilization (IVF) procedures are another important feature of the new reproductive technologies. Rather than being a population control technology for limiting fertility, IVF is designed to bypass infertility in a woman or couple and thus promote fertility. This technique is highly sought after by many couples in Western countries, especially middle- and upper-class couples, among whom infertility is inexplicably high. It is also increasingly available in urban centers around the world (Inhorn 2003). As this new technology spreads throughout the world, people reframe it within their own cultural logics. In much of the United States and the United Kingdom, where *in vitro* fertilization first became available, people tend to view it as "reproduction gone awry," because it is non-natural and a sign of one's natural inadequacy and failure (Jenkins and Inhorn 2003). Research on local cultural understandings of NRTs is emerging. In Athens, Greece, women who seek *in vitro* fertilization see it as natural because it helps them realize a key aspect of their feminine nature through pregnancy and birth (Paxson 2003). Many of these middle-class urban women commented that becoming a mother is the purpose of a woman's life, so IVF allows a woman's natural destiny to unfold. Husbands felt less positive about IVF because they believe that their important role in conception is bypassed by the process.

Medical institutional culture also varies worldwide in terms of its attitudes toward IVF. In the United States, it is medically acceptable to provide IVF services. In Japan, a doctor who performed an IVF procedure was expelled by the leading obstetric society there in 1998 (Jordan 1998). Japanese societal values in relation to reproduction are complicated: They oppose surgery because it cuts the body, but they support abortion. Birth control pills are illegal. There is, however, growing public demand in Japan for new reproductive techniques—a demand that is opposed by the medical profession. Religious institutions are also reacting to the NRTs, including *in vitro* fertilization, and formulating policies. Within the global religions, debate and diversity exist. Within Islam, for example, Sunnis allow IVF if the woman is fertilized with her husband's semen and recognize the resulting offspring as the legal child of the couple. Shiites, however, do not (*Women's Health Weekly* 2003)

The globalization of IVF is driven by many factors, including pronatalism, the stigma of childlessness, and adoption restrictions. Behind all these factors lurks the fact of rising infertility in both men and women, conditions more likely to go untreated among poorer populations. Infertility does seem to have class distributions, as does access to infertility treatment, including IVF. Estimates are that infertility affects 8–12 percent of couples worldwide (Inhorn 2003). Sub-Saharan Africa, referred to as the "infertility belt," has the highest rate of infertility in the world; about one-third of couples unable to conceive. Given the poverty of this region, infertility services are also least available there.

CULTURE AND DEATH

Cultural anthropologists have done many studies of fertility, but their research on mortality is relatively scant (Bledsoe and Hirschman 1989). This difference is partly because mortality is more difficult to research in a typical fieldwork period in the traditional fieldwork setting of a village or urban neighborhood. In a year, several births might occur in a village of 1000 people, but fewer infant deaths will occur and perhaps no murders or suicides. (Of course, if one did fieldwork in a home for the aged in the United States, then death would be far easier to study than birth.) Another reason for the difference in research emphasis between fertility and mortality is the greater availability of funding for fertility studies, given the worldwide concern with population growth and family planning.

Death may occur randomly and from biological causes that impair the body's functioning. However, cultural factors often put certain people more at risk than others of dying from a certain cause and at a particular age. Consider statistics on deaths from car accidents. According to many studies, the rate of severe accidents is higher among men, and men exhibit more high-risk driving behavior, such as driving at high speeds and driving under the influence of alcohol (Hakamies-Blomqvist 1994). Among older male and female drivers in Finland, an increase in fatal accidents occurs among older female drivers because they have had substantially less driving experience in terms of mileage and conditions. The lower experience level of women drivers is related to more men having held jobs to which they commuted. Women's relative lack of driving experience places them at a disadvantage when it comes to coping with the effects of aging on driving. If the division of labor were to change and more women had jobs to which they commuted, the accident pattern of older women drivers might also change.

Causes of death can be analyzed on several levels. For example, if an infant living in a poor, tropical country dies of dehydration, what might be the cause? Levels of causality considered in population studies are *proximate,* *intermediate,* and *ultimate.* A proximate cause is the one that is closest to the actual outcome. In the case of this infant, dehydration was the proximate cause of death and one that might be written on the death certificate. Why was the baby dehydrated? A closer look into the situation might show that the baby was malnourished. Malnutrition leads to diarrhea and subsequent dehydration. Malnutrition could be considered the intermediate cause of death. Why was the baby malnourished? This question takes us down a complex pathway of inquiry—maybe the family was very poor and could not afford adequate food for the baby. Perhaps the baby died during a period of extreme food scarcity in the area. Perhaps the baby was an unwanted third daughter and was fed less than she needed in order to thrive. The question of ultimate causation entails an analysis of the deeper economic, political, and social factors that put a particular individual at increased risk of dying. In the next section, we review how culture shapes death.

Infanticide

Deliberate killing of offspring has been widely documented cross-culturally, although it is not usually a frequent or common practice in any society (Dickemann 1975, 1979; Divale and Harris 1976; Scrimshaw 1984). Infanticide takes different forms and can be **direct infanticide** or **indirect infanticide** (Harris 1977). Direct infanticide is the death of an infant or child resulting from actions such as beating, smothering, poisoning, or drowning. Indirect infanticide, a more subtle process, may involve prolonged practices such as food deprivation, failure to take a sick infant to a clinic, or failure to provide warm clothing in winter.

The most frequent motive for direct infanticide reported cross-culturally is that the infant was "deformed" or very ill (Scrimshaw 1984:490–491). Other motives for infanticide include sex of the infant, an adulterous conception, an unwed mother, the birth of twins, and too many children in the family. A study of 148 cases of infanticide in contemporary Canada found that the mothers convicted of killing their offspring were likely to have given birth at a young age and may have had few supportive resources to help them (Daly and Wilson 1984).

Family Resource Constraints and Child "Fitness"

In all cultures, parents have expectations for their children—what roles they will play as children, their future marital status, and their roles as adults. If an infant appears to be unable to meet these expectations, parental disappointment and detachment may occur. As yet, no general theory has been formulated to explain precisely the relationship between resource constraints and perceived child "fitness." Not all people living in poverty practice infanticide, nor do all people practice infanticide when a child is born with certain disabilities.

Culturally accepted infanticide has long existed among the Tarahumara, a large group of indigenous peoples of northern Mexico (Mull and Mull 1987). The approximately 50,000 Tarahumara live in a rugged mountainous area. Most live in log houses with dirt floors and no running water and electricity. They grow corn and beans and raise sheep and goats, mainly for their own use. Human strength is valued in children as well as in adults, because children begin helping with herding and child care early in their lives. The possible existence of infanticide first became apparent to anthropologist Dennis Mull when he was working as a volunteer physician in a hospital. A twelve-month-old girl who had been admitted several months earlier developed a complication requiring the amputation of half her foot. During her recovery period, her mother's visits became less frequent. In conversations with the medical staff, the mother expressed a restrained but deep anger about the fact that her daughter had lost half her foot. After the child was dismissed from the hospital, she reportedly "failed" and died. One member of the community interpreted her death this way: "Well, after all, with only half a foot she'd never be able to walk right or work hard. She might never find a husband" (116–117).

Among the poor of urban Brazil, there exists a similar pattern of indirect infanticide that is driven by poverty (Scheper-Hughes 1992). Life is hard for the poor residents of the shantytown called Bom Jesus. Life expectancy is low, although precise information on mortality is not available for these shantytown dwellers. Available data on infant and child mortality in Bom Jesus since the 1960s led anthropologist Nancy Scheper-Hughes to coin the ironic phrase the "modernization of mortality." The modernization of mortality in Brazil reflects a deep division between mortality patterns of the rich and the poor. Economic growth in Brazil has brought rising standards of living for many. The national **infant mortality rate** (deaths of children under the age of one year per 1000 births) has declined substantially in recent decades, but the decline is unevenly distributed. High infant death rates are concentrated among the poorest classes of society. Poverty forces mothers to selectively (and unconsciously) neglect babies that seem sickly or weak, sending them to heaven as "angel babies" rather than trying to keep them alive. The people's religious beliefs, a form of Catholicism, provide ideological support for this practice of indirect infanticide because it allows mothers to believe that their dead babies are now safe in heaven.

When the infant's gender is the basis for infanticide, females tend to be the target (Miller 1997 [1981]: 42–44). Among foraging groups, female infanticide is rare, being found mainly among some circumpolar groups of North America. Presumably, this practice is related to the greater importance of raising males who will provide food through large-game hunting. Among horticultural societies, a correlation exists between the level of intergroup warfare and the practice of female infanticide (Divale and Harris 1976). Warfare places high value on raising males, to the detriment of investing care and resources in females.

Indirect female infanticide exists in contemporary times in much of China, the Republic of Korea, Hong Kong, India, Pakistan, and parts of the Middle East. (See the Unity and Diversity box on page 120.) In these countries, female infanticide is related to a complex set of factors, including the gender division of labor and marriage practices and costs.

A temple in Rajasthan, northern India, dedicated to women who have committed sati. ■ *Consider various examples of suicide in different cultures and be prepared to debate whether explanations of structure or agency seem more relevant.* (Source: © Lindsey Hebberd/CORBIS)

Suicide

Suicide is known in all societies, but the degree to which it is viewed as a positive or negative act varies. In some cultures, suicide is legally or religiously defined as a crime. Catholicism defines suicide as a sin, and suicide rates tend to be lower in Catholic countries than in Protestant countries (Durkheim 1951:152). Buddhism does not condone suicide, nor does it consider attempted suicide a punishable crime. Indeed, Buddhists have sometimes used suicide to make a political statement.

Suicide terrorism is a term that has become prominent since the September 11, 2001, attacks on the United States. Those attacks, as well as many others carried out in the Middle East and elsewhere by people of several different religious and political persuasions, involve the suicide of one or more people with the intention of killing other people as well (Andriolo 2002). Many religions put a positive value on martyrdom, or a person facing and accepting death for a sacred cause. Linking personal martyrdom with killing others is also found in some religions and secular political movements. The young Tamil woman who blew herself up, along with India's former prime minister Rajiv Gandhi (Indira Gandhi's eldest son), is an example of a political martyr–assassin. Her cause was ethnic Tamil separatism in Sri Lanka. Islam condemns suicide and teaches that hell awaits those who commit it. But certain reinterpretations, among Philippine Muslims, for example, see purposeful suicide killings as being outside Islamic teachings but nonetheless justi-

Unity and Diversity

FEMALE INFANTICIDE IN INDIA

THE INDIAN population has 55 million fewer females than males. Much of this gap is caused by indirect female infanticide and sex-selective abortion. Most of the scarcity of girls is located in northern India, where baby girls are breastfed less often and for a shorter period of time than baby boys, and they are taken to clinics for treatment of illnesses less frequently. Hospital admissions in the North are 2:1 boys to girls, and that is not because more boys are sick than girls but because family decision makers are more willing to allocate time and money to the health of boys than of girls (Miller 1997 [1981]).

Why is discrimination against daughters and in favor of sons in terms of household allocations of food, health care, and even attention, more marked in northern India than in its southern and eastern regions? This regional pattern corresponds with two features of the economy: production and marriage exchanges. The northern plains are characterized by dry-field wheat cultivation, which requires intensive labor inputs for plowing and field preparation and then moderate amounts of field labor for sowing, weeding, and harvesting, with women assisting in the latter tasks as unpaid family labor. Production in southern and eastern India relies more on wet rice cultivation, in which women form the bulk of the paid agricultural labor force. In much of southern India, women of the household sometimes participate on an equal footing with men in terms of agricultural planning and decision making.

Paralleling this regional difference in labor patterns is a contrast in costs related to marriage. In the North, marriage typically requires, especially among the propertied groups, **groomprice** or **dowry**—the transfer of large amounts of cash and goods from the bride's family to the groom's family. Marriage costs in the South among both propertied and unpropertied groups are more likely to emphasize **brideprice**—the transfer of cash and goods from the groom's side to the bride's father, along with a tradition of passing gold jewelry through the female line from mother to daughter. From a parent's perspective, the birth of several daughters in the northern system is a financial drain. In the South, a daughter is considered a valuable laborer and source of wealth. Importantly, much of northern dowry and southern bridewealth circulates:

An incoming dowry can be used to finance the marriage of the groom's sister, and bridewealth received in the South at the marriage of a daughter can be used for the marriage of her brother. Logically, in the North, the more sons per daughter in the household the better, because more incoming dowries will allow for a "better" marriage of a daughter.

The economic costs and benefits to a household of having sons versus daughters in India also vary by class. This variation is related to both work patterns and marriage patterns. Middle- and upper-class families, especially in the North, tend to keep girls and women out of the paid labor force more than the poor. Thus daughters are a greater economic liability among the better-off than among the poor where girls, as well as boys, may earn money in the informal sector—for example, doing piece-work at home. This class difference is mirrored in marriage costs. Among the poor, marriage costs are less than among the middle and upper classes, and they often involve balanced exchange between the bride's and groom's families. Thus, marriage costs of daughters are lower and the benefits of having sons are not that much greater than those of having daughters.

Poverty is therefore not the major driving factor of son preference and daughter disfavor in India. This combination, instead, is driven by the desire to maximize status and wealth. If one has two sons and one daughter in the North Indian marriage system of huge dowries, then two dowries will come in with the brides of the sons and only one dowry will be expended. Incoming dowries can be used to finance the dowry of one's own daughter, so one can provide a huge outgoing dowry that will attract a high status husband. If, on the other hand, one has two daughters and one son, the ratio of incoming to outgoing wealth changes significantly. This situation would impoverish a family rather than enrich it.

FOOD FOR THOUGHT

Have you experienced, or has anyone you know experienced, a feeling of being less valued as a child than other children in the family? If you are an "only child," you will need to ponder experiences related by friends.

fiable on other grounds. A few pages in the manual that the September 11 hijackers had with them related their actions to raids that the prophet Muhammad conducted to consolidate his position, thus portraying their actions as acceptable and even heroic and the end for them as entry into paradise instead of hell. Many Islamic scholars, however, do not accept the validity of this reasoning.

Throughout much of Asia and the South Pacific, suicide is considered a noble and honorable act. When Cheyenne Brando, daughter of Marlon Brando and Tahitian actress Tarita, committed suicide in Tahiti, the local mayor called her suicide "a beautiful gesture" (Gliotto 1995:70). Honorable suicide is also found in Japan, where it seems to result from a strong commitment to group goals and a feeling of failure to live up to those goals (Lebra 1976). In this way, suicide is a way of "saving face."

Sati (pronounced SUT-TEE), or the suicide of a wife upon the death of her husband, has been practiced in parts of India for several hundred years and, on occasion, into the present. According to Hindu scriptures, a woman whose husband dies does an act of great personal and group honor if she voluntarily joins his corpse on the funeral pyre and thus burns to death. No one knows how common this was in the past, but its ideal is still upheld by conservative Hindus. The most recent reported sati took place in the northern state of Rajasthan, in 1987, by a young widow named Roop Kanwar. Historians and social scientists have debated the degree of agency, or free will, involved in such suicides, as there is evidence of direct coercion in some cases—the widow was drugged or physically forced onto the pyre. Indirect coercion is also culturally embedded in the belief that a woman whose husband dies is to blame for his death: Perhaps she didn't serve him with enough devotion, pray or fast for him enough, or give him enough food. The life of surviving widows is difficult, involving loss of status, shame, and material deprivation. Knowing this, a new widow may believe herself to be better off dead.

In terms of sheer numbers, suicide has long been most prevalent in the industrialized, urbanized societies of Europe. However, in several developing nations, such as Sri Lanka and Samoa, suicide rates have risen steeply in recent decades. The usual explanation for cross-cultural variation in suicide rates is that rapid social changes brought about by industrialism, the spread of education, and global change in consumer values encourage new aspirations that may be impossible to achieve. French sociologist Emile Durkheim (1951 [1897]) used the term *anomie* to refer to the feelings of dislocation and dissatisfaction caused by rapid social change and thwarted ambitions. The concept of anomic suicide seems to apply well to the rising trend of youth suicide worldwide.

Epidemics

The chapter on medical anthropology (Chapter 8) will discuss disease in more depth, but for our purposes here, it is important to introduce the massive impact of HIV/AIDS on mortality in the past two decades as a primary example of epidemic-related death. At the present time, sub-Saharan countries have been the most affected by the HIV epidemic (Nyambedha, Wandibba, and Aagaard-Hansen 2003). Most of the deaths have occurred among adults of parent age. These deaths are tragic in themselves, and they also leave behind them huge numbers of orphaned children. Global estimates are that 10 million children under the age of fifteen years have lost their mother or both parents to AIDS. In Kenya alone, it is likely that there will be 1.5 million orphaned children by 2005. Some families in Kenya are now headed by children as young as ten to twelve years old. Community-based interventions to help these disadvantaged children suffer from several weaknesses, including lack of attention to local cultural factors (see the Lessons Applied box on page 122).

Violence

Violent death can be the result of private, interpersonal conflict, or it can occur in a public arena, either through informal conflict between individuals or groups, such as gang fights, or formal conflict such as war. Throughout history, millions of people have died from private and public violence. Often their deaths have culturally defined patterns.

Private Violence: Spousal Abuse

Throughout the world, private violence resulting in death is all too common. One example, infanticide, was discussed above. Lethal spousal violence is known to exist throughout most of the world in varying degrees, although it is difficult to pinpoint cross-cultural rates because statistics are undependable or unavailable. In the case of spouses, far more women are killed by husbands or male partners than vice versa. Anecdotal evidence suggests that in much of the Middle East, a husband may kill his wife or daughter without fear of punishment, as though it is within his rights in terms of protecting family honor. The United States has high rates of lethal spousal violence, with Kentucky having the highest reported rates of wife killing.

In India, beginning in the 1980s, many cases of an apparently new form of **femicide**, or murder of a person based on the fact of being female, were reported in the media. Called *dowry death*, such murders were characteristically committed by a husband, often in collusion

Lessons Applied

RESEARCH ON LOCAL CULTURAL PATTERNS FOR IMPROVED ORPHAN CARE IN KENYA

THE DRAMATIC increase in the numbers of orphans in Africa—an increase attributable to the AIDS epidemic—calls for new thinking about how to care for these children, because traditional mechanisms are inadequate. Child care patterns in many parts of the world, and especially in many African kinship systems, involve grandparents and other family members. But now, even this social safety net is not enough.

Many non-governmental agencies have become involved in helping to design community-based services for AIDS orphans. Cultural anthropologists can help make these services more effective by offering insights about local cultural practices and beliefs so that programs can be tailored to fit particular communities. Anthropologists have long known that "one-size-fits-all" programs, designed by outsiders without attention to local culture, may operate less effectively than they could or, at worst, fail disastrously.

One anthropological study undertaken to provide such needed cultural information was conducted in western Kenya in an area bordering Lake Victoria (Nyambedha, Wandibba, and Aagaard-Hansen 2003). The Luo are the predominant ethnic group in the region. The area is poor, and most Luo practice small-scale farming and obtain some additional income from fishing, migrant labor, and informal gold mining. Recurrent droughts lead to frequent crop failures. Children are important in the local economy: They work on farms planting, weeding, and harvesting and do such other important tasks as collecting firewood, herding animals, fetching water, and fishing. Clean water is scarce. Health services provided by a Christian mission and the government are of poor quality and not affordable for most people.

The Luo define an orphan as someone under the age of eighteen years who has lost either one or both parents; thus they refer to single and double orphans. (The Luo definition differs from the usual international definition: someone under the age of fifteen years who has lost both parents.) The Luo say that the neediest are double orphans.

The research involved both quantitative and qualitative data-gathering techniques (review Chapter 2). Questionnaires were administered to a random sample of households, and then in-depth interviews were conducted with a subsample of twenty orphans and orphan caretakers from the first survey. Other interviews were conducted with key informants in a range of social roles, such as village elders, teachers, members of women's groups, and staff of the local children's home. Fourteen focus group discussions (FGDs) were held with a cross section of people to explore further the main themes of the study. Last, five households where orphans lived were monitored for six months to obtain longitudinal information on household resources, changes in household membership, coping mechanisms, and outside support.

Analysis of the data reveals many useful findings. First, they provide information on the population of

---

with his mother, and carried out by throwing a flammable substance over the victim and then lighting her on fire. These murders are especially prevalent in northern cities. They are spurred by an obsessive material interest in extracting wealth from the wife's family first through her dowry and later through a continuing stream of demanded gifts. If the bride's family cannot comply with these demands, the bride's life is endangered. This form of femicide is related to the overall low value of women in India, especially in the North and among the status-aspiring middle and upper classes.

Public Violence

Two forms of lethal public violence that anthropologists study are warfare and genocide. These topics are discussed in greater depth in Chapter 11. In this section, we focus on their effects on mortality. The few anthropological studies that have addressed mortality from warfare cross-culturally reveal that among horticultural societies, warfare accounts for the highest proportion of male deaths and functions as a major mechanism of population control (Divale and Harris 1976). Horticulture's requirement for large territories puts many groups in conflict with one another. In recent decades, conflicts with outsiders have increased; for example, the Yanomami of the Brazilian and Venezuelan Amazon region are squeezed by outsiders such as cattle ranch developers and miners (Ferguson 1990). This external pressure impels them to engage in intergroup raids that often result in the deaths of male fighters and also sometimes of women, who may be captured and killed. In some especially vulnerable groups of Yanomami, up to one-third of all adult males die as a result of intergroup raids and warfare.

---

orphans. About one out of three children (34 percent) had lost one or both parents. Of these, about half had lost their father, about 20 percent had lost their mother, and 30 percent were double orphans.

Second, the study provided information on the orphans' needs. The main problems the orphans faced were food shortage, lack of money for school fees, and inadequate medical care and clothing. In Luo culture, fathers are responsible for paying children's school fees. Thus paternal orphans tended to drop out of school. Maternal orphans are considered more vulnerable than paternal orphans, because their father is likely to remarry and his new wife will favor her own biological children. About half of the orphans remained with one parent. Others moved in with relatives, especially grandparents, whose resources were already stretched but who felt they could not refuse to take in their grandchild. Many orphans taken in by better-off relatives ended up providing free labor for that family. Alternatively, they took on wage work for nonrelatives. In either case, their school participation suffered.

The large and sudden increase in the number of orphans creates larger strains on the community as people come to realize that their traditional pattern of caring for orphans within the kinship structure is not adequate. The traditional generosity of kin seems to be declining. At the same time, a longstanding pattern of spending a lot of money on funerals means that resources that could go to orphans go to burial and after-burial rituals instead.

Community-based organizations such as churches and women's groups in this region are doing little to help the orphans, although in other areas they are more active. The study provides a baseline of the population of orphans, information about their specific needs and coping strategies, and insights about community views of the problem. It points to the particular needs of different types of orphans and the varying strengths of different family structures in caring for orphans.

The authors reject the idea of constructing an orphanage as a way of dealing with the problem. They offer no specific suggestions for community-based programs, but it is easy to see that the following would help: financial support to single-parent and grandparent caretakers, waiving or community funding of the school fees for orphans, and a social movement to divert some of the money used for funerals to orphan care.

FOOD FOR THOUGHT

Has the issue of AIDS orphans in Africa come to your attention before? If so, how—television, newspapers, or what? How was the issue presented? If it had not come to your attention, what might explain its relative invisibility as a globally significant issue?

In contrast, in industrialized societies, the death rates of males actively involved in warfare constitute a much smaller proportion of total death rates, being replaced by such causes as automobile accidents and heart disease. The Vietnam–American War of the 1960s and 1970s resulted in the death of about 60,000 Americans in Vietnam (mostly males) and of many times that number of Vietnamese.

Some scholars distinguish **genocide,** the destruction of a culture and its people through physical extermination, from **ethnocide,** the destruction of a culture without physically killing its people. The Chinese occupation of Tibet, the Khmer Rouge's massacres in Cambodia, the Serbian-Bosnian conflict, the Hutu-Tutsi conflict in Rwanda, and the Indonesian government's actions in East Timor are examples of politically motivated genocide.

The history of Native American demography can also be interpreted as one of genocidal destruction and has been called "the American holocaust." It is likely that well over 50 million Amerindians died as a result of contact with the Europeans from 1492 through the seventeenth century (Stannard 1992). For example, the European presence in Central America had the following results:

Before the coming of the Europeans, central Mexico, radiating out from the metropolitan centers over many tens of thousands of square miles, had contained about 25 million people—almost ten times the population of England at that time. Seventy-five years later hardly more than one million were left. And central Mexico, where 60 out of a hundred people perished, was typical. . . . In western and central Honduras 95 percent of the native

Refugees fleeing the late 1990s violence in Rwanda on their way to neighboring Zaire. Many refugees did not survive the ordeal, although we do not have statistics adequate to assess their mortality rate. ■ *Use the Internet to search for mortality rates from a recent conflict and speculate on how accurate the data might be.* (Source: © Allan Tannenbaum/The Image Works)

people were exterminated in half a century. In western Nicaragua the rate of extermination was 99 percent—from more than one million people to less than 10,000 in just sixty years. (430)

The indigenous population of the Caribbean islands was exterminated. Only archaeological evidence and Spanish archival documents recording fragments of the original peoples' culture remain.

Genocide against indigenous peoples has been occurring for centuries as imperialist powers and profit-seeking explorers and settlers have intentionally brought about the extinction of entire peoples (Maybury-Lewis 2002). During the nineteenth century, British settlers in Tasmania carried out an overt campaign to exterminate the indigenous Tasmanians. In other cases, mass killings were used as means of terrorizing survivors into performing forced labor, as, for example, in the rubber plantations of Peru and the Congo. These historical examples of "imperialist genocide" were driven by greed and supported by a racist ideology that considered indigenous people less than human. Today, greed-driven and carelessly planned development projects such as large dams (Chapter 16) often prove to be an indirect form of genocide when they completely disrupt where indigenous people live, force them to resettle, and subject them to new diseases and suicidal despair.

Politically motivated examples of genocide of indigenous peoples also can be easily found. Since the middle of the twentieth century, the government of India has waged a campaign of terror against many groups in its states bordering Burma to prevent separatist movements from gaining strength. One tribe, the Nagas, numbers about two and a half million; the Indian government has placed 200,000 troops in their area to quell the tribe's attempts to join with Nagas in Burma to form a separate Naga country. The Naga people voted overwhelmingly for independence in 1951, and India invaded the region in 1954. There are no mortality data available for this situation, but one can only assume that the casualties are far higher on the Naga side than on the government side.

KEY CONCEPTS

SUGGESTED READINGS

Kamran Asdar Ali. *Planning the Family in Egypt: New Bodies, New Selves*. Austin: University of Texas Press, 2002. This ethnographic study conducted by a Pakistani doctor and anthropologist, examines the policies and practices of family planning programs in Egypt to see how this elitist, Western-influenced state creates demographically compliant citizens. His findings reveal the dilemma created for women as family planning programs pressure them to think of themselves as individual decision makers acting in their own and the nation's interest by limiting their fertility, even though they are still bound by their wider families and religion to pronatalism.

Caroline Bledsoe and Barney Cohen, eds. *Social Dynamics of Adolescent Fertility in Sub-Saharan Africa*. Washington, DC: National Academy Press, 1993. An anthropologist and a demographer examine national survey data on cultural factors related to high fertility rates among adolescents in sub-Saharan Africa. Attention is given to patterns of adolescent sexuality, attitudes toward marriage, women's status, knowledge and practice of contraception, and the role of education in change.

John D. Early and Thomas N. Headland. *Population Dynamics of a Philippine Rain Forest People: The San Ildefonso Agta*. Gainesville: University of Florida Press, 1998. This comprehensive study of population dynamics of an Agta group living on Luzon Island in the Philippines draws on a forty-four-year quantitative database on fertility, mortality, and migration from the time when the Agta were forest foragers to the present (they are now small-scale farmers in rural Philippine society). It profiles a minority people without economic and political power and documents the impact of international logging interests on their lives.

Thomas E. Fricke. *Himalayan Households: Tamang Demography and Domestic Processes*. New York, Columbia University Press, 1994. An example of demographic anthropology, this is a local study of population patterns and change in one region of Nepal. The book includes chapters on the subsistence economy, fertility and mortality, the life course, household dynamics, and recent changes.

W. Penn Handwerker, ed. *Births and Power: Social Change and the Politics of Reproduction*. Boulder, CO: Westview Press, 1990. An overview chapter by the editor is followed by eleven case studies, including studies of the Inuit of Canada, the Bariba of West Africa, the Mende of Sierra Leone, Hungary, and Bangladesh, along with studies from the United States addressing teen pregnancy and an essay on AIDS in Africa.

Nancy Howell. *Demography of the Dobe !Kung*. New York: Academic Press, 1979. This classic book describes the demography of a group of South African foragers before they were sedentarized. The text considers how anthropological methods contribute to demographic analysis of small-scale societies, causes of illness and death, fertility and sterility, and population growth rates.

Marcia C. Inhorn. *Infertility and Patriarchy: The Cultural Politics of Gender and Family Life in Egypt*. Philadelphia: University of Pennsylvania Press, 1996. Based on fieldwork in Alexandria, this book uses narratives from several infertile Egyptian women to show the different ways in which these women and their families deal with cultural pressures to bear children.

Leith Mullings and Alaka Wali. *Stress and Resilience: The Social Context of Reproduction in Central Harlem*. New York: Kluwer Academic, 2001. Documenting the daily efforts of African Americans to contend with oppressive conditions, this ethnography focuses on the experiences of women especially during pregnancy and details the strategies they use to address the strains that their economic and social context place on them.

Nancy Scheper-Hughes *Death Without Weeping: The Violence of Everyday Life in Brazil*. Berkeley: University of California Press, 1993. This book is a landmark "ethnography of death," based on fieldwork in a Brazilian shantytown over several periods of time. The author argues that poverty drives a demographic system of very high infant mortality rates and high fertility.

Nancy Scheper-Hughes and Carolyn Sargent, eds. *Small Wars: The Cultural Politics of Childhood*. Berkeley: University of California Press, 1998. Following an introduction by the co-editors, eighteen chapters explore aspects of infant and child mortality and health in a wide array of contexts, including Japan, Ecuador, the United States, Israel, Mexico, Portugal, the Dominican Republic, Cuba, England, Croatia, and Brazil.

Soraya Tremayne, ed. *Managing Reproductive Life: Cross-Cultural Themes in Sexuality and Fertility*. New York: Bergahn Books, 2001. Twelve chapters are organized under three headings: agency and identity, fertility and parenthood, and policy and vulnerable groups. Cases are from India, Thailand, the United Kingdom, Burkino Faso, Peru, Nigeria, and Hong Kong, and topics include motherhood among prostitutes, the stigma of infertility, how male migration affects fertility, and the reproductive health of refugees.

HOW are modes of reproduction related to modes of production?

The modes of reproduction, or the dominant pattern of fertility in a culture, are everywhere shaped by culture. The various modes of production are basic structures to which reproduction responds. For thousands of years, foragers maintained a balanced level of population through direct and indirect means of fertility regulation. As sedentarization increased and food surpluses became more available and storable, population increased as well, culminating in the highest rates of population growth in human history among settled agriculturalists. In industrial economies, most fertility rates are low or at a below-replacement level. Within countries, economic inequalities are linked to differing patterns of fertility and mortality.

HOW does culture shape fertility in different contexts?

Cross-culturally, many techniques exist for increasing fertility, reducing it, and regulating its timing. Anthropological studies of indigenous fertility-regulating mechanisms reveal hundreds of different methods, including the use of herbs and other natural sources for inhibiting or enhancing fertilization and for inducing abortion if an undesired pregnancy occurs. In nonindustrial societies, the knowledge and practice of fertility regulation were largely unspecialized and available to all women. Early specializations included midwives and herbalists. In the industrial mode of reproduction, scientific and medical specialization abounds, and most knowledge and expertise is no longer in the hands of women themselves. Class-stratified access to fertility-regulating methods exists globally and within nations.

HOW does culture shape mortality in different contexts?

Population growth and change are also affected through the cultural shaping of death. The practice of infanticide is of ancient origin, and it still exists today. It may be done in response to family resource limitations, perceptions of "fitness" of the child, or preferences about the gender of offspring. Deaths from suicide, and from public and private violence, also reflect cultural patterns that "target" certain people or groups. Thus, birth and death, far from being random, natural events, are cultural events to a large extent.

THE BIG QUESTIONS

- **WHAT** is the scope of psychological anthropology?

- **HOW** does culture shape personality and identity from birth through adolescence?

- **HOW** does culture shape personality and identity in adulthood through old age?

6

PERSONALITY, IDENTITY, AND HUMAN DEVELOPMENT

Young boys of the Shan people, Thailand, participating in the Poi Sang Long festival. This annual event culminates in the initiation of young boys into the Buddhist monkhood for a minimum of two years. (*Source: Kevin R. Morris/CORBIS*)

The Mehinaku are peaceful horticulturalists of the Brazilian Amazon whose society, thus far, is mainly intact (Gregor 1981). Nonetheless, they are aware of the presence and power of Brazilians (non-Indians).

An analysis of 385 dreams of the Mehinaku indicates that they have deep anxieties about the outsiders. Of the total set of dreams, over half contained indications of some level of anxiety. In 31 of the dreams, Brazilians were central characters, and most of these dreams were tinged with fear.

Recurrent themes in the dreams with outsiders as key characters were fire, assault, and disorientation. Although the Mehinaku's land and culture are still intact, their inner tranquility is gone.

The study of people's dreams in different cultural contexts is just one of the many approaches that psychological anthropologists pursue in their attempt to understand psychological processes.

Psychological anthropology addresses many of the topics of contemporary Western psychology: learning, perception, cognition, memory, intelligence, the emotions, sexuality and gender, personality, identity, and mental health problems. Studying these topics cross-culturally reveals the ethnocentrism involved in applying Western psychological concepts universally, including definitions of what is "normal." An enduring question in psychological anthropology is whether and how much human psychology is the same cross-culturally or whether variation overrides universals.

This chapter provides background on how cultural anthropology has approached the study of the individual within culture—particularly how cultures shape **personality**, an individual's patterned and characteristic way of behaving, thinking, and feeling. We also consider how cultures create people's sense of identity: who they think they are in relation to others, their sense of self. The material is presented in terms of general stages of the life cycle, from birth through death in old age.

The subject matter of this chapter is referred to as **ethnopsychology**, the study of how various cultures define and create personality, identity, and mental health. This chapter focuses on "normal" human development, as defined culturally. Problematic aspects of human development, including what Western psychology defines as mental illness, are discussed in Chapter 7.

CULTURE, PERSONALITY, AND IDENTITY

Most Cultural anthropologists think that personality is formed through enculturation, or socialization, the process of cultural transmission to infants and other new members. They seek answers to these questions: Do different cultures enculturate their members into different personalities? If so, how and why?

The Culture and Personality School

The American-based Culture and Personality School began in the 1930s and persisted through the 1970s. Cultural anthropologists who were part of this group adopted some aspects of Freudian theories, especially the concept of the unconscious; the importance of childhood experiences in shaping personality and identity; and the symbolic analysis of people's dreams, words, and stories. Members of the Culture and Personality School, however, differed from Freud in rejecting universalism. These anthropologists, working within the Boasian tradition of historical particularism (Chapter 1), believed that each culture has a unique history that affects its values, behavior, and personality types.

Two directions that the Culture and Personality School took were, first, understanding how child-rearing practices affect personality and, second, describing national-level personality patterns. The first of these is still accepted, whereas the second is largely discredited.

Personality and Child Rearing

In the early 1930s, Margaret Mead went to the Sepik River area of northern New Guinea. Her subsequent book, *Sex and Temperament in Three Primitive Societies* (1963 [1935]), revealed striking differences in how male and female roles and personalities were defined and acted out. Mead's findings seemed to prove that nature is subservient to culture—that culture, not nature, dictates what is male and what is female. Among the Arapesh, the first group she studied, both men and women had nurturant and gentle personalities. Both valued parental roles and both participated equally in child care. Arapesh males and females all behaved according to what is stereotypically defined as "female" in Western cultures. Among the Mundugumor, in contrast, both males and females corresponded to the Western stereotype of "male" behavior. Adults in general were assertive, aggressive, loud, and even fierce. Children were treated indifferently by their parents, and neither mothers nor fathers expressed nurturance. The situation among the Tchambuli was equally surprising to Mead and her readers: The men fussed about their looks, gossiped with each other most of the day, and did little in the way of productive work. The women were competent and responsible, providing most of the food through fishing and gardening, and managing the household. The women played a dominant role in the culture, and their personalities reflected this importance. These findings suggest that gender is an arbitrary matter, defined culturally and shaped through child-rearing patterns. Mead's descriptions of child care, including differences in tenderness or neglect during breastfeeding, provide evidence of how children in different contexts learn patterns of personality and behavior.

Cultural Patterns and National Character

Ruth Benedict, a leading figure of the Culture and Personality School, argued that personality types characterize whole cultures or even nations. In her book *Patterns of Culture* (1959 [1934]), she proposed that cultures are formed through the unconscious selection of a few cultural traits from the "vast arc" of potential traits. For example, one culture may emphasize monetary values whereas another overlooks them. The selected traits

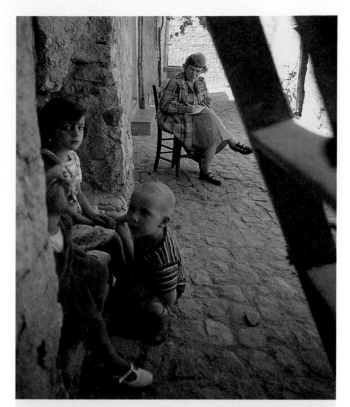

Margaret Mead, during her later years of fieldwork, observes children's interactions in Sicily. ■ *Have you ever attempted to observe small children's behavior for research purposes? How would such research differ from doing research among teenagers or adults?* (Source: © Ken Heyman/Woodfin Camp & Associates)

"interweave" to form a cohesive pattern, a **cultural configuration,** characteristic of the thoughts and behaviors of everyone in the culture. Benedict first formulated her theories while doing research on Native American cultures. In her view, the Pueblo Indians of the American Southwest had personalities that exemplified a "middle road," involving moderation in all things and avoiding excess and violence. She termed the Pueblo an "Apollonian" culture, after the Greek deity Apollo. In contrast, she labeled the Kwakwaka'wakw Indians of the Pacific Northwest "Dionysian," after the Greek god of revelry and excess (and drinking wine), mainly because of their potlatches and high levels of expressive emotionality. Looking back on this approach, one is struck by the Western ethnocentrism of using classical Greek labels and by the tendency to label an entire culture with one term.

During World War II the United States Office of War Information commissioned Benedict to analyze Japanese personality structure and submit reports to the government to help defeat the Japanese. During the war she could not do fieldwork, so she did "anthropology at a distance." She consulted secondary sources (newspapers, magazines, movies) and interviewed Japanese Americans. Her resulting book, *The Chrysanthemum and the Sword* (1969 [1946]), presents a set of essential features of Japanese character: importance of *on* (obligation, the necessity to repay gifts and favors), the concept of virtue, the value of self-discipline, keeping one's name "clear" or honorable, and rules of etiquette.

Following Benedict's work on Japan, **national character studies** that defined personality types and core values of entire nations became a prominent pursuit of psychological anthropologists. Contemporary anthropological standards, however, find three major faults with national character studies. They are ethnocentric: They classify cultures according to Western psychological values and features. They are reductionist: They emphasize only one or two features. They are totalizing: They obscure intranational variation in their construction of a single national character: *the* French, *the* English, *the* Japanese.

Class and Personality

Two cultural anthropologists of the mid-twentieth century proposed theories about how poverty shapes personality. George Foster (1965), who did research among small-scale farmers in Mexico, proposed a model called the **image of the limited good.** People who have this world view believe that the resources or wealth available within a particular social group are finite. If someone increases his or her wealth, other people necessarily lose out. The pie analogy illustrates how the image of the limited good works. If a group of eight people equally divides a pie into eight pieces, everyone gets the same share. But if one person takes two pieces, only six pieces remain for everyone else. One person's gain is another's loss. The image of the limited good, according to Foster, is found along with a "status quo" mentality that prevents people from trying to improve their economic condition. Major personality traits associated with the image of the limited good are jealousy, suspiciousness, and passivity.

Oscar Lewis (1966) proposed a related concept, the **culture of poverty,** to explain the personality and behavior of the poor and why poverty persists. He typified poor Mexican people as, among other things, "improvident," lacking a future time-orientation, and sexually promiscuous. Because of these personality characteristics, poor people are trapped in poverty and cannot change their situation.

Nearly fifty years after the writing of Foster and Lewis, the prevailing view of their theories is that they were eth-

nocentric, reflecting the position of Foster and Lewis as privileged people living in the context of mid-twentieth-century capitalist growth in the United States. The prevailing values of economically successful people in that context included self-assertion, aggressive competitiveness, and a belief that resources are infinite. Opposite traits and values were attributed to the poor as negative features to explain why poverty persisted. These scholars considered neither structurist nor human agency perspectives to try to understand people's lifestyles in poverty. In spite of the limits of their theories, Lewis is remembered for his many rich ethnographies of lower-class people's lives in Mexico, Puerto Rico, and the United States, and Foster contributed valuable work in medical anthropology.

Recent ethnopsychology studies have tried to be less ethnocentric in their interpretations. Some new work considers the many cases of revolution and resistance among poor and marginalized people, completely reversing the models proposed by Foster and Lewis about passivity.

At the opposite end of the class spectrum, psychological anthropologists are beginning to "study up" the class structure. An examination of how corporate culture shapes personality of middle- and upper-class urban men in Japan shows how child care patterns and the demands of the corporate business world fit together to create compliant male workers. (See the Unity and Diversity box.)

Person-Centered Ethnography

The newest direction in psychological anthropology is called **person-centered ethnography;** it is research that focuses on the individual and how the individual's psychology and subjective experience both shape and are shaped by her or his culture (Hollan 2001). In terms of its methods, person-centered ethnography relies heavily on what people say about their perceptions and experiences. Thus, like Western psychology and psychiatry, it is fundamentally discourse-based rather than observation-based. Gaining an emic view about individual people and their perceptions is the paramount goal. Yet most person-centered ethnographies situate details about individuals and what they say about their experience within the wider cultural context, because individuals and cultures are interactive.

One such contextualized study considers notions of the self and selfhood in a mountainous village in Nepal (Hardman 2000). The context provided is mainly about family relations, religion and concepts of the ancestors, and rituals, but some discussion is provided of land rights and the egalitarian principle of exchange. The emphasis, however, is on the local conception of *niwa,* or individ-

Unity and Diversity

CORPORATE INTERESTS AND MALE PERSONALITY FORMATION IN JAPAN

RESEARCH IN Japan on the personality of "salarymen," males employed in the fast-paced corporate world, links male personality with the demands of the business world (Allison 1994). Salarymen work long hours for the company. They leave home early in the morning and return late at night and thus are nicknamed "7–11 men." Many Tokyo salarymen eat dinner with their family only a few times a year. After work, they typically spend many hours with fellow workers at expensive nightclubs. Groups of about five to ten men go out together after work. A few drinks and light snacks can result in a tab in the hundreds of dollars for one hour. The corporation picks up the bill. At the club, men relax and have fun after a long day at work. This is ensured by having a trained hostess sit at the table, keeping the conversation moving along in a lightly playful tone. Her job is to flatter and flirt with the men and to make them feel good.

Anne Allison did participant observation while working as a hostess. She found that conversations are full of teasing and banter, with much of it directed at the hostess and most of it derogatory: The hostess's breasts are too small, her hair is not right, and so on. The hostess must take all of this with a smile, and even joke along with it: "Yes, I have no breasts at all." Allison calls this type of banter "breast talk." How should this focus on the female breast be interpreted? Salarymen's night club behavior appears to be linked with their upbringing. Given the near total absence of the father from the home scene, children are raised mainly by the mother.

The concentration of maternal attention is especially strong toward sons and their school achievements. The goal is that the boy will do well in school, get into a top university, and then secure a job with a large corporation. These corporations pay well, guarantee lifelong employment, and provide substantial benefits after retirement. In the corporation, hierarchies are clear, total loyalty is required, work hours are long, and the pressure to perform is high. Regular socializing at the club solidifies bonds between salarymen and strengthens their loyalty to the corporation.

Salarymen's behavior in night clubs can also be viewed as a reaction to their upbringing, with its total control by the mother. Club culture puts the man in control, reversing the power differential of his childhood. At the club, he has guaranteed control over a desirable woman who flatters him and flirts with him. She will never control him because after an hour or so of fun, he leaves and there is no enduring relationship. Club culture provides only temporary ego gratification for a salaryman: He needs to return again and again for reinforcement. This fact keeps salarymen away from their homes, leaving their own sons in the isolated care of the mother.

FOOD FOR THOUGHT

Can you think of examples of how other cultures socialize males—or females—to be compliant corporate employees?

uality and personality in terms of desires and wishes. In opposition to many broad statements from nonanthropologists about "Asian mentalities" and the lack of a concept of an autonomous self in "Asian societies," this study found clear evidence of a concept of individuality and interpersonal difference in *niwa*. As one villager commented, there are as many different *niwa* as there are faces. Interestingly, individual *niwa* is generally not to be expressed in public. With increasing social change, however, it is exhibited more often. Women are demonstrating their initiative and agency by selling beer and liquor. Young people are expressing opinions in public. At the level of wider society, individuality should not go so far as to upset socially shared views of propriety, which

include frugality, charitable giving, and feelings of conscience and shame. The self and individualism can exist but must do so within cultural bounds.

As many psychological anthropologists direct their attention to the details of individual perceptions and experience, others insist that the comparative method cannot be abandoned (Moore and Mathews 2001). For example, how does the Nepali villager's concept of *niwa* compare to notions of the self in other contexts? Are there private/public notions of self elsewhere, and, if so, how does that distinction play out? We see here the fruitful tension between ethnography (of the most peopleclose variety) and ethnology, the need to place detailed local cases in a wider frame.

THE ROLE OF CULTURAL KNOWLEDGE IN CONFLICT MEDIATION IN A U.S. HOSPITAL NURSERY

A NEW hospital had been built in a suburban community in the United States to provide services for its rapidly growing immigrant population (Deitrick 2002). Most of the nurses on staff were long-time residents of the community and had graduated from a local community college, where their training included no attention to cultural differences.

Cultural conflict arose upon the birth of a baby to a Turkish immigrant family. The infant had not yet been brought to the mother's room, and members of her family arrived to welcome the new baby. Along with them came a Muslim religious leader to administer the usual honey blessing to the infant before his first feeding. This ritual ensures a sweet life for the baby.

The nurse in charge denied the family access to the baby, saying that he first must have a medical examination and that unpasteurized honey could not be given to him. The baby's father was upset and claimed that the blessing must be administered because whatever the baby first tastes determines the quality of its life.

Fortunately, a nurse who also had training in cultural anthropology, Lynn Deitrick, entered into the discussions and was able to act as a **cultural broker,** a person—often but not always an anthropologist—who is familiar with the practices and beliefs of two different cultures and can promote cross-cultural understanding to prevent or mediate conflicts. She listened to the views of the Turkish family and learned that only a tiny amount of honey would be placed on the baby's tongue for the blessing. She suggested a compromise to the medical staff whereby the baby would be taken for ten minutes to the mother's room, where the family would be present and the Muslim cleric could administer the blessing. The attending physician agreed, saying that she was not "on record" as approving the blessing but that she understood its importance. Deitrick took the baby to the family and returned ten minutes later to find a smiling mother and father. The baby then underwent blood tests and other medically mandated procedures and was discharged in good health—*and* assured of a sweet life—two days later.

FOOD FOR THOUGHT

Did Lynn Deitrick do the right thing by acting as a cultural broker in this case, or should the medical model have been followed with no compromise?

PERSONALITY AND IDENTITY FORMATION FROM INFANCY THROUGH ADOLESCENCE

In the United States, commonly accepted life stages include infancy, childhood, adolescence, middle age, and old age (psychologists and other experts concerned with human development construct even finer substages). Western life-cycle stages are based on biological features such as the ability to walk, puberty, and capacity for parenthood (Bogin 1988). These stages are not cultural universals. Whereas the biological model assumes that all its life-cycle markers should form the basis of universal stages, cultural anthropologists find striking variation in how different cultures construct life stages and how such stages may be quite unrelated to biology (Johnson-Hanks 2002). The cultural construction of life stages thus can ignore or override what Western biology would dictate.

Birth and Infancy

This section on how culture shapes personality and identity considers first the social context of birth itself. We then consider the issue of parent–infant co-sleeping patterns and how they may shape personality and identity. Last, we take up the topic of gender identity formation at this early stage of the life cycle.

The Birth Context

Cultural anthropologists have asked whether the cultural context of the event of birth itself has psychological effects on the infant. Cross-cultural research does in fact reveal that variations in the birth experience affect an infant's psychological development. Brigitte Jordan (1983), a pioneer in the cross-cultural study of birth, conducted

In Bom Jesus, a shantytown in northeastern Brazil, this mother was told by a doctor at the local clinic that her son was dying of anemia and that she needed to feed him red meat. The mother said, "Now, where am I going to find the money to feed my hopeless son rich food like that?" ■ *What is your perspective on Western bonding theory, and how did you come to have this view?* (Source: Nancy Scheper-Hughes)

should be present, along with other female kin such as her mother-in-law, godmother and sisters, and her friends. Thus, a Mayan mother is surrounded by a large group of supportive people.

In the United States, hospital births are the norm. The newborn infant is generally taken to the nursery, where it is wrapped in cloth and placed in a plastic crate under bright lights rather than being cared for by a family member. Some critics argue that the hospital-based system of highly regulated birth is extremely technocratic and too managed, alienating the mother—as well as other members of the family and the wider community—from the birthing process and the infant (Davis-Floyd 1992). Such criticism has led to consideration of how to improve the way birth is conducted. The Western medical model of birth and non-Western practices contrast sharply—and sometimes comes into serious conflict. In a Western hospital birthing situation where immigrant families have views on proper infant care, providing an anthropological perspective on their culture may serve to mediate conflict between the medical culture and the immigrant people's culture (see the Lessons Applied box).

Bonding

Many contemporary Western psychological theorists say that parent–infant contact and bonding at the time of birth is crucial for setting in motion parental attachment to the infant. Western specialists say that if this bonding is not established at the time of the infant's birth, it will not develop later. Explanations for juvenile delinquency or other unfavorable child development problems often include reference to lack of proper infant bonding at birth.

Nancy Scheper-Hughes (1992), whose research in a Brazilian shantytown was discussed in Chapter 5, questions Western bonding theory. She argues that bonding does not necessarily have to occur at birth to be successful. Her observations in Brazil show that many mothers do not exhibit bonding with their infants at birth. Bonding occurs later, if the child survives infancy, when it is several years old. She proposes that this pattern of later bonding is related to the high rate of infant mortality among poor people of Brazil. If women were to develop strong bonds with their infants, they would suffer untold amounts of grief. Western bonding is adaptive in low-mortality/low-fertility societies in which strong maternal attachment is reasonable because infants are likely to survive.

Sleeping Patterns

Related to bonding theory is the question of where and with whom the infant sleeps. The underlying hypothesis motivating much of the research on sleeping patterns is

research on birth practices in Mexico, Sweden, Holland, and the United States. She studied the birth setting, including its location and who is present, the types of attendants and their roles, the birth event, and the postpartum period. Among Mayan women in Mexico, the midwife is called in during the early stages of labor. One of her tasks is to give a massage to the mother-to-be. She also provides psychological support by telling stories, often about other women's birthing experiences. The husband is expected to be present during the labor so that he can see "how a woman suffers." The woman's mother

that little or no infant–parent co-sleeping promotes "strong ego formation" (in other words, an autonomous person with a high degree of independence and sense of self), whereas long periods of parent–infant co-sleeping foster "weak ego formation" (a person with a low sense of personal autonomy and a high degree of interpersonal connectivity). This hypothesis finds apparent confirmation in Japanese culture, in which mothers and infants sleep together for a long time. Indeed, one survey found that Japanese people rarely sleep alone at any time during their lives (Caudill and Plath 1966). The correlation between long periods of parent–infant co-sleeping and weak ego formation, however, is not confirmed in a study of personality formation among the Basque people of Spain (Crawford 1994). Interviews with 217 Basque women probed topics such as their attitudes about parenting; their religious beliefs, dreams, and personality characteristics; and their childhood sleeping patterns. Of these women, 167 had slept in their parents' room for two to three years. Compared to the women who had not been co-sleepers as children, the women who had been co-sleepers had both greater ego strength and a greater sense of connectedness. Thus, ethnology shows that co-sleeping does not necessarily prevent the development of a strong ego.

Gender and Infancy

As noted in Chapter 1, cultural anthropologists distinguish between sex and gender. Sex is something that everyone is born with. In the view of Western science, it has three biological markers: genitals, hormones, and chromosomes. Males are defined as people who have a penis, more androgens than estrogens, and the XY chromosome. Females have a vagina, more estrogens than androgens, and the XX chromosome. Increasingly, however, scientists are finding that these two categories are not air-tight. In all populations, some people are born with indeterminate genitals, similar proportions of androgens and estrogens, and chromosomes with more complex distributions than simply XX and XY. Thus, a continuum model of gender is more accurate than a strict binary model.

Gender, in contrast, reflects the learned behavior and beliefs associated with maleness and femaleness and thus varies culturally (Miller 1993). Individuals acquire their gender identity, roles, and status through learning, much of which is unconscious. From the moment of birth, an infant's life course is shaped by whether it is labeled male or female and what the defined roles and status of "male" and "female" are in a particular culture. Most cultural anthropologists believe in the high degree of human "plasticity" (or personality malleability and flexibility), as demonstrated by Mead's early work on gender roles and personality in New Guinea, and that gender social-

ization can to a large extent override sex-linked features such as hormones.

Many other researchers continue to insist that a wide range of supposedly sex-linked personality characteristics are innate. A major problem arises in trying to test for innate characteristics. First, one needs data on infants before they are subject to cultural treatment. But culture starts shaping the infant from birth through handling and treatment by others (this may begin even in the womb, through exposure to sound and motion). Second, studying and interpreting the behavior of infants is fraught with potential bias.

Studies of infants have focused on assessing the potential innateness of three major Euro-American personality stereotypes: whether infant males are more aggressive than infant females, whether infant females are more social than infant males, and whether males are more independent (Frieze et al. 1978:73–78). Boy babies cry more than girl babies, and some people believe this is evidence of higher levels of inborn aggression in males. An alternative interpretation is that baby boys on average tend to weigh more than girls. They therefore are more likely to have a difficult delivery from which it takes time to recover, so they cry more, but not out of aggressiveness. In terms of socialness, baby girls smile more often than boys. Does this mean girls are born to be people pleasers? Evidence of caretakers smiling more at baby girls shows that the more frequent smiling of girls is a learned, not an innate, response. In terms of independence or dependence, studies thus far reveal no clear gender differences in how upset babies are when separated from their caretakers.

Taken as a whole, studies seeking to document innate gender differences through the behavior of infants are not convincing. Two questions continue to be important: If gender differences are innate, why do cultures go to so much trouble to instill them? Second, if gender differences are innate, then they should be similar throughout history and cross-culturally, which they aren't. Throughout this chapter, we explore cultural constructions of gender at various stages of the life cycle.

Socialization during Childhood

The concept of "the child" as a special age category may have emerged first in Europe in the last few centuries (Ariès 1962). In art, portraits of children became commonplace only in the seventeenth century. Other changes occurred at the same time: new interests in children's habits, more elaborate terminology about children and childhood, and special clothing for children instead of small-sized versions of adult clothing. The special focus on "the child" is associated with the emergence of industrial capitalism's need for an ever-expanding market.

"The child" became a new niche for sales, which allowed for the production and sale of clothes, books, and toys specifically for that niche. In less industrialized cultures, "the child" is not regarded as having such specialized needs. In these societies, children are expected to take on adult tasks at an earlier age. These different expectations about what a child should do and be have implications for personality formation.

Mode of Production and Child Personality

The Six Cultures Study is a renowned cross-cultural study designed to provide comparative data on children's personalities in relation to their activities and tasks (Whiting and Whiting 1975). Researchers observed sixty-seven children between the ages of three and eleven years. They recorded many forms of behavior, such as being supportive of other children; hitting other children; and performing tasks such as child care, cooking, and errands. These behaviors were analyzed in the following personality dimensions: "nurturant-responsible" or "dependent-dominant." Nurturant-responsible personalities are characterized by caring and sharing acts toward other children. The dependent-dominant personality involves fewer acts of care-seeking and more acts that asserted dominance over other children. Six teams of researchers were trained in the methodology and conducted intensive research in six contexts (see Table 6.1).

The Gusii children of Kenya had the highest prevalence of a nurturant-responsible personality type, whereas the children in Orchard Town had the lowest. Orchard Town children had the highest prevalence of the dependent-dominant personality type. The range of variation follows a general pattern correlating with the mode of production. "Group A" cultures (Kenya, Mexico, Philippines) all had more nurturant-responsible children. Their economies are similar: They are more reliant on horticulture and other forms of less intensive production. The economies of "Group B" cultures (Okinawa, North India, New England) were based on either intensive agriculture or industry.

How does the mode of production influence child tasks and personality? The key underlying factor is differences in women's work roles. In Group A cultures, women are an important part of the labor force and spend much time working outside the home. In these cultures, children take on more family-supportive tasks and thereby develop personalities that are nurturant/responsible. When women are mainly occupied in the home, as in Group B cultures, children have fewer tasks and less responsibility. They develop personalities that are more dependent/dominant. Gusii children were responsible for the widest range of tasks and at earlier ages than children in any other culture in the study, often performing tasks that an Orchard Town mother does. Some children in all six cultures took care of other children, but Gusii children (both boys and girls) spent the most time doing so. They also began taking on this responsibility at a very young age, between five and eight years old.

This study has implications for Western child development experts. In one direction, we can consider what happens when the dependent-dominant personality develops to an extreme level—into a narcissistic personality. A narcissist is someone who constantly seeks self-attention and self-affirmation, with no concern for other people's needs. The Western consumer-oriented economy supports the development of narcissism through its inculcation of identity formation through ownership of self-defining goods (clothing, electronics, cars) and access to self-defining services (vacations, therapists, fitness salons). The Six Cultures Study suggests that involving children more in household responsibilities might result in less self-focused personality formation.

TABLE 6.1 Modes of Production and Child Personality: Six Cases

Culture	Location	High Scores: Nurturant-Responsible Low Scores: Dependent-Dominant Personality
Group A: Horticulture or Family Farming		
Gusii	Kenya	+1.14
Oaxaca	Mexico	+0.54
Tarong	Philippines	+0.48
Group B: Intensive Agricultural or Industrial		
Taira	Japan	−0.24
Rajputs	India	−0.75
Orchard Town	United States	−1.04

Source: From *Children of Six Cultures: A Psycho-Cultural Analysis*, p. 71, by B. B. Whiting and J. W. M. Whiting. Copyright © 1975 by the President and Fellows of Harvard College. Reprinted by permission of Harvard University Press, Cambridge, MA.

Sibling caretaking, as shown here in Ghana, is a common task of older children cross-culturally, but especially in nonindustrial societies. ■ *What tasks do children in your microculture(s) regularly do?* (Source: Roshani Kothari)

Informal Learning

Games and toys shape personality. Among hunting peoples such as the Yanomami, young boys learn to be future hunters by shooting small arrows from small bows at small targets such as beetles. They learn to kill animals without sentimentality. In contrast, caring for animals as pets is a prominent part of child socialization in the West, where many animals are taboo as food. Some games, such as chess, teach strategic thinking that appears to be correlated with social-political patterns of hierarchy and obedience.

The media are another important area for child socialization and personality acquisition. One study considered children's cartoon shows aired on American television in the 1980s (Williams 1991). Content analysis reveals two types of shows, one featuring interpersonal relationships and one featuring battles:

One was aimed at little girls and included groups of characters joined by relational values. "Rainbow Brite" had a set of multicolored friends; both friends and kin sur-

rounded "My Little Pony. . . ." "Strawberry Shortcake" presided over a group, mostly little girls. . . . At the other extreme are programs that toy companies intended for boys. . . . All presented heroes on teams. . . . Teammates had no common ties or work other than those involving fighting. Each good team faced an evil team that chased, attacked, captured, and deceived them. (114–115)

Boy-focused cartoons emphasized the importance of group identity in the face of "the enemy." Enemy teams look different from the heroes: the Thundercats (heroes) battle the Mutants (enemies), and He-Man (hero) takes on Skeletor (enemy).

Formal Schooling

Universal primary education exists in most nations, but not all. For example, in Mali, one of the world's poorest countries, only 25 percent of children attend primary school (United Nations Development Programme 1994). Poorer children cross-culturally face more problems enrolling and remaining in school. In some countries, the school system is inadequate, with too few local schools available. In poor families, children are needed to work. The schooling experience is also diminished for the poor because malnourished and exhausted children have more difficulty concentrating in class. Their level of achievement is likely to be lower than that of better-off children because of economic factors. Teachers, however, may interpret their performance as a sign of "bad attitude," apathy, and laziness.

In Malawi, a poor nation of southern Africa, all children face obstacles in completing primary education, but it is especially difficult for girls (Davison and Kanyuka 1992). An ethnographic study of this situation included eighty students (forty boys and forty girls) at two grade levels. It was conducted in four poor rural districts where girls' school participation rates were among the lowest and their drop-out rates the highest. Most of the children came from agricultural families. Both boys and girls face the same constraints in terms of the quality of the schools and teachers. Girls also had to contend with negative attitudes from male teachers about the value of schooling for them. This discouragement of their academic achievement in the schools is mirrored by their home situation, where parents indirectly discourage girls from valuing schooling and instead instill in them the values of domesticity. Girls are supposed to learn to assume the traditional roles of wife and mother.

School systems that offer little in the way of creative learning experiences, home situations that are unsupportive of girls' achievement, and conservative political elements in the wider society combine to constrain cognitive achievements and the attainment of independent, autonomous personalities among women. "Tracking" female students into domestic roles characterizes formal

Left: A Yanomami boy acquiring skills necessary for hunting and warfare through play. Right: An American boy playing a video game. ■ *Consider examples of children's games that may provide learning and skills related to adult roles in the culture.* (Sources: © Napoleon A. Chagnon/AnthroPhoto, left; © Bill Varie/CORBIS, right)

education throughout much of the world. Students in these situations may experience conflicts about such tracking and resist it to varying degrees.

In Israel, all-girl Zionist-Orthodox boarding schools are aimed at strengthening the religiosity of girls and preparing them for family life. They also emphasize academic excellence, and the girls are highly motivated to achieve. The curriculum includes lectures, lessons, religious activities, and volunteer community work. Religious study excludes the canonic texts, promoting instead everyday religious practice and emphasis on morality, wifehood, childrearing, and purity. A study of the socialization of girls in these schools takes into account the interplay of religion, gender, and adolescent education (Rapoport, Garb, and Penso 1995). Close supervision of the girls is maintained by teachers, peers, and older girls who serve as "big sisters." Even during "free time," the girls are supposed to discuss religion. According to the school teachings, a woman's modesty is part of her essence. The ideal of selfhood involves invisibility, with no suggestion of an affirmative self-presence. A woman is to be mute in the outside, public world. The girls are taught that their sexuality should be treated as a secret, hidden treasure, with self-restraint a key virtue in contrast to how girls behave in the secular world. One student commented, "For example, I walk by some [secular] girl with exposed legs, so she has no value, she simply presents herself as an object, she doesn't say, first look for my character. . . . and I feel very proud that I am modest" (54). However, some girls expressed ambivalent feelings about the value placed on modesty and self-restraint. The strong Zionist-Orthodox emphasis on family roles conflicts with the simultaneous pressure for academic achievement. Some girls resolve the dilemma of career aspirations and achievement versus the domestic role by opting for career paths that will accommodate their family role or by giving up further studies.

Adolescence and Identity

Puberty is a time in the human life cycle that occurs universally and involves a set of biological markers. In males, the voice deepens and facial and body hair appear; in females, menarche and breast development occur; in both males and females, pubic and underarm hair appear and sexual maturation is achieved. **Adolescence,** in contrast, is a culturally defined period of maturation from around the time of puberty until the attainment of adulthood, usually marked by becoming a parent, getting married, or becoming economically self-sufficient.

Is Adolescence a Universal Life-Cycle Stage?

Some scholars say that all cultures define a period of adolescence. One comparative study using data on 186 societies indicated the "ubiquity" of a culturally defined phase of adolescence (Schlegel 1995; Schlegel and Barry 1991). Cultures as diverse as the Navajo and the Trobriand Islanders, among others, have special terms comparable to the American term *adolescent* for a person between puberty and marriage. This apparent ubiquity has been taken by some sociobiologists as grounds for generating a theory that adolescence is a response to the biological onset of reproductive capacity and is biologically adaptive because it provides "training" for becoming a parent (Schlegel 1995:16).

In contrast to the sociobiological view, other anthropologists view adolescence as culturally constructed. They dispute the claims of universal adolescence and its function as reproductive training. In many cultures, they point out, there is no recognized period of adolescence. In others, recognition of an adolescent phase is recent. Moroccan anthropologist Fatima Mernissi (1987), for example, states that adolescence was not a recognized life-cycle phase for females in Morocco until the late twentieth century. "The idea of an adolescent unmarried woman is a completely new idea in the Muslim world, where previously you had only a female child and a menstruating woman who had to be married off immediately so as to prevent dishonorable engagement in premarital sex" (xxiv).

In different cultures, the length of adolescence, or whether it exists at all, is related to gender roles. In many horticultural and pastoral societies where men are valued as warriors, as among the Maasai, a lengthy period between childhood and adulthood is devoted to training in warfare and developing solidarity among males. Females, on the other hand, move directly from being a girl to being a wife. A Maasai girl learns her adult roles while she is a child, assisting in the care of cattle and doing other tasks. In other cultures, females have long periods of separation between girlhood and womanhood, marked by seclusion from general society, during which they learn special skills and lore, and then re-emerge into society as marriageable (J. Brown 1978). Such evidence of variation seems to speak against any theory of universality.

Schoolchildren in Japan exhibiting eagerness to participate in class. ■ *What else can you read from this photograph about these Japanese schoolchildren? How does that compare to your school experience at this age?* (Source: © Nichol Katz/Woodfin Camp & Associates)

Cultural materialism provides an explanation that takes into account the variable distribution of adolescence cross-culturally. Cross-cultural analysis of the relationship between adolescence and mode of production indicates that a prolonged period of adolescence is likely to be preparation for such culturally valued adult roles as worker, warrior, or reproducer (in contrast to the sociobiological explanation that focuses on reproductive roles alone). Adolescence for females in many nonindustrial societies, accompanied by years of training and seclusion, is found where adult females have high rates of participation in food production (J. Brown 1978). This correlation can be explained by the need to train young women for their adult roles. Likewise, certain areas of employment in industrialized societies, especially in most of the professions such as medicine and law and the upper echelons of the corporate world, require a university education. The many years of study in a context outside mainstream society can be considered a key part of the adolescent period that precedes the assumption of adult roles.

During the latter half of the twentieth century, industrialization and economic globalization were accompanied by the spread of Western notions of adolescence among the middle and upper classes in countries around the world. The age at marriage has risen as young people attempt to complete their educations and find employment before starting a family (Xenos 1993). At the same time, class differences exist. Those who are poor tend to have shorter adolescent phases: They spend less time in formal education, and they are likely to become parents at younger ages.

Coming of Age and Gender Identity

Margaret Mead made famous the phrase "coming of age" in her book *Coming of Age in Samoa* (1961 [1928]). It can refer generally to the period of adolescence or specifically to a ceremony or set of ceremonies that marks the boundaries of adolescence. What are the psychological aspects of this phase of life when children become adults?

Among the Sambia, a highland New Guinea group, people do not believe that a young boy "naturally" grows into a man (Herdt 1987). Instead, a boy's healthy maturation requires that he join an all-male initiation group. In this group, he becomes a partner of a senior male, who regularly transfers his semen to the youth orally. The Sambia believe that ingesting semen nourishes the youth. After a period in this initiation group, the youth will rejoin society, form a heterosexual relationship, and raise children.

Ceremonies that provide the transition from youth to adulthood often involve marking of the body in some way as if, through this, to impress the person undergoing it with a clear sense of gender identity and group identity. Such marking includes scarification, tattooing, and genital surgery. In many societies, adolescent males undergo genital surgery that involves removal of part of the skin around the tip of the penis. Without this operation, the boy would not become a full-fledged male. A young Maasai male, in a first-person account of his initiation into manhood, describes the "intolerable pain" he experienced following the circumcision, as well as his feeling of accomplishment two weeks later when his head was shaved and he became a warrior: "As long as I live, I will never forget the day my head was shaved and I emerged a man, a Maasai warrior. I felt a sense of control over my destiny so great that no words can accurately describe it" (Saitoti 1986:71).

For girls, the physical fact of menstruation is marked by rituals in some cultures; in others it is not noted publicly at all. In Turkey, and elsewhere in the Middle East, menstruation is not even mentioned to young girls, who are thus surprised and shocked at menarche (Delaney 1988:79). Turkish girls generally feel ashamed and embarrassed by menstruation. Their Islamic culture teaches them that menstruation is the result of Eve's disobedience against Allah. Eve allowed herself to be persuaded by Satan to eat a forbidden fruit, so she was punished by being made to bleed monthly. In contrast, Hindus have elaborate feasts and celebrations for girls on their first menstruation in South India, though not in the North (Miller 1997 [1981]). In the absence of studies on the psychological impact of these differences, one can only speculate that being made the person of honor at a celebration

A Maasai warrior's mother shaves his head during part of his initiation ceremony into adulthood. ■ *Think of other rites of passage and how they do or do not involve changes in head hair style or headdress.* (Source: © Robert Caputo/National Geographic Image Collection)

would have positive effects on a girl's sense of self-esteem, whereas ignoring menstruation or linking it with shamefulness would have the opposite effect.

The Western term **female genital cutting (FGC)** refers to several forms of genital cutting practiced on females (Gruenbaum 2001). These practices may include the excision of part or all of the clitoris, part or all of the labia, and (the least common practice) infibulation, the stitching together of the vaginal entry, leaving a small aperture for drainage of menstrual blood. These procedures are performed when the girl is between seven and fifteen years of age. Some form of genital cutting is most common in the Sahelian countries of Africa, from the west coast to the east coast. It is also found in Egypt, in some groups of the Middle East (particularly among Bedu tribes), and among some Muslim groups in South and Southeast Asia. Genital cutting occurs in many groups in which female labor participation is high, but also in others where it is not. In terms of religion, genital cutting is often, but not always, associated with people who are Muslim. In Ethiopia, some Christian groups practice it. Scholars have yet to provide a convincing explanation for the regional and social distribution of female genital cutting.

Many young girls have been reported to look forward to the ceremony so that they will be free from childhood tasks and can take on the more respected role of an adult woman. In other cases, anthropologists have reported hearing statements of resistance. Among the Ariaal, pastoralists of northern Kenya, a new bride's genitals are cut on the day of her wedding (Fratkin 1998:60). The Ariaal practice involves removal of the clitoris and part or all of the labia majora. At one wedding, a bride-to-be was heard to say: "I don't want to do this, I don't even know this man, please don't make me do this." The older women told her to be strong and that it would soon be over. The bride-to-be is expected to emerge in a few hours to greet the guests and join the wedding ceremony. Fewer issues have forced the questioning of cultural relativism more clearly than female genital cutting (see the Critical Thinking box).

Sexual Identity

Puberty is the time when sexual maturity is achieved and sexual orientation becomes more apparent. Scholars have long debated whether sexual preferences are biologically determined (somehow mandated by genetic or hormonal factors) or culturally constructed and learned. Biological anthropologist Melvin Konner (1989) takes a middle position, saying that both factors play a part, but simultaneously warning us that no one has a simple answer to the question of who becomes gay:

Neither science nor art has yet produced a single answer. Yet perhaps that in itself is the answer: that anything so complicated and various and interesting could have a single origin seems wrongheaded. Socrates and Tennessee Williams, Sappho and Adrienne Rich, to take only four people, representing only two cultures, seem so certain to have come to their homosexuality in four such different ways as to make generalizations useless. (60)

Lesbian feminist poet Adrienne Rich's (1980) approach combines attention to both biology and culture in her view that all people are biologically bisexual but that patriarchal cultures try to mold them into being heterosexual. This "compulsory heterosexual project," she says, will never be completely successful in overcoming innate bisexuality, so some people will always opt out of the heterosexual mold and become either homosexual or bisexual.

The cultural constructionist position emphasizes socialization and childhood experiences as the most powerful factors shaping sexual orientation. Support for this position comes from a recent study in the United States suggesting that later-born male children are more likely than earlier-born children to be homosexual (Blanchard et al. 1995). For lesbians, fewer studies are available, but those indicate that lesbians tend to be later-born and to have more sisters than heterosexual women. A hypothesis worth investigating is whether parents unconsciously promote "girl"-like behavior in the last-born when they have several sons, in order to have a child to fulfill female roles, and "boy"-like behavior in a last-born girl who follows several sisters.

Another indication of the role of culture in sexual identity is that many people change their sexual orientation more than once during their lifetime. In the Gulf state of Oman, the *xanith* is a male who becomes more like a female, wearing female clothing and having sex with other men for several years, but then reverts to a standard male role by marrying a woman and having children (Wikan 1977). Similar fluidity during the life cycle between homosexuality and heterosexuality occurs among Sambia males (Herdt 1987). These examples indicate that, given the same biological material, some people can assume different sexual identities over time.

No matter what theoretical perspective one takes on the causes of sexual preferences, it is clear that homosexuals are discriminated against in contexts where heterosexuality is the norm of mainstream society. Homosexuals in the United States have frequently been victims of violence, legal biases, housing discrimination, and problems in the work place, including wage discrimination. They often suffer from being stigmatized by parents, other students, and the wider society. The psychological damage done to their self-esteem is related to the fact that homosexual youths in the United States have substantially higher suicide rates than heterosexual youths.

Some cultures explicitly allow for more than two strictly defined genders and permit the expression of varied forms of sexual orientation without societal condem-

Critical Thinking

CULTURAL RELATIVISM AND FEMALE GENITAL CUTTING

IN CULTURES THAT PRACTICE female genital cutting, like male circumcision, it is a necessary step toward full womanhood. It is required for a woman to be considered marriageable in societies in which marriage is the normal path for women. Fathers say that an uncircumcised daughter is unmarriageable and will bring no brideprice. Aesthetically, supporters claim that removal of the labia makes a woman beautiful and that removing her "male" parts makes her a complete woman.

The more prevalent Western view, which is increasingly shared by many people who traditionally practiced what is perhaps best labeled female genital cutting (FGC), is that FGC is both a sign of low female status and an unnecessary cause of women's suffering.

FGC has been linked with a range of health risks, including those related to the surgery itself (shock, infection) and future genito-urinary complications (Gruenbaum 2001). Infibulation causes scarring and malformation of the vaginal canal that obstruct delivery and may cause lacerations to the mother and even death of the infant and mother. The practice of having a new bride's husband "open" her, using a stick or knife to loosen the aperture, is both painful and an opportunity for infection. After giving birth, a woman is usually reinfibulated, and the process begins again. Health experts have suggested that this repeated trauma to the woman's vaginal area could increase the risk of contracting HIV/AIDS. The Western view argues that the effects of both clitoridectomy and infibulation on a woman's sexual enjoyment are highly negative—that clitoral orgasm, for one thing, is no longer possible. Some experts have also argued that FGC is related to the high level of infertility in many African countries (Chapter 5). A recent study of fertility data from the Central African Republic, Côte d'Ivoire, and Tanzania, however, found no clear relationship between FGC and fertility levels.

This widespread and enduring practice (though no one knows its precise beginnings) has all too often become viewed in oversimplified terms and modeled on the basis of its most extreme forms. What are the views of insiders? Is there any evidence for agency? Or is it all structure and should anthropologists support FGC liberation movements?

One new voice that transcends insider/outsider divisions is that of Fuambai Ahmadu, born and raised in Washington, DC. She is descended from a prominent Kono lineage in Sierra Leone and is getting a doctorate in anthropology for research on female genital cutting in the Gambia (2000). In 1991 she traveled to Sierra Leone with her mother and several other family members for what she refers to as her "circumcision." In a powerful and insightful essay, she describes Kono culture as gender-complementary, with strong roles for women. She also describes her initiation and subsequent reflections. Although the physical pain was excruciating (in spite of the use of anesthetics), "the positive aspects have been much more profound" (p. 306). Through the initiation she became part of a powerful female world. Her analysis addresses the effects of genital cutting on health and sexuality and argues that Westerners have exaggerated these issues by focusing on infibulation (which she says is rarely practiced) rather than on the less extreme forms. However, she adds that if global pressures against the practice continue, she will go along with that movement and support "ritual without cutting" (p. 308).

CRITICAL THINKING QUESTIONS

Why do you think that FGC is a prominent issue in human rights debates in the West, whereas other forms of initiation (such as fraternity and sorority hazing) are condoned?

Where do you stand on the issue and why?

What is your perspective on FGC?

---

nation. Most such "third genders" are neither purely "male" nor purely "female," according to a particular culture's definition of those terms. These gender categories offer ways for "males" to cross gender lines and assume more "female" behaviors, personality characteristics, and dress. In some Native American cultures, a **berdache** is a male (in terms of genital configuration) who opts to wear female clothing, may engage in intercourse with a man as

well as a woman, and female tasks such as basket weaving and pottery making (Williams 1992). The berdache constitutes an accepted and admired third gender role. A particular person may become a berdache in a variety of ways. Some people say that parents, especially if they have several sons, choose one to become a berdache. Others say that a boy who shows interest in typically female activities or who likes to wear female clothing is allowed to

A Zuni berdache, We'wha, wearing the ceremonial costume of Zuni women and holding a pottery bowl with sacred corn meal. ■ *Generate an hypothesis about why most cultural examples of cross-gender roles involve males assuming female roles and dress, rather than the other way around?* (Source: © The National Anthropological Archive/Smithsonian Institution)

ing out to their families, will sometimes have an elderly relative who takes them aside and tells them about the berdache tradition. A part-Choctaw gay man recalls that his full-blooded Choctaw grandmother realized he was gay and it was totally acceptable . . . This respectful attitude eliminates the stress felt by families that harbor homophobia" (p. 225).

In India, the counterpart of the Native American berdache is termed a **hijira.** Hijiras dress and act like women but are neither truly male nor truly female (Nanda 1990). Many hijiras were born with male genitals or with genitals that were not clearly male or female. Hijiras have the traditional right to visit the home of a newborn, inspect its genitals, and claim it for their group if the genitals are neither clearly male nor clearly female. Hijiras born with male genitals may opt to go through an initiation ceremony that involves cutting off the penis and testicles. Hijiras roam large cities of India, earning a living by begging from store to store (and threatening to lift their skirts if not given money). Because women do not sing or dance in public, the hijiras play an important role as performers in public events, especially as dancers or musicians. Given this public role and the hijira's association with prostitution, people in the mainstream do not admire or respect hijiras, and no family would be delighted to hear that their son has decided to become a hijira. In contrast to the berdache among Native American groups, the hijiras form a separate group from society.

In Thailand, three gender categories have long existed: *phuuchai* (male), *phuuyung* (female), and *kathoey* (transvestite/transsexual/hermaphrodite) (Morris 1994). Like the berdache and hijira, a kathoey is "originally" a male who crosses into the body, personality, and dress defined as female. Sexual orientation of kathoeys is flexible, including either male or female partners. In contemporary Thailand, explicit discussion and recognition of homosexuality exists, usually couched in English terms, conveying a sense of its foreignness. The words for lesbian are *thom* (from the word "tomboy") and *thut* (an ironic usage from the American movie *Tootsie* about a heterosexual male transvestite). As in many parts of the world, reflecting the widespread presence of patriarchal norms, lesbianism in Thailand is a more suppressed form of homosexuality than male homosexuality.

become a berdache. Such a child is a focus of pride for the family, never a source of disappointment or stigma. Throughout decades of contact with Euro-American colonizers, including Christian missionaries, the institution of the berdache became a focus of disapproval and ridicule by the outsiders (Roscoe 1991). Under the influence of the negative reactions of the Euro-Americans, many Native American cultures began to suppress their berdache traditions in favor of mainstream White values and practices that promote less gender fluidity. In the 1980s, as Native American cultural pride began to grow, the open presence of the berdache and the **amazon** (a woman who takes on male roles and behaviors) has returned. Native American cultures in general remain accepting of gender role fluidity and the contemporary concept of being gay: "Younger gay Indians, upon com-

PERSONALITY AND IDENTITY IN ADULTHOOD

Adulthood for most of the world's people means the likelihood of entering into some form of marriage, or long-term domestic relationship, and having children. This section considers how selected aspects of adulthood, such as parenthood and aging, affect mature people's psychological status and identity.

Becoming a Parent

Biologically, a woman becomes a mother when she gives birth to an infant and is transformed from a pregnant woman into a mother. Motherhood, the cultural process of becoming a mother, has been termed **matrescence** (Raphael 1975). Like adolescence, matrescence varies cross-culturally in terms of duration and meaning. In some cultures, a woman is transformed into a mother as soon as she thinks she is pregnant. In others, she becomes a mother and is granted full maternal status only when she delivers an infant of the "right" sex, as in much of northern India.

Among the Beti people of Southern Cameroon, West Africa, motherhood is not merely or clearly defined by having a child (Johnson-Hanks 2002). The Beti are both an ethnic group and a social status group of educated professionals within the wider society. "School girl" is one category of young Beti women. If a school girl becomes pregnant, this is a matter of great shame, and the girl is not considered to have entered a phase of motherhood even though she has borne a child. In this case, a biological marker does not bring about movement into a new life stage but instead contributes to ambiguity in categories.

In nonindustrial cultures, matrescence occurs in the context of supportive family members. Some cultures promote prenatal practices, abiding by particular food taboos, which can be regarded as part of matrescence. Such rules make the pregnant woman feel that she has some role in helping to make the pregnancy turn out right. In the West, medical experts increasingly define the prenatal period as an important phase of matrescence, and they have issued many scientific and medical rules for potential parents, especially mothers (Browner and Press 1995, 1996). Pregnant women are urged to seek prenatal examinations; be under the regular supervision of a doctor who monitors the growth and development of the fetus; follow particular dietary and exercise guidelines; and undergo a range of tests such as ultrasound scanning. Some anthropologists think that such medical control of pregnancy leads to the greater likelihood of post-partum depression among mothers as a result of their lack of control in matrescence.

Patrescence, or becoming a father, usually is less socially noted than matrescence. The practice of **couvade** is an interesting exception to this generalization. Couvade consists of "a variety of customs applying to the behavior of fathers during the pregnancies of their wives and during and shortly after the births of their children"

(Broude 1988:902). The father may take to his bed before, during, or after the delivery. He may also experience pain and exhaustion during and after the delivery. More common is a pattern of couvade that involves a set of prohibitions and prescriptions for male behavior. For example, an expectant father may not hunt a certain animal, eat certain foods, cut objects, or engage in extramarital sex. Early theories of why the couvade exists relied on Freudian interpretations that men were seeking cross-sex identification (with the female role) in contexts where the father role was weak or fathers were absent. But cross-cultural data on the existence of couvade indicates the opposite: Couvade occurs in societies where paternal roles in child care are prominent. This interpretation views couvade as one phase of men's participation in parenting: Their good behavior as expectant fathers helps ensure a good delivery for the baby. Another interpretation of couvade is that it offers support for the mother. In Estonia, a folk belief is that a woman's birth pains will be less if her husband helps by taking some of them on himself (Oinas 1993).

The widespread pattern of women being the major caretakers of infants and children has led many people to think there is something innate about females as causal in care taking roles. Most cultural anthropologists agree that child care is predominantly the responsibility of females worldwide—but not universally. They point to differences in the degree of involvement and other possible caretakers besides the biological mother. In many cultures of the South Pacific, child care is shared across families, and women breastfeed other women's babies. Paternal involvement varies as well. Among the Aka pygmy hunter–gatherers of the Central African Republic, paternal child care is prominent (Hewlett 1991). Aka fathers are intimate, affectionate, and helpful, spending about half of their time each day holding or within arm's reach of their infants. While holding their infants, they are more likely to hug and kiss them than mothers are. The definition of good fatherhood among the Aka means being affectionate toward children and assisting the mother when her workload is heavy. Among the Aka, gender equality prevails, and violence against women is unknown. The high level of paternal involvement in child care helps explain this pattern.

Middle Age

In industrial countries, the boundaries of "middle age" are typically defined as being between thirty and seventy years of age (Shweder 1998). A major turning point is now the fortieth birthday. Stanley Brandes explores the meanings of turning forty to American middle-class men in a book entitled *Forty: The Age and the Symbol* (1985). The "forty syndrome" comprises feelings of restlessness,

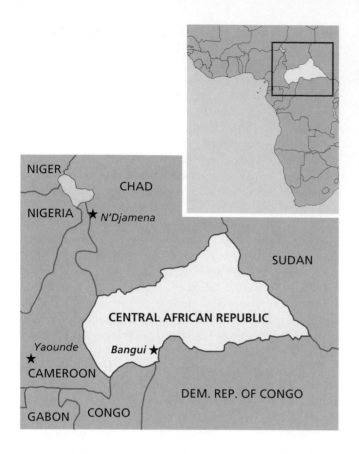

An Aka father and his son. Aka fathers are affectionate caretakers of infants and small children. Compared to mothers, they are more likely to kiss and hug children. ■ *How does this compare to a microculture with which you are familiar?* (Source: Barry Hewlett)

rebelliousness, and unhappiness that often lead to family break-ups. One possible reason behind this emphasis on forty as a turning point for males is that it reflects the current midpoint of a "typical" life span for a middle-class American man. In cultures with shorter lifespans, a "midlife" crisis would necessarily occur at some point other than the age of forty years, if it were to happen at all. Such a "crisis" seems strongly embedded in contemporary United States culture and its pervasive fear and denial of death (Shore 1998:103).

Menopause is a significant aspect of middle age for women in some, but not all, cultures. A comparative study examined differences in perception and experience of menopause among Mayan women of Mexico and rural Greek women (Beyene 1989). Among the Mayan women, menopause is not a time of stress or crisis. They associate menstruation with illness and look forward to its end. Menopause among these women is not associated with physical or emotional symptoms. None of the women reported hot flashes or cold sweats. No role changes were associated with menopause. In contrast, the rural Greek women recognized menopause as a natural phenomenon that all women experience and one that causes temporary discomfort, *exapi,* which is a phase of hot flashes especially at night, that may last about a year. The women did not think exapi was terribly serious and certainly did not regard it as worthy of medical atten-

tion. Postmenopausal women emphasized the relief and freedom they felt. Postmenopausal women can go into cafes by themselves, something they would never do otherwise, and they can participate more fully in church ceremonies. In Japan, also, menopause is a minimally stressful experience and is rarely considered something that warrants medical attention (Lock 1993).

The Senior Years

The "senior" life-cycle stage may be a development of contemporary human society because, like most other mammals, our early ancestors rarely lived beyond their reproductive years (Brooks and Draper 1998 [1991]). The category of the aged, like several other life-cycle stages we have discussed, is variably recognized, defined, and valued. In many cultures, elders are highly revered and their life experiences are valued as the greatest wisdom. In others, aged people become burdens to their families and to society. In general, the status and well-being of the elderly is higher where they continue to live with their families (Lee and Kezis 1979). This pattern is more likely to be found in nonindustrial societies than in industrialized ones, where the elderly are increasingly experiencing a shift to "retirement homes." In such age-segregated settings, people have to create new social roles and ties and find new ways of gaining self-esteem and personal satisfaction. Research in a rural central New York retirement home shows that being allowed to have pets has a positive effect on people's adjustment (Savishinsky 1991).

The Final Passage

It may be that no one in any culture welcomes death, unless he or she is in very poor health and suffering greatly. The contemporary United States, with its dependence on medical technology, appears to play a leading role in resistance to death, often at high financial and psychological cost. In many other cultures, a greater degree of acceptance prevails. A study of attitudes toward death and dying among Alaskan Inuits revealed a pervasive feeling that people are active participants in their death rather than passive victims (Trelease 1975). The person near death calls friends and neighbors together, is given a Christian sacrament, and then, within a few hours, dies. The author comments, "I do not suggest that everyone waited for the priest to come and then died right away. But the majority who did not die suddenly did some degree of planning, had some kind of formal service or celebration of prayers and hymns and farewells" (35).

In any culture, loss of a loved one is accompanied by some form of sadness, grief, and mourning. The ways of expressing such emotions vary from extended and public grieving that is expressively emotional to no visible sign of grief being presented. The latter pattern is the norm in Bali, Indonesia, where people's faces remain impassive at funerals and no vocal lamenting occurs (Rosenblatt, Walsh, and Jackson 1976). No one knows how different modes of expression of loss are related to the actual experience of loss itself (Brison and Leavitt 1995). Does highly expressive public mourning contribute to a "faster" healing process, or does a quietly repressed sense of grief play an adaptive role? The domain of emotional suffering surrounding death is a relatively new area of study for psychological anthropologists—one that promises to provide intriguing insights. The expression of grief surrounding death is also of interest to anthropologists who study religion (Bowen 1998). Research shows that beliefs about the dead, and how the dead may affect the living, shape people's experience of death and mourning.

KEY CONCEPTS

adolescence, p. 140
amazon, p. 144
berdache, p. 143
couvade, p. 145
cultural broker, p. 134
cultural configuration, p. 131

culture of poverty, p. 132
ethnopsychology, p. 130
female genital cutting (FGC), p. 142
hijira, p. 144
image of the limited good, p. 132
matrescence, p. 145

national character studies, p. 132
patrescence, p. 145
person-centered ethnography, p. 132
personality, p. 130
puberty, p. 139

SUGGESTED READINGS

Evalyn Blackwood, ed. *The Many Faces of Homosexuality: Anthropological Approaches to Homosexual Behavior.* New York: Harrington Park Press, 1986. This text contains chapters on anthropological writings about lesbianism, and case studies of ritualized male homosexuality in Irian Jaya, the berdache in North America, hijiras of India, lesbian relationships in Lesotho, and Mexican male homosexual interaction patterns in public.

Ellen Gruenbaum. *The Female Circumcision Controversy: An Anthropological Perspective.* Philadelphia: University of Pennsylvania Press, 2001. The author draws on her more than five years of fieldwork in Sudan, and discusses how change is occurring through economic development, the role of Islamic activists, health educators, and educated African women.

Charlotte E. Hardman. *Other Worlds: Notions of Self and Emotion among the Lohorung Rai.* New York: Berg, 2000. The author conducted fieldwork in a mountainous region of Nepal to learn about one community's perception of what it means to be a person.

Judith Schachter Modell. *Ruth Benedict: Patterns of a Life.* Philadelphia: University of Pennsylvania Press, 1983. This biography of a prominent psychological anthropologist provides insights into Benedict's development as an anthropologist, her research and writings, and her role in the Culture and Personality School.

Michael Moffatt. *Coming of Age in New Jersey: College and American Culture.* New Brunswick: Rutgers University Press, 1991. Based on a year's participant observation in a college dormitory in a university in the eastern United States, this study offers insights on sexuality, race relations, and individualism.

Mimi Nichter. *What Girls and Their Parents Say About Dieting.* Cambridge, MA: Harvard University Press, 2000. The author collected and analyzed interview data with adolescent girls in the United States, focusing on perceptions of weight, attachment to dieting, and the influence of their mothers' views and comments on weight.

Richard Parker. *Bodies, Pleasures and Passions: Sexual Culture in Contemporary Brazil.* Boston: Beacon Press, 1991. This ethnographic study of contemporary sexual culture in Brazil addresses such topics as sexual socialization, bisexuality, sadomasochism, AIDS, prostitution, samba, the symbolism of breasts, courting, and carnival.

Joel S. Savishinsky. *Breaking the Watch: The Meanings of Retirement in America.* Ithaca, NY: Cornell University Press, 2000. Fieldwork in a nursing home in a small town in central New York state sheds light on the retirees themselves through vivid portraits of several, along with their own words on friendship in the home, finding purpose in life, and dealing with finances.

Joseph J. Tobin, David Y. H. Wu, and Dana H. Davidon. *Preschool in Three Cultures: Japan, China, and the United States.* New Haven: Yale University Press, 1989. This book offers comparative insights about parents' reasons for sending children to preschool, including a shared concern for learning cooperation in all three contexts and a contrast between the emphasis on academic learning in the United States and on social learning in Japan.

John W. Traphagan. *Taming Oblivion: Aging Bodies and the Fear of Senility in Japan.* Albany: State University of New York Press, 2000. The author conducted fieldwork in a small town north of Tokyo to investigate people's attitudes and practices related to old age, especially as aging people attempt to prevent the onset of the *boke* condition, or what English-speaking Westerners would call senility.

WHAT is the scope of psychological anthropology?

Psychological anthropology is devoted to the study of individuals and their personality and identity, within particular contexts. In North American anthropology, psychology has its roots in the Culture and Personality School that emerged in the early part of the twentieth century. These anthropologists studied how different child-rearing patterns shape personality, national patterns of personality, and the relationship between poverty and personality. More recently, psychological anthropologists have begun studying personality formation in Western and industrial cultures. The latest turn in psychological anthropology is an emphasis on person-centered ethnography and close attention to individual perceptions and experiences. Compared to the Western discipline of psychology, psychological anthropology takes a much wider view of key concepts such as personality and the self—a perspective gained through ethnographic research.

HOW does culture shape personality and identity from birth through adolescence?

Human psychological development begins from the moment of birth, if not before. Margaret Mead was a pioneer in showing how infant care practices such as breastfeeding, how the baby is held, and how much contact the infant has with others can affect personality formation, including gender identity. Her study of the Arapesh, Mundugumor, and Tchambuli peoples of New Guinea indicates that gender is a largely "plastic" (or malleable) aspect of human personality. Cross-cultural studies show that children's work roles and family roles correspond to personality patterns. Informal and formal learning, depending on cultural context, shapes young people's sense of identity in various ways.

Adolescence, a cultural time around puberty and before adulthood, varies cross-culturally from being nonexistent to being long in duration and involving detailed training and elaborate ceremonies. "Coming of age" ceremonies sometimes involve bodily cutting, which denotes membership of the initiate in a particular gender. In contrast to the sharp distinction between "male" and "female" laid out in Western science, many cultures have longstanding traditions of third gender identities, most prominently for males or people of indeterminate biological sex markers, to become more like females in those cultures.

HOW does culture shape personality and identity in adulthood through old age?

Reflecting the fact that women tend to be more involved than males in child care, cultures generally provide more in the way of enculturation of females for this role. In nonindustrial societies, learning about motherhood is embedded in other aspects of life, and knowledge about birthing and child care is shared among women. In industrialized cultures, science and medicine play a large part in defining the maternal role. This change reduces women's autonomy and fosters their dependence on external, non-kin-based structures.

The senior years are, in general, shorter in nonindustrialized societies than in industrialized societies, in which lifespans tend to be longer. Elder men and women in nonindustrial cultures are treated with respect, are considered to know the most, and retain a strong sense of their place in the culture. Increasingly in industrialized societies, elderly people either remove themselves or are removed from their families and spend many years in age-segregated institutions. This transition tends to have negative implications for their psychological well-being.

THE BIG QUESTIONS

- **WHAT** is ethnomedicine?
- **WHAT** are three major theoretical approaches in medical anthropology?
- **HOW** are illness and healing changing during globalization?

7

ILLNESS AND HEALING

Steven Benally, Jr., an apprentice medicine man, practices for a ceremony in his hogan on the Navajo Reservation near Window Rock, Arizona. An apprentice often studies for a decade or more. (Source: © Kevin Fleming/CORBIS)

Primatologist Jane Goodall witnessed a polio epidemic among the chimpanzees she was studying in Tanzania (Foster and Anderson 1978:33–34). A group of healthy animals watched a stricken member try to reach the feeding area but did not help him. Another badly paralyzed chimpanzee was simply left behind when the group moved on.

Humans also sometimes resort to isolation and abandonment, as in the Inuit practice of leaving aged and infirm people behind in the cold, the stigmatization of HIV/AIDS victims, and the ignoring of the homeless mentally ill in the United States. Compared to our nonhuman primate relatives, though, humans have created more complex and variable ways of interpreting health problems and highly creative methods of preventing and curing them.

Since the 1970s, medical anthropology has been one of the most rapidly growing areas of research in all of anthropology's four fields. This chapter presents a selection of findings from this exciting subfield. We first learn about **ethnomedicine**, or the health systems of particular cultures. This section is mainly descriptive of various cultural approaches to health, illness, and healing from an emic perspective. In the second section, we consider three important theoretical approaches in medical anthropology, each with a different view of how best to study and interpret health systems and health problems. In the last section, we address key topics in contemporary change, including new health challenges and how healing has changed, especially as indigenous systems increasingly interact with Western medicine.

ETHNOMEDICINE

Medical anthropologists have long been interested in studying ethnomedicine, or cross-cultural health systems. A health system encompasses many areas: perceptions and classifications of illness, prevention measures, diagnosis, healing (magical, religious, scientific, healing substances), and healers. In addition to these core topics, ethnomedicine has recently expanded its focus to new topics such as the anthropology of the body, culture and disability, and change in indigenous or "traditional" healing systems, especially change resulting from the effects of globalization and the growth of multiple and mixed healing systems.

In the 1960s when the term *ethnomedicine* first came into use, it referred only to non-Western health systems and was synonymous with *folk medicine, popular medicine,* and even the abandoned term *primitive medicine.* Two major problems exist with using the term *ethnomedicine* in this way. First, it is "totalizing"—that is, excessively generalizing. Labeling all non-Western medicine as "folk" or "popular," in contrast to "scientific" or "professional" Western medicine, overlooks such highly developed and specialized non-Western systems as those of India and China, to name just two examples. It is also totalizing in terms of implying that all Western health systems are "professional" and thus overlooks much thinking and practice in the West that could well be labeled "folk" or "popular." Second, the early meaning of *ethnomedicine* is ethnocentric, because Western medicine is an ethnomedical system too, intimately bound to Western culture and its values. We must nonetheless recognize that, especially since the 1950s and the increasing spread of Western culture and science globally, Western biomedicine is more appropriately termed a global or "cosmopolitan" system.

The current use of the term *ethnomedicine* thus embraces all cultural health systems. Within any of them, a range of variations may exist—from more local practices and beliefs held by laypeople to more widespread practices that require skills that must be learned over many years of training available only to a few.

Perceptions of the Body

Cultures have various ways of defining the body and its parts in relation to illness and healing. The highland Maya of Chiapas, southern Mexico, have a detailed vision of the exterior body but do not focus much attention on internal organs, a fact related to the nonexistence of surgery as a healing technique among them (Berlin and Berlin 1996). Separation of the mind from the body has long characterized Euro-American popular and scientific thinking. Thus Western medicine has a special category called "mental illness," which addresses certain health problems as though they were located only in the mind. In many cultures where such a mind–body distinction does not exist, there is no category of "mental illness."

Cross-cultural variation exists in perceptions of which bodily organs are most critically involved in the definition of life versus death. In the West, a person may be declared dead while the heart is still beating if the brain is judged "dead." In many other cultures, this definition of brain death is not accepted, perhaps an indication of the relatively great value accorded to the brain in Western culture (Ohnuki-Tierney 1994).

In Japan, attitudes against cutting the body explain the much lower rates of surgery there than in the United States. The Japanese concept of *gotai* refers to the value of maintaining bodily intactness in life and death to the extent that ear piercing is devalued: "Newspapers reported that one of the qualifications of a bride for Crown Prince Naruhitao was that she not have pierced ears" (Ohnuki-Tierney 1994:235). An intact body ensures rebirth. Historically, the warrior's practice of beheading the victim was the ultimate form of killing because it violated the integrity of the body and prevented the enemy's rebirth. Gotai is also an important reason for the widespread popular resistance to organ transplantation in Japan.

Another area of study related to the body is whether the body is considered to be a bounded physical unit, with disease treatment thus focused on just the body, or is considered to be connected to a wider social context, in which case treatment addresses the wider social sphere (Fabrega and Silver 1973). Western biomedicine typically addresses a clearly defined, individual physical body or mind. In contrast, many non-Western healing systems encompass the social context within which an individual's physical body is situated. Diagnoses that address

South African healer Magdaline Ramaota speaks to clients in Durban. In South Africa, few people have enough money to pay for AIDS drugs. The role of traditional healers in providing psychological and social support for victims is extremely important. ■ *Do Internet research to learn about the current and projected rates of HIV/AIDS in African countries.* (Source: © AFP/CORBIS)

the "social body" in nonindustrial, non-Western medical systems may include the family or community members as responsible, or they may look to the supernaturals as being in some way unhappy. A cure is brought about by holding a family or community ritual that seeks to restore correct social relations or to appease the deities.

Defining Health Problems

Medical anthropologists often sound like philosophers, devoting much attention to defining concepts and delineating the object of study. Because medical anthropologists have conducted many studies of emic perceptions of health and health problems, they have found that their own (usually Western) concepts do not fit well with other cultural definitions. Cross-cultural knowledge forces us to broaden our own definitions. Consider, for example,

Tshampa Xiganang, a practitioner of traditional Tibetan medicine living in Nepal. ■ *Note similarities and differences in this setting compared to one that you might visit for a checkup or minor health complaint.* (Source: © Macduff Everton/CORBIS)

the term *dore* as used by the Desana people of the Colombian rainforest, a group of forager–horticulturalists (Reichel-Dolmatoff 1971 cited in Hahn 1995:23). This term refers to a complex set of symbols related to the verb "to order" or "to send." Among the Desana, falling sick is the result of an order, a mandate, sent by or through a supernatural agent—a rather different definition from any found in Western biomedicine.

An approach commonly used in medical anthropology to help sort through the richness of cultural labels and perceptions is the **disease/illness dichotomy.** This dichotomy is parallel to etic and emic understandings of health problems. The term *disease* refers to a biological pathology that is objective and universal (Kleinman 1995:31). A virus is a virus no matter where it lands. Disease is thus a scientific, etic concept. In contrast, the term *illness* refers to the culturally specific understandings and experiences of a health problem or some more generalized form of suffering. A viral infection may be differently understood and experienced in different cultures. In some it may not be perceived as a health problem at all or may be thought of as "sent" by a supernatural force. Culture thus provides the framework within which disease and other forms of suffering become illness (Rubel, O'Nell, and Collado-Ardón 1984). Medical anthropologist and physician Arthur Kleinman suggests that Western biomedicine focuses narrowly on disease and neglects illness (1995). He urges medical anthropologists to continue to do research on illness and bring its importance to the attention of biomedicine.

Another important concept reflects the attempt of medical anthropologists to broaden ethnomedicine and remove it even further from narrow biological definitions of health problems: **structural suffering,** also known as structural affliction. The term *structural* refers to certain devastating forces that cause suffering, such as economic and political situations like war, famine, forced migration, and poverty. These conditions affect health in many ways, inducing effects that range from depression to outright death. They also include the negative effects of disruption of one's family life, livelihood, and sense of home and security. The usual approaches in Western biomedicine are not designed to deal with the effects of structural suffering. Western disease classifications do not encompass structural suffering. For example, following the attacks on the United States of September 11, 2001, medical personnel had to classify the health status of survivors and the causes of deaths. In some cases their usual coding system was inadequate.

Medical anthropologists study how people of different cultures label and classify illness and suffering. The term *nosology* refers to the classification of health problems. The term **ethno-nosology** refers to cross-cultural systems of classification of health problems. Western biomedicine defines and labels diseases according to its diagnostic criteria and sets these guidelines down in thick manuals used by physicians when treating patients. In nonstate societies, verbal traditions are the repository of such information. A range of bases for classifications exist cross-culturally: causal agent, vector (the means of transmission, such as mosquitoes), the body part that is affected, symptoms, the pathological process itself, the stage of the disease, the victim's behavior, and combinations of any of these.

Locally specific disorders are referred to as **culture-bound syndromes** (see Table 7.1 on page 155). A culture-bound syndrome is a collection of signs and symptoms that is restricted to a particular culture or a limited number of cultures (Prince 1985:201). Many culture-bound syndromes are caused by psychosocial factors such as

TABLE 7.1 Selected Culture-Bound Syndromes

Syndrome	Cultural/Geographic Location	Symptoms
aiyiperi	Yoruba (Nigeria)	hysterical convulsive disorders, posturing and tics, psychomotor seizures
amok	Malaysia and Indonesia	dissociative episodes, outbursts of violent and aggressive or homicidal behavior directed at people and objects, persecutory ideas, amnesia, exhaustion
anfechtung	Hutterites (Manitoba, Canada)	withdrawal from social contact, feeling of having sinned, feeling of religious unworthiness, temptation to commit suicide
brain fag	Nigerian and East African students	pain, heat or burning sensations, pressure or tightness around head, blurring of vision, inability to concentrate when studying, anxiety and depression, fatigue and sleepiness
cholera	Guatemala	nausea, vomiting, diarrhea, fever, severe temper tantrums, unconsciousness and dissociative behavior
ghost sickness	Navajo of the southwestern United States	weakness, bad dreams, feelings of danger, confusion, feelings of futility, loss of appetite, feelings of suffocation, fainting, dizziness, hallucinations and loss of consciousness
koro	South China, Chinese and Malaysian populations in southeast Asia, Hindus of Assam	in males, anxiety that the penis will recede into the body; in females, anxiety that the vulva and breasts will recede into the body.
latah	Malaysia and Indonesia	afflicted person becomes flustered and may say and do things that appear amusing, such as mimicking people's words and movements
mal de ojo (evil eye)	Mediterranean and Latin American Hispanic populations	fitful sleep, crying without apparent cause, diarrhea, vomiting, fever in a child or infant
pibloktoq (Arctic hysteria)	Inuit of the Arctic, Siberian groups	brooding, depressive silences, loss or disturbance of consciousness during seizure, tearing off of clothing, fleeing or wandering, rolling in snow, speaking in tongues or echoing other people's words
windigo	Cree, Ojibwa, and related Native American groups of central and northeastern Canada	depression, nausea, distaste for usual foods, feelings of being possessed by a cannibalistic monster, homicidal or suicidal impulses
shinkeishitsu	Japan	fear of meeting people, feelings of inadequacy, anxiety, obsessive-compulsive symptoms, hypochondriasis

Source: Adapted from Simons and Hughes 1985:91–110.

stress or shock, but they may have biophysical symptoms. For example, *susto,* or "fright disease," is a widely distributed culture-bound syndrome of Latino cultures. People afflicted with susto attribute it to shock, such as losing a loved one or experiencing a frightening accident (Rubel, O'Nell, and Collado-Ardón 1984).

In the Chiapas area of Mexico, a woman reported that her susto was brought on by an accident in which pottery she had made was broken on its way to market, and a man said that his susto came on after he saw a dangerous snake. Susto symptoms include appetite loss, loss of motivation, breathing problems, generalized pain, and nightmares. Analysis of many cases of susto in three vil-

lages showed that the people most likely to be afflicted were those who were socially marginal or experiencing a sense of role failure. The woman whose pottery had broken, for example, had also suffered two spontaneous abortions and was worried that she would never have children. People with susto have higher mortality rates than the unafflicted population. This finding indicates that a deep sense of social failure places a person at a higher risk of dying.

Medical anthropologists first studied culture-bound syndromes in non-Western cultures. This focus has led to a bias in thinking that all culture-bound syndromes are found in "other" cultures. Now, anthropologists rec-

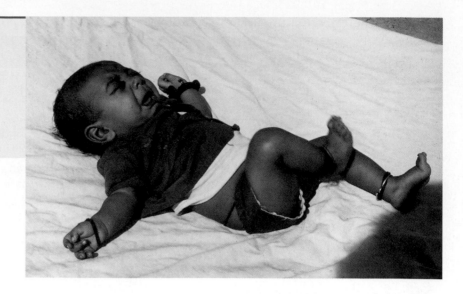

Throughout northern India, people believe that the tying on of strings provides protection from malevolent spirits and forces. This baby has five protective strings. ■ *What parallel forms of protection for infants would Western biomedicine require?* (Source: Barbara Miller)

ognize that some afflictions of the West are also culture-bound syndromes. Examples include agoraphobia, an obsessive fear of leaving one's home and going to public places, and eating disorders such as anorexia nervosa and bulimia.

Anorexia nervosa and a related condition, bulimia, are examples of culture-bound syndromes found predominantly among Euro-American adolescent girls of the United States (Brumberg 1988), although some cases have been documented among African American girls in the United States, and in Japan, Hong Kong, and India (Fabrega and Miller 1995). Anorexia nervosa's cluster of symptoms includes self-perceptions of fatness, aversion to food, hyperactivity, and, as the condition progresses, continuous wasting of the body and often death. The association between anorexia and industrial culture suggests that as industrialism and westernization spread throughout the world, it is likely that the associated culture-bound syndromes will, too.

No one has found a biological cause for anorexia nervosa, and thus it stands as a clear example of a culturally constructed affliction. It is difficult to cure with either medical or psychiatric treatment (Gremillon 1992), which is a logical result of its cultural foundations. Pinpointing what the cultural causes are, however, has also not proved easy. Many experts cite the societal pressures on young girls in the United States toward excessive concern with their looks, especially body weight. Others feel that anorexia is related to girls' unconscious resistance to over-controlling parents. To such girls, their food intake may appear to be the one thing they have power over. This need for self-control through food deprivation becomes addictive and entrapping. Although the primary cause may be rooted in culture, the affliction becomes intertwined with the body's biological functions. Extreme

fasting leads to the body's inability to deal with ingested food. Thus, some medical treatments involve intravenous feeding to override the biological block.

Preventive Practices

Many different practices based in either religious or secular beliefs exist cross-culturally for preventing misfortune, suffering, and illness. Among the Maya of Guatemala, one of the major illnesses is called *awas* (Wilson 1995). Children born with awas show symptoms such as lumps under the skin, marks on the skin, or albinism. Causes of awas are related to events that happen to the mother during her pregnancy: She may have been denied food she desired or have been pressured to eat food she didn't want, or she may have encountered a rude, drunk, or angry person (usually a male). In order to help prevent awas in babies, Mayan people go out of their way to be careful around pregnant women. A pregnant woman, like land before planting, is considered sacred and is treated in special ways: She is always given the food she wants, and people behave with respect in her presence. In general, the ideal is to keep a pregnant woman in a state of contentment and optimism.

Common forms of ritual health protection include charms, spells, and strings tied around parts of the body. After visiting a Buddhist temple in Japan, one might purchase a small band to tie around the wrist to prevent future problems related to health and fertility. Wrist ties are commonly placed on infants in rural areas in India, especially by Hindus. Tying strings onto a tree or part of a shrine when undertaking a pilgrimage is another way that people attempt to secure their wishes for a healthy future.

An anthropologist working in rural northern Thailand learned of the display of carved wooden phalluses throughout a village as protection against a certain form of sudden death among men (Mills 1995). In 1990, fear of a widow ghost attack spread throughout the area. The fear was based on several radio reports of unexplained deaths of Thai migrant men working in Singapore. People interpreted these sudden deaths as caused by widow ghosts. Widow ghosts are believed to roam about, searching for men whom they take as their "husbands." Mary Beth Mills was conducting research in Baan Naa Sakae village at the time of the fear:

> I returned to Baan Naa Sakae village after a few days' absence to find the entire community of two hundred households festooned with wooden phalluses in all shapes and sizes. Ranging from the crudest wooden shafts to carefully carved images complete with coconut shell testicles and fishnet pubic hair, they adorned virtually every house and residential compound. The phalluses, I was told, were to protect residents, especially boys and men, from the "nightmare deaths" (*lai tai*) at the hands of malevolent "widow ghosts" (*phii mae maai*). (249)

In the study area, spirits (*phii*) are a recognized source of illness, death, and other misfortunes. One variety of phii, a widow ghost is the sexually voracious spirit of a woman who has met an untimely and perhaps violent death. When a seemingly healthy man dies in his sleep, a widow ghost is blamed. The wooden phalluses hung on the houses were protection against a possible attack:

> [I]nformants described these giant penises as decoys that would attract the interest of any *phii mae maai* which might come looking for a husband. The greedy ghosts would take their pleasure with the wooden penises and be satisfied, leaving the men of that household asleep, safe in their beds. (251)

As the radio reports ceased, villagers' concerns about the widow ghosts died down, and the phalluses were removed.

Diagnosis

If an affliction has been experienced and the person with the condition decides to seek help for it, diagnosis is the first stage in treatment. Diagnosis is the result of efforts to find out what is wrong and to label the affliction in order to determine the proper form of treatment. It includes magical-religious techniques such as **divination,** in which a specialist attempts to gain supernatural insights, and secular techniques such as asking the ill person to supply detailed descriptions of symptoms. Among the Navajo, hand trembling is an important diagnostic technique (W. Morgan 1977). The hand trembling diagnosis works this way: The specialist enters the home of the afflicted person and, with friends and relatives present, discusses the problem. The specialist sits facing the patient, closes his eyes, and thinks of all the possible causes. When the correct one comes to mind, the specialist's arm involuntarily shakes, revealing the diagnosis. In all three forms of Navajo diagnosis, the specialist goes into a trance-like state that lends authority to the outcome.

Among the urban poor of Bahia in Brazil, a flexible approach exists to ascertaining the cause of disease (Ngokwey 1988). In Feira de Santana, the second largest city in the state of Bahia, illness causation theories fit into the following domains: natural, socioeconomic, psychological, and supernatural. Natural causes include exposure to the environment. Thus "too much cold can provoke gripe; humidity and rain cause rheumatism; excessive heat can result in dehydration. . . . Some types of winds are known to provoke *ar do vento* or *ar do tempo,* a condition characterized by migraines, hemiplegia, and 'cerebral congestion'" (795). Other natural explanations for illness take into account the effects of aging, heredity, personal nature (*natureza*), and gender. Contagion is another "natural" explanation, as are the effects of certain foods and eating habits. Popular knowledge connects the lack of economic resources, proper sanitation, and health services with illnesses. "One informant said, 'There are many illnesses because there are many poor'" (796). In the psychosocial domain, certain emotions are attributed to illnesses: "Anger and hostile feelings (*raiva*), anxiety and worry are possible causes of various illnesses ranging from *nervoso,* a folk illness characterized by 'nervousness,' to heart problems and *derrame* (cerebral hemorrhage)" (796). In the supernatural domain, illness is caused by spirits and magical acts.

The African-Brazilian religious systems of the Bahia region encompass a range of spirits who can inflict illness, including spirits of the dead and devil-like spirits. Some spirits cause specific illnesses; others bring general misfortune. Spells cast by envious people with the evil eye (*ohlo grosso*) are a well-known cause of illness. People recognize multiple levels of causality. In the case of a stomach ache, for example, they might blame a quarrel (the ultimate cause), which prompted the aggrieved party to seek the intervention of a sorcerer, who cast a spell (the instrumental cause), which led to the illness. This multiple etiology then calls for a range of possible treatments.

Emic perceptions of symptoms and explanations for why illness occurs often directly contradict the teachings of Western biomedicine. This divergence may lead, on one hand, to people's rejection of Western biomedicine and, on the other, to frustration among medical care providers who accuse such people of "noncompliance." We return to this issue in the last section of this chapter.

Ways of Healing

This section considers two ways of conceptualizing and dealing with healing: the public and participatory group healing of the Ju/wasi and the humoral system of bodily balance through food intake in Malaysia. We also consider healers and healing substances.

Community Healing Systems

A general distinction can be drawn between private and **community healing.** The former addresses bodily ailments more in isolation, and the latter emphasizes the social context as crucial to healing. Compared to Western biomedicine, many non-Western systems involve greater use of public healing and community involvement. An example of public or community healing comes from the Ju/wasi foragers of the Kalahari desert in southern Africa. Ju/wasi healing emphasizes the mobilization of community "energy" as a key element in the cure:

> The central event in this tradition is the all-night healing dance. Four times a month on the average, night signals the start of a healing dance. The women sit around the fire, singing and rhythmically clapping. The men, sometimes joined by the women, dance around the singers. As the dance intensifies, *num* or spiritual energy is activated by the healers, both men and women, but mostly among the dancing men. As num is activated in them, they begin to *kia* or experience an enhancement of their consciousness. While experiencing kia, they heal all those at the dance. . . .
>
> The dance is a community event at which the entire camp participates. The people's belief in the healing power of num brings substance to the dance. (Katz 1982:34–36)

Thus an important aspect of the Ju/wasi healing system is its openness—everyone has access to it. The role of healer is also open: There is no special class of healers with special privileges. In fact, more than half of all adult men and about 10 percent of adult women are healers.

Humoral Healing Systems

Humoral healing systems are based on a philosophy of balance among certain natural elements within the body (McElroy and Townsend 1996). In this system, food and drugs have different effects on the body and are classified as either "heating" or "cooling" (the quotation marks indicate that these properties are not the same as thermal measurements per se). Diseases are the result of bodily imbalances—too much heat or coolness—which must be counteracted through dietary changes or medicines that will restore balance.

Humoral healing systems have been practiced for thousands of years in the Middle East, the Mediterranean, and much of Asia and spread to the New World

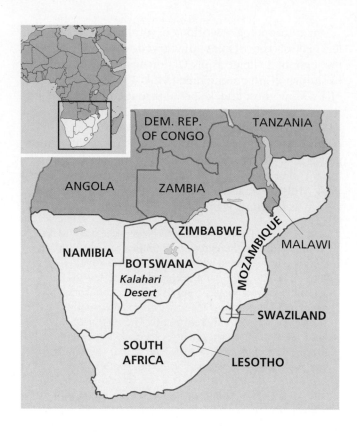

through Spanish colonization. They have shown substantial resilience in the face of Western biomedicine, often incorporating it into their own framework—for example, in the classification of biomedical treatments as either heating or cooling.

In Malaysia, several different humoral traditions coexist, reflecting the region's history of contact with outside cultures. Malaysia has been influenced by trade and contact between its indigenous culture and that of India, China, and the Arab-Islamic world for around two thousand years. Indian, Chinese, and Arabic medical systems all define health as the balance of opposing elements within the body, although each has its own variations (Laderman 1988:272). Indigenous belief systems may have been especially compatible with these imported models because they also were based on concepts of heat and coolness.

Insights about what the indigenous systems were like before outside contact comes from ethnographic accounts about the Orang Asli, indigenous peoples of the interior who are relatively less affected by contact. A conceptual system of hot-cold opposition dominates Orang Asli cosmological, medical, and social theories. The properties and meanings of heat and coolness differ from those of Islamic, Indian, or Chinese humoralism in several ways. In the Islamic, Indian, and Chinese systems, for example, death is the ultimate result of too much coolness. Among the Orang Asli, excessive heat is the primary cause of mortality. Heat emanates from the sun, and it is

A Ju/wasi healer in a trance, in the Kalahari desert, southern Africa. Most healers are men, but some are women. ■ *In your microculture, what are the patterns of gender, ethnicity, and class among various kinds of healers?* (Source: © Irven DeVore/ AnthroPhoto)

by tying around her waist sashes that contain warmed leaves or ashes, and she lies near a fire.

Healers

In an informal sense, everyone is a "healer" because self-treatment is always the first consideration in dealing with a perceived health problem. Yet in all cultures, some people become recognized as having special abilities to diagnose and treat health problems. Notable specialists include midwife, bonesetter (someone who resets broken bones) **shaman** (a healer who mediates between humans and the spirit world), herbalist, general practitioner, psychiatrist, acupuncturist, chiropractor, and dentist. Cross-cultural evidence indicates some common features of healers (Foster and Anderson 1978). See Table 7.2.

TABLE 7.2   Criteria for Becoming a Healer

- *Selection:* Certain individuals may show more ability for entry into healing roles. In Western medical schools, selection for entry rests on apparently objective standards, such as pre-entry exams and college grades. Among the Ainu of northern Japan, healers were men who had a special ability to go into a sort of seizure called *imu:* (Ohnuki-Tierney 1980).

- *Training:* This often involves years of observation and practice, and the period of training may be extremely arduous, even dangerous. In some non-Western traditions, a shaman must make dangerous journeys, through trance or use of drugs, to the spirit world. In Western biomedicine, medical school involves immense amounts of memorization, separation from family and normal social life, and long periods of work without sleep.

- *Certification:* Legal certification or ritual certification, such as a shaman going through a formal initiation ritual announcing his or her competence.

- *Professional image:* The healer role is demarcated from ordinary people through behavior, dress, and other markers, such as the white coat in the West and the Siberian shaman's tambourine for calling the spirits.

- *Expectation of payment:* Compensation in some form whether in kind or in cash, is expected for all formal healers. Payment level may vary depending on the status of the healer and other factors. In northern India, strong preference for sons is reflected in payments to the midwife for helping with the delivery; in rural areas, the payment is twice as great if a son is born. In the United States, medical professionals in different specializations receive markedly different salaries.

associated with excrement, blood, misfortune, disease, and death. Humanity's hot blood makes people mortal, and their consumption of meat speeds the process. Heat causes menstruation, violent emotions, aggression, and drunkenness. Coolness, in contrast, is vital for health.

Health is protected by staying in the forest to avoid the harmful effects of the sun. This belief justifies the rejection of agriculture by some groups because it exposes people to the sun. Treatment of illness is designed to reduce or remove heat. If someone were to fall ill in a clearing, the entire group would relocate to the coolness of the forest. The forest is also a source of cooling leaves and herbs. Healers are cool and retain their coolness by bathing in cold water and sleeping far from the fire. Extreme cold, however, can be harmful. Dangerous levels of coolness are associated with the time right after birth, because the mother is believed to have lost substantial heat. The new mother should not drink cold water or bathe in cold water. She increases her body heat

Ingredients for traditional medicines available in a shop in Singapore include deer and antelope horns, monkey gall bladders, amber, freshwater pearls, and ginseng. ■ *Have you ever gone to a pharmacy in a non–Euro-American context? If so, what did you notice? And similarities?* (Source: © William & Deni McIntyre/Photo Researchers, Inc.)

Healing Substances

Around the world, thousands of different natural or manufactured substances are used as medicines for preventing or curing health problems. Anthropologists have spent more time studying the use of medicines in non-Western cultures than that in the West, although a more fully cross-cultural approach is emerging that examines the use of Western pharmaceuticals (van der Geest, Whyte, and Hardon 1996). **Ethnobotany** explores the cultural knowledge of local plants and their use for a variety of purposes in different settings. Increasing awareness of the range of potentially useful plants worldwide provides a strong incentive for protecting the world's cultural diversity, because it is people who are the repositories of knowledge about different botanical resources (Posey 1990). Leaves of the coca plant, for example, have for centuries been a key part of the medicinal systems of the Andean region, although this plant

has broader uses in ritual, in masking hunger pains, and in combatting the cold (Carter, Morales, and Mamani 1981). Coca is used for gastrointestinal problems and also for sprains, swellings, and colds. A survey of coca use in Bolivia showed a high prevalence rate: Of the 3501 people asked whether they used coca medicinally, about 85 percent answered yes. The leaf may be ingested alone (chewed), and it is frequently combined with other substances in a *maté*, or drink composed of any of a variety of herbs in a water base. Specialized knowledge about preparing some of the matés is reserved for trained herbalists. One maté, for example, is for treating asthma. Made of a certain root and coca leaves, it should be taken three to four times a day until the patient is cured.

Minerals are also widely used for prevention and healing. For example, bathing in water that contains high levels of sulphur or other minerals has wide popularity for promoting health and curing several ailments, including arthritis and rheumatism. About 40,000 people a year go to the Dead Sea, which lies beneath sea level between Israel and Jordan, for treating skin diseases (Lew 1994). The adjacent sulfur springs and mud from the shore are believed to be helpful for people with skin ailments such as psoriasis. In fact, expenses for a therapeutic trip to the Dead Sea are tax deductible in the United States. German studies conclude that it is more cost-effective to pay for a trip to the Dead Sea than to hospitalize a psoriasis patient. Whereas these practices seem clearly to show therapeutic value, instances of people's eating dirt appear to be less understandable within the framework of therapy (see the Critical Thinking box).

Western patent medicines have gained popularity worldwide. There are benefits to the use of these medicines, as well as detriments, including use without prescription and overprescription. Often, the sale of patent medicines is unregulated, and they are available for purchase from local markets by self-treating individuals. The popularity of capsules and even injections has led to overuse in many cases. Medical anthropologists are assessing the distribution channels of medicines, the increased commodification of medicine, and cross-cultural perceptions of the efficacy of various types of medicines.

THEORETICAL APPROACHES IN MEDICAL ANTHROPOLOGY

Here we consider three theoretical approaches to understanding health systems. The first emphasizes the importance of the environment in shaping health problems and

Critical Thinking

WHY DO PEOPLE EAT DIRT?

GEOPHAGIA, THE eating of earth, is a special form of "pica," or the "habitual consumption of items not commonly considered to be food or the compulsive consumption of otherwise normal food items" (Reid 1992). It presents a fascinating puzzle that has been studied by medical anthropologists, cultural geographers, historians, and medical experts. Geophagia has been documented in several Native American groups of South America and the American Southwest, in the Mediterranean region, among women and children in India, among pregnant African American women and children, and in some African cultures. There is typically a preference for certain kinds of earth or clay, and the clay is often baked before consumption, or formed into tablets, or mixed with other substances such as honey.

Medical experts offer explanations based on pathology; in other words, they believe people eat earth or clay because there is something wrong with them. Some pathologies implicated in geophagia are colon perforation, fecal impaction, severe tooth abrasion, and, especially, anemia. According to this view, anemic persons consume earth as an unconscious way of increasing iron levels. Therefore, geophagia can be "cured" through iron therapy. Other experts argue that the arrow of causation points in the opposite direction: Clay consumption reduces the body's ability to absorb iron, so it causes anemia. The anemia arguments are complex and the data often inconclusive because of small samples or lack of good control groups. Thus, although an association

between geophagia and anemia seems often (but not always) to exist, the direction of causation is undetermined.

Some medical anthropologists propose that geophagia may have a positive adaptive value. Eating clay, they say, may function as a supplement to dietary minerals. Clay from markets in Ghana, for example, has been found to contain phosphorus, potassium, calcium, magnesium, copper, zinc, manganese, and iron. Another adaptive role for geophagia is in traditional antidiarrheal preparations. Many clays of Africa have compositions similar to that of Kaopectate, a Western commercial antidiarrheal medicine.

A third hypothesis is that consuming clay may act as a detoxicant, preventing the nausea or indigestion that would otherwise result from eating plant materials that contain certain toxins. This hypothesis receives support from the fact that clay is commonly eaten during famines to help people digest leaves, bark, and other unaccustomed and hard-to-digest foods. In addition, laboratory rats react to exposure to chemical toxins or new flavors by eating clay.

CRITICAL THINKING QUESTIONS

Is it likely that only one of the above explanations for geophagia is correct in all cases? Why or why not?

Could all of the above explanations be correct?

Could none be correct? Why?

---

their spread. The second highlights symbols and meaning as critical in people's expression of suffering and how healing occurs. The third underlines the need to look at economic and political structural factors as deep causes of health problems and as related to certain features of Western biomedicine.

The Ecological/Epidemiological Approach

The **ecological/epidemiological approach** examines how aspects of the natural environment interact with culture to cause health problems and to influence their spread throughout the population. According to this approach,

research should focus on gathering information about the environmental context and social patterns that affect health, such as food distribution within the family, sexual practices, hygiene, and population contact. Research tends to be quantitative and etic, although this approach is often combined with qualitative and emic methods to provide richer results (as discussed in Chapter 2).

The ecological/epidemiological approach yields findings relevant to public health programs by revealing causal links between environmental context and health problems. It also helps by providing socially targeted information about groups "at risk" for specific problems. For example, although hookworm is extremely common throughout rural China, researchers learned that rice cultivators have the highest rates of all. This pattern is

Women working in padi fields near Jinghong, China. Agricultural work done in standing water increases the risk of hookworm infection. ■ *Is hookworm a threat where you live? What is the major infectious disease in your home region?* (Source: © Peter Menzel/Stock Boston, LLC)

related to the fact that the disease is spread through night soil (human excrement used as fertilizer) that is applied to the fields where the cultivators work.

Settled populations living in dense clusters are more likely than mobile populations to experience certain health problems, including declining diet quality and infectious disease (Cohen 1989). Many contemporary studies in the ecological/environmental mode attest to the importance of this distinction. As more and more mobile populations choose, or are forced, to settle into agricultural or urban lives, it is increasingly urgent that the often negative health consequences of sedentariness be recognized and mitigated. One recent study compared the health status of two groups of Turkana people in northwest Kenya (Barkey, Campbell, and Leslie 2001). Some of the Turkana are still pastoralists, whereas others have settled into a town where they no longer keep animals.

The two groups differ strikingly in diet, activities, and social organization. Pastoralist Turkana eat mainly animal foods (milk, meat, and blood), spend much time in rigorous physical activity, and live in large family groups. Settled Turkana men eat mainly maize and beans. Although the study provided no information on physical activity, it is logical to assume that sedentariness means less. Settled Turkana no longer live with large family groups. Instead, they live near strangers. A comparison of the health of men in the two groups revealed that the settled men reported more eye infections, chest infections, backache, and cough/cold. This does not mean that the pastoralist Turkana men had no health problems. For example, a quarter of the pastoralist men reported eye infections. But one-half of the settled men did so. In terms of nutrition, the settled Turkana were shorter and had greater body mass than the pastoral Turkana.

Colonialism and Disease

Anthropologists have applied the ecological/epidemiological approach to the study of the impaired health and survival of indigenous peoples as a result of colonial contact. A basic question is how the introduction of European pathogens (disease-producing organisms) varies in relation to the size of the indigenous population involved (Larsen and Milner 1994). Overall, findings about the effects of colonial contact are negative, ranging from the quick and outright extermination of indigenous peoples to resilient adjustment, among other groups, to drastically changed conditions.

In the Western hemisphere, colonialism brought a dramatic decline in the indigenous populations they contacted, although disagreement exists about the numbers involved (Joralemon 1982). In coordination with archaeologists and colonial historians, medical anthropologists have tried to estimate the role of disease in depopulation, relative to other factors such as warfare, harsh labor practices, and general cultural disruption, and to discover which diseases were most important. Research along these lines indicates that the precontact New World was largely free of the major European infectious diseases such as smallpox, measles, and typhus, and perhaps also of syphilis, leprosy, and malaria. The exposure of indigenous peoples to these infectious diseases, therefore, was likely to have a massive impact, given the people's complete lack of resistance. One analyst compared contact to a "biological war":

Smallpox was the captain of the men of death in that war, typhus fever the first lieutenant, and measles the second lieutenant. More terrible than the conquistadores on horseback, more deadly than sword and gunpowder, they made the conquest by the whites a walkover as compared to what it would have been without their aid. They were

Unity and Diversity

AN AYURVEDIC DOCTOR AND HIS AGING PATIENT IN SOUTH INDIA

MARGARET TRAWICK in her study of Ayurvedic healing in India, follows the "healing is in the meaning" approach in interpreting some aspects of the efficacy and appeal of Ayurvedic treatments (1988). Ayurvedic medicine is a widely used Indian health system based on texts composed from the beginning of the Christian era to about AD 1000. Based on humoral principles, Ayurvedic diagnoses take into account whether bodily "channels" controlling the flow of life in the human body are blocked or open and clear. An interview between an Ayurvedic physician and an old woman of a poor caste group in southern India reveals the themes of channels, processes of flow, points of connection (the heart is believed to be the center of all channels), and everyday activities that regulate the flow of life.

Here are some clips from the doctor–patient conversation:

D: Let's see your eyes. Let's see your pulse. Is your age over sixty?

P: Probably.

D: . . . Is there chest pain?

P: A little.

D: Does your heat flutter?

P: It flutters . . .

D: Is there pain in the joints?

P: Yes. . . .

D: Have you taken any treatment for this?

P: I have taken no treatment at all. . . . (138–139)

After the interview, the doctor offers dietary prescriptions to "quicken" the patient's body—such as avoidance of tamarind, because that causes "dullness," and consumption of light food so that it won't get crowded inside her. In addition to general advice about what to eat and what to avoid, he gives her a detailed daily regimen to follow: "Drink two coffees, in the morning a coffee and in the evening a coffee. Add palm sugar to the coffee, filter it and remove the dirt, add cow's milk and drink it. . . . Eat wheat grain made soft. At three o'clock drink only one cup of coffee. Eat more food than coffee" (138–139). Finally, he gently tells her that, basically, she is growing old.

In this interaction, the meanings conveyed through the interview offer the client a sense that she is being taken seriously by the caregiver and give her some self-efficacy in that there are things she can do to alleviate her distress, such as carefully following a dietary regime.

FOOD FOR THOUGHT

Provide an interpretivist view of an interaction that you have had with a healer/doctor.

---

the forerunners of civilization, the companions of Christianity, the friends of the invader. (Ashburn 1947:98, quoted in Joralemon 1982:112)

This quotation emphasizes the importance of the three major diseases in Latin American colonial history: smallpox, measles, and malaria. A later arrival, cholera, also had severe effects because its transmission through contaminated water and food thrives in areas of poor sanitation.

The Interpretivist Approach

Some medical anthropologists examine health systems as systems of meaning. They study how people in different cultures label, describe, and experience illness and how healing modalities offer meaningful responses to individual and communal distress. These interpretivist anthropologists have examined aspects of healing, such as ritual trance, as symbolic performances. Claude Lévi-Strauss established this approach in a classic essay called "The Effectiveness of Symbols" (1967). He examined how a song sung during childbirth among the Kuna Indians of Panama lessens the difficulty of childbirth. His main point was that healing systems provide meaning to people who are experiencing seemingly meaningless forms of suffering. The provision of meaning offers psychological support and courage to the afflicted and may enhance healing through what Western science calls the *placebo effect*, a healing effect obtained through the positive power of believing that a particular method is effective. Anthropological research suggests that between 10 and 90 percent of the efficacy of medical prescriptions lies in the placebo effect (Moerman 1979, 1983, 1992). Several features may be involved: the power of the person prescribing a particular treatment, the very act of prescription, and concrete details about the medicine, such as its color, name, and place of origin (van der Geest, Whyte, and Hardon 1996). (See the Unity and Diversity box.)

Critical Medical Anthropology

Critical medical anthropology is an approach that, like structurism, focuses on the analysis of how economic and political power structures shape people's health status, their access to health care, and the prevailing healing systems. They show how economic and political systems create and perpetuate social inequality in health status. Critical medical anthropologists also take a cultural constructionist position, arguing that illness is more often a product of one's culturally defined position than of something "natural." Critical medical anthropologists have exposed the power of **medicalization,** or the labeling of a particular issue or problem as medical and requiring medical treatment when, in fact, it may be economic or political.

Critical medical anthropologists tend to look first at how larger structural forces determine the distribution of illness and people's responses to it. But they are also concerned to see how individuals may, through personal agency, resist such forces. Critical medical anthropology also examines Western biomedicine itself, viewing it as a global power structure, critiquing Western medical training, and looking at doctor–patient relationships as manifestations of social control rather than social liberation.

The Role of Poverty

Broad distinctions exist between the most prevalent afflictions of the richer, more industrial nations and those of the poorer, less industrial nations. In the former, the major categories of death are circulatory diseases, malignant cancers, AIDS, alcohol consumption, and tobacco consumption (United Nations Development Programme 1994:191). For developing countries, a different profile appears: Tuberculosis, malaria, and AIDS predominate. There is substantial empirical evidence that poverty is a major cause of morbidity (sickness) and mortality (death) in both industrial and developing countries. It may be manifested in different ways—for example, by causing extreme malnutrition in Chad or Nepal and high death rates from street violence among the poor of affluent nations.

Throughout the developing world, rates of childhood malnutrition are inversely related to income. As income increases, calorie intake as a percent of recommended daily allowances also increases (Zaidi 1988:122). Thus increasing the income levels of the poor may be the most direct way to influence health and nutrition. Yet, in contrast to this seemingly logical approach, many health and nutrition programs around the world have been focused on treating the outcomes of poverty rather than its causes.

The widespread practice of addressing the health outcomes of poverty and social inequality with pills or other medical options has been documented by critical medical anthropologists. An example is Nancy Scheper-Hughes's research in Bom Jesus, northeastern Brazil, mentioned in Chapter 5 (1992). The people who experienced symptoms of weakness, insomnia, and anxiety were given pills by a local doctor. Scheper-Hughes is convinced that the people were hungry and needed food. This system serves the interests of pharmaceutical companies and, more generally, helps to keep inequitable social systems in place. Similar critical analyses have shown how psychiatry treats symptoms and serves to keep people in their places, rather than addressing the root causes of affliction, which may be powerlessness, unemployment, and thwarted social aspirations. High rates of depression among women in Western societies, and their treatment with a range of psychotropic drugs and personal therapists, are an example.

Western Medical Training Examined

Since the 1980s, critical medical anthropologists have pursued the study of Western biomedicine as a powerful cultural system. Much of their work critiques Western medical school training and its emphasis on technology. They often advocate for greater recognition of social factors in diagnosis and treatment, reduction of the spread of biomedical technology, and diversification of medical specialists to include alternative healing, such as massage, acupuncture, and chiropractic (Scheper-Hughes 1990).

Robbie Davis-Floyd (1987) examined the culture of obstetric training in the United States. She interviewed twelve obstetricians, ten male and two female. As stu-

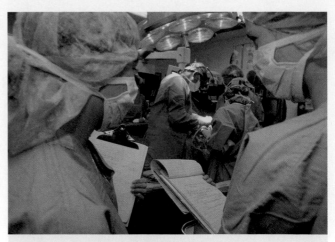

Medical students in training in a Western biomedical setting. These students are observing brain surgery. ■ *What does this scene convey about values and beliefs of Western medicine?* (Source: © Lara Jo Regan/Getty Images)

dents, they absorbed the technological model of birth as a core value of Western obstetrics. This model treats the body as a machine (recall the discussion of the technological model of birth in Chapter 5). The physician-technician uses the assembly-line approach to birth in order to promote efficient production and quality control. As one of the residents in the study explained, "We shave 'em, we prep 'em, we hook 'em up to the IV and administer sedation. We deliver the baby, it goes to the nursery and the mother goes to her room. There's no room for niceties around here. We just move 'em right on through. It's not hard to see it like an assembly line" (292). The goal is the "production" of a healthy baby. The doctor is in charge of achieving this goal, and the mother takes second place. One obstetrician said, "It is what we all were trained to always go after—the perfect baby. That's what we were trained to produce. The quality of the mother's experience—we rarely thought about that. Everything we did was to get that perfect baby" (292).

This goal involves the use of sophisticated monitoring machines. One obstetrician said, "I'm totally dependent on fetal monitors, 'cause they're great! They free you to do a lot of other things. . . . I couldn't sit over there with a woman in labor with my hand on her belly, and be in here seeing 20 to 30 patients a day" (291). In addition, use of technology conveys status: "Anybody in obstetrics who shows a human interest in patients is not respected. What *is* respected is interest in machines" (291).

How does obstetrical training socialize medical students into accepting this technological model? First, medical training involves a lengthy process of *cognitive retrogression* in which the students go through an intellectual hazing process. During the first two years of medical school, most courses are basic sciences, learning tends to be rote, and vast quantities of material must be memorized. The sheer bulk of memorization forces students to adopt an uncritical approach to it. Mental overload socializes students into a uniform pattern, giving them a *tunnel vision* in which the knowledge of medicine assumes supreme importance. As one informant put it,

> Medical school is not difficult in terms of what you have to learn—there's just so much of it. You go through, in a six-week course, a thousand-page book. The sheer bulk of information is phenomenal. You have pop quizzes in two or three courses every day the first year. We'd get up around 6, attend classes till 5, go home and eat, then head back to school and be in anatomy lab working with a cadaver, or something, until 1 or 2 in the morning, and then go home and get a couple of hours of sleep and then go out again. And you did that virtually day in and day out for four years, except for vacations. (298–299)

The second phase, which could be termed *dehumanization,* is one in which medical school training succeeds in overriding humanitarian ideals through its emphasis on technology and objectification of the patient. One informant explained, "Most of us went into medical school with pretty humanitarian ideals. I know I did. But the whole process of medical education makes you inhuman . . . by the time you get to residency, you end up not caring about anything beyond the latest techniques you can master and how sophisticated the tests are that you can perform" (299). The physical aspect of hazing through exhaustion intensifies during the residency years. The last two years of medical school and the four years of residency are devoted primarily to hands-on experience. The obstetrical specialization involves intensive repetition and learning of technical skills, including surgery. One obstetrician summed up the entire process of transformation: "It doesn't seem to matter—male or female, young or old, wealthy or poor—it is only the most unusual individual who comes through a residency program as anything less than a technological clone" (307).

This study emphasizes how biomedical caregivers are trained to become dependent on technology as the basis of their expertise. Similar studies of other biomedical specialists, such as surgeons, make the same point (Cassell 1991) and show how the power of physicians is correlated with the complexity of the technology they use. Other studies reveal the detriments of reliance on technology when the healing issue requires human understanding and interaction rather than machines (Fadiman 1997).

GLOBALIZATION AND CHANGE

Perhaps no other aspect of Western society except the capitalist market system, and the English language, has so permeated the rest of the world as Western biomedicine. As biomedicine is adopted in other contexts, it undergoes localization and change. Medical anthropologists study how and why such change occurs and what the effects are on the people involved.

Globalization trends in the past decade have brought not only economic and political changes but also medical changes. The arrow of influence has mainly gone in the direction of spreading aspects of Western biomedicine to many parts of the world. More minor changes have spelled increasing appreciation in the West for some aspects of non-Western healing, such as acupuncture. In this section we consider new and emerging health challenges, changes in healing, and applied medical anthropology's growing role.

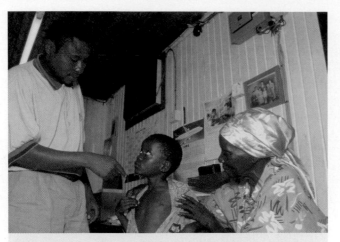

A woman takes her eight-year-old grandson, who has HIV/AIDS, to a clinic in Dar es Salaam, Tanzania. Throughout the world, increasing numbers of children are infected and are, at the same time, orphans because their parents have died of the disease. ■ *In your culture, what is the prevalence of HIV/AIDS among children, and what services are provided for them?* (Source: © Sean Sprague/Stock Boston, LLC)

The New Infectious Diseases

The 1950s brought hope that infectious diseases were being controlled through Western scientific advances such as antibiotic drugs, vaccines against childhood diseases, and improved technology for sanitation. In North America, death from infections common in the late nineteenth and early twentieth centuries was no longer a major threat in the 1970s. In tropical countries, pesticides lowered rates of malaria by controlling the mosquito populations. Since the 1980s, however, we have entered an era of shaken confidence. Besides the spread of the HIV/AIDS epidemic, another challenge is presented by the fact that many infectious microbes have reappeared in forms that are resistant to known methods of prevention and treatment. New contexts for exposure and contagion are being created through increased international travel and migration, expansion of populations into previously uninhabited forest areas, changing sexual behavior, and overcrowding in cities. Several new and re-emerging diseases are related to unsafe technological developments. For example, the introduction of soft contact lenses has caused eye infections from the virus *acanthamebiasis.*

Many medical anthropologists are contributing their expertise to understanding the causes and distribution of the new infectious diseases by studying social patterns and cultural practices. Research about HIV/AIDS addresses factors such as intravenous drug use, sexual behavior, and condom use among different groups and how intervention programs could be better designed and tar-

geted. For example, one study assessed attitudes toward condom use among White, African American, and Hispanic respondents in the United States (Bowen and Trotter 1995). Whites were most likely to use condoms, followed by Hispanics, with the lowest use among African Americans. Across all groups, people with "main partners" (as opposed to "casual partners") were more likely to use condoms, as were older people and people classified as having a higher level of personal assertiveness. Recommendations for increasing condom usage include self-awareness programs and assertiveness training, especially for younger people in casual relationships.

Diseases of Development

Diseases of development are diseases that are caused or increased by economic development activities (Hughes and Hunter 1970). Examples of diseases in this category are schistosomiasis, river blindness, malaria, and tuberculosis (Foster and Anderson 1978:27).

In many developing countries, dramatically increased rates of schistosomiasis (a disease caused by the presence of a parasitic worm in the blood system) have been traced to the construction of dams and irrigation systems. Over 200 million people suffer from this debilitating disease (Foster and Anderson 1978). The larvae of this particular form of worm hatch from eggs and mature in slow-moving water such as lakes and rivers. Upon maturity, they can penetrate human (or other animal) skin with which they come into contact. People who wade or swim in infected waters are very likely to become infected. Once inside the human body, the adult schistosomes breed in the veins around the human bladder and bowel. They send fertilized eggs through urine and feces into the environment. These eggs then continue to contaminate water in which they hatch into larvae. Anthropologists' research has documented steep increases in the rates of schistosomiasis at high dam sites over the past three decades of dam construction in developing countries (Scudder 1973). This increased risk is caused by the dams slowing the rate of water flow. Stagnant water systems offer an ideal environment for development of the larvae. Anthropologists have used this information to speak out against the construction of large dams.

Formerly unidentified diseases of development continue to appear. One of these is Kyasanur forest disease, or KFD (Nichter 1992). This viral disease was first identified in 1957 in southern India:

> Resembling influenza, at onset KFD is marked by sudden chills, fever, frontal headaches, stiffness of the neck, and body pain. Diarrhea and vomiting often follow on the third day. High fever is continuous for five to fifteen days, during which time a variety of additional symptoms may manifest themselves, including gastrointesti-

nal bleeding, persistent cough with blood-tinged sputum, and bleeding gums. In more serious cases, the infection progresses to bronchial pneumonia, meningitis, paralysis, encephalitis, and hemorrhage. (224)

In the early 1980s, an epidemic of KFD swept through over thirty villages near the Kyasanur forest. Mortality rates in hospitals ranged between 12 and 18 percent of those admitted. Investigation revealed that the KFD especially affected agricultural workers and cattle tenders who were most exposed to newly cleared areas near the forest. In the cleared areas, international companies established plantations and initiated cattle raising. Ticks, which had long existed in the local ecosystem, increased in number in the cleared area and found inviting hosts in the cattle and their tenders. Thus, human modification of the ecosystem through deforestation and introduction of cattle raising caused the epidemic and shaped its social distribution.

Changes in Healing: Medical Pluralism

Contact between cultures sometimes leads to a situation in which aspects of both cultures coexist: two (or more) different languages, religions, systems of law, or health systems, for example. The term *pluralism* expresses the presence of multiple cultural options within a society. When anthropologists discuss health systems, **medical pluralism** is the term they use to refer to a situation in which more than one medical/health system exists in a given culture.

Medical pluralism provides both options and complications. First, something may be classified as a health problem in some cultures and not in others. For example, spirit possession is welcomed in some cultures but would be considered schizophrenia according to Western psychiatry. Second, the same issue may be classified as having a different cause (such as supernatural versus germ theories) and therefore require different treatments. Third, certain treatment modalities may be rejected as violating cultural rules. All of these issues affect how a particular culture will react to exogenous (outside) medical practices.

In some cases, we find the coexistence of many forms of healing that offer clients a range of choices. In other cases, conflicting explanatory models of illness and healing result in serious misunderstandings between healers and clients.

Selective Pluralism: The Case of the Sherpas

The Sherpas of Nepal offer an unusual example of a newly capitalizing context in which preference for traditional healing systems remains strong, along with the

Among the many forms of medical treatment available to the Sherpa of Nepal, shamanic healing remains a popular choice. ■ *Why might many Sherpa people continue to see a shaman for illness rather than a biomedical doctor?* (Source: Vincanne Adams)

adoption of certain aspects of biomedicine (V. Adams 1988). Formerly pastoralist–farmers, the Sherpas now provide services for international tourism. They work as guides, porters, cooks, and administrators in trekking agencies and as staff at hotels and restaurants. The variety of healing therapies available in the Upper Khumbu region fit into three categories:

- Orthodox Buddhist practitioners, such as lamas, who are consulted for both prevention and cure through their blessings and *amchis;* they practice Tibetan medicine, a system largely derived from India's Ayurvedic medicine;

- unorthodox religious or shamanic practitioners, who perform divination ceremonies for diagnosis; and

- biomedical practitioners, who at first used their diagnostic techniques and medicines mainly for tourists and later established a permanent medical facility in 1967.

In Khumbu, traditional healers are thriving and in no way threatened by wider economic changes brought by the tourist trade and influx of wealth. The reason is that high-mountain tourism is a particular form of capitalist development that does not radically change the social relations involved in production. This type of tourism brings in money but does not require large-scale capital investment from outside. Thus the Sherpas maintain control of their productive resources, their family structures remain largely the same, and wider kinship ties remain important in the organization of tourist business.

When Explanatory Models Conflict

The disjuncture between biomedicine and local cultural patterns has been documented by many anthropologists. In some instances, miscommunication occurs between biomedical doctors and clients in matters as seemingly simple as a prescription that should be taken with every meal. The doctor assumes that this means three times a day, but some people do not eat three meals a day and thus unwittingly do not follow the doctor's instructions.

One anthropological study of a case in which death resulted from cross-cultural differences shows how complex the issue of communication across medical cultures is.

The "F family" are Samoan immigrants living in Honolulu, Hawaii (Krantzler 1987). Neither parent speaks English. Their children are "moderately literate" in English but speak a mixture of English and Samoan at home. Mr. F was trained as a traditional Samoan healer. Mary, a daughter, was first stricken with diabetes at the age of sixteen. She was taken to the hospital by ambulance after collapsing, half-conscious, on the sidewalk near her home in a Honolulu housing project. After several months of irregular contact with medical staff, she was again brought to the hospital in an ambulance, unconscious, and she died there. Her father was charged with causing Mary's death through medical neglect.

Nora Krantzler analyzes this case from the perspectives of the Western medical providers and Samoan culture. Here is the medical sector view, beginning with Mary's first admission to the hospital:

> At that point, her illness was "discovered" and diagnosed as juvenile onset diabetes mellitus. She was initially placed in the Pediatric Intensive Care Unit for 24 hours, then transferred to a pediatric ward for about a week until her diabetes was "under good control." She, her parents, and her older sister were taught how to give insulin injections, and Mary was shown how to test her urine for glucose and acetone. She was given a 1-month supply of insulin. . . . She was further "counseled" about her diet. . . . She was then to be followed up with visits to the outpatient clinic. Following the clinic's (unoffi-

cial) policy of linking patients with physicians from their own ethnic group, she was assigned to see the sole Samoan pediatric resident. (326–327)

Over the next few months, she was seen once in the clinic by a different resident (a physician at the stage of training following internship). She missed her next three appointments, came in once without an appointment, and was readmitted to the hospital on the basis of test results from that visit. At that time, she, her parents, and her older sister were once again advised about the importance of compliance with the medical advice they were receiving. Four months later, she returned to the clinic with blindness in one eye and diminished vision in the other. She was diagnosed with cataracts, and Dr. A, the Samoan physician, again advised her about the seriousness of her illness and the need for compliance. He wanted her to be admitted to the hospital to have the cataracts removed. Her father initially refused but then was persuaded. Dr. A wrote in Mary's chart:

> Her diabetes seemed to be very much out of control at the time but I was having a very difficult time with the patient and her father. . . . I consented to the father's wishes to have him supplement the insulin with some potion of his that he had prepared especially to control her sugar. . . . He did not believe that there was such an illness which would require daily injection for the rest of one's life and thanked me for my efforts but claimed that he would like to have total control of his daughter's illness at this time. (328–329)

The medical experts increasingly judged that "cultural differences" were the basic problem and that in spite of all their attempts to communicate with the F family, they were basically incapable of caring for Mary. Legal sanctions were used to force her family to bring her to the hospital for surgery.

The family's perspective, in contrast, was grounded in *fa'a Samoa*, the Samoan way. Their first experience in a large hospital occurred after Mary's collapse:

> When Mr. F first arrived at the hospital, he spoke with different hospital staff (using a daughter as a translator) and was concerned that there was no single physician caring for Mary. (Since it was a teaching hospital, she was seen by residents as well as by attending physicians.) He felt that the hospital staff members gave him different interpretations of Mary's illness, including discrepant results, leading him to perceive her care as experimental and inconsistent. The family also observed a child die while Mary was in the Intensive Care Unit, further reinforcing this perception and instilling fear over Mary's chance of surviving in this hospital. Partly due to language difficulties, they felt they did not get an adequate explanation of her problem over the course of her treat-

A Korean mansin performs the Tale of Princess Pari, a female hero who braves the perils of the underworld in quest of an herb that will restore her dying parents. Twenty years ago, this segment of the kut for the dead would have been performed outside the house gate. In urban Korea, it is performed inside to avoid complaints about noise and traffic obstruction. ■ *How has modernization affected the practice of Western biomedicine in terms of where it is practiced, and what are the social implications of such change?* (Source: Laurel Kendall)

ment. When they asked what was wrong with her, their perception was that "everyone said 'sugar.'" What this meant was not clear to the family; they were confused about whether she was getting too much sugar or too little. Mary's mother interpreted the explanations to mean she was not getting enough sugar, so she tried to give her more when she was returned home. Over time, confusion gave way to anger, and a basic lack of trust of the hospital and the physicians there developed. The family began to draw on their own resources for explaining and caring for Mary's illness, relying heavily on the father's skills as a healer. (330)

From the Samoan perspective, the F family behaved logically and appropriately. The father, as household head and healer in his own right, felt he had authority. Dr. A, although Samoan, had been resocialized by the Western medical system and alienated from his Samoan background. He did not offer the personal touch that the F family expected. Samoans believe that children above the age of twelve are no longer children and can be expected to behave responsibly. Assigning Mary's twelve-year-old sister to assist her with her insulin injections and recording results made sense to them. Also, appointments are not required at the hospital in American Samoa.

Clinical Medical Anthropology

Clinical medical anthropology or **applied medical anthropology,** is the application of anthropological knowledge to further the goals of health care providers—for example, in improving doctor–patient communication in multicultural settings, making recommendations about culturally appropriate health intervention programs, and providing insights about factors related to disease that medical practitioners do not usually take into account. In their work, different clinical medical anthropologists draw on ethnomedical knowledge and on any of the three theoretical approaches or a combination of them.

Although critical medical anthropology and clinical medical anthropology may seem diametrically opposed to each other (the first seeking to critique and even limit the power and range of the medical establishment and the second seeking to make it more effective), some medical anthropologists are building bridges between the two perspectives.

An example of a clinical medical anthropologist who combines the first two approaches is Robert Trotter (1987), who conducted research on lead poisoning among children in Mexican American communities. The three most common sources of lead poisoning of children in the United States are eating lead-based paint chips, living near a smelter where the dust has high lead content, and eating or drinking from pottery made with an improperly treated lead glaze. The discovery of an unusual case of lead poisoning by health professionals in Los Angeles in the early 1980s prompted investigations that produced understanding of a fourth cause: the use of a traditional healing remedy, *azarcon,* which contained lead, by people of the Mexican American community. Azarcon is used to treat a culture-bound syndrome called *empacho,* which is a combination of indigestion and constipation, believed to be caused by food sticking to the abdominal wall.

Trotter was called on by the U.S. Public Health Service to investigate the availability and use of azarcon. His research took him to Mexico, where he surveyed the con-

Lessons Applied

PROMOTING VACCINATION PROGRAMS

VACCINATION PROGRAMS, especially as promoted by UNICEF, are often introduced in countries with much fanfare, but they are sometimes met with little enthusiasm by the target population. In India, many people are suspicious that vaccination programs are clandestine family planning programs (Nichter 1996). In other instances, fear of foreign vaccines prompts people to reject inoculations. Overall, acceptance rates of vaccination have been lower than Western public health planners expected. What factors have limited vaccination acceptance?

Public health planners have not paid enough attention to broad reasons why certain innovations are accepted or rejected. There have been problems in supply (clinics do not always have vaccines on hand). Cultural understandings of illness and the role of inoculations have not been considered. Surveys show that many mothers have a partial or inaccurate understanding of what the vaccines protect against. In some cases, people's perceptions and priorities did not match what the

vaccines were supposed to address. In others, people did not see the value of multiple vaccinations. In Indonesia, a once-vaccinated and healthy child was not considered to be in need of another inoculation.

Key features in the overall communication strategy are promoting trust in the public health program and providing locally sensible understandings of what the vaccinations do and do not do. Another important role that applied medical anthropologists play in promoting more effective public health communication is to work with public health specialists in enhancing their understanding of and attention to local cultural practices and beliefs.

FOOD FOR THOUGHT

Are all vaccines of unquestionable benefit to the recipients? Search the Internet for information on new vaccines—for example, the vaccine against hookworm—in terms of their pros and possible cons.

---

tents of herbal shops and talked with *curanderos* (local healers). He learned about an alternative name for azarcon, *greta*, which helped him trace the distribution of this lead-based substance in the United States. His work led to U.S. government restrictions on azarcon and greta to prevent their further use, to recommendations about the need to provide a substitute remedy for the treatment of empacho that would not have harmful side effects, and to ideas about how to advertise this substitute. Throughout his involvement, Trotter played several roles: researcher, consultant, and program developer, and he was able to garner anthropological knowledge applicable to the solution of a health problem.

Much work in clinical medical anthropology involves health communication (Nichter and Nichter 1996: 327–328). Anthropologists can help health educators in the development of more meaningful messages through

- addressing local ethnophysiology and acknowledging popular health concerns;
- taking seriously all local illness terms and conventions;
- adopting local styles of communication;
- identifying subgroups within the population that may be responsive to different types of messages and incentives;

- monitoring the response of communities to health messages over time and facilitating corrections in communication when needed; and
- exposing possible victim-blaming in health messages.

These principles helped health care officials understand local response to public vaccination programs in several countries of Asia and Africa (see Lessons Applied box).

Since 1978, the World Health Organization has endorsed the incorporation of traditional medicine, especially healers, in national health systems (Velimirovic 1990). This policy emerged in response to increasing pride, among nations, in their own medical traditions and in response to shortages of trained biomedical personnel. Debates continue about the efficacy of many traditional medical practices as compared to biomedicine. For instance, opponents of the promotion of traditional medicine claim that it has no effect on such infectious diseases as cholera, malaria, tuberculosis, schistosomiasis, leprosy, and others. They insist that it makes no sense to allow for or encourage ritual practices against malaria, for example, when a child has not been inoculated against it. Supporters of traditional medicine as one aspect of a planned, pluralistic medical system point out that biomedicine neglects a person's mind and soul,

---

whereas traditional medicine is socially contextualized. Also, indigenous curers are more likely to know clients and their families, thus facilitating therapy.

One area where progress has been made in maintaining positive aspects of traditional health care is in midwifery. Many governments of developing countries have designed training programs that equip traditional birth attendants (TBAs) with rudimentary training in germ theory and provide them with basic "kits" that include a clean razor blade for cutting the umbilical cord. The many thousands of TBAs working at the grassroots level around the world thus are not squeezed out of their work but continue to perform their important role with some enhanced skills and tools.

KEY CONCEPTS

clinical or applied medical anthropology, p. 169
community healing, p. 158
critical medical anthropology, p. 164
culture-bound syndromes, p. 154
diseases of development, p. 166

disease/illness dichotomy, p. 154
divination, p. 157
ecological/epidemiological approach, p. 161
ethnobotany, p. 160
ethno-nosology, p. 154

ethnomedicine, p. 152
humoral healing systems, p. 158
medicalization, p. 164
medical pluralism, p. 167
shaman, p. 159
structural suffering, p. 154

SUGGESTED READINGS

Eric J. Bailey. *Medical Anthropology and African American Health*. New York: Greenwood Publishing Group, 2000. This book explores the relationship between cultural anthropology and African American health care issues. One chapter discusses how to do applied research in medical anthropology.

Nancy N. Chen. *Breathing Spaces: Qigong, Psychiatry, and Healing in China*. New York: Columbia University Press, 2003. Taking a critical medical anthropology approach, this ethnography explores *qigong*, a charismatic form of healing based on meditative breathing exercises. The author places her study within the impact of capitalist globalization and Western psychiatric globalization on the lives of people in China.

Paul Farmer. *AIDS and Accusation: Haiti and the Geography of Blame*. Berkeley: University of California Press, 1992. This book combines discussion of the global structures related to the spread of HIV/AIDS with in-depth study in one village in Haiti where HIV/AIDS is locally interpreted as one more phase in people's long-term exposure to afflictions and suffering.

Paul Farmer. *Infections and Inequalities: The Modern Plagues*. Berkeley: University of California Press, 1999. Farmer blends interpretive medical anthropology with critical medical anthropology in this comparative study of how poverty kills through diseases such as tuberculosis and AIDS. Trained as a Western biomedical physician and as an anthropologist, Farmer takes an activist position.

Stephanie Kane. *AIDS Alibis: Sex, Drugs and Crime in the Americas*. Philadelphia: Temple University Press, 1998. Kane provides an interpretive study of the combined forces of sex, drugs, and crimes in two contexts: Chicago and Belize, Central America. An activist anthropologist as well, she critiques the war on drugs, the war on crime, and current public health programs in the hope that serious reconsiderations of these systems can lead to useful reform.

Richard Katz. *Boiling Energy: Community Healing among the Kalahari Kung*. Cambridge: Harvard University Press, 1982. This account of the healing practices of the Ju/wasi [!Kung] of the Dobe area between Namibia and Botswana focuses on several different healers, their training, and their styles.

Emily Martin. *The Woman in the Body: A Cultural Analysis of Reproduction*. Boston: Beacon Press, 1987. This book explores how Western medical textbooks represent women's reproductive experiences and how these descriptions compare to a sample of Baltimore women's perceptions and experiences of menstruation, childbirth, and menopause.

Carol Shepherd McClain, ed. *Women as Healers: A Cross-Cultural Perspective*. New Brunswick, NJ: Rutgers University Press, 1989. This collection of eleven studies is preceded by a general overview. Case studies include Ecuador, Sri Lanka, Mexico, Jamaica, the United States, Serbia, Korea, Southern Africa, and Benin.

Valentina Napolitano. *Migration, Mujercitas, and Medicine Men: Living in Urban Mexico*. Berkeley: University of California Press, 2002. This is an ethnography of Guadalajara, western Mexico, with a focus on how immigrants from surrounding areas adapt to urban life. The author describes their roles in the Catholic Church, the diverse health systems available, and life-cycle rituals as a focus of meaning.

Sherry Saggers and Dennis Gray. *Dealing with Alcohol: Indigenous Usage in Australia, New Zealand and Canada*. New York: Cambridge University Press, 1998. This comparative study looks at structural issues such as European colonialism, the interests of liquor companies in creating and sustaining high rates of alcohol consumption among many indigenous groups, and the people's own understandings of their situation.

WHAT is ethnomedicine?

Ethnomedicine is the study of health systems of specific cultures. Health systems include categories and perceptions of illness and approaches to prevention and healing. Research in ethnomedicine shows how perceptions of the body differ cross-culturally and reveals both differences and similarities across health systems in perceptions of illness and symptoms. Culture-bound syndromes are illnesses that are locally specific in the way symptoms are clustered and causes are ascribed, but some formerly culture-bound syndromes are now undergoing globalization. Ethnomedical studies of healing, healing substances, and healers reveal a wide range of approaches. Community healing systems are more characteristic of small-scale nonindustrial societies. They emphasize group interaction and treating the individual within the social context. In industrial societies, biomedicine emphasizes the body as a discrete unit, and treatment addresses the individual body or mind.

WHAT are three major theoretical approaches in medical anthropology?

Ecological/epidemiological medical anthropology emphasizes the systemic links between environment and health. Anthropologists working in this framework have shown how certain categories of people are at risk of contracting particular diseases within various contexts in historical times and the present. The interpretivist approach focuses on studying illness and healing as a set of symbols and meanings. Research in this framework shows how, cross-culturally, definitions of health problems and healing systems for these problems are embedded in meanings. Critical medical anthropologists focus on health problems and healing within their economic and political contexts and ask what power relations are involved and who benefits from particular forms of healing. Critical medical anthropologists analyze the role of inequality and poverty in health problems and have critiqued Western biomedicine as a system of social control.

HOW are illness and healing changing during globalization?

Health systems everywhere are facing accelerated change in the face of globalization, which includes the spread of Western capitalism as well as new diseases and new medical technologies. The "new infectious diseases" are a challenge to health care systems in terms of prevention and treatment. "Diseases of development" are new health problems caused by development projects (such as dams) that change the physical and social environments. In terms of healing systems, the spread of Western biomedicine to non-Western contexts is a major direction of change, and as a consequence, medical pluralism exists in all countries. Clinical or applied medical anthropologists play a role in promoting forms of change in health systems. They may inform medical care providers of more appropriate forms of intervention and/or inform local peoples about their increasingly complex medical choices.

THE BIG QUESTIONS

- **HOW** do cultures create kinship ties through descent, sharing, and marriage?

- **WHAT** is a household and what do anthropologists study about household life?

- **HOW** are kinship and households changing?

8

KINSHIP AND DOMESTIC LIFE

Some members of a bedu household in Yemen.
(Source: © Norbert Schiller/The Image Works)

Learning another culture's kinship system is as challenging as learning another language. This was true for Robin Fox (1995 [1978]) during his research among the Tory Islanders of Ireland. Some of the Irish kinship terms and categories he encountered were similar to American English usage, but others were not. For example, the word *muintir* can mean "people" in its widest sense, as in English. It can also refer to people of a particular social category, as in "my people," or close relatives.

Another similarity is with *gaolta*, the word for "relatives" or "those of my blood." In its adjectival form, gaolta refers to kindness like the English word "kin," which is related to "kindness." Tory Islanders have a phrase meaning "children and grandchildren," also like the English term "descendants."

The word for "friend" on Tory Island is the same as the word for "kin," reflecting the cultural circumstances on Tory Island with its small population, all living close together: Everyone is related by kinship, so, logically, friends are kin.

Studying kinship systems and domestic life offers surprising discoveries. In some cultures, an uncle has a closer relationship with his sister's children than with his own children. In others, a child considers his or her mother's sisters as mothers and is close to all of them. Cousins, including first cousins (offspring of one's mother's and father's siblings), are preferred as marriage partners in much of the Middle East and in parts of South Asia where cousin marriages are both common and legal. In some cultures, a person may have more than one spouse. Increasing numbers of people in Europe and North America choose to cohabit with a partner and never get married.

The closest and most intense human relationships often involve people who consider themselves linked to each other through **kinship**, or a sense of being related to another person or persons. All cultures have ideas about what a kinship is and have rules for appropriate behavior between kin. These rules can be informal or formally defined by law, such as the United States law forbidding marriage between first cousins. From infancy, people begin learning about their particular culture's **kinship system**—that is, the combination of ideas about who are kin and what kinds of behavior kinship relationships involve. Like one's first language, one's kinship system becomes so ingrained that it tends to be taken for granted as something "natural" rather than cultural.

This chapter first considers cross-cultural variations in kinship systems. We then examine a key unit of domestic life: the household. The last section of the chapter provides examples of change in kinship patterns and household organization.

THE STUDY OF KINSHIP

In all cultures, kinship links modes of production, reproduction, and ideology. Depending on the type of economy, kinship shapes children's personality development, influences a person's marriage options, and affects the status and care of the aged. In small-scale nonindustrial cultures, kinship is the primary, and often only, principle that organizes people into coherent and meaningful groups. The kinship group performs the functions of ensuring the continuity of the group by arranging marriages; maintaining social order by setting moral rules and punishing offenders; and providing for the basic needs of members by regulating production, consumption, and distribution. In large-scale industrial societies, kinship ties exist, but other forms of social affiliation draw people together into groups that have nothing to do with kinship.

Early anthropologists documented the importance of kinship in the societies they researched. Lewis Henry Morgan and others argued that kinship was the most important organizing principle in non-state cultures. They also discovered that definitions of who counts as kin differed from those of contemporary Europe and the United States. For example, Western cultures emphasize "blood" relations as primary—that is, relations between people linked by birth from a biological mother and father (Sault 1994). Yet not all cultures define who is a "blood" relative in the same way. In some, males in the family are of one "blood" (or "substance"), females of another. This view contrasts with the Euro-American definition that all biological children of the same parents share the same "blood."

Among a group of Inuit living in northern Alaska, the word for kin literally means "addition" (Bodenhorn 2000). In their kinship system, the kin of anyone considered kin are also one's kin. Thus the network of people who feel related to each other is extensive. These people define kin as people who act like kin. If a person ceases to act like a kinsperson, he or she stops being a kinsperson. Hence you might hear people comment that someone *used to be* their cousin.

We first review how cultural anthropologists represent and analyze information on kinship. We then consider three bases on which people cross-culturally define kinship relationships. The first involves being born from someone, the second arises through sharing important substances, and the third involves marriage or marriage-like arrangements.

Kinship Analysis

Early anthropological work on kinship tended to focus on finding out who is related to whom and in what way. Typically, the anthropologist would interview one or two people, asking questions such as: What do you call your brother's daughter? Can you (as a man) marry your father's brother's daughter? What is the term you use to refer to your mother's sister? In another approach, the anthropologist would ask an individual to name all his or her relatives, explain how they are related to the interviewee, and provide the terms by which they refer to him or her.

From this kind of reported information, the anthropologist would construct a **kinship diagram,** a schematic way of presenting data on the kinship relationships of an individual, called "ego" (see Figure 8.1). This diagram depicts all of ego's relatives, as remembered by ego and reported to the anthropologist. Strictly speaking, information gained from the informant for his or her kinship diagram is not supplemented by asking other people to fill in where ego's memory failed (in contrast to a genealogy; see below). In cultures where kinship plays a greater role in social relations, it is likely that an informant will be able to provide information on more relatives than in cultures where kinship ties are less important in comparison to other networks such as friendships and work groups. When I took a research methods course as an undergraduate, I interviewed my Hindi language teaching assistant about his kin for a class assignment. From an upper-class family in India, he remembered a total of over sixty relatives in his father's and mother's families, thus providing a much more extensive kinship diagram than I would have been able to for my Euro-American family.

FIGURE 8.1 Symbols Used in Kinship Diagrams

Characters		Relationships		Kin Abbreviations	
○	female	=	is married to	**Mo**	mother
△	male	≈	is cohabiting with	**Fa**	father
⊘	deceased female	⊬	is divorced from	**Br**	brother
⧄	deceased male	≉	is separated from	**Z**	sister
●	female "ego" of the diagram	⊙	adopted-in female	**H**	husband
▲	male "ego" of the diagram	⧄	adopted-in male	**W**	wife
		|	is descended from	**Da**	daughter
		⌐	is the sibling of	**S**	son
				Co	cousin

In contrast to a kinship diagram, a **genealogy** is constructed by beginning with the earliest ancestors (rather than starting with ego) that can be traced, then working down to the present. The Tory Islanders were not comfortable beginning with ego when Robin Fox was attempting to construct kinship diagrams. They preferred to proceed genealogically, so he followed their preference. Tracing a family's complete genealogy may involve archival research in the attempt to construct as full a record as possible. In Europe and the United States, Christians often record their "family tree" in the front of the family Bible.

Decades of anthropological research have produced a mass of information on kinship terminology, or the terms that people use to refer to people they consider to be kin of various types. For example, in Euro-American kinship, children of one's father's sister and brother and one's mother's sister and brother are all referred to by the same kinship term: cousins. Likewise, one's father's sister (aunt) and brother (uncle) and one's mother's sister and brother have the same terms. And the terms *grandmother* and *grandfather* can refer to the ascending generation on either one's father's or one's mother's side. In some cultures, different terms are used for kin on one's mother's and father's sides. In North India, one's father's father is *baba* and one's mother's father is *nana*. Another type of kinship system emphasizes solidarity along lines of siblings of the same gender so that one's mother and mother's sisters all have the same term, which translates as "mother." This system is found among the Navajo, for example.

Anthropologists have classified the cross-cultural variety in kinship terminology into six basic types, named after groups that were first discovered to have that type of system; for example, there is an "Iroquois" type and an "Eskimo" type (see Figure 8.2). Cultures that have similar kinship terminology are placed into one of the six categories. The Yanomami, in this way, are identified as having an Iroquois naming system. (My opinion is that memorizing these six types of terminology is not a fruitful way to promote understanding of actual kinship dynamics, so this text avoids going into detail on them.)

Toward Kinship in Action

The formalism of early kinship studies led many students of anthropology—and some of their professors—to think that kinship is a boring subject. Fortunately, a renewed interest in kinship has led to consideration of it in the context of other topics, such as power relations, reproductive decision making, women's changing work roles, and ethnic identity (Carsten 2000). We can leave much of the terminology behind, but some of the complexity of kinship systems cross-culturally must be faced.

FIGURE 8.2 **Two Kinship Naming Systems**

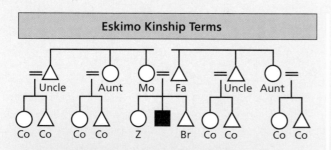

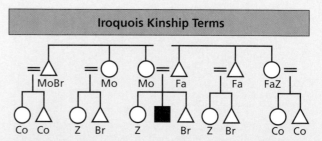

Eskimo kinship terminology, like that of most Euro-Americans, has unique terms for kin within the nuclear family that are not used for any other relatives: mother, father, sister, brother. This fact is related to the importance of the nuclear family. Another feature is that the same terms are used for relatives on both the mother's side and the father's side, a property that is related to bilineal descent.

Iroquois kinship terminology operates in unilineal systems. One result is that there are different terms for relatives on the mother's and father's sides and distinctions between cross and parallel cousins. Another feature is the "merging" of one's mother with one's mother's sister (both are referred to as "mother") and of one's father with one's father's brother (both are referred to as "father").

FIGURE 8.3 Modes of Production, Kinship, and Household Structure

FORAGING	HORTICULTURE	PASTORALISM	AGRICULTURE	INDUSTRIALISM (CAPITALIST)
Descent and Inheritance				**Descent and Inheritance**
Bilineal		Unilineal (matrilineal or patrilineal)		Bilineal
Marital Residence				**Marital Residence**
Neolocal or bilocal		Matrilocal or patrilocal		Neolocal
Household Type				**Household Type**
Nuclear		Extended		Nuclear or single-parent or single-person

As anthropologists attempt to study kinship as a dynamic aspect of life, they are increasingly turning to varied sources of data gathering, rather than simply interviewing informants. Participant observation is extremely valuable for learning about who interacts with whom, how they interact with each other, and why their relationship has the content it has. Observations can provide understanding, for example, of the frequency and intensity of people's kinship interactions and the degree to which they have supportive social networks. Another approach, the life history method (see Chapter 2), reveals changes through an individual's lifetime and the way they are related to events such as migration, a natural disaster, or political change. "Focused life histories" are useful in targeting key events related to kinship, such as marriage or cohabitation, divorce, and widowhood/widowerhood. Anthropologists interested in population dynamics, for example, use focused life histories, interviews, and questionnaires to gather information on personal demographics to learn at what age a woman commenced sexual relations, how many pregnancies she had, if and when she had an abortion or bore a child, whether the child lived or died, and when she stopped having children.

Descent

Descent is the tracing of kinship relationships through parentage. It is based on the fact that everybody is born from someone else. Descent creates a line of people from whom someone is descended, stretching through history. But not all cultures reckon descent in the same way. Some cultures have a **bilineal descent** system, in which a child is recognized as being related by descent to both parents. Others have a **unilineal descent** system, which recognizes descent through only one parent, either the father or the mother. The distribution of bilineal and unilineal systems is roughly correlated with different modes of production (see Figure 8.3 above). This correspondence makes sense because economies—production, consumption, and exchange—are closely tied to the way people and their labor power are organized and how commodities are used and transferred.

Unilineal Descent Unilineal descent systems are the basis of kinship in about 60 percent of the world's cultures and hence are the most common form of descent. In general, unilineal systems are found in societies with a "fixed" resource base, such as crop land or herds, over which people have some sense of ownership. Inheritance rules that regulate the transmission of property through only one line help maintain cohesiveness of the resource base. Unilineal systems thus are most closely associated with pastoralism, horticulture, and agricultural modes of production.

Two patterns of unilineal descent are **patrilineal descent**, in which kinship is traced through the male line alone, and **matrilineal descent**, in which kinship is traced through the female line alone. In a patrilineal system, only male children are considered members of the kinship lineage. Female children "marry out" and become members of the husband's lineage. The same applies in matrilineal descent systems, in which only daughters are considered to carry on the family line.

Jack Goody (1976), a leading kinship theorist of the later twentieth century, advanced our thinking in this area. He developed a comparative approach that reveals differences between the descent systems of rural sub-Saharan Africa and Eurasia. In sub-Saharan African groups that rely on horticultural production, women are prominent as producers, reproducers, marketers, and decision makers. Their matrilineal descent system recognizes and perpetuates the importance of women. In rural Eurasia, in contrast, plough agriculture has long been the mode of production. As discussed in Chapter 3, males are primarily involved with plough agricultural systems, and women play complementary roles in animal care, food processing, weeding, and harvesting. The patrilineal descent system associated with this mode of production does not give women's tasks high value. Members of the gender that controls the resources (both productive and reproductive) tend to have higher status. Thus, in general, women have higher status in matrilineal societies, and men have higher status in patrilineal societies. The question of *why* a particular culture is matrilineal or patrilineal has not been resolved.

Patrilineal descent is found among about 44 percent of all cultures. It is prevalent throughout much of India,

East Asia, the Middle East, Papua New Guinea, northern Africa, and some horticultural groups of sub-Saharan Africa. Margery Wolf's book, *The House of Lim* (1968), is a classic ethnography of a patrilineal system. Wolf lived for two years with the Lims, a Taiwanese farming household (see Figure 8.4). Wolf describes first the village setting and then the Lims' house, giving attention to the importance of the ancestral hall with its family altar, where the household head meets guests. She next provides a chapter on Lim Han-ci, the father and household head, and then a chapter on Lim Hue-lieng, the eldest son. She next introduces the females of the family: wives, sisters, and an adopted daughter. The ordering of the chapters reflects the importance of the "patriarch" (senior, most powerful male) and his eldest son, who will, if all goes according to plan, assume the leadership position as his father ages and dies. Daughters marry out into other families. In-marrying females (wives, daughters-in-law) are always considered outsiders and are never fully merged into the patrilineage. The Lim's kinship system exemplifies strong patrilineality in that it heavily weights position, power, and property with males. In such systems, girls are raised "for other families" and are thus not fully members of their natal (birth) family; however,

FIGURE 8.4   The Lim Family of Taiwan

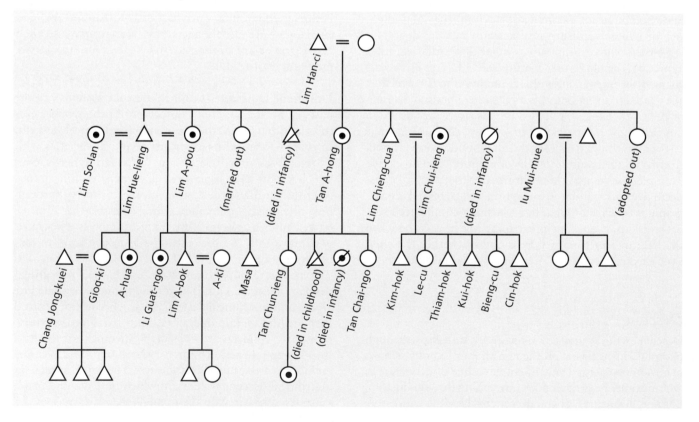

they never become fully merged into their marriage family either and hence are always considered somehow "outsiders." Residence of married couples is typically **patrilocal,** with or near the husband's natal family. The world's most strongly patrilineal systems are found in East Asia, South Asia, and the Middle East. (See the Unity and Diversity box on page 182.)

Matrilineal descent exists in about 15 percent of all cultures. It traces kinship through the female line exclusively, and children belong to their mother's group. It is found among many Native North American groups; across a large band in central Africa; among many groups of Southeast Asia and the Pacific, and Australia; in parts of eastern and southern India; in a small pocket of northern Bangladesh; and in localized parts of the Mediterranean coast of Spain and Portugal. Matrilineal societies vary greatly, from foragers such as the Tiwi of northern Australia to settled ranked societies such as the Nayar of southern India (Lepowsky 1993:296). The majority, however, are found in horticultural systems where women have primacy in production and distribution of food and other goods. Married couples tend to reside **matrilocally,** with or near the wife's natal family. Often, but not always, matrilineal kinship is associated with recognized public leadership positions for women, as among the Iroquois and Hopi.

The Minangkabau (pronounced mee-NAN-ka-bow, the last syllable rhyming with "now") of Indonesia are the largest matrilineal group in the world (Sanday 2002). They are primarily agriculturalists, producing substantial amounts of surplus rice, but many of them also participate in migratory labor, working for wages in Indonesian cities for a time and then returning home. In their matrilineal kinship system, women hold power through their control of lineage land and its products and of agricultural employment on their land and through their preeminent position in business (especially having to do with rice). Inheritance passes from mothers to daughters, making the matrilineal line the enduring controller of property. Each submatrilineage, constituting several generations, lives together in a lineage house or several closely located houses. The senior woman has the power—her decisions are sought in all economic and ceremonial matters. The senior male of the sublineage has the role of representing its interests to other groups, but he is only a representative, not a powerful person in his own right.

Double Descent   A minority of cultures have double descent systems (also called double unilineal descent) that combine patrilineal and matrilineal descent. In these systems, offspring are believed to inherit different personal attributes and property from both their father's line and their mother's line. For example, the Bangangté of Cameroon in West Africa have a double descent system (Feldman-Savelsberg 1995). Through the maternal line, one inherits movable property (such as household goods and cattle), personality traits, and a type of witchcraft substance that resides in the intestines. Patrilineal ties determine physical resemblance and rights to land and village residence.

Bilineal Descent   Bilineal descent traces kinship from both parents equally to the child. Family groups tend to be nuclear, with strong bonds linking father, mother, and their children. Marital residence is predominantly **neolocal,** or involving residence for the married couple somewhere away from the residence of both the bride's and the groom's parents. Neolocality offers more flexibility than what is usual in unilineal systems. Inheritance of property from the parental generation is allocated equally among all offspring regardless of their gender. In bilineal descent systems, conception theories emphasize an equal biological contribution to the child from the mother and father. For example, contemporary Western science states that the sperm contributed by the male and the ovum contributed by the female are equally important in the formation of a new person.

Bilineal descent is found in less than one-third of the world's cultures (Murdock 1965 [1949]:57). The highest frequency of bilineal descent is found at the opposite ends of the production continuum (refer to Figure 8.3 on page 179). For example, the Ju/wasi have bilineal descent, and most people think bilineal descent is the prevalent pattern in the United States. (See the Critical Thinking box on pge 184.) A minority pattern of bilineal descent is called **ambilineal descent.** This system recognizes that a person is descended from both parents but allows individuals to decide which descent group to be more closely affiliated with. Such a culture is therefore characterized by **bilocal** residence. For example, in Tahiti, newly married couples choose to live either with or near cither the bride's or the groom's family, with no particular preference involved (Lockwood 1993).

Given that most of the world's people recognize the biological connection between a baby and both parents, it is puzzling why the majority of kinship systems are unilineal and thus emphasize only one parent. Evolutionists of the late 1800s (Chapter 1) claimed that in early societies, the father was not known. Bilineal kinship, they said, emerged as "higher civilization" and male dominance emerged, granting the male greater recognition in paternity. Thus, unilineal kinship systems are remnants of earlier times. This argument is weak on two grounds. First, it is ethnocentric to claim that contemporary bilineal cultures, especially Euro-American cultures, are the only ones that recognize the father's biological role. Evidence from many unilineal cultures indicates widespread recognition of paternity. Second, foraging peoples tend

Unity and Diversity

THE NAMED AND THE NAMELESS IN A CANTONESE VILLAGE

THE VILLAGE of Ha Tsuen is located in the northwest corner of a rural area of Hong Kong (Watson 1988). About 2500 people live in the village. All the males belong to the same patrilineage and have the same surname of Teng. They are descended from a common ancestor who settled in the region in the twelfth century. In Ha Tsuen, as in its wider region, kinship is patrilineal. Daughters of Ha Tsuen marry out of the village. Sons of Ha Tsuen marry brides who come in from other villages, and marital residence is patrilocal.

Women do not own property, and they have no direct control of the means of production. Few married women are employed in wage labor; rather, they depend on their husbands for financial support. Local politics is a male domain, as is all public decision making.

A woman's status as a new bride is low, and the transition from daughter to bride can be difficult psychologically. Women's primary role is in reproduction, especially of sons. As a woman bears children, especially sons, her status in the household increases.

The naming system reflects the greater power, importance, and autonomy of males. A child is first given a name referred to as his or her *ming* when it is thirty days old. Before that time, the mother and infant are secluded to prevent soul loss in the infant. The thirty-day ceremony is as elaborate as the family can afford if the baby is a boy, including a banquet for neighbors and village elders and the presentation of red eggs to everyone in the community. For a girl, the thirty-day ceremony likely involves just a special meal for close family members. Paralleling this bias toward sons in monetary expenditure is the amount of thinking that goes into the selection of the ming and its meaning. A boy's ming is distinctive and flattering, perhaps having a literary or classical connection. A girl's ming often has negative connotations, such as "Last Child," "Too Many," "Little Mistake," or "Joined to a Brother," which implies hope that she will be a lucky charm to bring the birth of a son

next. Uncomplimentary names may be given to a boy, but the goal is for protection: to trick the spirits into thinking he is only a worthless girl so that they won't take him. Thus, a precious son may be given the ming "Little Slave Girl."

Marriage is the next formal naming occasion. When a male marries, he is given or chooses for himself a *tzu,* or marriage name. Gaining a tzu is an integral part of the marriage ceremony and a key marker of male adulthood. The tzu is not used in everyday address, but appears mainly on formal documents. A man also has a *wai hao,* "outside name," which is his public nickname. As he enters middle age, he may take a *hao* or courtesy name, which he chooses and which reflects his self-aspirations and self-perceptions. In the case of a woman, her ming ceases to exist upon her marriage. She no longer has a name, but instead her husband refers to her as *nei jen,* "inner person," since now her life is restricted to the domestic world of household, husband's family, and neighborhood. In her married life, she is referred to by **teknonyms,** or names for someone based on their relationship to someone else, such as "Wife of So and So," "Mother of So and So." Her personhood and identity are rigidly defined by the kinship system, and her names are derived from her place in that system. In old age, she becomes *ah po,* "Old Woman," like every other aged female in the village.

Throughout their lives, men accumulate more and better names than women, and they can choose many of these names themselves. Over the course of their lives, women have fewer names than men. Women's names are standardized rather than personalized, and they have no control over them.

FOOD FOR THOUGHT

Do you know of any examples of naming biases determined by a child's gender, or birth order, or other factor?

to have bilineal kinship, suggesting that the world's earliest humans may have also had bilineal kinship.

In attempting to explain the relative scarcity of bilineal systems, cultural materialists suggest that the mode of production influences the type of kinship system. They point out that bilineal kinship systems are associated mainly with two modes of production: foraging and industrialism. Both modes of production rely on a flexi-

ble gender division of labor in which both males and females contribute, relatively equally, to production and exchange. Logically, then, a bilineal kinship system recognizes the strengths of both the mother's and father's side. Bilineal kinship is adaptive for foraging and industrial populations because it fits with small family units that are spatially mobile. Bilineal kinship offers the most flexibility in terms of residence, keeping open opportunities related to making a living. As the world becomes increasingly urbanized and industrialized, and if the gender division of labor and resource entitlements were to become more equal, then bilineal kinship might increase in distribution.

As noted earlier, residence rules often match the prevailing "direction" of descent rules (refer to Figure 8.3). Thus, in most patrilineal societies, marital residence is patrilocal (with or near the male's kin). In most matrilineal societies, it is matrilocal (with or near the woman's kin) or **avunculocal** (with or near the groom's mother's brother). Common in Western industrialized society is the practice of neolocality. These residence patterns have political, economic, and social implications. The combination of matrilineal descent and matrilocal residence, for example, is often found among groups that engage in long-distance warfare (Divale 1974). Strong female household structures maintain the domestic scene while the men are absent on military campaigns, as among the Iroquois of upstate New York and the Nayar of southern India. Patrilineal descent and patrilocal residence promote the development of cohesive male-focused lineages that are associated with frequent local warfare, which requires the presence of a force of fighting men on the home front.

Sharing

Many cultures give priority to kinship that is based not on biologically defined birth but on acts of sharing and support. These relationships may be informal or formally certified, as in legalized adoption. Ritually formalized kinship fits in this category, including godparenthood (kinship based on ritual ties) and blood brotherhood (kinship based on sharing of "blood" or some other substance).

Food Sharing Sharing-based kinship is common throughout much of Southeast Asia, New Guinea, and Australia (Carsten 1995). On an island of Malaysia, the process of developing sharing-based relatedness starts in the womb and continues throughout a person's life. The first food sharing is when the fetus is fed by the mother's blood. After birth, the infant is fed from its mother's breast. Breast milk is believed to derive from the mother's blood, and thus "blood becomes milk." This tie is crucial. A child who is not breastfed will not "recognize" its mother. Breastfeeding is the basis of the incest rule: Kin who have been fed from the same breast may not marry. After the baby is weaned, its most important food is cooked rice. Sharing cooked rice, like breast milk, becomes another way the kinship ties are created and maintained, especially between mothers and children. Men are often away—on fishing trips, in coffee shops, or at the mosque—and so they are less likely to have these rice-sharing bonds.

Adoption and Fostering Transferring children from their birth parent to the care of others through adoption and fostering is found in all cultures. Adoption offers a cultural solution to the natural unevenness in human reproduction. Common motivations for adopting a child include infertility and the desire to obtain a particular kind of child (often a son). Motivations for the birth parent to transfer the child to someone else's care include having a premarital pregnancy in cultures that do not condone children being born outside a marriage relationship, having "too many" children as defined in that culture, and having "too many" of a particular gender of child. For example, among the Maasai, if a woman has several children, she might "give" one of hers to a friend, neighbor, or aged person who has no children or no one to care for her or him.

Fostering a child is sometimes similar to a formal adoption in terms of permanence and a developed sense of a close relationship. Or it may involve a temporary placement of a child with someone else for a specific purpose, with little development of a sense of kinship. Child fostering is common throughout sub-Saharan Africa. Parents foster out children to enhance their chances for formal education or to help them learn a skill such as marketing through apprenticeship. Most fostered children go from rural to urban areas and from poorer to better-off households. What are the lives of these fostered children like? Insights about the lives of fostered children comes from fieldwork conducted in a neighborhood in the city of Accra, Ghana (Sanjek 1990b). Child fostering in the neighborhood is common: About one-fourth of the children were foster children. Twice as many of the fostered children were girls as boys. School attendance rates, however, were biased toward boys. All of the boys were attending school, but only four of the thirty-one girls were. An important factor affecting the treatment of the child involves whether the fostered child is related to his or her sponsor. As a whole, 80 percent of the children were kin of their sponsors, but among girls, only 50 percent were kin. People who sponsor non-kin fostered girls often use the girls as maids, and they make a cash payment to the girl's parents. These child maids cook and do housecleaning. Some assist their sponsors in market work by carrying goods or watching the trading area when the market woman is elsewhere. Fostered boys do not perform such tasks because they are attending school.

A study in two villages of East Java, Indonesia, reveals that informal child fostering, or "borrowing," is common (Beattie 2002). The initiative for a child transfer is usually out of the parents' hands: The borrower approaches the parents and tells them of a dream he or she had—of rescuing a child from a flood, for example—which, in the Javanese view, gives the parents no choice but to "lend" their child. The arrangement is quite informal when children are borrowed by non-kin, and the

Critical Thinking

HOW BILINEAL IS AMERICAN KINSHIP?

"AMERICAN KINSHIP" is a general model based on the bilineal system of Euro-Americans of the 1960s (Schneider 1968). According to this model, children are considered to be descended from both mother and father, and general inheritance rules suggest that property is divided equally between sons and daughters. Given the rich cultural diversity of the United States and Canada, most would now consider the label "American kinship" and its characterization as bilineal to be overgeneralized.

In reality, aspects of both patrilineality and matrilineality exist. Indicators of patrilineality include the practice of a wife dropping her surname at marriage and taking her husband's surname, and using the husband's surname for offspring. Although inheritance is supposedly equal between sons and daughters, often it is not. In many business families, the business is passed from father to sons, while daughters are given a different form of inheritance such as a trust fund. On the other hand, a degree of **matrifocality** (a domestic system in which the mother is the central figure) arises from another source: high rates of divorce and the resulting trend of more young children living with the mother than with the father. A matrifocal emphasis creates

mother-centered residence and child-raising patterns. It may also affect inheritance patterns.

In order to explore descent patterns in the United States, each student in the class should draw his or her own kinship diagram. Students should note their microculture or ethnicity at the top of the chart, choosing the label that they prefer. Then each student should draw a circle around the relatives who are "closest" to ego, including parents, grandparents, aunts, uncles, cousins—whoever fits in this category as defined by ego. As a group, students in the class should then consider the following questions about the kinship diagrams.

CRITICAL THINKING QUESTIONS

How many students drew equal circles around relatives on both parents' sides? How many emphasized the mother's side? How many emphasized the father's side?

Do microcultural or ethnic patterns emerge in terms of the circled kin?

From this exercise, what can be said about "American kinship"?

child takes turns spending time with both families, having a meal or nap here and there. When a child is borrowed by a kinsperson, though, the arrangement is more likely to be ritually sealed. Foster parents are renamed "mother" and "father," and the child calls the natural mother "elder sister." Whether or not a child is fostered, Javanese children have flexible living arrangements, spending time in different houses, eating and sleeping wherever they feel at home. This kinship fluidity mirrors fluidity in other aspects of life, such as gender roles and religion. No strict dichotomy in gender roles exists between "male" and "female." Rather, there is a wide spectrum of possibilities, with much room in the middle, androgynous ground. A similar flexibility exists in the realm of religion; people are either Hindu or Muslim, but not rigidly so in either case. It is possible to transfer from one to the other, depending on political circumstances. For example, many Muslims became Hindu during the Suharto regime, even though a strict interpretation of Hinduism would say that one has to be born a Hindu.

Legalized Adoption in the United States

Currently, about one of every ten couples in the United States is infertile, and many of these couples would like to have children. Some use fertility drugs, *in vitro* fertilization, or surrogate child bearing. Many people, including those who have biologically recognized children, choose to adopt. Since the mid-1800s, adoption has been a legalized form of child transfer in the United States. It is "a procedure which establishes the relationship of parent and child between persons not so related by nature" (Leavy and Weinberg 1979, quoted in Modell 1994:2). Judith Modell, cultural anthropologist and adoptive parent, studied people's experiences of adoptees, birth parents, and adoptive parents. According to Modell, the biological relationship of kinship is so pervasive in the United States that the legal process of adoption attempts to construct the adoptive relationship to be as much like a biological one as possible. The adopted child is given a new birth certificate, and the birth parent ceases to have any relationship to the child. This pattern is called

An orphanage in Shanghai, China. Human rights activists have claimed that abuse—especially of children with physical handicaps—was widespread in Chinese orphanages. Following this allegation, foreign media were invited to visit the Shanghai Children's Welfare Institute. ■ *Have you ever visited an orphanage? If so, what were your impressions? If not, do you know of the existence of orphanages in your microculture?* (Source: © Reuters/Will Burgess)

"closed adoption." A recent trend is toward "open adoption," in which adoptees and birth parents have access to information about each other's identity and have freedom to interact with one another. Of the twenty-eight adoptees Modell talked with, most, but not all, were interested in searching for their birthparents. For many adoptees, a search for birth parents involves an attempt to discover "who I really am." For others, such a search is backward-looking and not a path toward formulating one's identity. Thus, in the United States, adoption legalizes sharing-based kinship but does not completely replace a sense of descent-based kinship for everyone involved.

Ritually Established Sharing Bonds Ritually defined "sponsorship" of children descended from other people is common throughout the Christian—especially Catholic—world from South America to Europe and the Philippines. Relationships between godparents and godchildren often involve strong emotional ties and financial flows from the former to the latter. In Arembepe, a village in Bahia state in northeastern Brazil, "Children asked their godparents for a blessing the first time they saw them each day. Godparents occasionally gave cookies, candy, and money, and larger presents on special occasions" (Kottak 1992:61).

In the village of Santa Catalina in the Oaxaca Valley of southern Mexico, godparenthood is both a sign of the sponsor's status and the means to increased status (Sault 1985). A request to be a sponsor is acknowledgment of a person's ability to care for the child and reflects well on one's entire family. It also gives the godparent influence over the godchild. Because the godparent can call on the godchild for labor, being a godparent of many children increases power by bestowing the ability to amass a labor force when needed. Most sponsors are male–female couples, but a notable number of sponsors are women alone. This pattern reflects the important role and high status of women in the Mayan culture of the Oaxaca region.

Marriage

The third major basis for forming close interpersonal relationships is through marriage or other forms of "marriage-like" relationships, such as long-term cohabitation. This section discusses mainly formal marriage.

Toward a Definition Anthropologists recognize that marriage exists in all cultures, though it may take different forms and serve different functions. However, what constitutes a cross-culturally valid definition of marriage is open to debate. A standard definition from 1951 is now discredited: "Marriage is a union between a man and a woman such that children born to the woman are the recognized legitimate offspring of both parents" (Barnard and Good 1984:89). This definition says that the partners must be of different genders. It implies that a child born outside a marriage is not socially recognized as legitimate. Exceptions exist to both these features cross-culturally. Same-gender marriages are legal in Denmark, Norway, and Holland. In the United States in 2000, the state of Vermont passed a law giving legal

A Khasi couple in their wedding clothes. The Khasi, who live in the hilly regions of northeastern India and northern Bangladesh, trace descent through women, and children take the last name of their mothers. ■ *What information on matrilineal cultures can you discover on the Internet?* (Source: © Reuters/Utpal Baruha)

108–109). In this type of marriage, a woman with economic means gives gifts to obtain a "wife," goes through the marriage rituals with her, and brings her into the residential compound just as a man would who married a woman. This wife contributes her productive labor to the household. The two women do not have a sexual relationship. Instead, the in-married woman will have sexual relations with a man. Her children will belong to the compound into which she married, however. This arrangement supplies the adult woman's labor and her children's labor to the household compound.

The range of practices that come under the heading of marriage make it impossible to find a definition that will fit all cases. One might accept the following as a working definition of **marriage**: a more or less stable union, usually between two people, and who are likely to be, but are not necessarily, coresident, sexually involved with each other, and procreative with each other.

Selecting a Spouse   All cultures have preferences about whom one should and should not marry or with whom one should and should not have sexual intercourse. Sometimes these preferences are informal and implicit, and other times they are formal and explicit.

Rules of Exclusion

Some sort of **incest taboo,** or a rule prohibiting marriage or sexual intercourse between certain kinship relations, is one of the most basic and universal rules of exclusion.

In his writings of the 1940s, Claude Lévi-Strauss dealt with the question of why all cultures have kinship systems. In his classic ethnological study, *The Elementary Structures of Kinship* (1969 [1949]), he argues that incest avoidance motivated men to exchange women between families (recall discussion of this topic under "Rights in People" in the discussion of exchange in Chapter 4). This exchange, he says, is the foundation for social networks and social solidarity beyond the immediate group. Such networks allow for trade between areas with different resources and the possibility that peaceful relations will exist between bride-exchangers.

Western genetic research suggests an alternative theory about why there is a universal incest taboo: Larger breeding pools help reduce the frequency of certain genetically transmitted conditions. Both theories are functional, in that they attribute the universal existence of incest taboos to their adaptive contribution, although in two different ways. No one has resolved the question of why incest taboos exist.

The most basic and universal form of incest taboo is against marriage or sexual intercourse between fathers and their children, and mothers and their children. In most cultures, brother–sister marriage has also been for-

rights to same-sex couples, as did Ontario, Canada, in 1999.

In many cultures no distinction is made between legitimate and illegitimate children on the basis of whether they were born within a marriage. Many women in the Caribbean region, for example, do not marry until later in life. Before that, a woman has sequential male partners with whom she bears children. None of her children is considered more or less "legitimate" than any other.

Other definitions of marriage focus on rights over the spouse's sexuality. But not all forms of marriage involve sexual relations; for example, the practice of woman–woman marriage exists among the Nuer of the Sudan and some other African groups (Evans-Pritchard 1951:

The marriage of two gay men in the United States in 1996. Ceremonies uniting people of the same sex are now legally recognized in some parts of the United States, Canada, and Europe. ■ *What have you read recently in newspapers about same-sex marriage?* (Source: © Jim West)

brother—the term *cross* indicates the different genders of the linking siblings. Parallel-cousin marriage is favored by many Islamic groups, especially the subform called *patrilateral parallel-cousin marriage*, which indicates a tendency for cousin marriage in the direction of the father's line rather than the mother's. Hindus of southern India favor cross-cousin marriages, especially between matrilateral cross cousins (through the mother's line). But although cousin marriage is the preferred form, it nonetheless constitutes a minority of all marriages in the region. A survey of several thousand couples in the city of Chennai [formerly called Madras, see map] in southern India showed that three-fourths of all marriages involved unrelated people, whereas one-fourth were between first cross cousins (or between uncle and niece, which is considered the same relationship as that between cross cousins) (Ramesh, Srikumari, and Sukumar 1989). Readers who are unfamiliar with cousin marriage systems may find them objectionable on the basis of the potential genetic disabilities from "close inbreeding." A study of thousands of such marriages in south India, however, revealed only a very small difference in rates of

bidden. But there are exceptions. The most well-known example of brother–sister marriage being allowed comes from Egypt at the time of the Roman Empire (Barnard and Good 1984:92). Between 15 and 20 percent of marriages were between full brothers and sisters, not just within a few royal families, as is popularly believed. In other cultures, such as the Nuer of Sudan, the incest taboo extends to the extended lineage, which may include hundreds of people. The question of cousins is dealt with in highly contrasting ways cross-culturally. Notably, incest taboos do not universally rule out marriage or sexual intercourse with cousins. In fact, some kinship systems promote cousin marriage, as discussed in the next section.

Preference Rules

In addition to incest taboos, many other rules of exclusion exist, such as prohibiting marriage with people of certain religions, races, or ethnic groups. Such exclusionary rules are often stated in the inverse—as rules of preference for marriage *within* a particular religion, race, or ethnic group.

A variety of preference rules exist cross-culturally concerning whom one should marry. Rules of **endogamy,** or marriage within a particular group, stipulate that the spouse must be chosen from within a defined pool of people. In kin endogamy, certain relatives are preferred, often cousins. Two major forms of cousin marriage exist. One is marriage between **parallel cousins,** children of either one's father's brother or one's mother's sister—the term *parallel* indicates that the linking siblings are of the same gender. The second is marriage between **cross cousins,** children of either one's father's sister or one's mother's

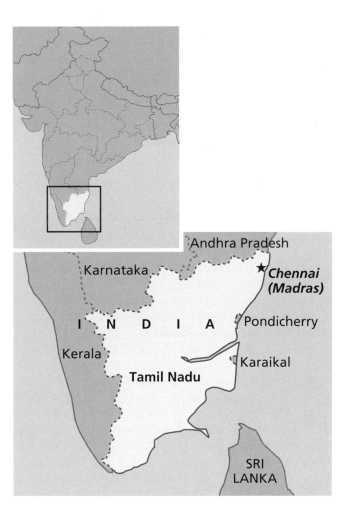

Males and females throughout much of Southeast Asia are approximately the same size, as is the case with this couple from Bali, Indonesia. ■ *What are your cultural perceptions of the height of an ideal partner for you?* (Source: © Rick Smolan/Stock Boston, LLC)

certain "birth defects" as compared to cultures in which cousin marriage is not practiced (Sundar Rao 1983). But marriage pools in South India are in fact quite diffuse, offering many options for "cousins," in contrast to a closed pool such as one village.

Endogamy may also be based on location. Village endogamy is a basis of arranging marriages throughout the eastern Mediterranean among Christians and Muslims. Village endogamy is the preferred pattern among Muslims throughout India and among Hindus of southern India. Hindus of northern India, in contrast, forbid village endogamy and consider it a form of incest. Instead, they practice village **exogamy** ("marriage out"). For them, a preferred spouse should live in a far-off village or town. Thus marriage distance is greater in the north than in the south, and brides are far less likely to maintain regular contact with their natal kin in the north. Many songs and folktales of north Indian women convey sadness about being separated from their natal families, a theme that may not make much sense in a situation of village endogamy, where the bride's parents are likely to be close by.

Status considerations often shape spouse selection. The rule of **hypergyny** requires the groom to be of higher status than the bride; in other words, the bride "marries up." Hypergyny is a strong rule in northern India, especially among upper-status groups. It is also implicitly followed among many people in the United States, where females "at the top" have the hardest time finding an appropriate partner because there are so few options "above them." Women medical students are a prime population experiencing an increased marriage squeeze because of status hypergyny. The opposite is **hypogyny**, when the female "marries down." Status hypogyny is rare cross-culturally, as is age hypogyny, in which the groom is younger than the bride. Age hypogyny, though rare as a preferred pattern, is increasing in the United States because of the marriage squeeze on women who would otherwise prefer a husband of equal age or somewhat older. **Isogamy**, marriage between equals, is found in cultures where male and female roles and status are more equal.

Physical features, such as ability, looks, and appearance, are factors that may be explicitly or implicitly recognized. Facial beauty, skin color, hair texture and length, height, and weight are variously defined as important. Height hypergyny (in which the groom is taller than the bride) is more common in male-dominated contexts. Height-isogamous marriages are common in cultures where gender roles are relatively equal and where sexual dimorphism (differences in shape and size of the female body compared to the male body), is not marked, as in much of Southeast Asia.

People with physical disabilities, particularly women, face constraints in marrying nondisabled partners (Sentumbwe 1995). Nayinda Sentumbwe, a blind researcher, conducted fieldwork with participants in education and rehabilitation programs for blind people in Uganda. He realized that all of the married women in his study had blind spouses, but few of the married men did. In exploring the reason for this pattern, Sentumbwe considered Ugandan perceptions of blind people and gender relations, especially the housewife role. Most Ugandans consider blindness to be the worst of all physical disabilities. In their perception, blindness decreases women's competence as wives and mothers and reduces their desirability as spouses. Ugandan housewives have many roles: mother, hostess, housekeeper, homestead-keeper, provider of meals, and provider of home-grown food, among others. It is important for men to have "competent" wives, and so they avoid blind women as partners. Instead, men often choose blind women as lovers. The relationship between lovers is private and does not involve social competence in the woman.

The importance of romantic love as a requirement for marriage is a matter of debate between biological determinists and cultural constructionists. Biological determinists argue that feelings of romantic love are universal among all humans because they play an adaptive role in uniting males and females in care of offspring. Cultural constructionists, in contrast, argue that romantic love is far from universal—that it is an unusual, even "aberrant," factor influencing spouse selection (Little 1966, quoted in Barnard and Good 1984:94). In support of a cultural constructionist position, anthropologists point to variations in male and female economic roles to explain cross-cultural differences in an emphasis on romantic love. Romantic love is more likely to be an important factor in relationships in cultures where men contribute more to subsistence and where women are therefore economically dependent on men. Whatever the cause of romantic love, it is a common basis for marriage in many cultures (Levine et al. 1995).

Within the United States, microcultural variations exist in the degree to which women value romantic love as a basis for marriage. Dorothy Holland and Margaret Eisenhart (1990) conducted a study of young American women just entering college in 1979–1981 and again in 1987 after the women had graduated and begun their adult lives. Their research sites were two southern colleges in the United States, one attended predominantly by White Euro-Americans and the other by African Americans. They found a contrast between the women of the two colleges. The White women were much more committed to notions of romantic love than the Black women. This pattern matched differences in career goals and expectations of future earning ability. White women were less likely to have strong career goals and more likely to expect to be economically dependent on their spouse. The Black women expressed self-dependence and stronger career goals. The ideology of romantic love apparently "derails" many young White women from competing with men in the job market. The theme of romantic love supplies young women with a model of the heroic male provider as the ideal, with her role being one of attracting him and offering the domestic context for their married life. Black women are socialized to be more economically autonomous, a pattern that stems from African traditions in which women earn and manage their own earnings.

Arranged marriages, are formed, instead, as a link between the two families involved and on the basis of considerations of what constitutes a "good match" between the families. Arranged marriages are common in many Middle Eastern, African, and Asian countries. Some theorists have claimed that arranged marriages are "traditional" whereas love marriages are "modern." They believe arranged marriages will disappear with modernity. Japan presents a case of a highly industrialized economy with a highly educated population in which arranged unions constitute a substantial proportion of all marriages, about 25 to 30 percent (Applbaum 1995). In earlier times, marriage partners would be found through personal networks, perhaps with the help of an intermediary who knew both families. Now, in large cities such as Tokyo and Osaka, professional matchmakers are important sources for finding marriage partners. The most common considerations in one's search for a spouse

The Taj Mahal, located in Agra, north India, is a seventeenth-century monument to love. It was built by the Mughal emperor Shah Jahan as a tomb for his wife, Mumtaz Mahal, who died in childbirth in 1631. ■ *What other architectural monuments to love or marriage can you name?* (Source: Jack Heaton)

are the family's reputation and social standing, the absence of undesirable traits such as a case of divorce or mental illness in the family, and the potential spouse's education, income, and occupation.

Marriage Gifts Most marriages are accompanied by gift-giving, of goods or services, between the partners, members of their families, or friends. The major forms of marital exchanges cross-culturally are dowry and brideprice (defined in Chapter 5). Dowry involves the transfer of goods, and sometimes money, from the bride's side to the new conjugal unit for their use. This "classic" form of dowry includes household goods such as furniture, cooking utensils, and sometimes rights to a house. Dowry is the predominant form of marriage transfer in a broad region of Eurasia, from Western Europe through the northern Mediterranean and into China and India (Goody 1976). In northern India, dowry is more appropriately termed *groomprice* because the goods and money pass not to the new couple but rather to the groom's family (Billig 1992). In China during the Mao era, marriage gifts of any type were viewed as a sign of women's oppression and made illegal. Now, marriage gifts are becoming more common with the recent increase in consumerism (Whyte 1993).

Brideprice, or the transfer of goods or money from the groom's side to the bride's parents, is more common in horticultural and pastoral cultures, whereas dowry is associated with intensive agricultural societies. In cultures where dowry and brideprice are given, recent decades have brought an inflation in the required amounts, making it difficult in some cases for young people to marry. **Bride-service,** less common than brideprice, is still practiced in some horticultural societies, especially in the Amazon. Bride-service involves the groom working for his father-in-law for a certain period of time before returning home with the bride. Bride-service is paid in labor rather than in goods.

Many marriages involve gifts from both the bride's and the groom's side. For example, a typical pattern in the United States is for the groom's side to be responsible for paying for the rehearsal dinner the night before the wedding and for the bride's side to be responsible for everything else.

The woman on the lower right is part of a polyandrous marriage, which is common among Tibetan peoples. She is married to several brothers, two of whom stand behind her. The older man with the sash in the front row is her father-in-law. ■ *For people who have grown up in monogamous cultures, the daily dynamics of polyandry are difficult to imagine. Ask yourself why this is so.* (Source: © Thomas L. Kelly/Woodfin Camp & Associates)

Forms of Marriage   Cultural anthropologists distinguish two forms of marriage on the basis of the number of partners involved. **Monogamy** is marriage between two people—a male or female if the pair is heterosexual, two people of the same gender in the case of a homosexual pair. Heterosexual monogamy is the most common form of marriage cross-culturally, and in many countries, is the only legal form of marriage.

Polygamy is marriage with multiple spouses, a pattern allowed by the majority of the world's cultures, even though the majority of people within such cultures may not practice plural marriage (Murdock 1965:24 [1949]). Two forms of polygamous marriage exist. The predominant pattern is **polygyny,** marriage of one man with more than one woman. Within cultures that allow polygyny, the majority of unions nevertheless are monogamous. **Polyandry,** or marriage between one woman and more than one man, is rare. However, it has been practiced among groups as diverse as the Kaingang of the Amazon, the Todas of southern India, and the Chukchee of Siberia. One region in which polyandry occurs over a large area includes Tibet, the Himalayan region of India, and parts of Nepal.

Anthropologists have asked why polygyny exists in some cultures and not in others (White and Burton 1988). Evolutionary theorists suggested that polygyny constituted a middle stage. Engels's three stages, for example,

went from "group marriage" (in which everyone was supposedly married to everyone else, a hypothetical situation unknown ethnographically for the past or the present), polygyny, and then monogamy. Biological determinists say that polygyny contributes to males' reproductive success by allowing them to maximize the spread of their genes in future generations. But neither evolutionary nor biological determinist models can explain the cross-cultural variation in the distribution of polygyny. Economic theories have been proposed. One economic hypothesis states that polygyny is more likely where women's contribution to the economy is more important. Political and demographic factors have also been examined, especially the role of warfare in reducing the ratio of males to females, and the taking of female captives in warfare. Data for 142 societies show that one factor alone cannot explain the presence or absence of polygyny (White and Burton 1988). Instead, support for a set of interrelated views emerges:

■ Polygyny fits with an expansionist economic strategy in homogeneous and high-quality environments.

■ Polygyny is associated with warfare for plunder and/or female captives.

■ Polygyny is associated with the presence of strongly bonded groups of males linked through ties between brothers.

- Polygyny is constrained in the context of plow agriculture or by high dependence on fishing.

Some support was found for the hypothesis about the effect of female contribution to subsistence, but not at such a strong level as for these factors.

HOUSEHOLDS AND DOMESTIC LIFE

In casual conversation, North Americans might use the words *family* and *household* interchangeably to refer to people who live together. Social scientists have proposed a distinction between the two terms, both of which may refer to a *domestic group*, or people who live together. A **family** includes people who consider themselves related through kinship—descent, marriage, or sharing. In North American English, the term *family* includes both close or immediate relatives and more distant relatives. One may live with some members of one's family every day and see them but see others only once a year on a major holiday, or less. People who are considered close family relatives may be scattered in several different residences, including grandparents, aunts, uncles, cousins, and children of divorced parents who may live with different parents. The notion of the family as a clearly defined unit with firm boundaries thus often misrepresents the fluidity of this category (Lloyd 1995).

In contrast, the term **household** refers to a domestic group who may or may not be related by kinship and who share living space, including perhaps a kitchen and certain budgetary items such as food and rent. Most households around the world consist of family members who are related through kinship, but an increasing number do not. An example of a non-kin household is a group of friends who live in the same apartment. A single person living alone also constitutes a household.

In this section of the chapter, we look at household forms and household organization cross-culturally. We also examine relationships between and among household members.

The Household: Variations on a Theme

In this section, we consider three major forms of households and then examine the concept of household headship. The topic of female-headed households receives detailed attention because this pattern of headship is of considerable contemporary policy interest.

Household Forms

Household organization can be categorized into several types according to how many married adults are involved. Single-person households comprise only one member, living alone. A single-parent household comprises an adult with offspring. The **nuclear household** (which many people call the nuclear family) contains one adult couple (married or "partners"), with or without children. **Extended households** contain more than one adult married couple. These couples may be related through the father–son line (making a patrilineal extended household such as the Lims of Taiwan, Figure 8.4) through the mother–daughter line (a matrilineal extended household), or through sisters or brothers (a collateral extended household). Polygynous (multiple wives) and polyandrous (multiple husbands) households are complex households in which one spouse has multiple partners. They may all live together in one residence or, as is the case in many African polygynous households, each wife has a separate residential unit within the overall household compound.

The precise cross-cultural distribution of these various types is not known. However, some broad generalizations can be offered. First, nuclear household units are found in all cultures (Murdock 1965:2 [1949]). The nuclear household as the exclusive household type is characteristic of about one-fourth of the world's cultures. One-half of all cultures are characterized by the presence of extended households. The distribution of nuclear versus complex household forms roughly corresponds with modes of production (Figure 8.3 on page 179). The nuclear form is most characteristic of economies at the two extremes of the continuum: in foraging groups and in industrialized societies, reflecting the need for spatial mobility and flexibility in making a living. Polygynous or polyandrous households and extended households constitute a substantial proportion of households in horticultural, pastoral, and nonindustrial agricultural economies. Throughout Asia—China, Japan, India—in much of Africa, and among Native North Americans, some form of complex or extended households is the ideal and frequently the reality.

In India, where extended households are the preferred form, the household may contain fifty or more members. Property provides the material base to support many people, and in turn, large land holdings require a large labor force to work the land. In northern India, more households own property than in southern and eastern India, where rates of landlessness are higher. In addition to property differences, the unbalanced sex ratio in the North means there are more sons available to bring in wives and establish patrilineal extended households (see Chapter 5). Logically, then, patrilineal extended households are more common in the northern part of the coun-

In China, the stem household system is undergoing change as many people have one daughter and no son as a result of the One Child Policy and generally lowered fertility. ■ *Speculate about what the next generation of this household might contain.* (Source: © Keren Su/Stock Boston, LLC)

try (Kolenda 1968). (Recall, however, the existence of matrilineal extended households, mainly in the southern state of Kerala.)

In Japan, the extended household structure has endured within the context of an industrial and urban economy. The *ie,* or "stem household," has a long history in Japan and is still important (Skinner 1993). A variant of an extended household, a **stem household** contains two (and only two) married couples related through the males. Thus only one son remains in the household, bringing in his wife, who is expected to perform the important role of caretaker for the husband's parents as they age. The patrilineal stem household is still widely preferred, yet it is increasingly difficult to achieve. The rising aspirations of children often mean that no child is willing to live with and care for the aging parents. In this context, parents sometimes exert considerable pressure on an adult child to come and live with them (Traphagan 2000). One compromise solution is for an adult child and his or her spouse to live near the parents but not with them.

Household Headship

The question of who heads a household is often difficult to answer. This section reviews some of the approaches to this question and provides insights into how cross-cultural perceptions about household headship differ.

The *head* is the primary person (or people) in charge of supporting the household financially and making decisions. Cultural anthropologists realize that the concept of household head is an ethnocentric, Euro-American definition of one person who makes most of the money, controls most of the decision making, and was traditionally a man. European colonialism spread the concept of the male head of household around the world, along with laws that vest household authority in male headship.

The model of one male head has influenced the way official statistics are gathered and reported worldwide. The result is that if a household has a coresident male and female, there will be a tendency to report the household as "male-headed," regardless of the actual internal dynamics. In Brazil, the official definition considers only a husband to be head of the household, regardless of whether he contributes to the household budget and is married to the woman. Thus "[S]ingle, separated or widowed women who house and feed their children, grandchildren and elderly or handicapped parents are deprived of the title of head of the family. If they have a partner with them on the day when the census official arrives, he is considered to be the head of the family, whether or not he is the father of any of the children, contributes to the family income, or has been living there . . . only a few months" (de Athayde Figueiredo and Prado 1989:41). Similarly, according to official reports, 90 percent of households in the Philippines are headed by males (Illo 1985). Anthropological research shows, however, that women play a prominent role in income generation and budgetary control, and both male and female domestic partners tend to share decision making. Thus coheadship would be a more appropriate label for many households in the Philippines and elsewhere.

Many early anthropologists overlooked household headship patterns that did not conform to their Eurocentric view of male headship. Nancie González was one of the first anthropologists to define and study matrifocality, a domestic pattern in which a woman (or women) is the central, stable figure around whom other members cluster (1970:233). The mother is likely to be the primary or only income provider. The concept of matrifocality does not exclude the possibility that men may be part of the household, but they are not the central income providers or decision makers.

There has been much public discussion in the United States recently about women as household heads. Concern has arisen because the number of such households is increasing, and these households are more likely to be poorer than households that contain a married couple. What causes the formation of woman-headed households? A woman-headed household can come about if a partner existed at one time, but for some reason—such as separation, divorce, or death—is no longer part of the household, or if a partner exists but is not coresident because of migration, imprisonment, or some other form of separation. (Most thinking about woman-headed households assumes a heterosexual relationship and thus

Members of a matrifocal household in rural Jamaica: two sisters and their children. ■ *What kind of household formation pattern is prevalent in your microcultural experience?* (Source: Barbara Miller)

does not account for woman-headed households formed by a single woman with children either adopted or conceived through artificial insemination, with or without a visiting woman partner.) See Table 8.1 on page 194 for information on three theories that have been proposed to account for the absence of a male spouse or partner. The three theories about why woman-headed households exist can be labeled "compensatory theories." They suggest that a woman-headed household emerges as a default system when "something is wrong" or men are unavailable as spouses. This view is based on the assumption that the heterosexual nuclear household is the "normal" pattern. Cultural anthropology suggests, instead, that a variety of household forms are to be expected, depending on such factors as men's and women's economic roles, especially access to work, wages, and the distribution of productive resources such as property.

Intrahousehold Dynamics

How do household members interact with each other? What are their emotional attachments, rights, and responsibilities? What are the power relationships between and among members of various categories, such as spouses, siblings, and those of different generations?

Kinship systems define what the content of these relationships should be. In everyday life, people may conform more or less to the ideal. The important dimension of how people may or may not diverge from ideal roles and relationships is, oddly, one that has been neglected for a long time by cultural anthropology and has only recently attracted some attention.

Spouse/Partner Relationships

Anthropologists who study relationships between spouses and partners consider a range of topics: decision making, power relationships, degree of attachment and commitment, duration of commitment, and the possibility of intimate relationships outside the primary relationship. This section presents findings on levels of emotional satisfaction between spouses and how they may be related to extramarital relationships.

A landmark sociological study of marriages in Tokyo in 1959 compared marital satisfaction of husbands and wives in love marriages and arranged marriages (Blood 1967). In all marriages, marital satisfaction declined over time, but differences between the two types emerged. The decline was greatest for wives in arranged marriages and least for husbands in arranged marriages. In love-match marriages, husbands' satisfaction dropped dramatically and a bit later than their wives' satisfaction, but both husbands and wives have nearly equal levels of satisfaction by the time they had been married nine years and more.

Sexual activity of couples can be both an indication of marital satisfaction and a cause of marital satisfaction. Anthropologists have not studied this topic much, but help from sociologists working with survey data is available. Analysis of reports of marital sex from a 1988 survey in the United States shows that frequency per month declines with duration of marriage, from an average of twelve times per month for people aged nineteen to twenty-four years, to less than once a month for people seventy-five years of age and older (Call, Sprecher, and Schwartz 1995). Older married people have sex less frequently, as do those who report being less happy. Within each age category, sex is more frequent among three categories of people: those who are cohabiting but not married, those who cohabited before marriage, and those who are in their second or later marriage.

Sibling Relationships

Sibling relationships are another understudied aspect of kinship dynamics. Suad Joseph (1994) provides an example of research on this topic in her study of a working-class neighborhood of Beirut, Lebanon. She got to know several families well and became especially close to Hanna, the oldest son in one of these families. Hanna was an attractive young man, considered a good marriage choice, with friends across religious and ethnic groups. He seemed peace-loving and conscientious. Therefore, the author reports, "I was shocked . . . one sunny afternoon to hear Hanna shouting at his sister Flaur and slapping her across the face" (50). Aged twelve, Flaur was the oldest daughter. "She seemed to have an opinion on most things, was never shy to speak her mind, and welcomed guests with boisterous laughter. . . . With a lively sense of humor and good-natured mischief about her, neighbors thought of her as a

TABLE 8.1 Households Headed by Women: Three Theories and Cultural Critique

Slavery Theory	Poverty Theory	Unbalanced Sex Ratio Theory
The high frequency of woman-headed households among African Americans in the Western hemisphere is often said to be the heritage of slavery, which intentionally broke up marital ties. This theory has several problems. If slavery were the cause of woman-headed households, one would predict that all peoples who experienced slavery would have this household form. But this is not the case. In Jamaica, which is populated mainly by descendants of African slaves, percentages of woman-headed households vary between rural and urban areas (Miller and Stone 1983). Yet both urban and rural people have the same heritage. Likewise, in the United States, no generic "Black household" exists, just as there is no generic "White household." Homes with two coresiding parents were the norm among Black Americans following the Civil War through the mid-twentieth century. It is true that the slave system denied legal standing to adult pairings because owners did not want their slaves committed to lifetime relationships. Slaves were subject to sale, and wives and husbands, parents and children, were separated. Although such circumstances would seem to have led to a "break-up" of a conjugal [married] household tradition, it is now clear that the slaves themselves never accepted the arrangements imposed by the owners: "Once freed, blacks sought the durable unions they had been denied" (Hacker 1992:69). In the United States, percentages of woman-headed households have increased in roughly the same proportion among Blacks and Whites. Thus similar factors may underlie the changes for both populations. The distribution of woman-headed households throughout the world is more widespread than the distribution of slavery. Clearly, other factors must be involved in promoting the formation of this pattern.	Woman-headed households are said to be adaptations to poverty, because in many societies, the poor have a higher frequency of woman-headed households. If so, it is only one of many possible adaptations, because not all low-income populations worldwide are characterized by high rates of woman-headed households. Within the United States, significant ethnic differences exist: Low-income Chinese, Japanese, and other Asian peoples generally have low frequencies of single-parent households, and many low-income Mexican American communities have dual-parent families (Pelto, Roman, and Liriano 1982:40). As an explanatory factor, poverty needs to be considered along with male and female income-earning capabilities, other resources available, and other support systems. In the Caribbean region and throughout Latin America, the association between poverty and woman-headed households is strong. But beneath this seemingly negative association, some positive findings appear. In the Caribbean region, about one-third of all households have been woman-headed over the past few decades (Massiah 1983, Marcoux 2000). These women have "visiting unions," involving a steady sexual relationship but separate residences. Many women who were interviewed in a study conducted in several islands (Massiah 1983) commented that they sometimes expect and hope for financial support from their male partner or "baby father." But many others emphasized the value they place on freedom from a husband or permanent partner. One woman said, "Being single fits in with my independent thinking" (41). Another commented on her visiting union: "I like freedom, so I'm keeping it like it is."	Woman-headed households are said to occur in contexts of high male emigration or other situations causing a shortage of males. The sheer unavailability of partners limits marriage. In Spanish Galicia, the local economy, inheritance rules, and household formation are related (Kelley 1991). This coastal region has a high percentage of households headed by unmarried women. In the village of Ezaro, about one-fourth of all baptisms in the latter half of the nineteenth century were of "illegitimate" children. This proportion declined in the twentieth century, but the region still stands out from the rest of Spain. In Ezaro, households headed by unmarried mothers constitute over 10 percent of the total. Little or no stigma is attached to unwed motherhood in Galicia, in contrast to the generally high value that the Mediterranean kinship system places on marriage and male honor through control of the sexuality of female family members. Women household heads often hold honored positions. What accounts for this system? The answer lies in Galicia's high rates of male emigration. The scarcity of males promotes flexible attitudes toward unwed motherhood. In Ezaro, women are in charge of agricultural work. They inherit land and gain prestige and power from owning and managing agricultural land: "Women's work is considered so critical to the prestige of the household in Ezaro that success at work is the single most important factor in the community's evaluation of a woman's character (and in her own self-evaluation). The good woman in Ezaro is the hardworking woman" (572). Thus a woman's work is more important than her marital status. Inheritance practices reflect the importance of women's agricultural work. The goal is to ensure continuity of the *casa*, the house, which includes both the physical structure and its members. Parents usually award one of their children with a larger share of the inheritance, making that child the principal heir. Daughters are often chosen, and thus a single woman can become head of an estate. Her children ensure that the estate has continuity.

live wire" (50). Further consideration of the relationship between Hanna and Flaur indicated that Hanna played a fatherly role to Flaur. He would be especially irritated with her if she lingered on the street near their apartment building, gossiping with other girls: "He would forcibly escort her upstairs to their apartment, slap her, and demand that she behave with dignity" (51). Adult family members thought nothing was wrong and said that Flaur enjoyed her brother's aggressive attention. Flaur herself commented, "It doesn't even hurt when Hanna hits me," and said that she hoped to have a husband like Hanna.

An interpretation of this common brother–sister relationship in Arab culture is that it is part of the socializing process that maintains and perpetuates patriarchal family relationships: "Hanna was teaching Flaur to accept male power in the name of love . . . loving his sister meant taking charge of her and that he could discipline her if his action was understood to be in her interest. Flaur was reinforced in learning that the love of a man could include that male's violent control and that to receive his love involved submission to control" (52). This close and unequal sibling relationship persists throughout life. Even after marriage, a brother maintains a position of responsibility toward his sister and her children, as does a married sister toward her brother and his children. This loyalty can lead to conflict between husband and wife as they vie for support and resources from their spouse in competition with their siblings.

Domestic Violence

Domestic violence can occur between domestic partners, parents and children, and siblings. This section concerns the first of these. Violence between domestic partners, with males dominating as perpetrators and women as victims, seems to be found in nearly all cultures, although in varying forms and frequencies (J. Brown 1999). A cross-cultural review revealed that wife beating is more common and more severe where men control the wealth and is less common and less severe where women's work groups are prominent (Levinson 1989). (See the Lessons Applied box on page 196.) The presence of women's work groups is related to a greater importance of women in production and matrifocal residence. These factors provide women with the means to leave an abusive relationship. For example, among the Garifuna, an African-Indian people of Belize, Central America, incidents of spouse abuse occur, but they are infrequent and not extended (Kerns 1992). Women's solidarity in this matrifocal society limits male violence against women.

Increased domestic violence worldwide throws into question the notion of the house as a refuge or place of security. In the United States, for example, there is evidence of high and increasing rates of intrahousehold abuse of children (including sexual abuse), violence between spouses or partners, and abuse of aged family members. More cross-cultural research is needed to help policy makers understand the factors affecting the safety of individuals within households.

Household Transformations

The composition and sheer existence of a particular household can change as a consequence of several factors, including divorce, death, and possible remarriage. This section reviews some anthropological findings on these topics.

Divorce and Kinship Patterns   Divorce and separation, like marriage and other forms of long-term union,

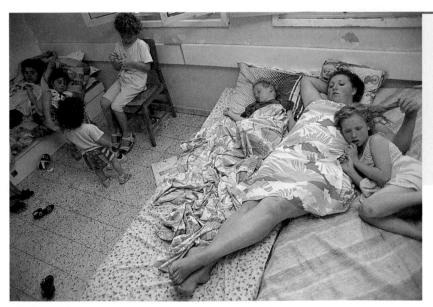

A shared bedroom in a battered woman's shelter, Tel Aviv, Israel. Many people wonder why abused women do not leave their abusers. Part of the answer lies in the unavailability and low quality of shelters throughout much of the world. ■ *Think of other factors that might prevent women from leaving their abusers.* (Source: © David Wells/The Image Works)

Lessons Applied

WIFE ABUSE IN RURAL KENTUCKY

DOMESTIC VIOLENCE in the United States is reportedly highest in the state of Kentucky. An ethnographic study of domestic violence in Kentucky revealed several cultural factors that make it difficult to prevent wife abuse in this region (Websdale 1995). The study included interviews with fifty abused wives in eastern Kentucky as well as with battered women in shelters, police officers, shelter employees, and social workers.

Three categories of isolation exist in rural Kentucky and make domestic violence particularly difficult to prevent:

- *Physical isolation* The women reported a feeling of physical isolation in their lives. Abusers' tactics were more effective because of geographical isolation:

  The batterer's strategies, according to the women, included removing the phone from the receiver (for example, when leaving for work) . . . locking the thermostat, especially in winter, as a form of torture; disabling motor vehicles to reduce or eliminate the possibility of her leaving the residence; destroying motor vehicles; closely monitoring the odometer reading on motor vehicles (a simple yet effective form of control due to the lack of alternative means of transportation); driving recklessly to intimidate his partner; discharging firearms in public (for example, at a battered woman's pet). (106–107)

  It is difficult to leave an abusive home located many miles from the nearest paved road, especially if the woman has children. No public transportation serves even the paved road. Nearly one-third of households had no phones. Getting to a phone to report abuse results in delay and gives police the impression that the call is less serious.

  Physical remoteness delays response time to calls for help and increases a woman's sense of hopelessness. "Sheriffs have acquired a very poor reputation among battered women in the region for not attending domestic calls at all.

- *Social isolation* Aspects of rural family life and gender roles lead to a system of "passive policing." In rural Kentucky, men are seen as providers and women are strongly tied to domestic work and child rearing.

When women do work, their wages are about 50 percent of men's wages. Residence is often in the vicinity of the husband's family, which creates isolation of a woman from the potential support of her natal family and restricts help-seeking in the immediate vicinity because the husband's family is likely to be nonsupportive. Police officers, especially local ones, view the family as a private unit, a man's world. They are less inclined to intervene and arrest husbands whom they feel should be dominant in the family. In some instances, the police take the batterer's side, share the batterer's understandings of the situation, and have similar beliefs in a man's right to control his wife.

- *Institutional isolation* Battered women in rural areas face special problems in using the limited services of the state. The fact that abused women often know the people who run the services ironically inhibits the women from approaching them, given values of family privacy. In addition, social services for battered women in Kentucky are scarce. Other institutional constraints include less schooling for rural women than urban women, lack of day care centers to allow mothers the option to work outside the home, inadequate health services with doctors appearing unfamiliar with domestic violence, and religious teaching of fundamentalist Christianity that supports patriarchal values, including the idea that it is women's duty to stay in a marriage, to "weather the storm."

The analysis suggests some recommendations. Women need more and better employment opportunities to reduce their economic dependency on abusive partners. Rural outreach programs should be strengthened. Expanded telephone subscriptions might decrease rural women's institutional isolation. Because of the complexity of the social situation in Kentucky, no single solution will suffice.

FOOD FOR THOUGHT

Think of some ways in which the structural conditions in Kentucky differ from or resemble those in another context where wife beating occurs.

A widow of Maderia, Portugal, wearing the typical black, modest clothing required in the Mediterranean region as a sign of widowhood. ■ *What changes are required for widows and widowers in your microculture?* (Source: © Andy Levin/Photo Researchers, Inc.)

fluid way both of joining and of breaking up. The same is true for the contemporary United States with its (more or less) bilineal system. The patrilineal kinship systems of Pakistan and northern India seem related to the low divorce rates there.

How durable are marriages with multiple spouses? Concerning the relationship between polygyny and divorce, a case study in Nigeria found that two-wife arrangements are the most stable and that unions with three or more wives have the highest rates of disruption (Gage-Brandon 1992).

Widow(er)hood   The position of a widow or widower carries altered responsibilities and rights. Women's position as widows is often marked symbolically. In Mediterranean cultures, a widow must wear modest, simple, and black-colored clothing, sometimes for the rest of her life. Her sexuality is supposed to be virtually dead. At the same time, her new "asexual" status allows her greater spatial freedom than before. She can go to public coffeehouses and taverns, something not done by women whose husbands are living.

Extreme restrictions on widows are recorded for parts of South Asia where social pressures on a widow enforce self-denial and self-deprivation, especially among the propertied class. A widow should wear a plain white sari, shave her head, eat little food, and live an asexual life. Many widows in India are abandoned, especially if they have no son to support them. They are considered polluting and inauspicious. In a similar fashion, widows there experience symbolic and life-quality changes much more than do widowers in South Africa:

> A widower is encouraged to take on the challenge of picking up the pieces and to face life again. He is reminded that he must be strong and swallow his pain. His body is not marked in any significant way except to have his head shaved, as is the custom in most African communities. He also is required to wear a black button or arm band. The period of mourning for widowers is generally six months, compared to at least one year for widows. . . . The fear of the ritual danger embodied in widows is expressed in terms of "heat," "darkness," and "dirt." . . . Her body is marked in different communities by some or all of the following practices: shaving her head, smearing a mixture of herbs and ground charcoal on her body, wearing black clothes made from an inexpensive material, and covering her face with a black veil and her shoulders with a black shawl. A widow may express her liminal status in a variety of ways, [such as by] eating with her left hand, wearing clothes inside out, wearing one shoe, or eating out of a lid instead of a plate (Ramphele 1996:100).

Remarriage   Remarriage patterns are influenced by economic factors and gender-linked expectations that shape a person's desirability as a partner. In the United

are cultural universals, even though they may be frowned on or forbidden. Marriages may break up for several reasons: The most common are voluntary separation and death of one of the partners. Globally, variations exist in the legality and propriety of divorce. Some religions, such as Roman Catholicism, prohibit divorce. In some cultures, such as Islamic societies, divorce is easier for a husband to obtain than for a wife. Important questions about marital dissolution include the causes for it, the reasons why divorce rates appear to be rising worldwide, and the implications for the welfare of children of divorced parents.

Why do divorce rates vary cross-culturally? One hypothesis suggests that divorce rates will be lower in cultures with unilineal descent, where a large descent group has control over and interests in offspring (Barnard and Good 1984:119). Royal lineages, with their strong vested interests in maintaining the family line, are examples of groups especially unlikely to favor divorce, because divorce generally means losing control of offspring.

How does this theory hold up in the face of evidence? In bilineal foraging societies, couples generally have a

A newly married husband and wife and their relatives in front of a church in Seoul, Republic of Korea. ■ *How does this wedding group resemble or differ from a wedding you have attended?* (Source: © Noboro Komine/Photo Researchers, Inc.)

States, divorce is frequently followed by remarriage for both males and females, with a slight edge for men. In Japan, the tendency to remarry is significantly greater for males than for women (Cornell 1989). A marked age distribution in nonremarriage for women exists: "[W]hile divorced Japanese women, up to age 40, are already about 15% more likely to remain divorced than are their U.S. white female counterparts of the same age, after age 40 their situation grows rapidly more unfavorable for remarriage. In the subsequent decade it rises to 25% more divorced at age 45, 40% more at age 48, more than half again as many at age 50, and 65% more at age 51" (460). Older women's lower rates of remarriage are the result of age-hypergynous marriage and males' greater access to economic and political resources that increase their attractiveness as marriage partners in spite of their increasing age.

CHANGING KINSHIP AND HOUSEHOLD DYNAMICS

This section provides examples of how marriage and household patterns are changing. Many of these changes have roots in colonialism whereas others are more the result of recent changes effected by globalization and increased population movements.

Change in Marriage

Although the institution of marriage in general remains prominent, many of its specific details are changing. Nearly everywhere, the age at first marriage is rising. This change is related to increased emphasis on completing a certain number of years of education before marriage and to rising aspirations about the potential spouse's economic status before contemplating marriage. Marriages between people of different nations and ethnicity are increasing, partly because of increased rates of international migration. Migrants take with them many of their marriage and family practices. They also adapt to rules and practices in their area of destination. Pluralistic practices evolve, such as conducting two marriage ceremonies—one based on the "original" culture and the other conforming to norms in the place of destination.

Style changes in weddings abound. Globalization of Western-style "white weddings" promotes the adoption of many features that are familiar in the West: a white wedding gown for the bride, a many-layered wedding cake, and certain kinds of floral arrangements. What the bride and groom wear is an expression of both the bride's and the groom's personal identity and also the cultural identity of their family and larger social group. Clothing choice may reflect adherence to "traditional" values or may reject those in favor of more "modern" values. Euro-American trends are prominent worldwide. Throughout much of East and Southeast Asia, advertisements and upscale stores display the Western-style white wedding gown (though less so much in India, where white clothing for women signifies widowhood and is inauspicious). On the other hand, some resurgence of local "folk" styles is occurring in some contexts, such as in Morocco, where there is a trend for "modern" brides to wear a Berber costume (long robes and jewelry characteristic of the rural, mountain people) at one stage of the wedding ceremony.

Matrilineal kinship appears to be declining worldwide in the face of both colonialism and globalization. European colonial rule in Africa and Asia contributed to the decline in matrilineal kinship by registering land and other property in the names of assumed male heads of household, even where females were the heads (Boserup 1970). This process eroded women's previous rights and powers. Western missionary influence also transformed matrilineal cultures into more patrilineal systems (Etienne and Leacock 1980). European influences have led to the decline of matrilineal kinship among Native North

Americans (which long constituted one of the largest distributions of matrilineal descent worldwide, although not all Native North American groups were matrilineal). A comparative study of kinship among three areas of the Navajo reservation in Arizona shows that matrilineality exists where conditions most resemble the pre-reservation era (Levy, Henderson, and Andrews 1989).

In the case of the Minangkabau of Indonesia, matrilineal kinship was undermined by Dutch colonialism, which promoted the image of male-led nuclear families as an ideal; by the Islamic faith, which currently promotes female domesticity and male household dominance; and by the modernizing Indonesian state, which insists on naming males as heads of households (Blackwood 1995).

Changing Households

Changing economic opportunities in recent times have led to rapid change in household structures and dynamics.

Some anthropologists argue that the frequency of extended households will decline with industrialization and urbanization, which are considered key factors of modernity. This argument is based on an assumed European model of reduced numbers of extended farming households and increased numbers of nuclear households. Taking the nuclear household as a key marker of modernity, though, has its problems. First, historical evidence indicates that nuclear households characterized nonindustrial, premodern northwestern Europe (Goody 1996). Thus the apparent transformation from extended households to nuclear households with modernity is not universal. Asian data clearly do not fit the model. In India, urban areas have a higher percentage of extended households than rural areas (Freed and Freed 1969). Further, data from India on literacy rates, often taken as an indicator of modernity and exposure to change, again show contradictory findings. A study in West Bengal state of eastern India found that heads of extended households are more likely to be literate than heads of nuclear households (Dasgupta, Weatherbie, and Mukhopadhyay 1993).

Employment of daughters in electronics factories in Malaysia has changed intrahousehold power structures (Ong 1987). The girls' mothers encourage them to take up factory work and urge them to contribute a proportion of their earnings to the household economy. This frees up daughters from their father's control (a control traditional among Malaysian Muslims), while giving greater control to the mother.

International migration is another major cause of change in household formation. Dramatic changes in reproductive patterns can occur in one generation when members of a farming household in, for example, Taiwan or India migrate to England, France, or the United States. Having many children makes economic sense in their homeland, but it does not in their new destination. These migrants decide to have only one or two children and live in small, isolated nuclear households. International migration creates new challenges for relationships between parents and children. The children often become strongly identified with the new culture and have little connection with their ancestral culture, and this pattern can be a source of anxiety for their parents. Often, values in the new culture conflict with those of the culture of origin, putting children in conflict with their parents over issues such as dating, dress, and career goals.

In 1997, the people of Norway were confronted with a case of kidnapping of an eighteen-year-old Norwegian citizen named "Nadia," who was taken by her parents to Morocco and held captive there (Wikan 2000). The full story is a complicated one, but the core issues revolve around conflict between Moroccan family values and Norwegian ones. Nadia's parents felt that she should be under their control and that they had the right to arrange her marriage in Morocco, whereas Nadia held a Norwegian concept of personal autonomy. In the end, Nadia and her parents returned to Norway, where the courts ruled that, for the sake of the family, the parents would not be jailed on grounds of kidnapping their daughter. The case brought stigma to Nadia among the Muslim community of Norway, who viewed her as a traitor to her culture. She now lives at a secret address and avoids publicity. An anthropologist close to this case who served as an expert cultural witness during the trial of her parents reports that, in spite of her seclusion, she has offered help to other young women who have sought her out.

What about domestic life in this new millennium? Basic outlines of the near future indicate the reduced economic dependence of women and the weakening of marriage in industrialized societies (Cherlin 1996: 478–480). These changes, in turn, will lead to increased movement away from nuclear household living and to increased diversity in household forms.

During the second half of the twentieth century, household size in the United States shrank from an average of 3.3 to 2.6 persons (U.S. Bureau of the Census 1999:60). The current situation contains several seemingly contradictory patterns first noted in the early 1980s by two sociologists (Cherlin and Furstenberg 1992 [1983]): (1) the number of unmarried couples living together has more than tripled since 1970, and (2) one out of four children is not living with both parents. At current rates, half of all American marriages begun in the 1980s will end in divorce.

At the start of the twenty-first century, three kinds of households are most common in the United States: households composed of couples living in their first marriage, single-parent households, and households formed through remarriage (Cherlin and Furstenberg 1992 [1983]:3). A new fourth category is the **intergenerational household,** in which an "adult child" returns to live with his or her parents. About one in three unmarried adults between the ages of twenty-five and fifty-five share a home with their mother or father or both (*Psychology Today* 1995 [28]:16). Currently, in the United States, adult offspring spend over two hours a day doing household chores, with daughters contributing about 17 hours a week and sons 14.4 hours. The daughters spend most of their time doing laundry, cooking, cleaning, and washing dishes, whereas sons are more involved in yard work and car care. Even so, the parents still do three-quarters of the housework.

Kinship and household formation are certainly not dull and static concepts. Just trying to keep up to date on their changing patterns in the United States is a daunting task, to say nothing of the rest of the world.

KEY CONCEPTS

ambilineal descent, p. 181
avunculocal, p. 183
bilineal descent, p. 179
bilocal, p. 181
bride-service, p. 190
cross cousin, p. 187
descent, p. 179
endogamy, p. 187
extended households, p. 191
family, p. 191
exogamy, p. 188
genealogy, p. 178
household, p. 191
hypergyny, p. 188
hypogyny, p. 188
incest taboo, p. 186
intergenerational household, p. 200
isogamy, p. 188
kinship, p. 176

kinship diagram, p. 177
kinship system, p. 176
marriage, p. 186
matrifocality, p. 184
matrilineal descent, p. 179
matrilocally, p. 181
monogamy, p. 190
neolocal, p. 181
nuclear household, p. 191
parallel cousin, p. 187
patrilineal descent, p. 179
patrilocal, p. 181
polyandry, p. 190
polygamy, p. 190
polygyny, p. 190
stem household, p. 192
teknonyms, p. 182
unilineal descent, p. 179

SUGGESTED READINGS

Irwin Altman and Joseph Ginat, eds. *Polygynous Families in Contemporary Society.* Cambridge: Cambridge University Press, 1996. Based on research conducted with twenty-six Mormon families in Utah, this book provides a detailed account of polygyny as practiced in two fundamentalist communities, one rural and the other urban. Topics covered include Mormon history, how polygynous marriages are arranged, how couples manage their time and finances, and emotional relationships within the household.

John Borneman. *Belonging in the Two Berlins: Kin, State and Nation.* New York: Cambridge University Press, 1992. This book considers two levels of analysis: people's changing perceptions of the family and the government's policies related to the family.

Dorothy Ayers Counts, Judith K. Brown, and Jacquelyn C. Campbell, eds. *To Have and to Hit: Cultural Perspectives on Wife Beating.* Champaign/Urbana: University of Illinois Press, 1999. This book includes case studies plus an introductory overview and a concluding comparative essay. One chapter considers the possible evolutionary origin of wife abuse. Cases are from Australia, southern Africa, Papua New Guinea, India, Central America, the Middle East, and the Pacific.

Irene Glasser and Rae Bridgman. *Braving the Street: The Anthropology of Homelessness. Public Issues in Anthropological Perspective,* vol. 1. New York: Bergahn Books, 1999. Fieldwork with homeless people reveals complexities of the problem that have been overlooked by public officials. The authors propose solutions.

Laurel Kendall. *Getting Married in Korea: Of Gender, Morality and Modernity.* Berkeley: University of California, 1996. This ethnographic study examines preferences about desirable spouses, matchmaking, marriage ceremonies and their financing, and the effect of women's changing work roles on their marital aspirations.

Judith S. Modell. *A Sealed and Secret Kinship: The Culture of Policies and Practices in American Adoption.* New York, Bergahn Books, 2002. This books focuses on the increasing debate about adoption by reviewing case examples of parents, children, kin, and non-kin of adoptive families in the United States. The author addresses topics such as adoption reform, adoptee experiences of searching for their birth parents, current practices of placing children, and changes in welfare policy.

Robert McC. Netting, Richard R. Wilk, and Eric J. Arnould, eds. *The Household: Comparative and Historical Studies of the Domestic Group.* Berkeley: University of California Press, 1984. This book includes comparative chapters on changing forms and functions of the household; case studies of contemporary Thailand, Niger, Belize, and the United States; and historical analyses of the Baltic region and Sweden.

Ellen Oxfeld. 1993. *Blood, Sweat, and Mahjong: Family and Enterprise in an Overseas Chinese Community.* Ithaca, NY: Cornell University Press. Situated in Calcutta, this ethnography provides insights about a Chinese family business and how it is organized.

Sulamith Heins Potter. *Family Life in a Northern Thai Village: A Structural Study in the Significance of Women.* Berkeley: University of California Press, 1977. This ethnography of matrifocal family life in rural Thailand focuses on work roles, rituals, and intrafamily relationships.

Nancy Tapper. *Bartered Brides: Politics, Gender and Marriage in an Afghan Tribal Society.* New York: Cambridge University Press, 1991. Based on fieldwork before the Soviet invasion, this study examines marriage among the Maduzai, a tribal society of Turkistan. The book looks at the way marriage is related to productive and reproductive aspects of society and the role it plays in managing political conflict and competition.

Margaret Trawick. *Notes on Love in a Tamil Family.* Berkeley: University of California Press, 1992. This reflexive ethnography takes a close look at the daily dynamics of kinship in one Tamil (South Indian) family. Attention is given to sibling relationships, the role of older people, children's lives, and the way love and affection are played out.

Michael Young and Peter Willmott. *Family and Kinship in East London.* New York: Penguin Books, 1979. This classic study of kinship relationships among the working class of "Bethnal Green" focuses on the importance of married women's continued close relationships with their mothers, as maintained through residential proximity and visiting.

HOW do cultures create kinship ties through descent, sharing, and marriage?

Key differences exist between unilineal and bilineal descent systems. Within unilineal systems, further important variations exist between patrilineal and matrilineal systems in terms of property inheritance, residence rules for married couples, and the relative status of males and females. Worldwide, unilineal systems are more common than bilineal systems. Within unilineal kinship systems, patrilineal kinship is more common than matrilineal kinship. A second important basis for kinship is sharing. Sharing one's child with someone else through either informal or formal processes is probably a cultural universal. Sharing-based kinship is created through food transfers, including breast feeding (in at least one culture, children breast-fed by the same woman are considered kin and cannot marry). Ritualized sharing creates kinship, as in the case of godparenthood. The third basis for kinship is marriage, another universal factor, even though definitions of marriage may differ substantially. All cultures have rules of exclusion and preference rules for spouses.

WHAT is a household and what do anthropologists study about household life?

A household may consist of a single person living alone or may be a group comprising more than one person who may or may not be related by kinship; these individuals share a living space and, often, financial responsibilities for the household. Nuclear households consist of a mother and father and their children, but they also can be just a husband and wife without children. Nuclear households are found in all cultures but are most common in foraging and industrial societies. Extended households include more than one nuclear household. They are most commonly found in cultures with a unilineal kinship system. Stem households, which are most common in East Asia, are a variant of an extended household in which only one child, usually the first-born, retains residence with the parents. Household headship can be shared between two partners or can be borne by a single person, as in woman-headed households. Intrahousehold dynamics, between parents and children and among siblings, reveals complex power relationships as well as security, sharing, and sometimes violence. Household break-up comes about through divorce, separation of cohabiting partners, or death of a spouse or partner.

HOW are kinship and households changing?

The increasingly connected world in which we live is having marked effects on kinship formation and household patterns and dynamics. Matrilineal systems have been declining in distribution since European colonialist expansion beginning in the 1500s. Many aspects of marriage are changing, including a trend toward later age at marriage in many developing countries. Although marriage continues to be an important basis for the formation of nuclear and extended households, other options (such as cohabitation) are increasing in importance in many contexts, including urban areas in developed countries. The implications of changes in household forms and dynamics for the care of dependent members (such as children, the aged, and disabled members) raise key questions for the future.

THE BIG QUESTIONS

- **WHAT** is the range of cross-cultural variation of social groups?
- **WHAT** is social stratification, and what are its effects on people?
- **WHAT** is civil society?

9

SOCIAL GROUPS AND SOCIAL STRATIFICATION

Immigrant farm workers from India pick strawberries on a commercial fruit farm in Kent, southern England. Immigrants from Great Britain's former colonies constitute a large and growing percentage of the population (*Source: © Caroline Penn/Panos Pictures*)

In the early 1800s, when French political philosopher Alexis de Tocqueville visited the United States and characterized it as a "nation of joiners," he implied that people in some cultures are more likely to join groups than others.

The questions of what motivates people to join groups, what holds people together in groups, and how groups deal with leadership and participation have intrigued scholars in many fields for centuries.

This chapter focuses on non-kin groups and microculture formation. In Chapter 1, we defined several factors related to microcultures: class, race, ethnicity, gender, age, region, and institutions such as prisons and retirement homes. Thus far, we have looked at how these factors affect fieldwork and at how they vary in different economies and reproductive and kinship systems. This chapter looks again at these key factors of social differentiation in order to see how they affect group formation and the relationships among groups in terms of hierarchy and power. It first examines a variety of social groups ranging from more small-scale to larger-scale and then considers inequalities among certain social groups.

SOCIAL GROUPS

A **social group** is a cluster of people beyond the domestic unit who are usually related on grounds other than kinship, although kinship relationships may exist between people in the group. Two basic categories exist: the **primary group,** consisting of people who interact with each other and know each other personally, and the **secondary group,** consisting of people who identify with each other on some common ground but who may never meet with one another or interact with each other personally.

Members of all social groups have a sense of rights and responsibilities in relation to the group which, if not maintained, could mean loss of membership. Because of its face-to-face nature, membership in a primary group involves more direct accountability about rights and responsibilities than secondary group membership. When discussing different kinds of groups, social scientists also draw a distinction between informal groups and formal groups (March and Taqqu 1986:5):

- Informal groups are smaller and less visible.

- Members of informal groups have close, face-to-face relationships with one another; members of formal groups may or may not know each other.

- Organizational structure is less hierarchical in informal groups.

- Informal groups do not have legal recognition.

Modes of economies affect the formation of social groups, the greatest variety being found in agricultural and industrial societies (see Figure 9.1). One theory suggests that mobile populations, such as foragers and pastoralists, are less likely to develop enduring social groups beyond kin relationships. It may be true that foragers and pastoralists have less variety of social groups, but they do not completely lack social groupings. A prominent form of social group among foragers and pastoralists is an **age set,** a group of people close in age who go through certain rituals, such as circumcision, at the same time.

FIGURE 9.1 Modes of Social Organization

FORAGING	HORTICULTURE	PASTORALISM	AGRICULTURE	INDUSTRIALISM (CAPITALIST)

Characteristics

Informal and primary
  Egalitarian structure
  Ties based on balanced exchange

Ritual ties

Characteristics

Formal and secondary
  Recognized leadership
  Dues and fees

Functions

Companionship

Functions

Special purposes
  Work, war, lobbying government

Types of Social Groups

Friendship

Friendship
Age-based work groups
Gender-based work groups

Types of Social Groups

Friendship
  Urban youth gangs
  Clubs, associations

Status Groups:
  Class, race, ethnicity, caste, age, gender
Institutional Groups:
  Prisons, retirement homes
Quasi-Political Groups:
  Human rights, environmental groups

A related hypothesis is that settled and densely populated areas will have more social groups as a way to organize society. Again, this may be generally true, but important variations exist. Both informal and formal groups appear to be varied and active in Africa, Latin America, and Southeast Asia, but less so in South Asia (Uphoff and Esman 1984). In Bangladesh, a densely populated and agrarian country of South Asia, indigenous social groups are rare. The most prominent ties beyond the immediate household are kinship-based (Miller and Khan 1986). In spite of the lack of indigenous social groups, however, Bangladesh has gained world renown for its success in forming local credit groups through an organization called the Grameen Bank, which gives loans to poor people to help them start small businesses.

In northern Thailand's Chiangmai region, in contrast, many social groups exist (Potter 1976). The village, as a group, supports the Buddhist temple, the temple library, the monastery and school, irrigation canals, the cremation grounds, and the village roads. Within this overall structure, several more formal and focused groups exist: the temple committee that arranges festivals; the school committee; the Young People's Club (youth from about the age of fifteen until their marriage who assist at village ceremonial functions); the village dancers (about a dozen young, unmarried women who host intervillage affairs); the funeral society (which provides financial aid for funeral services); neighborhood groups that take turns sending food to the temple for the monks; and irrigation work groups. The reasons why some cultures have strong and enduring social groups and others do not await further exploration.

In the following sections, we will encounter a variety of social groups. We begin with the most face-to-face, primary groups of two or three people based on friendship and move to larger groups with explicit goals, such as countercultural groups and activist groups.

Friendship

Friendship falls in the category of a primary social group that is informal. One question that cultural anthropologists ask is whether friendship is a cultural universal. Two factors make it difficult to answer this question. First, insufficient cross-cultural research exists to answer the question definitively. Second, defining friendship cross-culturally is problematic. It is likely, however, that something like "friendship" (close ties between non-kin) is a cultural universal, though shaped in different degrees from culture to culture (see the Unity and Diversity box).

Social Characteristics of Friendship

Friends are chosen on a voluntary basis, but even so, the criteria for who qualifies as a friend may be culturally structured. For instance, gender segregation may prevent cross-gender friendships and promote same-gender friendships, and racial segregation limits cross-race friendships. Another characteristic of friendship is that friends are supportive of each other, psychologically and sometimes materially. Support is mutual, shared back and forth in an expectable way (as in balanced exchange, see Chapter 4). Friendship generally occurs between social equals, although there are exceptions, such as friendship between older and younger people, a supervisor and a staff worker, or a teacher and a student.

Sharing stories is often a basis of friendship groups. In a study of male peer groups focused on interactions in rumshops in Guyana, South America, Indo-Guyanese men who have known each other since childhood reaffirm their solidarity through spending time, every day, at the rumshop eating, drinking, and regaling each other with stories (Sidnell 2000). Through shared storytelling about village history and other aspects of local knowledge, men display their equality with each other. The pattern of storytelling, referred to as "turn-at-talk," in which efforts are made to include everyone as a storyteller in turn, also serves to maintain equality and solidarity. These friendship groups are tightly knit, and the members can call on one another for economic, social, political, and ritual help. We will return to the importance of shared stories in social bonding when we discuss activist groups.

Friendships in Prison

Prisons, like colleges and universities, are social institutions with limited populations among whom friendship relationships may develop. In the case of colleges and universities, people are there voluntarily and have a good idea about how long they will be there. It makes sense to form enduring bonds with friends and classmates. In the context of prisons, people are not there voluntarily, and the formation of social ties is limited.

One factor that affects the formation of friendship in prisons is the duration of the sentence. A study that explored this issue first had to deal with the difficulty of doing participant observation. A research team of two people included an "insider" and an "outsider" (Schmid and Jones 1993). The "insider" was an inmate serving a short-term sentence who did participant observation, conducted interviews, and kept a journal. The "outsider," a sociologist, met with this inmate weekly to discuss find-

ings (he also did the analysis). The inmate researcher was a male, so this study deals only with male prisoners. Furthermore, because his was a short-term sentence, the study's findings concern the effects of short-term sentencing (of one or two years) on social relationships among inmates.

Three stages of short-term inmate adaptation are typical. First, inmates experience uncertainty and fear based on their images of what life is like in prison. They avoid contact with other prisoners and guards as much as possible. The next stage involves the creation of a survival niche. The prisoner has selective interactions with other inmates and may develop a "partnership" with another inmate. Partners hang around together and watch out for each other. In the third phase, the prisoner anticipates his eventual release, transfers to a minimum security area, increases contact with outside visitors, and begins the transition to the outside. In this stage, partners begin to detach from each other as one of the pair moves toward the outside world.

Friendship Among the Urban Poor

Carol Stack's study of how friendship networks promote economic survival among low-income African Americans is a landmark contribution (1974). Her research was conducted in the late 1960s in "The Flats," the poorest section of a Black community in a midwestern city. She found extensive networks of friends "supporting, reinforcing each other—devising schemes for self help, strategies for survival in a community of severe economic deprivation" (28). Close friends, in fact, are referred to by kin terms.

Unity and Diversity

MALE AND FEMALE FRIENDSHIPS IN RURAL SPAIN

THE PREVAILING gender division of labor and spatial gender segregation found in southern Spain shape differences in men's and women's friendship patterns (Uhl 1991). Women's lives are taken up mainly with unpaid household work within the domestic domain. Men's lives involve the two activities of work and leisure outside the house. This dichotomy is somewhat fluid, however, for women's domestic roles do take them into the public domain—markets, town hall, taking children to school—with some time for visiting friends.

Women often referred to their friends either with kin terms or as *vecina,* "neighbor," reflecting women's primary orientation to family and neighborhood. For men, an important category of friend is an *amigo,* a friend with whom one casually interacts. This kind of casual friendship is the friendship of bars and leisure-time male camaraderie. It grows out of work, school, common sports and hobbies, and drinking together night after night. Women do not have such friendships. Men also are more likely than women to have *amigos(as) de trabajo,* friendships based on work activities. Differences between men and women also emerge in the category of "true friends," or *amigo(as) del verdad* or *de confianza.* True friends are those with whom one shares secrets without fear of betrayal. Most men claimed to have many more true friends than the women claimed to have, a circumstance that reflects their wider social networks.

FOOD FOR THOUGHT

What different categories of friends do you have? Are some kinds of friends "closer" or "truer" than others?

People in the Flats, especially women, maintain a set of friends through exchange: "swapping" goods (food, clothing) needed by someone at a particular time, sharing "child keeping," and giving or lending food stamps and money. Such exchanges are part of a clearly understood pattern—gifts and favors go back and forth over time. Friends thus bound together are obligated to each another and can call on each other in time of need. In opposition to theories that suggest the breakdown of social relationships among the very poor, this research documents how poor people strategize and cope through social ties.

Clubs and Fraternities

Clubs and fraternities define membership in terms of some sense of shared identity. Thus they may comprise people of the same ethnic heritage (such as the Daughters of the American Revolution in the United States), occupation or business, religion, or gender. Although many clubs appear to exist primarily to serve functions of sociability and psychological support, deeper analysis often shows that these groups have economic and political roles as well.

Women's clubs in a lower-class neighborhood in Paramaribo, Suriname, have multiple functions (Brana-Shute 1976). Here, as is common elsewhere in Latin America, clubs raise funds to sponsor special events and support individual celebrations, meet personal financial needs, and send cards and flowers for funerals. Members attend each other's birthday parties and death rites as a group. The clubs thus offer the women psychological support, entertainment, and financial help. A political aspect exists, too. Club members often belong to the same political party and attend political rallies and events together. These women constitute political interest groups that can influence political outcomes. Politicians and party workers confirmed that real pressure is exerted on them by women individually and in groups.

College fraternities and sororities are highly selective groups that serve a variety of explicit functions, such as entertainment and social service. They also form bonds between members that may help in securing jobs after graduation. Unlike sociologists, few anthropologists have studied the "Greek system" on American campuses. One exception is Peggy Sanday, who was inspired to study college fraternities after the gang rape of a woman student by several fraternity brothers at the campus where she teaches. In her book, *Fraternity Gang Rape: Sex, Brotherhood, and Privilege on Campus* (1990), she explores initiation rituals; the role of pornography, ritual dances, and heavy drinking at parties; and how they are related to a pattern of male bonding solidified by victimization and ridicule of women. Gang rape, or a "train," is a prevalent practice in some, not all, fraternities. Fraternity party invitations may hint at the possibility of a "train." Typically, the brothers seek out a "party girl"—a somewhat vulnerable young woman who may be especially seeking of acceptance or especially high

on alcohol or other substances (her drinks may even have been "spiked"). They take her to one of the brother's rooms, where she may or may not agree to have sex with one man—often she passes out. Then a "train" of men have sex with her. Rarely prosecuted, the male participants reinforce their sense of privilege, power, and unity with one another through this group ritual involving abuse of a female outsider.

Cross-culturally, men's clubs in which strong male–male bonds are created and reinforced by the objectification and mistreatment of women are common, but not universal. They are especially associated with cultures where male–male competitiveness is an important feature of society (Bird 1996) and in which warfare and group conflict are frequent. In many indigenous Amazonian groups, the men's house is fiercely guarded from being entered by women. If a woman trespasses on male territory, she is punished by gang rape. One interpretation is that males have a high degree of anxiety about their identity as fierce warriors and as sexually potent males (Gregor 1982). Maintaining their identity as fierce males toward outsiders involves taking an aggressive position in relation to women of their own group. Parallels of gynophobic ("women-hating" or otherwise anti-woman) men's clubs do not exist among women. College sororities are not mirror images of college fraternities. Women's groups and organizations, even if vocally anti-male, do not involve physical abuse of males or ritualized forms of derision.

Countercultural Groups

Several kinds of groups are formed by people who seek consciously to resist conforming to the dominant cultural pattern, as in the "hippie" movement of the 1960s. This section considers examples of countercultural groups. One similarity among these groups is the importance of bonding through shared rituals.

Youth Gangs

The term *gang* can refer to a variety of groups, such as one's friends, as in "I think I'll invite the gang over for pizza" (Short 1996:325). The more specific term **youth gang** refers to a group of young people, found mainly in urban areas, who are often considered a social problem by adults and law enforcement officials (Sanders 1994:5–15).

Youth gangs vary in terms of how formally they are organized. Gangs—like clubs and fraternities—often have a recognized leader, formalized rituals of initiation for new members, and symbolic markers of identity such as tattoos or special clothing. An example of an informal youth gang with no formal leadership hierarchy or initiation rituals is that of the "Masta Liu" in Honiara, the capital city of the Solomon Islands, the South Pacific (Jourdan 1995). The primary unifying feature of the male youth who become Masta Liu is the fact that they are unemployed. Most have migrated to the city from the countryside to escape what they consider an undesirable lifestyle there: working in the fields under control of their elders. Some *liu* live with extended kin in the city, others organize liu-only households. They spend their time wandering around town (*wakabaot*) in groups of up to ten: "They stop at every shop on their way, eager to look at the merchandise but afraid to be kicked out by the security guards; they check out all the cinemas only to dream in front of the preview posters . . . not even having the $2 bill that will allow them to get in; they gaze for hours

Members of a fraternity at the University of Texas at Austin engage in public service by planting trees at an elementary school. ■ *What knowledge do you have of the positive and negative social aspects of college fraternities and sororities? How could anthropological research provide a clearer picture?* (Source: © Bob Daemmrich/Stock Boston, LLC)

on end, and without moving, at the electronic equipment displayed in the Chinese shops, without saying a word: one can read in their gaze the silent dreams they create" (210).

"Street gangs" are a more formal variety of youth gang. They generally have leaders and a hierarchy of membership roles and responsibilities. They are named, and their members mark their identity with tattoos or "colors." Much popular thinking associates street gangs with violence, but not all are involved in violence. An anthropologist who did research among nearly forty street gangs in New York, Los Angeles, and Boston learned much about why individuals join gangs, providing insights that also contradict popular thinking (Jankowski 1991). One common perception is that young boys join gangs because they are from homes with no male authority figure with whom they could identify. In the gangs studied, just as many gang members were from intact nuclear households. Another common perception is that the gang replaces a missing feeling of family. This study showed that the same number of gang members reported having close family ties as those who didn't.

What, then, might be the reasons behind joining a male urban gang? A particular personality type characterized many gang members, a type that could be called a "defiant individualist." The defiant individualist type has five traits: intense competitiveness, mistrust or wariness, self-reliance, social isolation, and a strong survival instinct. A structurist view suggests that poverty, especially urban poverty, leads to the development of this kind of personality structure. Within the context of urban poverty, such a personality structure becomes a reasonable response to the prevailing economic obstacles and uncertainty.

In terms of explaining the global spread of urban youth gangs, structurists point to global economic changes in urban employment opportunities. In many countries, the declining urban industrial base has created persistent poverty in inner-city communities (Short 1996:326). At the same time, aspirations for a better life have been promoted through schooling and the popular media. Urban gang members, in this view, are the victims of large structural forces beyond their control. Yet research with gang members shows that they are not passive victims of structural forces: Many of these youths want to be economically successful, but social conditions channel their interests and skills into illegal pursuits rather than into legal pathways to achievement.

Body Modification Groups

One of the many countercultural movements in the United States includes people who have a sense of community strengthened through forms of body alteration. James Myers (1992) did research in California among people who feel they are a special group because of their interest in permanent body modification, especially genital piercing, branding, and cutting. Fieldwork involved participant observation and interviews. Myers was involved in six workshops organized especially for the San Francisco SM (sadomasochist) community; attended the Fifth Annual Living in Leather Convention held in Portland, Oregon, in 1990; and spent time in tattoo and piercing studios, as well as talking with students and others in his home town who were involved in these forms of body modification. The study population included males and females, heterosexuals, gays, lesbians, bisexuals, and SMers. The single largest group was SM homosexuals and bisexuals. The study population was mainly White, and most had either attended or graduated from college.

Myers witnessed many modification sessions at workshops: Those seeking modification go up on stage and have their chosen procedure done by a well-known expert. Whatever the procedure, the volunteers exhibit little pain (usually a sharp intake of breath at the moment the needle passes through or the brand touches skin). After that critical moment, the audience breathes an audible sigh of relief. The volunteer stands up and adjusts clothing, and members of the audience applaud. This public event is a kind of initiation ritual that binds the expert, the volunteer, and the group together. Pain has long been recognized as an important part of rites of passage, providing an edge to the ritual drama. The audience in this case witnesses and validates the experience and also becomes joined to the initiate through witnessing.

A prominent motivation for seeking permanent body modification was a desire to identify with a specific group of people. As one informant said,

> It's not that we're sheep, getting pierced or cut just because everyone else is. I like to think it's because we're a very special group and we like doing something that sets us off from others. . . . Happiness is standing in line at a cafeteria and detecting that the straight-looking babe in front of you has her nipples pierced. I don't really care what her sexual orientation is, I can relate to her. (292)

Work Groups

Work groups are organized to perform specific tasks, although they also may have other functions, including sociality and friendship among members. They are found in all modes of production, but they are more prominent in nonindustrialized horticultural and agricultural communities where land preparation, harvesting, or repair of irrigation canals requires large inputs of labor that exceed the capability of a single household unit. In her classic study of the Bemessi people of the Cameroon, West Africa, Phyllis Kaberry (1952) describes a labor group system (called a *tzo*, which is translated as "working bee"). Among the Bemessi, women were responsible mainly for horticulture. Reflecting this role, women were also responsible for collective work. For preparing corn beds, about ten to twelve women worked on each others' plots, whereas for weeding, smaller groups of three to four women formed. At the end of the day, the women have a meal of fish provided by their husbands. A woman who fails to provide shared work is reported to the chief.

Youth work groups are common in African regions south of the Sahara, particularly in settled, crop-growing areas. The major responsibility of the youth groups is providing field labor. The group members work one or more days in the village chief's fields for no reward or pay. They also maintain public paths and the public meeting area, construct and maintain roads between villages, build and repair canals, combat brush fires, maintain the village mosque, and prevent animals from grazing where they aren't allowed (Leynaud 1961). Girls' groups exist, but in patrilocal contexts they are less durable because marriage and relocation break girls' ties with childhood companions (Hammond 1966:133). As adults, however, women in African cultures have many types of associations such as mothers' groups, savings groups, and work groups.

Irrigation organizations are formal groups devoted to maintaining irrigation canals and distributing the water. These organizations are responsible for a highly valued good, and they tend to develop formal leadership and membership rules and roles. Because watershed systems cross large regions, irrigation organizations often provide links among many local groups.

The important role these organizations play is illustrated in the Chiangmai region of northern Thailand. At the village level, care of the irrigation canals is a constant concern (Potter 1976). Each year the main dam across the Ping River is washed away by floods and must be rebuilt. This task requires two weeks of concentrated labor by all the farmers who use the system. The main canal has to be cleared at least once a year and the smaller ones more often. These tasks require much organization. In the Chiangmai region, the administration has three tiers. At the highest level is the overall leader of the irrigation group, who is chosen by three local political leaders. At the time of Potter's study, the head was a wealthy man of high social status who had been in the position for twenty years. He had two assistants. At the next lower

Left: A Tahitian chief wears tattoos that indicate his high status. Right: A woman with tattooed arms and pierced nose in the United States. ■ *In your microcultural experience, what do tattoos mean to you when you see someone with them?* (Sources: © Charles & Josette Lenars/CORBIS, left; © Royalty-Free/CORBIS, right)

tier are the heads of each major canal in the system. At the most local level was the village irrigation leader, chosen by the village farmers. Irrigation leaders have many duties, including keeping detailed records and arbitrating disputes. They receive some benefits, such as exemption from either furnishing irrigation labor or paying a proportion of their land tax, or they can keep part of the revenues from fines levied against those who are delinquent in providing labor.

Allocating the water from the canals requires careful administration. As is often the case, water is allocated proportionally according to land holdings (Coward 1976, 1979). But farmers who are downstream are more likely to be deprived of their fair share than farmers who are upstream and can divert more water to their fields. In order to deal with conflicts that arise from this built-in inequity in one area of the Philippines, subgroups of farmers formed to meet and discuss distribution problems.

Another administrative issue is corruption such as water theft, in which a particular farmer will tap off water out of turn (Price 1995). In one area of Egypt, water theft is more common as distance from the main canal increases. These farmers feel they are justified because they tend to get less water through the distribution system than farmers closer to the source.

Cooperatives

Cooperatives are a form of economic group with two key features: Surpluses are shared among the members, and decision making follows the democratic principle of one person, one vote (Estrin 1996). Agricultural and credit cooperatives are the most common forms of cooperatives worldwide, followed by consumer cooperatives. We will look at two examples of cooperatives to see how human agency, within different structures, can bring about positive results. In the first case, the cooperative gives its members economic strength and checks the power of the richest farmers in one region of India. In the second case, women craft producers in Panama achieve economic position within the world market and also build social ties and political leadership skills.

Farmers' Cooperatives in Western India

In India's western state of Maharashtra, the sugar industry is largely owned and operated through farmer cooperatives (Attwood 1992). Most shareholders are small farmers, producing just one or two acres of sugar cane. Yet the sugar industry, owned and managed cooperatively, is huge, almost as large as the state's iron and steel industry. In contrast, in the northern states where sugar cane is grown, cooperatives are not prominent.

How and why are sugar cooperatives so successful in this region? The answer lies in the different pattern of social stratification. The rural social stratification system in Maharashtra is simpler than in northern India (see pp. 219–222). In most villages, the Marathas are the dominant caste, but here they constitute even more of a majority and control even more village land than is typical of dominant castes. They also have stronger local ties with each other because their marital arrangements are locally centralized. Thus they have a better basis for cooperating with each other in spite of class differences among themselves. Large farmers dominate the elected board of directors of the cooperatives. These "sugar barons" use their position to gain power in state politics. However, within the cooperatives their power is held in check. They do not form cliques that exploit the cooperatives to the detriment of the less wealthy. In fact, large farmers cannot afford to alienate the small and mid-size farmers, for that would mean economic ruin for the cooperative and the loss of their own profits. The technology of sugar cane processing requires wide participation of the farmers. Mechanization involves investing in expensive heavy equipment. The machinery cannot be run at a profit unless it is used at full capacity during the crushing season. If small and mid-size farmers were displeased with their treatment, they might decide to pull out of the cooperative and put their cane into other uses. Then capacity would be underused and profits would fall.

Craft Cooperatives in Panama

In Panama's east coastal region, indigenous Kuna women have long sewn beautiful *molas*, or cloth with appliqued designs. This cloth is made for their own use as clothing (Tice 1995). Since the 1960s, molas have been important items for sale both on the world market and to tourists who come to Panama. Revenue from selling molas is now an important part of the household income of the Kuna. Some women continue to operate independently, buying their own cloth and thread and selling their molas either to an intermediary who exports them or in the local

Kuna Indian woman selling molas, San Blas Islands, Panama. ■ *Learn more about molas from the Web.* (Source: © Wolfgang Koehler)

tourist market. But many other women have joined cooperatives that offer them greater economic security.

The cooperative buys cloth and thread in bulk and distributes it to the women. The women are paid almost the entire sale price for each mola, with only a small amount of the eventual sale prices being taken out for cooperative dues and administrative costs. Their earnings are steadier than what the fluctuating tourist season offers.

Beyond the initial economic reasons for joining the cooperative, other benefits include the use of the cooperative as a consumer's cooperative (buying rice and sugar in bulk for members), as a source of mutual strength and support, and as a place for women to develop greater leadership skills and to take advantage of opportunities for political participation in the wider society.

Self-Help Groups

Recent years have seen a proliferation, worldwide, of self-help groups, or groups formed to achieve specific personal goals, such as coping with illness or bereavement, or lifestyle change, such as trying to exercise more or lose weight. Self-help groups also increasingly use the Internet to form virtual support communities. Anthropologists who study these groups focus on why members join, on rituals of solidarity, and on leadership and organization patterns.

An ethnography of Alcoholic Anonymous groups in Mexico City reports that most members are low-income working-class males (Brandes 2002). Most of these men migrated to Mexico City from rural areas several decades earlier to find work and improve their standard of living. Their drinking problems are related both to their poverty and to the close links between alcohol consumption and male gender identity in Mexico (a "real man" consumes a lot of alcohol). Through a dynamic of shared stories and regular meetings, AA members in Mexico City achieve a high rate of sobriety. The success of AA in Mexico is leading to a rapid proliferation of groups. Membership is growing at about 10 percent a year, a remarkably high rate of growth for a self-help organization. By the end of the twentieth century, Latin America accounted for almost one-third of the world AA membership. Thus a model of a middle-class self-help organization that originated in the United States has been culturally localized by low-income men throughout Latin America.

SOCIAL STRATIFICATION

Social stratification consists of hierarchical relationships between different groups—as though they were arranged in layers or "strata." Stratified groups may be unequal on a variety of measures, including material resources, power, human welfare, education, and symbolic attributes. People in groups in higher positions have privileges not experienced by those in lower-echelon groups, and they are likely to be interested in maintaining their privileged position. Social stratification appeared late in human history, most clearly with the emergence of agriculture. Now some form of social stratification is nearly universal.

Analysis of the categories—such as class, race, gender, and age—that form stratification systems reveals a crucial difference among them: the degree to which membership in a given category is an **ascribed position,** based on qualities of a person gained through birth, or an **achieved position,** based on qualities of a person gained through action. Ascribed positions include one's race, ethnicity, gender, age, and physical ability. These factors are generally out of the control of the individual, although some flexibility exists for gender (through surgery and hormonal treatments) and for certain kinds of physical conditions. Also, one can sometimes "pass"

as a member of another race or ethnic group. Age is an interesting ascribed category because an individual goes through several different status levels associated with age. Achievement as a basis for group membership means that a person belongs on the basis of some valued attainment. Ascribed systems are thus more "closed" and achievement-based systems more "open" in terms of mobility within the system (either upward or downward). Some scholars of social status believe that increasing social complexity and modernization led to an increase in achievement-based positions and a decline in ascription-based positions.

In this section, we look at the way key social categories define group membership and relations of inequality among groups.

The Concept of Status Groups

Societies place people into categories—student, husband, child, retired person, political leader, or member of Phi Beta Kappa—which are referred to as a person's **status,** or position or standing in society (C. Wolf 1996). Each status has an accompanying **role,** which is expected behavior for someone of a particular status, and a "script" for how to behave, look, and talk. Some statuses have more prestige attached to them than others (the word *status* can be used to mean prestige, relative value, and worth). Groups, like individuals, have status, or standing in society. Noted German sociologist Max Weber called lower-status groups "disprivileged groups." These include, in different contexts and in different times, physically disabled people, people with certain illnesses such as leprosy or HIV/AIDS, indigenous peoples, minorities, members of particular religions, women, and others.

Within societies that have marked status positions, different status groups are marked by a particular lifestyle, including goods owned, leisure activities, and linguistic styles. The maintenance of group position by higher-status categories is sometimes accomplished by exclusionary practices in relation to lower-status groups through a tendency toward group in-marriage and socializing only within the group.

Class: Achieved Status

Social class (as defined in Chapter 1) refers to a person's or group's position in society defined primarily in economic terms. In many cultures, class is a key factor determining a person's status, whereas in others it is less important than, for example, birth into a certain family. However, class and status do not always match. A rich person may have become wealthy in disreputable ways and never gain high status. Both status and class groups are secondary groups, because a person is unlikely to know every other member of the group, especially in large-scale societies. In most instances, they are also informal groups; there are no recognized leaders or elected officials of the "urban elite" or the "working class." Subsegments of these large categories do organize themselves into formal groups, such as labor unions or exclusive clubs for the rich and famous. Class can be both ascribed and achieved because a person who is born rich has a greater than average chance of living an upper-class lifestyle.

In "open" capitalistic societies, the prevailing ideology is that mobility in the system is up to the individual. Some anthropologists refer to this ideology as meritocratic individualism—the belief that rewards go to those who deserve them. This ideology would seem to be most valid for people with decent jobs rather than menial workers or the unemployed, but in fact the ideology is widely held outside the middle class (Durrenberger 2001). In the United States, the pervasive popular belief in rewards for equal opportunity and merit, is upheld and promoted in schools and universities even in the face of substantial evidence to the contrary.

Conservative governments have long sought to weaken labor unions, and they continue to promote the fantasy of a classless society based on meritocratic individualism to support their anti-union policies. Anthropologists who take a structurist perspective point to the power of economic class position in shaping a person's lifestyle and his or her ability to choose a different one. Obviously, a person who was born rich can, through individual agency, become poor, and a poor person can become rich. But in spite of exceptions to the rule, a person born rich is more likely to lead a lifestyle typical of that class, just as a person born poor is more likely lead a lifestyle typical of that class.

The concept of class was central to the theories of Karl Marx. Situated within the context of Europe's Industrial Revolution and the growth of capitalism, Marx wrote that class differences, exploitation of the working class by the owners of capital, class consciousness among workers, and class conflict are forces of change that would eventually spell the downfall of capitalism. In contrast to Marx's approach, French sociologist Emile Durkheim viewed social differences (including class) as the basis for social solidarity (1966 [1895]). He distinguished two major forms of societal cohesion: **Mechanical solidarity,** which exists when groups that are similar join together, and **organic solidarity,** which prevails when groups with different abilities and resources are linked together in complementary fashion. Mechanical solidarity creates less enduring relationships because it involves little mutual need. Organic solidarity builds on need and creates stronger bonds. Durkheim placed these two concepts in an evolutionary framework, saying that in nonindustrial times, the division of labor was only minimally specialized: Everyone did what everyone else did. With increasing social complexity and economic specialization, organic solidarity developed.

Race, Ethnicity, and Caste: Ascribed Status

Three major ascribed systems of social stratification are based on divisions of people into unequally ranked groups on the basis of race, ethnicity (defined in Chapter 1) and **caste,** a ranked group, determined by birth, often linked to a particular occupation and to South Asian cultures. Like status and class groups, these three categories are secondary social groups, because no one can have a personal relationship with all other members of the entire group. Each system takes on local specificities depending on the context. For example, race and ethnicity are interrelated and overlap with conceptions of culture in much of Latin America, although differences in what they mean in terms of identity and status occur in different countries in the region (de la Cadena 2001). For some the concept of *mestizaje,* or racial mixture, refers to people who are disenfranchised and cut off from their Indian roots, but for others it can refer to literate and successful people who retain indigenous cultural practices. One has to know the local system of categories and meanings attached to them to understand the dynamics of inequality that go with them.

Yet systems based in difference defined in terms of race, ethnicity and caste share with each other, and with class-based systems, some important features. First, they relegate large numbers of people to particular levels of entitlement to livelihood, power, security, esteem, and freedom (Berreman 1979 [1975]:213). This simple fact should not be overlooked. Second, those with greater entitlements dominate those with lesser entitlements. Third, members of the dominant groups tend—consciously or unconsciously—to seek to maintain their position. Marvin Harris refers ironically to the maintenance of dominance as an "organizational challenge" that is met in two ways: through institutions that control ideology among the dominated and through institutions that physically suppress potential rebellion or subversion by the dominated (1971, quoted in Mencher 1974:469). Fourth, in spite of efforts to maintain systems of dominance, instances of subversion and rebellion do occur, indicating the potential for agency among the disprivileged.

Race

Racial stratification results from the unequal meeting of two formerly separate groups through colonization, slavery, and other large-group movements (Sanjek 1994). Europe's "age of discovery," beginning in the 1500s, ushered in a new era of global contact. In contrast, in rela-

Boys in a small town of Brazil exhibit the skin-color diversity in the Brazilian population. ■ *If you were a census taker and had to categorize the "race" of these boys on the basis of physical features, what categories would you use?* (Source: © David G. Houser/CORBIS)

tively homogeneous cultures, ethnicity is a more important distinction than race. In contemporary Nigeria, for example, the population is relatively homogeneous, and *ethnicity* is the more salient term (Jinadu 1994). A similar situation prevails in Rwanda and other African states.

A key feature of racial thinking is its insistence that behavioral differences among peoples are "natural," inborn, or biologically caused (in this, it resembles sexism, ageism, and casteism). Throughout the history of racial categorizations in the West, such features as head size, head shape, and brain size have been accepted as the reasons for behavioral differences. Writing early in the twentieth century, Franz Boas contributed to de-coupling supposed racial attributes from behavior (review Chapter 1). He showed that people with the same head size but from different cultures behaved differently and that people with different head sizes within the same cultures behaved similarly. For Boas and his followers, culture, not biology, is the key explanation for behavior. Thus race is not a biological reality; there is no way to divide the human population into races on the basis of certain biological features. Yet "social race" exists and continues to be a basis of social stratification. In spite of some progress in reducing racism in the United States in the twentieth century, racial discrimination persists. (See the Critical Thinking box on page 218.) One way of understanding this persistence is to see racial discrimination as linked to class formation, rather than separate from it (Brodkin 2000). In this view, racial stereotyping and discrimination function to keep people in less desirable jobs, or unemployed, as necessary aspects of advanced industrial capitalism, which depends on there being a certain number of low-paid workers and even a certain amount of unemployment.

Racial classifications in the Caribbean and in Latin America are complicated systems of status classification. This complexity results from the variety of contact over the centuries between peoples from Europe, Africa, Asia, and indigenous populations. Skin tone is one basis of racial classification, but it is mixed with other physical features and economic status as well. In Haiti, for example, racial categories take into account physical factors such as skin texture, depth of skin tone, hair color and appearance, and facial features (Trouillot 1994). They also include a person's income, social origin, level of formal education, personality or behavior, and kinship ties. Depending on how these variables are combined, a person occupies one category or another—and may even move between categories. Thus a person with certain physical features who is poor will be considered to be a different "color" than a person with the same physical features who is well-off.

An extreme example of racial stratification was the South African policy of apartheid, legally sanctioned segregation of dominant Whites from non-Whites. White dominance in South Africa began in the early 1800s with White migration and settlement. In the 1830s, slavery was abolished. At the same time, increasingly racist thinking developed among Whites (Johnson 1994:25). Racist images, including visions of Africans as lazy, out of control, and sex-driven, served as the rationale for colonialist domination in place of outright slavery. In spite of years of African resistance to White domination, the Whites succeeded in maintaining and increasing their control for nearly two centuries. In South Africa, Blacks

Critical Thinking

WHAT'S MISSING FROM THIS PICTURE?

READ THE following summary from a news item entitled "Baseball Team Members Who Used KKK Symbol Will Receive Multi-Cultural Training" (*Jet* 1996). Then consider how anthropological research could provide a fuller understanding of racism in its social context:

> A county school board in Virginia opted not to punish members of the state champion high school baseball team who used a Ku Klux Klan symbol. The team members drew the symbol in the dirt before games for good luck. Investigators believe that the symbol represents four hooded Klansmen looking down a hole, the last thing a Black victim would see after being dropped down a well by Klansmen. The school superintendent decided to reprimand the coaches, and the school board voted to send the students for "multi-cultural training."

This brief news item tells us some things about the case but provides little information that would lead to deeper understanding of the cultural context. If a cultural anthropologist decided to do in-depth fieldwork in the community, what kinds of research questions would be most important? Here are some examples:

- The racial composition of the team.
- The racial composition of the school leadership (superintendent), coaches, and other local leaders.
- The pattern of racial and class stratification in the community in which the school is located.
- Other possible forms of racist thinking and behavior in the community.

- Any generational differences that might exist in racist thinking and behavior in this community.
- The reactions of different community members to the behavior of members of the high-school baseball team; the reactions of the coaches; the reactions to the school superintendent's decision about how to treat the baseball players.
- Social programs in the schools and wider community that might reduce racism.

Ku Klux Klan symbol

CRITICAL THINKING QUESTIONS

How does cultural anthropology differ from journalism in terms of research goals?

In terms of research methods?

In terms of research results and how they are presented?

What are the comparative strengths and weaknesses of each approach?

---

constitute 90 percent of the population, a numerical majority dominated, through strict apartheid, by the White minority until only recently. Every aspect of life for the majority of Africans was far worse than for the Whites. Every measure of life quality—infant mortality, longevity, education—showed great disparity between the Whites and the Africans. In addition to physical deprivation, the Africans experienced psychological suffering through constant insecurity about raids from the police and other forms of violence.

Since the end of apartheid in South Africa in 1994, many social changes have taken place. One study describes the early stages of the dismantling of apartheid in the city of Umtata, the capital of the Transkei (Johnson 1994). Before the end of apartheid, Umtata "was like

other South African towns: all apartheid laws were in full force; public and private facilities were completely segregated; only whites could vote or serve in the town government; whites owned all the major economic assets" (viii). When the change came, Umtata's dominant Whites bitterly resisted at first. They did not want to lose their privileges, and they feared reprisals by the Africans. These things did not happen, however. The initial stages of transition brought "neoapartheid," in which White privilege was not seriously threatened. Then members of the dominant group began to welcome the less tense, "nonracial" atmosphere.

In contrast to the explicitly racist discrimination of South African apartheid, racism exists within contexts where no public discourse about race or racism is found—where instead there is silence about it (Sheriff 2000). In such a context, the silence works to allow racial discrimination to continue in ways that are as effective as a clearly stated policy such as apartheid, or perhaps even more so because it is more difficult to critique and dismantle an institution whose existence is denied.

Ethnicity

Ethnicity includes a shared sense of identity on some grounds and a set of relationships to other groups (Comaroff 1987). Identity is formed sometimes on the basis of a perception of shared history, territory, language, or religion. Thus ethnicity can be a basis for claiming entitlements to resources (such as land or artifacts) and for defending or regaining those resources.

States are interested in managing ethnicity to the extent that it does not threaten security. China has one of the most formalized systems for monitoring its many ethnic groups, and it has an official policy on ethnic minorities, meaning the non-Han groups (Wu 1990). The government lists a total of fifty-four groups other than the Han majority, which constitutes about 94 percent of the total. The other 6 percent of the population is made up of these fifty-four groups, about 67 million people. The non-Han minorities occupy about 60 percent of China's land mass and are located in border or "frontier" areas such as Tibet, Yunnan, Xinjiang, and Inner Mongolia. Basic criteria for defining an ethnic group include language, territory, economy, and "psychological disposition." The Chinese government establishes strict definitions of group membership and group characteristics; it even sets standards for ethnic costumes and dances. The Chinese treatment of the Tibetan people is especially severe and can be considered an attempt at ethnocide (annihilation of the culture of an ethnic group by a dominant group). The Chinese government's treatment of Tibetan traditional medicine over the past several decades illustrates how the Han majority uses certain aspects of minority cultures.

In 1951, China forcibly incorporated Tibet, and the Chinese government undertook measures to bring about the social and economic transformation of what was formerly a decentralized, Buddhist feudal regime. This transformation has brought increasing ethnic conflict between Tibetans and Han Chinese, including demonstrations by Tibetans and crackdowns from the Chinese. Traditional Tibetan medicine has become part of the Chinese–Tibetan conflicts because of its cultural significance and importance to religion in Tibetan society (Janes 1995:7). Previously based on a model of apprenticeship training, it is now westernized and involves several years of classroom-based, lecture-oriented learning followed by an internship. At Tibet University, only half of all formal lecture-based instruction is concerned with traditional Tibetan

medicine. Curriculum changes have reduced the integrity of Tibetan medicine: It has been separated from its Buddhist content, and parts of it have been merged with a biomedical approach. Some might say that overall, traditional Tibetan medicine has been "revived" in China, but stronger evidence supports the argument that the state has co-opted it and transformed it for its own purposes.

People of one ethnic group who move from one niche to another are at risk of exclusionary treatment by the local residents. Rom, or gypsies, are a **diaspora population,** a dispersed group living outside their original homeland, and are scattered throughout Europe and the United States. Their history is one of mobility and marginality since they first left India around AD 1000 (Fonseca 1995). Everywhere they live, they are marginalized and looked down on by the settled populations. Traditional Rom lifestyle is one of movement, and temporary camps of their wagons often appear overnight on the outskirts of a town. For decades, European governments have tried to force the Rom to settle down. In addition, Rom migration to cities in Central and Eastern Europe is increasing because of unemployment and declining standard of living. In Budapest, Hungary, the Rom minority is the most disadvantaged ethnic group (Ladányi 1993). Not all Rom in Budapest are poor, though. Some 1 percent have gained wealth. However, the vast majority live in substandard housing in the slum inner areas of Pest. Since the fall of state socialism, discrimination against Roms has increased. Rom houses have been torched, and their children have been harassed while going to school.

A less difficult but still not easy adjustment is being experienced by Indo-Canadians (immigrants from India to Canada). In research among a sample of nearly three hundred Indo-Canadians in Vancouver, British Columbia, about half of all the respondents reported experiencing some form of discrimination in the recent past (Nodwell and Guppy 1992). The percentage was higher among men (54 percent) than among women (45 percent). The higher level for men was consistent across the four categories: verbal abuse, property damage, workplace discrimination, and physical harm. Verbal abuse was the most frequent form of discrimination, reported by 40 percent of both men and women. Indo-Canadians of the Sikh faith who were born in India say that they experience the highest levels of discrimination in Canada. Apparently, however, their actual experience of discrimination is not greater than for other Indo-Canadians. The difference is that Sikhs who were born in India are more sensitive to discrimination than others. Sikhism, as taught and practiced in India, supports a strong sense of honor, which should be protected and, if wronged, avenged. This study helps explain differences in perception of discrimination among ethnic migrants. It does not explain why such high levels of discriminatory treatment exist in a nation committed to ethnic tolerance.

A Rom encampment in Romania's Transylvania region. Not all European Rom are poor, however. Some urban Rom have become wealthy and have therefore attracted the jealousy of the non-Rom population. ■ *Discuss any members of a socially outcast group that you may have encountered in your microculture.* (Source: © Bruno Barbey/ Magnum)

Caste

The caste system is a form of social stratification found in its clearest form in India, among its Hindu population, and in other areas of Hindu culture such as Nepal, Sri Lanka, and Fiji. It is particularly associated with Hindu peoples because ancient Hindu scriptures are taken as the foundational sources for defining the major social categories called *varnas* (a Sanskrit word meaning "color"). The four varnas are the *brahmans*, who were priests; the *kshatriya*, or warriors; the *vaishya*, or merchants; and the *shudras*, or laborers. Of these, men of the first three varnas could go through a ritual ceremony of "rebirth" and thereafter wear a sacred thread. These three categories are referred to as "twice-born," and their status is higher than that of the shudra varna. Beneath the four varna groups were people considered so low that they were outside the caste system itself (hence the word *outcast*). Throughout history, these people have been referred to by many names in Indian languages and by the English term *untouchable*. Mahatma Gandhi, himself a member of an upper caste, renamed them *harijans* (or "children of god") as part of his attempt to raise their status into that of the level above them. Currently, members of this category have adopted the term **dalit** (meaning "oppressed" or "ground down") as their favored name.

The dalit category and all of the varna contain many locally named groups called *castes*, or, more appropriately, *jatis*. The term *caste* is a Portuguese word meaning "breed" or "type" and was first used by Portuguese colonialists in the fifteenth century to refer to the closed social groups they encountered (Cohn 1971:125). *Jati* means "birth group" and conveys the meaning that a Hindu is born into his or her group. It is an ascribed status. Just as the four varnas are ranked relative to each other, so are all the jatis within them. For example, the jati of brahmans "may be subdivided into priestly and non-priestly subgroups, the priestly Brahmans into Household-priests, Temple-priests and Funeral-priests; the Household-priests into two or more endogamous circles; and each circle into its component clans and lineages . . . non-priestly Brahmans are superior in relation to priestly ones, and Household-priests in relation to Funeral-priests" (Parry 1966:77).

Status levels also exist among dalits. In western Nepal, which like India has a caste system, dalit artisans such as basket-weavers and ironsmiths are the highest tier (Cameron 1995). They do not touch any of the people beneath them. The second tier includes leatherworkers and tailors. The bottom tier comprises people who are "untouchable" to all groups, including other dalits, because their work is extremely polluting according to Hindu rules. This category includes musicians (because some of their instruments are made of leather and they perform in public) and sex workers.

Indian anthropologist M. N. Srinivas (1959) contributed the concept of the **dominant caste** to refer to the tendency for one caste in any particular village to control most of the land and, often, to be numerically preponderant as well. Brahmans are at the top of the social hierarchy in terms of ritual purity, and they are often, but not always, the dominant caste. Throughout northern India, it is common for jatis of the kshatriya varna to be the dominant village group. This is the case in Pahansu village, where a group called the Gujars is dominant (Raheja 1988). The Gujars constitute the numerical majority, and they control most of the land (see Table 9.1). Moreover, they dominate in the **jajmani system,** a patron-provider

TABLE 9.1 Caste Ranking in Pahansu Village, North India

Caste Name	Traditional Occupation	Number of Households	Occupation in Pahansu
Gujar	agriculturalist	210	owner cultivator
Brahman	priest	8	priest, postman
Baniya	merchant	3	shopkeeper
Sunar	goldsmith	2	silversmith, sugar cane press operator
Dhiman (Barhai)	carpenter	1	carpenter
Kumhar	potter	3	potter, tailor
Nai	barber	3	barber, postman
Dhobi	washerman	2	washerman
Gadariya	shepherd	4	agricultural laborer, weaver
Jhivar	water-carrier	20	agricultural laborer, basket-weaver
Luhar	ironsmith	2	blacksmith
Teli	oil-presser	2	beggar, cotton-carder, agricultural laborer
Maniharan	bangle-seller	1	bangle-seller
Camar	leatherworker	100	agricultural laborer
Bhangi	sweeper	17	sweeper, midwife

Source: Adapted from Raheja 1988:19.

system in which landholding patrons (*jajmans*) are linked, through exchanges of food for services, with brahman priests, artisans (blacksmiths, potters), agricultural laborers, and other workers such as sweepers (Kolenda 1978:46–54). In Pahansu, Gujars have power and status as the major patrons, supporting many different service providers who are beholden to them.

Some anthropologists have described the jajmani service system as one of mutual interdependence (organic solidarity, to use Durkheim's term) that provides security for the less well-off. Others argue that the system benefits those at the top to the detriment of those at the bottom. This perspective, from "the bottom up," views the patron-service system and the entire caste system as one of exploitation by those at the top (Mencher 1974). The benign interpretation is based on research conducted among the upper castes who present this view. From low-caste people's perspective, it is the patrons who have the power. Dissatisfied patrons can dismiss service providers, refuse them loans, or not pay them. Service providers who are dissatisfied with the treatment they receive from their patrons have little recourse. In addition, male patrons often demand sexual access to females of service-providing households.

Throughout South Asia, the growth of industrial manufacturing and marketing has reduced the need for some service providers, especially craftspersons such as tailors, potters, and weavers. With less need for their skills in the countryside, many former service providers have left the villages to work in urban areas. The tie that remains the strongest is between patrons and their brahman priests, whose ritual services cannot be replaced by machines.

The caste system involves several mechanisms that maintain it: marriage rules, spatial segregation, and ritual. Marriage rules strictly enforce jati endogamy. Marriage outside one's jati, especially in rural areas and particularly between a higher-caste female and lower-caste male, is cause for serious, even lethal, punishment by caste elders and other local power-holders. Among urban educated elites, a trend to allow inter-jati marriages is perceptible, but such marriages are still not preferred.

Spatial segregation functions to maintain the privileged preserve of the upper castes and to remind the lower castes continually of their marginal status. In many rural contexts, the dalits live in a completely separate cluster; in other cases, they have their own neighborhood sections into which no upper-caste person will venture. Ritual rules and practices also serve to maintain dominance. The rich upper-caste leaders sponsor important annual festivals, thereby regularly restating their claim to public prominence (Mines 1994).

Social mobility within the caste system has traditionally been limited, but instances have been documented of group "up-casting." Several strategies exist, including gaining wealth, affiliation or merger with a somewhat higher jati, education, migration, and political activism (Kolenda 1978). A group that attempts to gain higher jati status takes on the behavior and dress of twice-born

Only a special category of brahman priests can officiate at the Chidambaram temple in south India. Here, members of an age-mixed group sit for a moment's relaxation. ■ *Name some other groups in which membership cuts across age differences.* (Source: Barbara Miller)

jatis. These include men wearing the sacred thread, vegetarianism, non-remarriage of widows, seclusion of women from the public domain, and the giving of larger dowries for the marriage of a daughter. Some dalits have opted out of the caste system by converting to Christianity or Buddhism. Others are becoming politically organized through the Dalit Panthers, a social movement seeking greater power and improved economic status for dalits.

Discrimination on the basis of caste was made illegal by the Indian constitution of 1949, but constitutional decree did not bring an end to these deeply structured inequalities. The government of India has instituted policies to promote the social and economic advancement of dalits, such as reserving for them places in medical schools, seats in the government, and public-sector jobs. This "affirmative action" plan has infuriated many of the upper castes, especially brahmans, who feel most threatened. Is the caste system on the decline? Surely aspects of it are changing. Especially in large cities, people of different jatis can "pass" and participate on a more nearly equal basis in public life—if they have the economic means to do so.

CIVIL SOCIETY

Civil society consists of the social domain of diverse interest groups that function outside the government to organize economic, political and other aspects of life. It has a long history in Western philosophy, and many different definitions have been proposed by thinkers such as John Locke, Thomas Paine, Adam Smith, and Karl Marx (K. Kumar 1996:89). According to the German philosopher Hegel, civil society encompasses the social groups and institutions between the individual and the state. Italian social theorist Gramsci wrote that there are two basic types of civic institutions: those that support the state, such as the Church and schools, and those that oppose state power, such as trade unions, social protest groups, and citizens' rights groups.

Civil Society for the State: The Chinese Women's Movement

In many instances, governments seek to build civil society to further their goals. The women's movement in China is an example of such a state-created organization. Canadian anthropologist Ellen Judd conducted a study of the women's movement in China, within the constraints that the government imposes on anthropological fieldwork by foreigners. Under the Mao leadership, foreign anthropologists were not allowed to do research of any sort in China. The situation began to change in the 1980s when some field research, within strict limitations, became possible.

Judd has developed a long-term relationship with China over several decades, having lived there as a student from 1974 to 1977, undertaking long-term fieldwork there in 1986, and returning almost every year since for research or some other activity, such as being involved in a development project for women or attending the Beijing Fourth World Conference on Women. According to Judd, "These various ways of being in China all allowed me some interaction with Chinese women and some knowledge of their lives . . ." (2002:14). In her latest project to study the Chinese women's movement, she wanted to conduct research as a cultural anthropologist would normally do, through intensive participant observation over a long period of time.

But even now, the Chinese government prohibits such research, keeping foreigners at a distance from everyday life. Judd was not allowed to join the local women's organization or to speak privately with any of the women. Officials accompanied her on all household visits and interviews. She was allowed to attend meetings, however, and she had access to all the public information about the goals of the women's movement, which is called the

A march of the "Mothers of the Disappeared" in Argentina. This organization of women combines activism motivated by personal causes (the loss of one's child or children to political torture and death) and wider political concerns (state repressiveness in general). ■ *How many activist groups in your culture can you name, and what are their goals?* (Source: © Peter Menzel/Stock Boston, LLC)

Women's Federations. A policy goal of the Chinese government is to improve the quality of women's lives, and the Women's Federations were formed to address that goal. The government oversees the operation at all levels, from the national level to the township and village. The primary objective is to mobilize women, especially rural women, to participate in literacy training and market activities.

Judd's fieldwork, constrained as it was by government regulations and oversight, nevertheless yielded some insights. She learned, through interviews with women members, about some women who have benefited from the programs, and she discovered how important education for women is in terms of their ability to enter into market activities. The book she wrote is largely descriptive, focusing on the "public face" of the Women's Federations in one locale. Such a descriptive account is the most that can emerge from research in China at this time. Given that the women's organizations are formed by and for the government, this example stretches the concept of civil society to—and perhaps beyond—its limits.

Activist Groups

Activist groups are groups formed with the goal of changing certain conditions, such as political repression, violence, and human rights violations. In studying activist groups, cultural anthropologists are interested in learning what motivates the formation of such groups, what their goals and strategies are, and what leadership patterns they exhibit. Sometimes anthropologists join the efforts of activist groups and use their knowledge to support these groups' goals (see the Lessons Applied box on page 224).

Many, but certainly not all, activist groups are initiated and organized by women. CO-MADRES of El Salvador is an important, women-led social movement in Latin America (Stephen 1995). CO-MADRES is a Spanish abbreviation for an organization called, in English, the Committee of Mothers and Relatives of Political Prisoners, Disappeared and Assassinated of El Salvador. It was founded in 1977 by a group of mothers protesting the atrocities committed by the Salvadoran government and military. During the civil war that lasted from 1979 until 1992, a total of 80,000 people died and 7000 more disappeared—one in every 100 El Salvadorans.

The initial group comprised nine mothers. A year later, it had grown to nearly thirty members, including some men. In 1979 they made their first international trip to secure wider recognition. This developed into a fullfledged and successful campaign for international solidarity in the 1980s, with support in other Latin American countries, Europe, Australia, the United States, and Canada. The group's increased visibility earned it repression from the government. Its office was bombed in 1980 and then four more times after that. Forty-eight members of CO-MADRES have been detained since 1977; five have been assassinated. Harassment and disappearances continued even after the signing of the Peace Accords in January 1992: "In February 1993, the son and the nephew of one of the founders of CO-MADRES were assassinated in Usulutan. This woman had already lived through the experience of her own detention, the detention and gang rape of her daughter, and the disappearance and assassination of other family members" (814).

In the 1990s, CO-MADRES focused on holding the state accountable for human rights violations during the civil war, as well as some new areas, such as providing better protection for political prisoners, seeking assurances of human rights protection in the future, working

Lessons Applied

ANTHROPOLOGY AND COMMUNITY ACTIVISM IN PAPUA NEW GUINEA

A CONTROVERSIAL issue in applied anthropology is whether or not an anthropologist should take on the role of community activist or act as an advocate on behalf of the people among whom they have conducted research (Kirsch 2002). Some say that anthropologists should maintain a neutral position in a conflict situation and simply offer information on issues—information that may be used by either side. Others say that it is appropriate and right for anthropologists to take sides and help support less powerful groups against more powerful groups. Those who endorse anthropologists' taking an activist or advocacy role argue that neutrality is never truly neutral: By seemingly taking no position, one indirectly supports the status quo, and information provided to both sides will generally serve the interests of the more powerful side in any case.

Stuart Kirsch took an activist role after conducting field research for over fifteen years in a region of Papua New Guinea that has been negatively affected by a large copper and gold mine called the Ok Tedi mine. The mine releases 80,000 tons of mining wastes into the local river system daily, causing extensive environmental damage that in turn affects people's food and water sources. Kirsch has joined with the local community in their extended legal and political campaign to limit further pollution and to gain compensation for damages suffered. He explains his involvement with the community as a form of reciprocal exchange. The community members have provided him with information about their culture for over fifteen years. He believes that his knowl-

edge is part of the people's cultural property and that they have a rightful claim to its use.

Kirsch's support of the community's goals took several forms. First, his scholarly research provided documentation of the problems of the people living downstream from the mine. Community activists incorporated his findings in their speeches when traveling in Australia, Europe, and the Americas to spread awareness of their case and gather international support. During the 1992 Earth Summit, one leader presented the media with excerpts from an article by Kirsch during a press conference held aboard the Greenpeace ship *Rainbow Warrior II* in the Rio de Janeiro harbor. Second, he worked closely with local leaders, helping them decide how best to convey their views to the public and in the court. Third, he served as a cultural broker in discussions among community members, politicians, mining executives, lawyers, and representatives of NGOs in order to promote solutions for the problems faced by people living downstream from the mine. Fourth, he convened an international meeting of environmental NGOs in Washington, DC, in 1999 and secured funding to bring a representative from the community to the meeting.

In spite of official reports recommending that the mine be closed in 2001, its future remains uncertain. No assessment of past damages to the community has been prepared. As the case goes on, Kirsch will continue to support the community's efforts by sharing with them the results of his research, just as they have for so long

against domestic violence, educating women about political participation, and initiating economic projects for women. The work of CO-MADRES, throughout its history, has incorporated elements of both the "personal" and the "political," concerns of mothers and other family members for lost kin and for exposing and halting abuses of the state and military. The lesson learned from the case of CO-MADRES is that activist groups formed by women can be based on issues related to the domestic domain (murdered sons and other kin), but their activities can extend to the top of the public political hierarchy.

Another example of activist group formation under difficult conditions comes from urban Egypt (Hopkins and Mehanna 2000). The Egyptian government frowns

on overt political action outside the realm of the government. Although Egyptian citizens are deeply concerned about environmental issues such as waste disposal, clean air and water, and noise, group formation for environmental causes is not easily accomplished. People interviewed in Cairo reported that they rarely discuss environmental issues with one another. One example of environmental concern, however, did result in the closing of a highly polluting lead smelter. In this case, the people in the affected neighborhood banded together around this particular issue and called attention to the situation in the public media, prompting high-level officials to take up their case. They were successful partly because their target was localized—one relatively small industry—and also because the industry was so clearly guilty of pollut-

shared their culture with him. Indigenous people worldwide are increasingly invoking their rights to anthropological knowledge about themselves. According to Kirsch, these claims require anthropologists to rethink their roles and relationships with the people they study. It can no longer be a relationship in which the community provides knowledge and the anthropologist keeps and controls that knowledge for his or her intellectual development alone. Although the details are still being worked out, the overall goal must be one of collaboration and cooperation.

FOOD FOR THOUGHT

Consider the pros and cons of anthropological advocacy, and decide what position you would take on the Ok Tedi case. Be prepared to defend your position.

Yonggam people gather at a meeting in Atkamba village on the Ok Tedi River to discuss legal proceedings in 1996. At the end of the meeting, leaders signed an agreement to an out-of-court settlement, which was presented to the Victorian Supreme Court in Melbourne, Australia. The current lawsuit concerns the Yonggam people's claim that the 1996 settlement agreement has been breached. (Source: Courtesy of Stuart Kirsch)

ing the environment. This effort, however, did not lead to the formation of an enduring group.

In post-socialist states, concern about the environment has prompted the emergence of many nongovernmental groups. In Poland, youth activism related to the environment grew in strength beginning in the late 1980s (Glínski 1994:145). This was the first generation to come after Stalin that had not experienced martial law, so they had less fear of organizing than their parents. Furthermore, the government's policy of limited liberalization involves concessions to social groups and the interests they expressed, and the mass media have greater freedom of expression. In opposition to dominant values of the 1960s and 1970s, members of the early phase of the Polish green movement promoted nonviolence, distance

from the political system, and an ironic and gentle way of communicating their interests. The government promoted distance between it and the youth environmental groups in several ways: It ignored environmental issues, many political elites actively sought to marginalize the youth movement, and police units were dispatched against public protests of the youth groups, (for example, demonstrations in the late 1980s and early 1990s against construction of a nuclear power plant and a dam).

The 1990s brought a second phase in youth involvement when preliminary dialogue between some organizations and the Ministry of Environmental Protection took place. The ministry established a special office and organized monthly meetings with representatives of the youth groups. The groups themselves are becoming more formally organized as NGOs, and their activities receive support from national and international foundations and ecological groups. This example of the change in the role and organization of a social movement unfolded in the post-socialist context of Poland, but it shares general features with youth movements in other places, such as increased political involvement, organizational sophistication, and global linkages.

New Social Movements and Cyberpower

Social scientists have begun to use the term *new social movements* to refer to the many new groups that emerged in the late 1980s and 1990s, often as the result of post-socialist transitions, but in other contexts too (some examples are discussed in Chapter 16 in the context of international development). These groups are often constituted by disprivileged minorities—ethnic groups, women, the poor. Increasingly, they involve networks wider than the immediate social group, and most recently, they have taken advantage of cybertechnology to broaden their membership, exchange ideas, and raise funds (Escobar 2002). Cyber-enhanced social movements are important new political actors and the source of promising ways to resist, transform, and present alternatives to current political structures. The importance of cybernetworking has, of course, not been lost on formal political leaders, who are paying increased attention to their personal web sites and those of their parties.

KEY CONCEPTS

SUGGESTED READINGS

Sandra Bell and Simon Coleman, eds. *The Anthropology of Friendship*. New York: Berg, 1999. The editors provide an introductory chapter on enduring themes and future issues in the anthropological study of friendship. The nine essays that follow discuss friendship in contemporary Melanesia, historical friendship as portrayed in Icelandic sagas, friendship in the context of a game of dominoes in a London pub, how friendship creates support networks in North-East Europe, and the globalization of friendship ties revealed through an East African case.

Gerald Berreman. *Caste and Other Inequities: Essays on Inequality*. Delhi: Folklore Institute, 1979. These eighteen essays on caste and social inequality in India were written over a period of twenty years. Topics include caste and economy, caste ranking, caste and social interaction, and a comparison of caste with race in the United States.

Stanley Brandes. *Staying Sober in Mexico City*. Austin: University of Texas Press, 2002. This ethnography of Alcoholics Anonymous groups in Mexico City focuses on how these groups help low-income men remain sober through social support. Although emphasizing the role of human agency in these men's attempts to remain sober, the author reminds us that the high rate of alcoholism among poor Mexican men must be viewed in the context of structural conditions that make life very difficult.

Liliana Goldin, ed. *Identities on the Move: Transnational Processes in North America and the Caribbean Basin*. Austin: University of Texas Press, 2000. This collection offers essays on identity formation and change in the process of voluntary migration or displacement and on how states label and exclude transnationals, often in racialized ways.

Thomas A. Gregor and Donald Tuzin, eds. *Gender in Amazonia and Melanesia: An Exploration of the Comparative Method,* 2001. Two anthropologists, one a specialist on indigenous peoples of Amazonia and the other on Papua New Guinea, are the editors of this volume, which includes a theoretical overview chapter and then several chapters addressing similarities and differences between cultures of the two regions in domains such as fertility cults, rituals of masculinity, gender politics, and age-based gender roles.

Steven Gregory and Roger Sanjek, eds. *Race.* New Brunswick: Rutgers University Press, 1994. Each editor provides a useful introductory chapter. Seventeen other contributions cover aspects of racism in the United States and the Caribbean, how race articulates with other inequalities, and racism in higher education and anthropology.

Cris Shore and Stephen Nugent, eds. *Elite Cultures: Anthropological Perspectives.* New York: Routledge, 2002. This volume contains two introductory chapters and a concluding chapter framing twelve ethnographic cases from around the world. The major issues addressed are how elites in different societies maintain their positions, how elites represent themselves to others, how anthropologists study elites, and the implications of research on elites for the discipline of anthropology.

Kevin A. Yelvington. *Producing Power: Ethnicity, Gender, and Class in a Caribbean Workplace.* Philadelphia, PA: Temple University Press, 1995. This ethnography examines class, race, and gender inequalities as linked processes of social stratification within the context of a factory in Trinidad and in the wider social sites of households, neighborhoods, and global interconnections.

Karin Tice. *Kuna Crafts, Gender and the Global Economy.* Austin: University of Texas Press, 1995. This ethnographic study looks at how the tourist market has affected women's production of molas in Panama and how women have organized into cooperatives to improve their situation.

WHAT is the range of cross-cultural variation of social groups?

Groups can be classified in terms of whether all members have face-to-face interaction with one another, whether membership is based on ascription or achievement, and how formal the group's organization and leadership structure are. Thus groups extend from the most informal, face-to-face groups, such as those based on friendship, to groups that have formal membership requirements and whose members are widely dispersed and never meet each other. All groups have some criteria for membership, often based on a perceived notion of similarity. Many groups require some sort of initiation of new members, which in some cases involves dangerous or frightening activities that serve to bond members to one another through a shared experience of helplessness.

WHAT is social stratification, and what are its effects on people?

Social stratification consists of hierarchical relationships between and among different groups. Stratified intergroup relations are commonly based on categories such as class, race, ethnicity, gender, age, and ability. The degree of social inequality among different status groups is highly marked in agricultural and industrial societies, whereas status inequalities are not characteristic of foraging societies and are less significant in most pastoral and horticultural societies. India's caste-based system is an important example of a rigid structure of social inequality based on a person's birth group.

WHAT is civil society?

Civil society consists of groups and organizations that, although they are not part of the formal government, perform functions that are economic or political. Civil society groups can be roughly divided into those that support government policies and initiatives, and thus further the interests of government, and those that oppose government policies and actions, such as environmental protest groups. Some anthropologists who study activist groups decide to take an advocacy role and apply their knowledge to further the goals of the group. This direction in applied anthropology is related to the view that anthropological knowledge is partly the cultural property of the groups who have shared their lives and insights with the anthropologist.

THE BIG QUESTIONS

- **WHAT** does political anthropology cover?

- **WHAT** are the major cross-cultural forms of political organization and leadership?

- **HOW** are politics and political organization changing?

10

POLITICS AND LEADERSHIP

Gloria Macapagal-Arroyo, president of the Philippines, at a press conference where she presented the alleged terrorist, Taufek Refke, an Indonesian (back, left). She stated that Refke belongs to a large cell of terrorists in the southern Philippines. *(Source: AP/Wide World Photos)*

Headlines from the year 2003:

- Violence Continues in Afghanistan
- School Bus Fees Anger Parents
- Nigerian President Re-elected
- Rebels in Nepal Postpone Peace Talks
- U.S. Teams Hunt for Iraqi Weapons
- Canada Disputes SARS Travel Alert
- 1.7 Tons of Cocaine Seized Off Colombia
- North Korea Says It Has Nuclear Arms

These events are cultural happenings related to public power and politics. Anthropologists in all four fields address political and legal topics. Archaeologists study the evolution of centralized forms of political organization and the physical manifestations of power in monumental architecture, housing, and material possessions. Primatologists do research on dominance relationships, coalitions, and aggression among nonhuman primates. Linguistic anthropologists analyze power differences in interpersonal speech, the media, political propaganda, and more.

Political anthropology, a subfield of cultural anthropology, addresses the area of human behavior and thought related to power: who has it and who doesn't; degrees of power; the bases of power; abuses of power; relationships between political and religious power; political organization and government; social conflict and social control; and morality and law.

POLITICS AND CULTURE

When cultural anthropologists consider the concept of politics, they tend to take a broader view than a political scientist because their cross-cultural data indicate that many kinds of behavior and thought (in addition to formal party politics, voting, and government) are political. Cultural anthropologists offer important examples of political systems that might not look like political systems at all to people who have grown up in large states. This section explores basic political concepts from an anthropological perspective and raises the question of whether political systems are universal to all cultures.

British anthropologists, especially Bronislaw Malinowski and A. R. Radcliffe-Brown, long dominated theory-making in political anthropology. Their approach, referred to as functionalism (review the discussion of this concept in Chapter 1), emphasized how institutions such as political organization and law promote social cohesion. Later, the students of these two teachers developed divergent theories. For example, in the late 1960s, some scholars began to look at aspects of political organization that pull societies apart. The new focus on disputes and conflict prompted anthropologists to gather information on dispute cases and to analyze the actors involved in a particular conflict.

This approach has been countered by a swing toward a more macro view that examines politics, no matter how local, within a global context (Vincent 1996). The global perspective prompted studies of colonialism and neo-colonialism. Ann Stoler's book *Capitalism and Confrontation in Sumatra's Plantation Belt, 1870–1979* (1985), on the history and cultural impact of Dutch colonialism in Indonesia, is a pioneer study in the anthropology of colonialism. Since the 1980s, the experiences of "subaltern" peoples (those subordinated by colonialism) and "subaltern movements" in former colonized regions have attracted research attention, particularly from native anthropologists of decolonizing countries.

The history of political anthropology in the twentieth century illustrates the theoretical tensions between the individual-as-agent approach and the structurist perspective that sees people as constrained in their choices by larger forces.

Politics: The Use of Power, Authority, and Influence

What, first, do we mean by the word *politics*? This book uses the term *politics* to refer to the organized use of public power, as opposed to the more private micropolitics of family and domestic groups. **Power** is the ability to bring about results, often through the possession or use of

Unity and Diversity

SOCIALIZATION AND WOMEN POLITICIANS IN KOREA

PARENTAL ATTITUDES affect children's involvement in public political roles. Chunghee Sarah Soh's (1993) research in the Republic of Korea reveals how variation in paternal roles affects daughters' political leadership roles. Korean female members of the National Assembly can be divided into two categories: elected members (active seekers) and appointed members (passive recipients). Korea is a strongly patrilineal and male-dominated society, so female political leaders represent "a notable deviance from the usual gender-role expectations" (54). This "deviance" is not stigmatized in Korean culture; rather it is admired within the category of *yŏgŏl*. A *yŏgŏl* is a woman with "manly" accomplishments. Her personality traits include extraordinary bravery, strength, integrity, generosity, and charisma. Physically, a *yŏgŏl* is likely to be taller, larger, and stronger than most women and to have a stronger voice than other women. Why do some girls grow up to be a *yŏgŏl*?

Analysis of the life histories of elected and appointed female legislators offers clues about differences in their socialization. Elected female legislators were likely to have had atypical paternal experiences of two types: either an absent father or an atypically nurturant father. Both of these experiences facilitated a girl's socialization into *yŏgŏl* qualities, or, in the words of Soh, into developing an androgynous personality that combines both masculine and feminine traits. In contrast, the presence of a "typical" father results in a girl developing a more "traditional" female personality that is submissive and passive.

An intriguing question follows from Soh's findings: What explains the socialization of different types of fathers—those who help daughters develop leadership qualities and those who socialize daughters for passivity?

Representative Kim Ok-son greets some of her constituents who are members of a local Confucian club in Seoul, Republic of Korea. She is wearing a men's style suit and has a masculine haircut. ■ (Source: Chunghee Sarah Soh)

FOOD FOR THOUGHT

Given your microcultural experience, what socialization factors do you think might influence boys or girls to become politicians?

---

forceful means. Closely related to power are authority and influence. **Authority** is the right to take certain forms of action. It is based on a person's achieved or ascribed status or moral reputation. Authority differs from power in that power is backed up by the potential use of force and power can be wielded by individuals without their having authority in the moral sense.

Influence is the ability to achieve a desired end by exerting social or moral pressure on someone or some group. Unlike authority, influence may be exerted from a low-status and marginal position. All three terms are relational. A person's power, authority, or influence exists in relation to other people. Power implies the greatest likelihood of a coercive and hierarchical relationship, and authority and influence offer the most scope for consensual, cooperative decision making. Power, authority, and influence are all related to politics, power being the strongest basis for action and decision making—and potentially the least moral.

Politics: Cultural Universal?

Is politics a human universal? Some anthropologists would say "No." They point to instances of cultures with scarcely any institutions that can be called political, with no durable ranking systems, and with very little aggression. Foraging lifestyles, as a model for early human evolution, suggest that nonhierarchical social systems characterized human life for 90 percent of its existence. Only with the emergence of private property, surpluses, and other changes did ranking systems, government, formal law, and organized aggression emerge. Also, studies show how dominance-seeking and aggression are learned behaviors, emphasized in some cultures and among some segments of the population, such as the military, and de-emphasized among others, such as religious leaders, healers, and child care providers. Being a good politician or a five-star general is a matter of socialization. (See the Unity and Diversity box.)

FIGURE 10.1 Modes of Political Organization

FORAGING	HORTICULTURE	PASTORALISM	AGRICULTURE	INDUSTRIALISM (CAPITALIST)
Political Organization				**Political Organization**
Band	Tribe	Chiefdom	Confederacy	State / State
Leadership				**Leadership**
Band leader	Headman/Headwoman / Big-man / Big-woman	Chief / Paramount chief		King/queen/president prime minister/emperor

Social Change

More surpluses of resources and wealth ⟶
Increased population density and residential centralization ⟶
More social inequality/ranking ⟶
Less reliance on kinship relations as the basis of political structures ⟶
Increased internal and external social conflict ⟶
Increased power and responsibility of leaders ⟶
Increased burdens on the population to support political organization ⟶

Other anthropologists argue that despite a wide range of variation, politics is a human universal. Every society is organized to some degree by kinship relationships, and many anthropologists would not draw a clear boundary between how kinship organizes power and how political organization organizes power. This chapter takes the approach that there is a continuum of political structures, starting with the minimal forms found among foraging groups.

POLITICAL ORGANIZATION AND LEADERSHIP

Political organization is the existence of groups for purposes such as public decision making and leadership, maintaining social cohesion and order, protecting group rights, and ensuring safety from external threats. Power relationships situated in the private domain—within the household, for example—may be considered "political" and may be related to wider political realities, but they are not forms of political organization. Political organizations have several features, some of which overlap with those of the groups and organizations discussed in Chapter 9:

- *Recruitment principles:* Criteria for determining admission to the unit.

- *Perpetuity:* Assumption that the group will continue to exist indefinitely.

- *Identity markers:* Particular characteristics that distinguish it from others, such as costume, membership card, or title.

- *Internal organization:* An orderly arrangement of members in relation to each other.

- *Procedures:* Prescribed rules and practices for behavior of group members.

- *Autonomy:* Ability to regulate its own affairs. (Tiffany 1979:71–72)

Cultural anthropologists cluster the many forms of political organization that occur cross-culturally into four major types (see Figure 10.1). The four types of political organization correspond, generally, to the major economic modes (see Chapter 3). Recall that the categories of economies represent a continuum, which suggests that there is overlap between different types rather than clear boundaries; this overlap exists between types of political organization as well.

Bands

The term *band* refers to the political organization of foraging groups. Because foraging has been the predominant mode of production for almost all of human history, the band has been the most longstanding form of political organization. A **band** comprises between twenty people and a few hundred people at most, all related through kinship. These units come together at certain times of the year, depending on their foraging patterns and ritual schedule.

Band membership is flexible: If a person has a serious disagreement with another person or a spouse, one option is to leave that band and join another. Leadership is informal, with no one person named as a permanent leader. Depending on events, such as organizing the group to relocate or to send people out to hunt, a particular person may come to the fore as a leader for that time. This is usually someone whose advice and knowledge about the task are especially respected.

There is no social stratification between leaders and followers. A band leader is the "first among equals." Band leaders have limited authority or influence, but no power. They cannot enforce their opinions. Social leveling mechanisms prevent anyone from accumulating much authority or influence. Political activity in bands involves mainly decision making about migration, food distribution, and resolution of interpersonal conflicts. External conflict between groups is rare because territories of different bands are widely separated and the population density is low.

The band level of organization barely qualifies as a form of political organization because groups are flexible, leadership is ephemeral, and there are no signs or emblems of political affiliation. Some anthropologists argue that "real" politics did not exist in undisturbed band societies.

Chief Paul Payakan, leader of the Kayapo, a group of indigenous horticulturalists living in the rainforest of the Brazilian Amazon. Payakan was instrumental in mobilizing widespread resistance in the region against the construction of a hydroelectric dam. ■ *Have you read in newspapers, or seen on television, news about the Kayapo or other Amazonian tribes recently? If so, what was the issue? If not, locate an update about the Kayapo on the Web.* (Source: © Hank Wittemore/CORBIS SYGMA)

Tribes

A tribe is a more formal type of political organization than the band. Typically associated with horticulture and pastoralism, tribal organization developed about 10,000 to 12,000 years ago with the advent of these modes of production. A **tribe** is a political group that comprises several bands or lineage groups, each with similar language and lifestyle and occupying a distinct territory. These groups may be connected through a **clan** structure in which most people claim descent from a common ancestor, although they may be unable to trace the exact relationship. Kinship is the primary basis of membership. Tribal groupings contain from a hundred to several thousand people. Tribes are found in the Middle East, South Asia, Southeast Asia, the Pacific, and Africa and among Native Americans.

A tribal headman or headwoman (most are male) is a more formal leader than a band leader. Key qualifications for this position are being hardworking and generous and possessing good personal skills. A headman is a

political leader on a part-time basis only, yet this role is more demanding than that of a band leader. Depending on the mode of production, a headman will be in charge of determining the times for moving herds, planting and harvesting, and setting the time for seasonal feasts and celebrations. Internal and external conflict resolution is also his responsibility. A headman relies mainly on authority and persuasion rather than on power. These strategies are effective because tribal members are all kin and have loyalty to each other. Furthermore, exerting force on kinspersons is generally avoided.

Among horticulturalists of the Amazonian rainforest, for example, tribal organization is the dominant political pattern. Each local tribal unit, which is itself a lineage, has a headman (or perhaps two or three). Each tribal group is autonomous, but recently many have united temporarily into larger groups, in reaction to threats to their environment and lifestyle from outside forces.

Pastoralist tribal formations are often linked into a confederacy, with local units or segments maintaining substantial autonomy. The local segments meet together rarely, usually at an annual festival. But in case of an external threat, the confederacy gathers together. Once the threat is removed, local units resume their autonomy. The equality and autonomy of units, along with their ability to unite and then disunite, is referred to as a **segmentary model** of political organization. This form of tribal organization is found among pastoralists worldwide (Eickelman 1981). For example, the Qashqa'i, pastoralists of Iran, have three levels of political organization—subtribe, tribe, and confederacy (Beck 1986). Leaders at each level deal with wider authorities and external forces on behalf of the tribespeople and communicate information to other levels. Leaders also help people in time of economic need.

Leadership among the Qashqa'i combines both ascribed and achieved features. Subtribe headmen's positions were based mainly on achievement. Both *khans* (tribe leaders) and *ilkhanis* (confederacy leaders) were members of noble lineages and achieved their positions through patrilineal descent, with the eldest son favored. The role of the *ilkhani* merges into that of chiefs (described in the next section).

The increased power of the state in recent decades has undermined the role of leaders such as Borzu Qermezi, headman of one segment of the Qashqa'i tribe (Beck 1991). The state government formulated new policies regulating migratory schedules, pasture use, and prices of animal products. These new rules constrained the power of local leaders such as Borzu Qermezi and reduced his importance to his followers, who began to withdraw their support from him.

Big-Man and Big-Woman Leadership

In between tribal and chiefdom organizations is the **big-man system** or **big-woman system,** in which key individuals devote efforts to developing a political following through a system of redistribution based on personal ties and grand feasts (as mentioned in Chapter 4). Anthropological research in Melanesia, a large region in the South Pacific, established the existence of the big-man type of politics, and most references to it are from this region (Sahlins 1963, Strathern 1971). Personalistic, favor-based political groupings are, however, also found elsewhere.

Unlike a tribal headman, a big-man or big-woman has an expanded following that includes people in several villages. A big-man tends to have greater wealth than his followers, although people continue to expect him to be generous. The core supporters of a big-man tend to be kin, with extended networks including non-kin. A big-man has heavy responsibilities in regulating both internal affairs—cultivation—and external affairs—intergroup feasts, exchanges of goods, and war. In some instances, a big-man is assisted in carrying out his responsibilities by a group of other respected men. These councils include people from the big-man's different constituencies.

Big-man political organization is common in Papua New Guinea. In several tribes in the Mount Hagen area of the New Guinea highlands, an aspiring big-man develops a leadership position through making *moka* (Strathern 1971). Making moka involves exchanging gifts and favors with individuals and sponsoring large feasts where further gift-giving occurs. A crucial factor in big-manship in the Mount Hagen area is having at least one wife. An aspiring big-man urges his wives to work harder than ordinary women in order to grow more food to feed more pigs. (Pigs are an important measure of a man's status and worth.) The role of the wife is so important that a man whose parents died when he was young is at an extreme disadvantage. He has impaired chances of getting a wife or wives because he lacks financial support from his parents for the necessary bridewealth.

Using his wife's (or wives') production as an exchange base, the aspiring big-man extends his moka relationships, first with kin and then beyond. By giving goods to people, he gains prestige over them. The recipient, later, will make a return gift of somewhat greater value. The exchanges go back and forth, over the years. The more he gives, and the more people in his exchange network, the greater prestige the big-man develops.

Although big-manship is an achieved position, analysis of the family patterns of big-manship in the Mt. Hagen area shows that most big-men are the sons of big-men (see Table 10.1). This is especially true of major big-men,

TABLE 10.1   Family Background of Big-Men in Mt. Hagen, Papua New Guinea

	Father Was a Big-Man	Father Was Not a Big-Man	Totals
Major Big-Men	27	9	36
Minor Big-Men	31	30	61
Total	58	39	97

Source: From *The Rope of Moka: Big-Men and Ceremonial Exchange in Mount Hagen, New Guinea,* p. 209, by Andrew Strathern. Copyright © 1971. Reprinted by permission of Cambridge University Press.

Throughout much of the South Pacific, big-man and big-woman politics has long involved the demonstration of generosity on the part of the leaders, who are expected to be able to mobilize resources for impressive feasts such as this one on Tanna Island. ■ *How does this political system resemble or differ from a political system with which you are familiar?* (Source: © Kal Muller/ Woodfin Camp & Associates)

of whom over three-quarters were sons of former big-men. It is unclear whether this pattern results from the greater wealth and prestige of big-man families, from socialization into big-manship through paternal example, or from a combination of these aspects.

With few exceptions, the early anthropological literature about Melanesian tribal politics portrays men as dominating public exchange networks and the public political arenas. Women as wives are mentioned as important in providing the material basis for men's political careers. A study of Vanatinai, however, a Pacific island that is gender-egalitarian, reveals the existence of big-women as well as big-men (Lepowsky 1990). In this culture, both men and women can gain power and prestige by sponsoring feasts at which valuables are distributed, especially mortuary feasts (feasts for the dead). Although more Vanatinai men than women are involved in political exchange and leadership-building, some women are extremely active. These women lead sailing expeditions to neighboring islands to visit their exchange partners who are both male and female, and they sponsor lavish feasts attended by many people. On Vanatinai, big-women also include powerful sorcerers, famous healers, and successful gardeners.

Contact with European colonial culture gave men a political edge that they had not had before on Vanatinai. The Europeans traded with men for goods and approached women mainly for sexual relations. Formal government councils were established. Thus far, all councilors on Vanatinai have been male. In addition, some Vanatinai men have received training in the English language, the language of government, and thus have another advantage. In other cases, European domination led to more political equality between men and women with the imposition of "pacification," which ended local warfare and thereby eliminated one of the traditional paths to power for men.

Chiefdoms

A **chiefdom** is a political grouping of permanently allied tribes and villages under one recognized leader. Compared to most tribes, chiefdoms have larger populations, often numbering in the thousands, and are more centralized and socially complex. Hereditary systems of social ranking and economic stratification are found in chiefdoms, with social divisions existing between the chiefly lineage or lineages and non-chiefly groups. Chiefs and their descendants are considered superior to commoners, and intermarriage between the two strata is forbidden. Chiefs are expected to be generous, but they may have a more luxurious lifestyle than the rest of the people. The chiefship is an "office" that must be filled at all times. When a chief dies or retires, he or she must be replaced. In contrast, the death of a band leader or big-man or big-woman does not require that someone else be chosen as a replacement. A chief has more responsibilities than a band or tribal leader. He or she regulates production and redistribution, solves internal conflicts, and plans and leads raids and warring expeditions. Criteria for becoming a chief are clearly defined. Besides ascribed criteria (birth in a chiefly lineage, or being the first son or daughter of the chief), achievement is also important. Achievement is measured in terms of personal leadership skills, charisma, and accumulated wealth. Chiefdoms have existed throughout the world.

Anthropologists and archaeologists are interested in how and why chiefdom systems evolved as an intermediary unit between tribes and states and in what the political implications of this evolution are (Earle 1991). Several political strategies support the expansion of power in chiefdoms: controlling more internal and external wealth and distributing feasting and gift exchanges that create debt ties; improving local production systems; applying force internally; forging stronger and wider external ties; and controlling ideological legitimacy. Depending on local conditions, different strategies were employed. Internal control of irrigation systems was the most important factor in the emergence of chiefdoms in prehistoric southeastern Spain, whereas control of external trade was more important in the prehistoric Aegean region (Gilman 1991).

Gender and Leadership

Much evidence about leadership patterns in chiefdoms comes from historical examples. Prominent chiefs—men and women—are documented in colonial archives and missionary records. Many historical examples of women chiefs and women rulers come from West Africa, including the Queen Mother of the Ashanti of Ghana and of the Edo of Nigeria (Awe 1977).

Oral histories and archival records show that Yoruba women had the institution of the *iyalode,* chief of the women. The iyalode was the women's political spokesperson in the "council of king-makers," the highest level of government. She was a chief in her own right, with chiefly insignia including the necklace of special beads, wide-brimmed straw hat, shawl, personal servants, special drummers, and bell ringers. She had her own council of subordinate chiefs. The position of iyalode was based on achievement. The most important qualifications were her proven ability as a leader, economic resources to maintain her new status as chief, and popularity. Tasks included settling disputes via her court and meeting with women to formulate women's stand on such policy issues as the declaration of war and the opening of new markets. Although she represented all women in the group and had widespread support among women, she was outnumbered at the council of king-makers because she was the only female and the only representative of all women.

The Iroquois of central New York provide a case of women's indirect political importance (J. K. Brown 1975). Men were chiefs, but women and men councilors were the appointing body. Most adult males were gone for extended periods, waging war as far away as Delaware and Virginia. Women controlled production and distribution of the staple crop, maize. If the women did not want warriors to leave for a particular campaign, they would refuse to provide them with maize, thereby vetoing the plan. Some have said that the Iroquois are an example of a **matriarchy,** or a society in which women are dominant in terms of economics, politics, and ideology. But most anthropologists think that the Iroquois are better characterized as an egalitarian society, because women did not control the society to the exclusion of men nor did they oppress men as a group. Men and women participated equally on the councils.

Pocahontas played an important role in Native American–British relations during the early colonial period. ■ *Recall the images that you have seen of her—from books, movies, stories— and ask yourself whether they might be biased in any way.* (Source: North Wind Picture Archives)

Why do women play greater political roles in some chiefdoms than in others? The most satisfactory answers point to women's economic roles as the primary basis for political power, as among the Iroquois and many African horticultural societies. In contrast, the dominant economic role of men in Native American groups of the prairies, following the introduction of the horse by the Spanish and the increased importance of buffalo hunting by men, supported male-dominated political leadership in such groups as the Cheyenne.

A marked change in leadership patterns in chiefdoms in the past few hundred years is the decline of women's political status due to European and North American colonial and missionary influences (Etienne and Leacock 1980). For example, British colonialists redefined the institution of iyalode in Nigeria. Now "she is no longer a member of any of the important councils of government. Even the market, and therefore the market women, have been removed from her jurisdiction, and have been placed under the control of the new local government councils in each town" (146).

Ethnohistorical research on chiefdoms in Hawai'i provides another view of formerly powerful women chiefs (Linnekan 1990). Following Captain Cook's arrival in 1778, a Western-model monarchy was established. By the time the United States annexed the islands in 1898, indigenous Hawaiian leaders had been displaced by westerners.

Confederacies

An expanded version of the chiefdom occurs when several chiefdoms are joined in a confederacy headed by a chief of chiefs, "big chief," or paramount chief. Many prominent confederacies have existed—for example, in Hawai'i in the late 1700s, and, in North America, the Iroquois league of five nations that stretched across New York state, the Cherokee of Tennessee, and the Algonquins who dominated the Chesapeake region in present-day Virginia and Maryland. In the Algonquin confederacy, each village had a chief, and the regional council was composed of local chiefs and headed by the paramount chief. Powhatan, father of Pocahontas, was paramount chief of the Algonquins when the British arrived in the early 1600s. Confederacies were supported financially by contributions of grain from each local unit. Kept in a central storage area where the paramount chief lived, the grain was used to feed warriors during external warfare that maintained and expanded the confederacy's borders. A council building existed in the central location, where local chiefs came together to meet with the paramount chief to deliberate on questions of internal and external policy.

States

A **state** is a centralized political unit encompassing many communities and possessing coercive power. Earliest evidence of the state form of political organization comes from Mesopotamia, China, India, and Egypt, perhaps as early as 4000 BCE. States emerged in these several locations with the development of intensive agriculture, increased surpluses, and increased population density. The state is now the form of political organization in which all people live. Band organizations, tribes, and chiefdoms exist, but they are incorporated within state structures.

There are many theories about why the state evolved (Trigger 1996). Demographic theory says that population density drove the need for central mechanisms for social control. Economic theory argues that the state emerged in response to the increased surpluses of food production in the neolithic era, which produced sufficient wealth to support a permanent ruling class. Political theory says that the state arose as a necessary structure to manage increased competition for land and access to food surpluses. Marxist theory says that the state emerged to maintain the dominance of the ruling class. Rather than emphasizing a single causal factor, most scholars now include multiple causes in their theories.

Powers of the State

Most cultural anthropologists now ask "how" states become and remain states. In this inquiry, they focus on the enhanced power that states have over their domain:

■ *States define citizenship and its rights and responsibilities.* In complex nations, since early times, not all residents were granted equal rights as citizens.

■ *States monopolize the use of force and the maintenance of law and order.* Internally, the state controls the population through laws, courts, and the police. Externally, the state uses force defensively to maintain the nation's borders and offensively to extend its territory.

■ *States maintain standing armies and police* (as opposed to part-time forces).

■ *States keep track of their citizens in terms of number, age, gender, location, and wealth through census systems that are regularly updated.* A census allows the state to maintain formal taxation systems, military recruitment, and policy planning such as population settlement, immigration quotas, and social benefits such as old-age pensions.

■ *States have the power to extract resources from citizens through taxation.* All political organizations are supported by contributions of the members, but variations occur in the rate of contributions expected, the form in which they are paid, and the return that members get in terms of services. In bands, people voluntarily give time or labor for "public projects" such as a group hunt or a planned move. Public finance in states is based on formal taxation that takes many forms. **In-kind taxation** is a system of mandatory, non-cash contributions to the state. For example, the Inca state used the *corvee*, a labor tax, to finance public works such as roads and monuments and to provide agricultural labor on state lands. Another form of in-kind taxation in early states required that farmers pay a percentage of their crop yield. Cash taxes, such as the income tax that takes a percentage of wages, emerged only in the past few hundred years.

■ *States manipulate information.* Control of information to protect the state and its leaders can be done directly (through censorship, restricting access to certain information by the public, and promotion of favorable images via propaganda) and indirectly through pressure on journalists and television networks to present information in certain ways.

Symbols of State Power

Religious beliefs and symbols are often closely tied to the power of state leadership: The ruler may be considered to be a deity or part deity, or may be a high priest of the state religion, or may be closely linked with the high priest, who serves as advisor. Architecture and urban planning remind the populace of the greatness of the state. In pre-Columbian Mexico, the central plaza of city-states, such as Tenochtitlán (founded in 1345), was symbolically equivalent to the center of the cosmos and was thus the locale of greatest significance (Low 1995). The most important temples and the residence of the head of state were located around the plaza. Other houses and structures, in decreasing order of status, were located on avenues in decreasing proximity to the center. The grandness and individual character of the leader's residence indicate power, as do monuments—especially tombs to past leaders or heroes or heroines. Egypt's pyramids, China's Great Wall, and India's Taj Mahal are a few of the world's great architectural reminders of state power.

In democratic states where leaders are elected by popular vote and in socialist states where political rhetoric emphasizes social equality, expense and elegance are muted by the adoption of more egalitarian ways of dress (even though in private, these leaders may live relatively opulent lives in terms of housing, food, and entertainment). The earlier practice of all Chinese leaders wearing a "Mao jacket," regardless of their rank, was a symbolic statement of their anti-hierarchical philosophy. A quick glance at a crowd of people including the prime minister of Canada or Britain or the president of the United States would not reveal who was the leader because dress differences are avoided. Even members of British royalty wear "street clothes" on public occasions where regalia is not required.

Local Power and Politics in Democratic States

The degree to which states influence the lives of their citizens varies, as does the ability of citizens to influence the political policies and actions of their governments. Some anthropologists, as citizens, use their knowledge of culture at home or abroad to influence politics in their own countries (see the Lessons Applied box). So-called totalitarian states have the most direct control of local politics. In most other systems, local politics and local government are granted some degree of power. In highly centralized states, the central government controls public finance and legal institutions, leaving little power or autonomy in these matters to local governments. In decentralized systems, local governments are granted some forms of revenue generation (taxation) and the responsibility of providing certain services.

Local politics of varying types continues to exist within state systems, their strength and autonomy being dependent on how centralized the state apparatus is. This section considers examples of village politics in Japan, factional politics in Belize that link different localities, and

Afghanistan Prime Minister Hamed Karzai wears a carefully assembled collection of regional political symbols. The striped cape is associated with northern tribes. The Persian-lamb hat is an Uzbek style popular in the capital city, Kabul. He also wears a tunic and loose trousers, which are associated with villagers, and sometimes adds a Western-style jacket as well. His clothing implies a statement of unity and diversity about his country.
■ *Study clothing styles of other national leaders and see if you can "read" their symbolic messages.*
(Source: © Reuters NewMedia Inc./CORBIS)

local electoral politics in France to illustrate varying patterns of political goals and strategies.

In Japan, relatively egalitarian systems of local power structures exist in villages and hamlets. Families subtly vie for status and leadership roles through gift-giving, as is common in local politics worldwide (Marshall 1985). Egalitarianism prevails as a community value, but people strive to be "more than equal" by making public donations to the *buraku*, or hamlet. The custom of "giving a gift to the community" is a way that hamlet families can improve their positions in the local ranking system. In

Lessons Applied

CULTURAL KNOWLEDGE FOR ENGAGED CITIZENSHIP

Several times during the 1980s and 1990s, David Price conducted fieldwork on rural development and irrigation in Egypt. Following a trip to Egypt in October 2002, he, along with other Middle East scholars from his region in Washington State, held a series of meetings with their congressional representative (Price, personal communication, 2003). Their goal was to convince the congressman to change his upcoming vote from authorizing military action against Iraq to opposing it. In meetings with the congressman, Price emphasized his firsthand, street-level knowledge of Egyptian people's opinions about, and probable reactions to, such a war. He stressed how U.S. pressures on Egypt's president Mubarak could destabilize American interests in Egypt and how U.S. military action would strengthen the position of Islamic fundamentalists throughout the Middle East. Price gave his congressman (and the congressman's wife, a former World Bank economist) copies of editorials and other papers he had written.

A few weeks after the vote, Price happened to meet up with the congressman and his wife. They both remarked how his information on everyday Egyptians' interpretations of U.S. actions had prompted them to rethink the congressman's position. On the basis of Price's insights, the congressman was also inspired to ask probing questions of CIA and State Department briefing personnel regarding the instability that American military action in Iraq could bring to Egypt, as well as probing questions pertaining to American threats to withhold aid to Egypt if it opposed military action.

FOOD FOR THOUGHT

Choose a contemporary political issue, and compose a mock letter to the government representative of your home district supporting a position on that issue. Imagine that you are a cultural anthropologist with relevant knowledge to back up your position. What will you say in your letter?

---

one hamlet, all thirty-five households recently gave gifts to the community on specified occasions: the forty-second birthday of male family members, the sixty-first birthday of male family members, the seventy-seventh birthday of male family members, the marriage of male family members, the marriage of a female family member whose husband will be the household successor, the birth of the household head or successor couple's first child, and the construction of a new house. These occasions for public gift-giving always include a meal to which members of all hamlet households are invited. Since the 1960s, it has also become common to give an item that is useful for the hamlet, such as a set of fluorescent light fixtures for the hamlet hall, folding tables, space heaters, and vacuum cleaners.

Local politics within a democratic framework may involve another type of gift-giving and exchange in the interest of maintaining or gaining power. Here we see people in elected positions of power giving favors in expectation of political loyalty in return. In these cases, various **factions** vie with each other. A faction is a politically oriented group whose members are mobilized and maintained by a leader to whom the ties of loyalty are lateral—from leader to follower (Brumfiel 1994). Factions tend to lack formal rules and formal succession in their leadership.

Two villages in Belize show a contrast in the development and role of factional politics (Moberg 1991). One village, Mt. Hope, is faction-free; the other village, Charleston, has divisive factionalism. Economic differences between the two villages are important. In Mt. Hope, the government provided residents with land and established a marketing board to purchase villagers' crops. Farmers grow rice for the domestic market and citrus crops for export. Citrus growers account for about half of Mt. Hope's households, receive more than three-fourths of its total income, and control about 87 percent of the land. In Charleston, most men work in small-scale fishing augmented by part-time farming. Lack of a road that would allow export of agricultural crops has inhibited the development of commercial agriculture. Start-up costs for citrus cultivation (fertilizer, insecticide, tractors) are prohibitive for most Charleston households. Charleston is "racked by intense intergroup conflict," and that includes factional conflict that divides kin groups: "One of the village's most acrimonious political conflicts exists between two brothers whose relationship deteriorated when the allies of one brother were excluded from a cooperative that the other had organized" (221). Intense factionalism in Charleston is sustained by outside political party patronage and favor-giving. Local faction leaders vie with one another to obtain grants and other ben-

---

efits from the state. In return, national political parties look to Charleston as a base for developing political loyalties. The national parties have bypassed Mt. Hope because economic development created less dependence on state favors for projects such as a cooperative or a road. Charleston was ripe for political manipulation; Mt. Hope was not.

In rural France, family ties and family reputation influence who becomes an elected local leader (Abélès 1991). The department of Yonne, located in the Burgundy region southeast of Paris, is the "provincial heartland" of France. Fieldwork there was devoted to understanding how individuals gained access to local political office, and it involved interviewing local politicians, attending town council meetings, and following local elections. France is divided into 36,000 communes that are grouped in 96 departments. Communes and departments are the major arenas for local politics. At the commune level, elected officials are the mayor and town councilors. Several political parties contest the elections—the Socialist party, the Union for French Democracy, and others, including scattered support for the Communist party.

A successful candidate for either commune or department positions should have local roots and come from a distinguished family. Typically, the same family names recur again and again. In one town, the Truchots and the Rostains dominated public life for over a half century. Both families were grain and wine merchants. Another factor influencing electoral choice is a bias toward incumbents. The monopoly of political office by a certain family is perceived by local people to contribute to order and peace. Thus local roots, reputation, and networks combine with a value placed on continuity as the ingredients for electoral success in rural France (see the Critical Thinking box on page 244). This combination is summed up in the concept of legitimacy. "To enjoy legitimacy is to belong to a world of eligible individuals, those to whom responsibilities can be entrusted. Legitimacy is an elusive quality at first glance: certain individuals canvassing the votes of their fellow-citizens are immediately recognized as legitimate, while others, despite repeated efforts, are doomed to failure. . . . It is as though a candidate's legitimacy is something people instinctively recognize"(265).

Gender and Leadership

Most states are hierarchical and patriarchal, excluding members of lower classes and women from equal participation. Some contemporary states are less male-dominated than others, but none are female-dominated. One view of gender inequality in states suggests that increasing male dominance with the evolution of the state is based on male control of the technology of production and warfare (Harris 1993). Women in most cultures have been excluded from these areas of power, and they have not been able to reverse or equalize these longstanding power relationships except in states that are relatively peaceful, such as Finland, Norway, Sweden, and Denmark.

Strongly patriarchal contemporary states preserve male dominance through ideologies that restrict women's political power, such as purdah (female seclusion and segregation from the public world), as practiced in much of the Muslim Middle East, Pakistan, and north India. In China, scientific beliefs that categorize women as less strong and dependable than men have long been used to rationalize the exclusion of women from politics (Dikötter 1998). Socialist states usually pay some attention to increasing women's political roles. The proportion of female members of legislative bodies is higher in socialist states than in capitalist democracies, but still not equal.

A handful of contemporary states have or have recently had women as prime ministers or presidents. Such powerful women include Indira Gandhi in India, Golda Meir in Israel, Margaret Thatcher in the United Kingdom, and Benazir Bhutto in Pakistan. Female heads of state are often related by kinship (as wife or daughter) to former heads of state. Indira Gandhi, for example, was the daughter of the popular first prime minister of independent India, Jawaharlal Nehru (she was not related to Mahatma Gandhi). But it is unclear whether these women's leadership positions can be explained by their inheriting the role or through the political socialization they may have received, directly or indirectly, as a result of being born into political families.

Women's leadership roles can also be indirect, as mothers or wives of male rulers such as Eva Peron in Argentina and Hillary Clinton in the United States during her tenure as first lady. Women's indirect political power through their children, especially sons, is an important but understudied topic. One piece of information comes from contemporary Turkey, where most parents consider politics an undesirable career for their children. However, in a recent survey, more women than men stated that they would say "yes" to their sons' political ambitions (Güneş-Ayata 1995:238–239). The implication is that mothers of male leaders use their position as mothers to influence politics because direct political roles are largely closed to them.

CHANGE IN POLITICAL SYSTEMS

In the early days of political anthropology, researchers examined the varieties of political organization and leadership and created the categories of bands, tribes, chiefdoms, and states. Contemporary political anthropolo-

Supporters of independence for East Timor celebrate on the streets of Dili as Indonesian soldiers leave the capital in September 1999. ■ *Do Internet research to learn about the current political situation in East Timor. Who is the leader? What kind of government has been put in place?* (Source: © Reuters/ Jason Reed)

gists are more interested in political dynamics and change, especially in how the pre-eminent political form, the state, affects local people's lives. This section covers selected topics in the anthropological study of political change.

Emerging Nations and Transnational Nations

Many different definitions exist for a *nation,* and some of them overlap with definitions given for a *state* (Maybury-Lewis 1997b:125–132). One definition says that a **nation** is a group of people who share a language, culture, territorial base, political organization, and history (Clay 1990). In this sense, a nation is culturally homogeneous, and the United States would be considered not a nation but rather a unit composed of many nations. According to this definition, groups that lack a territorial base cannot be termed nations. A related term is the *nation-state,*

which some say refers to a state that comprises only one nation, whereas others think it refers to a state that comprises many nations. A clear example of a nation is the Iroquois nation of central New York state.

Depending on their resources and power, nations may constitute a political threat to states (examples include the Tamils in Sri Lanka, the Tibetans in China, and the Palestinians in the Middle East). In response to this (real or perceived) threat, states seek to create and maintain a sense of unified identity. Political scientist Benedict Anderson, in his widely read book *Imagined Communities* (1991 [1983]) writes about the efforts that state-builders employ to create a sense of belonging—"imagined community"—among diverse peoples. Strategies include the imposition of one language as *the* national language; the construction of monuments and museums; and the creation of songs, poetry, and other media messages about the "motherland." More recently, anthropologists inspired by Anderson's writings have added to his thinking by, for example, including state laws and other bureaucratic prac-

Critical Thinking

HOW "OPEN" IS DEMOCRATIC ELECTORAL POLITICS?

IN FRANCE, the only legal requirements for office are French citizenship and age. Other than that, elected positions are, in principle, "open" to anyone interested in contesting them. According to the perspective that emphasizes human agency in shaping behavior and events, one would hypothesize nearly complete openness in elections and low predictive value of "name" or "family" in determining electoral success. But such "openness" does not seem to be the case in rural Burgundy and may not exist elsewhere.

In comparison, consider the dynamics of the local political system(s) in which you have lived.

CRITICAL THINKING QUESTIONS

What are the criteria in your home country for eligibility to hold office?

Do all eligible people appear to run for office on an equal basis?

Do all eligible people appear equally successful in being elected?

How do the electoral success patterns of candidates resemble or differ from that described for rural Burgundy?

A political rally of indigenous people in Bolivia. ■
Do some research to discover what are the political concerns of indigenous peoples in Bolivia. (Source: Roshani Kothari)

tices as forms of secular ritual that seek to create a sense of unity (Bigenho 1999). State control of areas of life such as religion and language has been documented for many parts of the world.

As emerging states seek to build and maintain a sense of belonging among their plural populations, those groups are building their own solidarity and political momentum. The Kurds, for example, are a group of about 20 million people, most of whom speak some dialect of the Kurdish language (Major 1996). They live in a region that extends from Turkey into Iran, Iraq, and Syria. This area is mainly grasslands, interspersed with mountains, with no coastline. Oil reserves have been found in some places, but the main resource of international interest is the headland of the Tigris and Euphrates rivers: "These rivers give life to the surrounding region (including most of Iraq) and also provide power to Turkey, Syria, and Iraq, through hydroelectric generators built in and near Kurdistan" (C1). The 12 million Kurds in Turkey constitute 20 percent of the total population and live mainly in the southeastern portion of the country (J. Brown 1995). They have been battling for a separate state for years, with no success. The kurds want the right to have Kurdish-language schooling and television

and radio broadcasts; they would like to have their folklore recognized as well.

Attempts by nationalistic states to force homogenization of ethnic groups will prompt resistance of varying degrees from those who wish to retain autonomy. Cultural anthropologists are studying both local and global aspects of these struggles. Their data can contribute to "peace and conflict" studies and policy by providing case studies and theories based on comparative analysis.

With globalization and increased international migration, anthropologists claim that we must rethink the concept of the nation. The case of Puerto Rico is particularly illuminating because of its continuing status as a quasi-colony of the United States (Duany 2000). Puerto Rico is neither fully a state of the United States nor an autonomous political unit with its own national identity. Furthermore, Puerto Rican people do not co-exist in a bounded spatial territory. By the late 1990s, nearly as many Puerto Ricans lived in the United States mainland as on the island of Puerto Rico. Migration to Puerto Rico also occurs, creating cultural diversity there. Migrants include returning Puerto Ricans and others from the United States, such as Dominicans and Cubans. These migration streams—outgoing and incoming—complicate in two ways the sense of Puerto Rico as constituting a nation. First, half of the "nation" lives outside the home territory. Second, within the home territory, ethnic homogeneity does not exist because of the diversity of people who migrate there. The Puerto Ricans who are return migrants are different from the islanders because many have adopted English as their primary language. All of these processes foster the emergence of a transnational identity, which differs from a national identity centered in either the United States or Puerto Rico. (Chapter 15 provides additional material on transnationalism.)

Democratization

Democratization is the process of transformation from an authoritarian regime to a democratic regime. This process includes several features: the end of torture, the liberation of political prisoners, the lifting of censorship, and the toleration of some opposition (Pasquino 1996: 173). In some cases, what is achieved is more a relaxation of authoritarianism than a true transition to democracy, which would occur when the authoritarian regime is no longer in control. Political parties emerge, some presenting traditional interests and others oppositional. The variety of approaches to democratization is great, and outcomes are similarly varied (Paley 2002). Of the twenty-seven nations created from the former Soviet Union, nineteen are democracies, at least in name. All nations in Western Europe are democracies, as are the majority in the Americas. The percentage is about half in Asia and the Pacific. Africa, with less than one-third,

Aung San Suu Kyi is the leader of the Burmese democracy and human rights movement. The daughter of Burma's national hero, Aung San, who was assassinated just before Burma gained its independence from the British, she has frequently been placed under house arrest since 1989. She was awarded the Nobel Peace Prize becoming the eighth woman to receive the award. ■ *What can you learn about her and her writings from the Internet?* (Source: © Daniel Simon/Gamma Images)

has the lowest percentage. The transition to democracy appears to be most difficult when the change is from highly authoritarian socialist regimes. This pattern is partly explained by the fact that democratization implies a transition from a planned economy to one based on market capitalism (Lempert 1996).

Women in Politics: New Directions?

Two questions arise in the area of changing patterns of women in contemporary politics: Is the overall participation of women at varying political levels increasing? Do women in politics bring more attention to women's issues such as the division of labor and wages, access to health care, and violence? The answer to the first question is yes, at the international level, but modestly. In 2000, only 6 of a total of 190 world leaders were women. In terms of the second question, none of these leaders except Bruntland of Norway had a record of supporting women's issues. One interpretation of this pattern is that women political leaders in male-dominated contexts become "like men" or have to avoid "feminist issues" in order to maintain their position.

Women do not have political status equal to that of men in any country (Chowdhury et al. 1994:3). In general, women are still marginalized from formal politics and must seek to achieve their goals either indirectly (as wives or mothers of male politicians) or through channels other than formal politics, such as grassroots movements.

In contrast, in some Native American groups, recovery of former political power is occurring (B. G. Miller 1994). In several communities, female participation in formal politics is increasing, along with attention to issues that face women. This change is taking place within the context of women's greatly decreased roles, the result of colonialist policies. For example, until recently, only Native American men in the United States were allowed to vote. One explanation for the change is that women are obtaining newly available managerial positions on reservations. These positions give women experience in dealing with the outside world and authority for assuming public office. In addition, they face less resistance from men than women in more patriarchal contexts do. Most Native Americans do not view women's roles as contradictory to public authority roles.

The resurgence in women's political roles among the Seneca of New York state and Pennsylvania echoes these themes (Bilharz 1995). From women's precontact position of at least equal political power with men, Seneca women's status had declined in many ways. Notably, when the constitution of the Seneca nation was drawn up on a European model in 1848, men were granted the right to vote, but not women. In 1964, Seneca women finally gained the right to vote. Even before enfranchisement, women were politically active and worked on committees formed to stop the building of Kinzua Dam in Pennsylvania. For Seneca women, job creation through the Seneca Nation of Indians (SNI) brought new employment opportunities. Although no woman has run for president of the Seneca Nation as yet and only a few women have been head of a reservation, many women hold elective offices of clerk and judge, and many women head important service departments of the SNI, such as Education and Health. Women of the Seneca nation still retain complete control over the "clearing" (the cropland), and "their primacy in the home has never been challenged" (112). According to Bilharz, Seneca women have regained a position of equality.

Globalization and Politics

Since the seventeenth century, the world's nations have been increasingly linked in a hierarchical structure that is largely regulated through international trade. In the seventeenth century, Holland was the one core nation, dominating world trade. It was then surpassed by England and France, which remained the two most powerful nations up to around 1900. In the early part of the twentieth century, challenges for world dominance were made by the United States and later Germany and Japan. The outcome of World War II placed the United States as leader of the "core" (see Chapter 3). Most recently, Japan, the European Union, and China are playing larger roles.

Cultural anthropology's traditional strength has been the study of small, bounded local groups, so anthropologists have come late to the study of international affairs (Wilson 2000). Now, more anthropologists have enlarged their focus to the international level, studying both how global changes affect local politics and how local politics affects international affairs. Worldwide communication networks facilitate global politics. Ethnic politics, although locally initiated, increasingly has international repercussions. Migrant populations promote interconnected interests across state boundaries.

A pioneering study in "the anthropology of international affairs" is Stacia Zabusky's (1995) research on patterns of cooperation among international scientists at the European Space Agency. The ESA involves people from different European nations seeking to cooperate in joint ventures in space and, more indirectly, to promote peaceful relations in Europe. Zabusky attended meetings and interviewed people at the European Space Research and Technology Centre, ESA's primary production site, in the Netherlands. Focusing on people's work roles, their styles of reaching consensus at meetings, and the role of national differences in this cooperative effort, she found that language plays a key part in affecting cooperation. The official languages of the ESA are English and French, but most interactions take place in English. Some non-native English speakers felt that this gave the British an automatic advantage, especially in meetings where skill in speech can win an argument. A major divisive factor is the sheer geographic dispersal of the participants throughout Europe. This means that travel is a constant, as scientists and engineers convene for important meetings. Despite logistical problems, meetings are an important part of the "glue" that promoted cooperation above and beyond just "working together." Conversations and discussions at meetings allow people to air their differences and work toward agreement. Zabusky concludes that the ESA represents an ongoing struggle for cooperation that is motivated by more than just the urge to do "big" science. "In working together, participants were dreaming about finding something other than space satellites, other than a unified Europe or even a functioning organization at the end of their travails. Cooperation indeed appeared to participants not only as an achievement but as an aspiration" (197).

We know that culture exists at all levels of human interaction—local, national, international, and transnational and even in cyberspace, and power relations are embedded in culture at all these levels. Anthropologists are now contributing to debates about the definition and use of the term *culture* by international organizations such as UNESCO: Happy as we are that organizations pay attention to culture, our wish is that they would not use outdated concepts that portray cultures as nicely bounded entities with a simple list of traits, such as language, dress, and religion (Wright 1998, Eriksen 2001).

Anthropologists are also tackling the study of powerful international organizations such as NATO (Feldman 2003). Anthropologists must "study up," as Laura Nader urged us to do over three decades ago (1972), because people, power, and culture are "up" there. Anthropologists need to examine their own culture, which tends to be power-averse, to feel empathy with the powerless—with "the village people" and not the people who wield power at NATO. As one anthropologist urges, it is high time that anthropologists break their silence about institutions with lethal powers (Feldman 2003).

KEY CONCEPTS

authority, p. 233
band, p. 235
big-man or big-woman system, p. 236
chiefdom, p. 237
clan, p. 235

faction, p. 241
influence, p. 233
in-kind taxation, p. 239
matriarchy, p. 238
nation, p. 243

political organization, p. 234
power, p. 232
segmentary model, p. 236
state, p. 239
tribe, p. 235

SUGGESTED READINGS

Stanley R. Barrett. *Culture Meets Power.* Westport, CN: Praeger, 2002. The author examines why the concept of power has gained ascendancy in anthropology, seeming to eclipse the concept of culture. He argues that the concept of power is no less ambiguous than that of culture and that the two concepts both need to be considered in understanding contemporary affairs, including events such as the September 11, 2001, attacks on the United States.

Jane K. Cowan, Marie-Bénédicte Dembour, and Richard A. Wilson, eds. *Culture and Rights: Anthropological Perspectives.* New York: Cambridge University Press, 2001. This collection includes three overview/theoretical chapters, seven case studies that address issues such as child prostitution and ethnic and women's rights, and a chapter that critiques the UNESCO concept of culture.

Mona Etienne and Eleanor Leacock, eds. *Women and Colonization: Anthropological Perspectives.* New York: Praeger, 1980. This classic collection examines the impact of Western colonialism and missionary intervention on women of several indigenous groups of North America and South America, Africa, and the Pacific.

A. W. Johnson and Timothy Earle. *The Evolution of Human Societies: From Foraging Groups to Agrarian States.* Stanford, CA: Stanford University Press, 1987. This comprehensive synthesis provides links among ecology, economy, and political organization and includes detailed case studies of over a dozen cultures as illustrations.

David H. Lempert. *Daily Life in a Crumbling Empire.* New York: Columbia University Press, 1996. This two-volume ethnography is based on fieldwork conducted in Moscow before perestroika. It is the first comprehensive ethnography of urban Russia and its economic, political, and legal systems and reforms.

Mark Moberg. *Citrus, Strategy, and Class: The Politics of Development in Southern Belize.* Iowa City: University of Iowa Press, 1992. The theoretical debate of structure versus agency frames this ethnography of household and village economies within the world economy and the transformation from factional politics to class formation. The author provides quantitative data as well as insights from five individual lives in a chapter entitled "Keep on Fighting It."

Dan Rabinowitz. *Overlooking Nazareth: The Politics of Exclusion in Galilee.* New York: Cambridge University Press, 1997. This ethnographic study of Palestinian citizens in an Israeli new town examines specific situations of conflict and cooperation and provides theoretical insights into nationalism and ethnicity. Biographical accounts of three Palestinians—a medical doctor, a basketball coach, and a local politician—are included.

Katherine Verdery. *The Political Lives of Dead Bodies: Reburial and Postsocialist Change.* New York: Columbia University Press, 1999. Post-USSR political changes in Eastern Europe involved a rethinking and revision of the past and forward thinking about the present. An understudied aspect of post-Communist political change in Eastern Europe involved the disposition of the bodies of dead political leaders, heroes, artists, and regular people. Many bodies were exhumed and relocated and have been given a new political "life."

Joan Vincent. *Anthropology and Politics: Visions, Traditions and Trends.* Tucson: The University of Arizona Press, 1990. This text presents a definitive history of the emergence of political anthropology, with a detailed presentation of theories and findings through the late 1980s.

Joan Vincent, ed. *The Anthropology of Politics: A Reader in Ethnography, Theory, and Critique.* Malden, MA: Blackwell Publishers, 2002. Over forty essays are arranged in four broad historical sections to demonstrate the dynamic interplay among theory, ethnography, and critique. First come classics of the Enlightenment (Adam Smith, Karl Marx, others). There follows a section on early ethnographies (E. E. Evans-Pritchard, others), coupled with contemporary updates (such as Sharon Hutchinson). The third section is on colonialism and imperialism (Talal Asad, June Nash, others), and the last focuses on cosmopolitanism (Aihwa Ong, James Ferguson, others).

Jack M. Weatherford. *Tribes on the Hill.* New York: Rawson, Wade Publishers, 1981. This engagingly written analysis of politics within the United States Congress examines the effects of male privilege and seniority on ranking, lobbying tactics, and ritual aspects of the legislation process.

WHAT does political anthropology cover?

Political anthropology is the study of power relationships in the public domain and how they vary and change cross-culturally. Political anthropologists study the concept of power, as well as related concepts such as authority and influence. They have discovered differences and similarities between politics and political organization in small-scale societies and large-scale societies by examining issues such as leadership roles and responsibilities, the social distribution of power, and the emergence of the state.

WHAT are the major cross-cultural forms of political organization and leadership?

Patterns of political organization and leadership vary according to mode of production and global economic relationships. Foragers have a minimal form of leadership and political organization in the band. Band membership is flexible. If a band member has a serious disagreement with another person or a spouse, one option is to leave that band and join another. Leadership in bands is informal. A tribe is a more formal type of political organization than the band. A tribe comprises several bands or lineage groups, with a headman or headwoman as leader. Big-man and big-woman political systems are an expanded form of tribe, with leaders having influence over people in several different villages. Chiefdoms may include several thousand people. Rank is inherited, and social divisions exist between the chiefly lineage or lineages and non-chiefly groups. A state is a centralized political unit encompassing many communities and possessing coercive power. States arose in several locations with the emergence of intensive agriculture, increased surpluses, and increased population density. Most states are hierarchical and patriarchal. Strategies for building nationalism include imposition of one language as *the* national language, monuments, museums, songs, poetry, and other media-relayed messages about the homeland. Ethnic/national politics has emerged within and across states as groups compete for either increased rights within the state or autonomy from it.

HOW are politics and political organization changing?

The anthropological study of change in leadership and political organization has documented several trends, most of which are related to the influences of European colonialism or contemporary capitalist globalization. Post-colonial nations struggle with internal ethnic divisions and pressures to democratize. Women as leaders of states are still a tiny minority. In some groups, however, women leaders are gaining ground, as among the Seneca. Globalized communication networks promote the growth of global politics. Cultural anthropologists have rarely addressed the topic of international political affairs and the role of international organizations such as the United Nations. However, they are increasingly interested in demonstrating the usefulness of cultural anthropology in global peacekeeping and conflict resolution.

THE BIG QUESTIONS

- **WHAT** is the scope of legal anthropology?

- **WHAT** are cross-cultural patterns of maintaining social order and control?

- **WHAT** are cross-cultural patterns of social conflict?

11

SOCIAL ORDER AND SOCIAL CONFLICT

The antiglobalist movement has gained supporters worldwide. This is a scene from the Seattle demonstration during the Global Trade Meeting of 2000. *(Source: © Robert Sorbo/CORBIS)*

Socially agreed-upon ways of behaving shape people's everyday life in countless ways. We wait for our turn to get on a bus rather than pushing to the head of the line, and we pay for a sandwich at the deli instead of stealing it.

This chapter discusses options for maintaining peace and order, including informal arrangements that we hardly know exist and more formal laws and systems of crime prevention. It moves from the study of conformity and order to the study of situations in which normal expectations and laws are not followed, and conflict and violence occur. These issues of order and conflict cross-culturally constitute the important subfield of legal anthropology.

Anthropologists in all four fields have devoted attention to the subjects of social order and social conflict. Archaeologists have examined artifacts such as weapons, remains of forts, and the waxing and waning of political centers in order to understand group conflict in the past. Primatologists study nonhuman primate patterns of cooperation, coalitions, and conflict. Linguistic anthropologists have done research on social conflict related to national language policies and on how communication patterns within the courtroom and in international mediation influence outcomes. Over the course of the twentieth century, legal anthropology, like political anthropology, moved from its original foundations in functionalism (the way a particular practice or belief contributes to social cohesion) toward the study of internal divisiveness.

Launching the subfield through his classic book, *Crime and Custom in Savage Society* (1962 [1926]), functionalist Bronislaw Malinowski wrote that in the Trobriand Islands, social ties themselves promoted mutual social obligation and harmony. No separate legal institutions existed; instead, law was embedded in social life. This discovery that social relationships can perform the same functions as laws and courts was one of his important contributions.

Several new directions have emerged in legal anthropology: the study of legal discourse especially in courtroom settings, law in postcolonial settings, **critical legal anthropology** (an approach that examines how the law and judicial systems serve to maintain and expand the dominant power interests rather than protecting those who are marginal and less powerful), and law and human rights in cross-cultural perspective (Merry 1992).

The concept of social control has several meanings, depending on one's perspective. A generally accepted definition in anthropology is that **social control** is the process by which an orderly social life is maintained (Garland 1996:781). In contrast, others would emphasize the negative aspects of social control systems as institutions that support hierarchy and domination. Underlying both views are two premises:

- Social control systems exist to ensure a certain degree of social conformity to agreed-upon rules.

- Some people in all cultures violate the rules and resist conformity (what sociologists refer to as "deviant behavior").

SYSTEMS OF SOCIAL CONTROL

Social control systems include internalized social controls that exist through socialization for proper behavior, edu-

Amish men in a communal barn-raising in Pennsylvania. ■ *Think of an example of shared work from your microcultural experience.* (Source: © Paul Solomon/Woodfin Camp & Associates)

cation, and peer pressure. They may also include formal systems of codified rules about proper behavior and punishments for deviation. In the United States and Canada, the Amish and Mennonites (Christian immigrant groups from Europe) rely on internalized social controls more than most microcultural groups. These groups have no police force or legal system; the way social order is maintained is through religious teaching and group pressure. If a member veers from correct behavior, punishment such as ostracism ("shunning") may be applied.

Cultural anthropologists distinguish two major instruments of social control: norms and laws. **Norms** are generally-agreed-upon standards for how people should behave. All societies have norms. They are usually unwritten and learned unconsciously through socialization. Norms include, for example, the expectation that children should follow their parents' advice, that people standing in line should be orderly, and that an individual should accept an offer of a handshake (in cultures where handshakes are the usual greeting) when meeting someone for the first time. In rural Bali, etiquette dictates certain greeting forms between people of different status: "[P]ersons of higher status and power are shown very marked respect. . . . if [they are] seated, then others moving past them crouch" (Barth 1993:114).

Enforcement of norms tends to be informal; for example, a violation may simply be considered rude and the violator avoided in the future. In others, direct action may be taken, such as asking someone who disrupts a meeting to leave.

The categories of norm and law form a continuum in terms of how explicitly they are stated and how strongly they are enforced. A **law** is a binding rule created through enactment or custom that defines right and reasonable behavior. Laws are enforceable by threat of punishment. Systems of law are more common and more elaborate in state-level societies, but many non-state societies have formalized laws.

Often the legitimacy and force of law are based on religion. For example, Australian Aborigines believe that law came to humans during the "Dreamtime," a period in the mythological past when the ancestors created the world. Law and religion are synonymous in contemporary Islamic states. Secular Western states consider their laws to be religiously neutral, but in fact, much Western legal practice is heavily influenced by Judeo-Christian beliefs.

In this section, we consider forms of social control in small-scale societies as contrasted with large-scale societies, namely states. The former are more characterized by the use of norms. States rely more on legal sanctions, yet local-level groups, such as neighbors, still practice social sanctions among themselves. The last part of the section takes up findings from critical legal anthropology.

Social Control in Small-Scale Societies

Anthropologists distinguish between small-scale societies and large-scale societies in terms of prevalent forms of conflict resolution, social order, and punishment of offenses. Formal laws are rare among foraging groups, although indigenous circumpolar groups and Australian Aborigines are known for their more formalized, though unwritten, law systems. Because bands are small, close-knit groups, disputes tend to be handled at the interpersonal level through discussion or one-on-one fights. An observer's notes on his conversations with some Kalahari desert foragers lend insight into social order in small

Widespread looting of archaeological artifacts occurred in both Afghanistan and Iraq following U.S.-led military actions. In 2002, this Afgan man put himself in charge of an Islamic archaeological site and allowed local people to search for artifacts to be taken to shops and sold. ■ *See if artifacts from Afghanistan and Iraq are available for sale on the Internet.* (Source: © Kate Brooks/CORBIS)

groups (Ury 1990). They say that if a man takes your bow and arrows, go to the man and tell him not to do it again. If your daughter wants to go off with a man you don't like, try to convince her not to; if she doesn't agree, let her go, knowing that she'll learn her lesson and eventually come back. In the most serious disputes—when a man runs off with another man's wife—the husband should go and get her and then move far away so the other man can't get her again. And what if his wife goes off with another man? The husband should go and fetch her again. What if she refuses to come back? Then he should take the children and move far away, leaving her with the new man.

Group members may act together to punish an offender through shaming and ridicule. Emphasis is on maintaining social order and restoring social equilibrium, not hurtfully punishing an offender. Ostracizing an offending member (forcing the person to leave the group) is a common means of formal punishment. Capital punishment is rare but not nonexistent. For example, in some Australian Aboriginal societies, a law restricted access to religious rituals and paraphernalia to men who had gone through a ritual initiation. If an initiated man shared secrets with an uninitiated man, the elders would delegate one of their group to kill the offender. In such instances, the elders act like a court.

In non-state societies, punishment is often legitimized through belief in supernatural forces and their ability to affect people. Among the highland horticulturalists of the Indonesian island of Sumba, one of the greatest offenses is to fail to keep a promise (Kuipers 1990). Breaking a promise will bring on "supernatural assault" by the ancestors of those who have been offended by the person's misbehavior. The punishment may come in the form of dam-age to crops, illness or death of a relative, destruction of the offender's house, or having clothing catch on fire. When such a disaster occurs, the only recourse is to sponsor a ritual that will appease the ancestors.

Conflict resolution among horticulturalists relies on many of the same methods as among foragers, notably public shaming and ridicule. Discussing disputes in the Trobriand Islands in the early twentieth century, Malinowski provides a functional interpretation:

> The rare quarrels which occur at times take the form of an exchange of public expostulation (*yakala*) in which the two parties assisted by friends and relatives meet, harangue one another, hurl and hurl back recriminations. Such litigation allows people to give vent to their feelings and shows the trend of public opinion, and thus it may be of assistance in settling disputes. (1926: 60)

Village fission (breaking up) and ostracism are mechanisms for dealing with unresolvable conflict. The overall goal in dealing with conflict in small-scale societies is to return the group to harmony.

Social Control in States

In densely populated societies with more social stratification and more wealth, increased stress occurs in relation to the distribution of surplus, inheritance, and rights to land. In addition, increased social scale means that not everyone knows everyone else, and face-to-face accountability exists only in localized groups. Three important factors of state systems of social control are the increased specialization of roles involved in social control, the formalized use of trials and courts, and the use of power-enforced forms of punishment, such as prisons and the

Lessons Applied

LEGAL ANTHROPOLOGIST ADVISES RESISTANCE TO "COERCIVE HARMONY"

IN THIS example, an anthropologist uses her cross-cultural insights to provide a critique of her own culture, with an eye to producing improved social relations (Nader 2001). Laura Nader had conducted extensive fieldwork in Latin America, as well as in the World Court in Europe. Her main interest lies in cross-cultural aspects of conflict and conflict resolution. In terms of her observations of her home country, the United States, she points out that leading politicians are currently emphasizing the need for unity, consensus, and harmony among the American people. But the United States, she points out, was founded by dissenters, and democracy depends on people speaking out. Democracy, in her view, supports the right to be indignant and the idea that "indignation can make Americans more engaged citizens" (B13).

A professor of anthropology at the University of California at Berkeley, Nader fosters the expression of critique, opinion, and even indignation when she teaches. One of her students commented that "Dr. Nader is a pretty good professor, except she has opinions" (B13). She took that as a compliment.

Nader feels that Europeans are generally less concerned about social harmony than the United States is. Americans consider it bad manners to be contentious, whereas in Europe, debate—even bitterly contentious

debate—is valued. She uses the term *coercive harmony* to refer to the informal but strong pressure in the United States to agree, to be nice, to avoid digging beneath the surface, to stifle indignation at the lack of universal health care or the low voter turnout in presidential elections. The unstated, informally enforced policy of coercive harmony labels cultural critique as bad behavior, as negative rather than positive. Nader finds it alarming that in a country that proclaims freedom as its primary feature, coercive harmony in fact suppresses contrary views and voices through the idiom of politeness, niceness, and friendliness.

How can this insight be used to improve the situation in the United States? Nader suggests one step: Make sure that critique, dissent, and indignation are supported in schools. Teachers should avoid contributing to the informal enforcement of social harmony and consensus and should instead proactively encourage critique.

FOOD FOR THOUGHT

Watch several television interview shows with politicians on BBC, and compare the style to that seen on a U.S. station. (Try especially to see Jeremy Paxman, one of Britain's most infamous interviewers.) How do the interview styles compare?

---

death penalty. Yet informal mechanisms also exist. In the accompanying Lessons Applied box, one activist anthropologist provides a cultural critique of them.

Specialization

The specialization of tasks related to law and order—police, judges, lawyers—increases with the emergence of state organization. In non-state societies, society at large determines right from wrong and punishes offenders, or the elders may have special authority and be called on for advice. In chiefdoms, special advisors, such as the "leopard-skin chief" of the Nuer of Sudan, played a leading role in decision making about crime and punishment. Full-time professionals, however, such as judges and lawyers, emerged with the state. These professionals often come from powerful or elite social groups, a fact that perpetuates elite biases in the justice process itself. In the

United States, the legal profession is committed to opposing discrimination on the basis of gender and race, but it is nonetheless characterized by a lack of representation of women and minorities. Minority women, who face a double bind, are especially underrepresented (Chanen 1995:105).

Policing includes processes of surveillance and the threat of punishment related to maintaining social order (Reiner 1996). Police are the specific organization and personnel who discover, report, and investigate crimes. As a specialized group, police exist mainly in states. Japan's low crime rate has attracted the attention of Western law-and-order specialists, who think that it may be the result of the police system there. They are interested in learning whether solutions to America's crime problems can be found in such Japanese policing practices as neighborhood police boxes staffed by foot patrolmen and volunteer crime prevention groups organized on a neighborhood basis.

Fieldwork among police detectives in the city of Sapporo reveals aspects of Japanese culture and policing that promote low crime rates and would not transfer easily to the United States (Miyazawa 1992). First, the police operate under high expectations that no false arrests should be made and that all arrests should lead to confession. And, in fact, the rate of confession is very high. This may be because the police do a good job of targeting the guilty or because the police have nearly complete control of interrogation over isolated suspects for long periods of time, which can lead to wearing down resistance and potentially distorting the process of justice. In Japan, an "enabling legal environment" gives more power to the police and less to the defendant than in United States law. For example, the suspect's statements are not recorded verbatim or taped. The detectives write them up and the suspect is asked to sign them.

Trials and Courts

In societies where misdoing and punishment are defined by spirits and ancestors, a person's guilt is proved simply by the fact that misfortune has befallen him or her. If a person's crops were damaged by lightning, then that person must have done something wrong. In other instances, guilt may be determined through **trial by ordeal**, a form of trial in which the accused person is put through some kind of test that is often painful. In this case, the guilty person will be required to place a hand in boiling oil, for example, or to have a part of the body touched by a red-hot knife. Being burned is a sign of guilt, whereas not being burned means the suspect is innocent. The court system, with lawyers, judge, and jury, is used in many contemporary societies, although there is variation in how cases are presented and juries constituted. The goal of contemporary court trials is to ensure both justice and fairness. Analysis of actual courtroom dynamics and patterns of decision making in the United States and elsewhere, however, reveals serious problems in achieving these goals.

Prisons and the Death Penalty

Administering punishment involves doing something unpleasant to someone who has committed an offense. Cultural anthropologists have examined forms of punishment cross-culturally, as well as the relationship between types of societies and forms of punishment. In small-scale societies, punishment is socially rather than judicially managed. As noted earlier, the most extreme form of punishment is usually ostracism and only rarely death. Another common form of punishment, especially in Islamic cultures of the Middle East, is that in the case

Interior scene of the Cellular Jail in India's Andaman Islands, which was so-named because all prisoners had single cells, arranged in rows, to prevent them from engaging in social interaction and possible collusion to escape or rebel. ■ *Find out about how prisons in your home country are designed.* (Source: Barbara Miller)

of theft or murder, the guilty party must pay compensation to members of the harmed family. The prison, as a place where people are forcibly detained as a form of punishment, has a long history, but it probably did not predate the state. The dungeons and "keeps" of old forts and castles are vivid evidence of the power of some people to detain and inflict suffering on others. In general, such prisoners were not detained for long periods—they were tried and punished and their cell emptied. Long-term detention of prisoners did not become common until the seventeenth century in Europe (Foucault 1977). The first penitentiary in the United States was built in Philadelphia in the late 1700s (Sharff 1995). Cross-nationally and through history, percentages of imprisoned people vary widely. The United States and Russia have high percentages compared to other contemporary Western countries: 550 and 470 prisoners per 100,000 population, respectively. The British Isles rate is about 100, whereas the Scandinavian countries have among the lowest rates, under 60. In the United States, nearly two million people are in prison, and the "corrections industry" is a growing sector of society (Rhodes 2001).

The death penalty (capital punishment) is rare in non-state societies because condemning someone to death requires a great deal of power. A comparison of capital punishment in the contemporary United States with human sacrifice among the Aztecs of Mexico of the sixteenth century reveals striking similarities (Purdum and Paredes 1989). Both systems involve the death of mainly able-bodied males who are in one way or another socially marginal. In the United States, most people who are executed are non-White, have killed Whites, are poor, and have few social ties. Aztec sacrificial victims were mainly male war captives from neighboring states, but Aztec children were also sometimes sacrificed. The deaths in both contexts communicate a political message about the state's power and strength to the general populace, which is why they are highly ritualized and widely publicized events.

Social Inequality and the Law

Critical legal anthropologists examine the role of law in maintaining power relationships through discrimination against such social categories as indigenous people, women, and minorities within various judicial systems around the world, including longstanding democracies. This section presents an example from Australia.

At the invitation of Aboriginal leaders in Australia, Fay Gale and colleagues (1990) conducted research comparing the treatment of Aboriginal youth and that of White youth in the judicial system. The question posed by the Aboriginal leaders was: Why are our kids always in trouble? Two directions can be pursued to find the answer. First, structural factors such as Aboriginal displacement from their homeland, poverty, poor living conditions, and bleak future prospects can be investigated. These factors might make it more likely for Aboriginal youth to commit crimes than the relatively advantaged White youth. Second, the criminal justice system can be examined to see whether it treats Aboriginal and White youth equally. The researchers decided to direct their attention to the judicial system because little work had been done on that area by social scientists. Australia, a former colony of England, adopted the British legal system, which claims to administer the law equitably. Gale's research assesses this claim in one state, South Australia.

Results show that Aboriginal youth are overrepresented at every level of the juvenile justice system, from apprehension (being caught by the police) through pretrial processes to the ultimate stage of adjudication (the judge's decision) and disposition (the punishment): "A far greater proportion of Aboriginal than other young people follow the harshest route. . . . [A]t each point in the system where discretion operates, young Aborigines are significantly more likely than other young persons to receive the most severe outcomes of those available to the decision-makers" (3). At the time of apprehension (being caught by the police), the suspect can be either formally arrested or informally reported. A formal arrest is made to ensure that the offender will appear in court. Officers ask the suspects for a home address and whether they have a job. Aboriginal youths are more likely than White youths to live in a poor neighborhood in an extended family, and they are more likely to be unemployed. Thus they tend to be placed in a category of "undependable," and they are formally arrested more than nonaboriginal youths for the same crime (see Table 11.1). The next step determines whether the suspect will be tried in Children's Court or referred to Children's Aid Panels. The Children's Aid Panels in South Australia have gained acclaim worldwide for the opportunities they give to individuals to avoid becoming repeat offenders and take their proper place in society. But most Aboriginal youth offenders are denied access to them and instead have to appear in court, where the vast majority of youthful offenders end up pleading guilty. The clear and disturbing finding from this look at how Aboriginal youths fare is that the mode of arrest tends to determine each subsequent stage in the system.

TABLE 11.1 Comparison of Outcomes for Aboriginal and White Youth in the Australian Judicial System

	Aboriginal Youth (percent)	White Youth (percent)
Brought into system via arrest rather than police report	43.4	19.7
Referred to Children's Court rather than diverted to Children's Aid Panels	71.3	37.4
Proportion of Court appearances resulting in detention	10.2	4.2

Note: Most of these youths are males; data are from 1979 to 1984.

Source: From "Comparison of Outcomes for Aboriginal and White Youth in the Australian Judicial System," pg. 4, in *Aboriginal Youth and the Criminal Justice System: The Injustice of Justice?* by Faye Gale, Rebecca Bailey-Harris, and Joy Wundersitz. Copyright © 1990. Reprinted by permission of Cambridge University Press.

This scene occurred in Mantes-la-Jolie, France, in 1994. Female Muslim students who wish to wear a headscarf while attending public schools in France have been banned from doing so by the government. This ban has led to protests and court disputes for over a decade. ■ *What is the current position of the French government? What is the current position of your government on clothing allowed in public schools?* (Source: © Giry Daniel/CORBIS SYGMA)

Change in Legal Systems

Law-and-order systems, like other cultural domains, change over time. European colonialism since the seventeenth century has had major effects on indigenous systems. Legal systems of contemporary countries have to deal with social complexity that has its roots in colonialism and new patterns of migration.

European Colonialism and Indigenous Systems

Colonial governments, to varying degrees, attempted to learn about and rule their subject populations through what they termed "customary law" (Merry 1992). By seeking to codify customary law, colonial governments created fixed rules where flexibility and local variation had formerly existed. Often the colonialists ignored local customary law and imposed their own laws. Homicide, marriage, land rights, and indigenous religion were frequent areas of European imposition. Among the Nuer of Sudan, British legal interventions resulted in confusion among the Nuer about blood feuds (Hutchinson 1996). In case of homicide, Nuer practices involved either the taking of a life in repayment or payments in cattle, depending on the relationship between the victim and the assailant, the type of weapon used, and current rates of bridewealth as an index of value. In contrast, the British determined a fixed amount of indemnity, and they imprisoned people for committing a vengeful murder.

From the Nuer point of view, these practices were incomprehensible. They interpreted being put in prison as a way of protecting the accused person from a reprisal attack.

When European administrators and missionaries encountered aspects of marriage systems different from their own, they often tried to impose their own ways. Europeans tried in most cases to stop polygamy as un-Christian and uncivilized. In South Africa, however, British and Afrikaaner Whites tolerated the continuation of traditional marriage practices of South African peoples (Chambers 2000). So-called customary law, applying to the many diverse practices of South African Black communities, permits a number of marriage forms that, despite their variety, share two basic features. First, marriage is considered a union between two families, not two individuals. Second, bridewealth is paid in nearly all groups, though formerly in cattle and now in cash. These traditions made sense in a largely rural population in which men controlled the major form of movable wealth—cattle. In the latter part of the twentieth century, many people no longer lived in rural areas within extended families, and most of these people worked in the wage economy. In the view of South African Blacks of the 1990s, much of customary marriage law appeared inequitable to women, and so the 1994 Black-majority parliament that came to power adopted a new marriage law that eliminated a large part of the customary law. This change reflects a split between the views of "modernist" legislators, who favor gender equity in the law as provided for in the new constitution, and the views of especially rural elders, who feel that tradition has been forsaken.

Colonial imposition of European legal systems onto indigenous systems added another layer, and one that had pre-eminent power over others. **Legal pluralism** exists when more than one kind of legal process might be applied to identical cases (Rouland 1994:50). For example, should a case of murder in the Sudan be tried according to indigenous Sudanese principles or European ones? Post-colonial nations are now in the process of attempting to reform their legal systems and develop more unified codes (Merry 1992:363).

Law and Complexity

In situations where several different cultural groups are subject to a single legal code, misunderstandings between the perspectives of both legal specialists and the affected people are likely and may result in conflict. For example, in the United States and Canada, female genital cutting (recall Chapter 6) is against the law. Yet members of some immigrant groups wish to have their daughters' genitals altered. Cultural relativists (Ahmadu 2000, Shweder 2003) support people's freedom to pursue their traditional cultural practices.

The issue of whether Muslim girls can wear head scarves in school in non-Muslim countries is another example of group rights versus state laws (Ewing 2000). For many Muslims, the head scarf is a sign of proper Muslim society, a rejection of Western secularism, and an aspect of religious freedom. Westerners typically view the head scarf as a sign of women's oppression and as a symbol of rejection of the entire ethos of schooling and modernity. In France, beginning in 1989, disputes have erupted over girls wearing head scarves in school. In 1994, the French education director stated that head scarves would not be permitted in school, yet Jewish boys, at that point, had been allowed to wear yarmulkes (head caps). Muslim leaders responded by taking the issue to court, and as of 2004, the issue has not been settled.

SOCIAL CONFLICT AND VIOLENCE

All systems of social control have to deal with the fact that conflict and violence may occur. This section considers the varieties of social conflict as studied by cultural anthropologists. Conflict can occur at any social level, from the private microlevel of the household to the public situation of international warfare. Here we consider findings from anthropological research on conflict, moving from interpersonal conflict in the domestic domain to public conflict.

Interpersonal Conflict

Interpersonal conflict encompasses a wide range of behavior, from arguments to murder. At the most micro level, the household, interpersonal disputes are common (review Chapter 8's section on domestic violence). Some might say that it's easier to kill or be cruel to someone you don't know, an anonymous enemy. But abusive and lethal conflict between people who are intimately related as lovers or family members is frequent cross-culturally. Dating violence among high school and college students is an increasing problem (Makepeace 1997, Sanday 1996).

Beyond the household, interpersonal conflict occurs between neighbors and residents of the same town or village, often over resources or territory. Since the 1970s, villagers of the Gwembe Valley in Zambia, southern Africa, have kept diaries documenting economic and demographic information and reports of disputes (Colson 1995). Over the years, the number of disputes has increased. There are two possible reasons for this change: Disputing may actually be on the rise because of the increased availability of beer and guns, or the people have become more willing to disclose "the seamy side" of their communities, or both. One thing is clear: Disputes still occur over the same issues: cattle damage to growing crops, land encroachment, inheritance, elopement and impregnation damages, marriage payments and marriage difficulties, slander, accusations of sorcery, theft, physical violence, and the rights of senior people over the labor of younger men and women. One important new cause for disputes is debts.

A different pattern of interpersonal conflict emerges from interviews with one hundred middle-class, American suburbanites (Perin 1988). Dogs emerged as a major basis of conflict: "[I]n the first five minutes of listening to suburbanites discuss neighbors, it became clear that dogs are the most worrisome population. . . ." (108)

Problems include dogs roaming off the leash; barking; relieving themselves; chewing garbage bags; biting; and threatening children, joggers, and bicyclists. How do American suburbanites deal with conflicts about dogs? Some opt for a face-to-face solution, and others resort to the dog warden after trying to talk to the neighbor several times. In pursuing the issue to court, every complaint has to be substantiated. A building inspector in Houston said, "The barking dog isn't as cut and dried a thing as it might seem. We watch it for a week. If we're going to court, we have to prove it's excessive. We have to keep numbers. People's first reaction to a barking complaint is

Anthropologist Michael Herzfeld (far right) observes, and interacts with, Glendiot men at a coffeehouse while doing fieldwork on male bonding and banditry in Crete. ■ *Do you think a woman anthropologist could conduct fieldwork on the topic of male bonding in Crete?* (Source: Cornelia Mayer Herzfeld)

that they're not in violation." (113). Mutual hostility may continue for a long time. The seriousness of dog-related conflicts led to an expanded role of the courts. In Middlesex District Court in Massachusetts, one day each month is devoted to dog cases, and two days a month are needed in Portland, Oregon. In Santa Barbara, California, the city attorney's office provides professional mediation for dog-related disputes.

Banditry

Banditry is a form of aggressive conflict that involves socially patterned theft. It is usually practiced by a person or band of persons who are socially marginal and who gain a special social status from their illegal activity. Political scientists, sociologists, historians, and anthropologists have proposed various theories to explain why banditry appears at particular times and places more than others, why it is persistent in some contexts, and what sentiments inspire bandits. One theory is that bandits flourish in the context of weak states and decline as states grow stronger and increase their control of the use of violence (Blok 1972). Another view is that banditry is a form of protest, expressing a yearning for a just world (Hobsbawm 1969). Neither theory can explain, however, the surge of banditry in late-nineteenth-century Egypt during the time of British colonialism (Brown 1990). British control was not weak, nor was this banditry an expression of anti-British sentiment (banditry existed in Egypt long before the British arrived). Instead, the answer appears to be that the British chose to highlight the presence of banditry as a social problem so that they could justify their presence and role in imposing law and order.

One anthropologist has, somewhat humorously, termed banditry "adventurist capital accumulation" (Sant Cassia 1993:793), but it is much more than that. For example, banditry, male identity and status, and the creation of social alliances are closely associated on the Greek island of Crete (Herzfeld 1985). In this sheepherding economy, manhood and male identity depend on a local form of banditry—stealing sheep. "Coming out on the branch" is a metaphor for the attainment of manhood following a young male's first theft. This phrase implies that he is now a person to be reckoned with. To not participate in sheep raids is to be effeminate. Each theft, however, requires a countertheft in revenge, and so the cycle goes on. For protection of his flock from theft and to be able to avenge any theft that occurs, a shepherd relies heavily on male kin (both patrilineal kin and kin through marriage). Another important basis for social ties is sheep stealing itself. After a series of thefts and counterthefts and rising hostility between the two groups, a mediator is brought in to resolve the tension, the result being that the enemies swear to be loyal friends from then

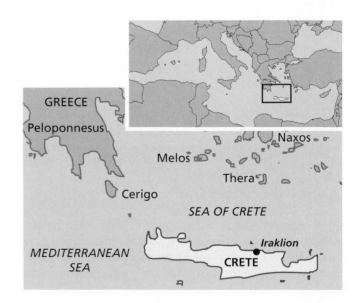

toralism, and raiding as honorable. Villagers have composed songs praising her, and a movie appeared in 1995 depicting her as a heroine who suffered, resisted, and ultimately triumphed.

Feuding

Feuding, or long-term, retributive violence that may be lethal between families, groups of families, or tribes, is a widely distributed form of intergroup aggression. A concept of revenge motivates such back-and-forth violence between two groups. Feuding long had an important role among the horticultural Ilongot people of the Philippine highlands (Rosaldo 1980). From 1883 to 1974, Ilongot feuds were structured around headhunting as redress for an insult or offense. Manhood was defined by the taking of a first head, and fathers were responsible for transferring the elaborate knowledge of headhunting to their sons. In 1972, the government banned headhunting and attempted to stop the Ilongot from practicing shifting horticulture. The repercussions were devastating. The banning of headhunting weakened father–son ties that had been solidified by the handing down of the elaborate techniques of headhunting. The people said they were no longer Ilongots.

Sometimes contemporary change may lead to increased feuding, as in the case of Thull, a Pakistani village of about 6000 people (Keiser 1986). "Blood feuds" (which involve the death of someone in the enemy group) increased in frequency and intensity over a fifteen-year period in the 1960s and 1970s. Previously, there had been fights, usually expressing hostility between members of three patrilineal clans, but they rarely involved deadly weapons. According to the traditional honor code in this region, an act of avenging should not exceed the original act: A blow should answer a blow, a death a death. For a murder, a man prefers to kill the actual murderer, but a father, adult brother, or adult son is a permissible substitute; killing women and children is unknown. Wrongs committed against a man through his wife, sister, or daughter are special, and whatever the transgression, the most appropriate response is to kill the offender: "For example, staring at a man's wife or his daughter or sister (if she is of marriageable age) demands a deadly retaliation. Thus, according to some people in Thull, Diliwar Khan killed Said Omar because Said Omar had come to Diliwar Khan's door "not to bring food, but rather to catch a glimpse of Diliwar Khan's attractive young wife" (327).

Why did blood feuds increase in Thull? The answer lies in the effects of economic change on the area. A new road changed the economy from a balanced blend of herding and cultivation to increased cultivation, especially of potatoes as a cash crop. The government initi-

Phulan Devi, India's "Bandit Queen" and heroine of the poor, became an elected Member of Parliament after eleven years in prison. Here she participates in Parliament in New Delhi in 2000. She was assassinated in 2001. ■ *For a class project, read a biography of her, watch the video called "The Bandit Queen," read commentary on the Internet, and be prepared to comment on the "mythic" aspects of her life's story.* (Source: AFP/CORBIS)

on. Male identity formation through sheep stealing in highland Crete is still strong, although it is declining somewhat as some shepherds take up farming. Another force of change is the government, which has sought, mainly unsuccessfully, to suppress the raiding and to define sheep stealing as a crime.

Analysis of many instances of banditry reveals that they often involve mythification of bandits (Sant Cassia 1993). In this process, the imagined character of the bandit becomes more significant than what the bandit actually did. The story of Phulan Devi, India's "Bandit Queen," contains many aspects of banditry mythification: her low socioeconomic status, traditions of pas-

The Hatfield clan in West Virginia in 1899. The longstanding feud between the Hatfields and the McCoys became part of American legend. ■ *What can you learn about the cultural context of this feud?* (Source: © Bettmann/CORBIS)

ated large-scale logging operations in the region (the reason for building the road), which involved local men in wage work and greatly increased the amount of cash available. Tension increased among males, and men grew more vigilant about defending their honor. Along with the increased cash came a dramatic increase in the number of firearms owned. Now even poor men can afford rifles. More guns mean more lethal feuding.

Ethnic Conflict

Ethnic pluralism is a characteristic of most states in the world today. Ethnic conflict and grievances may result from an ethnic group's attempt to gain more autonomy or more equitable treatment (Esman 1996). It may also be caused by a dominant group's actions to subordinate, oppress, or eliminate an ethnic group by genocide or ethnocide. In the past few decades, political violence has increasingly been enacted within states rather than between states and constitutes the majority of many "shooting wars" in the world today (Clay 1990). Political analysts and journalists often cite ethnicity, language, and religion as the causes of certain conflicts. It is true that ethnic identities give people an ideological sense of commitment to a cause, but one must look beneath these labels to see whether deeper issues exist, such as claims to land, water, ports, and other material resources.

Consider Central Asia, a vast region populated by many ethnic groups, none of whom has a pristine indigenous claim to the land. Yet in Central Asia, every dispute

appears on the surface to have an ethnic basis: "Russians and Ukrainians versus Kazakhs over land rights and jobs in Kazakhstan, Uzbeks versus Tajiks over the status of Samarkhand and Bukhara, conflict between Kirghiz and Uzbeks in Kyrghyzstan, and riots between Caucasian Turks and Uzbeks in the Fergana Valley of Uzbekistan" (Clay 1990:48).

Attributing all such problems to ethnic differences overlooks resource competition based on regional, not ethnic, differences. Uzbekistan has most of the cities and irrigated farmland, but small states like Kyrghyzstan and Tajikistan control most of the water. Turkmenistan has vast oil and gas riches. "No ethnic catalyst would be needed to provoke conflict in such situations; simple need or greed would more than suffice" (51). Ethnic conflicts are waged in many different ways, from the cruelest and most gruesome killings and rapes to more subtle forms. (See the Unity and Diversity box.)

Revolution

A **revolution** is a political crisis initiated by illegal and usually violent actions by subordinate groups that seek to change political institutions (Goldstone 1996:740). Revolutions have occurred in a range of societies, including monarchies, postcolonial Third World countries, and totalitarian states. Scholars who have compared revolutions in modern times—England 1640, France 1789, Mexico 1910, China 1911, Russia 1917, Iran 1979—say that interrelated factors, such as a military or fiscal crisis and a weak state military machine, may prompt a revolution. The process of revolution varies in terms of the degree of popular participation, the roles of radicals and moderates, and leadership.

Theorists also argue about the different roles of rural and urban sectors in fostering revolution. Many revolutions occurred in mainly agrarian countries and were propelled by rural participants, not urban radicalism (Skocpol 1979; E. Wolf 1969). Such agrarian-based revolutions include the French, Russian, and Chinese revolutions. A rural-based movement also characterizes many national liberation movements against colonial powers such as French Indo-China, Guinea-Bissau, Mozambique, and Angola (Gugler 1988). Algeria was a somewhat more urbanized country, but it was still about two-thirds rural in 1962 when the French finally made peace there. In all of these cases, the colonial power was challenged by a rural-based guerrilla movement that controlled crop production, processing, and transport and thus could strike at the heart of the colonial political economy.

On the other hand, some revolutions have been essentially urban in character, as in Bolivia, Iran, and Nicaragua. The case of Cuba is mixed; rural-based guerrillas played a prominent role and the cities provided cru-

Unity and Diversity

BOSNIAN REFUGEES' TRAUMA TESTIMONIES

REFUGEE SURVIVORS of violence are especially at risk to suffer from various mental health problems, including what Western psychiatrists term PTSD (post-traumatic stress disorder). PTSD can include symptoms such as depression, anxiety, sleep disorders, and changes in personality. In treating refugee survivors in North America, several approaches have been used, including the testimony method in conjunction with therapy such as support groups. One study of twenty Bosnian refugees who are now settled in the United States sheds light on the positive effects of having survivors narrate their "trauma testimonies," which are accounts of their experiences of terror and suffering (Weine et al. 1995). The testimony method involves asking the individual "to tell in detail the story of what happened to them and recording their narrative account verbatim. . . . many clinicians agree that having individuals tell the story of their traumatic experiences in a safe and caring interpersonal setting helps them to live better with traumatic memories" (536–537).

Ten of the refugees in the study were male and ten were female. They belonged to six families and ranged in age from 13 to 62 years. All but one were Muslims, and all adults were married and had worked either inside or outside the home. Analysis of the testimony showed that all had experienced a high number of traumatic events, the frequency increasing with a person's age. The number of traumatic events in the narratives did not differ by gender, but the qualitative aspects of the trauma did:

> Adult men were more likely to be separated from their families and to be held in concentration camps where they suffered extreme deprivation and atrocities. Adult women (as well as adolescents of both genders) were often held briefly in detention camps and

then they spent months fleeing from capture or being held in occupied territory where they were subjected to violence. (537)

Almost all the refugees experienced the destruction of their homes, forced evacuation, food and water deprivation, disappearance of family members, exposure to acts of violence or death, detainment in a refugee camp, and forced emigration: "Nearly all the refugees emphasized the shock that came with the sudden occurrence of human betrayal by neighbors, associates, friends, and relatives" (538).

The testimonies document the genocidal nature of the traumas directed at the entire Muslim Bosnian population. The traumas experienced were "extreme, multiple, repeated, prolonged and communal" (539). Some of the survivors carry with them constant images of death and atrocity. One man describes them as "films" that play in his head. In contrast, others have lost their memories of the events, and one woman was later unable to remember the trauma story she told three weeks earlier: "All kinds of things come together. Being expelled. Things we lost. Twenty years of work—then suddenly being without anything. . . . All the memories come at the same moment and it's too much" (541). The massiveness of their suffering, the psychiatrists report, extends beyond the bounds of the current diagnostic category of PTSD.

FOOD FOR THOUGHT

The Bosnian refugees described here have experienced diverse cultural interactions, from the violence in their homelands to Western therapeutic treatment in the United States. Have you ever experienced anything similar to either one of these situations? If so, what were your reactions and feelings?

cial support for the guerrillas. The importance of cities in these revolutions is related to the fact that the countries were highly urbanized. Thus, revolutionary potential exists where resources are controlled and where the bulk of the population is located. Given the rapid urban growth in Third World countries, it is possible that the world is entering "the age of urban revolutions" (Gugler 1988).

Warfare

Several definitions of war have been proposed (Reyna 1994). Is it open and declared conflict between two political units? This definition would rule out, for example, the American–Vietnam War because it was undeclared. Is it simply organized aggression? This definition is too broad because not all organized violence can be consid-

YANOMAMI: THE "FIERCE PEOPLE"?

THE YANOMAMI are a horticultural people living in dispersed villages of between 40 and 250 people in the Venezuelan rain forest (Ross 1993). Since the 1960s, sociobiological anthropologist Napoleon Chagnon has studied several Yanomami villages. He has written a widely read and frequently republished ethnography called *The Fierce People* (1992 [1968]) about the Yanomami and helped to produce several classic ethnographical films about them, including "The Feast" and "The Axe Fight."

Chagnon's writings and films have promoted a long-standing view of the Yanomami as exceptionally violent and prone to lethal warfare. According to Chagnon, about one-third of adult Yanomami males die violently, about two-thirds of all adults had lost at least one close relative through violence, and over 50 percent had lost two or more close relatives (205). He has reported that one village was raided 25 times during his first 15 months of fieldwork. Although village alliances are sometimes formed, they are fragile and allies may turn against each other unpredictably.

Chagnon's representation of the Yanomami world is one of danger, threats, and counterthreats. Enemies, human and supernatural, are everywhere. Support from one's allies is uncertain. All of this uncertainty leads to what Chagnon describes as the *waiteri* complex, a set of behaviors and attitudes that includes a fierce political and personal stance for men and forms of individual and group communication that stress aggression and independence. Fierceness is a dominant theme in socialization, as boys learn how to fight with clubs, participate in chest-pounding duels with other boys, and use a spear. Adult males are aggressive and hostile toward adult females, and young boys learn to be aggressive toward girls from an early age.

Chagnon provides a sociobiological explanation for the Yanomami's being so fierce. He reports that the Yanomami explain that village raids and warfare are carried out so that men may obtain wives. Although the Yanomami prefer to marry within their village, there is a shortage of potential brides because the Yanomami practice of female infanticide creates a scarcity of women. Although the Yanomami prefer to marry endogamously, taking a wife from another group is preferable to remaining a bachelor. Men in other groups, however, are unwilling to give up their women; hence the necessity for raids. Suspicion of sorcery or theft of food are other valid reasons for raids. Chagnon argues that within this system, warfare contributes to reproductive success because successful warriors are able to gain a wife or more than one wife (polygyny is allowed). Thus successful warriors will have higher reproductive rates than unsuccessful warriors. Successful warriors, Chagnon suggests, have a genetic advantage for fierceness, which they pass on to their sons, leading to a higher growth rate of groups with violent males through genetic selection for fierceness. Male fierceness, in this view, is biologically adaptive. This position has raised substantial controversy for many years.

Marvin Harris (1984), from the cultural materialist perspective, says that protein scarcity and population dynamics in the area are the underlying cause of warfare. The Yanomami lack plentiful sources of meat, which is highly valued. Harris suggests that when game in an area became depleted, pressure would rise to expand into the territory of neighboring groups, thus precipitating conflict. Such conflicts in turn resulted in high rates of adult male mortality. Combined with the effects of female infanticide, this meat-warfare complex kept population growth rates down to a level that the environment could support.

Another view depends on historical data. Brian Ferguson (1990) argues that the high levels of violence were caused by the intensified Western presence during the preceding one hundred years. Furthermore, diseases introduced from outside, especially measles and malaria,

ered warfare. Perhaps the best definition is that **war** is organized, group action directed against another group and involving lethal force (Ferguson 1994, quoted in Reyna 1994:30). A critical point is that lethal force during war is legal if it is conducted according to the rules of battle.

Cultural variation exists in the frequency and seriousness of wars. Intergroup conflicts between different bands of foragers are relatively rare. The informal, non-hierarchical political organization among bands is not conducive to waging armed conflict. Bands do not have specialized military forces or leaders.

Archaeological evidence indicates that warfare intensified during the Neolithic era. Plant and animal domestication required more extensive land use, and they were accompanied by increased population densities. The

severely depopulated the Yanomami and would have greatly increased their fears of sorcery (that is how they explain disease). The attraction to Western goods such as steel axes and guns would also increase intergroup rivalry. Thus Ferguson suggests that the "fierce people" are a creation of historical forces, especially contact and pressure from outsiders, as much as of factors internal to their society.

Following on Ferguson's position but with a new angle, journalist Patrick Tierney pointed the finger of blame at Chagnon himself (2000). Tierney maintained that it was the presence of Chagnon, with his team of co-researchers and many boxes of trade goods, that triggered a series of lethal raids because of increased competition for those very goods. In addition, Tierney argued that Chagnon intentionally prompted the Yanomami to act fiercely for his films and to stage raids that actually led to bad feelings where they had not existed before.

In 2001, the American Anthropological Association established the El Dorado Task Force, charging it to examine five topics related to Tierney's allegations that Chagnon's and others' representations of the Yanomami may have had a negative impact on them and that the activities of anthropologists and others may have contributed to "disorganization" among the Yanomami. The report of the El Dorado Task Force appears on the AAA website (*www.aaanet.org*). Overall, the AAA position repudiates all charges against Chagnon and instead emphasizes the harmfulness of false accusations that may jeopardize future scientific research.

Napoleon Chagnon (center) in the field with two Yanomami men, 1995. Chagnon has been accused of using lavish distribution of goods to the Yanomami to gain their cooperation in his research, but thereby markedly changing their culture. ■ (Source: © Antonio Mari)

CRITICAL THINKING QUESTIONS

Do you think that Chagnon's characterization of the Yanomami as the "fierce people" is accurate? [*Hint:* Are all Yanomami people equally fierce?]

Which perspective presented here appears most persuasive to you and why?

What relevance does this case have to the theory that violence is a universal human trait?

resulting economic and demographic pressures put more and larger groups in more direct and intense competition with each other. Tribal leadership patterns facilitate mobilization of warrior groups for raids (recall the discussion of the segmentary model in Chapter 10). But tribal groups do not have uniform levels of warfare. At one extreme are the Yanomami of the Venezuelan and Brazilian Amazon, who have been described as "the fierce peo-

ple." Some anthropologists, however, question whether this characterization of the Yanomami is correct. (See the Critical Thinking box.)

Many chiefdoms have high rates of warfare and high casualty rates. They have increased capacity for war in terms of personnel and surplus foods to support long-range expeditions. The chief could call on his or her retainers as a specialized fighting force as well as the gen-

Mahatma Gandhi (left), leader of the Indian movement for freedom from British colonial control, on his famous "Salt March" of 1930, in which he led a procession to the sea to collect salt in defiance of British law. He is accompanied by Sarojini Naidu, a noted freedom fighter. ■ *What are your images of Gandhi and how did you come by them?* (Source: © Bettmann/CORBIS)

attempts to extend boundaries, secure more resources, ensure markets, support political and economic allies, and resist aggression from other states. Others point to humanitarian concerns that prompt participation in "just wars," to defend values such as freedom or to protect human rights that are defined as such by one nation and are being violated in another.

Causes of war in Afghanistan have changed over time (Barfield 1994b). Since the seventeenth century warfare had increasingly become a way in which kings justified their power in terms of the necessity to maintain independence from outside forces such as the British and Czarist Russia. The last Afghan king was murdered in a coup in 1978. When the Soviet Union invaded in 1979, no centralized ruling group existed to meet it. The Soviet Union deposed the ruling faction, set up one of its own, and then waged war against the Afghan population, killing over one million people and causing three million Afghans to flee the country and millions of others to be displaced internally. Yet, in spite of the lack of a central command, ethnic and sectarian differences, and being outmatched in equipment by Soviet forces, Afghanistan mounted a war of resistance that eventually wore down the Soviets, who withdrew in 1989.

This case suggests that war was a more effective tool of domination in the premodern period when it settled matters more definitively. In premodern times, fewer troops were needed to maintain dominance after a conquest, because continued internal revolts were less common and the main issue was defense against rivals from outside. Success in the Soviet Union's holding of Afghanistan would have required more extensive involvement and commitment, including introduction of a new economic and political system and ideology that would win the population over. Current events show only too clearly that winning a war and taking over a country represent only the first stage in a process much more complicated than the term *regime change* implies. Afghanistan is now attempting to recover and rebuild after twenty-five years of war, although its problems of national integration and security have roots that go much deeper than the Soviet invasion (Shahrani 2002). These roots include powerful local codes of honor that value political autonomy and require vengeance for harm received, the superimposed moral system of Islam, the revitalized drug economy, and the effects of intervention from outside powers involving governments and corporations, including Unocal of California, Delta Oil of Saudi Arabia, and Bridas of Argentina. The difficulty of constructing a strong state with loyal citizens in the face of these conflicting internal and external factors is great.

In addition to studying the dynamics of war itself and post-conflict situations, cultural anthropologists also study the armed forces as social institutions, issues related to soldiers in the armed forces, and the effects of soldiers

eral members of society. Chiefs and paramount chiefs could be organized into effective command structures (Reyna 1994:44–45). The potential for more extensive and massive campaigns expanded as chiefdoms and confederacies evolved into state-level organizations. In states, standing armies and complex military hierarchies are supported by increased material resources through taxation and other forms of revenue generation. Greater state power allows for more powerful and effective military structures, which in turn increase the state's power. Thus a mutually reinforcing relationship emerges between the military and the state. States are generally highly militarized, but not all are, nor are all states equally militarized. Costa Rica does not maintain an army, whereas Turkey has one of the world's largest.

Examining the causes of war between states has occupied scholars in many fields for centuries. Some experts have pointed to common, underlying causes, such as

Representatives of ten NATO countries at the World Court in The Hague. This distinguished body of legal experts exhibits a clear pattern of age, gender, and ethnicity. ■ *What might be the implications of this pattern?* (Source: © Reuters/Fred Ernst)

on the wider society. Cultural anthropologists are, by and large, against war and have perhaps, therefore, shied away from studying the institutions of war. But now they are paying increased attention to the armed forces. Much of this research comes from a perspective of critique, viewing the armed forces as instruments of power and, often, repressive domination. Militarization in particular, or the intensification of labor and resources allocated to military purposes, is studied in order to provide insights that might lead to its control and reduction (Lutz 2002). In parallel with discussions elsewhere in this book, we could name this emerging area of study **critical military anthropology**, the study of the military as a power structure.

A study of the military in Bolivia reveals, for example, that the young, male soldiers are recruited from the most powerless sections of society—minority farming groups such as the Quechua and Aymara, and poor urban dwellers (Gill 1997). They serve as the foot soldiers who risk death in combat more than the members of more powerful social groups and who are more likely to suffer emotional abuse from their commanding officers. Military service is an obligation of all able-bodied Bolivian men, but many middle-class and upper-class men are able to avoid serving. It is also a prerequisite for many forms of urban employment. A more subtle, underlying motivation is that army service enables marginalized, powerless boys to express bravery, competence, and patriotism and thereby earn the respect and admiration of women as responsible adult males. The army instills a heightened sense of masculinity in its soldiers first through basic training, which lasts for three months and emphasizes the importance of male bonding and the link between

masculinity and citizenship. A soldier who completes his service receives a *libreta militar,* "military booklet," which documents his successful completion of duty and is used to help him obtain work in urban factories. The booklet is also useful in various transactions with the state and thus is a kind of ticket to citizenship. Better-off men simply pay a fee for the booklet. That is easy enough for them but impossible for poor men whose wages would not support the cost, which, in the late 1990s, ranged between $200 and $500.

In Israel, military service is a focal point of citizenship and nation-building (Khanaaneh 2002). Service in the military, for all Jewish citizens, is also a pathway to full citizenship. Non-Jews in Israel, notably Palestinians who constitute one-fifth of Israel's population, are normally excluded from the military. Nonetheless, about 5000 Palestinians living in Israel currently volunteer to serve in the Israeli military. Interviews with twenty-four Arab men and one Arab woman who have served in various Israeli security branches—the army, border patrol, and police force—reveal the complexities and contradictions involved in their motivations and their identities as military personnel. These people are socially marginal in Israeli society because they are Arabs, and are even feared as security threats, but in their roles in the military they often gain positions of power and physical force. Joining the military is a way for these people to achieve higher status through access to jobs, state land, educational subsidies, and low-interest loans. All of these entitlements are denied to non-serving Arabs. Being able to buy state land, however, raises a stark contradiction: The state policy of taking over Arab lands often involves confiscating land of Arabs who served in the military. In one instance in 2002, fifty homes of Arab Bedouins who had served were confiscated. Thus, military service enables Arabs to buy back land that was originally theirs. Other contradictions arise when Arab members of the Israeli army have to carry out operations against other Arabs. Some of the soldiers justify their role by saying that their presence makes for gentler treatment of Arabs than would otherwise be administered. Others say that they are "nationalists" and that their role is neither Zionist nor Arab.

Nonviolent Conflict

Mohandas K. Gandhi was one of the greatest designers of strategies for bringing about peaceful political change. Born in India, he studied law in London and then went to South Africa, where he worked as a lawyer serving the Indian community and evolved his primary method of civil disobedience through nonviolent resistance (Caplan 1987). In 1915 he returned to India, joined the nationalist struggle against British colonialism, and put into action

Women near Kabul, Afghanistan, look at replicas of land mines during a mining awareness program sponsored in 2003 by the International Committee of the Red Cross (ICRC). Afghanistan is still heavily mined and rates of injury and mortality from mines are high. ■ *Do Internet research to learn about international organizations involved in de-mining.* (Source: © Reuters NewMedia Inc./CORBIS)

his model of civil disobedience through nonviolent resistance, public fasting, and strikes.

Celibacy is another key feature of Gandhian philosophy because avoiding sex helps maintain one's inner strength and purity (recall the lost semen complex mentioned in Chapter 5). Regardless of whether one agrees with Gandhi's support of sexual abstinence, the methods he developed of nonviolent civil disobedience have had a profound impact on the world. Martin Luther King, Jr., and his followers adopted many of Gandhi's tactics during the U.S. Civil Rights Movement, as did members of the Peace Movement of the 1960s and 1970s in the United States.

Most subordinate classes throughout history have not had the luxury of open, organized political activity because of its danger. Instead, people have had to resort to ways of living with or "working" the system. Political scientist James Scott (1985) used the phrase *weapons of the weak* in the title of his book on rural people's resistance to domination by landlords and government through tactics other than outright rebellion or revolution. Weapons of the weak include "foot dragging," desertion, false compliance, feigned ignorance, and slander, as well as more aggressive acts such as theft, arson, and sabotage. Many anthropologists have followed Scott's lead and contributed groundbreaking studies of everyday resistance. One weapon of the weak that Scott overlooked is humor. Humor is an important part of Native American cultural resistance to domination by White society (Lincoln 1993). Instead of pitying themselves or lamenting the genocide that occurred as a result of European and Euro-American colonization, Native Americans have cultivated a sharp sense of humor. "Rez"

(reservation) jokes travel like wildfire. Charlie Hill, for example, is notorious for his one-liners:

> The first English immigrants, he snaps, were illegal aliens—"Whitebacks, we call 'em." Hill imagines the Algonquians asking innocently, "You guys gonna stay long?" His Custer jokes are not printable ("Look at all those f---ing Indians!"—a barroom nude painting of Custer's last words). (4–5)

Or, what did Native Americans say at Plymouth Rock? Answer: "There goes the neighborhood." Obviously, humor has not been the only source of strength for Native Americans, but humor surely must be added to the list of weapons of the weak.

MAINTAINING WORLD ORDER

Computer-operated war missiles, e-mail, the Internet, satellite television, and jet flights mean that the world's nations are more closely connected and better able to influence each other's fate than ever before. Modern weaponry means that such influences can be more lethal and more depersonalized. In the face of these realities, politicians, academics, and the public ponder the possibilities for world peace. Anthropological research on peaceful, local-level societies shows that humans are capable of living together in peace. The question is whether people living in larger groups that are globally connected can also live in peace. This section discusses two issues related to world order.

International Legal Disputes

Numerous attempts have been made, over time, to create institutions to promote world peace. The United Nations is the most established and respected of such institutions. One of the UN's significant accomplishments was its creation of the International Court of Justice, also known as the World Court, located in The Hague in the Netherlands (Nader 1995). In 1946, two-thirds of the Court's judges were American or Western European. Now the Court has many judges from developing countries. Despite this more balanced representation, there has been a decline in use of the World Court and an increased use of international negotiating teams for resolving disputes between nations. Laura Nader analyzed this decline and found that it follows a trend in the United States, beginning in the 1970s, to promote "alternate dispute resolution" (ADR). The goal was to move more cases out of the courts and to privatize dispute resolution. On the surface, ADR seems a more peaceful and more dignified option. Deeper analysis of actual cases and their resolution shows, however, that this bilateral process favors the stronger party. Adjudication (formal decree by a judge) would have resulted in a better deal for the weaker party than bilateral negotiation did. Thus less powerful nations are negatively affected by the move away from the World Court.

The United Nations and International Peace-Keeping

What role might cultural anthropology play in international peace-keeping? Robert Carneiro (1994) has a pessimistic response. Carneiro says that during the long history of human political evolution from bands to states, warfare has been the major means by which political units enlarged their power and domain. Foreseeing no logical end to this process, he predicts that war will follow war until superstates become ever larger and one megastate is the final result. He considers the United Nations powerless in dealing with the principal obstacle to world peace, which is national sovereignty interests. Carneiro indicts the United Nations for its lack of coercive power and its poor record of having resolved disputes through military intervention in only a few cases. If war is inevitable, there is little room for hope that anthropological knowledge can be applied to peace-making efforts.

But despite Carneiro's views, cultural anthropologists have shown that war is not a cultural universal and that different cultures have ways of solving disputes without resorting to killing. The cultural anthropological perspective of critical cultural relativism (review this concept in Chapter 1) can provide useful background on issues of conflict and prompt a deeper dialogue between parties.

One positive point emerges. The United Nations does provide an arena for airing disputes. This more optimistic view suggests that international peace organizations play a major role by providing analysis of the interrelationships among world problems and by helping others see what are the causes and consequences of violence (Vickers 1993:132). In addition, some people see hope for local and global peace-making through nongovernmental organizations and local grassroots initiatives that seek to bridge group interests.

KEY CONCEPTS

banditry, p. 260
critical legal anthropology, p. 252
critical military anthropology, p. 267
feuding, p. 261

law, p. 253
legal pluralism, p. 259
norm, p. 253
policing, p. 255

revolution, p. 262
social control, p. 252
trial by ordeal, p. 256
war, p. 264

SUGGESTED READINGS

John Carman, ed. *Material Harm: Archaeological Studies of War and Violence.* Glasgow, Scotland: Cruithne Press, 1997. The editor provides an introductory chapter on archaeological approaches to violence and a concluding chapter on the need to give archaeology a moral voice. Nine case study chapters consider topics such as the identification of head injuries, Irish Bronze Age swords, West Mediterranean hill forts, and warfare and the spread of agriculture in Borneo.

Jack David Eller. *From Culture to Ethnicity to Conflict: An Anthropological Perspective on International Ethnic Conflict.* Ann Arbor: University of Michigan Press, 1999. Two introductory chapters discuss terminology and the relationships among culture, ethnicity, and conflict, and subsequent chapters provide case studies of Sri Lanka, the Kurds, Rwanda and Burundi, Bosnia, and Québec.

R. Brian Ferguson and Neil L. Whitehead, eds. *War in the Tribal Zone: Expanding States and Indigenous Warfare.* Santa Fe, NM: School of American Research Press, 1992. Essays on tribal and pre-state warfare include examples from pre-Columbian Mesoamerica, early Sri Lanka, West Africa, the Iroquois, the Yanomami, and highland New Guinea.

Pamela Frese and Margaret Harrell, eds. *Anthropology and the United States Military: Coming of Age in the Twenty-First Century.* New York: Palgrave/Macmillan, 2003. This volume of collected essays contributes to knowledge in several core anthropological areas (such as kinship, the body, leadership, and meaning) by addressing army spouses, gender roles, weight control and physical readiness, anthrax vaccines, and the military advisor, among other topics.

Thomas Gregor, ed. *A Natural History of Peace.* Nashville: University of Tennessee Press, 1996. This book contains essays on "what is peace?" reconciliation among nonhuman primates, the psychological bases of violent and caring societies, community-level studies on Amazonia and Native America, and issues of peace and violence between states.

Hugh Gusterson. *Nuclear Rites: A Weapons Laboratory at the End of the Cold War.* Berkeley: University of California Press, 1996. This ethnographic study focuses on the nuclear research community of Livermore, California. It explores the scientists' motivations to develop nuclear weapons, the culture of secrecy in and around the lab, and prevalent metaphors in nuclear research, which often have to do with reproduction and birth.

Roger N. Lancaster. *Life Is Hard: Machismo, Danger, and the Intimacy of Power in Nicaragua.* Berkeley: University of California Press, 1992. This ethnography of everyday life in a barrio of Managua, Nicaragua, examines interpersonal violence as well as the wider issue of how living during a revolution affected people.

Sally Engle Merry. *Getting Justice and Getting Even: Legal Consciousness among Working-Class Americans.* Chicago: University of Chicago Press, 1990. Based on fieldwork among native-born, White, working-class Americans in a small New England town and their experiences in the court system, this book considers how the court system is perceived by the litigants as more often controlling than empowering.

Bruce Miller. *The Problem of Justice: Tradition and Law in the Coast Salish World.* Lincoln: University of Nebraska Press, 2001. The author compares several legal systems operating in the Northwest Coast region from Washington State to British Columbia. The effects of colonialism differ from group to group; some are strong and independent, and others are disintegrating.

Jeffrey Rubin. *Decentering the Regime: Ethnicity, Radicalism and Democracy in Jchitán, Mexico.* Durham, NC: Duke University Press, 1997. Written by a political scientist who adopted the methods of cultural anthropology, this study analyzes how the Mexican state defines, represents, and relates to indigenous peoples and how indigenous peoples struggle against the state.

Jennifer Schirmer. *The Guatemalan Military Project: A Violence Called Democracy.* Philadelphia: University of Pennsylvania Press, 1998. This book is an ethnography of the Guatemalan military, documenting its role in human rights violations through extensive interviews with military officers and trained torturers.

WHAT is the scope of legal anthropology?

Legal anthropology encompasses the study of cultural variation in social order and social conflict. Early legal anthropologists approached the subject from a functionalist viewpoint that stresses how social institutions promote social cohesion and continuity. In contrast, the more recent approach of critical legal anthropology points out how legal institutions often support and maintain social inequalities and injustice. Legal anthropologists also study the difference between norms and laws. Legal anthropologists are increasingly examining how legal systems change. Colonialism and contemporary globalization have changed indigenous systems of social control and law, often resulting in legal pluralism.

WHAT are cross-cultural patterns of maintaining social order and control?

Systems of social order and social control vary cross-culturally and over time. Legal anthropologists have examined systems of social control in small-scale societies and in large-scale societies, namely the state. Social control in small-scale societies seeks to restore order more than to punish offenders. In small-scale societies, common forms of punishment are social shaming and shunning. In states, imprisonment and capital punishment may exist, reflecting the greater power of the state. State systems of social control have a wide variety of legal and social control specialists.

WHAT are cross-cultural patterns of social conflict?

Cross-cultural data on levels and forms of conflict and violence indicate that high levels of lethal violence are not universal and are more often associated with the state than with other forms of political organization. Social conflict ranges from face-to-face conflicts, as among neighbors or domestic partners, to larger group conflicts between ethnic groups and states. Solutions that would be effective at the interpersonal level are often not applicable to large-scale, impersonalized conflict. Cultural anthropologists are turning their attention to global conflict and peace-keeping solutions. Key issues involve the role of cultural knowledge in dispute resolution and how international or local organizations can help achieve or maintain peace.

THE BIG QUESTIONS

- **WHAT** are the major features of human verbal language?
- **HOW** do language, thought, and society interact?
- **WHAT** is human paralanguage?

12

COMMUNICATION

Indigenous language dictionaries and usage guides are available on the Web and may help indigenous peoples preserve their cultures (check out The Internet Guide to Australian Languages). *(Source: © Robert Essel NYC/CORBIS)*

Many animals and insects such as chimpanzees, lions, and bees have sophisticated ways of communicating about where food is available or warning about an impending danger. People are in almost constant communication with other people, with supernaturals, with pets, or with other domesticated animals.

Communication is the conveying of meaningful messages from one person or animal or insect to another. Means of communication among humans include eye contact, body posture, position and movements of limbs, and language.

Language is a form of communication that is a systematic set of arbitrary symbols shared among a group and passed on from generation to generation. It may be spoken, signed, or written.

Linguistic anthropology is devoted to the study of communication—mainly, but not exclusively, among humans. This chapter presents material on human communication, drawing on work in linguistic anthropology, one of general anthropology's four fields. It discusses the characteristics of human language that set it apart from communication among other animals and considers what we know about the origins of languages. Then the role of language in our multicultural worlds is discussed: how language is related to thought and society. Last, we address the topic of communication without the use of words at all.

Linguistic anthropology began in the United States, inspired by the realization that Native American languages were rapidly disappearing through population decline and assimilation into Euro-American culture. Franz Boas gained eminence for recording many of the languages, myths, and rituals of these disappearing cultures (recall Chapter 1). Another force driving the development of linguistic anthropology was the discovery, through cross-cultural fieldwork, that many existing non-Western languages had never been written down. Study of non-Western languages revealed a wide range of different sounds and exposed the inadequacy of Western alphabets to represent such varied sounds. This gap prompted the development of the International Phonetic Alphabet, which contains symbols to represent all known sounds in human languages worldwide, such as the symbol "!" to indicate a click sound common in southern African languages.

Many anthropologists are designing practical applications of research findings to promote improved language learning among school children, migrants, and refugee populations. The modification of standardized tests to reduce bias against children from varied cultural backgrounds is an area where applied linguistic anthropologists are increasingly active. Linguistic anthropologists also study language use in deaf communities, including research on cross-cultural differences in sign language. This work helps to promote greater public understanding of the cultures of people who are deaf and contributes to improved teaching of sign language (see the Lessons Applied box).

HUMAN VERBAL LANGUAGE

This section begins with a discussion of some of the challenges facing researchers in linguistic anthropology (review Chapter 2 on research methods) and then discusses two distinctive features of human language that separate it from other animals' communication. A brief review of formal properties of language is followed by consideration of historical linguistics and language change.

Lessons Applied

ANTHROPOLOGY AND PUBLIC UNDERSTANDING OF THE LANGUAGE AND CULTURE OF PEOPLE WHO ARE DEAF

ETHNOGRAPHIC STUDIES of the communication practices and wider culture of people who are deaf have great importance and practical application (Senghas and Monaghan 2002). First, this research demonstrates the limitations and inaccuracy of the "medical model" that construes deafness as a pathology or deficit and sees the goal as curing it. Instead, anthropologists propose the "cultural model," which views deafness simply as one possibility in the wide spectrum of cultural variation. (In this context a capital D is often used: Deaf culture.) Studies clearly show that deafness leaves plenty of room for human agency. The strongest evidence of agency among people who are deaf is sign language itself, which exhibits adaptiveness, creativity, and change. This new view helps to promote a non-victim, non-pathological identity for people who are deaf and to reduce social stigma related to deafness. Third, anthropologists working in the area of Deaf culture studies are examining how people who are deaf become bilingual—for example, fluent in both English and Japanese sign languages. Their findings are being incorporated in markedly improved ways of teaching sign language.

FOOD FOR THOUGHT

Learn the signs for five words in English sign language, and then learn the signs for the same words in another sign language. Are they the same or different, and how might one explain the similarity or difference?

Fieldwork Challenges

Research in linguistic anthropology shares the basic methods of cultural anthropology (fieldwork and participant observation), but its more specialized areas require data gathering and analysis. The study of language in actual use relies on tape recordings or video recordings of people and events. The tapes are then analyzed qualitatively or quantitatively. Video recordings, for example, may be subjected to a detailed "frame analysis" that can pinpoint when communication breaks down or misunderstandings occur.

Linguistic anthropologists argue that the analysis of recorded data is best done when it is informed by broader knowledge about the culture. This approach derives from Malinowski's view that communication is embedded in its social context and must therefore be studied in relation to that context. An example of such a contextualized approach is a study in Western Samoa that gathered many hours of tape-recorded speech as well as conducting participant observation (Duranti 1994). Analysis of the transcriptions of the recorded talk revealed two major findings about how speech used in village council meetings is related to social status. First, turn-taking patterns reflected and restated people's power positions in the group. Second, people used particular grammatical forms and word choices that indirectly either praised or blamed others, thus shaping and reaffirming people's moral roles and status relations. Nonlinguistic data that helped the researchers form these interpretations included observa-tion of seating arrangements and the order of the distribution of kava (a ritually shared intoxicating beverage). The findings about the role of language in creating and maintaining social and moral order contribute to a richer understanding of the wider social context of status formation in Samoa.

Most cultural and linguistic anthropologists face the challenge of translation. One has to understand more about a language than just vocabulary in order to provide a reliable and meaningful translation. An anthropologist once translated a song that occurred at the end of a play in Zaire (Fabian 1995). The play was presented in the Swahili language, so he assumed that the final song was, too. Thus, he thought the repeated use of the word *tutubawina*, a Swahili word, indicated that it was a fighting song. A Swahili speaker assisting the anthropologist said, no, it was a soccer song. The puzzled anthropologist later learned, by writing to the theater performers, that the word *tutubawina* as used in this song was not a Swahili word at all and that it indicates a marching song.

Linguistic anthropologists who study ordinary language use face the problem of the **observer's paradox**, the impossibility of doing research on natural communication events without affecting the naturalness sought (McMahon 1994:234). The mere presence of the anthropologist with a tape recorder makes the speaker concentrate on speaking "correctly" and more formally. Several options exist for dealing with the paradox: recording informants in a group, observing and recording speech outside an interview situation, or using structured inter-

Chimpanzees have demonstrated a remarkable ability to learn aspects of human language. Here, trainer Joyce Butler signs "Nim" and Nim signs "Me."
■ *Consider examples of how animals other than humans communicate with each other.* (Source: © Susan Kuklin/ Photo Researchers, Inc.)

views in which the informant is asked to perform various speech tasks at varying levels of formality. In this last technique, the informant is first asked to read a word list and a short passage. The next stage is a question-and-answer session. Last, the interviewer encourages the informant, who may be more relaxed by now, to produce informal conversational speech by asking about childhood rhymes and sayings, encouraging digressions to get the informant to talk for longer periods, and posing questions that are likely to prompt an emotional response. Another strategy is to use "role plays" in which informants are asked to act out a particular scene, such as arguing about something. Data from semistructured techniques can be compared with the more casual styles of natural speech to assess the possible bias created.

Key Characteristics: Productivity and Displacement

Most anthropologists agree that nonhuman primates share with humans some ability to communicate through sounds and movements, and that some can be trained to recognize and use arbitrary symbols that humans use. Whatever progress will be made in teaching nonhuman primates aspects of sign language, it is unlikely that they could ever develop the range of linguistic ability that humans possess, because human language relies so heavily on two features that depend on the richness of arbitrary symbols.

Human language is said to have infinite **productivity,** or the ability to communicate many messages efficiently. In contrast, consider gibbon communication in the wild. Gibbons have nine calls that convey useful messages such as "follow me," "I am angry," "here is food," "danger," and "I am hurt." If a gibbon wants to communicate particular intensity in, say, the danger at hand, the only option is to repeat the "danger" call several times and at different volumes: "danger," *"danger," "DANGER,"*

and so on. This variation allows some productivity, but with greater degrees of danger, the system of communication becomes increasingly inefficient. By the time twenty danger calls have been given, it may be too late. In comparison, human language's capacity for productivity makes it extremely efficient. Different levels of danger can be conveyed in these ways:

"I see a movement over there."
"I see a leopard there."
"A leopard—run!"
"Help!"

Human language also uses the feature of **displacement,** which enables people to talk about displaced domains—events in the past and future—as well as the immediate present. According to current thinking, displacement is not a prominent feature of nonhuman primate communication. A wild chimpanzee is unlikely to be able to communicate the message "Danger: there may be a leopard coming here tonight." Instead, it communicates mainly what is experienced in the present. Even if nonhuman primates can learn to use displacement, its use among humans is far more prevalent. Among humans, the majority of language use is related to displaced domains, including reference to people and events that may never exist at all, as in fantasy and fiction.

Formal Properties of Verbal Language

Besides the above general characteristics, human language can be analyzed in terms of its formal properties: sounds, vocabulary, and grammar—all features that lie within formal or "structural" linguistics (Agar 1994). Learning a new language usually involves learning different sets of sounds. The sounds that make a difference for meaning in a language are called **phonemes;** the study of phonemes is called **phonetics.** Sharon Hutchinson comments on her

FIGURE 12.1 **Dental and Retroflex Tongue Positions** When making a dental sound, the speaker places the tongue against the upper front teeth (position A on the diagram). For making a retroflex sound, the speaker places the tongue up against the back of the palate (position B on the diagram).

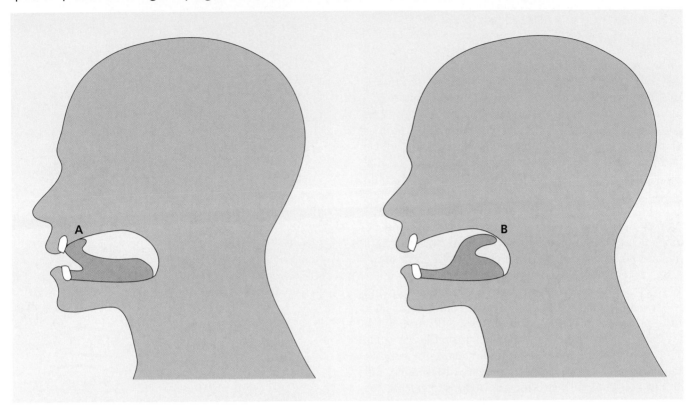

attraction to phonemes of the Nuer language spoken in the Sudan:

> As a native English speaker, I find the seeming airy lightness and rich melodic qualities of the Nuer language to be attractive. The language contains few "hard" consonants—and those that do exist are often softened or silenced at the ends of words. A terminal "k," for instance, often slides into a breathy "gh" sound . . . or a lighter "h" sound or is suppressed entirely. . . . The apparent "airiness" of the language stems from the fact that many Nuer vowels are heavily aspirated—that is, they are released with an audible bit of breath as in the English "hi" and "hea" in "behind" and "ahead." Indeed, one of the earliest obstacles I faced in trying to learn the language was to hear and to control the voice's "breathiness" or "nonbreathiness" in the pronunciation of various Nuer vowels. (1996:xv–xvi)

A native English-speaker trying to learn the north Indian language called Hindi is challenged to learn to produce and recognize several new sounds. For example, four different "d" sounds exist. None are the same as an English "d," which is usually pronounced with the tongue placed on the ridge behind the upper front teeth (try it). One "d" in Hindi, which linguists refer to as a "dental"

sound, is pronounced with the tongue pressed firmly behind the upper front teeth (try it). (See Figure 12.1.) Next is a dental "d" that is also aspirated (pronounced "with air"); making this sound involves the tongue being in the same position and a puff of air expelled during pronunciation (try it, and try the regular dental "d" again with no puff of air at all). Next is what is referred to as a "retroflex sound," accomplished by flipping the tongue back to the central dome of the roof of the mouth (try it, with no puff of air). Finally, there is the aspirated retroflex "d" with the tongue again in the center of the roof of the mouth and a puff of air. Once you can do this, try the whole series again with a "t," because Hindi follows the same pattern with this letter as with the "d." Several other sounds in Hindi require careful use of aspiration and placement of the tongue for communicating the right word. A puff of air at the wrong time can produce a serious error, such as saying the word for "breast" when you want to say the word for "letter."

Grammar consists of the patterns and rules by which words are organized to make sense in a string. All languages have a grammar, although they vary in form. Even within the languages of contemporary Europe, German is characterized by its placement of the verb at the end of the sentence (try to compose an English sentence with its main verb at the end). Phonemes, vocabulary, and grammar are the formal building blocks of language.

Origins and History

Did the first humans have language, and if so, what was it like? Did grunts and exclamations evolve into words and sentences? Did early humans attempt to imitate the sounds of nature? Did a committee meet and decide to put together a set of arbitrary symbols with meanings that everyone would accept? No one knows, nor will we ever know, how language started in the first place. The prevailing view is that early humans began to develop verbal language around 50,000 years ago, using calls, body postures, and gestures. Human **paralanguage,** a category that includes all forms of nonverbal communication (such as body posture, voice tone, touch, smells, and eye and facial movements), is thus a continuation of the earliest phase of human language.

No contemporary human language can be considered a "primitive" model of early human language. That would defy the principle of **linguistic relativism,** which says that all languages have passed through thousands of years of change, and all are equally successful forms of communication. Languages differ in their structure and in the meaning they ascribe to various concepts (or *semantics*), but all are equally capable of conveying subtle meanings and complex thoughts. There is no such thing as a "simple" language—one that is easy to learn because it is less complex than others. Early scholars of comparative linguistics were sometimes misled by ethnocentric assumptions that language structures of European languages were normative and that languages that did not have that same structure were somehow deficient. Many Westerners used to consider Chinese "primitive" on these grounds. Now we know that different languages have complexity in different areas—sometimes verb forms, sometimes noun formations.

Writing Systems

Archaeological data cannot provide insights on speech. Attempts to trace the beginnings of language are thus limited to working with records of written language. Evidence of the earliest written languages comes from Mesopotamia, Egypt, and China, with the oldest writing system in use by the fourth millennium BCE in Mesopotamia (Postgate, Wang, and Wilkinson 1995). Some scholars say that symbols found on pottery in China dated at 5000 to 4000 BCE should be counted as the earliest writing. At question here is the definition of a writing system: Does the presence of symbolic markings on pots constitute a "writing system" or not? Most schol-

FIGURE 12.2 **Logographic and Current Writing Styles in China** *(Source: Courtesy of Molly Spitzer Frost.)*

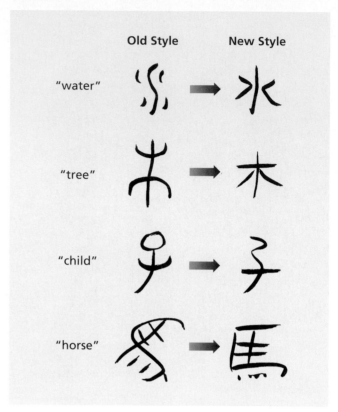

ars say that a symbolic mark that could refer to a clan name is not necessarily evidence of a writing system that involves the use of words in relation to each other in a systematic way. A similarity of forms in all early writing systems is the use of **logographs,** or symbols that convey meaning through a form or picture that resembles what is being referred to. Over time, some logographs retained their original meaning, others were kept but given more abstract meaning, and non-logographic symbols were added (see Figure 12.2).

The emergence of writing is associated with the political development of the state. Some scholars take writing as a key diagnostic feature that distinguishes the state from earlier political forms because recordkeeping was an essential task of the state. The Inca state is one exception to this generalization; it used *quipu,* or cords of knotted strings of different colors, for keeping accounts and recording events. Two interpretations of early writing systems exist. One is that the primary use of early writing was ceremonial because of the prevalence of early writing on tombs, bone inscriptions, or temple carvings. The other is that early writing was utilitarian: for gov-

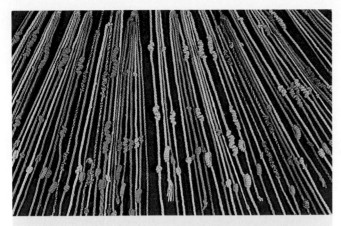

Quipu, or knotted strings, were the basis of state-level accounting in the Incan empire. The knots convey substantial information for those who could interpret their meaning. ■ *How does a quipu system compare to current technology that states use to keep track of official information? What do the differences suggest about contemporary states?* (Source: © M. Vautier, Anthropological & Archaeological Museum, Lima, Peru/Woodfin Camp & Associates)

ernment recordkeeping and trade. In this view, the archaeological record, is biased toward durable substances, and this bias favors the preservation of ceremonial writing (because durable substances such as stone were more likely to be used for ceremonial writing that was intended to last). Utilitarian writing is more likely to have been done on perishable materials because people would be less concerned with permanence—consider the way we treat shopping lists. Thus, no doubt much more utilitarian writing existed than what has been preserved.

Historical Linguistics

Historical linguistics is the study of language change through history via methods that compare shifts over time and across space in formal aspects of language such as phonetics, grammar, and semantics. This approach originated in the eighteenth century with a discovery made by Sir William Jones, a British colonial administrator working in India. During his spare time in India, he studied Sanskrit, an ancient language of India. He was the first to notice strong similarities among Sanskrit, Greek, and Latin in vocabulary and grammar. For example, the Sanskrit word for "father" is *pitr*, in Greek it is *patér*, and in Latin, *pater*. This was an astounding discovery for the time, given the prevailing European mentality that placed its cultural heritage firmly in the clas-

sical Graeco-Roman world and depicted the "Orient" as completely separate from "Europe" (Bernal 1987).

Following Jones's discovery, other scholars began comparing lists of words and grammatical forms in different languages: the French *père*, the German *Vater*, the Italian *padre*, the Old English *faeder*, the Old Norse *fadhir*, the Swedish *far*. With these lists, scholars could also determine degrees of closeness and distance in their relationships—for example, that German and English are closer to each other, and French and Spanish are closer to each other. Later scholars contributed the concept of "language families," or clusters of related languages. Attempting to reconstruct the ancient ancestral languages of family trees was a major research interest of the nineteenth century. Comparison of contemporary and historical Eurasian languages and shifts in sound, vocabulary, and meaning yielded a model of a hypothetical early parent language called Proto-Indo-European (PIE). For example, the hypothetical PIE term for "father" is p#ter (the "#" symbol is pronounced like the "u" in *mutter*). Linguistic evidence suggests that PIE was located somewhere in Eurasia, either north or south of the Black Sea. From its area of origin, PIE speakers subsequently spread out in waves toward Europe, central and eastern Asia, and South Asia. The farther they moved from the PIE center in terms of time and space, the more their language diverged from original PIE.

Current methods of linguistic analysis support the possibility of the original homeland of Proto-Indoeuropean either among pastoralists in an area north of the Black Sea about 6,000 years ago, or in central Turkey among farmers over 8,000 years ago.

Colonialism, Globalization, and Language Change

Languages change constantly, sometimes slowly and in small ways, other times rapidly and dramatically. Most of us are scarcely conscious of such changes. Colonialism was a major force of change. Not only did colonial powers declare their own language as the language of government, business, and higher education, but they often took direct steps to suppress indigenous languages and literatures.

A **pidgin** is a contact language that emerges when different cultures with different languages come to live in close proximity and therefore need to communicate (McMahon 1994:253). Pidgins are generally limited to highly functional domains, such as trade, because that is what they were developed for. A pidgin therefore is no one's first language. Many pidgins of the Western hemisphere developed out of slavery, where owners needed to communicate with their slaves. A pidgin is always learned as a second language. Tok Pisin, the pidgin language of

Papua New Guinea, consists of a mixture of many languages: English, Samoan, Chinese, and Malayan. Tok Pisin has been declared one of the national languages of Papua New Guinea, where it is transforming into a **creole**, or a language that is descended from a pidgin, has its own native speakers, and involves linguistic expansion and elaboration. About two hundred pidgin and creole languages exist today, mainly in West Africa, the Caribbean, and the South Pacific.

National policies of cultural assimilation of minorities have also led to the extinction of many indigenous and minority languages. The Soviet attempt to build a USSR-wide commitment to communism after the 1930s included mass migration of Russian speakers into remote areas, where they eventually outnumbered indigenous peoples (Belikov 1994). In some cases, Russian officials visited areas and burned books in local languages. Children were forcibly sent away to boarding schools, where they were taught in Russian. The Komi, an indigenous group who spoke a Finno-Ugric language, traditionally formed the majority population in their area north of

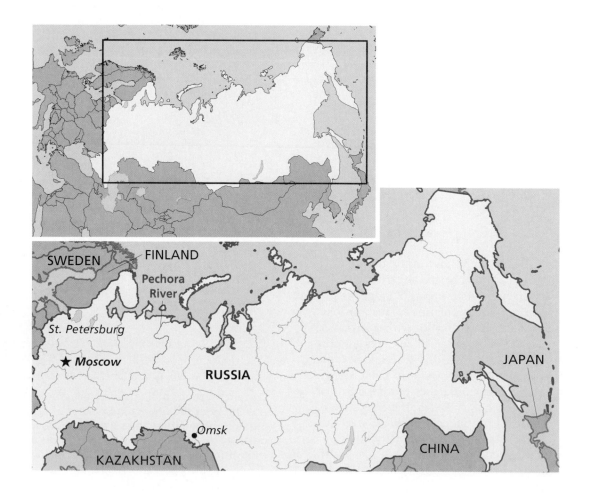

European Russia on the banks of the lower Pechora River. Russian immigration brought in greater numbers of people than the original population—and the use of Russian in schools. All Komi became bilingual. The Komi language was so heavily influenced by Russian that it now may be extinct.

Anthropologists are concerned about the rapid loss of languages throughout the world—one result of accelerated globalization, including Western economic and media expansion (Hill 2001). **Language decay** occurs when speakers use, in some contexts, a new language in which they may be semifluent and when they have limited vocabulary in their native language. **Language extinction** occurs at the point when language speakers abandon their language in favor of another language, and the original language no longer has any competent users. Language extinction is a serious problem in Australia and North and South America and is becoming more serious in Siberia, Africa, and South and Southeast Asia. As discussed in Chapter 3 (the Lessons Applied box), linguistic anthropologists are playing an important role in documenting decaying and dying languages.

Languages that are gaining currency over decaying and dying languages are called **global languages,** or world languages. They are languages that are spoken worldwide in diverse cultural contexts, notably English and Spanish. As these global languages spread to areas and cultures beyond their home area and culture, they take on new, localized identities. One scholar says that there are now many "Englishes," or plural English languages (Bhatt 2001). England's English was transplanted through colonial expansion to the United States, Canada, Australia, New Zealand, South Asia, Africa, Hong Kong, and the Caribbean. English became the dominant language in the colonies; it was used in government and commerce and was taught in schools. Over time, regional and subregional varieties of English have developed, often leading to a form of English that a native speaker from England cannot understand at all.

Efforts to revive or maintain local languages face a difficult challenge. Political opposition often comes from national governments that may fear local identity movements and may not wish to support administratively or financially bilingual or multilingual policies and programs. The English-only movement among political conservatives in the United States is an example of attempts at suppressing linguistic diversity (Neier 1996). Because language is such a vital part of culture, linguistic suppression can be equivalent to cultural suppression or ethnocide.

Ski enthusiasts use a more elaborate set of terms to differentiate forms of snow than most English speakers, among whom "powder" and "corn," for example, are not familiar concepts for snow. ■ *What other focal vocabularies can you think of?* (Source: © Jeff Greenberg/Photo Researchers, Inc.)

LANGUAGE, THOUGHT, AND SOCIETY

This section presents material that illuminates the relationships among language, thought, and society. First, we discuss two theoretical approaches to these relationships. Then we look in greater depth at how different "levels" of language are related to thought and society.

Two Models

During the twentieth century, two theoretical perspectives were influential in the study of how language, thought, and society are related. They are presented here as two separate models, but some anthropologists draw on both (Hill and Mannheim 1992).

Edward Sapir and Benjamin Whorf formulated an influential model called the **Sapir-Whorf hypothesis,** which claims that differences in language predetermine differences in thinking. For example, if a language has no word for what in English is called "snow," then a person who has been brought up in that language cannot think of "snow" as it is meant in English. Whorf first began developing this theory through study of different languages' vocabulary and grammar. He was so struck by the differences that he is often quoted as having said that people who speak different languages inhabit different "thought worlds." This catchy phrase became the basis for what is called **linguistic determinism,** which states that language determines consciousness of the world and behavior. Extreme linguistic determinism implies that the frames and definitions of a person's primary language are so strong that it is impossible to learn another language fully or to truly understand another culture (Agar 1994:67).

An alternative model to the Sapir-Whorf hypothesis is proposed by scholars working in the area of **sociolinguistics,** the study of language in relation to society. These theorists argue that a person's social position determines the content and form of language.

William Labov's (1966) research of the 1960s established this approach. Labov conducted studies of the use of particular speech sounds among people of different socioeconomic classes in New York City. He hypothesized that class differences would be reflected in the use of certain sounds. For example, pronunciation of the consonant "r" in words such as *car, card, floor,* and *fourth* tends to be associated with upper-class people, whereas its absence ("caw," "cawd," "flaw," "fawth") is associated with lower-class people. In order to obtain data on discourse without the formalizing effects of taped interviews, Labov relied on the use of rapid and anonymous observations of sales clerks' speech in three Manhattan department stores. The stores were chosen to represent three class levels: Saks the highest, then Macy's, then S. Klein. His assumption was that the clerks in these stores represented different class levels and statuses. Labov would approach a clerk and inquire about the location of some item that he knew was on the fourth floor. The clerk would respond, and then Labov would say, "Excuse me?" in order to prompt a more emphatic repeat of the word *fourth.* His analysis of the data confirmed the hypothesis. The higher-status "r" was pronounced both the first and second times by 44 percent of the employees in Saks, by 16 percent of the employees in Macy's, and by 6 percent of the employees in S. Klein. In the rest of the cases, some of the clerks used the "r" in the emphatic, repeat response, but most uses were without the "r." The following section reviews major contributions in the area of sociolinguistics and its study of language in use.

The topic of focal vocabularies illustrates the connections between the Sapir-Whorf hypothesis and sociolinguistics. **Focal vocabularies** are clusters of words that refer to important features of a particular culture. Studying focal vocabularies shows how language is both a thought-world (according to the Sapir-Whorf hypothesis) and a cultural construction responsive to a particular cultural context. For example, many languages of the polar north recognize many different forms of snow and have many specific terms for these varieties. Environmental conditions that make snow such an important factor, in conjunction with economic adaptations, drive this amplification and therefore shape how Inuit people actually think about the weather. Similarly, English speakers of the United States who are avid skiers have a richer focal vocabulary related to forms of cold-weather precipitation than people who grew up in Florida and have never seen snow or gone skiing.

Multiple Levels of Language

One characteristic of contemporary language change is the increasing numbers of people who speak more than one language. Much of this change is the result of colonialism and, now, increased migration related to economic globalization. Another characteristic is the existence of variation within a single language in such matters as word choice, intonation, and even grammar, which is tied to multicultural diversity.

Bilingualism

Global culture contact since the era of colonial expansion beginning in 1500 has meant that people have been increasingly exposed to more than one language. One result is that more people are bilingual. Bilingualism is simply the capacity to speak two languages. A true bilingual has "native" speaking abilities in two languages.

Many world populations are bilingual because their country was colonized and a second language was introduced. As a result of their close proximity and high exposure to many languages, Europeans often grow up learning more than one language. The emergence of large populations speaking multiple languages has led to heated debates about the value of more than one "standard" language. Can **linguistic pluralism** (the presence of linguistic diversity within a particular context) be supported in terms of cost to the educational system? The effort to foster linguistic pluralism or bilingualism arises out of the belief that it will help reduce economic disparities between native speakers of the first language and non-native speakers.

Language testing of bilingual people seems to support the contention that even if people are fluent in their adopted language, they are still at a disadvantage. According to one theory, a person who has to use two languages to communicate everyday does not really have full capabilities in either language, because each one fills in for the other to create a unitary whole out of two partial languages (Valdés and Figueroa 1994:7). Thus, if such

The presence of both French and Arabic cultural influences in Morocco results in the frequent use of bilingual shop signs. ■ *Where have you seen bilingualism in public use? What languages were used and why?* (Source: Barbara Miller)

Interviewer: What were the other kinds of diseases that people talked about in the past?

Informant: Hmm . . . That [tuberculosis] . . . was mostly, it well . . . they always said cirrhosis. . . . *It seems* like no matter what anybody died from . . . if they drank, it was cirrhosis. *I don't know* if anybody *really* knew a long time ago what anybody *really* died from. Even if the doctor requested an autopsy, the people would just say no . . . you know . . . it won't be done. So *I don't* think it was . . . you know . . . it was just what the doctor thought that would go down on the death certificate. (506)

The many cues appear to health care practitioners as indecisiveness or noncooperation. These interpretations are incorrect, given the rules that the speakers are following about the validity of statements, humility, and religious belief.

Dialects

Linguists jokingly say that a dialect is a language without an army, suggesting power differentials between speakers of a language and speakers of a dialect. A **dialect** is a way of speaking in a particular place, or, more precisely, a subordinate variety of a language arising from local circumstances (R. Williams 1983:105). Thus there is standard English, and there are dialects of English. For example, the British singing group the Beatles originated in the city of Liverpool, known for its distinct dialect called "Scouse." Cockney, spoken in London, is another prominent dialect. Speakers of these dialects are able to understand each other, but with some difficulty.

Standard forms of a language will have the stamp of authority of the state and will be taught using standardized textbooks. Dialects may appear in literature or films as a way of adding "local color." Dialect speakers are often considered second-class because they do not speak the standard language. For many years, language experts have argued about whether Black English is a dialect of standard English or a language in its own right. So-called Black English has been looked down on by "linguistic conservative" champions of a standard English tradition. To them, Black English was a broken, haphazard, ungrammatical form of English that needed to be "corrected." In a more understanding vein, many educators realize that Black children in the United States learn one language at home and are then confronted with another language in school. Effectively, they are expected to be bilingual because they must develop proficiency in standard English. Political scientist Andrew Hacker says that recognition of this issue is what is needed, not the teaching of Black English in schools, as was proposed by the city of Oakland in early 1997, with its promo-

a person is evaluated in one of these languages, he or she will appear to have a low level of linguistic competence: "When a bilingual individual confronts a monolingual test, developed by monolingual individuals, and standardized and normed on a monolingual population, both the test taker and the test are asked to do something that they cannot. The bilingual test taker cannot perform like a monolingual. The monolingual test cannot 'measure' in the other language" (87). Given the monolingual content of existing tests, bilingual students are likely to test lower than monolingual students. This finding may explain why, in U.S. schools in several states, Latino students are "overrepresented" in special education classes. Such a pattern of linguistic and ethnic discrimination has a long history in the United States.

Health care providers in the United States who speak standard English often misinterpret messages conveyed to them. In Mohawk English, linguistic cues are words or phrases that preface a remark to indicate the speaker's attitude toward what is being said, especially the degree of confidence in it (Woolfson et al. 1995). For example, standard English includes cues such as *maybe* and *in my opinion*. Three functions of cuing exist in Mohawk English. They may indicate the speaker's unwillingness or inability to verify the certainty of a statement; respect for the listener; or the view of Mohawk religion that health is in the hands of the creator and that any statement about health must acknowledge human limitations. A striking feature of medical interviews conducted among the Akwesasne (St. Regis) people of upper New York was cuing. Here is a typical example:

tion of teaching in "Ebonic" or Black English (1992: 171).

Another thing that White teachers need to understand is that Black children may have culturally distinct styles of expression that should be valued. For example, Black children should be given more opportunities for expressive talking because, as Hacker notes, Black culture gives attention to both style and substance. In terms of narrative style, Black children tend to use a spiral pattern, skipping around to various topics before addressing the theme, whereas White children use a linear style. In terms of literature assignments, if more Black authors were read in classrooms, this would help provide a cultural anchor to their heritage for Black children, signal respect for their traditions, and at the same time enrich White children, who might otherwise not get such exposure.

Language Codes

Within a single language, particular microcultures have distinctive **codes,** or ways of speaking, that may include marked vocabulary, grammar, and intonation depending on age, gender, occupation, and class of the speaker and listener. (Speakers of the same language should generally be able to understand different codes within it but are less likely to understand different dialects within it.) Most people know more than one code and are able to *code-switch,* or move from one code to another as needed. For example, consider how you talk to your college friends when you are in a group, compared to how you might speak to a physician or potential employer. Code-switching can be an intentional strategy used to further the interests of the speaker. In the decolonizing nations, people may express their resistance to the colonial powers by avoiding complete switching to the colonial language, but instead using code-mixing. In *code-mixing,* the speaker starts in the native language and then introduces words or phrases from the colonial language (Myers-Scotton 1993:122).

Gender codes exist in most languages. North American English female codes possess several features: more politeness, rising intonation at the end of sentences, and the frequent use of **tag questions,** which are questions seeking affirmation that are placed at the end of sentences: "It's a nice day, *isn't it?*" (Lakoff 1973). Male codes are less polite, maintain a flat, assertive tone in a sentence, and do not use tag questions. One conversational characteristic is that men interrupt women more than women interrupt men. In general, the female code is a subservient, complementary, "weak" form, whereas the male code is dominating, hierarchical, and "strong."

Sociolinguist Deborah Tannen's popular book *You Just Don't Understand* (1990) shows how differences in male and female communication styles in the United States may lead to miscommunication. She says that "women

speak and hear a language of connection and intimacy, while men speak and hear a language of status and independence" (42). Sometimes men and women use similar linguistic styles, such as indirect response, but their differing motivations create different meanings that are embedded in their speech. For example, many husbands saw their role as one of protector in explaining why they used an indirect rather than a direct response to a question:

Michele: What time is the concert?
Gary: You have to be ready by seven-thirty. (289)

Michele feels that Gary is withholding information by not answering her directly, thus maintaining a power position. He feels that he is simply "watching out for her" by getting to the real point of her question. A similarly indirect response given by a wife to a husband is shaped around her goal of being helpful by anticipating the husband's real motivation:

Ned: Are you just about finished?
Valerie: Do you want to have supper now? (289)

Gender codes in spoken Japanese also reflect and reinforce gender differences and hierarchies (Shibamoto 1987). Certain words and sentence structures convey femininity, humbleness, and politeness. A common contrast between male and female speech is the attachment, by females, of the honorific prefix "o-" to nouns (see Table 12.1). This addition gives female speech a more refined and polite tone. Polite forms of speech, cross-culturally, are more associated with female gender codes than male gender codes. This gender difference carries over into related areas of speech. For example, a study of apologizing carried out on the Pacific Island of Vanuatu found that women apologize more frequently than men (Meyerhoff 1999).

Discourse, Identity, and Power

Some sociolinguists study discourse (or talk) in particular domains in order to learn about power dynamics, how

TABLE 12.1   Male-Unmarked and Female-Marked Nouns in Japanese

	Male	Female
Box lunch	bentoo	obentoo
Money	kane	okane
Chopsticks	hasi	ohasi
Book	hon	ohon

Source: From "The Womanly Woman: Manipulation of Stereotypical and Nonstereotypical Features Japanese Female Speech," pg. 28, by Janet Shibamoto in *Language, Gender, and Sex in Comparative Perspective,* ed. by S.U. Philips, S. Steel, and C. Tanz. Copyright © 1987. Reprinted by permission of Cambridge University Press.

Unity and Diversity

MOTHER–INFANT TALK IN WESTERN SAMOA AND THE UNITED STATES

BABY TALK is culturally widespread and shares features with other *simplified registers* such as "teacher talk," "foreigner talk," and talk to the elderly, lovers, and pets. Elinor Ochs (1993) compared hundreds of hours of mother-infant "conversations" among Western Samoans and White middle-class (WMC) North Americans. Among the WMC Americans, mothers used three basic verbal strategies: baby talk or other forms of simplification, guessing and negotiating meaning of messages that the child conveys, and praising the child's accomplishments. The WMC American mothers' baby talk included restricted vocabulary, baby talk words (the child's own version of words), shorter sentences, simplification of sounds (for example, avoiding consonant clusters in favor of consonant-vowel pairs), avoidance of complex sentences, topical focus on the here-and-now, exaggerated intonation, slower pace, repetition, and providing sentence frames for the child to complete. Baby talk is an important register in WMC American society because the culture is so child-centered, yet it is primarily a register used by mothers and female caretakers.

Child-centeredness also promotes use of mothers' second strategy, strong verbal accommodation of the adult to the child. The WMC mothers, for example, often participated in conversation-like interactions with tiny infants, including greeting exchanges with a newborn. This pattern indicates the mother's willingness to take on the conversational work of both infant and mother. The WMC mothers responded to children's unintelligible speech by attempting to guess at the meaning: "Guessing involves attempting to formulate the child's intended message, which in turn may entail taking into consideration what the child is looking at, holding, what the child has just said and other clues" (162).

In the third strategy, WMC mothers praised their children for activities beyond their competence, things they could not have done without the mother. For example, in joint activities such as a mother and child building a block tower together, the mother praised the child as the sole builder, thus denying her participation and raising the position of the child.

Western Samoan mothers do not use a simplified register when talking with their infants and young children. Instead, Samoan has a simplified register used toward foreigners, who historically were missionaries, government representatives, and other people in high social positions. Thus accommodation of the speaker to the listener is appropriate, "just as a host accommodates to a guest" (160). In the case of a child's unintelligible utterances, Western Samoan mothers ignore them or point out that they are unintelligible. In terms of praising:

> There is a strong expectation that the first one to be praised will in turn praise the praiser. Typically the praise consists of the phrase "*Maaloo!*" ("Well done!"). Once the first *maaloo* is uttered, a second *maaloo* is to be directed to the producer of the original *maaloo*. . . . Children in Western Samoa households are socialized through such bidirectional praising practices to articulate the contributions of others, including mothers. (164)

Samoan women have a position of prestige in their relationships with their children. They are accommodated to by their children.

FOOD FOR THOUGHT

Reflect on your own use of simplified registers, perhaps in speaking with your siblings or best friends. What gets simplified—word length, sentence structure?

---

people of different groups convey meaning, and how miscommunication occurs. Anthropologists have studied thousands of conversations in varied contexts, from cursing someone out to telephone conversations to chiefly speeches. (See the Unity and Diversity box.) Discourse styles and content provide clues about a person's social background, age, gender, and status. Consider what cultural information can be gleaned simply from the following bit of a conversation:

"So, like, you know, Ramadan?"
"Yeah."
"So I'm like talking to X, you know, and like she goes, 'Hey Ramadan starts next week.'"
"And I'm like, what do you say, Happy Ramadan, Merry Ramadan?" (Agar 1994:95).

If you thought that the speakers were college students, you were correct. They were young women who were probably born in the United States, native English speakers likely to be White, and non-Muslim.

The following examples are chosen to illustrate how discourse is related to identity and power relationships in two quite different domains: children's arguments and teenage girls' everyday talk.

Children's dispute styles in different cultures reveal how argumentation is learned and how power dynamics are played out. Cross-cultural research on children's disputes shows that argument style is culturally learned. For example, among Hindi-speaking Indian children of Fiji, overlapping is the norm, with little regard for strict turn-taking (Lein and Brenneis 1978). In other cultural contexts, offended feelings can arise when turn-takers try to converse with overlappers. The turn-taker feels that the overlapper is rude, and the overlapper feels that the turn-taker is distant and unengaged.

An article entitled "You Fruithead!" presents an analysis of children's arguments using data gathered among White, middle-class children of western Massachusetts (Brenneis and Lein 1977). The children were asked to do role plays, arguing about issues such as giving back a ball or who is smarter. Prominent stylistic strategies during an argument included use of volume, speed, and stress and intonation. Elevated volume was prominent, although sometimes an echo pattern of a soft statement followed by a soft response would occur. Acceleration of

In many North American microcultures, teenage girls frequently discuss body weight. The girl on the scale points out the fat under her arm. ■ *What are your views on female body weight? How might your views affect whom you choose for friendship or other close relationships?* (Source: © Richard Lord/ PhotoEdit)

speed was common among older children, less so among younger children. Strict adherence to turn-taking was followed, with no overlapping. Stress and intonation were used in rhythmical patterns, sometimes with a demand for rhyming echoes, as in

You're skinny.
You're slimmy.
You're scrawny.
You're . . . I don't know.

The last line indicates defeat because the child was unable to come up with a meaningful term that echoed the word "scrawny." In terms of content, most arguments began with an assertion such as "I'm stronger," which calls for an identical or escalated assertion such as "*I'm* Stronger," or "I'm the strongest in the world." Many of the children's arguments involved insults and counterinsults. Often the argument ends with the loser being unable to respond.

In the United States, Euro-American adolescent girls' conversations exhibit a high level of concern with their body weight and image (Nichter 2000). A study of 253 girls in the eighth and ninth grades in two urban high schools of the Southwest reveals the contexts and meanings of "fat talk." Fat talk usually starts with a girl commenting, "I'm so fat." The immediate response from her friends is "No, you're not." Girls in the study say that fat talk occurs frequently throughout the day. The following representative conversation between two fourteen-year-olds was recorded during a focus-group discussion:

> *Jessica:* I'm so fat.
> *Toni:* Shut up, Jessica. You're not fat—you know how it makes you really mad when Brenda says she's fat?
> *Jessica:* Yeah.
> *Toni:* It makes me really mad when you say that cuz it's not true.
> *Jessica:* Yeah, it is.
> *Toni:* Don't say that you're fat. (Nichter and Vuckovic 1994:112)

Yet girls who use fat talk are typically not overweight and are not dieting. The weight of the girls in the study was within "normal" range, and none suffered from a serious eating disorder. Fat talk sometimes functions as a call for positive reinforcement from friends that the initiator is an accepted group member. In other cases, it occurs at the beginning of a meal, "especially before eating a calorie-laden food or enjoying a buffet-style meal where an individual is faced with making public food choices" (115). In this context, fat talk is interpreted as functioning to absolve the girl from guilt feelings and to give her a sense that she is in control of the situation.

Media Anthropology

Media anthropology is the cross-cultural study of communication through electronic media such as radio, television, film, and recorded music and print media, including newspapers, magazines, and popular literature (Spitulnik 1993). Media anthropology is an important emerging area that links linguistic and cultural anthropology (Allen 1994). Media anthropologists study the media process and content, the audience response, and the social effects of media presentations. Media anthropology brings together the interests and goals of anthropology and the media by promoting a contextualized view. In journalism, for example, media anthropology promotes going beyond the reporting of crises and other events to presenting a more holistic, contextualized story. Another goal is to disseminate anthropology's findings to the general public via radio, television, print journalism, magazines, and the Internet. **Critical media anthropology** asks to what degree access to media messages is mind-opening and liberating or propagandizing and controlling, and whose interests the media are serving.

The Media Process: Studying War Correspondents

Mark Pedelty has studied who creates media messages and how they are disseminated. In *War Stories* (1995), he examines the culture of war correspondents in El Salvador. He finds that their culture is highly charged with violence and terror: "War correspondents have a unique relationship to terror, however, a hybrid condition that combines voyeurism and direct participation. . . . They need terror to realize themselves in both a professional and spiritual sense, to achieve and maintain their cultural identity as 'war correspondents'" (2). Pedelty probes the psychological ambivalence of war correspondents, who are often accused of making a living from war and violence and who become dependent on the continuation of war for their livelihood. (Even the Salvadoran correspondents, whose country was being wracked by violence, worried that the end of the war would also mean the end of their ability to support their families.) He also addresses media censorship, direct and indirect, and how it affects what stories readers receive and the way events are described. (See the Critical Thinking box on page 288.)

Media Institutions and Gender: Inside a Japanese Television Station

Ethnographic research within the Japanese television station ZTV provided one anthropologist with insights into the social organization of the workplace and how it mirrors the messages put forth through television programming (Painter 1996). Gender dynamics form the basis of his analysis, although that was not his original research topic. He had planned to conduct a study of power dynamics and everyday behavior at the station, not thinking that, in fact, gender is the main factor shaping those dynamics.

Nonverbal communication in Japanese culture is especially marked by the frequent use of bowing. Two Japanese men in business meet each other, bow, and exchange business cards. ■ *Describe some important forms of nonverbal communication in your cultural world(s).* (Source: © Olympia/ PhotoEdit)

Critical Thinking

A TALE OF TWO NEWS STORIES

MARK PEDELTY talked with an experienced European reporter about how she alters her story depending on which newspaper she is writing for (1995). She showed him computer printouts of two reports she had written about the same event, one for a European news institution and the other for a U.S. newspaper.

The U.S. Report

Leftist rebels in El Salvador have admitted that one of their units may have executed two U.S. servicemen after their helicopter was shot down last Wednesday. An official FLMN rebel statement issued yesterday said two rebel combatants had been detained, "under the charge of suspicion of assassinating wounded prisoners of war. "

The U.S. helicopter was downed in the conflictive eastern province of San Miguel as it was flying back to its base in Honduras. One pilot was killed in the crash, but a Pentagon autopsy team concluded that the other two servicemen in the helicopter were killed execution-style afterwards. Civilians confirmed that the two servicemen had survived the crash, although no one actually saw the actual execution.

"The FMLN has concluded that there are sufficient elements to presume that some of the three, in the condition of wounded prisoners, could have been assassinated by one or various members of our military unit," said the rebel statement. It also said that their investigations had determined that their initial information from units on the ground was false.

At first the guerrillas said the bodies of the Americans had been found in the helicopter. Then they said that two of the three had survived the crash but later died of wounds. Salvadoran officials have said that if the Americans were executed the guerrillas should hand over those responsible. The call was echoed by Rep. Joe Moakley (D-Mass), the Chairman of a congressional special task force on El Salvador.

"We should expect and we should demand that the FMLN turn over to the judicial authorities those

responsible, if not this lack of action will have serious consequences," he said.

But the rebel statement made no promises to do that. "If responsibility for the crime is proved, the FMLN will act with all rigor, in conformity with our normal war justice," read the statement. The rebels said that because of the nationality of the victims, the investigations would be carried out publicly. The rebels also defended shooting down the helicopter, which they said was flying in "attack position" in a conflict zone. The UH1H Huey helicopter is the same model as those used by the Salvadoran army and was flying very low to evade anti-aircraft missiles.

The rebel statement did not say whether those detained were in charge of the guerrilla unit which shot down the helicopter. Western diplomats believe it unlikely the unit would have time to radio for orders. The hilly terrain also made radio communication over any distance difficult.

A U.S. embassy spokesman in San Salvador said State Department and embassy officials are studying the rebel statement . . .

The killings have opened up a debate in Washington as to whether another $42.5 million in military aid to El Salvador, frozen by Congress last October, should be released. The money was withheld in protest at the lack of progress in investigating the murders of six Jesuit priests by elite army soldiers a year ago. [The final four paragraphs concern the Jesuit murder case.]

The European Report

Nestled amid the steep mountains of Northern Chalatenango province, a simple wooden cross on a hill marks the grave of a teenage guerrilla fighter. There is no name on the grave. None of the villagers from the nearby settlement of San Jose Las Flores who buried his body two years ago knew what he was called. In life the young guerrilla had little in common with three North American servicemen who were killed last month after the rebels shot down their heli-

At ZTV, men outnumber women, with close to 90 percent of the full-time employees (*shain*) being men. Shain women rarely occupy positions of power or even minimal authority. At the time of the research, no woman had reached the level of section manager, the lowest managerial position in the company. An ideology pervasive among the male employees, especially the senior ones,

depicts women as inherently inferior workers. As the president of ZTV commented one afternoon, "[B]asically, compared to men, women are less intelligent, they have less physical strength, even their bodily structures are different—that is the philosophy I hold to—but in order to show that the company president is *not* a male chauvinist, we are also hiring women. They are people too, after

copter. They were enemies on opposite sides of a bitter war. But they shared a common death. They were all killed in cold blood after being captured.

When the young rebel was killed two years ago, I remember taking cover behind the wall of the church of San Jose Las Flores. One moment I was watching two adolescent guerrilla fighters sipping from Coke bottles and playing with a yo-yo. Then I remember seeing soldiers running, crouching, and shooting across the square. The crack of automatic rifle fire and the explosion of grenades was deafening in the confined space.

The whole incident lasted about twenty minutes. As soon as the soldiers left, whooping and yelling victory cries, we ran across the square to find the body of one of the teenage guerrillas still twitching. The villagers said that he had been wounded and surrendered. The soldiers had questioned him—and then finished him off at close range in the head. The bullet had blown off the top of his skull.

I remember clearly the reaction of the then U.S. ambassador when asked about the incident. "That kind of incident cannot be condoned," he said, "but I was a soldier, I can understand—it happens in a war." In a country where tens of thousands have been killed, many of them civilians murdered by the U.S. backed military or by right-wing death squads, there was no suggestion of any investigation for the execution of a prisoner.

At the beginning of January of this year a U.S. helicopter was shot down by rebel ground fire in Eastern El Salvador. The pilot died in the crash. But two other U.S. servicemen were dragged badly wounded from the wreckage by the rebels. Before the guerrillas left they finished off the two wounded Americans execution style with a bullet in the head.

The present U.S. ambassador referred to the guerrillas in this incident as "animals." The killings made front page news internationally and provided the climate needed by President Bush to release forty-two and a half million dollars of military aid, which was frozen

last October by Congress. U.S. lawmakers wanted to force the Salvadoran army to make concessions in peace talks and clean up its human rights record.

The two incidents highlight a fact of political life in El Salvador, recognized by all, that it is not worth killing Americans. Until the helicopter incident, in more than a decade of civil war the rebels have killed only six U.S. personnel. They have a deliberate policy of not targeting Americans, despite the fact that most guerrillas have a deep hatred of the U.S. government. As many have been killed by the U.S.' own allies. Extreme groups in the military, who resent U.S. interference, murdered four U.S. church workers and two government land reform advisers in the early 1980s.

In fact the rebels, because of the outcry and the policy implications in Washington, have had to admit guilt in the helicopter incident. They have arrested two of their combatants and say they will hold a trial. They have clearly got the message.

Up until the Gulf War El Salvador had easily seen the most prolonged and deepest U.S. military commitment since Vietnam. However, it is a commitment for which few Americans have felt the consequences.

Source: Mark Pedelty, *War Stories: The Culture of Foreign Correspondents*, pp. 9–12. Copyright © 1995. Reprinted by permission of Routledge/Taylor & Francis Books, Inc.

CRITICAL THINKING QUESTIONS

What are the major differences in content between the U.S. and the European news reports? (Consider the use and order of "facts," writer's voice, frame, and use of quotations.)

Are these two reports giving the same message in two different ways, or are they contradictory?

What might be the audience response to each, and how might the writing of each report lead to a different response?

all. While they may have certain limitations, there must also be 'territories' where they can make use of their abilities, too" (47). Many of the female employees at ZTV are temporary workers, pretty women who "adorned every office, tending the three pseudo-domestic zones of the Japanese workplace: the copy machine, the tea area, and the word processors" (51). These "flowers of the workplace" were occupied with answering the phone, sorting postcards from viewers, serving tea, and generally making the male employees feel important. Their behavior was consistently pleasant and subservient, and their dress stylish (compare this with the discussion of Japanese hostess clubs in Chapter 6). Although these women had the lowest status in the station, they also had some freedom to joke about social hierarchies in a way that no permanent woman employee would.

A parallel appears between the way female temporary workers are employed to complement and serve men and be harmonious and beautiful, and women's portrayal on Japanese television as listening to and agreeing with men. Women on television provide harmony through their roles in maintaining warm human relations, not (like men) struggling for dominance and superiority. Like the temporary workers, some women presented on television make fun of the status quo through parody and play—as long as it does not go too far. The limits are clearly defined.

The primary audience for Japanese television is the category of *shufu*, housewives. People at ZTV were preoccupied with the characteristics and preferences of shufu. They devised six categories, ranging from the strongly self-assertive "almighty housewife" to the "tranquil and prudent" housewife. A popular form of programming for housewives is the *hōmu dorama*, the "home drama" or domestic serial. These serials represent traditional values such as filial piety and the proper role of the daughter-in-law in regard to her mother-in-law. Caring for the aged has become a prominent theme that supplies the central tension for many situations in which women have to sort out their relationships with each other. In contrast, television representations of men emphasize their negotiation of social hierarchies within the workplace and other public organizations.

Although most programming presents women in traditional domestic roles, many women in contemporary Japan are rejecting such shows. In response, producers are experimenting with new sorts of dramas in which women are shown as active workers and aggressive lovers—anything but domesticated housewives. One such show is a ten-part serial aired in 1992 called *Selfish Women*. The story concerns three women: an aggressive single businesswoman who faces discrimination at work, a young mother who is raising her daughter alone while her photographer husband lives with another woman, and an ex-housewife who divorced her husband because she found home life empty and unrewarding. There are several male characters, but except perhaps for one, they are depicted as less interesting than the women. The show's title is ironic. In Japan, women who assert themselves are often labeled "selfish" by men. The lead women in the drama use the term in a positive way to encourage each other: "Let's become even more selfish!" Painter comments that, "though dramas like *Selfish Women* are perhaps not revolutionary, they are indicative of the fact that telerepresentations of gender in Japan are changing, at least in some areas." (69)

BEYOND WORDS: HUMAN PARALANGUAGE

Human communication involves many nonverbal forms, including tone of voice, silence, and the full gamut of body language from posture to dress to eye movements. Referred to as *paralanguage*, these ways of communication follow patterns and rules just as verbal language does. Like verbal language, they are learned—often unconsciously—and without learning, one will be likely to experience communication errors, sometimes funny and sometimes serious. Like verbal language, they vary cross-culturally and intraculturally.

Silence

The use of silence can be an effective form of communication. Like those of verbal language, its meanings differ cross-culturally. In Siberian households, the lowest-status

Tuareg men in Niger, West Africa, greeting each other. Tuareg men's greetings involve lengthy handshaking and close body contact. ■ *Compare this greeting with how adult males in your microculture greet each other.* (Source: © Charles O. Cecil)

person is the in-marrying daughter, and she tends to speak very little (Humphrey 1978). However, silence does not always indicate powerlessness. In American courts, comparison of speaking frequency among the judge, jury, and lawyers shows that lawyers, who have the least power, speak most, whereas the silent jury holds the most power (Lakoff 1990:97–99).

Native Americans tend to be silent more often than Euro-American speakers. Many outsiders, including social workers, have misinterpreted this as either reflecting their sense of dignity, or, more insultingly, signaling a lack of emotion or intelligence. How wrong and ethnocentric such judgments are is revealed by a study of silence among the Western Apache of Arizona (Basso 1972 [1970]). The Western Apache use silence in four contexts. First, when meeting a stranger (someone who cannot be identified), especially at fairs, rodeos, or other public events, it is considered bad manners to speak right away. That would indicate interest in something like money, or work, or transportation, which are possible reasons for exhibiting such bad manners. Second, silence is important in the early stages of courting. Sitting in silence and holding hands for several hours is appropriate. Speaking "too soon" would indicate sexual willingness or interest. That would be immodest. Third, when children come home after a long absence at boarding school, parents and children should meet each other with silence for about fifteen minutes rather than rushing into a flurry of greetings. It may be two or three days before sustained conversations are initiated. Last, a person should be silent when "getting cussed out," especially at drinking parties. An underlying similarity of all these contexts is the uncertainty, ambiguity, and unpredictability of the social relationships. Rather than chattering to "break the ice," the Apache response is silence. The difference between the Apache style and the Euro-American emphasis on quick and continuous verbal interactions in most contexts can cause cross-cultural misunderstandings. Outsiders, for example, have misinterpreted Apache parents' silent greeting of their returning children as bad parenting or as a sign of child neglect.

Kinesics

Kinesics is the study of communication that occurs through body movements, positions, facial expressions, and spatial behavior. This form of nonverbal language also has rules for correct usage, possibilities for code-switching, and cross-cultural variation. Misunderstandings of body language can easily happen because, like verbal language and international forms of sign language, it is based on arbitrary symbols. Different cultures emphasize different "channels" more than others; some are more touch-oriented than others, for example, or use

A satellite dish now dominates the scene in a village in Niger, West Africa. Throughout the world, the spread of electronic forms of communication have many and diverse social effects. ■ *Pretend you are a cultural anthropologist doing research on communication in this village. What do you want to study in order to assess the effects of satellite communication on the people and their culture?* (Source: © Charles O. Cecil)

facial expressions more. Eye contact is valued during Euro-American conversations, but in many Asian contexts, direct eye contact could be considered rude or possibly also a sexual invitation. Nonverbal communication is important in communicating about social relationships, especially dominance and accommodation, or positive versus negative feelings.

Dress and Looks

Manipulation of the body is another way of sending messages. Marks on the body, clothing, and hair styles convey a range of messages about age, gender, sexual interest

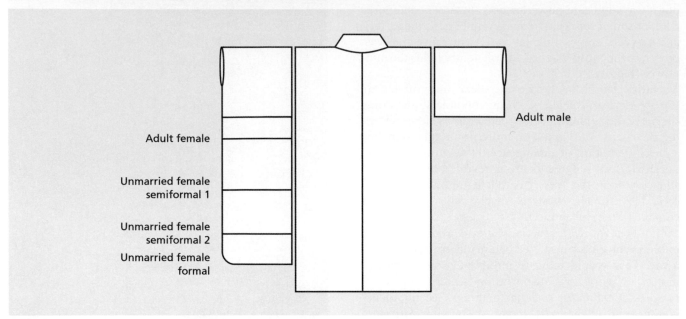

or availability, profession, wealth, and emotions. In the United States, gender differentiation begins in the hospital nursery with the color coding of blue for boys and pink for girls. In Japan, the kimono provides an elaborate coding system for gender, life-cycle stage, and formality of the occasion (see Figure 12.3). The more social responsibility and status one has, which depends on age and gender, the shorter the sleeve of one's kimono. An interesting contrast exists with the academic gowns worn by professors in the United States at special events such as graduation ceremonies. Professors with a doctorate (Ph.D.) wear gowns with full-length sleeves, whereas professors with a master's degree wear gowns with sleeves cut above the elbow.

Messages conveyed through dress, like other linguistic cues, have the property of arbitrariness. Consider the different meaning of the new veiling in just two cases, Egypt and Kuwait (MacLeod 1992). The "new veiling"

of Kuwaiti women distinguishes them as relatively wealthy, leisured, and honorable, in contrast to poor, laboring, immigrant women workers. The new veiling in Egypt is done mainly by women from the lower and middle economic levels, where it has been adopted as a way for working-class women to accommodate to pressures from Islamic fundamentalism to veil, while preserving their right to keep working outside the home. The message of the head covering is "I am a good Muslim and a good wife/daughter." In Kuwait, the headscarf says, "I am a wealthy Kuwaiti citizen."

Human communication is a vast and exciting field. It includes verbal language and paralanguage. It varies across cultures and has rich and complex meanings. It touches every aspect of our lives from our hair styles to our jobs. A time allocation study of hours per day spent in some form of communication among the "Nacirema" would be quite revealing.

KEY CONCEPTS

SUGGESTED READINGS

William Frawley, Kenneth C. Hill, and Pamela Munro, eds. *Making Dictionaries: Preserving Indigenous Languages of the Americas.* Berkeley: University of California Press, 2002. An introductory chapter by the editors presents ten issues in the making of a dictionary, and fourteen subsequent chapters address particular topics such as how to standardize spelling in formerly unwritten languages, and case studies of dictionary making in languages such as Hopi and Nez Perce.

Faye D. Ginsburg, Lila Abu-Lughod, and Brian Larkin, eds. *Media Worlds: Anthropology on New Terrain.* Berkeley: University of California Press, 2002. The editors offer an introductory chapter on media anthropology and new directions in the field. The remaining nineteen chapters provide cultural examples organized in five themes: cultural activism and minority claims, the cultural politics of nation–states, transnational circuits, media industry and institutions, and media technology.

Marjorie H. Goodwin. *He-Said-She-Said: Talk as Social Organization among Black Children.* Bloomington: Indiana University Press, 1990. A study of everyday talk among children of an urban African American community in the United States, this book shows how children construct social relationships among themselves through verbal interactions including disputes, pretend play, and stories.

Jack Goody. *The Power of the Written Tradition.* Washington, DC: The Smithsonian Institution, 2000. This book focuses on how writing confers power on societies that have it, compared to those that rely on oral communication. Goody's analysis encompasses the changing power of books in the age of the Internet.

Fadwa El Guindi. *Veil: Modesty, Privacy, and Resistance.* New York: Berg, 1999. El Guindi argues that veiling in Arab-Islamic states has many functions and is more complicated than most Western stereotypical views of shame and persecution suggest. The veil may signal group identity and resistance to Western values such as materialism.

Joy Hendry. *Wrapping Culture: Politeness, Presentation and Power in Japan and Other Societies.* New York: Oxford University Press, 1993. This book explores the pervasive idiom and practice of "wrapping" in Japanese culture, including verbal language, gift-giving, and dress. In verbal language, wrapping involves the use of various forms of respect, indicating social levels of the speakers, and the use of linguistic forms of beautification, which have the effect of adornment.

Fern L. Johnson. *Speaking Culturally: Language Diversity in the United States.* Thousand Oaks, CA: Sage Publications, 2000. This book describes a variety of discourse styles in the United States, paying special attention to gender and ethnicity. Chapters address language patterns among African Americans, Latinos, and Asian Americans and within institutional contexts such as health care settings, the legal system, schools, and workplaces. The final chapter considers the issue of bilingual education.

Robin Toimach Lakoff. *Talking Power: The Politics of Language in Our Lives*. New York: Basic Books, 1990. Lakoff explores strategies of communication and language power-plays in English in the United States, providing examples from courtrooms, classrooms, summit talks, and joke-telling.

William L. Leap. *Word's Out: Gay Men's English*. Minneapolis: University of Minnesota Press, 1996. Fieldwork among gay men in the Washington, DC, area produced this ethnography. It addresses gay men's speech as a cooperative mode of discourse, bathroom graffiti, and discourse about HIV/AIDS.

Catherine A. Lutz and Jane L. Collins. *Reading National Geographic*. Chicago: University of Chicago Press, 1993. This study presents the way *National Geographic*'s editors, photographers, and designers select text and images of Third World cultures and how middle-class American readers interpret the material.

Purnima Mankekar. *Screening Culture, Viewing Politics: An Ethnography of Television, Womanhood, and Nation in Postcolonial India*. Durham, NC: Duke University Press, 1999. This ethnographic study of mass media in India shows how modernity interacts with core cultural values, especially those related to the family and gender.

Daniel Miller and Don Slater. *The Internet: An Ethnographic Approach*. New York: Berg, 2000. This is the first ethnography of Internet culture. Based on fieldwork in Trinidad, it offers an account of the political and social contexts of Internet use, individual experiences of being online, and the impact of the Internet on Trinidadian people and their culture

Susan U. Philips, Susan Steele, and Christine Tanz, ed. *Language, Gender and Sex in Comparative Perspective*. New York: Cambridge University Press, 1987. An introductory essay, followed by eleven chapters, explores women's and men's speech in Japan, Western Samoa, and Mexico; children's speech in American preschools and in Papua New Guinea; and sex differences in how the brain is related to speech.

Lisa Philips Valentine. *Making It Their Own: Ojibwe Communicative Practices*. Toronto: University of Toronto Press, 1995. This ethnographic study examines a variety of speech events in a small community of Ojibwe people in northern Ontario, Canada. It considers speech variations among speakers, code-switching, and multilingualism, as well as connections between spoken language and church music.

WHAT are the major features of human verbal language?

Linguistic anthropologists point to two features that appear to distinguish human verbal language from communication that other animals use: productivity and displacement. Some study the formal, or structural, properties of verbal language, especially the basic units of meaningful sound, or phonemes. Others focus on historical linguistics, including the emergence of writing as a distinctly human form of verbal communication. Early historical linguists such as Sir William Jones discovered the relationships among languages previously thought to be unrelated, such as German and Sanskrit, and this discovery contributed to greater insights about human history and settlement patterns across Asia and Europe. The recent history of language change has been influenced by the colonialism of past decades or centuries and by the Western globalization of the current era. Many indigenous and minority languages have become extinct, and many others are in danger of doing so. National policies of cultural integration sometimes involve the repression of minority languages. Western globalization supports the spread of English as an increasingly powerful global language with emerging localized variants that have their own distinctive character.

HOW do language, thought, and society interact?

Language, thought, and society are intimately connected in all cultural contexts. One model, the Sapir-Whorf hypothesis, places emphasis on how our language structures our cultural worlds. Another model, called sociolinguistics, emphasizes how our cultural and social worlds shape our language. Many anthropologists draw on both models. Linguistic anthropologists realize how arbitrary the boundaries are between languages, dialects, and even particular linguistic codes that gain prominence. More important than hard and fast definitions of these categories is the context within which modes of communication change and the way speech may be related to the social status and treatment of the speakers. Linguistic anthropologists increasingly study power issues in their attempt to understand how language is linked to dominance, agency, and identity. Media anthropology is an emerging area of interest in anthropology. Research in media anthropology sheds light on how culture shapes media messages and the social dynamics in media institutions.

WHAT is human paralanguage?

We use many forms of nonverbal language to communicate with each other. These include silence, body placement in relation to other people, and our physical appearance—the way we dress, hair styles, and body marking such as tattoos and other ornamentation. Like verbal language, paralanguage involves the use of arbitrary symbols, so speakers must learn it in order to communicate effectively in particular cultural contexts.

THE BIG QUESTIONS

- **WHAT** is religion and what are the basic features of religions?

- **HOW** do world religions illustrate globalization and localization?

- **WHAT** are some important aspects of religious change in contemporary times?

13

RELIGION

Probably the most famous archaeological site in the world, England's Stonehenge is the focus of conflict about its use and management. Archaeologists view it as a monument requiring preservation while religious groups view it as a temple to be used for rituals. *(Source: © Jan Stromme/Bruce Coleman, Inc.)*

When studying the religious life of people of rural northern Greece, anthropologist Loring Danforth observed rituals in which participants walk across several yards of burning coals (1989). They do not get burned, they say, because their faith and a saint protect them.

Upon his return to the United States, Danforth met an American who regularly walks on fire as part of his New Age faith and also organizes training workshops for people who want to learn how to firewalk. Danforth himself firewalked in a ceremony in rural Maine.

Not every anthropologist who studies religion undertakes such challenges during fieldwork, but they do all share an interest in enduring questions about humanity's understanding of the supernatural realm and relationships with it: Why do some religions have many gods and others just one? Why do some religions advocate animal sacrifice? Why do some religions give greater room for women's participation? How do different religions respond to changing conditions in the political economy?

Religion has been a cornerstone topic in cultural anthropology since the beginnings of the discipline. Over many decades, a rich collection of material has accumulated. The early focus was on religions of indigenous and tribal peoples. More recently, anthropologists have devoted attention to the major religions of state-level societies. With increasing globalization and population movements, religious traditions are also moving and changing as they adapt to new cultural contexts.

RELIGION IN COMPARATIVE PERSPECTIVE

This section sets the stage for the following sections by discussing core areas in the anthropology of religion, including how we define religion, given the cross-cultural diversity in belief systems, and theories about why religion began and why it is so pervasive. We then cover types of religious beliefs, ritual practices, and religious specialists.

What Is Religion?

Since the earliest days of anthropology, various definitions of religion have appeared. One of the simplest, offered by British anthropologist Edward Tylor in the late 1800s, is that religion is the belief in spirits. The definition favored by a more holistic approach is that **religion** is both beliefs and actions related to supernatural beings and forces (what Tylor referred to as spirits). In defining religion so that it can be applied cross-culturally, anthropologists avoid a narrow definition that says religion is the belief in a supreme deity. In many religions, no concept of a supreme deity exists, and others have multiple deities. Religion is related to, but not the same as, a people's **world view,** or way of understanding how the world came to be, its design, and their place in it. World view is a broader concept and does not include the criterion of concern with a supernatural realm. An atheist has a world view, but not a religious one.

Magic versus Religion

In the late 1800s, Edward Tylor wrote that magic, religion, and science are alike in that they are different ways in which people have tried to explain the physical world and events in it. Tylor thought that magical laws were false and scientific laws were true, and that religion is based on the false assumption that the world operates under the control of supernaturals. James Frazer (1978[1890]), writing at about the same time as Tylor, defined **magic** as people's attempt to compel supernat-

Christian firewalkers in northern Greece express their faith by walking on hot coals and reaffirm divine protection by not getting burned. Speculate on why some religious rituals involve physical and mental challenges. ■ *How do these challenges compare to physical and mental challenges in secular life, such as certain sports?* (Source: © Loring Danforth)

ural forces and beings to act in certain ways, in contrast to religion, the attempt to please supernatural forces or beings. After reviewing many practices cross-culturally that he considered magical, Frazer deduced two general principles of magic. First is the "law of similarity," the basis of what he called *imitative magic*. It is founded on the assumption that if person or item X is like person or item Y, then actions done to person or item X will affect person or item Y. A familiar example is a voodoo doll. If someone sticks pins into a doll X that represents person Y, then person Y will experience pain or suffering. The second is the "law of contagion," which is the basis for *contagious magic*. The law of contagion says that persons or things once in contact with a person can still have an effect on that person. Common items for working contagious magic include a person's hair trimmings, nail clippings, teeth, spit, blood, and fecal matter and the placenta of a baby. In cultures where contagious magic is practiced, people are careful about disposing of their personal wastes so that no one else can get hold of them.

Such scholars of religion as Tylor and Frazer supported an evolutionary model (Chapter 1), with magic as the predecessor of religion. They evaluated magic as less spiritual and ethical than religion and therefore more "primitive." They assumed that, in time, magic would be completely replaced by the "higher" system of religion and then, ultimately, by science as the most rational way of thinking. They would be surprised to see the widespread presence of magical religions in the modern world, as evidenced, for example, by a recent ethnographic

study of magic and witchcraft in contemporary London (Luhrmann 1989).

In fact, magic exists in all cultures. In different situations, people turn to magic, religion, or science. For example, magic is prominent in sports (Gmelch 1997 [1971]). American baseball players repeat actions or use charms (including a special shirt or hat) to help them win—on the assumption that if it worked before, it may work again. They are following Tylor's law of contagion. Such magical thinking is most common in contexts where uncertainty is greatest. In baseball, pitching and hitting involve more uncertainty than fielding, and pitchers and hitters are more likely to use magic. Magical practices are also prominent in farming, fishing, the military, and love. Thus we can no longer subscribe to an evolutionary model by which religion has replaced magic, because magic still widely exists. In a similar fashion, one cannot argue that science has replaced religion.

Theories of the Origin of Religion

Why did religion come into being? The existence of some form of religion in all contemporary cultures has prompted many theorists to adopt a functionalist approach. According to this view, religion provides ways of explaining and coping with universal "imponderables of life" such as birth, illness, misfortune, and death.

Tylor's theory, as proposed in his book *Primitive Culture* (1871), was based on his assumption that early people had a need for explanation, especially of the difference between the living and the dead. They therefore developed the concept of a soul that exists in all living things and departs from the body after death. Tylor named this way of thinking **animism**, the belief in souls or "doubles." Eventually, Tylor speculated, the concept of the soul became personified until, later, human-like deities were conceived. For Tylor, religion evolved from animism to polytheism (the belief in many deities) to monotheism (the belief in one supreme deity). Beliefs characteristic of animism still exist; they include, for example, beliefs about angels and visitations of the dead and the New Age religious use of crystals (Stringer 1999).

In contrast to Tylor, Frazer suggested that religion developed out of the failure of magic. Neither scholar suggested a place or time period during which these developments may have occurred, and both based their theories on speculation rather than on archaeological or other empirical data.

Later, functional theories emerged. Emile Durkheim, in his book *The Elementary Forms of the Religious Life* (1915), offered a functional explanation for how and why religion came into being. He reviewed ethnographical data on "primitive" religions cross-culturally and was struck by their social aspects: Durkheim speculated that early humans realized, through clan gatherings, that

A stone sculpture at Mamallapuram, south India, dating from the eighth or ninth century, depicts the triumph of the goddess Durga (riding the lion, left of center) over the bull-headed demon Mahishasura. The story of her saving the world through the killing of Mahishasura has inspired countless works of art in India. ■ *Think of an example from your culture in which a myth is portrayed graphically.* (Source: Simon Hiltebeitel)

contact with one another made them feel uplifted and powerful. This positive feeling, arising from social solidarity, became attached to the clan totem, an emblem of their group that became the first of many future objects of worship. Religion therefore originated to serve society by giving it cohesion through shared symbols and group rituals. Malinowski said that rituals help reduce anxiety and uncertainty. Marx, taking a *class conflict* rather than a functional approach, emphasized religion's role as an "opiate of the masses." By this phrase, Marx meant that religion provides a superficial form of comfort to the poor, masking the harsh realities of class inequality and thereby preventing uprisings of the poor against the rich.

A third major theoretical thread, *symbolic analysis,* informs Freud's theory of the role of the unconscious. Many anthropologists agree with Freud that religion is a "projective system" that expresses people's unconscious thoughts, wishes, and worries. Anthropologists have also applied Freudian analysis of symbols, and their underlying or hidden meanings in dreams, to the analysis of myths.

A fourth theoretical theme, which combines Durkheimian functionalism with symbolic analysis, comes from Clifford Geertz (1966) who proposed that religions are primarily *systems of meaning*. In this view, religion offers a conception of reality, "a model of life," and a pattern for how to live.

Varieties of Religious Beliefs

Religions comprise beliefs and behavior. Scholars of religion generally address belief systems first because they appear to inform patterns of religious behavior. Religious beliefs tend to be shared by a group, sometimes by very large numbers of people. Through the centuries, people have found ways to give their beliefs permanence. Elders teach children the group's songs and tales, artists paint the stories on rocks and walls, and sculptors create images in wood and stone that depict aspects of religious belief.

In this section, we consider cross-cultural variation in religious beliefs. We discuss major forms in which religious beliefs are transmitted from one generation to the next. We then review a range of beliefs about supernatural beings.

How Beliefs Are Expressed

Beliefs are expressed and transferred over the generations in two main forms: **myth,** narrative stories about supernatural forces or beings, and **doctrine,** direct statements about religious beliefs.

A myth is a narrative that has a plot with a beginning, middle, and end. The plot may involve recurrent motifs, the smallest units of narrative. Myths convey messages about the supernaturals indirectly, through the story itself, rather than by using logic or formal argument. Greek and Roman myths, such as the stories of Zeus, Athena, Orpheus, and Persephone, are world-famous. Some people would say that the Bible is a collection of myths; others would object to that categorization as suggesting that the stories are not "real" or "sacred."

Myths are distinguished from folktales, which are secular stories. Borderline cases between the categories of myth and folktale exist. For example, some people would classify "Cinderella" as a folktale, whereas others would quickly point out that the fairy godmother is not an ordinary human and so "Cinderella" is a myth. Such arguments are more entertaining than important.

Celebration of Holi, a spring festival popular among Hindus worldwide. In this scene in New Delhi, a young woman sprays colored water on a young man as part of the joyous event. The deeper meaning of Holi is tied to a myth about a demon. ■ *How is the arrival of spring marked in your microculture?* (Source: © AFP/CORBIS)

Myths have long been part of people's oral tradition. Only with the emergence of writing were these stories recorded, and then only if they were of great importance, perhaps part of a royal or priestly tradition. Many of the world's myths are still unwritten.

Anthropologists have asked why myths exist. Malinowski said that a myth is a "charter" for society in that it expresses core beliefs and teaches morality. Thus, for Malinowski, myths serve to maintain society itself by helping people. In contrast, Claude Lévi-Strauss, probably the most famous mythologist, saw myths as functional but in a philosophical and psychological way. Myths help people deal with the deep conceptual contradictions between, for example, life and death and good and evil, by providing stories in which these dualities find a solution in a mediating third factor. These mythological solutions are buried within a variety of surface details in the myth. For example, many Pueblo Indian myths juxtapose grass-eating animals (vegetarians) with predators (carnivores). The mediating third character is the raven, who is a carnivore but, unlike other creatures, does not have to kill to eat meat because it is a scavenger. A third functional view takes a cultural materialist perspective and says that myths store and transmit information related to making a living and managing economic crises (Sobel and Bettles 2000). Analysis of twenty-eight myths of the Klamath and Modoc, Native Americans of Oregon and California, revealed that subsistence risk are a consistent theme in all of them. The myths also emphasize ways to cope with hunger, such as skill in hunting and fishing, food storage, resource diversification, resource conservation, spatial mobility, reciprocity, and the role of supernatural forces. Thus myths may promote economic survival and success of groups in the short run by imparting knowledge about crisis management, and they may contribute to long-term economic sustainability by transmitting knowledge about environmental management and conservation.

Epics are longer than myths and focus more on heroic traditions. Many epics are associated with particular ethnic groups or nations, such as the *Odyssey* and the *Iliad* of Greece. Less well known in North America are India's two great Hindu epics, the *Mahabharata* and the *Ramayana*. Iceland's *eddas* of the thirteenth century are grouped into two categories: mythic (dealing with gods) and heroic (dealing with humans).

Doctrine, the other major form in which beliefs are expressed, explicitly defines the supernaturals—who they are, what they do, and how to relate to them through religious practice; the world and how it came to be; and people's roles in relation to the supernaturals and to other humans. Doctrine, which is written and formal, is close to law in some respects because it links incorrect beliefs and behaviors with punishments for each. Many religious scriptures incorporate both myth and doctrine.

Doctrine is associated with institutionalized, large-scale religions rather with than small-scale "folk" religions. Doctrine, however, can and does change (Bowen 1998:38–40). Over the centuries, various Popes have pronounced new doctrine for the Catholic church. A papal declaration of 1854, made with the intent of reinvigorating European Catholicism, bestowed authenticity on the concept of the Immaculate Conception, an idea with substantial popular support.

Muslim doctrine is expressed in the Qu'ran, the basic holy text of the Islamic faith, which consists of revelations made to the prophet Muhammed in the seventh century, and in collections of Muhammed's statements and deeds (Bowen 1998:38). In Kuala Lumpur, Malaysia, a small group of highly educated women called the Sisters in Islam regularly debate with members of the local *ulama*, religious authorities who are responsible for interpreting Islamic doctrine especially concerning families, education, and commercial affairs (Ong 1995). In recent years, the debates have concerned such issues as polygamy, divorce, women's work roles, and women's clothing.

Beliefs about Supernatural Forces and Beings

In all cultures, some concept of otherworldly beings or forces exists, even though not all members of the culture believe in their existence. Supernaturals range from impersonal forces to those that look just like humans. Supernaturals can be supreme and all-powerful creators or smaller-scale, annoying spirits that take up residence in people through "possession."

The term **animatism** refers to belief systems in which the supernatural is conceived of as an impersonal power. A well-known example is *mana,* a concept widespread throughout the Melanesian region of the South Pacific. Mana is a force outside nature that works automatically; it is neither spirit nor deity. It manifests itself in objects and people and is associated with personal status and power, because some people accumulate more of it than others. Some supernaturals are **zoomorphic**—deities that appear in the shape, or partial shape, of animals. No satisfactory theory has appeared to explain why some religions develop zoomorphic deities, and for what purposes, and why others do not. Religions of classical Greece and Rome and ancient and contemporary Hinduism are especially rich in zoomorphic supernaturals.

Anthropomorphic supernaturals, deities in the form of humans, are common but not universal. The human tendency to perceive of supernaturals in their own form was noted 2500 years ago by the Greek philosopher Xenophanes (who lived sometime between 570 and 470 BCE). He said, "If cattle and horses, or lions, had hands, or were able to draw with their feet and produce the worlds which men do, horses would draw the forms of gods like horses, and cattle like cattle, and they would make the gods' bodies the same shape as their own" (*Fragment* 15). But why some religions do and others do not have anthropomorphic deities is a question that is impossible to answer fully. Such deities are more common in sedentary societies than among foragers.

Anthropomorphic supernaturals, like humans, can be moved by praise, flattery, and gifts. They can be tricked. They have emotions: They get irked if neglected, they can be loving and caring, or they can be distant and nonre-

sponsive. Most anthropomorphic supernaturals are adults. Few are very old or very young. Humans and supernaturals have similar marital and sexual patterns. Divine marriages tend to be heterosexual. In societies where polygyny occurs, male gods also have multiple wives. Deities have sexual intercourse, within marriage and sometimes extramaritally. Gods of the Greek and Roman pantheon, the entire collection of deities, often descended to earth and kidnapped and raped human women. So far, however, legal divorce has not occurred among supernaturals. Although many supernaturals have children, grandchildren are not prominent.

In pantheons (collectivities of deities), a division of labor exists by which certain supernaturals are responsible for particular domains. This greater specialization among the supernaturals reflects the greater specialization in human society that emerged with agriculture. There may be deities of forests, rivers, the sky, wind and rain, agriculture, child-

Religion provides an important source of social cohesion and psychological support for many new immigrant groups, whose places of worship attract both worshippers and cultural anthropologists interested in learning how religion fits into migrants' adaptation. This is a scene at a Lao Buddhist temple in Virginia. ■ *See what you can find out about Buddhism in North America from the Internet.* (Source: Ruth Krulfeld)

birth, disease, warfare, and marital happiness. Some gods are more effective for material wealth and others for academic success. The supernaturals have political roles and hierarchies. High gods, such as Jupiter and Juno of classical Roman religion, are distant from humans and hard to contact. The more approachable deities are below them in the hierarchy. Next, one finds a collection of spirits, good and bad, often unnamed and uncounted.

Deceased ancestors can also be supernaturals. In some religions, spirits of the dead can be prayed to for help, and in turn they may require respect and honor from the living (Smith 1995:46). Many African, Asian, and Native American religions have a cult of the ancestors, as did religions of ancient Mesopotamia, Greece, and Rome. In contemporary Japan, ancestor veneration is the principal religious activity of many families. Three national holidays recognize the importance of the ancestors: the annual summer visit of the dead to their home and the visits by the living to graves during the two equinoxes.

Humans may also, after their death, be transformed into deities. This process, called **euhemerism,** is named after the philosopher Euhemerus of Messene (ca. 340–260 BCE), who suggested that classical Greek deities had once been earthly people.

Beliefs about Sacred Space

Beliefs about the sacredness of certain spaces are probably found in all religions, but such beliefs are more prominent in some religions than others. Sacred spaces may or may not be marked in a permanent way. Unmarked spaces include rock formations or rapids in a river (Bradley 2000). The fact that unmarked spaces in prehistory may have been religious sites poses a major challenge to archaeologists interested in reconstructing early religion. Sometimes, though, archaeologists can find evidence of sacrifices at such sites to attest to their ritual importance.

Among the indigenous Saami people of northern Norway, Sweden, and Finland, religious beliefs were, before Christian missionary efforts, strongly associated with sacred natural sites, which were often unmarked (Mulk 1994). These sites included rock formations resembling humans, animals, or birds. The Saami sacrificed animals and fish at these sites until strong pressures from Christian missionaries forced them to repress their practices and beliefs. Although many Saami today still know where the sacred sites are, they will not reveal them to others.

Another important form of sacred space that has no permanent mark occurs in an important domestic ritual conducted by Muslim women throughout the world called the *khatam quran,* the "sealing" or reading of the holy book, the Koran (Werbner 1988). A study of Pakistani migrants living in the city of Manchester, England, reveals that this ritual involves a gathering of mostly women who read the Qu'ran and then share a ritual meal. The reason for gathering can be to give thanks or to seek divine blessing. During the ritual, the otherwise nonsacred space of the house becomes sacred. A "portable" ritual such as this one is especially helpful in migrant adaptation, because it can be conducted without a formally consecrated ritual space. All that is required is a supportive group of kin and friends and the Qu'ran.

Religions of many of the Aboriginal people of Australia are closely tied to sacred space. During a mythological past, called the Dreamtime, the ancestors walked the earth and marked out the territory belonging to a particular group. People's knowledge of where the ancestors roamed is secret. In several cases that have recently been brought to the courts, Aboriginal peoples have claimed title to land that is being sought by business interests such as mining companies. Anthropologists have sometimes become involved in these disputes, providing expert testimony documenting the validity of the Aboriginal claims to their sacred space.

In one such case, secret Aboriginal knowledge about a sacred place and its associated beliefs was gender-specific: It belonged to women and could not be told to men. The anthropologist who was hired to support the women's claims was a woman and could therefore be told about the sacred places, but she would not be able to convey that knowledge in court to the male judge. These cultural nuances demanded considerable ingenuity on the part of the anthropological consultant (see the Lessons Applied box on page 304).

Ritual Practices

Rituals are patterned forms of behavior that have to do with the supernatural realm. Many rituals are the enactment of beliefs expressed in myth and doctrine, such as the Christian ritual of communion. Rituals are distinct from *secular rituals,* such as a sorority or fraternity initiation or a common-law wedding, which are patterned forms of behavior with no connection to the supernatural realm. It is not always easy to distinguish ritual from secular ritual. Consider the American holiday of Thanksgiving, which originated as a sacred meal, its primary purpose being to give thanks to god for the survival of the pilgrims (Siskind 1992). Its original Christian meaning is not maintained by everyone who celebrates the holiday now. It may even be rejected—for example, by Native Americans, who are not likely to consider the arrival and survival of the pilgrims a cause for thankfulness.

Anthropologists and scholars of religion have categorized rituals in many ways. One division is based on how regularly the ritual is performed. Regularly performed rituals are called *periodic rituals.* Many periodic rituals

ABORIGINAL WOMEN'S CULTURE, SACRED SITE PROTECTION, AND THE ANTHROPOLOGIST AS EXPERT WITNESS

A GROUP of Ngarrindjeri (prounounced NAR-en-jeery) women and their lawyer hired Diane Bell to serve as a consultant to them in supporting their claims to a sacred site in southern Australia (Bell 1998). The area was threatened by the proposed construction of a bridge that would cross sacred waters between Goolwa and Hindmarsh Island. The women claimed protection for the area and sought prevention of the bridge building on the basis of their secret knowledge of its sacredness—knowledge that had been passed down from mother to daughter over generations. The High Commission formed by the government to investigate their claim considered it to be a hoax perpetrated to block a project important to the country. Helping the women prove their case to a white, male-dominated court system was a challenging task for Diane Bell, an anthropologist teaching in the United States but also a white Australian by birth, with extensive fieldwork experience among Aboriginal women.

Bell conducted research over many months to marshal evidence for the validity of the women's claims—including newspaper archives, early recordings of ritual songs, and oral histories of Ngarrindjeri women. She prepared reports for the courtroom about women's sacred knowledge that were general enough to avoid violating the rule of women-only knowledge but detailed enough to convince the High Court judge that the women's sacred knowledge was authentic. In the end the judge was convinced, and the bridge project was canceled in 1999.

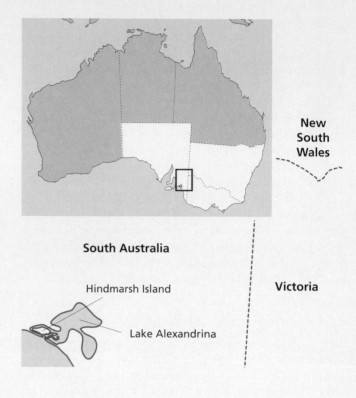

FOOD FOR THOUGHT

On the Internet, learn more about this case and other disputes in Australia about sacred sites.

---

are performed annually to mark a seasonal milestone such as planting or harvesting or to commemorate some important event. For example, an important periodic ritual in Buddhism, Visakha Puja, or Buddha's Day, commemorates the birth, enlightenment, and death of the Buddha (all on one day). On this day, Buddhists gather at monasteries, hear sermons about the Buddha, and perform rituals such as pouring water over images of the Buddha. Calendrical events such as the shortest day of the year, the longest day, the new moon, and the full moon often shape ritual cycles. Nonperiodic rituals, in contrast, occur irregularly, at unpredictable times, in response to unscheduled events such as a drought or flood, or to events in a person's life such as illness, infertility, birth, marriage, or death.

Life-Cycle Rituals

Belgian anthropologist Arnold van Gennep (1960 [1908]) first proposed the category of life-cycle rituals in 1909. **Life-cycle rituals**, or rites of passage, mark a change in status from one life stage to another of an individual or group. Victor Turner's (1969) fieldwork among the Ndembu, horticulturalists of Zambia, provided insights about the phases of life-cycle rituals. Turner found that, among the Ndembu, and cross-culturally, life-cycle rituals have three phases: separation, transition, and reintegration. In the first phase, the initiate (the person undergoing the ritual) is separated physically, socially, or symbolically from normal life. Special dress may mark the separation—for example, a long white gown for a

An Apache girl's puberty ceremony (the initiate is on the left). Cross-cultural research indicates that the celebration of girls' puberty is more likely to occur in cultures in which adult women have valued productive and reproductive roles. ■ *Can you generate a hypothesis about why this is the case? How does this theory apply to your microcultural experience?* (Source: © John Annerino)

ing that the baby has gotten through the most dangerous period and is likely to survive. In contrast is the increasingly common practice in the United States of pregnant women purchasing an ultrasound video of their unborn fetus, a secular ritual that declares the "personhood" of the fetus before it is born. This practice is related to a context of low infant mortality.

Differences in the cross-cultural distribution of puberty rituals for boys and girls may reflect the economic value and status of males and females. Most societies have some form of puberty ceremony for boys, but puberty ceremonies for girls are less common. In societies where female labor is important and valued, girls have elaborate (and sometimes painful) puberty rites (J. Brown 1978). Where their labor is not important, menarche is unmarked and there is no puberty ceremony. Puberty rites function to socialize the labor force, among other things (review Chapter 6 on puberty rites). For example, among the Bemba of southern Africa, during initiation, a girl learns to distinguish thirty or forty different kinds of mushrooms and to know which ones are edible and which are poisonous.

Pilgrimage

Pilgrimage is round-trip travel to a sacred place or places for purposes of religious devotion or ritual. Prominent pilgrimage places are Varanasi in India (formerly called Banaras) for Hindus; Mecca in Saudi Arabia for Muslims; Bodh Gaya in India for Buddhists; Jerusalem in Israel for Jews, Christians, and Muslims; and Lourdes in France for Christians. Pilgrimage often involves hardship, with the implication that the more suffering that is involved, the more merit the pilgrim accumulates. Compared to a weekly trip to church or synagogue, pilgrimage removes a person further from everyday life, is more demanding, and therefore is potentially more transformative.

Victor Turner applied his three sequences of life-cycle rituals to pilgrimage as well: The pilgrim first separates from everyday life, then enters the liminal stage during the actual pilgrimage, and finally returns to be reintegrated into society in a transformed state. Indeed, in many pilgrimage traditions, a person who has gone on certain pilgrimages gains enhanced public status—for example, the status of *haji* (someone who has done the *haj,* or pilgrimage to Mecca) in the Islamic faith.

Connections among myth sacred sites, and pilgrimage are strong. For example, in the Hindu goddess tradition, the story of Sati is the basis for the sanctity of four major and forty-six minor pilgrimage sites in India (Bhardwaj 1973). Because of an argument with her father over whether her husband Shiva was welcome at a big sacrifice her family was holding, the unhappy Sati committed suicide. When Shiva heard about her death, he was distraught. He picked up her body and carried it over his shoulder as he wandered across India, grieving. Along

baby that is to be baptized in a church. In many cultures of the Amazon and in East and West Africa, adolescents are secluded for several years in separate huts or areas away from the village. The transition phase, or *liminal phase,* is the time when the person is no longer in the previous status but is not yet a member of the next stage. Liminality often involves the learning of specialized skills that will equip the person for the new status. Reintegration, the last stage, occurs when the initiate emerges and is welcomed by the community in the new status.

How can we explain variations in the occurrence and elaboration of such rituals? Consider an example of explanation related to the mode of reproduction. Ritual marking of a baby's entry into society as a human is a common practice, but it varies in terms of how soon after birth the ceremony is performed. Where infant mortality rates are high, the ceremony tends to be done late, when the baby is a year old or even older. Until the ceremony has been performed, the baby is not named and is not considered "human." This timing may be a way of ensur-

A young Bosan man dressed as an oversexualized woman, one of the most common costumes in the carnival street-theater masquerades in the Sardinian town of Bosa. ■ *Consider what might be the meaning of the object he is holding.* (Source: Lorenzo Pezzatini)

the way, parts of her body fell to the ground. The places where they dropped became holy. Some of these include her tongue at Jwala Mukhi and her throat at Vaishno Devi, both in the Himalayas, and her genitals in the eastern state of Assam.

Pilgrimage, especially among Hindus in India, may involve bathing in a sacred river, in a pond near a temple, or even in the ocean (Gold 1988). Flowing water is believed to have great powers of purification. Many of India's most famous pilgrimage sites are located on rivers, such as Varanasi (Banaras), the most prominent place of Hindu pilgrimage, which is located on the Ganges River.

Rituals of Inversion

In some rituals, normal social roles and relations are temporarily inverted. Scholars who adopt a functionalist perspective say these rituals allow for social "steam" to be let off temporarily and may also provide a reminder about the propriety of normal, everyday roles and practices to which people must inevitably return once the ritual is over.

These **rituals of inversion** are common cross-culturally, one of the best-known in the West being Carnival. Carnival is celebrated throughout the northern Mediterranean region, North and South America, and the Caribbean. It is a period of riotous celebration before the Christian fast of Lent (Counihan 1985). Carnival begins at different times in different places, but always ends on Mardi Gras (or Shrove Tuesday), the day before the fasting period of Lent begins. The word *Carnival* is

derived from Latin and means "flesh farewell," referring to Lent.

In Bosa, a town in Sardinia, Italy, Carnival involves several aspects of social role reversal and relaxing of usual social norms: "The discotheques extend their hours, and mothers allow their daughters to attend more often and longer than at other times of the year. Men and women play sexually, fondling and flirting with each other in the discotheques and [performing] masquerades that are totally illicit at other times of the year" (14). Carnival in Bosa has three major phases. The first is impromptu street theater and masquerades that take place over several weeks, usually on Sundays. The theatrical skits are social critiques of current events and local happenings. The masquerades mainly involve men dressing up as exaggerated women:

> Young boys thrust their padded breasts forward with their hands while brassily hiking up their skirts to reveal their thighs. . . . A youth stuffs his shirt front with melons and holds them proudly out. . . . The high school gym teacher dresses as a nun and lifts up his habit to reveal suggestive red underwear. Two men wearing nothing but bikinis, wigs, and high heels feign a stripper's dance on a table top. (15)

The second phase occurs during the morning of Mardi Gras, when hundreds of Bosans, mostly men, dress in black like widows and flood the streets. They accost passersby, shaking in their faces dolls and other objects that are maimed in some way or bloodied. They shriek at the top of their lungs as if mourning, and they say, "Give us milk, milk for our babies. . . . They are dying, they are neglected, their mothers have been gallivanting since St. Anthony's Day and have abandoned their poor children" (16). The third phase, called *Giolzi,* takes place during the evening. Men and women dress in white, wearing sheets for cloaks and pillow cases for hoods. They blacken their faces. Rushing into the street, they hold hands and chant the word "Giolzi." They storm at people, pretending to search their bodies for Giolzi and then say "Got it!" It is not clear what Giolzi is, but whatever it is, it represents something that makes everyone happy. How does an anthropologist interpret these events? Carnival allows people to act out roles that are normally closed off to them, for a short time, before they have to go back to their normal positions. It also provides a time in which everyone has fun. In this way, rituals of inversion can be seen to function as mechanisms for maintaining social order: After the allotted days of revelry, everyone returns to his or her original place for another year.

Sacrifice

Many rituals involve **sacrifice,** or the offering of something for transfer to the supernaturals. Sacrifice has a long history throughout the world and is probably one of the oldest forms of ritual. It may involve killing and offering animals; or making human offerings (of whole people, parts of a person's body, or even bloodletting); or offering vegetables, fruits, grains, flowers, or other products. One anthropologist suggests that flowers are symbolic replacements for former animal sacrifices (Goody 1993).

Spanish documents from the sixteenth century describe Aztec state-sponsored sacrifices in which priests made offerings of humans and other animals, ostensibly to "feed" the gods on behalf of the welfare of the state. Apparently the gods were fond of human blood—as well as of quails, crocodiles, jaguars, ducks and salamanders. One of the most widely offered items for important events, such as a coronation or the naming of newborn babies, was a limited amount of ritually induced bleeding. Symbolic anthropologists accept the religious logic involved in pleasing the gods as a sufficient explanation for blood sacrifice. Cultural materialists are inclined to propose an explanation for the practice that is tied to resources, particularly sources of protein. (See the Critical Thinking box on page 308.)

Religious Specialists

Not all rituals require the presence of a religious specialist, or someone with special and detailed training, but all require some level of knowledge on the part of the performer(s) about how to do them correctly. Even the daily, household veneration of an ancestor requires some knowledge gained through informal learning. At the other extreme, many rituals cannot be done without a highly trained specialist.

Shamans and Priests

General features of the categories of shaman and priest illustrate key differences between these two types of specialists (many other specialists fit somewhere in between). Shamans or shamankas (the female form with the "-ka" ending derives from the original Siberian usage) are part-time religious specialists who gain their status through direct relationships with the supernaturals, often by being "called." A potential shaman may be recognized by special signs, such as the ability to go into a trance. Anyone who demonstrates shamanic abilities can become a shaman; in other words, this is an openly available role. Shamans are more often associated with non-state societies, yet in many ways, faith healers and evangelists of the United States could be considered to fit in this category. One of the most important functions of shamanic religious specialists is in healing (review Chapter 7).

In states, the more complex occupational specialization in religion means that there is a wider variety of types of specialists, especially what anthropologists refer to as "priests" (not the same as the specific modern role of the Catholic priest) and promotes the development of religious hierarchies and power structures. The terms **priest** and **priestess** refer to a category of full-time religious specialists whose position is based mainly on abilities gained through formal training. A priest may receive a divine call, but more often the role is hereditary, passed on through priestly lineages. In terms of ritual performance, shamans are more involved with nonperiodic rituals. Priests perform a wider range of rituals, including periodic state rituals. In contrast to shamans, who rarely have much secular power, priests and priestly lineages often do.

Other Specialists

Certain other specialized roles are widely found. Diviners are specialists who are able to discover the will and wishes of the supernaturals through techniques such as reading animal entrails. Palm readers and tarot card readers fit into the category of diviners. Prophets are specialists who convey divine revelations usually gained through visions or dreams. They often possess charisma, an especially attractive and powerful personality, and may be able to perform miracles. Prophets have founded new religions, some longlasting and others shortlived. Witches use psychic powers and affect people through emotion and thought. Mainstream society often condemns witchcraft as negative. Some scholars of ancient and contemporary witchcraft differentiate between positive forms that involve healing and negative forms that seek to harm people.

Critical Thinking

WHY DID THE AZTECS PRACTICE HUMAN SACRIFICE AND CANNIBALISM?

EVIDENCE OF state-sponsored human sacrifice and cannibalism of the victims among the Aztecs of Mexico comes from accounts written by the Spanish conquistadors (Harris 1977, 1989; Sanday 1986). The Aztec gods required human sacrifice—they "ate" human hearts and "drank" human blood. Most of the victims were prisoners of war, but many others were slaves, and sometimes young men and women, and even children.

The victims were marched up the steep steps of the pyramid, held lying on their backs over a stone altar, and slit open in the chest by a priest, who wrenched out the heart (said to be still beating), which was then burned in offering to the gods. The body was rolled down the other side of the temple, where it was retrieved by butchers and prepared for cooking. The skull was returned to the temple area to be put on display racks. Although no one knows for sure how many victims were sacrificed, estimates are in the hundreds of thousands. At a single site, a chronicler reported that the display racks contained more than one hundred thousand skulls (Harris 1977:106). At one especially grand event, victims were arranged in four lines, each two miles long. Priests worked for four days to complete the sacrifices.

Human sacrifice and cannibalism of any scale might seem to invite the question "Why?" Certainly one must ask "why" about sacrifice and cannibalism as practiced on the grand scale of the Aztecs. Of the many attempted explanations, two perspectives are compared here: an etic view and an emic view.

Michael Harner (1977) and Marvin Harris (1977, 1989) propose a cultural materialist explanation based on references to factors in the regional ecology and the politics of Aztec expansionism. The region of the Aztec empire lacked sufficient amounts of animal sources of protein to satisfy its growing population. Although the ruling classes managed to maintain their supply of delicacies such as dog, turkey, duck, deer, rabbit, and fish, little was available for the poor. Yet the rulers needed to support and retain the loyalty of their army in order to protect and expand the empire's boundaries, and they needed to keep the masses happy. Providing the gods with human hearts and blood was a powerful statement of the empire's strength. It had the additional benefit of yielding huge amounts of meat for soldiers and commoners. Such "cannibal redistribution" could be manipulated by the state to reward particular groups and to compensate for periodic shortages in the agricultural cycle.

Peggy Sanday (1986) rejects the materialist perspective and provides an interpretive one based on texts describing the Aztec people's own rationale and motives. Sacrifice and cannibalism, she says, followed religious logic and symbolism and were practiced to satisfy the gods' hunger, not human hunger. Aztec religion says that the gods require certain sacrifices in order for the universe to continue to operate. Human flesh was consumed not as an "ordinary meal" but as part of a religious identification with the gods, just as people would wear the skins of sacrificed victims in order to participate in their sacredness. Sanday says that the etic explanation, in focusing on the "business" aspects of Aztec sacrifice and cannibalism, has overlooked the tradition's religious meaning for the Aztecs.

CRITICAL THINKING QUESTIONS

How do the two explanations differ in the data they use?

Which do you find more convincing, and why?

Is there any other way to explain Aztec human sacrifice and cannibalism?

WORLD RELIGIONS

The term **world religions** was coined in the nineteenth century to refer to religions with many followers that crossed national borders and had a few other specific features, such as a concern with salvation (the belief that human beings require deliverance from an imperfect world). At first, the term referred only to Christianity, Islam, and Buddhism. It was later expanded to include Judaism, Hinduism, Confucianism, Taoism, and Shintoism. The category of world religions is less appropriate now, because many more religions cross national boundaries and therefore have "world" reach. Nonetheless, because college religion courses teach entire semesters of material on these "world religions," this chapter provides an anthropological perspective on five of them. In addition, because of the global importance of the African diaspora that began with the European colonial slave trade, a sixth category of world religions is included that describes key elements shared among the diversity of traditional African belief systems.

Cultural anthropologists emphasize that no world religion exists as a single monolithic entity. Rather, each comprises many variants due to microcultural and regional variations, as well as doctrinal differences between reformist and fundamentalist interpretations. The world religions have long traveled outside their original borders through intentional attempts to expand and gain converts, or through migration of believers to new locales. European colonialism was a major force of expansion of Christianity, especially (but not exclusively) through missionary work of various Protestant sects. Now, the increased rate of population movements (Chapter 15) and the rapid expansion of television and the Internet have given even greater impetus to religious movement and change. One anthropologist says that the world religions face a "predicament" in terms of how to maintain a balance between standardization based on core beliefs and the increasingly local variants emerging everywhere (Hefner 1998). From Christian televangelism to Internet chat rooms, contemporary religion appears to be more dynamic and interactive than ever before, raising doubt about the validity of claims that modernity means the decline of religious belief and the rise of secularism.

The five world religions of long-standing that are considered here are discussed first in terms of their general history, distribution, and teachings. Then examples are given of how they vary in different contexts to show how the same texts and teachings are localized. Often, when a world religion moves into a new cultural region, it encounters indigenous religious traditions. The two world religions that emphasize proselytizing, or seeking converts, are Christianity and Islam. Their encounters with indigenous religions have often been violent and have included physical destruction of local sacred places and objects (Corbey 2003). Common approaches include burning, overturning, dismantling, or cutting up things, dumping them into the sea, and hiding them in caves. European Christian missionaries in the 1800s often confiscated sacred goods and shipped them to Europe for sale to private owners or museums. Both Christian and Islamic conversion efforts frequently involved the destruction of local sacred sites and the construction of their own places of worship on top of the original site.

In many cases, incoming religions and local religions coexist as separate traditions, either as complements or as competitors, in what is called **religious pluralism.** In **syncretism,** elements of two or more religions blend together. Syncretism is most likely to occur when elements of two religions form a close match with each other. For example, if a local myth involves a hero who has something to do with snakes, there may be a syncretistic link with the Catholic belief in St. Patrick, who is believed to have driven snakes out of Ireland.

Many situations of non-fit can also be provided. Christian missionaries have had difficulty translating the Bible into indigenous languages because of lack of matching words or concepts, and because of differing kinship and social structures. Some Amazonian groups, for example, have no word that fits the Christian concept of "heaven" (Everett 1995, personal communication). In other cases, matrilineal peoples have found it difficult to understand the significance of the Christian construct of "god the father."

Hinduism

Over 650 million people in the world are Hindus (Hiltebeitel 1995). The majority live in India, where Hinduism accounts for about 80 percent of the population. The other 20 million, the Hindu diaspora, live in the United States, Canada, the United Kingdom, Malaysia, Fiji, Trinidad, Guyana, and Hong Kong. A Hindu is typically born a Hindu, and Hinduism does not actively seek converts. The four Vedas, composed in Sanskrit in northern India between 1200 and 900 BCE, are the core texts of Hinduism. Many other scholarly texts and popular myths and epics, especially the Mahabharata (the story of a war between two lineages, the Pandavas and the Kauravas) and the Ramayana (the story of king Rama and his wife Sita), also serve as unifying scriptures. Throughout India, a multiplicity of local traditions exist, some of which carry forward elements from pre-Vedic times. Thus Hinduism incorporates a diversity of ways to be a Hindu. It offers a rich polytheism and at the same time a philosophical tradition that reduces the multiplicity of deities into oneness. Deities range from simple stones (in Hinduism, stones can be gods) placed at the foot of a tree to elegantly carved and painted icons of gods such as Shiva, Vishnu, and the goddess Durga. Everyday worship of a deity involves lighting a lamp in front of the god, chanting hymns and mantras (sacred phrases), and taking *darshan* (sight of) the deity (Eck 1985). These acts bring blessings to the worshipper.

Although certain standard features of Hinduism exist, such as acceptance of key texts and worship of important, well-known deities, many localized versions of Hinduism throughout India involve the worship of deities and practice of rituals unknown elsewhere. For example, firewalking is an important part of goddess worship in southern and eastern India (Freeman 1981; Hiltebeitel 1988) and among some Hindu groups living outside India, notably Fiji (C. Brown 1984). Besides regional variations, caste differences in beliefs and practices are marked, even within the same area or village. Lower-caste deities prefer offerings of meat sacrifices and alcohol; upper-caste deities prefer offerings of flowers, rice, and fruit. Temple structures range from magnificent buildings to a simple canopy placed over the deity for shade. Yet the "unity in diversity" of Hinduism has long been recognized as real, mainly because of the shared acceptance of elements of Vedic thought.

A Nayar Fertility Ritual

The matrilineal Nayars of Kerala, South India, perform a nonperiodic ritual as a remedy for the curse of the serpent deities who cause infertility in women (Neff 1994). This ritual exemplifies the unity of Hinduism in several ritual elements, such as the use of camphor and incense, the importance of serpent deities, and offering flowers to the deity. The all-night ritual includes, first, women painting a sacred design of intertwined serpents on the floor. Several hours of worshipping the deity follow. Ritual elements include a camphor flame, incense, and flowers. Music comes from drumming, cymbals, and singing. All of these please the deity. The presence of the deity, though, is fully achieved when a Nayar woman goes into trance. Through her, matrilineal family members may speak to the deity and be blessed.

Thus, along with universal elements of Hindu ritual, we find that the role of matrilineal kin among the Nayars provides local variation in ritual. Among the Nayars, a woman's matrilineal kin—mother, uncles, brothers—are responsible for ensuring that her desires for motherhood are fulfilled. They share her interest in her reproductive success in continuing the matrilineage. What the women say during the trance is important. They typically draw attention to family disharmonies or neglect of the deities. This message diverts blame from the infertile woman for whom the ritual is being held. It reminds family and lineage members of their responsibilities for each other.

Hindu Women and Karma in Great Britain

One of Hinduism's basic concepts is that of *karma*, translated as "destiny" or "fate." A person's karma is determined at birth on the basis of his or her previous life and how it was conducted. The karma concept has prompted many outsiders to judge Hindus as fatalistic, lacking a sense of agency. But anthropological research on how people actually think about karma in their everyday lives reveals much individual variation from fatalism to a strong sense of being in charge of one's destiny. One study looked at women's perceptions of karma among Hindus living in Britain (Knott 1996). Some Hindu women are fatalistic in their attitudes and behavior, but others are not. One woman who had a strongly fatalistic view of karma said,

> [W]hen a baby's born . . . we have a ritual on the sixth day. That's when you name the baby, you know. And on that day, we believe the goddess comes and writes your future . . . we leave a blank white paper and a pen and we just leave it [overnight]. . . . So I believe that my future—

whatever happens—is what she has written for me. That tells me [that] I have to do what I can do, and if I have a mishap in between I have to accept that. (24)

Yet another woman said that her sufferings were caused by the irresponsibility of her father and the "bad husband" to whom she had been married. She challenged her karma and left her husband: "I could not accept the karma of being with Nirmal [her husband]. If I had done so, what would have become of my children?" (25). Because Hindu women's karma dictates being married and having children, leaving one's husband is a major act of resistance. For some young women informants, questioning the role of karma was the same as questioning their parents' authority. Such intergenerational conflicts create feelings of ambiguity and confusion.

Options for women seeking support when questioning or changing their roles can be either religious (praying more and fasting) or secular (seeking the advice of a psychological counselor or social worker). Some Hindu women in Britain have themselves become counselors and help support other women's independence and self-confidence. This work involves clear subversion of the traditional rules of karma for women.

Buddhism

Buddhism originated in a founding figure, Siddhartha Gautama (ca. 566–486 BCE), revered as the Buddha, or Awakened One (Eckel 1995:135). It began in northern India, where the Buddha grew up. From there, it spread throughout the subcontinent, into Inner Asia and China, to Sri Lanka, and on to Southeast Asia. In the past two hundred years, Buddhism has spread to Europe and North America. Buddhism's popularity subsequently faded in India, and Buddhists now constitute less than 1 percent of India's population. Its global spread is matched by a great diversity of doctrine and practice, to the extent that it is difficult to point to a single essential feature (for example, no single text is accepted as authoritative for all forms of Buddhism), other than the importance of Gautama Buddha. Many Buddhists worship the Buddha as a deity, but others do not—they honor his teachings and follow the pathway he suggested for reaching nirvana, or release from worldly life.

Buddhism first arose as a protest against certain features of Hinduism, especially caste inequality, yet it retained and revised several Hindu concepts, such as karma. In Buddhism, everyone has the potential for achieving nirvana (enlightenment and the overcoming of human suffering in this life), the goal of Buddhism. Good deeds are one way to achieve a better rebirth with each incarnation, until finally, release from samsara (the cycle of birth, reincarnation, death, and so on) is achieved. Compassion toward others, including animals, is a key

Buddhism gained an established footing in Japan in the eighth century. The city of Nara was an important early center of Buddhism. Here an emperor sponsored the casting of a huge bronze statue of the Buddha. ■ *Is there a Buddhist temple where you live? If so, have you visited it? If not, find out where the nearest one is, and visit it if possible.* (Source: Jack Heaton)

virtue. Branches of Buddhism have different texts that they consider their canon. The major division is between the Theravada Buddhism practiced in Southeast Asia and the Mahayana Buddhism of Tibet, China, Taiwan, Korea, and Japan. Buddhism is associated with a strong tradition of monasticism through which monks and nuns renounce the everyday world and spend their lives meditating and doing good works. Buddhists have many and varied annual festivals and rituals. Some events bring pilgrims from around the world to India—to Sarnath, where the Buddha gave his first teaching, and Gaya, where he gained enlightenment.

Local Spirits and Buddhism in Southeast Asia

One theory says that wherever Buddhism exists outside India, it is never the exclusive religion of the devotees because it arrived to find established local religions already in place (Spiro 1967). In Burma, Buddhism and indigenous traditions coexist without one being dominant. Indigenous Burmese beliefs remained strong because they offer a way of dealing with everyday problems. According to Burmese Buddhism, a person's karma (as in Hinduism) is a result of previous births and determines his or her present condition. If something bad happens, the person can do little but suffer through it. Burmese supernaturalism, on the other hand, says that the bad thing happened because of the actions of capricious spirits called *nats*. Ritual actions can combat the influence of nats. In other words, nats can be dealt with,

but karma cannot. The continuity of belief in nats can be seen as an example of human agency and creativity. People kept what was important to them from their traditional beliefs but also adopted aspects of the new religion. Buddhism, however, became an important cultural force and the basis for social integration in Burma. One village, for example, had three Buddhist monasteries, with four resident Buddhist monks and several temporary monks. Every male child was ordained as a temporary member of the monastic order. Almost every villager observed Buddhist holy days. Although Buddhism is held to be the supreme truth, the spirits retain control when it comes to dealing with everyday problems such as a toothache or a monetary loss. Other studies of religion in Southeast Asia provide examples in which there appears to be more blending of local religions with Buddhism, rather than their separate but complementary existence (See the Unity and Diversity box on page 312.)

Buddhism and Abortion in Japan

Buddhist teachings about the "fluidity" of the supernatural and human realms are important in contemporary Japan, especially in relation to the widespread practice of abortion there. In Japanese Buddhism, fetuses, like newborn infants, are not considered to be full-fledged, solid lives (LaFleur 1992). They are fluid creatures who can be "returned" through abortion (or, in previous centuries, infanticide) to the supernatural realm. People believe that a "returned" fetus may come back at a more convenient time. Women who have had an abortion commonly go to a Buddhist temple and perform a special ritual in which they pray for the good fortune of the rejected fetus. They dedicate a small statue to it that may be placed, along with hundreds of other such statues, in a cemetery-like setting (refer to the photo on page 116 in Chapter 5). It is periodically adorned with clothing, cheap jewelry, and trinkets. These practices may have a positive psychological effect on the parents by diverting feelings of sadness. Thus doctrine and ritual fit with the reproductive goal of many Japanese families to have few children, within the context of abortion being the predominant way of limiting the number of offspring.

Judaism

The first and basic Judaic religious system was defined around 500 BCE, following the destruction of the Temple in Jerusalem by Babylonians in 586 BCE (Neusner 1995). The early writings, called the Pentateuch, established the theme of exile and return as a paradigm for Judaism that endures today. The Pentateuch is also called the Five Books of Moses, or the Torah.

Followers of Judaism share in the belief in the Torah (the Five Books of Moses, or Pentateuch) as the revela-

Unity and Diversity

TATTOOS AND SACRED POWER IN RURAL THAILAND

FIELDWORK AMONG Shan people in an irrigated rice area of Thailand revealed the importance of tattooing, a tradition shared with much of Southeast Asia (Tannenbaum 1987). Shan tattooing blends aspects of Buddhism with local spirit beliefs and even elements of Hinduism as practiced by some groups in neighboring Burma.

The Shan have three general classes of tattoos:

1. Tattoos that act on other people, causing them to like or fear the bearer, and that cause the spirits to be kind (*acun*).

2. Tattoos that act on the bearer, increasing the bearer's skill (*yapeya*).

3. Tattoos that create a barrier around the person that prevents animals from biting, knives from cutting, and bullets from entering the body (*kat* or *pik*).

Tattoos are done in two colors—red and blue/black. The first two types tend to be done in red; the third type tends to be done in blue/black. Different designs are associated with each type. For example, the two-tailed lizard is a common tattoo in the first type.

The first type is popular among many people, because it brings health to the bearer. It is the main type of tattoo among women, used for illness prevention as well as for curing an illness. A person who falls ill may get a tattoo incorporating a letter of the Shan alphabet in the design, either on the calf, around a body joint, around the mouth, or on the top of the tongue. Some of the most powerful designs in this category are placed on the back or over the heart. The most powerful tattoo in this category, called the Five Buddha tattoo, is not allowed for women. Men who get this tattoo have to follow five Buddhist precepts at all times: refrain from killing, stealing, improper sexual behavior, lying, and intoxication. This tattoo is red, but it also includes exfoliated skin from a Buddhist monk. That makes this tattoo different from all others and makes its bearer like a monk. Whereas most tattoos in the first category cause other people to look favorably on the bearer, the Five Buddha tattoo inspires fear and awe.

Tattoos in the second category, worn by men, are all related to words. Some increase people's memory and help them on exams. Others strengthen a person's speaking ability. The most powerful tattoos in this group give a person such great verbal skills that they can intimidate others. They increase courage as well. One tattoo in this category is the Saraswati tattoo, which depicts, among other things, the head of Saraswati, the Hindu goddess of knowledge, on the bearer's right shoulder. To call on Saraswati for help, the person brushes his lips on the tattoo.

The third category of tattoos, those that provide a protective barrier, has one subset that prevents bites from insects, snakes, dogs, cats, tigers, and so on. If the person has the tattoo and gets bitten nonetheless, the tattoo helps reduce the pain. A general anti-bite tattoo is a cat on the lower arm. More powerful tattoos in this third category protect people from weapons. They seal off the body. A person should be careful not to get too many of these tattoos, however, because they seal the body off completely and can also prevent good fortune from entering it. Someone with many of these tattoos is likely to be poor or unlucky.

The Shan people do not question why or how their tattoos work. They simply believe that they do. They blend what anthropologists classify as magic with religious beliefs from Buddhism—as well as Hinduism, in the case of the Saraswati tattoo. Sacred power is the key that links all these beliefs together into a coherent system for the Shan.

FOOD FOR THOUGHT

Consider what kinds of things people do in your microculture to get people to like them, to do well on exams, and to protect the body from harmful intrusions.

---

tion of God's truth through Israel, a term for the "holy people." The Torah explains the relationship between the supernatural and human realms and guides people in how to carry out the world view through appropriate actions. A key feature of all forms of Judaism is the identification of what is wrong with the present and how to escape, overcome, or survive that situation. Jewish life is symbolically interpreted as a tension between exile and return, given its foundational myth in the exile of the Jews from Israel and their period of slavery in Egypt.

Judaism is monotheistic, teaching that God is one, unique, and all-powerful. Humans have a moral duty to follow Jewish law, to protect and preserve life and health, and to follow certain duties such as observing the Sabbath. The high regard for human life is reflected in the general opposition to abortion within Jewish law and in

The kotel (or Western Wall) in Jerusalem is a sacred place of pilgrimage, especially for Jews. Males pray at a section marked off on the left, women at the area on the right. Both men and women should cover their heads, and women should take care, when leaving the wall area, to keep their faces toward it and avoid turning their backs to it. ■ *Think of some behavioral rules at another sacred place you know of.* (Source: Barbara Miller)

opposition to the death penalty. Words, both spoken and written, have unique importance in Judaism: There is an emphasis on truth-telling in life and on the use of established literary formulas at precise times during worship. These formulas are encoded in a *sidur,* or prayer book. Dietary patterns also distinguish Judaism from other religions; for example, rules of kosher eating forbid the mixing of milk or milk products with meat.

Contemporary varieties of Judaism range from conservative Hasidism to Reform Judaism, which emerged in the early 1800s. One difference between these two perspectives concerns the question of who is Jewish. Jewish law traditionally defined a Jewish person as someone born of a Jewish mother. In contrast, reform Judaism recognizes as Jewish the offspring of a Jewish father and a non-Jewish mother. Currently the Jewish population numbers about 18 million worldwide, with about half living in North America, a quarter in Israel, and another 20 percent in Europe and Russia. Smaller populations are scattered across the globe.

Who's Who at the Kotel

The most sacred place to all Jews is the kotel, or Western Wall in Jerusalem. Since the 1967 war, which brought Jerusalem under Israeli rule, the kotel has been the most important religious shrine and pilgrimage site of Israel. The kotel is located at one edge of the Temple Mount (or Haram Sharif), an area sacred to Jews, Muslims, and Christians. According to Jewish scriptures, god asked Abraham to sacrifice his son Isaac on this hill. Later, King Solomon built the First Temple here in the middle of the tenth century BCE. It was destroyed by Nebuchadnessar in 587 BCE, when the Jews were led into captivity in Baby-

lon. Around 500 BCE, King Herod built the Second Temple on the same site. The kotel is a remnant of the Second Temple. Jews of all varieties and non-Jews come to the kotel in vast numbers from around the world. The kotel plaza is open to everyone, pilgrims and tourists. The wall is made of massive rectangular stones weighing between two and eight tons each. At its base is a synagogue area partitioned into men's and women's sections.

An ethnographic study of what goes on at the kotel reveals how this single site brings together a variety of Jewish worshippers and secular visitors. There is great diversity among the visitors, evident in the various styles of dress and gesture:

> The Hasid . . . with a fur *shtreimel* on his head may enter the synagogue area alongside a man in shorts who utilizes a cardboard skullcap available for "secular" visitors. American youngsters in jeans may ponder Israeli soldiers of their own age, dressed in uniform, and wonder what their lot might have been if they [had been] born in another country. Women from Yemen, wearing embroidered trousers under their dresses, edge close to the Wall as do women accoutred in contemporary styles whose religiosity may have been filtered through a modern education. . . . (Storper-Perez and Goldberg 1994:321)

In spite of plaques that state the prohibition against begging, there are beggars who offer to "sell a blessing" to visitors. They may remind visitors that it was the poor who built the wall in the first place. Another category of people is young Jewish men who, in search of prospective "born again" Jews, "hang around" looking for a "hit" (in their words). Most of the hits are young Americans who are urged to take their Jewishness more seriously and, if male, to be sure to marry a Jewish woman. Other regulars are Hebrew-speaking men who are available to organize a prayer service. One of the most frequent forms of religious expression at the kotel is the insertion of written prayers into the crevices of the wall.

The social heterogeneity of the Jewish people is thus transcended in a single space, creating some sense of what Victor Turner (1969) called *communitas,* a sense of collective unity out of individual diversity.

Passover in Kerala

The Jews of the Kochi area (formerly called Cochin) of Kerala, south India, have lived there for about 1000 years (Katz and Goldberg 1989). The Maharaja of Kochi had respect for the Jewish people, who were mainly merchants. He relied on them for external trade and contacts. In recognition of this, he allowed a synagogue, which is still standing, to be built next to his palace. Syncretism is apparent in Kochi Jewish lifestyle, social structure, and rituals. Basic aspects of Judaism are retained, along with adoption of many aspects of Hindu practices. Three aspects of syncretism with Hinduism are apparent in passover, one of the most important annual rituals of the Jewish faith. First, the Western/European passover celebration is typically joyous and a time of feasting. In contrast, the Kochi version has adopted a tone of austerity and is called "the fasting feast." Second, Kochi passover allows no role for children, whereas at a traditional *seder* (ritual meal) children usually ask four questions as a starting-point of the narrative. The Kochi Jews chant the questions in unison. (In Hinduism, children do not have solo roles in rituals.) Third, a Kochi seder stresses purity even more than standard Jewish requirements. Standard rules about maintaining the purity of kosher wine usually mean that no gentile (non-Jew) should touch it. But Kochi Jews expand the rule to say that if the shelf or table on which the wine sits is touched by a gentile, the wine is impure. This extra level of "contagion" is influenced by Hindu concepts of pollution.

Christianity

Christianity has many ties with Judaism, from which it sprang, especially in terms of the Biblical teachings of a coming savior, or messiah. It began in the eastern Mediterranean in the second quarter of the first century (Cunningham 1995:240–253). Most of the early believers were Jews who took up the belief in Jesus Christ as the "messiah" (annointed one) who came to earth in fulfillment of prophesies contained in the Hebrew scriptures. Today, Christianity is the largest of the world's religions with about 1.5 billion adherents, or nearly one-third of the world's population. It is the majority religion of Australia, New Zealand, the Philippines, Papua New Guinea, and most countries of Europe and of North and South America and about a dozen southern African countries. Chris-

A celebration of the Christian holy day of Palm Sunday in Port-au-Prince, Haiti. European colonialism brought African slaves to the "New World" and to Christianity through missionary efforts. Many forms of Christianity are now firmly established in the Caribbean region. ■ *Discover through a Web site or other source what the major Christian denominations in Haiti are.* (Source: Edward Keller)

tianity is a minority religion throughout Asia, but Asian Christians constitute 16 percent of the world's total Christians and are thus a significant population.

Christians accept the Bible (Old and New Testaments) as containing the basic teachings of their faith, believe that a supreme God sent his son to earth as a sacrifice for the welfare of humanity, and look to Jesus as the model to follow for moral guidance. The three largest branches of Christianity are Roman Catholic, Protestant, and Eastern Orthodox. Within each of these branches, various denominations exist. Christianity has existed the longest in the Near East and Mediterranean regions. In contemporary times, the greatest growth in Christianity is occurring in sub-Saharan Africa, parts of India, and Indonesia. It is currently experiencing a resurgence in Eastern Europe.

Protestantism among White Appalachians

Studies of protestantism in Appalachia describe local traditions that outsiders who are accustomed to standard, urban versions may view as "deviant." For example, some churches in rural West Virginia and North Carolina, called Old Regulars, practice three obligatory rituals: footwashing, communion (a ritual commemorating the "Last Supper" that Jesus had with his disciples), and baptism (Dorgan 1989). The footwashing ceremony occurs once a year in conjunction with communion, usually as an extension of the Sunday service. An elder is called to the front of the church, and he preaches for ten to twenty minutes. Then there is a round of handshaking and embracing. Two deaconesses come forward to "prepare the table" by uncovering the sacramental elements placed there earlier under a white tablecloth (unleavened bread, serving plates for the bread, cups for the wine, a decanter or quart jar or two of wine). The deacons come forward and break the bread into pieces while the moderator pours the wine into the cups. Men and women form separate groups as the deacons serve the bread and wine. After the deacons serve each other, it is time for the footwashing. The moderator may begin this part of the service by quoting from the New Testament (the book of John, chapter 13, verse 4): "He riseth from supper, and laid aside his garments; and he took a towel and girded himself." He then takes a towel and basin from the communion table and puts water in it, selects a senior elder and removes his shoes and socks, and then washes his feet slowly and attentively. Other members come forward and take towels and basins. Soon "the church is filled with crying, shouting, and praising as these highly poignant exchanges unleash a flood of emotions . . . and literally scores of high-pathos scenes will be played out" (106). Participants take turns washing and being washed. A functional interpretation of the ritual of footwashing is that it helps maintain social cohesion.

Another feature of worship in some small, Protestant subdenominations in West Virginia involves the handling of poisonous snakes. This practice finds legitimation in the New Testament (Daugherty 1997 [1976]). According to a passage in Mark (16:15–18), "In my name shall they cast out devils; they shall speak with new tongues; they shall take up serpents; and if they drink any deadly thing, it shall not hurt them; they shall lay hands on the sick, and they shall recover." Members of "Holiness-type" churches believe that the handling of poisonous snakes is the supreme act of devotion to God. Biblical literalists, these people choose serpent-handling as their way of celebrating life, death, and resurrection and of proving that only Jesus has the power to deliver them from death. Most serpent handlers have been bitten many times, but few have died. One interpretation of this ritual practice says that the risks of handling poisonous rattlesnakes and copperheads mirror the risks of the environment. The people are poor, with high rates of unemployment and few prospects for improvement. Outsiders might ask whether such dangerous ritual practices indicate that the people are somehow psychologically disturbed. Psychological tests indicate, however, that they are more emotionally healthy, on average, than members of mainline Protestant churches.

The Last Supper in Fiji

Among Christians in Fiji, the image of the "Last Supper" is a dominant motif (Toren 1988). This scene, depicted on tapestry hangings, adorns most churches and many houses. People say, "Christ is the head of this household, he eats with us and overhears us" (697). The image's popularity is the result of its fit with Fijian notions of communal eating and kava drinking. Seating rules at such events place the people of highest status, such as the chief and others close to him, at the "above" side of the room, away from the entrance. Others sit at the "lower" end, facing the highly ranked people. Intermediate positions are located on either side of the person of honor, in ranked order. Da Vinci's rendition of the Last Supper places Jesus Christ in the position of a chief, with the disciples in an ordered arrangement around him. "The image of an ordered and stratified society exemplified in people's positions relative to one another around the kava bowl is encountered virtually every day in the village" (706). The disciples and the viewers "face" the chief and eat and drink together, as is appropriate in Fijian society.

Islam

Islam is based on the teachings of the prophet Muhammed (AD 570–632) and is thus the youngest of the world religions (Martin 1995:498–513). The Arabic word *Islam* means "submission" to the will of the one god, Allah, through which peace will be achieved. Islam also implies acceptance of Muhammed as the last and final messenger of god, "the seal of the prophets." Muslim-majority nations are located in northern Africa; the Middle East, including Afghanistan, Pakistan, and Bangladesh in South Asia; and several nations in Central Asia and Southeast Asia. In fact, the majority of the world's Muslims (60 percent) live in South Asia or Southeast Asia. Although Islam originally flourished among pastoral nomads, only 2 percent of its adherents now are in that category.

A common and inaccurate stereotype of Islam among many non-Muslims is that wherever it exists, it is the same. This erroneously monolithic model tends to be based on some imagined version of Arab Islam as practiced in Saudi Arabia. A comparison of Islam in highland Sumatra, Indonesia, and Morocco, North Africa, reveals culturally constructed differences (Bowen 1992). The annual Feast of Sacrifice is celebrated by Muslims around the world. It commemorates god's sparing of Abraham's son Ishmael (Isaac in Christian and Jewish traditions). It takes place everywhere on the tenth of the last month of the year, also called Pilgrimage Month. The ritual reminds Muslims of their global unity within the Islamic faith. One aspect of this event in Morocco involves the king publicly plunging a dagger into a ram's throat, a reenactment of Muhammad's performance of the sacrifice on the same day in the seventh century. Each male head of household follows the pattern and sacrifices a ram. Size and virility of the ram are a measure of the man's power and virility. Other men of the household stand to witness the sacrifice, while women and children are absent or in the background. After the ram is killed, they come forward and dab its blood on their faces. In some villages, women play a more prominent role before the sacrifice by daubing the ram with henna (red dye), thus sanctifying it, and using its blood afterward in rituals to protect the household. These national and household rituals are highly symbolic of male power in the public and private domains—the power of the monarchy and the power of patriarchy.

The degree of local adaption to Moroccan culture becomes clear when it is compared with the ritual's enactment in Sumatra, which has a less patriarchal culture than Morocco and a political structure that does not emphasize monarchy. In Isak, a traditionalist Muslim village, people have been Muslims since the seventeenth century. They sacrifice all kinds of animals, including chickens, ducks, sheep, goats, and water buffalo. As long as the throat is cut and the meat is eaten, it satisfies the demands of god. Before cutting the victim's throat, the sacrificer dedicates it to one or more relatives. In contrast to Morocco, most sacrifices receive little notice and are done mainly in the back of the house with little fanfare. Both women and men of the household refer to it as "their" sacrifice, and there are no signs of male dominance. Women may sponsor a sacrifice, as did one wealthy woman trader who sacrificed a buffalo (the actual cutting, however, is done by a man). The Moroccan ritual emphasizes fathers and sons. The Isak ritual includes attention to a wider range of kin on both the husband's and wife's side, daughters as well as sons, and dead relatives, too. In the Indonesian context, no centralized dynastic meanings are given to the ritual.

The differences in the way the same ritual is practiced in two cultural contexts do not arise because Moroccans know the scriptures better than Sumatrans. The Isak area has many Islamic scholars who consult the scriptures and discuss issues. Rather, the cultural context, including kinship and politics, into which the same scriptural tradition is placed shapes it to local interests and needs.

African Religions

The distinction between the world religions and "local religions" is blurry because many local religions are now practiced by people who have migrated to other nations, so they aren't just "local." This is true for African religions, many of which spread outside Africa through the enforced movements of people as slaves, and for religions such as Confucianism that have been diffused by voluntary migration. This section attempts to summarize some key features of African religions and then

A sacred altar in a local African religion in Togo, West Africa. ■ *Can you distinguish some of the ritual elements displayed here? Are some incomprehensible to you? How would an anthropologist begin to learn about the beliefs involved in this religion?* (Source: © Gerd Ludwig/ Woodfin Camp & Associates)

offers an example of a new religion with African roots, Ras Tafari.

Features of African Religions

As of 1994, Africa's total population comprised 341 million Christians, 285 million Muslims, and about 70 million people practicing indigenous religions (Smith 1995:15–16). With its diverse geography, cultural variation, and history, Africa encompasses a wide range of indigenous religions. Some common, but not universal, features of indigenous African religions are

- Myths about a rupture that once occurred between the creator deity and humans.
- A pantheon that includes a high god and many secondary supernaturals ranging from powerful gods to lesser spirits.
- Elaborate initiation rituals.
- Rituals involving animal sacrifices and other offerings, meals, and dances.
- Altars within shrines as focal places where humans and deities meet.
- Close links with healing.

Although these general features are fairly constant, African indigenous religions are rethought and reshaped with variable results (Gable 1995). Furthermore, as African religions have moved around the world to new locations with the movement of African peoples, they have been adapted in various ways to their new contexts, as discussed in the following section on the Ras Tafari religion.

Ras Tafari

Also called Rastafarianism, Ras Tafari is a relatively new religion of the Caribbean, the United States, and Europe. It is not known how many Rastafarians there are because they refuse to be counted (Smith 1995:23). Ras Tafari is an unorthodox, protest religion that shares few of the features of African religions mentioned above. Ras Tafari traces its history to several preachers of the early twentieth century who taught that Ras ("Prince") Tafari, then the Ethiopian emperor Haile Selassie, was the "Lion of Judah" who would lead Blacks to the African promised land. Rastafarianism does not have an organized set of doctrines, and there are no written texts or enforced orthodoxy. Shared beliefs of the many diffuse groups include the belief that Ethiopia is heaven on earth, that Haile Selassie is a living god, and that all Blacks will be able to return to the homeland through his help. Since the death of Haile Selassie in 1975, greater emphasis has been placed on pan-African unity and Black power, and less on Ethiopia. Rastafarianism is particularly strong in Jamaica, where it is associated with reggae music, dreadlocks, and *ganja* (marijuana) smoking. Variations within the Rastafarian movement in Jamaica range from beliefs that one must fight oppression to the position that living a peaceful life brings victory against evil.

DIRECTIONS OF CHANGE

All religions have established mythologies and doctrines that provide a certain degree of continuity and, often, conservativism in religious beliefs and practices. Yet nowhere are religions frozen and unchanging. Cultural anthropologists have traced the resurgence of religions that seemed to have been headed toward extinction through colonial forces, and they have documented the emergence of seemingly new religions. Likewise, they are observing the contemporary struggle of once-suppressed religions in socialist states to find a new position in the post-socialist world. Religious icons (carvings or other artistic renderings of Mary, for example), once a prominent feature in Russian Orthodox churches, had been removed and placed in museums. Now, the churches want them back. Indigenous people's beliefs about the sacredness of their land are an important part of their attempts to protect their territory from encroachment and development by outside commercial interests. The world of religious change offers these examples, and far more, as windows into wider cultural change.

Revitalization Movements

Revitalization movements are social movements that seek to bring about positive change, either through reestablishing all or parts of a religion that has been threatened by outside forces or through adopting new practices and beliefs. Such movements often arise in the context of rapid cultural change and appear to represent a way for people to try to make sense of their changing world and their place in it. One such movement that emerged as a response of Native Americans to the invasion of their land by Europeans and Euro-Americans was the Ghost Dance movement (Kehoe 1989). In the early 1870s, a shaman named Wodziwob of the Paiute tribe in California declared that the world would soon be destroyed and then renewed: Native Americans, plants, and animals would come back to life. He instructed people to perform a circle dance, known as the "Ghost Dance," at night.

This movement spread to other tribes in California, Oregon, and Idaho but ended when the prophet died and his prophecy was unfulfilled. A similar movement emerged in 1890, led by another Paiute prophet, Wovoka, who had a vision during a total eclipse. His message was the same: destruction, renewal, and the need to perform circle dances in anticipation of the impending event. The dance spread widely and had various effects. Among the Pawnee, it provided the basis for a cultural revival of old ceremonies that had fallen into disuse. The Sioux altered Wovoka's message and adopted a more overtly hostile stance toward the government and White people. Newspapers began to carry stories about the "messiah craze," referring to Wovoka. Ultimately, the government took action against the Sioux, killing Chief Sitting Bull and Chief Big Foot and about three hundred Sioux at Wounded Knee. In the 1970s, the Ghost Dance was revived again by the American Indian Movement, an activist organization that seeks to advance Native American rights.

Cargo cults are a type of revitalization movement that emerged in much of Melanesia (including Papua New Guinea and Fiji), and in New Zealand among the indigenous Maori peoples, in response to Western influences. Most prominent in the first half of the nineteenth century, cargo cults emphasize the acquisition of Western trade goods, or "cargo" in local terms. Typically, a prophetic leader emerges with a vision of how the cargo will arrive. In one instance, the leader predicted that a ship would come, bringing not only cargo but also the people's dead ancestors. Followers set up tables for the expected guests, complete with flower arrangements.

John Frum Movement supporters stand guard around one of the cult's flag poles at Sulphur Bay village (Tanna, Vanuatu).
■ *What does this scene remind you of from your own cultural experience?* (Source: Lamont Lindstrom)

Later, after World War II and the islanders' experiences of aircraft arrivals bringing cargo, the mode of anticipated arrival changed to planes. Once again, people would wait expectantly for the arrival of the plane. The cargo cults emerged as a response to the disruptive effects of new goods being suddenly introduced into indigenous settings. The outsiders imposed a new form of exchange system that emphasized the importance of Western goods and denied the importance of indigenous valuables such as shells and pigs. This transformation undermined traditional patterns of status-gaining through the exchange of indigenous goods. Cargo cult leaders sought help, in the only way they knew, in obtaining Western goods so that they could gain social status in the new system.

Contested Sacred Sites

Religious conflict often becomes focused on sacred sites. One place of recurrent conflict is Jerusalem, where many religions and sects within religions compete for control of sacred terrain. Three major religions claim they have primary rights: Islam, Judaism, and Christianity. Among the Christians, several different sects vie for control of the Church of the Holy Sepulchre. In India, frequent conflicts over sacred sites occur between Hindus and Muslims. Hindus claim that Muslim mosques have been built on sites sacred to Hindus. On some occasions, the Hindus have destroyed the mosques. Many conflicts that involve secular issues surrounding sacred sites also exist worldwide. In the United States, White racists have

burned African American churches. In Israel, some Jewish leaders object to archaeological research because the ancient Jewish burial places should remain undisturbed. The same situation exists for Native Americans, whose burial grounds have often been destroyed for the sake of urban development in the United States and Canada. Around the world, large-scale development projects such as dams and mines have destroyed indigenous sacred areas. Resistance to such destruction is growing—for example, among Australian Aborigines, as discussed earlier in this chapter.

Religious Freedom as a Human Right

According to a United Nations Declaration, freedom from religious persecution is a universal human right. Yet violations of this right by countries and by competing religions are common. Sometimes people who are persecuted on religious grounds can seek and obtain sanctuary in other places or nations. Thousands of Tibetan Buddhist refugees, including their leader the Dalai Lama, fled Tibet after it was taken over by the Chinese. Several Tibetan communities have been established in exile in India, the United States, and Canada, where the Tibetan people attempt to keep their religion, language, and heritage alive.

The post-9/11 policy enactments in the United States related to the "campaign against terrorism" are seen by many as dangerous steps against constitutional principles of personal liberty—specifically, as infringements on the religious rights of practicing Muslims. The prevalent mentality in the government, and in much of the general populace, links the whole of Islam with terrorism and thereby stigmatizes all Muslims as potential terrorists. Physical attacks against people assumed to be Muslim were another aspect of such extreme thinking. Many anthropologists (for example, Mamdani 2002) have spoken out against the wrong-headedness and indecency of labeling an entire religion dangerous and putting all its members under the shadow of suspicion.

KEY CONCEPTS

animatism, p. 302

animism, p. 299

anthropomorphic, p. 302

cargo cult, p. 317

doctrine, p. 300

euhemerism, p. 303

life-cycle rituals, p. 304

magic, p. 298

myth, p. 300

priest/priestess, p. 307

religion, p. 298

religious pluralism, p. 309

revitalization movements, p. 317

rituals, p. 303

rituals of inversion, p. 306

sacrifice, p. 307

syncretism, p. 309

world religions, p. 308

world view, p. 298

zoomorphic, p. 302

SUGGESTED READINGS

Nadia Abu El-Haj. *Archaeological Practice and Territorial Self-Fashioning in Israeli Society.* Chicago: University of Chicago Press, 2001. A cultural anthropologist writes about the political aspects, specifically nation-building, of archaeology in Israel. Attention is focused on contested sacred sites, how secular interests are linked to sacred site archaeology, and debates about excavation of grave sites.

Diane Bell. *Ngarrindjeri Wurruwarrin: A World That Is, Was, and Will Be.* North Melbourne, Australia: Spinifex, 1998. This is an ethnography about Australian Aboriginal women's struggles to protect their sacred land from encroachment by developers. It devotes attention to the women's own voices, the perspective of the Australian government, the media, and even disputes among anthropologists about what constitutes truth and validity.

Thomas D. Blakely, Walter E. A. van Beek, and Dennis L. Thompson. *Religion in Africa: Experience and Expression.* Portsmouth, NH: Heinemann, 1994. This book contains an introductory overview and twenty chapters on topics that include the impact of Islam and Christianity on African religious systems, women's spirit cults, myth and epic, and new religious movements.

Karen McCarthy Brown. *Mama Lola: A Vodou Priestess in Brooklyn.* Berkeley: University of California Press, 1991. The life story of Mama Lola, a Vodou practitioner, is set within an ethnographic study of a Haitian community in New York.

David L. Carmichael, Jane Hubert, Brian Reeves, and Audhold Schanche, eds. *Sacred Sites, Sacred Places.* New York: Routledge, 1994. This volume contains an introductory essay and twenty-one chapters, some by archaeologists and others by cultural anthropologists, on sacred places in California, Ireland, Cameroon, Sweden, Poland, Kenya, and New Zealand, among others. The authors discuss methods applied in studying sacred sites, as well as policy issues related to site preservation.

Susan Greenwood. *Magic, Witchcraft and the Otherworld: An Anthropology.* New York: Berg, 2000. This book examines modern magic as practiced by Pagans in Britain, focusing on the Pagan view of the essence of magic as communication with an otherworldly reality. Chapters address witchcraft, healing, Goddess worship, and the relationship between magic and morality.

Klara Bonsack Kelley and Harris Francis. *Navajo Sacred Places.* Bloomington: Indiana University Press, 1994. The authors report on the results of a research project undertaken to learn about Navajo cultural resources, especially sacred sites, and the stories associated with them in order to help protect these places.

Lorna J. Marshall. *Nyae Nyae !Kung: Beliefs and Rites.* Cambridge, MA: Peabody Museum of Archaeology and Ethnology, Harvard University, 1999. This book provides detailed descriptions of Ju/wasi [!Kung] religious beliefs, including characteristics of supernaturals and rituals for childbirth and healing. The ethnographic data are from the 1950s, when Marshall did extensive fieldwork in the Nyae Nyae area of Namibia.

Anna S. Meigs. *Food, Sex, and Pollution: A New Guinea Religion.* New Brunswick, NJ: Rutgers University Press, 1983. This book provides an analysis of taboos surrounding food, sex, and vital bodily essences among the Hua people of Papua New Guinea.

Fatima Mernissi. *Beyond the Veil: Male–Female Dynamics in Modern Muslim Society.* Bloomington: Indiana University Press, revised edition, 1987. The author considers how Islam perceives female sexuality and seeks to regulate it on behalf of the social order. This edition contains a new chapter on Muslim women and fundamentalism.

WHAT is religion and what are the basic features of religions?

Early cultural anthropologists defined religion in contrast to magic and suggested that religion was a more evolved form of thinking about the supernatural realm. They collected information on religions of non-Western cultures and constructed theories about the origin and functions of religion. Since then, ethnographers have described the basic features of religious systems and documented a rich variety of beliefs, many forms of ritual behavior, and different types of religious specialists. Beliefs are expressed in either myth or doctrine and often are concerned with defining the roles and characteristics of supernatural beings and how humans should relate to them. Rituals, or the action side of beliefs, include life-cycle rituals, pilgrimage, rituals of inversion, and sacrifice. In some sense, all rituals are transformative for the participants. Many rituals, but not all, require the participation of a trained religious specialist such as a shaman/shamanka or priest/priestess. Religious specialist roles are fewer, less formalized, and carry less secular power and status in non-state societies. In states, religious specialists are often organized into hierarchies, and many specialists gain substantial secular power.

HOW do world religions illustrate globalization and localization?

The five world religions of long standing are based on a coherent and widely agreed-upon set of teachings, but as members of these religions move around the globe, the religious beliefs and practices are contextualized into localized variants. When a new religion moves into a culture, it may be blended with indigenous systems (syncretism), may coexist with indigenous religions in a pluralistic fashion, or may take over and obliterate the original beliefs.

WHAT are some important aspects of religious change in contemporary times?

Cultural anthropologists have documented religious change and sought to explain why and how it occurs. Religious movements of the past two centuries have often been prompted by colonialism and other forms of social contact. In some instances, indigenous religious leaders and cults arise in the attempt to resist unwanted outside forces of change, in other cases, they evolve as ways of incorporating selected outside elements. Issues of contemporary importance include the seemingly increasing amount of conflict surrounding sacred sites and hostilities related to the effects of secular power interests on religious institutions and spaces. The importance of considering religion as a human right, according to United Nations policy, was brought to the fore following the 9/11 attacks on the United States, when the "campaign against terrorism" jeopardized the rights of Muslim citizens.

THE BIG QUESTIONS

- **HOW** is culture expressed through art?
- **WHAT** do play and leisure activities tell us about culture?
- **HOW** is expressive culture changing in contemporary times?

14

EXPRESSIVE CULTURE

The decorated façade of a domestic dwelling in Kano, northern Nigeria. *(Source: © Robert Frerck/Odyssey Productions, Inc.)*

In the year 2004, the Louvre in Paris, one of the most well-known art museums in the world, will open a huge new museum in the shadow of the Eiffel Tower that will display so-called tribal art of Africa, Asia, the South Pacific, and the Americas (Corbey 2000). This project reflects the interest of France's president, Jacques Chirac, in non-Western art. It also reflects a new appreciation for the role of cultural anthropologists in helping museums to provide cultural context for objects that are displayed, because Maurice Godelier, a specialist on New Guinea, is closely involved in planning the new exhibits.

This new museum elevates "tribal" objects to the level of art, rather than placing them in a museum of natural history, as is so often the case in the United States. Yet, at the same time, it places "tribal" art in a museum that is clearly separate from the Louvre. The age-old conceptual division in European and Euro-American thinking, beginning with the Enlightenment, links the West with "civilization" and non-Western peoples with that which is uncivilized. It will prove most interesting to see how this new museum handles the challenge of moving beyond such a dichotomy.

In this chapter, we consider a vast area of human behavior and thought called **expressive culture**, which consists of learned and patterned ways of creativity that include art, leisure, and play (definitions of these terms are provided below). We start with a discussion of what the anthropology of art encompasses and some theoretical perspectives about cross-cultural art. The types of art discussed are sculpture, music, theater, architecture, and interior design. The next section reviews findings from the field of museum studies, in which scholars are seeking appropriate ways of representing culture in a museum context. We then take a cross-cultural look at another area of expressive culture: play and leisure activities. Last, we consider directions of change in expressive culture.

ART AND CULTURE

Compared to questions raised in art history classes you may have taken, you will find in this section that cultural anthropologists have a rather different view of art and how to study it (see the Critical Thinking box). Their findings, here as in other cultural domains, stretch and subvert the Western concepts and categories and prompt us to look at art within its context. Thus anthropologists consider many products, practices, and processes to be art. They also study the artist and the artist's place in society. In addition, they ask questions about how art, and expressive culture more generally, is related to microcultural variation, inequality, and power.

What Is Art?

Are ancient rock carvings art? Is subway graffiti art? An embroidered robe? A painting of a can of Campbell's soup? Philosophers, art critics, anthropologists, and art lovers have all struggled with the question of what art is. The issue of how to define art involves more than mere word games. The way art is defined affects the manner in which a person values and treats artistic creations and those who create art. Anthropologists propose broad definitions of art to take into account emic definitions cross-culturally. One definition says that **art** is the application of imagination, skill, and style to matter, movement, and sound that goes beyond the purely practical (Nanda 1994:383). The anthropological study of art considers both the process and the products of such human skill, the variation in art and its preferred forms cross-culturally, and the way culture constructs and changes artistic traditions. The skill that is involved is recognized as such in a particular culture. Such culturally judged skill can be applied to any number of substances and activities and the product can be considered art: for example, a beautifully presented meal, a well-told story, or a per-

Critical Thinking

PROBING THE CATEGORIES OF ART

PROBABLY EVERY reader of this book, at one time or another, has looked at an object on display in a museum or in an art book or magazine and exclaimed, "But that's not art!" As a critical thinking research project on "what is art," visit two museums, either in person or on the Internet. One of these should be a museum of either fine art or modern art. The other should be a museum of natural history. In the former, examine at least five items on display. In the latter, examine several items on display that have to do with human cultures (that is, skip the bugs and rocks).

Take notes on all the items that you are examining. Then answer the following questions.

CRITICAL THINKING QUESTIONS

What is it?

What contextual explanation does the museum provide about the object?

Was the object intended as a work of art or as something else?

In your opinion, is it art or not, and why or why not?

Last, compare your notes on the objects in the two types of museums. What do your notes tell you about categories of art?

---

fectly formed basket. In this sense, art is a human universal, and no culture can be said to lack artistic activity.

Within the general category of art, subcategories exist, sometimes denoting certain eras such as palaeolithic or modern art. Other subcategories are based on the medium of expression—for example, graphic or plastic arts (painting, drawing, sculpture, weaving, basketry, and architecture); the decorative arts (interior design, landscaping, gardens, costume design, and body adornment such as hairstyles, tattooing, and painting); performance arts (music, dance, and theater); and verbal arts (poetry, writing, rhetoric, and telling stories and jokes). All these are Western, English-language categories.

A long-standing distinction in the Western view exists between "fine art" and "folk art." This distinction is based on a Western-centric judgment that defines fine art as rare, expensive art produced by artists usually trained in the Western classical tradition. This is the kind of art that is included in college courses called Fine Arts. The implication is that all other art is less than fine and is more appropriately called folk art, ethnic art, primitive art, or crafts. Characteristics of Western fine art are as follows: It is created by a formally schooled artist, the product is made for the market (for sale or on commission), the product is clearly associated with a particular artist, the product's uniqueness is valued, and the product is not primarily utilitarian but is rather "art for art's sake." In contrast, all the rest of the world's art that is non-Western and nonclassical is supposedly characterized by the opposite features: It is created by an artist who has not received formal training, it is not produced for the market, the artist is anonymous and does not sign or individually

In South Africa, women paint colorful designs on the outside of houses ■ *What kind of domestic art do you know how to do?* (Source: Roshani Kothari)

---

claim the product, and it is made primarily for use in food storage and preparation, ritual, or war. However, examination of the adequacy of these two categories is in order.

All cultures have art, and all cultures have a sense of what makes something art versus non-art. The term *esthetics* refers to agreed-upon notions of quality (Thompson 1971:374). Before anthropologists proved otherwise, however, Western art experts considered that esthetics either did not exist or was poorly developed in non-Western cultures. We now know that esthetic principles, or established criteria for artistic quality, exist everywhere, whether or not they are written down and formalized. Franz Boas, from his wide review of many forms of art in pre-state societies, deduced principles that he claimed were universal for these cultures, especially symmetry, rhythmic repetition, and naturalism. (Jonaitis 1995:37). These principles do apply in many cases, but they are not as universal as Boas thought.

Ethno-esthetics consists of local cultural definitions of what is art. The set of standards concerning wood carving in West Africa illustrates the importance of considering cross-cultural variation in the criteria for art (Thompson 1971). Among the Yoruba of Nigeria, esthetic guidelines include the following:

- Figures should be depicted midway between complete abstraction and complete realism so that they resemble "somebody," but no one in particular (portraiture in the Western sense is considered dangerous).
- Humans should be depicted at their optimal physical peak, not in infancy or old age.
- There should be clarity of line and form.
- The sculpture should have the quality of luminosity achieved through a polished surface and the play of incisions and shadows.
- The piece should exhibit symmetry.

Some anthropological studies have documented intracultural differences in esthetic standards as well as cross-cultural variation. For example, one anthropologist showed computer-generated graphics to the Shipibo Indians of the Peruvian Amazon and learned that the men liked the abstract designs, whereas the women thought they were ugly (Roe in Anderson and Field 1993:257). If you are wondering why this difference would exist, consider the interpretation of the anthropologist: Shipibo men are the shamans and take hallucinogenic drugs that may give them familiarity with more "psychedelic" images.

Studying Art in Society

The anthropological study of art seeks to understand not only the products of art but also who makes it and why,

the role of art in society, and its wider social meanings. Franz Boas, was the first anthropologist to emphasize the importance of studying the artist in society. A significant thread in anthropology's theoretical history—functionalism—also dominated work of the early twentieth century on art. Anthropologists wrote about how paintings, dance, theater, and songs serve to socialize children into the culture, provide a sense of social identity and group boundaries, and promote healing. Art may legitimize political leaders and enhance efforts in war through magical decorations on shields and weapons. Art may serve as a form of social control, as in African masks worn by dancers who represent deities visiting humans to remind them of the moral order. Or art, to take a more current view, like language, can be a catalyst for political resistance or a rallying point for ethnic solidarity in the face of the state.

With its breadth of topical interest, the anthropology of art relies on a range of methods in data gathering and

Yoruba wood carving is done according to esthetic principles that require clarity of line and form, a polished surface that creates a play of light and shadows, symmetry, and the depiction of human figures that are neither completely abstract nor completely realistic. ■ *Have you ever seen African sculptures that follow these principles? Visit an African art museum on the Web for further exploration.* (Source: Courtesy of the Peabody Museum, Harvard University)

analysis. For some research projects, participant observation provides most of the necessary data. In others, participant observation is complemented by collecting and analyzing oral or written material such as video and tape recordings. Some anthropologists have become apprentices in a certain artistic tradition. For example, in undertaking one of the earliest studies of Native American potters of the Southwest, Ruth Bunzel (1972 [1929]) learned how to make pottery and thereby gained important data on what the potters thought constituted good designs. For John Chernoff, learning to play African drums was an important part of building rapport during his fieldwork in Ghana and an essential aspect of his ability to gain an understanding of the importance of music in Ghanaian society (1979). His book *African Rhythm and African Sensibility* is one of the first reflexive ethnographies (recall Chapter 2), taking into account the position and role of the ethnographer and how they shape what the ethnographer learns. Reading the introduction to this book is the best way to become convinced that fieldwork in cultural anthropology is far more than simply gathering the data you think you need for the project you have in mind, especially if your project concerns processes of creativity and expression, which are difficult to study through purely scientific methods.

Chernoff makes the case that only by turning scientific approaches upside down can a researcher learn about creativity and how it is related to society. As one of his drumming teachers said, "The heart sees before the eyes." Chernoff had to do more than practice participant observation. His heart had to participate, too. During his early months in the field, Chernoff often found himself wondering why he was there. To write a book? To tell people back in the United States about Ghana? No doubt many of the Ghanaians he met wondered the same thing, especially given that his early efforts at drumming were pretty bad, although he didn't realize it because he always drank copious amounts of gin before playing. Eventually, he became the student of a master drummer and went through a formal initiation ceremony. For the ceremony, he had to kill two chickens himself and eat parts of them in a form that most Americans will never see in a grocery store. Still, he was not playing well enough. He went through another ritual to make his wrist "smart" so that it would turn faster, like a cat chasing a mouse. For that ritual, he had to go into the bush, ten miles outside town, and collect ingredients. The ritual worked. Having a cat's hand was a good thing, but anthropologically it was more important to Chernoff that he had begun to gain an understanding of drumming in its social and ritual contexts.

He learned about Ghanaian family life and how it is connected to individual performers and to rituals that have to do with music. He also grew to see where his performance fell short and what he needed to do to improve. He gained great respect for the artists who taught him and admiration for their striving for respectability. Chernoff's personality was an important ingredient of the learning process. He comments that "I assumed that I did not know what to do in most situations. I accepted what people told me about myself and what I should be doing . . . I waited to see what people would make of me. . . . By staying cool I learned the meaning of character" (170).

Focus on the Artist

In the early twentieth century, Boas urged his students to go beyond the study of the products of art and study the artists. One role of the anthropologist, he said, is to add to the understanding of art by studying art from the artist's perspective. Ruth Bunzel's (1972 [1929]) research on Pueblo potters is a classic example of this tradition. She paid attention to the variety of pot shapes and motifs employed and also interviewed individual potters about their personal design choices. One Zuni potter commented, "I always know the whole design before I start to paint" (49). A Laguna potter said, "I made up all my designs and never copy. I learned this design from my mother. I learned most of my designs from my mother" (52).

The social status of artists is another aspect of the focus on the artist. Artists may be revered and wealthy as individuals or as a group, or they may be stigmatized and economically marginal. In ancient Mexico, goldworkers were highly respected. In Native American groups of the Pacific Northwest coast, male carvers and painters had to be initiated into a secret society, and they had higher status than other men. Often a gender division of artistic involvement exists. Among the Navajo, women weave and men do silversmithing. In the Caribbean, women of

In Sumba, Indonesia, Joel Kuipers interviews a ritual speaker who is adept at verbal arts performance. ■ *What is a form of verbal art in a microculture you know?* (Source: Joel Kuipers)

African descent are noted for their carvings of calabashes (large gourds). In the contemporary United States, most famous and successful graphic artists are male, although the profession includes many women. The lives of artists and performers are often outside the boundaries of mainstream society or challenge the social boundaries.

In Morocco, a *shikha* is a female performer who sings and dances at festivities, including life-cycle ceremonies such as birth, circumcision, and marriage (Kapchan 1994). These performers appear in a group of three or four with accompanying musicians. Their performance involves suggestive songs and body movements, including reaching a state of near-possession when they loosen their hair buns. With their long hair waving, they "lift the belt," a technique accomplished through an undulating movement that rolls the abdomen up to the waist. Their entertainment creates a lively atmosphere. "Through the provocative movements and loud singing of the shikhat, the audience is drawn up and into a collective state of celebration, their bodies literally pulled into the dance" (93). In their private lives, shikhat are on the social fringes, leading lives as single women who transgress limits applied to proper females. For example, they own property, drink alcohol, smoke cigarettes, and may have several lovers. Most of the shikhat have been rejected by their families. Middle- and upper-class women consider them vulgar and distance themselves from them. Yet shikhat who become successful, widening their performance spheres to larger towns and cities, manage to save money and become landowners and gain economic status. Furthermore, the modern mass media are contributing to an increased status of shikhat as performers. Recordings of shikhat music are popular in Morocco. State-produced television broadcasts carry performances of regional shikhat groups as a way of presenting the diverse cultures of the country.

Like those who pursue other occupations, artists are more specialized in state-level societies. Generally, among foragers, artistic activity is open to all, and artistic products are shared equally by all. Some people, however, may be singled out as especially good singers, storytellers, or carvers. With increasing social complexity and a market for art, specialized training is required to produce certain kinds of art, and the products are sought after by those who can afford them. Class differences in artistic styles and preferences emerge along with the increasingly complex division of labor.

Microcultures, Art, and Power

Art forms and styles, like language, are often associated with microcultural groups' identity and sense of pride. For example, the Berbers of highland Morocco are associated with carpets, Mayan Indians with woven and embroidered blouses, and the Inuit with stone carving.

A Mayan woman of Guatemala works at her hand loom. Mayan identity is closely linked with weaving styles and motifs, especially evidenced in women's blouses, which are embroidered as well. Three decades of warfare have threatened Mayan culture in Guatemala, but Mayan expressive culture is revitalizing. ■ *Locate a library or Internet reference on ethnic variations in styles and motifs in Mayan weaving.* (Source: © Douglas Mason/Woodfin Camp & Associates)

Cultural anthropologists provide many examples of linkages between various microcultural dimensions (ethnicity, gender, race) and power issues. In some instances, more powerful groups appropriate the art forms of less powerful groups. In others, forms of art are said to be expressive of resistance. One study reveals how political interests in Israel take ownership of ethnic artistic expression. (See the Unity and Diversity box.)

Gender relations are also played out in expressive culture. A study of a form of popular performance art in a Florida town, male strip dancing, shows how societal power relations between men and women are reinforced in this form of leisure activity (Margolis and Arnold 1993). Advertisements in the media tell women that seeing a male strip dancer is "their chance," "their night

Unity and Diversity

INVISIBLE HANDS CRAFTING ISRAELI SOUVENIRS

TOURISTS WHO buy arts and crafts souvenirs rarely learn much about the people who actually made the items. Yet they probably have some mental image of, for example, a village potter sitting at the wheel or a silversmith hammering at a piece of metal in a quaint workshop. Souvenir shops come in different varieties, from street stalls that sell a few items such as embroidered clothing or "ethnic" jewelry to national emporiums that seek to represent the full range of arts and crafts. An upscale store of the latter category in Israel, called Maskit, caters mainly to tourists (Shenhav-Keller 1993:183). Ethnographic study shows how the sellers "put Israeli society on display via its souvenirs." It also reveals how certain artists and craftspeople are selectively rendered invisible.

The tourist artifact, or souvenir, can be analyzed like a "text" that contains social messages. Looking at souvenirs this way reveals what both marketeers and tourists choose to preserve, value, and exchange (Clifford 1988:221). In the Maskit stores, three central themes in Israeli society are expressed in the choice and presentation of souvenirs: Israel's attitudes toward its ancient and recent past, its view of its religion and culture, and its approach to Arab Israelis and Palestinians. Shelly Shenhav-Keller (1993) conducted participant observation in the original Maskit store in Tel Aviv and interviewed Jewish Israeli, Arab Israeli, and Palestinian artists and artisans whose crafts were sold there. She provides some historical background on the shop:

> Maskit—The Israel Center for Handicrafts—was founded by Ruth Dayan (then the wife of Moshe Dayan) as a Ministry of Labor project in 1954, . . . Its stated purpose was "to encourage artisans to continue their native crafts in the new surrounding . . . to retain and safeguard the ancient crafts." (183)

Maskit was a success, and a chain of shops was eventually opened. As its status increased, Maskit came to be perceived as an "ambassador of Israel." Dignitaries who traveled from Israel abroad were loaded with gifts from the shop. Official visitors to Israel were given Maskit gifts.

The original shop had two floors. The top floor, where the entrance was located, had five sections: fash-ion (women's clothing, wedding gowns, and dresses with three different styles of Arab embroidery), jewelry, ritual articles (candlesticks, goblets, incense burners), decorative items, and books. The larger lower floor had five thematic sections: the Bar-Mitzvah Corner with prayerbooks and other ritual items, the children's corner (with clothing, games, toys, and T-shirts), the embroidery section (tablecloths, linens, pillow covers, wallets, eyeglass cases), the carpet section, and a large area for ceramics, glassware, and copperware.

Over the years, changes have occurred in who is producing the art sold in Maskit. Many of the original Jewish Israeli artists gained eminence and opened their own shops. Those that continue to supply Maskit specialize in ceramics, jewelry, carpet design, and ritual articles. These pieces are considered to have the status of art and may be displayed as an "individual collection" within the store. The amount of Jewish ethnic art—mainly Yemenite and Bukharan—has diminished as the older artists have aged and their descendants have not taken up the craft. This is most marked in Yemenite embroidery and silversmithing, the crafts that once dominated Maskit. Now, Arab embroidery is sought as a replacement.

After the 1967 Six-Day War, Arab Israeli and Palestinian craftsmanship became increasingly available with the incorporation of new areas within Israel, including the Occupied Territories. Most of the Arabs who were absorbed into the souvenir industry became hired laborers in factories and workshops owned by Maskit or by Israeli artisans who sold their works to Maskit.

Yet Maskit provides no information about the role of Israeli Arabs or Palestinians. The carpets, for example, are presented simply as handwoven Israeli carpets, even though Arab Israelis wove them.

FOOD FOR THOUGHT

Do you know of another example in which something attributed to one ethnic group or culture is actually produced by people not part of that group? Or do you think the Maskit use of Arab craftsmen to make "Israeli" souvenirs is unique?

out." Going to a male strip show is thus presumably a time of reversal of traditional gender roles in which men are dominant and women submissive. The researchers asked whether gender roles are reversed in a male strip-per bar. The short answer was "no." Women customers are treated like juveniles, controlled by the manager (who tells them how to tip as they stand in line waiting for the show to open) and symbolically humbled in relation to the dancers, who take on the role of lion-tamers, for example. The "dive-bomb" is further evidence that the women are not in charge. The dive-bomb is a particular form of tipping the dancer. The woman customer gets on her hands and knees and tucks a bill held between her teeth into the dancer's g-string.

Not all forms of popular art and performance are mechanisms of social control and hierarchy maintenance, however. In the United States, for example, urban Black youths' musical performance through rap music can be seen as a form of protest through performance. Their lyrics report on their experience of economic oppression, the danger of drugs, and men's disrespect for women.

Performance Arts

The performance arts include music, dance, theater, rhetoric (public speech-making) and narrative (such as storytelling). Because so much research has been done on music, this area has developed its own name: **ethnomusicology**, the cross-cultural study of music. Ethnomusicologists study a range of topics including the form of the music itself, the social position of musicians, how music interacts with other domains of culture, and change in musical traditions. This section provides a case study of the parallels between musical patterns and the gender division of labor in a foraging group in Malaysia. We next turn to an example of how anthropologists study theater, and in this case, we see how theater and religion fit together.

Music and Gender among the Temiar of Malaysia

An important topic for ethnomusicologists is gender differences in access to performance roles in music (for readers interested in approaching this topic as a research question, see Table 14.1). A cultural materialist analysis of this issue would predict that in cultures where gender roles and relationships in society are relatively egalitarian, access to and meanings in music would tend to be more egalitarian as well. This is the case, for example, among the Temiar, a group of foragers of highland Malaysia, whose musical traditions emphasize balance and complementarity between males and females (Roseman 1987). Among the Temiar, kinship and marriage rules are relatively flexible and open. Marriages are not arranged but instead are based on the mutual desires of the partners. Descent is bilineal, and marital residence follows no particular rule after a period of bride service. Marriages often end in separation, with the usual pattern for everyone being serial monogamy. Men, however, have a certain edge over women in political and ritual spheres. Men dominate as headmen and as spirit mediums who sing the songs that energize the spirits (although historical records indicate that women have been spirit mediums in the past). In most performances, individual

TABLE 14.1 Five Ethnographic Questions about Gender and Music

If you were doing an ethnographic study of gender roles in musical performance, the following questions would be useful in starting the inquiry. But they would not exhaust the topic. Can you think of questions that should be added to the list?
1. Are men and women equally encouraged to use certain instruments and repertoires?
2. Is musical training available to all?
3. Do male and female repertoires overlap, where, and for what reasons?
4. Are the performances of men and women public, private, or both? Are women and men allowed to perform together? In what circumstances?
5. Do members of the culture give equal value to the performances of men and women? On what criteria are these evaluations based, and are they the same for men and women performers?

Source: From "Power and Gender in the Musical Experiences of Women," pp. 224–225, by Carol E. Robertson in *Women and Music in Cross-Cultural Perspective*, ed. by Ellen Koskoff. Copyright © 1987. Reprinted by permission of Greenwood Publishing Group, Inc., Westport, CT.

male singers are the nodes through which the songs of spirit-guides enter the community, but women's performance role is significant. Overall, the male spirit-medium role is not necessarily of higher priority or status. The distinction between leader and chorus establishes some priority for males, but gender distinctions are blurred through overlap between phrases and repetition. The performance is one of general community participation with

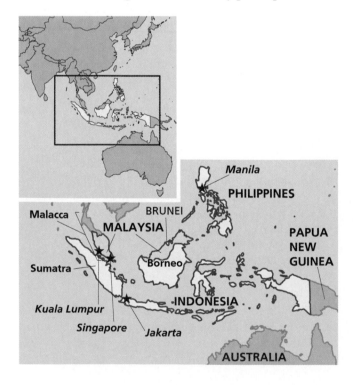

Many forms of theater combine the use of facial makeup, masks, and costumes to transform an actor into someone (or something) else. This is a Kathakali dancer applying makeup before a performance in Kerala, south India. ■ *What forms of dance or theater in your microculture involve the use of facial makeup to depict a particular character?* (Source: Roshani Kothari)

basic character types at their first entrance by "reading" the costuming and makeup. Six makeup types exist to depict characters ranging from the most refined to the most vulgar. Characters such as kings and heroes have green facial makeup, reflecting their high degree of refinement and moral uprightness. The most vulgar characters are associated with black facial makeup and occasionally black beards. Female demons are in this category: Their black faces are dotted with red and white, and they are the most grotesque of Kathakali characters.

Architecture and Decorative Arts

Like all art forms, architecture is interwoven with other aspects of culture. Architecture may reflect and protect social rank and class differences as well as gender, age, and ethnic differences (Guidoni 1987). Decorative arts—including interior decoration of homes and buildings, and external design features such as gardens—likewise reflect people's social position and "taste." Local cultures have long defined preferred standards in these areas of expression, but global influences from the West and elsewhere, such as Japan and other non-Western cultures, have been adopted and adapted by other traditions.

Architecture and Interior Design

Foragers, being nomadic, build dwellings as needed and then abandon them. Owning little and having no surplus goods, they need no permanent storage structures. The construction of dwellings does not require the efforts of groups larger than the family unit. Foragers' dwellings are an image of the family and not of the wider society. The dwellings' positioning in relation to each other reflects the relations between families.

More elaborate shelters and greater social cohesiveness in planning occur as foraging is combined with horticulture, as in the semipermanent settlements in the Amazon rainforest. People live in the settlement part of the year but break up into smaller groups that spread out into a larger area for foraging. Important decisions concern location of the site in terms of weather, availability of drinking water, and defensibility. The central plaza must be elevated for drainage, and drainage channels must be dug around the hearths. The overall plan is circular. In some groups, separate shelters are built for extended family groups; in others, they are joined into a continuous circle with connected roofs. In some cases, the headman has a separate and larger shelter.

Pastoralists have designed ingenious portable structures such as the teepee and yert. The teepee is a conical tent made with a framework of four wooden poles tied at the top with thongs, to which are joined other poles to complete the cone; this frame is then covered with buffalo hide. A yert is also a circular, portable dwelling, but

integrated male and female roles—just as in Temiar society.

Theater and Myth in South India

Theater is a type of enactment that seeks to entertain through conscious forms of acting, movement, and words related to dance, music, parades, competitive games and sports, and verbal art (Beeman 1993). Cross-culturally, strong connections exist among myth, ritual, and performance.

One theatrical tradition that offers an exuberant blend of mythology, acting, and music is Kathakali ritual dance-drama of southern India (Zarrilli 1990). Stylized hand gestures, elaborate makeup, and costumes contribute to the attraction of these dramas, which dramatize India's great Hindu epics, especially the Ramayana and the Mahabharata. Costumes and makeup transform the actor into one of several well-known characters from Indian mythology. The audience easily recognizes the

Yerts in Pamir, Afghanistan. The yert form of domestic architecture is widespread across Asia among pastoralists. ■ *How does a yert resemble, and how does it differ from, domestic architecture that you know?* (Source: © R. & S. Michaud/Woodfin Camp & Associates)

orate. In settled agricultural communities and urban centers where permanent housing is the norm, decoration is more likely to be found in homes. Wall paintings, sculptures, and other features distinguish the homes of more wealthy individuals. One study of interior decoration in contemporary Japan examined the contents of home decorating magazines and also involved participant observation within homes (Rosenberger 1992). A recurrent theme is how aspects of Western decorating styles are incorporated and localized (given a particularly Japanese flavor). Home decorating magazines target middle- and upper-class housewives who seek to express their status through new consumption styles. A trend is the abandonment of three features of traditional Japanese design: *tatami, shoji,* and *fusuma.* Tatami are two-inch-thick mats, about three feet by six feet. A room's size is measured in terms of the number of tatami mats it holds. Shoji are the sliding screen doors of tatami rooms, one covered with glass and the other with translucent rice paper often printed with a design of leaves or waves. Fusuma are sliding wall panels made of thick paper; they are removable so that rooms can be enlarged for gatherings. The tatami room usually contains a low table with pillows for seating on the floor. A special alcove may contain a flower arrangement, ancestors' pictures, and a Buddhist altar. Futons are stored in closets around the edges and brought out at night for sleeping.

In distancing themselves from the old style, a Japanese housewife makes these changes: The kitchen is given a central rather than marginal location and is merged with a space called the DK (dining-kitchen) or LDK (living-dining-kitchen), with wood, tile, or carpeting on the floor. Western products such as carpeting and curtains (instead of the fusuma, the tatami, and shoji) are used to cover surfaces and to separate rooms. Westernness is stated in the addition of a couch, dining set, VCR, and stereo and an array of small items—Western-style teapots, cuckoo clocks, and knick-knacks such as the Seven Dwarfs.

These changing design choices accompany deeper social changes that involve new aspirations about marriage and family relationships. Home decorating magazines promote the idea that the new style brings with it happier children with better grades and closer husband–wife ties. Tensions exist, however, between these ideals and the realities of middle- and upper-class life in Japan. Women feel compelled to work either part time or full time to be able to contribute income for satisfying their new consumer needs. Yet Japanese women are discouraged from pursuing careers and are urged to devote more time to domestic pursuits, including home decorating and child care, in order to provide the kind of life portrayed in the magazines. Children are placed in the conflicting position of being indulged as new consumer targets, while the traditional value of self-discipline still holds. Hus-

its roof is flatter than that of a teepee. The covering is made of cloth. This extremely lightweight structure is easy to set up, take down, and transport, and it is highly adaptable to all weather conditions. Encampments often arranged the teepees or yerts in several concentric circles. Social status was the structuring principle, and the council of chiefs and the head chief were located in the center.

With the development of the state, urban areas grew larger and showed the effects of centralized planning and power—for example, in grid-style street planning rather than haphazard street placement. The symbolic demonstration of the power, grandeur, and identity of states was—and still is—expressed architecturally through the construction of impressive monuments: temples, administrative buildings, memorials, and museums. Interior decoration of domestic dwellings also became more elab-

bands are put in the conflicting position of needing to be more attentive to wife and home while the corporate world calls them for a "7–11" working day. Furthermore, the Western-style, happy nuclear family image contains no plan for the aged. The wealthiest Japanese families manage to satisfy both individualistic desires and filial duties because they can afford a large house in which they dedicate a separate floor for the husband's parents, complete with tatami mats. Less wealthy people have a more difficult time dealing with these conflicting values.

Gardens and Flowers

Gardens for use, especially for food production, can be differentiated from gardens for decoration. Not all cultures have developed the concept of the decorative garden. Inuit peoples cannot construct gardens in the snow. Purely nomadic peoples have no gardens because they are on the move. The decorative garden seems to be a product of state-level societies, especially in the Middle East, Europe, and Asia (Goody 1993). Within these contexts, variation exists in what are considered to be the appropriate contents and design of a garden. A Japanese garden may contain no blooming flowers, focusing instead on the shape and placement of trees, shrubs, stones, and bodies of water (Moynihan 1979). Elite Muslim culture, with its core in the Middle East, has long been associated with formal decorative gardens. A garden, enclosed with four walls, is symbolically equivalent to the concept of "paradise." The Islamic garden pattern involves a square design with symmetrical layout, fountains, waterways, and straight pathways, all enclosed within walls. Islamic gardens often surrounded the tombs of prominent people. India's Taj Mahal, built by a Muslim emperor, follows this pattern, with one modification: The tomb was placed at one edge of the garden rather than in the center. The result is a dramatic stretch of fountains and flowers leading from the main gate up to the monument.

The contents of a personal garden, like a dinner menu with all its special ingredients or a collection of souvenirs from around the world with all their memories and meanings, makes a statement about its owner's identity and status. For example, in Europe during the height of colonialism, imperial gardens contained specimens from remote corners of the globe, collected through scientific expeditions. Such gardens are created through the intentional collection and placement of otherwise diverse plants in one place, creating a **heterotopia,** or the pulling together of different "places" into one (Foucault 1970). These gardens expressed the owner's worldliness and intellectual status.

Cut flowers are now important economic products; they provide income for gardeners throughout the world. They are also exchange items. In France, women receive

Worldwide, Hilton hotels look much like each other and do not reflect local cultural architectural styles.
■ *In your view, is this uniformity a good thing, or should Hiltons and other international hotels try to become more "vernacular"?* (Source: © Paul Conklin/PhotoEdit)

flowers from men more than any other kind of gift (Goody 1993:316). In much of the world, special occasions require gifts of flowers: In the West, as well as in East Asia, funerals are times for displays of flowers. Ritual offerings to the deities in Hinduism are often flowers such as marigolds woven into a chain or necklace.

Flowers are prominent motifs in Western and Asian secular and sacred art, but not in African art. Jack Goody (1993) tried to understand the absence of flowers in the religion and graphic arts of Africa (except for in Islamicized cultures of Africa, where flowers are prominent). Some possible answers include ecological and economic factors: Eurasia possesses a greater variety of blooming plants than Africa. Also, African horticulture, in general, is limited because less space is available for the production of luxury items. In many African kingdoms, luxuri-

Women practicing the art of flower arrangement in Japan. ■ *Are there art forms in your culture that are specific to women?* (Source: © Catherine Karnow/ Woodfin Camp & Associates)

ous goods include fabrics of various design, gold ornaments, and wooden carvings rather than flowers.

Museums and Culture

In this section we consider the concept of the museum and the debates about the role of museums in exhibiting and representing culture. Museum studies, in anthropology, include both anthropologists who work in museums helping to prepare exhibits and anthropologists who study museums—what they choose to display and how they display it—as important sites of culture itself.

What Is a Museum?

A museum is an institution that collects, preserves, interprets, and displays objects on a regular basis (Kahn 1995:324). Its purpose may be esthetic or educational. The idea of gathering and displaying objects goes back at least to the Babylonian kings of the sixth century BCE (Maybury-Lewis 1997a). The term comes originally from a Greek word referring to a place for the muses to congregate, where one would have philosophical discussions or see artistic performances. In Europe, the term *museum* came to denote a place where art objects were housed and displayed. Ethnographic and science museums came later, inspired by Europe's emerging interests in exploration in the 1500s and the accompanying scientific urge to gather specimens from around the world and classify them into an evolutionary history. The concept of the museum and its several forms has now diffused to most parts of the world.

The Politics of Exhibits

Within anthropology, "museum anthropology" emerged in the 1980s as a subfield concerned with studying how and why museums choose to collect and display particular objects (Ames 1992; A. Jones 1993; Stocking 1985).

Museum anthropologists are now at the forefront of serious debates about who gets to represent whom, the ownership of particular objects, and the public-service role of museums versus their possible elitism. A major issue is whether objects from non-Western cultures should be exhibited, like Western art objects, with little or no ethnographic context (Clifford 1988, Watson 1997). Most anthropologists would support the need for context, and not just for non-Western objects but for all objects on display. But the view that all forms of expressive culture are context-bound and can be better understood and appreciated within their social context is unfortunately rare among Western art historians and critics (Best 1986). For example, the museum label of Andy Warhol's hyperrealistic painting of a can of Campbell's soup should include information on the social context in which such art was produced and some background on the artist.

Debates also exist about who should have control of objects in museums that may have been claimed through colonial and neocolonial domination. The issue of **repatriation,** or returning objects to their original homes, is a matter of international and intranational concern.

In the United States and Canada, many Native American groups are lobbying successfully for the return of ancestral bones, grave goods, and potlatch goods. In 1990, the United States passed the Native American

Graves Protection and Repatriation Act (NAGRPA) after two decades of lobbying by Native American groups (Bray 1996; Rose, Green, and Green 1996). This act requires universities, museums, and federal agencies in the United States to inventory their archaeological holdings in preparation for repatriating skeletons to their Native American descendants. One survey indicates that museums alone hold over 14,000 Native American skeletons (not including Hawai'i), and unofficial estimates go as high as 600,000. Unknown numbers of other items are being inventoried as well, a process that is stretching thin museum resources (Watson 1997).

The break-up of the Soviet Union prompted claims from several independent states that wished to retrieve artistic property that originated in their locale and had been taken to Soviet national museums in Moscow and St. Petersburg. For example, Central Asian republics lost medieval carpets to Moscow and St. Petersburg museums; there are Georgian arms in the Armory of the Moscow Kremlin; and Ukrainians seek the return of objects of historical interest, such as the ceremonial staff of their national hero, Mazepa, who fought for Ukrainian independence against Peter the Great (Akinsha 1992a). In all, Ukraine has demanded the return of about two million art objects that originated in Ukrainian territory (Akinsha 1992b). Many of these objects were the pride of Russian museums, such as the Hermitage in St. Petersburg, which now faces the loss of many key objects.

Another dimension of dispute about art in Russia concerns the state and the church. The Soviet state put many icons and other religious objects in museums and turned churches into museums. Now the Russian Orthodox Church is campaigning for the return of church property. Churches are demanding that "all sacred objects of the church, all church buildings, and masterpieces of church art that were confiscated by the state after 1917 must be returned without exception to the ownership of the Russian Orthodox Church" (Akinsha 1992a:102). Art historians and museum officials worry that the churches have neither the resources nor the experience to care for these treasures. On the other hand, there are threats of theft and violence to museums from those who wish to return the icons to churches and monasteries. In response, some museums have removed certain pieces from display.

PLAY, LEISURE, AND CULTURE

This section turns to another area of expressive culture: what people do "for fun." It is impossible to draw a clear line between the concepts of play or leisure and art or performance, however, because they often overlap. For example, a person could paint watercolors in her leisure time, yet simultaneously be creating a work of art. In most cases, though, play and leisure can be distinguished from other activities by the fact that they have no direct, utilitarian purpose for the participant. Dutch historian Johan Huizinga, in the 1930s, proposed some features of play: It is unnecessary and thus free action; it is outside of ordinary life; it is closed and limited in terms of time; it has rules for its execution; and it contains an element of tension and chance (as summarized in Hutter 1996).

Leisure activities often overlap with play, but many leisure activities, such as reading or lying on a beach, would not be considered play because they lack rules, tension, and chance. Often, the same activity, depending on the context, could be considered work instead of play. For example, gardening as a hobby would be classified as a leisure activity, even though weeding, pruning, and watering are activities that could be considered work for someone else. Playing a game with a child might be considered recreational, but if one has been hired as the child's babysitter, then it is work. Professional sports are an area where the line between play and work breaks down completely because the "players" are paid to "play." Further, while play and leisure may be pursued from a nonutilitarian perspective, they are often surrounded by a wider context of commercial and political interests. For example, nonprofessional athletes competing in the Olympic games are part of a wider set of powerful interests, from advertisers to host cities to athletic equipment companies.

Within the broad category of play and leisure activities, several subcategories exist, including varieties of games, hobbies, and recreational travel. Cultural anthropologists study play and leisure within their cultural contexts as part of social systems. They ask, for example, why some leisure activities involve teams rather than individuals; what the social roles and status of people involved in particular activities are; what the "goals" of the games are and how they are achieved; how much danger or violence is involved; how certain activities are related to group identity; and how such activities link or separate different groups within or between societies or nations.

Games and Sports as Cultural Microcosm

Games and sports, like religious rituals and festivals, can be interpreted as reflections of social relationships and cultural ideals. In Clifford Geertz's terms, they are both "models of" a culture, depicting basic ideals, and "models for" a culture, socializing people into certain values and ideals. American football can be seen as a model for corporate culture in its clear hierarchy with leadership vested in one person (the quarterback), and its major goal of territorial expansion by taking over areas from the competition.

Wrestlers in the village of Sonepur, India. These wrestlers follow a rigorous regimen of dietary restrictions and exercise in order to keep their bodies and minds under control. Like Hindu ascetics, they seek to build up and maintain their inner strength through such practices. ■ *Think of another sport that emphasizes dietary restrictions.* (Source: © CORBIS. All Rights Reserved.)

A comparison of baseball as played in the United States and in Japan reveals core values about social relationships (Whiting 1979). These differences emerge dramatically when American players are hired by Japanese teams. The American players bring with them an intense sense of individualism, which promotes the value of "doing your own thing." This conflicts with a primary value that influences the playing style in Japan: *wa*, meaning discipline and self-sacrifice for the good of the whole. In Japanese baseball, players must seek to achieve and maintain team harmony, so extremely individualistic, egotistical plays and strategies are frowned upon.

Sports and Spirituality: Male Wrestling in India

In many non-Western settings, sports are closely tied to aspects of religion and spirituality. Asian martial arts, for example, require forms of concentration much like meditation, leading to spiritual self-control. Male wrestling in India, a popular form of entertainment at rural fairs and other public events, involves a strong link with spiritual development and asceticism (Alter 1992). In some ways these wrestlers are just like other members of Indian society. They go to work, and they marry and have families, but their dedication to wrestling involves important differences.

A wrestler's daily routine is one of self-discipline. Every act—defecation, bathing, comportment, devotion—is integrated into a daily regimen of discipline. Wrestlers come to the *akhara* (equivalent to a gymnasium) early in the morning for practice under the supervision of a guru or other senior akhara member. They practice moves with different partners for two to three hours. In the early evening, they return for more exercise. In all, a strong young wrestler will do around 2000 push-ups and 1000 deep kneebends a day in sets of 50 to 100.

The wrestler's diet is prescribed by the wrestling way of life. Wrestlers are mainly vegetarian and avoid alcohol and tobacco, although they do consume *bhang*, a beverage made of blended milk, spices, almonds, and concentrated marijuana. In addition to regular meals, wrestlers consume large quantities of milk, *ghee* (clarified butter), and almonds. These substances are sources of strength, because according to traditional dietary principles, they help to build up the body's semen.

Several aspects of the wrestler's life are similar to those of a Hindu *sannyasi,* or holy man who renounces life in the normal world. The aspiring sannyasi studies under a guru and learns to follow a strict routine of discipline and meditation called *yoga,* and he adheres to a restricted diet to achieve control of the body and its life force. Both wrestler and sannyasi roles focus on discipline to achieve a controlled self. In India, wrestling does not involve the "dumb jock" stereotype that it sometimes does in North America; rather, the image is of perfected physical and moral health.

Play, Pleasure, and Pain

Many leisure activities combine pleasure and pain because they may involve physical discomfort. Serious injuries may result from mountain climbing, horseback riding, or playing touch football in the backyard. A more intentionally dangerous category of sports is **blood sports,** competition that explicitly seeks to bring about a flow of blood or even death: Blood sports may involve human contestants, humans contesting against animal competitors, or humans hunting animal targets (Donlon 1990). In the United States and Europe, professional boxing is an example of a highly popular blood sport that has not yet been analyzed by anthropologists. Cultural anthropologists have looked more at the use of animals in blood sports such as cockfights and bullfights. These sports have been variously interpreted as providing sadistic pleasure, as offering vicarious self-validation (usually of males) through the triumph of their representative pit bulls or fighting cocks, and as the triumph of culture over nature in the symbolism of bullfighting.

Even the seemingly pleasurable leisure experience of a Turkish bath can involve discomfort and pain. One phase involves scrubbing the skin roughly several times with a rough natural sponge, a pumice stone, or a piece of cork wood wrapped in cloth (Staats 1994). The scrubbing removes layers of dead skin and "opens the pores" so that the skin will be beautiful. In Turkey, an option for men is a massage that can be quite violent, involving deep probes of leg muscles, cracking of the back, and being walked on by the (often hefty) masseur. In Ukraine, being struck repeatedly on one's bare skin with birch branches is the final stage of the bath. However, violent scrubbing, scraping, and even beating of the skin, along with radical temperature changes in the water, are combined with valued social interaction at the bathhouse.

Leisure Travel

Anthropologists who study leisure travel, or tourism, have often commented that their work is taken less seriously than it should be because of the perspective that they are just "hanging out" at the beach or at five-star hotels. Research on tourism, however, can involve as much conflict and danger as anthropological study of any other topic. Violence is not unknown in tourist destinations—for example, in Sri Lanka and the former Yugoslavia in the 1990s. Even when the research site is a peaceful one, anthropological investigation of tourism involves the same amount of effort as any other fieldwork.

Tourism is now one of the major economic forces in the world, it is growing, and it has dramatic effects on people and places in tourist destination areas. Expenditure of money, time, and effort for nonessential travel is nothing new. In the past, pilgrimage to religious sites has been a major preoccupation of many people (Chapter 13). A large percentage of worldwide tourism involves individuals from the industrialized nations of Europe, North America, and Japan traveling to the less industrialized nations. Ethnic tourism, cultural tourism, and off-the-beaten-path tourism are attracting increasing numbers of travelers.

These new kinds of tourism are often marketed as providing a view of "authentic" cultures. Images of indigenous people as the "Other" figure prominently in travel brochures and advertisements (Silver 1993). Tourist promotional literature often presents a "myth" of other peoples and places and offers travel as a form of escape to a mythical land of wonder. In fact, research on Western travel literature shows that from the time of the earliest explorers to the present, it has been full of "primitivist"

images about indigenous peoples (Pratt 1992). They are portrayed as having static or "stone age" traditions, remaining largely unchanged by the forces of Western colonialism, nationalism, economic development, and tourism itself (Bruner 1991). Tourists often seek to find the culture that the tourist industry defines rather than gaining a genuine, more complicated, and perhaps less photogenic view of it (Adams 1984). For the traveler, obtaining these desired cultural images through mass tourism involves packaging the "primitive" with the "modern" because most tourists want comfort and convenience along with their "authentic experience." Thus advertisements minimize the foreignness of the host country, noting, for example, that English is spoken and that the destination is remote yet accessible, while simultaneously promoting primitivist imagery. For example, "The Melanesian Discoverer" is a ship that cruises the Sepik River in Papua New Guinea, providing a way for affluent tourists to see the "primitive" while traveling in luxury.

The anthropology of tourism has focused most of its attention on the impact of global and local tourism on indigenous peoples and places. Such impact studies are important in exposing the degree to which tourism helps or harms local people. For example, the formation of Amboseli National Park in Kenya negatively affected the access of the Maasai to strategic water resources for their herds (Honadle 1985, as summarized in Drake 1991). The project staff promised certain benefits to the Maasai if they stayed off the reserve, but many of those benefits (including shares of the revenues from the park) never materialized. In contrast, in Costa Rica local people were included in the early planning stages of the Guanacaste National Park and have played a greater role in the park management system there.

Other studies, discussed in the following section of this chapter, document how local residents are exercising agency and playing an active role in transforming the effects of tourism to their advantage, as well as localizing outside influences to make them relevant to local conditions and frameworks of meaning.

CHANGE IN EXPRESSIVE CULTURE

Nowhere are forms and patterns of expressive culture frozen in time. Change is universal, and much change is influenced by Western culture through globalization. However, influence does not occur in only one direction. African musical styles have transformed the American musical scene since the days of slavery. Japan has exerted a strong influence on upper-class garden styles in the United States. Cultures in which tradition and conformity have been valued in pottery-making, dress, or theatre may find themselves having to make choices about whether to innovate, and if so, how. Many contemporary artists (including musicians and playwrights) from Latin America to China are fusing ancient and "traditional" motifs and styles with more contemporary themes and messages.

Western interest in indigenous arts as art is quite recent; their aesthetic value was not widely recognized until the early twentieth century. Before that, the typical Western reaction to non-Western art was often one of either horror or curiosity (Mitter 1977). Given current global exchanges and influences in art and play (especially organized sports), we can distinguish between those activities and products made for internal consumption and those made for the external world (Graburn 1976).

Changes occur through the use of new materials and technology and through the incorporation of new ideas and tastes. These changes often accompany social change, such as colonialism, global tourism, or political change.

Colonialism and Syncretism

Western colonialists had dramatic effects on the expressive culture of indigenous peoples with whom they came into contact. In some instances, colonial disapproval of particular art forms and activities resulted in their extinction. For example, when colonialists banned head-hunting in various cultures, this change also meant that body decoration, weapon decoration, and other related expressive activities were abandoned. This section provides an in-depth example of how colonial repression of indigenous forms succeeded only temporarily.

Western colonialist powers often acted directly to change certain indigenous art and leisure practices. In the Trobriand Islands, now part of Papua New Guinea, British administrators and missionaries sought to eradicate the frequent tribal warfare as part of a pacification process. One strategy was to replace it with intertribal competitive sports (Leach 1975). In 1903 a British missionary introduced the British game of cricket in the Trobriands as a way of promoting a new morality, separate from the former warring traditions. As played in England, cricket involves particular rules of play and a very proper look of pure white uniforms. In the early stages of the adoption of cricket in the Trobriands, the game followed the British pattern closely. As time passed and the game spread into more regions, it became increasingly localized. Most important, it was merged into indigenous political competition between big-men. Big-men leaders would urge their followers to increase production in anticipation of a cricket match because the matches were followed by a redistributive feast. The British missionaries had discouraged traditional magic in favor of Christianity, but the Trobriand Islanders transferred war-related magic into cricket. For example, spells are used to help one's team win, and the bats are ritually treated in the way that war weapons were. Weather magic is also important. If things are not going well for one's team, a spell to bring rain and force cancellation of the game may be invoked.

Other changes occurred. The Trobrianders stopped wearing the crisp white uniforms and instead donned paint, feathers, and shells. They announced their entry into the opposing village with new songs and dances, praising their team in contrast to the opposition. Many of the teams, and their songs and dances, draw on Western elements such as the famous entry song of the "P-K" team. (P-K is the name of a chewing gum. This team chose the name because the stickiness of gum is likened to the ability of their bat to hit the ball.) Other teams incorporated sounds and motions of airplanes, objects that they had never seen until World War II. Songs and dances are explicitly sexual and are enjoyed by all, in spite of missionary attempts to suppress such "immoral" aspects of Trobriand culture. The Trobrianders have changed some of the rules of play as well. The home team should always win, but not by too many runs. In this way, guests show respect to the hosts. Winning, after all, is not the major goal. The feast after the match is the climax for the Trobrianders.

Tourism's Complex Effects

Global tourism has had varied effects on indigenous arts. Often, tourist demand for ethnic arts and souvenirs has led to mass production of sculpture or weaving or jewelry of a lesser quality than was created before the demand. Tourists' interests in seeing an abbreviated form of traditionally long dance or theater performances has led to the presentation of "cuts" rather than an entire piece. Some scholars say, therefore, that tourism leads to the transformation of indigenous arts in a negative sense.

Tourist support for indigenous arts, however, is often the sole force maintaining them, because local people in a particular culture may themselves be more interested in foreign music, art, or sports. Vietnamese water puppetry is an ancient performance mode, dating back at least to the Ly Dynasty of 1121 ad (Contreras 1995). Traditionally, water puppet shows took place in the spring during a lull in the farm work, or at special festival times. Now, water puppet shows are performed mainly for foreign tourists in large cities. Vietnamese people tend to prefer imported videos (Brownmiller 1994).

One positive side effect of global tourism is the growing support for preservation of **material cultural heritage**, sometimes referred to as simply "cultural heritage," which includes entire sites (for example, an ancient city), monuments (buildings as well as monumental sculpture,

Classical dancers perform in Thailand. The intricate hand motions, with their impact augmented by the wearing of metal finger extenders, have meanings that accompany the narrative being acted out. International tourism is a major support for such performance arts in Thailand. ■ *Learn about UNESCO's recent declaration about "intangible" cultural heritage and speculate on what it may mean for the preservation of particular cultural forms.* (Source: © Dallas and John Heaton/CORBIS)

painting, and cave temples), and movable objects considered of outstanding value in terms of history, art, and science (Cernea 2001). UNESCO proposed the basic definition of material cultural heritage in 1972. Since then, many locations worldwide have been placed on its World Heritage List for preservation. In the Middle East and North Africa alone, 60 places are on UNESCO's list. Many invaluable sites and other aspects of material cultural heritage are lost to public knowledge through destructive engineering projects, war, looting, and private collecting. Applied anthropologists are involved in promoting better stewardship of material cultural heritage. Some are motivated by a desire to preserve the record of humanity for future generations, or for science. Others see that material cultural heritage, especially in poorer countries, can serve to promote improvements in human welfare, and they endorse forging a link between material cultural heritage and development (see the Lessons Applied box on page 340).

The preservation of indigenous forms of expressive culture can also occur as a form of resistance to outside development forces. One example of this phenomenon is the resurgence of the hula, or Hawai'ian dance (Stillman 1996). Beginning in the early 1970s, the "Hawai'ian Renaissance" grew out of political protest. Hawai'ian youth began speaking out against encroaching development from the outside that was displacing the indigenous people from their land and their resources. They promoted a concerted effort to revive the Hawai'ian language, the hula, and canoe paddling, among other things.

Since then, hula schools have proliferated, and hula competitions among the islands are widely attended. The 1990s, saw the inauguration of the International Hula Festival in Honolulu, which attracts competitors from around the world. The hula competitions have helped ensure the continued survival of this ancient art form, although some Hawai'ians have voiced concerns. First, they feel that allowing non-Hawai'ians to compete is compromising the quality of the dancing. Second, the format of the competition violates traditional rules of style and presentation, which require more time than is allowed, so important dances have to be cut.

Post-Communist Transitions

Major changes have occurred in the arts in the post-communist states of the former USSR for two reasons: loss of state financial support and removal of state controls over subject matter and creativity. "A new generation of talented young artists has appeared. Many are looking for something new and different—art without ideology" (Akinsha 1992c:109). Art for art's sake—art as independent from the socialist project—is now possible. A circle of artists called the Moscow Conceptualists had been the dominant "underground" (nonofficial) school of art. These artists focused on political subject matter and poverty. In contrast, the new underground finds its inspiration in nostalgia for the popular culture of the 1950s and 1960s, a pack of Yugoslav chewing gum, or the cover of a Western art magazine. Commercial galleries are

Lessons Applied

A STRATEGY FOR THE WORLD BANK ON CULTURAL HERITAGE

THE WORLD Bank, with headquarters in Washington, DC, and offices throughout the world, is an international organization funded by member nations that works to promote and finance economic development in poor countries. Even though most of its permanent professional staff are economists, the Bank has begun to pay more attention to noneconomic factors that affect development projects. One of the major moves in that direction occurred in 1972 when the Bank hired its first anthropologist, Michael Cernea. For three decades, Cernea has drawn attention to the cultural dimensions of development, especially in terms of the importance of local participation in development projects and people-centered approaches to project-forced resettlement (when, for example, large dams are being planned). His most recent campaign is to convince top officials at the World Bank that the Bank should become involved in supporting cultural heritage projects as potential pathways to development.

The World Bank already has in place a "do no harm" rule when it approves and financially supports construction projects. Cernea agrees that a "do no harm" rule is basic to preventing outright destruction, but it is a passive rule and does nothing to provide resources to preserve sites. He wants the Bank to move beyond its "do no harm" rule. He has written for the World Bank a strategy that is active, not passive. The strategy has two major objectives: (1) The World Bank should support cultural heritage projects that promote poverty reduction and cultural heritage preservation by creating employment and generating capital from tourism. (2) These projects should emphasize the educational value to both local people and international visitors on the grounds that cultural understanding has value for good will and relations at all levels—local, national, and international.

Cernea also offers two suggestions for better management of cultural heritage projects: (1) selectivity in site selection on the basis of the impact in reducing poverty, and (2) building partnerships for project planning and implementation among local, national, and international institutions.

FOOD FOR THOUGHT

Find, on the Internet, the UNESCO World Heritage Site that is nearest to where you live. What does the site contain, and what can you learn about its possible or potential role in generating income for the local people?

---

springing up, and a museum of modern art in Moscow may become a reality in the near future.

Theater in China is passing through a transition period with the recent development of some features of capitalism. Since the beginning of the People's Republic in 1949, the arts have gone through different phases, from being suppressed as part of the old feudal tradition to being revived under state control. China's theater companies have experienced financial crises in recent times (Jiang 1994:72). Steep inflation means that actors can no longer live on their pay. Theater companies are urging their workers to find jobs elsewhere, such as in making movies or videos, but this is not an option for provincial troupes. Local audience preferences have changed: "People are fed up with shows that 'educate,' have too strong a political flavor, or convey 'artistic values.' They no longer seem to enjoy love stories, old Chinese legends, or Euro-American theater. Most of the young people prefer night-clubs, discos, or karaokes. Others stay at home watching TV" (73). The new materialism in China means that young people want to spend their leisure time having fun.

For the theater, too, money now comes first. One trend is toward the production of Western plays.

For example, Harold Pinter's *The Lover* was an immediate success when it was performed in Shanghai in 1992. Why was it so successful?

> Sex is certainly a big part of the answer. Sex has been taboo in China for a long time; it is still highly censored in theater and films. The producers warned, "no children," fueling speculation about a possible sex scene. . . . Actually, *The Lover* contains only hints of sexuality, but by Chinese standards the production was the boldest stage show in China. The actress's alluring dress, so common in the west, has seldom, if ever, been seen by Chinese theatregoers. Also, there was lots of bold language—dialog about female breasts, for example. (75–76)

Another important feature is the play's focus on private life, on interiority, thoughts, and feelings. This emphasis corresponds with increasing interest in private lives in China. Change in the performing arts in China is being shaped both by global changes and by changes in the local political economy.

KEY CONCEPTS

SUGGESTED READINGS

Eduardo Archetti. *Football, Polo and the Tango in Argentina.* New York: Berg, 1999. An Argentinian anthropologist examines interlinking aspects of expressive culture in Buenos Aires and how they are related to elite tastes, gender, and international competitiveness. The overarching theme is the strong connections between football (soccer) as ritual violence and masculine identity formation.

Shirley F. Campbell. *The Art of Kula.* New York: Berg, 2002. This ethnography of art provides insights about the contemporary importance of kula trading among men in the Trobriand Islands. Kula trading and kula art continue to be important aspects of men's culture. The author focuses on designs painted on canoes and finds that kula art and its associated male ideology linked to the sea competes with female ideology and symbolism that is linked to the earth.

Rebecca Cassidy. *The Sport of Kings: Kinship, Class, and Thoroughbred Breeding in Newmarket.* New York: Cambridge University Press, 2002. This study of the British thoroughbred racing industry is based on fieldwork conducted in Newmarket, England. Findings about how people discuss the horses, their breeding, and their capabilities reflect more widely on the British class system and the hierarchy between humans and animals.

Michael M. Cernea. *Cultural Heritage and Development: A Framework for Action in the Middle East and North Africa.* Washington, DC: The World Bank, 2001. This document provides an overview of cultural heritage projects and possibilities in the Middle East and North Africa and a proactive strategy linking efforts to reduce poverty with high-impact cultural heritage projects. The strategy was adopted for use by the Middle East and North Africa group within the World Bank.

John Miller Chernoff. *African Rhythm and African Sensibility: Aesthetics and African Musical Idioms.* Chicago: University of Chicago Press, 1979. This book describes shared features of music style and musical performance throughout Africa and also explains links to key African cultural values.

Eugene Cooper and Yinho Jiang (contributor). *The Artisans and Entrepreneurs of Dongyang County: Economic Reform and Flexible Production in China.* Armonk, NY: M. E. Sharpe, 1998. This ethnography links economic change and artistic change in China through its description of traditional and contemporary woodcarving in two villages and one town.

Alice C. Fletcher. *Indian Games and Dances with Native Songs: Arranged from American Indian Ceremonials and Sports.* Boston: Bison Books, 1994 [1915]. This book is a reprint of a classic study of dances, songs, and games from many tribes by the anthropologist who coined the term *Native American*. The adaptations allow readers to perform these activities themselves.

Nelson H. H. Graburn, ed. *Ethnic and Tourist Arts: Cultural Expressions from the Fourth World.* Berkeley: University of California Press, 1976. Organized regionally, twenty chapters explore the survival, revival, and reinvention of the arts of indigenous peoples in North America, Mexico and Central America, South America, Asia, Oceania, and Africa. Graburn's introduction to the book and his introductory essays preceding the sections offer theoretical and comparative insights.

Jay R. Mandle and Joan D. Mandle. *Caribbean Hoops: The Development of West Indian Basketball.* Amsterdam: Gordon and Breach Publishers, 1994. This concise description and analysis of the emergence of basketball (mainly men's basketball) as a popular sport in several

Caribbean nations also explores regional differences within the Caribbean.

Timothy Mitchell. *Blood Sport: A Social History of Spanish Bullfighting*. Philadelphia: University of Pennsylvania Press, 1991. Based on fieldwork and archival study, this book presents a well-rounded view of bullfighting within the context of annual Spanish village and national fiestas, consideration of the role of the matador in society, and a psychosexual interpretation of the bullfight, with comparison to blood sports in ancient Rome.

Stuart Plattner. *High Art Down Home: An Economic Ethnography of a Local Art Market*. Chicago: University of Chicago Press, 1996. Based on participant observation and interviews with artists, art dealers, and collectors in St. Louis, Missouri, this book explores concepts of value related to contemporary art and constraints that the market places on artists.

Stacy B. Schaefer. *To Think with a Good Heart: Wixárike Women, Weavers, and Shamans*. Salt Lake City: University of Utah Press, 2002. Weaving woolen textiles is a woman-centered activity among the Wixárike of western Mexico. Women generate income from weaving, and master weavers gain domestic and public status. Most previous ethnographers of the Wixárike have studied men, so this book provides new insights into the world of women.

R. Anderson Sutton. *Calling Back the Spirit: Music, Dance and Cultural Politics in Lowland South Sulawesi*. New York: Oxford University Press, 2002. The author describes a wide variety of performance modes in South Sulawesi, Indonesia, from village ceremonies to studio-produced popular music. One chapter examines the role of village schools in institutionalizing local forms of music and dance; another considers the effects of mass media. Accompanying the book is a CD with examples of music that complement points made in the book.

Roxanne Waterson. *The Living House: An Anthropology of Architecture in South-East Asia*. New York: Oxford University Press, 1990. This richly illustrated book covers a range of topics related to domestic architecture in Southeast Asia, including how house forms and decorations are related to religious symbolism, kinship, social relationships, political status, and population migration.

THE BIG QUESTIONS REVISITED

HOW is culture expressed through art?

Cultural anthropologists question the narrowness of Western definitions of art. Anthropologists choose a broad definition that takes into account cross-cultural variations. In the anthropological perspective, all cultures have art and all cultures have a concept of what good art is. Ethnographers document the ways in which art is related to many aspects of culture: economics, politics, human development and psychology, healing, social control, and entertainment. Art may serve to reinforce social patterns, but it may also be a vehicle of protest and resistance. In state societies, people began collecting art objects in museums. Later, ethnographic museums were established in Europe as the result of scientific and colonialist interest in learning about other cultures. Anthropologists study museum displays as a reflection of cultural values as well as sites where perceptions and values are formed.

WHAT do play and leisure activities tell us about culture?

Anthropological studies of play and leisure examine these activities within their cultural context. Games reflect and reinforce dominant social values and have thus been analyzed as cultural microcosms. Sports and leisure activities, though engaged in for nonutilitarian purposes, are often tied to economic and political interests. In some cultures, sports are also related to religion and spirituality.

HOW is expressive culture changing in contemporary times?

Major forces of change in expressive culture include Western colonialism and international tourism. In some cases, outside forces have led to the extinction of local forms, whereas in other cases, outside forces have promoted continuity or the recovery of practices that had been lost. The effects of change are not always on the "receiving" culture's side, however, because expressive cultures in colonial powers and in contemporary core states have also changed through exposure to other, less powerful cultures.

THE BIG QUESTIONS

- **WHAT** are the major categories of migration?

- **WHAT** are examples of the new immigrants in the United States and Canada?

- **HOW** do anthropologists contribute to migration policies and programs?

15

PEOPLE ON THE MOVE

The so-called Marsh Arab people suffered from government projects that drained their region under the rule of Saddam Hussein as well as political repression. Many who fled the country as refugees are now returning. (*Source: © Nik Wheeler/CORBIS*)

The current generation of North American youths will experience more moves during their lives than previous generations. College graduates are likely to change jobs an average of eight times during their careers, and these changes may require relocation.

Ecological, economic, familial, and political factors are causing population movements at seemingly all-time high levels. Research in anthropology has shown, however, that frequent moves during a person's life and mass movements of peoples are nothing new; they have occurred throughout human evolution. Foragers, horticulturalists, and pastoralists relocate frequently as a normal part of their lives.

Migration is the movement of a person or people from one place to another (Kearney 1986:331). It is related to aspects of life such as job and family status. It may also affect health and social relationships. Thus migration is of great interest to many academic subjects and professions. Migration is one of three core areas of demography, along with fertility and mortality (recall Chapter 5). Historians, economists, political scientists, sociologists, and scholars of religion, literature, art, and music have studied migration. The professions of law, medicine, education, business, architecture, urban planning, public administration, and social work have specialties that focus on the process of migration and the period of adaption following a move. Experts working in these areas share with anthropologists an interest in such issues as the kinds of people who migrate, causes of migration, processes of migration, health and psychosocial adaptations to new locations, and implications for planning and policy.

Cultural anthropologists have addressed a wide range of issues surrounding migration. They have studied how migration is related to economic and reproductive systems, health and human development over the life cycle, marriage and household formation, politics and social order, and religion and expressive culture. There is no domain of human life that is not affected by migration; hence this topic pulls together much of the earlier material in this book. Given the breadth of migration studies, cultural anthropologists have used the full range of methods available, from individual life histories to large-scale surveys.

Three differences distinguish migration studies from other areas of research in cultural anthropology. First, anthropologists studying migration are more likely to have fieldwork experience in more than one location in order to understand the places of origin and estimation. Maxine Margolis (1994), for example, first did fieldwork in Brazil and then later studied Brazilian immigrants in New York City. Second, a greater emphasis on using both macro and micro perspectives characterizes anthropology's approach to migration studies. Studying migration has challenged traditional cultural anthropology's focus on one village or neighborhood and created the need to take into account national and global economic, political, and social forces (Basch, Glick Schiller, and Szanton Blanc 1994; Lamphere 1992). Third, anthropologists who work with migrants are more likely to be involved in applied anthropology. Many opportunities exist for anthropologists to contribute their knowledge and insights to help improve government policies and programs related to migration. Anthropologists have been at the forefront of efforts to improve the situation of people forced to move by war, environmental destruction, and massive building projects such as dams.

This chapter first presents information on the most important categories of migrants and the opportunities and challenges they face. The second section provides descriptions of several examples of immigrants to the United States and Canada. The last section considers urgent issues related to migration, such as human rights and risk assessment and prevention programs.

CATEGORIES OF MIGRATION

Migration encompasses many categories, depending on the distance involved; on the migration's purpose, duration, and degree of voluntarism (was the move forced or more a matter of choice?); and on the migrant's status in the new destination. There are major differences between **internal migration** (movement within national boundaries) and international migration. Moving between nations is likely to create more challenges both in the process of relocation and in adjustment after arrival.

Categories Based on Spatial Boundaries

This section reviews the basic features of three categories of population movement defined in terms of the spatial boundaries crossed: internal migration, international migration, and the new category of transnational migration. **Transnational migrants** are migrants who regularly move back and forth between two or more countries and form a new identity that transcends a single geopolitical unit (recall the discussion of transnationalism in Chapter 1).

Internal Migration

Rural-to-urban migration was the dominant form of internal population in most countries during the twentieth century. A major reason why people migrate to urban areas is the availability of work. According the **push–pull theory** of labor migration, rural areas are increasingly unable to support population growth and rising expectations about the quality of life (the push factor). Cities (the pull factor) attract people, especially youth, for employment and lifestyle reasons. The push–pull model makes urban migration sound like a simple function of rational decision making by people who have information on the costs and benefits of rural versus urban life, weigh that information, and then opt for going or staying (recall the approach to understanding culture that emphasizes human agency, Chapter 1). But many instances of urban migration are more likely to be the result of structural forces (economic need or political factors such as war) that are beyond the control of the individual.

Chinese Canadians mainly live in urban areas such as Vancouver and Toronto. In Vancouver, they constitute about 16 percent of the population. Vancouver's Chinatown is a vibrant tourist site as well as a place where Chinese Canadians reaffirm their cultural heritage as in the celebration shown here of Chinese New Year. ■ *When does Chinese New Year take place, and how is the date determined? Think of other "New Year" celebrations, when they occur, and what determines the timing.* (Source: © Annie Griffiths Belt/CORBIS)

The anonymity and rapid pace of city life and the likelihood of "psychosocial discontinuity" caused by relocation pose special challenges for migrants from rural areas. Urban life increases the risk of hypertension (elevated blood pressure through stress or tension), and hypertension is related to coronary heart disease. For example, hypertension is more prevalent in urban migrant populations than in settled rural groups (Hackenberg et al. 1983). This finding applied to both men and women. The relationship between elevated health risks resulting from psychosocial adjustment problems in rural-to-urban

migration exists among international immigrants as well—for example, among Samoans living in California (Janes 1990).

International Migration

International migration has grown in volume and significance since 1945 and especially since the mid-1980s (Castles and Miller 1993). It is estimated that nearly 2 percent of the world's population lives abroad (outside of their home countries). This is about 100 million people, including legal and undocumented immigrants. Migrants who move for work-related reasons constitute the majority of people in this category. At least 35 million people from developing countries have migrated to industrialized countries in the past three decades. The driving forces behind this trend are economic and political changes that affect labor demands and human welfare.

The "classic" countries of early international immigration are the United States, Canada, Australia, New Zealand, and Argentina. The immigration policies that these nations applied in the early twentieth century are labeled "White immigration" because they explicitly limited non-White immigration (Ongley 1995). In the 1960s in Canada, changes made immigration policies less racially discriminatory and more focused on skills and experience. The "White Australia" policy formally ended in 1973. In both the Canadian and Australian cases, a combination of changing labor needs and interest in improving their international image prompted the reforms. During the 1980s and the 1990s, the United States, Canada, and Australia experienced large-scale immigration from new sources, especially from Asia, and—to the United States—from Latin America and the Caribbean.

Long-time areas of out-migration of Northern, Western, and Southern Europe are now receiving many immigrants (often refugees from Asia). Hungary, Poland, and Czechoslovakia are new migrant destinations. International population flows in the Middle East are complex, with some nations (such as Turkey) experiencing substantial movements in both directions. Millions of Turks have emigrated to Germany, while ethnic Turks in places such as Bulgaria have returned to Turkey. Turkey has also received Kurdish and Iranian refugees. Several million Palestinian refugees now live mainly in Jordan and Lebanon. Israel has attracted Jewish immigrants from Europe, northern Africa, the United States, and Russia.

Transnational Migration

Transnational migration appears to be increasing along with other aspects of globalization. We must keep in mind, however, that transnationalism is a function of the creation of nation–state boundaries. Pastoralist people with extensive seasonal herding routes were "transnational" migrants long before national boundaries cut across their pathways.

Much contemporary transnational migration is motivated by economic factors. The spread of the global corporate economy is the basis for the growth of one category of transnational migrants nicknamed "astronauts," businesspeople who spend most of their time flying among different cities as investment bankers or corporate executives. At the lower end of the income scale are transnational migrant laborers who spend substantial amounts of time working in different places and whose movements depend on the demand for their labor.

An important feature of transnational migration is how it affects the migrant's identity and sense of citizenship. Constant movement among different places weakens the sense of having one home and promotes instead a sense of belonging to a diffused community of similar transnational migrants whose lives "in between" locations take on a new transnational cultural reality.

As a response to the increased rate of transnational migration, many of the "sending" countries (countries that are the source of emigrants) are making explicit efforts to redefine themselves as transnational nations (Glick Schiller and Fouron 1999). These countries, which have high proportions of emigrants, include Haiti, Colombia, Mexico, Brazil, the Dominican Republic, Portugal, Greece, and the Philippines. They confer continuing citizenship on emigrants and their descendants in order to foster a sense of belonging and willingness to continue to provide financial support in the form of **remittances**, or economic transfers of money or goods from migrants to their family back home. For example, at least 60 percent of the gross domestic product of the small Pacific island country of Tonga comes from remittances (Lee 2003:32).

Categories Based on Reason for Moving

In this section, we consider categories of migrants that are based on the reason for relocating. Readers should keep in mind that the spatial categories that we have already discussed overlap with the categories based on reason for moving. An international migrant, for example, may also be a person who moved for employment reasons. Displaced persons can be either internal or international. In other words, migrants experience different kinds of spatial change and, at the same time, have various different reasons for moving.

Labor Migrants

Thousands of people migrate each year to work for a specific period of time. They do not intend to establish permanent residence and are often explicitly barred from doing so. This form of migration, when legally contracted, is called *wage labor migration*. The period of work may be brief or it may last several years, as among rural Egyptian men who go to Middle Eastern countries to work for an average period of four years (Brink 1991).

Asian women are the fastest-growing category among the world's 35 million migrant workers (International Labour Office 1996). About 1.5 million Asian women are working abroad; most are in domestic service jobs, and some work as nurses and teachers. Major sending countries are Indonesia, the Philippines, Sri Lanka, and Thailand. Main receiving countries are Saudi Arabia and Kuwait, and, to a lesser degree, Hong Kong, Japan, Taiwan, Singapore, Malaysia, and Brunei. Such women are usually alone and are not allowed to marry or have a child in the country where they are temporary workers.

International migrant workers are sometimes illegally recruited and have no legal protection in their working conditions.

Circular migration is a common form of labor migration involving movement in a regular pattern between two or more places. Circular migration may occur either within or between nations. In the latter case, it is also referred to as transnational migration. Internal circular migrants include, for example, female domestic workers throughout Latin America and the Caribbean. These women have there permanent residence in the rural areas, but they work for long periods of time in the city for better-off people. They tend to leave their children in the care of their mother in the country and to send regular remittances for the children's support.

Displaced Persons

Displaced persons are people who, for one reason or another, are evicted from their homes, communities, or countries and forced to move elsewhere (Guggenheim and Cernea 1993). Colonialism, slavery, war, persecution, natural disasters, and large-scale mining and dam building are major causes of population displacement.

Refugees are a category of internationally displaced persons. Many refugees are forced to relocate because they are victims or potential victims of persecution on the basis of their race, religion, nationality, ethnicity, gender, or political views (Camino and Krulfeld 1994). Refugees constitute a large and growing category of displaced persons. An accurate count of all categories of refugees globally is unavailable, but it probably exceeds 10 million people. As of 2000, about one of every five hundred people were refugees (Lubkemann 2002). The lack of accurate data is compounded by political interests, which, in some cases, inflate numbers and, in others, to deflate numbers.

Internally displaced persons (IDPs) is the fastest-growing category of displaced people. IDPs are people who are forced to leave their home and community but who remain within their country. Current estimates are that the number of IDPs is double that of refugees, over 20 million people (Cohen 2002). Africa is the continent with the most IDPs, and within Africa, Sudan is the country with the highest number (around 4.5 million). Because IDPs do not cross national boundaries, they do not come under the purview of the United Nations or any other international body. These institutions deal with international problems and have limited authority over problems within countries. Francis Deng, former Sudanese ambassador, has taken up the cause of IDPs and is working to raise international awareness of the immensity of the problem. His efforts led to the formal definition of IDPs and to legal recognition of their status. In his role as UN Secretary-General for Internally Displaced Per-

Dr. Francis Deng, who earned a doctor of law degree from Yale University, is Representative of the United Nations Secretary-General on Internally Displaced Persons and directs a program on displaced persons at the Brookings Institution in Washington, DC. He has been instrumental in gaining international recognition of the plight of internally displaced persons. ■ *Do research on a case of IDPs in your home state or country, and report on it to the class.* (Source: AP/Wide World Photos)

sons, Deng coordinates a global coalition of institutions (including the UN, governments, and nongovernmental organizations) to provide more timely and effective assistance for IDPs. Many IDPs, like refugees live for extended periods in camps under miserable conditions with no access to basic supports such as health care and schools.

Development projects are often the reason why people become IDPs. Large dam construction, mining, and other projects have displaced millions in the past several decades. Dam construction alone is estimated to have displaced perhaps 80 million people in the past fifty years (Worldwatch Institute 2003). Forced migration due to development projects is termed **development-induced displacement (DID)**. Development-induced displacement is usually internal displacement and thus has typically fallen outside international legal frameworks. Mega-dam projects are now attracting the attention of concerned people worldwide who support local resistance to massive relocation. One of the most notorious cases is India's construction of a series of high dams in its Narmada river valley, which cuts across the middle of the country from the west coast. This massive project involves relocating hundreds of thousands of people—no one has a reliable estimate of the numbers. The relocation is against the residents' wishes, and government compensation to the "oustees" for the loss of the homes, land, and livelihood is completely inadequate. Thousands of people in the Narmada valley have organized protests over the many years of construction, and international environmental organizations have lent their support. A celebrated Indian novelist, Arundhati Roy, joined the cause by learning everything she could about the twenty years of government

planning for the Narmada dam projects, interviewing people who have been relocated, and writing a passionate statement called *The Cost of Living* (1999) against this massive project. A man now living in a barren resettlement area told how he used to pick fruit in the forest, forty-eight kinds. In the resettlement area he and his family have to purchase all their food, and they cannot afford any fruit at all (pp. 54–55). In the other Asian giant, China, the equally infamous Three Gorges Dam project will, when completed, have displaced perhaps 2 million (McCully 2003). Mega-dam projects are always promoted by governments as important to the national interest. But costs are always high for the local people who are displaced, and the benefits are always skewed toward corporate profits, energy for industrial plants, and water for urban consumers who can pay for it.

The manner in which displaced persons are relocated affects how well they will adjust to their new lives. Displaced persons in general have little choice about when and where they move; refugees typically have the least choice of all. Cultural anthropologists have done substantial research with refugee populations, especially those related to war (Camino and Krulfeld 1994; Hirschon 1989; Manz 1988). They have helped discover the key factors that ease or increase relocation stresses. One major issue is the extent to which the new location resembles or differs from the home place in several features such as climate, language, and food (Muecke 1987). Generally, the more different the places of origin and destination are, the greater the adaptational demands and stress. Other major factors are the refugee's ability to get a job commensurate with his or her training and experience, the

Unity and Diversity

SCHOOL GIRLS AND SPIRIT POSSESSION IN MADAGASCAR

ETHNOGRAPHIC RESEARCH conducted among adolescent boarding school children in Ambanja, a town in Madagascar, showed that girls experience more adjustment strains than boys (Sharp 1990). Ambanja is a "booming" migrant town characterized by rootlessness and anomie. Boarding school children in this town constitute a vulnerable group because they have left their families and come alone to the school.

Many of the boarding school girls, who were between the ages of thirteen and seventeen, experienced bouts of spirit possession. Local people say that the "prettiest" girls are the ones who become possessed. The data on possession patterns showed, instead, that possession is correlated with a girl's being unmarried and pregnant. Many of these school girls become the mistresses of older men, who shower them with expensive gifts such as perfume and gold jewelry. Such girls attract the envy of both other girls and school boys, who are being passed over in favor of adult men. Thus the girls have little peer support among their schoolmates. If a girl becomes pregnant, school policy requires that she be expelled. If the baby's father refuses to help her, she faces severe hardship. Her return home will be a great disappointment to her parents.

Within this context, a girl's spirit possession may be understood as an expression of distress. Through the spirits, girls act out their difficult position between country and city and between girlhood and womanhood.

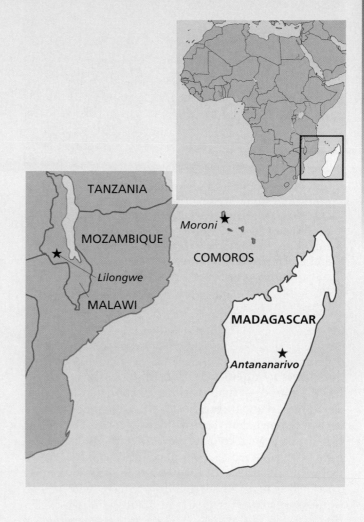

FOOD FOR THOUGHT

Consider the patterns of psychological stress among college students and their possible gender dimensions. How do these patterns of stress differ from or resemble the situation described here?

---

presence of family members, and whether people in the new location are welcoming or hostile to the refugees.

Institutional Migrants

Institutional migrants are people who move into a social institution, either voluntarily or involuntarily. They include monks and nuns, the elderly, prisoners, and boarding school or college students. This section considers examples of students and soldiers within the category of institutional migrants.

Studies of student adjustment reveal similarities to many other forms of migration, especially in terms of risks for mental stress (see the Unity and Diversity box). International students face serious challenges of spatial and cultural relocation. Like the school girls of Madagascar, they are at greater risk of adjustment stress than are local students. Many international students report mental health problems to varying degrees, depending on age, marital status, and other factors. Spouses who accompany international students also suffer the strains of dislocation.

United States marines wearing gas masks as protection from oil fumes during the 1990–1991 Gulf War. Many poorly understood illnesses afflict veterans of "Desert Storm" including skin conditions, neurological disorders, chronic fatigue, and psychological-cognitive problems ■ *Do research to learn about current medical thinking on the causes of Gulf War illnesses.* (Source: © David Leeson/The Image Works)

Soldiers are often sent on long-distant assignments for lengthy periods of time. Their destination may have negative physical and mental health effects on them, in addition to the fact that they may face combat. During the British and French colonial expansion, thousands of soldiers were assigned to tropical countries (Curtin 1989). Colonial soldiers faced new diseases in their destination areas. Their death rates from disease were twice as high as those of soldiers who stayed home, with two exceptions—Tahiti and Hawaii—where soldiers experienced better health than soldiers at home. Most military personnel were male, but in some colonial contexts, many wives accompanied their husbands. In India, mortality rates were higher for females than for males. This finding may be explained by the fact that the men had to pass a physical exam before enlistment, whereas their dependents did not.

As Chapter 11 noted, military anthropology is an emerging specialty, along with focus areas within it such as front-line anthropology. Little has been published by anthropologists on how military migration affects people's lives and sense of identity. One thing that is clear, however, is that U.S. military people on assignment lack in-depth training in how to communicate with local people and in the importance of respecting local people's cultures. A pocket-size handbook on Iraqi etiquette used by some U.S. troops in Iraq provides some extremely basic guidelines (Lorch 2003). For example, one should avoid arguments and should not take more than three cups of coffee or tea if you are someone's guest. One should also avoid the "thumbs up" gesture (it's obscene in the Middle East) and should not sit with one's feet on a desk. Such basics are helpful, but they do little to provide the cultural understanding that is critical in conflict and post-conflict situations. Soldiers during wartime are trained primarily to seek out and destroy the enemy, not to engage in cross-cultural communication. Winning a war in contemporary times often hinges on what the conquerors do following the outright conflict, and that often means keeping troops stationed in foreign cultures for extended periods of time. Such extended assignments take a heavy toll on military personnel's mental health.

THE NEW IMMIGRANTS TO THE UNITED STATES AND CANADA

The term **new immigrants** refers to international migrants who have moved since the 1960s. New immigrants worldwide include increasing proportions of refugees, many of whom are destitute and desperate for asylum. Three trends are apparent in the new international migration that began in the 1990s.

- *Globalization:* More countries are involved in international migration, leading to increased cultural diversity in sending and receiving countries.

- *Acceleration:* Quantitative growth of migration has occurred in all major regions.

- *Feminization:* Women are playing a greater role in migration to and from all regions and in all types of migration, and some forms exhibit a majority of women.

These three trends raise new challenges for policy makers and international organizations as the cultural practices of immigrant groups and the areas of destination increasingly come in contact, and sometimes, in conflict, with each other.

In the United States, the category of *new immigrants* refers to people who arrived following the 1965 amendments to the Immigration and Naturalization Act. This change made it possible for far more people from developing countries to enter, especially if they were professionals or trained in some desired skill. Later, the "family reunification" provision allowed permanent residents and naturalized citizens to bring in close family members. Most of the new immigrants in the United States are from Asia, Latin America, and the Caribbean, although increasing numbers are from Eastern Europe, especially Russia. The United States offers two kinds of visas for foreigners: immigrant visas (also called residence visas) and nonimmigrant visas for tourists and students (Pessar 1995:6). An immigration visa is usually valid indefinitely and allows its holder to be employed and to apply for citizenship. A nonimmigrant visa is issued for a limited time period and usually bars its holder from paid employment. Some immigrants are granted visas because of their special skills in relation to labor market needs, but most are admitted under the family unification provision.

The New Immigrants from Latin America and the Caribbean

Since the 1960s, substantial movements of the Latino population (people who share roots in former Spanish and Portuguese colonies in the Western hemisphere) have occurred, mainly but not entirely in the direction of the United States. Compared to numbers of legal immigrants in the 1960s, numbers doubled or tripled in the 1980s and then declined in the 1990s. For example, legal immigrants from Central America numbered about 100.000 in the 1960s, nearly 900,000 in the 1980s, and about 270,000 in the 1990s (Parrillo 1997:398). Excluding the residents of Puerto Rico, Latinos totaled about 2.4 million people, or about 9 percent of the United States population, in the 1990 census (Mahler 1995:xiii). In the United States as a whole, and in some cities, such as Los Angeles, Miami, San Antonio, and New York, Latinos are the largest minority group. Within the category of Latino new immigrants, the three largest subgroups are Mexicans, Puerto Ricans, and Cubans. Large streams also come from the Dominican Republic, Colombia, Ecuador, El Salvador, Nicaragua, and Peru.

Mexico is by far the major source of foreign-born immigrants to the United States (Grieco 2003). There are currently around 10 million foreign-born Mexicans living in the United States, a number that doubled from 1990 to 2000. Most live in traditional destination states such as California, Texas, and Illinois, although many more are now settling in states such as Georgia and North Carolina. Mexico also continues to be the leading source of unauthorized immigration into the United States.

Chain Migration of Dominicans

The Dominican Republic has ranked among the top ten source countries of immigrants to the United States since the 1960s (Pessar 1995). Dominicans are one of the fastest-growing immigrant groups in the United States. They are found in clusters in a few states, with their highest concentration in New York state. Within New York

A Dominican Day parade in New York City. ■ *Learn about some ethnic festival or event that is being held in the near future. Attend it and observe what signs and symbols of ethnicity are displayed, who attends, and what major messages about identity are conveyed.* (Source: © Stephen Ferry/Getty Images)

City, Washington Heights is the heart of the Dominican community. Unlike many other new-immigrant streams, the Dominicans are mainly middle- and upper-class. Most have left their homeland "in search of a better life." Many hope to return to the Dominican Republic, saying that in New York, "There is work but there is no life."

Patricia Pessar conducted fieldwork in the Dominican Republic and in New York City, and thus she has a transnational view. She studied the dynamics of departure (such as getting a visa), the process of arrival, and adaptation in New York. Like most anthropologists who work with immigrant groups, she became involved in helping many of her informants: "Along the way I also endeavored to repay people's help by brokering for them with institutions such as the Immigration and Naturalization Service, social service agencies, schools, and hospitals." (xv).

For Dominican immigrants, as for most other immigrant groups, the *cadena*, or chain, links one immigrant to another. **Chain migration** is the process by which a first wave of migrants then attracts relatives and friends to join them in the destination place. Most Dominicans who are legal immigrants have sponsored other family members, so most legal Dominicans have entered through the family unification provision. The U.S. policy defines a family as a nuclear unit, and thus, it excludes important members of Dominican extended family networks such as cousins and ritual kin (compadres). To overcome this

Hillary Clinton visits an orphanage in El Salvador in 1998. Many children were orphaned because their parents were killed during the civil war of the 1980s. Others were abducted by the Salvadoran military and still have not been reunited with their parents, two decades later. ■ *What do you think governments can do to help ensure children's safety and rights during war?* (Source: © Yuri Cortez/CORBIS)

barrier, some Dominicans use the technique of the "business marriage." In a business marriage, an individual pays a legal immigrant or citizen a fee of perhaps $2000 to enter into a "marriage." He or she then acquires a visa through the family unification provision. Such a "marriage" does not involve cohabitation or sexual relations; it is meant to be broken.

Dominicans have found employment in New York's manufacturing industries, including the garment industry. Dominicans are more heavily employed in these industries than any other ethnic group. Recent declines in the numbers of New York City's manufacturing jobs and the redefining of better positions into less desirable ones through restructuring have disproportionately affected them. Dominicans also work in retail and wholesale trade, another sector that has declined since the late 1960s. Others have established their own retail businesses, or *bodegas*. A problem with this line of work is that many bodegas are located in unsafe areas and some owners have been assaulted or killed. Declining economic opportunities for Dominicans have also been aggravated by arrivals of newer immigrants, especially from Mexico and Central America, who are willing to accept even lower wages and worse working conditions.

Although many families of middle and high status in the Dominican Republic initially secured fairly solid employment in the United States, they have declined economically since then. Dominicans now have the highest poverty rate in New York City, 37 percent, compared with an overall city average of 17 percent. Poverty is concentrated among women-headed households with young children.

The gender gap in wages is high, and women are more likely than men to be on public assistance. On the other hand, Dominican women in the United States are more often regularly employed than they would be in the

Dominican Republic. This pattern upsets a patriarchal norm in which the nuclear family depends on male earnings and female domestic responsibilities. A woman's earning power means that husband–wife decision making is more egalitarian. A working Dominican women is likely to obtain more assistance from the man in doing household chores. All of these changes help explain why Dominican men are more interested in returning to the Dominican Republic than women are. As one man said, "Your country is a country for women; mine is for men" (81).

Salvadorans: Escaping War to Struggle with Poverty

Salvadorans are the fourth largest Latino population in the United States, numbering 868,000 people in 2002 (Migration Information Source 2003). The civil war in El Salvador, which began in 1979 and continued for a decade, was the major stimulus for Salvadoran emigration (Mahler 1995). Most of the refugees from the war came to the United States, and many settled in New York City. About 60,000 chose to live on Long Island, where they are a rarely studied example of international migration to suburban areas. Middle- and upper-class Salvadorans were able to obtain tourist or even immigration visas relatively easily, but the poor could not. Many entered the United States illegally as *mojados* ("wetbacks"), or undocumented immigrants.

Like Mexicans, they use the term *mojado* to describe their journey, but for the Salvadorans there were three rivers to cross instead of one. These three crossings are a prominent theme of their escape stories, which are full of physical and psychological hardship, including hunger, arrests, and women being beaten and raped along the way. Once they arrive, things are not easy, especially in the search for work and housing. Lack of education and paucity of marketable skills limit the job search. For those who are undocumented immigrants, getting a decent job is even harder. These factors make it more likely that Salvadorans will work in the informal sector, where they are easy targets for economic exploitation.

Salvadorans who find work on Long Island receive low wages and work in poor conditions. Jobs involve providing services to better-off Long Island households. Men do outside work such as gardening, landscaping, construction, and pool cleaning. Women work as nannies, live-in maids, house cleaners, restaurant help, and caregivers for the elderly. They often hold down a variety of jobs—for example, working at a McDonalds in the morning and cleaning houses in the afternoon. Men's pride prevents them from taking lowly ("female") jobs such as washing dishes. Women are more flexible and hence are more likely than men to find work. For the poorest of Salvadoran refugees, even exploitive jobs may be an economic improvement compared to back home, where they could not support their families.

The Salvadorans were attracted to Long Island by its thriving informal economy, a sector where checking for visas was less likely to occur. Unfortunately, the cost of living on Long Island is higher than in many other places. The combination of low wages and high costs of living has kept most Salvadorans in the category of the working poor, with few prospects for improvement. They attempt to cope with high housing costs by crowding many people into units meant for a small family. Compared to El Salvador, where most people except for the urban poor owned their own homes, only a few Salvadorans on Long Island own homes. Residential space and costs are shared among extended kin and non-kin who pay rent. This situation causes intrahousehold tension and stress.

The Catholic Church has recognized that the Salvadorans are a substantial population, and it holds services in Spanish for this community of refugees. Still, the refugees carry with them memories of the war and their escape from it. In spite of all these difficulties, however, most Salvadorans evaluate their experience in the United States positively.

The New Immigrants from East Asia

Koreans: Economic Achievement and Political Identity

In 1962 the South Korean government began encouraging massive emigration (Yoon 1993). This change was motivated by perceived population pressure and an interest in gaining remittances from persons working abroad. Before 1965, most Korean immigrants were wives of American servicemen and children being adopted by

Korean Americans clean up the debris from attacks on their businesses after the Los Angeles riots of May 1992. ■ *Compare the situation in Los Angeles to that of Baghdad in March 2003 in terms of the social cleavages involved in looting of museums and destruction of other forms of public property.* (Source: © David Young-Wolff/PhotoEdit)

American parents. After 1965, most immigrants were members of nuclear families or family members being unified with earlier "pioneer" migrants already in the United States. During the peak years of 1985 and 1987, more than 35,000 Koreans immigrated to the United States annually, making South Korea the largest immigrant source nation after Mexico and the Philippines.

Many of the migrants were displaced North Koreans who had fled their homeland to avoid communist rule there between 1945 and 1951. They had difficulty gaining an economic foothold in South Korea. When the opportunity arose to emigrate to South America or the United States, they were more willing to do so than many established South Koreans. In 1981 North Koreans constituted only 2 percent of the population of South Korea, but they were 22 percent of the Korean population of Los Angeles. Most of these immigrants were entrepreneurial, Christian, and middle-class. In the 1990s the number of lower-class migrants increased, and many lower-class Korean immigrants moved to Los Angeles (Sonenshein 1996). In this city, Whites constitute less

Latino immigrants studying English in a program in Virginia. ■ *Besides learning a new language, what other kinds of learning is important for international immigrants?* (Source: © David H. Wells/CORBIS)

than 40 percent of the population, whereas Asian Americans and Latinos account for 50 percent. The proportion of Blacks is 14 percent. Electoral politics is mainly a matter of Blacks and Whites, with Hispanics involved to a lesser degree. In the area called South Central, a low-income section of the city shared by Blacks, Latinos, and Korean Americans, the Blacks are the only politically active group. Their views are liberal, and they are mainly Democrats. A wide gap separates Black politics from interests of the Korean Americans. Although the Korean Americans are arguably exploited by larger economic interests, especially in their role as small shop owners, within South Central they are seen by other people as exploitive. One issue over which conflict has arisen, especially between Blacks and Korean Americans, is liquor store ownership. Over the years, many bank branches, large grocery stores, and movie theaters have left South Central. The gap was filled by stores in which the most valuable commodity sold is liquor. In South Central there are far more liquor licenses per square mile than in the rest of Los Angeles County. Given this background, it is perplexing that no one foresaw the 1992 riots in which thousands of Korean businesses were damaged, including 187 liquor stores. (The Latino population also suffered severe losses. One-third of all deaths resulting from the riot were Latinos). For the Koreans, one outcome was an increased sense of ethnic unity and political awareness.

Changing Patterns of Consumption among Hong Kong Chinese

Studies of how international migrants change their behavior in the new destination have addressed, among other things, the question of whether consumption patterns change and, if so, how, why, and what effects such changes have on other aspects of their culture.

A study in Canada focused on the topic of consumption patterns among four groups: Anglo-Canadians, new Hong Kong immigrants (who had arrived within the previous seven years), long-time Hong Kong immigrants, and Hong Kong residents (Lee and Tse 1994). Since 1987, Hong Kong has been the single largest source of migrants to Canada. The new immigrant settlement pattern in Canada is one of urban clustering. The Hong Kong Chinese have developed their own shopping centers, television and radio stations, newspapers, and country clubs. Because of generally high incomes, the Hong Kong immigrants have greatly boosted Canadian buying power.

For most migrants, however, the move brought a lowered economic situation, reflected in consumption patterns. New immigrants may have to reduce spending on entertainment and expensive items. Primary needs of the new immigrants include items that only about half of all households owned: car, VCR, carpets, microwave oven, family house, and multiple TVs. Items in the second-needs category were dining room set, barbecue stove, deep freezer, and dehumidifier. Long-time immigrants tend to own more secondary products, suggesting that, with time and increased economic standing, expanded consumption of Anglo-Canadian products occurs.

At the same time, businesses in Canada have responded to immigrant tastes by providing Hong Kong style restaurants, Chinese branch banks, and travel agencies. Supermarkets have specialized Asian sections. Thus traditional patterns and ties are maintained to some extent. Two characteristics of Hong Kong immigrants distinguish them from other groups discussed in this section: their relatively secure economic status and their high level of education. Still, in Canada, they often have a difficult time finding suitable employment. Some have named Canada "Kan Lan Tai," meaning a difficult place to prosper, a fact that leads many to become "astronauts," or transnational migrants.

The New Immigrants from Southeast Asia

Three Patterns of Adaptation among the Vietnamese

Over one and a quarter million refugees left Vietnam during and after the wartime 1970s. Although most were relocated to the United States, many went to Canada, Australia, France, Germany, and Britain (Gold 1992). Vietnamese immigrants in the United States constitute the nation's third largest Asian American minority group. Three distinct subgroups are the 1975-era elite, the boat people, and the ethnic Chinese. Although they interact frequently, they have retained distinct patterns of adaptation.

The first group avoided many of the traumatic elements of flight. They were U.S. employees and members of the South Vietnamese government and military. They left before having to live under the communist regime, and they spent little time in refugee camps. Most came with intact families and received generous financial assistance. Using their education and English language skills, many found good jobs quickly and adjusted rapidly.

The boat people began to enter the United States after the outbreak of the Vietnam–China conflict of 1978. Mainly of rural origin, they lived for three years or more under communism, working in reeducation camps or "new economic zones." Their exit, either by overcrowded and leaky boats or on foot through Cambodia, was dangerous and difficult. Over 50 percent died on the way. Those who survived faced many months in refugee camps in Thailand, Malaysia, the Philippines, or Hong Kong before being admitted to the United States. Many more males than females escaped as boat people, so they are less likely to have arrived with intact families. They were less well educated than the earlier wave, half had no competence in English, and they faced the depressed American economy of the 1980s. By the time of their arrival, refugee cash assistance had been cut severely and other benefits canceled. They have had a much more difficult time adjusting to life in the United States than the 1975-era elite.

The ethnic Chinese, traditionally a distinct and socially marginalized class of entrepreneurs in Vietnam, arrived mainly as boat people. Following the 1987 outbreak of hostilities between Vietnam and China, the ethnic Chinese were allowed to leave Vietnam. Some have used contacts in the overseas Chinese community and have been able to reestablish their roles as entrepreneurs, but most have had a difficult time in the United States because they did not have a Western-style education. They were also sometimes subject to discrimination from other Vietnamese in the United States.

The general picture of Vietnamese adjustment in the United States shows high rates of unemployment, welfare dependency, and poverty, even after several years. Interviews with Vietnamese refugees in southern California reveal generational change and fading traditions among the younger generation.

Many Vietnamese teenagers in southern California have adopted the lifestyle of other low-income American teenagers. Their American friends are of more significance than their Vietnamese heritage in defining their identities. Given social variations and regional differences in adaptation throughout the United States, however, generalizations about "Vietnamese Americans" can be made only with caution.

Khmer Refugees' Interpretation of Their Suffering

Since the late 1970s, over 150,000 people from Kampuchea (formerly Cambodia) have come to the United States as refugees of the Pol Pot regime (Mortland 1994). They survived years of political repression, a difficult escape, and time in refugee camps before arriving in the United States.

Most Khmer refugees were Buddhist when they lived in Kampuchea. They have attempted to understand, within the Buddhist framework of karma, why they experienced such disasters. According to their beliefs, good actions bring good to the individual, family, and community; bad actions bring bad. Thus, many Khmer Buddhists blame themselves for the suffering endured under the Pol Pot regime, thinking that they did something wrong in a previous life. Self-blame and depression characterize many Khmer refugees. Others feel that Buddhism failed, and so they turn in large numbers to Christianity, the dominant faith of the seemingly successful Americans. In recent years, a resurgence of Khmer Buddhism has occurred. Many temples have been constructed, and popular public rituals and celebrations are held in them. For these reviving Buddhists, Christianity either becomes a complementary religion or is rejected as a threat to Buddhism. Changing interpretations arise over time and with new generations. It is difficult to say what the future holds for either the adults who are still trying to make sense of their suffering or for the new generation.

The New Immigrants from South Asia

Hindus of New York City Maintain Their Culture

With the 1965 change in legislation in the United States, a first wave of South Asian immigrants dominated by male professionals from India arrived (Bhardwaj and Rao 1990). Members of this first wave settled primarily in eastern and western cities. Subsequent immigrants from India have been less well educated and less wealthy, and they tend to be concentrated in New York and New Jersey. New York City has the largest population of South Asian Indians in the United States, with about one-eighth of the total number of South Asians in the United States (Mogelonsky 1995).

Members of the highly educated first wave are concentrated in professional fields such as medicine, engineering, and management (Helweg and Helweg 1990). One of the major immigrant groups in Silicon Valley, California, is South Asian Indian. Members of the less educated, later wave find work in family-run businesses or services industries. Indians dominate some trades, such as convenience stores. They have penetrated the ownership of budget hotels and motels and operate nearly half of the total number of establishments in this niche. More than 40 percent of New York City's licensed cab drivers are Indians, Pakistanis, or Bangladeshis (Mogelonsky 1995).

The South Asian Indian population in the United States is one of the better-off immigrant groups, and they are considered an immigrant success story. They place high value on their children's education and urge them to pursue higher education in fields such as medicine and engineering. In the United States, they tend to have small families and to invest heavily in their children's schooling and social advancement.

A continuing concern of many members of the first wave is the maintenance of Hindu cultural values in the face of conflicting patterns prevalent in mainstream American culture, such as dating, premarital sex, drinking, and drugs (Lessinger 1995). The Hindu population increasingly supports the construction of Hindu temples that offer Sunday school classes for young people and cultural events as a way of passing on the Hindu heritage to the next generation. They also attempt to appeal to the youth by accommodating to their lifestyles and preferences in terms of things like the kind of food served after rituals. Vegetarian pizza is now a common menu item for the young people.

Another challenge for Hinduism in the United States and Canada is to establish temples that offer ritual diversity that speaks to Hindus of many varieties. In New York City, the growth of one temple shows how its ritual flexibility helped it to expand. The Ganesha Temple was founded in 1997 under leadership from Hindus from southern India. Temple rituals at first were the same as those conducted in south Indian temples. Over the years, though, in order to widen its reach, the temple expanded its rituals to include those that would appeal to Hindus from other regions of India. The congregation has grown, and the physical structure has expanded to provide for this growth. The daily and yearly cycle had become more elaborate and more varied than what one would find at a typical Hindu temple in south India. The Ganesha temple is a major pilgrimage destination for Hindus who come to New York City from throughout India.

Among the Chinese ethnic population in Canada, the majority come from Hong Kong with much smaller proportions from Taiwan and China. The Hong Kong Chinese immigrants tend to be well-off in economic terms. Many of the male heads of household are "astronauts," leaving their families in Canada while they fly back and forth from Hong Kong to Canada. ■ *Is this a radically new form of household economy and structure, or is it similar to more longstanding patterns?* (Source: © Annie Griffiths Belt/CORBIS)

The New Immigrants from the Former Soviet Union

The breakup of the Soviet Union into fifteen separate countries spurred the movement of over 9 million people throughout Eastern Europe and Central Asia. Many are of Slavic descent and had lived in Central Asia during the existence of the Soviet Union and seek to return to their homelands. Another large category includes people who were forcibly relocated to Siberia or Central Asia. Since 1988, people from the former Soviet Union have been the largest refugee nationality to enter the United States (Littman 1993, cited in Gold 1995).

Soviet Jews Flee Persecution

A sizable proportion of the refugees from the former Soviet Union are Soviet Jews. The largest number of Soviet Jews live in Israel, but since the mid-1960s, over 300,000 have settled in the United States, especially in California (Gold 1995). There are several distinguishing features of the experience of Soviet Jewish refugees. First, their origins in the Soviet Union accustomed them to the fact that the government controlled almost every aspect of life. They were used to a wide range of government services, including jobs, housing, day care, and other basic needs. They have had to find new ways of meeting these needs in a market economy. Second, Soviet Jews, as White Europeans, are members of the dominant racial majority group in the United States. Although Soviet Jews have suffered centuries of discrimination in Eastern Europe, they are much closer to the racial mainstream in the United States. Their education also places them in the elite of new immigrant groups. Third, they have access to established and prosperous communities of American Jews. They have well-connected sponsors when they arrive. Most other new immigrant groups do not have these advantages.

Soviet Jewish immigrants, however, face several challenges. Many have a difficult time finding a job commensurate with their education and previous work in the Soviet Union. In Pittsburgh, Pennsylvania, many Soviet Jewish immigrants remain unemployed or accept menial labor jobs far beneath their qualifications. This is especially true for women who were employed as professionals in the Soviet Union but who can find no work in the United States other than house cleaning or baby sitting. Another major challenge involves marriage options. Cultural norms promote intraethnic marriage, and few Soviet Jews are interested in marrying Americans. However, the number of Soviet Jews in the marriage pool is small. As a result, marriage brokerage businesses have developed that pair young women in Russia with established immigrants in America.

MIGRATION POLICIES AND POLITICS IN A GLOBALIZING WORLD

Globalization and the increase in migration have attracted more attention to this issue on the part of anthropologists and other social scientists. The major questions raised concern national and international policies of inclusion and exclusion of particular categories of people. The human rights of various categories of migrants vary dramatically. Migrants of all sorts, including long-standing migratory groups such as pastoralists and horticulturalists, seek to find ways of protecting their lifestyles, maintaining their health, and building a sense of the future.

Inclusion and Exclusion

National policies that set quotas on the quantity and types of immigrants who are welcome and that determine how they are treated are largely dictated by political and economic interests. Even in the cases of seemingly humanitarian quotas, governments undertake a cost–benefit analysis of how much will be gained and how much will be lost. Governments show their political support or disapproval of other governments through their immigration policies. One of the most obvious economic factors affecting policy is labor flow. Cheap—even illegal—immigrant labor is used around the world to maintain profits for businesses and services for the better-off. Flows of such labor undermine labor unions and the status of established workers.

In the United States, immigration law specifies who will be allowed entry and what benefits the government will provide. A court case from 1915 presents issues that still prevail today (*Gegiow* v. *Uhl*, 1915). The case concerned a number of Russian laborers seeking to enter the United States. Only one member of the group spoke some English, and all had very little money. Their intention was to settle in Portland, Oregon. The acting commissioner of immigration in the port of New York denied them entry on the grounds that they were "likely to become public charges" because employment conditions in Portland were such that they probably would be unable to obtain work. The "aliens" seeking entry obtained legal counsel, and the case eventually went to the Supreme Court, where the decision was handed down by Chief Justice Oliver Wendell Holmes. He focused on "whether an alien can be declared likely to become a public charge on the ground that the labor market in the city of his immediate . . . destination is overstocked." The relevant statute, Holmes declared, deals with admission to the United States, not to a particular city within it. Further, Holmes commented that a commissioner of immigration is not empowered to make decisions about possible overstocking of labor in all of the United States, for that is a matter in the hands of the President.

National immigration policies are played out in local communities. In some instances, local resentments are associated with a so-called **lifeboat mentality**, which seeks to limit enlarging a particular group because of perceived resource constraints. Influxes of immigrants who compete for jobs have led to hostility in many parts of Europe and North America. Some observers have labeled this *working-class racism* because it emerges out of competition with immigrants for jobs and other benefits (Cole 1996).

The number of immigrants has grown substantially in southern Italy since the early 1980s. In the city of Palermo, with a total population of 800,000, there are between 15,000 and 30,000 immigrants from Africa, Asia, and elsewhere. Does the theory of working-class racism apply to the working class in Palermo? Two conditions seem to predict that it would: large numbers of foreign immigrants and a high rate of unemployment. However, instead of expressing racist condemnation of the immigrants, working-class residents of Palermo accept the immigrants as fellow poor people. One critical factor may be the lack of competition for jobs, which derives from the fact that working Palmeritans and immigrants occupy different niches. Immigrant jobs are less desirable, more stigmatized, and less well-paying. African immigrant men work in bars and restaurants, as building cleaners, or as itinerant street vendors. African and Asian women work as domestic servants in the better-off neigh-

borhoods. Sicilians do refer to immigrants by certain racial/ethnic names, but these seem to be used interchangeably and imprecisely. For example, a common term for all immigrants, Asian or African, is *tuichi*, which means *Turks*. The word can be applied teasingly to a Sicilian as well and in conversation may connote alarm, as in "Mom, the Turks!" Other loosely applied terms are the Italian words for Moroccans, Blacks, and Tunisians. In a questionnaire given to school children, the great majority agreed with the statement that "a person's race is not important." The tolerance among Palermo's working class may be only temporary. Nonetheless, it suggests that researchers take a closer look at cases elsewhere that require a loosening up of the theory of working-class racism against immigrants.

Recent politically conservative trends in the United States have succeeded in rolling back more progressive policies about immigration and minorities. Police raids in areas thought to have many undocumented migrants have brought mass expulsion. Reversals of affirmative action in college admissions, initiated in California in the late 1990s, gained widespread support among "nativist" Americans. This lifeboat mentality of exclusiveness and privilege is held mainly by the dominant White majority and others who have "made it."

Migration and Human Rights

Several questions arise in the context of anthropological inquiry about migration and human rights. One important question is whether migration is forced or voluntary (see the Critical Thinking box). Forced migration itself may be considered a violation of a person's human rights.

In January 2004, more than 50,000 Russian immigrants to Israel returned to Russia. Motivations for the move back include the difficult living conditions for many Russian immigrants in Israel, violence, and the improving economic situation in Russia. Nonetheless, people from Russia continue to migrate to Israel, and they now number over one million people, about 13 percent of the population. ■ *Learn how many people left Russia after the break-up of the Soviet Union in 1989 and where they went.* (Source: © David H. Wells/CORBIS)

Critical Thinking

HAITIAN CANE CUTTERS IN THE DOMINICAN REPUBLIC—A CASE OF STRUCTURE OR HUMAN AGENCY?

THE CIRCULATION of male labor from villages in Haiti to work on sugar estates in the neighboring Dominican Republic is the oldest and perhaps largest continuing population movement within the Caribbean region (Martínez 1996). Beginning in the early twentieth century, Dominican sugar cane growers began to recruit Haitian workers called *braceros*. Between 1852 and 1986, an agreement between the two countries' governments regulated and organized the labor recruitment. Since then, recruitment has become a private matter, with men crossing the border on their own or with recruiters working in Haiti without official approval.

Many studies and reports have addressed this system of labor migration. Two competing perspectives exist. The structurist position (View 1) says that the bracero system is neo-slavery and a clear violation of human rights. The human agency position (View 2) says that braceros are not slaves because they migrate voluntarily.

View 1

Supporters of this position point to interviews with Haitian braceros in the Dominican Republic that indicate, they say, a consistent pattern of labor rights abuses. Haitian recruiters approach poor men, and boys as young as seven years old, and promise them easy, well-paid employment in the Dominican Republic. Those who agree to go are taken to the frontier on foot and then either transported directly to a sugar estate in the Dominican Republic or turned over to Dominican soldiers for a fee for each recruit and then passed on to the sugar estate. Once there, the workers are given only one option for survival: cutting sugar cane, for which even the most experienced workers can earn only about US$2 a day. Working and living conditions on the estates are bad. The cane cutters are coerced into working even if they are ill, and working hours start before dawn and extend into the night. Many estate owners prevent Haitian laborers from leaving by having armed guards patrol the estate grounds at night. Many of the workers say that they cannot save enough from their meager wages to return home.

View 2

According to this view, reports of coercion are greatly exaggerated and miss the point that most Haitian labor migrants cross the border of their own volition. On the basis of his fieldwork in Haiti, anthropologist Samuel Martínez comments that "Recruitment by force in Haiti seems virtually unheard of. On the contrary, if this is a system of slavery, it may be the first in history to *turn away* potential recruits" (20). Some recruits have even paid bribes to recruiters in order to be hired. Most people, even young people, are aware of the terrible working conditions in the Dominican Republic, so they are exercising informed choice when they decide to migrate. Repeat migration is common and is further evidence of free choice. The major means of maintaining labor discipline and productivity on the sugar estates is not force but wage incentives, especially piece-work. The life histories of braceros show that many of them move from one estate to another; this discredits the view that the estates are "concentration camps."

However, Martínez does raise the issue of how free the "choice" to migrate to the Dominican Republic really is, given the extreme poverty in which many Haitians live. In Haiti few work opportunities exist, and the prevailing wage for rural workers is US$1 a day. Thus the poor are not truly free to choose to work in their home country: Labor migration to the Dominican Republic becomes a necessity. What looks like a free choice to participate in the bracero system is actually "illusory" or structured choice. It is based on the unavailability of the option to work for a decent wage in Haiti and on the forced, or structured, choice to work in the Dominican Republic.

CRITICAL THINKING QUESTIONS

What are the comparative strengths of View 1 and View 2?

What does each perspective support in terms of policy recommendations?

How does the concept of structured choice change those policy recommendations?

Another question concerns whether members of a displaced group have a guaranteed **right of return**, or repatriation, to their homeland. The right of return, which has been considered a basic human right in the West since the time of the Magna Carta, is included in the United Nations General Assembly Resolution 194 passed in 1948. It was elevated by the UN in 1974 to an "inalienable right."

The right of return is an enduring issue for Palestinian refugees, of whom hundreds of thousands fled or were driven from their homes during the 1948 war (Zureik 1994). They went mainly to Jordan, the West Bank/East Jerusalem, Gaza, Lebanon, Syria, and other Arab states. Jordan and Syria have granted Palestinian refugees rights equal to those of their citizens. In Lebanon, where estimates of the number of Palestinian refugees range between 200,000 and 600,000, the government refuses them such rights (Salam 1994). The lower number is favored by Israel because it makes the problem seem less severe; the higher number is favored by the Palestinians to highlight the seriousness of their plight and by the Lebanese government to emphasize its inability to absorb so many. Palestinians know that they are not welcome in Lebanon, but they cannot return to Israel because Israel denies them the right of return. Israel responds to the Palestinians' claims by saying that their acceptance of Jewish immigrants from Arab countries constitutes an equal exchange.

Protecting Migrants' Health

The health risks to migrants are many and varied because of the wide variety of migrant types and situations. Migrants whose livelihood depends on long-standing migratory economic systems, such as foraging, horticulture, and pastoralism, constitute one area of concern. Given the frequency in recent decades of drought and food shortages in the Sahel region of Africa, anthropologists are conducting studies to see how such conditions can be prevented, monitored, and more effectively coped with through humanitarian aid (see the Lessons Applied box).

Lessons Applied

STUDYING PASTORALISTS' MOVEMENTS FOR RISK ASSESSMENT AND SERVICE DELIVERY

PASTORALISTS ARE often vulnerable to malnutrition as a consequence of climate changes, fluctuations in food supply, and war and political upheaval. Because of their spatial mobility, they are difficult to reach with relief aid during a crisis. Cultural anthropologists are devising ways to gather and manage basic information about pastoralists' movements and nutritional needs in order to provide improved service delivery (Watkins and Fleisher 2002). The data required for such proactive planning include

1. Information on the number of migrants and the size of their herds in a particular location and at a particular time. Such data can inform planners about the level of services required for public health programs, educational programs, and veterinary services. This information can be used to assess the demand on particular grazing areas and water sources and is therefore important in predicting possible future crises.

2. Information on patterns of migratory movements. This information can enable planners to move services to where the people are rather than expecting people to move to the services. Some NGOs, for example, are providing mobile banking services and mobile veterinary services. Information about pastoralist movements can be used as an early warning to prevent social conflicts that might result if several groups arrived in the same place at the same time. And con-

flict resolution mechanisms can be put in place more effectively if conflict does occur.

The data collection involves interviews with pastoralists, often with one or two key informants, whom the anthropologists select for their specialized knowledge. Interviews cover topics such as the migratory paths followed (both typical and atypical), population levels, herd sizes, and the nutritional and water requirements of people and animals. Given the complex social systems of pastoralists, the data gathering must also include group leadership, decision-making practices, and concepts about land and water rights.

The anthropologists organize this information into a computerized database, linking the ethnographical data with geographic information systems (GIS) data on the environment and climate information from satellites. The anthropologists can then construct various scenarios and assess the relative risks that they pose to the people's health. Impending crises can be foreseen, and warning can be provided to governments and international aid agencies.

FOOD FOR THOUGHT

The tracking system described here remains outside the control of the pastoralists themselves. How might it be managed so that they participate more meaningfully and gain greater autonomy?

KEY CONCEPTS

SUGGESTED READINGS

Rogaia Mustafa Abusharaf. *Wanderings: Sudanese Migrants and Exiles in North America*. Ithaca, NY: Cornell University Press, 2002. This book explores the topic of Sudanese migration to the United States and Canada. The author provides historical background on the first wave, information on various Sudanese groups who have migrated, and an interpretation of Sudanese identity in North America as more unified than it is in the homeland.

Linda Basch, Nina Glick Schiller, and Christina Blanc Szanton. *Nations Unbound: Transnational Projects, Postcolonial Predicaments, and Deterritorialized Nation–States*. Langhorne, PA: Gordon and Breach Science Publishers, 1994. Eight chapters explore theoretical issues in transnational migration and present detailed analyses of cases of migration from the Caribbean, including St. Vincent, Grenada, and Haiti.

Colin Clarke, Ceri Peach, and Steven Vertovic, eds. *South Asians Overseas: Migration and Ethnicity*. New York: Cambridge University Press, 1990. The text includes fifteen chapters plus introductory essays that place the case studies in a broader context. Chapters are divided into two sections: South Asians in colonial and post-colonial contexts and South Asians in contemporary Western countries and the Middle East.

Sherri Grasmuck and Patricia R. Pessar. *Between Two Islands: Dominican International Migration*. Berkeley: University of California Press, 1991. Based on fieldwork in the Dominican Republic and New York City, this volume focuses on social ties and networks facilitating migration from rural areas in the Dominican Republic to Santo Domingo and from the Dominican Republic to the United States, and on how employment opportunities shape the migration experience.

Josiah McC. Heyman. *Finding a Moral Heart for U.S. Immigration Policy: An Anthropological Perspective*. Washington, DC: American Ethnological Society, Monograph Series, Number 7, 1998. An applied anthropology perspective inspires this critique of current U.S. immigration policy, finding it to be basically anti-immigrationist. The author suggests steps toward a more inclusive policy and discusses unresolved challenges and dilemmas.

Helen Morton Lee. *Tongans Overseas: Between Two Shores*. Honolulu: University of Hawai'i Press, 2003. The author, who had done fieldwork in Tonga, turns her attention to young Tongan migrants in Australia. She combines fieldwork in Melbourne with extensive research of the messages on a Tongan Internet forum called Kava Bowl, complemented with e-mail interviews of people who participate in the forum. The book focuses on the changing and varied aspects of young Tongan migrants' identify, ties to family in Tonga, and changing aspirations.

Beatriz Manz, *Refugees of a Hidden War: The Aftermath of Counterinsurgency in Guatemala*. Albany: State University of New York Press, 1988. This study was conducted to assess whether conditions would allow the return to Guatemala of 46,000 Indian peasant refugees living in camps in Mexico. It focuses on aspects of family and community life in the camps and in resettled villages in Guatemala where the Indians face discrimination and harassment from the military.

Jennifer Robertson. *Native and Newcomer: Making and Remaking a Japanese City*. Berkeley: University of California Press, 1991. This ethnography addresses the social and symbolic adjustments of native residents of Kodaira city and the many residents who moved to Kodaira beginning in the 1950s. Detailed attention is given to the role of a community festival in expressing links between the natives and newcomers, while also stating and maintaining group boundaries.

Archana B. Verma. *The Making of Little Punjab in Canada: Patterns of Immigration*. Thousand Oaks, CA; Sage Publications, 2002. This book traces the historical connections between Hindu migrants from Paldi village, in India's northern state of Punjab, to Vancouver Island, British Columbia. Strong family and kinship ties continue to link the migrants to their home area. Caste group solidarity among the migrants provides support in the face of discrimination on the part of the wider Canadian society.

WHAT are the major categories of migration?

Migrants are classified as internal, international, or transnational. Another category is based on the migrants' reason for moving. On this dimension, migrants are classified as labor migrants, institutional migrants, or displaced persons. People's adjustment to their new situations depends on the degree of voluntarism involved in the move, the degree of cultural difference between the place of origin and the destination, and how closely expectations about the new location are met especially in terms of making a living and establishing social ties. Displaced persons are one of the fastest-growing categories of migrants. Refugees, fleeing from political persecution or warfare face serious adjustment challenges because they often leave their home countries with few material resources and frequently have experienced much psychological suffering. The number of internally displaced persons is growing even faster than the number of refugees. Dams and other large-scale development projects result in thousands of people becoming IDPs. Internally displaced persons do not fall under the purview of international organizations such as the United Nations, but their situation is attracting the attention of a global consortium of governments and nongovernmental organizations.

WHAT are examples of the new immigrants in the United States and Canada?

Worldwide, the "new immigrants" are contributing to growing transnational connections and to the formation of increasingly multicultural populations within states. In the United States, the new immigrants from Latin America are the fastest-growing category. Immigrants from East and South Asia, who are more likely than others to have immigrated to the United States voluntarily, have achieved greater levels of economic success than most other new immigrant groups. Immigrant groups throughout the world are likely to face certain forms of discrimination in their new destinations, although the degree to which it occurs varies with the level of perceived resource competition from residents already settled.

HOW do anthropologists contribute to migration policies and programs?

Anthropologists have studied national and international migration policies and practices in terms of social inclusion and exclusion. Fieldwork in particular contexts reveals a range of patterns between local residents and immigrants. Working-class resentment among local people against immigrants is not universal and varies with the overall amount and type of employment available. Anthropologists study possible infringements of the human rights on migrants, especially in terms of the degree of voluntarism in their move and the conditions they face in the destination area. Gathering data on migratory movements of long-mobile people, such as pastoralists, can help make humanitarian aid programs more timely and effective.

THE BIG QUESTIONS

- **HOW** do cultural anthropologists study change?

- **WHAT** are various approaches to development?

- **WHAT** does cultural anthropology contribute to understanding some major issues in development?

16

DEVELOPMENT ANTHROPOLOGY

Rock paintings in Arnhemland, Australia, an important site for the Kunwinjku people. Arnhemland stretches across the northern part of the country and is the largest Aboriginal reserve in Australia. *(Source: © Penny Tweedy/Panos Pictures)*

We have had many visitors to Walpole Island since the French 'discovered us' in the seventeenth century in our territory, Bkejwanong. In many cases, these visitors failed to recognize who we were and to appreciate our traditions. They tried to place us in their European framework of knowledge, denying that we possessed our indigenous knowledge. They attempted to steal our lands, water, and knowledge. We resisted. They left and never came back. We continued to share our knowledge with the next visitors to our place . . . . It was a long-term strategy that has lasted more than three hundred years" (Dr. Dean Jacobs, Executive Director of Walpole Island First Nation, from his Foreword in VanWynsberghe 2002:ix).

The Walpole Island First Nation, located in Ontario, Canada, north of Michigan, has taken strong action in recent decades to protect its culture and environment. Its citizens have organized themselves and successfully fought to control industrial waste that was polluting its water source and land. They have regained their pride and integrity.

All cultures go through change, but the causes, processes, and outcomes are varied. Cultural change can be intentional or accidental, forward-looking or backward-looking, rapid or gradual, obvious or subtle, beneficial or harmful.

Anthropologists contribute to the understanding of how humanity has changed and how it continues to change. Biological anthropologists who study human evolution and humanity's relationship with nonhuman primates have the longest view. They look back many thousands—even millions—of years to learn how human biology and culture emerged. Archaeologists examine human cultural remains, from both prehistory and history, to discover how and when people migrated throughout the world and how social complexity developed. Linguistic anthropologists study the evolution of communication patterns and capabilities in prehistoric times, the spread and change in verbal and written languages with the emergence of settled life and of the state, and change in contemporary patterns of communication, including the effects of mass media.

In contrast to these three fields of anthropology, cultural anthropology's roots lie in the **synchronic** study of culture, or a "one-time" snapshot view of culture with minimal or no attention to the past. This early approach led to a static view of culture, perpetuating the images of cultures presented by ethnographers of, say, the 1960s or 1970s as though they had continuing validity decades later. Cultural anthropologists are still attempting to move away from such time-static approaches. They are paying more attention to cultural history and to studying cultures through time, replacing the synchronic approach with a **diachronic** (across-time) approach.

This chapter focuses on the topic of contemporary cultural change as shaped by development, which is directed change to achieve improved human welfare. The subject matter constitutes the important subfield of **development anthropology**, or the study of how culture and development interact. We consider general processes of cultural change in the first part of the chapter and contemporary theories and models in the second part. In the last section, we look in detail at three major issues in development anthropology: indigenous people, women, and human rights.

TWO PROCESSES OF CULTURAL CHANGE

When all is said and done, two basic processes drive all cultural change. The first is internal: the discovery of something new. The second is external: incorporation of something new from the outside. In this section, we consider some examples of cultural change brought about by each of these general processes.

Invention

The invention of something new may prompt cultural change. Inventions usually evolve gradually, through stepwise experimentation and accumulation of knowledge, but some appear suddenly. We can all name many technological inventions that have created cultural change—for example, the printing press, gun powder, polio vaccine, and satellite communication. Concepts, such as Jeffersonian notions of democracy, are also inventions.

Not all inventions have positive social outcomes. Even innovations inspired by a socially positive goal may turn out to have mixed or even negative social effects. (See the Critical Thinking box on page 370.)

Diffusion

Diffusion is the spread of culture—including technology and ways of behaving and thinking—through contact. It is logically related to invention because new discoveries are likely to spread. Diffusion can occur in several ways. First, in mutual borrowing, two societies that are roughly equal in power and level of development exchange aspects of their culture. For example, in the mid-twentieth century, the United States exported rock and roll music to England, and England in turn exported the Beatles to the United States. Second, diffusion may occur between unequal societies, involving a transfer from a dominant culture to a less powerful culture. This process may occur through force or, more subtly, through education or marketing processes that promote adoption of new practices and beliefs. For example, through the Peace Corps, the United States spreads many American practices and beliefs to developing countries. Third, a more powerful culture may appropriate aspects of a less powerful culture (the latter process is called cultural imperialism). For example, the Tower of London in England is full of priceless jewels from India.

In each of these types of diffusion, the result is some degree of *acculturation,* or change in one culture as a result of contact with another culture. At one extreme, a culture may become so thoroughly acculturated that it has become **assimilated,** no longer distinguishable as having a separate identity. In many cases, cultural change through diffusion has led to extreme change in the "receiving" culture, which becomes "deculturated," or extinct. Such deculturation has occurred among many indigenous people as the result of the introduction of new technology. (See the Lessons Applied box on page 372.) Other responses to acculturative influences include partial acceptance of something new with reformulation and reshaping, as in the case of cricket in the Trobriands (Chapter 14), or resistance and rejection. The study of international development is, in fact, concerned with the dynamics and results of a particular form of diffusion—that of Western goods, behavior, and values through international aid.

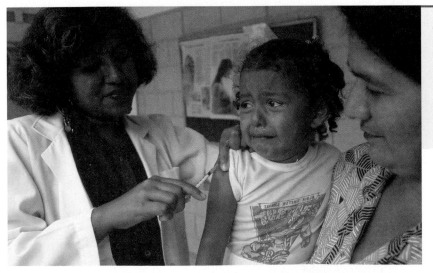

A doctor administering polio vaccine in Ecuador. The Pan American Health Organization (PAHO) established a plan in 1985 for eradicating the poliovirus from the Americas by 1990. ■ *Did they achieve their goal? If yes, when? If no, what is the current status of their effort?* (Source: © Jeremy Horner/CORBIS)

Critical Thinking

SOCIAL EFFECTS OF THE GREEN REVOLUTION

AGRICULTURAL SCIENTISTS of the 1950s, inspired by the laudable goal of eliminating world hunger, developed genetic variations of wheat, rice, and corn. These high-yielding varieties (HYV) of seeds were promoted to farmers throughout the developing world as part of the "Green Revolution" that would feed the planet by boosting production per acre. In most places where Green Revolution agricultural practices were adopted, grain production did increase. Was world hunger conquered? The answer is no, because world hunger is not merely a problem of production; it also involves distribution.

Analyses of the social impact of the Green Revolution in India reveal that one of its results was to increase disparities between the rich and the poor (Frankel 1971). How did this happen? Green Revolution agriculture requires several expensive inputs: purchased seeds (HYV seeds cannot be harvested from the crop and saved until the next year bcause they are hybridized), the heavy use of commercial fertilizers, and dependable irrigation sources. Thus farmers who could use HYV seeds successfully tended to be those who were already better off than others; they were selected for the innovation because they could afford such inputs. Small farmers who tried planting HYV seeds but could not provide these inputs experienced crop failure, went deeper into debt, and ended up having to sell the small amounts of land they had. Larger and better-off farmers took advantage of these new openings in the land market to accumulate more land and expand their holdings. With the acquisition of tractors and other mechanized equipment, large farmers became even more productive. Small farm-

ers were unable to compete and continued to be squeezed out financially. They became hired day laborers, dependent on seasonal employment by large farmers, or they migrated to cities where they became part of the urban underclass.

Looking at the Green Revolution from a critical thinking perspective, we may see more clearly whose interests were served, whether this was the original intention or not. The big winners included the companies involved in selling chemical fertilizers (largely petroleum-based) and HYV seeds; companies that manufactured and sold mechanized farm equipment; the larger farmers whose income levels improved; and the research scientists themselves, who gained funding for their research and world fame for their discoveries. In retrospect, it is difficult to imagine that early planners in the 1950s could have been so naive as not to realize whom they would be helping and whom they might end up hurting.

CRITICAL THINKING QUESTIONS

Is it likely that the original innovators of HYV grains considered what social transformations might occur in developing countries' agriculture as a result of their invention?

Would they have been likely to stop their research if they had realized that it would lead to the "rich getting richer and the poor getting poorer"? Should they have done so?

How does this example shed light on current debates about genetically modified food?

APPROACHES TO DEVELOPMENT

In this section we consider the theories of and approaches to international development that are applied by various kinds of institutions, from large-scale ones to small grass-roots organizations. We look closely at the development project as the main mechanism that such organizations use in their efforts to bring about change. Special meth-

ods employed by anthropologists who work in the field of development are the last topic in this section.

Theories and Models

This section discusses five theories or models of change that influence approaches to international development. They differ mainly in terms of the importance that they attach to economic growth versus equitable distribution of resources, in which measures of development they assume are most meaningful (for example, income versus health or education), and in the degree to which they take into account the environmental and financial sustainability of particular development goals.

Modernization

Modernization theory refers to change marked by industrialization, consolidation of the nation–state, bureaucratization, market economy, technological innovation, literacy, and options for social mobility. It derives from a period in Western European history beginning in the seventeenth century, which emphasized the importance of secular rationality and the inevitable advance of scientific thinking (Norgaard 1994). Modernization appears as almost an inevitable process that will, given the insights of science and rationality, spread throughout the world and lead to improvement in people's lives everywhere. Overall, the emphasis of modernization is on material progress and individual betterment.

Supporters and critics of modernization are found in both rich and poor countries. Supporters claim that the benefits of modernization (improved transportation; electricity; domestic comforts such as air conditioning; and technology such as washing machines, biomedical health care, and telecommunications) are worth the costs—whether those costs are calculated in terms of environmental or social costs. Other scholars in many disciplines—from literary studies to anthropology—regard modernization as problematic. Most cultural anthropologists are critics of modernization as a general process of social change because it leads to increased social inequality, the destruction of indigenous cultures, ecological ruin, and an overall decline in global cultural diversity (selected aspects of modernity, however, such as electricity and antibiotics, may be accepted as positive). In spite of strong cautionary critiques from anthropologists and environmentalists about the negative effects of modernization, nations around the world have not slowed their attempts to achieve it.

Growth-Oriented Development

International development emerged as a prominent theory about change after World War II, at the same time that the United States began to expand its role as a world leader. One can think of **development** as the attempt, through conscious planning and intervention, to bring the benefits of modernization to the developing world. Indeed, international development, as conceived by major development institutions such as the World Bank, is similar to modernization in terms of its ultimate goals. The process, however, emphasizes economic growth as the most crucial element in development. According to this theory, investments in economic growth in some sectors of the population will subsequently support (through the

"trickle-down" effect) wider achievement of improved human welfare, such as health and education. Since the 1950s, the United States has emphasized economic development in its foreign aid packages, especially the transfer of Western economic expertise (in the form of advisors) and technology (such as agricultural equipment) to developing countries. Promoting growth-oriented development in poor nations, as practiced by most large-scale development organizations, includes two major economic strategies:

- Increasing economic productivity and trade through, for example, new forms of agriculture, irrigation, and markets.

- Reducing government expenditures on public services such as schools and health in order to reduce debt and reallocate resources to uses perceived to be more directly related to increased production. This strategy, called **structural adjustment**, has been promoted by the World Bank since the 1980s.

The growth-oriented development model is being powerfully spread throughout the world under the current intensified pattern of economic and political globalization along the lines of the U.S. patterns. As noted in Chapter 1, cultural anthropologists are now taking up the research challenge presented by intensified globalization to study its effects on local cultures—and the effects of those cultures on efforts at globalization.

Distributional Development

In contrast to the growth-oriented approach, a distributional approach to development views poverty as the result of global economic and political factors such as world trade imbalances between nations and unequal distribution of resources within nations and communities. This approach, which takes a structural view, rejects the claim of other approaches that poverty is caused by some inadequacy on the part of poor people or poor countries themselves (Rahnema 1992). In terms of poverty reduction, its position is based on evidence that growth-oriented strategies applied without concern for distribution result in increased social inequality, with the "rich getting richer and the poor getting poorer."

The distributional approach takes a critical view of structural adjustment as promoted by those favoring the growth model, because it further undermines the welfare of the poor by removing the few entitlements they had in the form of services. Advocates of the distributional model insist on the need to readjust access to crucial resources within countries in order to enhance the ability of the poor to produce and provide for their own needs. Within a particular country, this perspective involves the following strategies, which differ markedly from the growth approach (Gardner and Lewis 1996).

Lessons Applied

THE SAAMI, SNOWMOBILES, AND THE NEED FOR SOCIAL IMPACT ANALYSIS

HOW WILL adoption of a new belief or practice benefit or harm a particular culture and its various members? This question is difficult to answer, but it must always be asked. A classic study of the "snowmobile disaster" among a Saami group in Finland offers a careful response to this question in a context of rapid techno-logical diffusion (Pelto 1973). In the 1950s, the Saami of Finland (previously referred to by outsiders as Lapps, which, in the Saami language, is a derogatory term) had an economy based on fishing and reindeer herding, which provided most of their diet. Reindeer had several other important economic and social functions. They were used as draft animals, especially in the hauling of wood for fuel. Their hides were made into clothing and their sinews used for sewing. Reindeer were key items of exchange, both in external trade and internal gift-giv-ing. A child was given a reindeer to mark the appear-ance of its first tooth. When a couple became engaged, they exchanged a reindeer with each other to mark the commitment. Reindeer were the most important wed-ding gift. Each summer the herds were let free, and then they were rounded up in the fall, a time of communal festivity.

By the 1960s, all this had changed because of the introduction of the snowmobile. Previously, the men had tended the reindeer herds on skis. The introduction of snowmobiles into herd management had several results.

The herds were no longer kept closely domesticated for part of the year, during which they became tame. Instead, they were allowed to roam freely all year and thus became wilder. On snowmobiles, the men would cover larger amounts of territory at round-up time to bring in the animals, and sometimes several round-ups occurred instead of one.

Herd size declined dramatically. The reasons for the decline included the stress inflicted on the reindeer by the extra distance traveled during round-ups, the multi-ple round-ups instead of a single one, and the fear aroused by the noisy snowmobiles. Round-ups were held at a time when the females were near the end of their pregnancy, another factor inducing reproductive stress. As the number of snowmobiles increased, the number of reindeer decreased.

Another economic change involved dependence on the outside through links to the cash economy. Cash was needed in order to purchase a snowmobile, to buy gaso-line, and to pay for parts and repairs. This delocalization of the economy led to social inequality, which had not existed before:

- The cash cost of effective participation in herding exceeded the resources of some families, who there-fore had to drop out of serious participation in herding.

The first step—called *resource assessment*—is to do research on the social distribution of access to critical resources (see Table 16.1 on page 374). The next step, called *cultural assessment*, involves research on the pos-itive or negative effects of development projects on the culture, with special attention to internal social variation (see Table 16.2 on page 374 for an example using a reset-tlement project). The third step is *redistribution of criti-cal resources*, especially land, to take into account inequities discovered in the first two steps. The last step is implementation of *assistance programs*, which are another way to achieve greater social equity through the targeted provision of services such as health care and edu-cation.

Many conservative economists argue on economic grounds that redistribution is not a realistic or a feasible strategy. Nevertheless, anthropologists have reported

cases in which the redistribution model has worked. Anthropological research in Nadur village, Kerala, posed the question of whether redistribution was an effective and realistic development strategy (Franke 1993). The answer was yes. Kerala's per capita income is low in comparison to the rest of India and to the rest of the world. Yet although income remained low and stagnant, substantial material improvements occurred in many people's lives, including some of the poorest of the poor. How did this happen? Redistribution was not the result of a socialist revolution; it took place through democrat-ic channels—protests and pressure on the government by people's groups and labor unions. These groups forced the state to reallocate land ownership, shifting some land to the landless and thereby reducing inequal-ity (although not eradicating it completely). In other instances, people pressured government leaders to

- The use of snowmobiles changed the age pattern of reindeer herding in favor of youth over age; thus older herders were squeezed out.
- The snowmobile pushed many Saami into debt.
- The dependence on cash and indebtedness forced many Saami to migrate to cities for work.

Pertti Pelto, the anthropologist who documented this case, terms these transformations a disaster for Saami culture. He offers some recommendations that might be helpful for the future: The lesson of the Saami, and of some other groups, should be presented to communities that are confronting development issues before they adopt new technology so that they will better understand the potential consequences; any group facing change should have a chance to weigh evidence on the pros and cons and make an informed judgment—something that the Saami had no opportunity to do. Pelto's work is thus one of the early warnings from anthropology about the need for **social impact assessments**, studies that gauge the potential social costs and benefits of particular innovations before the change is undertaken.

FOOD FOR THOUGHT

Speculate about what the Saami might have done if they had been able to consider a social impact assessment of the effects of snowmobiles on their culture.

The Saami are an indigenous Nordic people currently living in the two countries of Norway and Finland. Since the 1980s they have been fighting for legal rights in the countries where they live and, more broadly, in the Nordic Council, a regional association in which they have no representation. Saami activists are working on many issues including land rights, water rights, natural resource rights, language rights, other cultural rights, and political representation. ■ *Find out about the Nordic Council—its membership and goals—and get an updated status report on the Saami people's relationship to the Council.* (Source: © Staffan Widstrand/CORBIS)

improve village conditions by improving the schools, providing school lunches for poor children, and increasing attendance by dalit children. Throughout the 1960s and 1970s, Nadur village became a better place to live, for many people.

Human Development

Yet another contrast to "growth-first" strategies is called **human development**, the strategy that emphasizes investing in human welfare. The United Nations adopted the phrase *human development* to emphasize the need for improvements in human welfare in terms of health, education, and personal security and safety. According to this approach, improvements in human welfare will lead to overall development of the nation. We know that the reverse is not invariably true: The level of economic

growth of a country (or region within a country) is not necessarily correlated with its level of human development. Obviously, the relationship between poverty and development is more complex than one might assume. Some poor countries—and some areas within countries, such as India's Kerala state—have achieved higher levels of human development than their GNP or GDP would predict. Thus, in this view, economic growth is not an end in itself. The goal of development should be improved levels of human welfare.

Sustainable Development

A fourth position questions the long-term financial and environmental viability of the single-minded pursuit of economic growth. According to this view, the economic growth achieved by the wealthy nations has occurred at

TABLE 16.1 Key Questions in Assessing Resources

What are the most important resources available in the society?

How is access to these resources organized?

- Are key resources shared in the community, or do some people or groups have greater access than others?
- Are there obvious economic differences within the community? If so, what are they?
- Are key resources shared within the household, or do some members have greater access than others?

What is the distribution of decision-making power?

- Are some people or groups denied a voice?
- Do some people or groups have particular interests? If so, what are they?

Are these factors taken into consideration in the development policy or project?

Source: Adapted from Gardner and Lewis 1996:86.

TABLE 16.2 Key Questions in Assessing the Cultural Effects of a Resettlement Project

How are local property relations organized in the original location?

- What access do different groups have to property or other key resources?
- What goods are highly valued?
- What are the inheritance patterns?

How is work organized?

- What are the main tasks done and during what seasons?
- What is the division of labor by gender and age?
- What is the role of kinship in allocating labor?

How is the household organized?

- Who lives where and with whom?
- How is decision making allocated within the household?
- Are there notable differences in household organization within the community? If so, what are they and how do they change over time?

What is the local political structure?

- Do some people or groups monopolize power?
- Are some groups marginalized?

How suitable is the proposed relocation site and plan, given the above economic, social, and political findings?

Source: Adapted from Gardner and Lewis 1996:89.

great cost to the environment and cannot be sustained at its present level. Since the 1980s, the term **sustainable development**, or forms of development that do not destroy nonrenewable resources and are financially supportable, has gained prominence in international development circles.

Institutional Approaches to Development

Cultural anthropologists have become increasingly aware of the importance of examining the institutions and organizations involved in international development. This knowledge helps cultural anthropologists have a greater impact on how development is done. They have studied the management systems of large-scale institutions such as the World Bank, as well as "local" management systems found in diverse settings. They have also examined several aspects of behavior within the institutions themselves, including internal hierarchies and inequalities, social interactions, symbols of power, and institutional discourse. This section first describes some of the major development institutions and then discusses smaller, grassroots institutions.

Large-Scale Institutions

Large-scale development institutions can be separated into the *multilaterals* (those that include several nations as donors) and the *bilaterals* (those that involve a relationship between only two countries, a donor and a recipient). The major multilaterals are the United Nations and

the World Bank, each constituting a vast and complex social system. The United Nations, established in 1945, includes over 160 member states, each contributing an amount of money assessed according to its ability and each given one vote in the General Assembly (Fasulo 2003). The United States, Germany, and Japan are major contributors. Several UN agencies exist, fulfilling a range of functions (see Table 16.3). In all its units combined, the UN employs about 50,000 people.

The World Bank is supported by contributions from over 150 member countries. Founded in 1944 at a conference called by President Roosevelt in Bretton Woods, New Hampshire, "the Bank" is dedicated to promoting the concept of economic growth and expanded purchasing power throughout the world (Rich 1994). The main strategy is to promote international investment through loans. The World Bank is guided by a Board of Governors made up of the finance ministers of member countries. Rather than following the UN's approach of one country–one vote, the World Bank system assigns each country a number of votes based on the size of the country's financial commitment: "There is no pretense of equality—the economic superpowers run the show" (Hancock 1989:51).

TABLE 16.3 **Major Agencies within the United Nations Related to Development**

Agency	Headquarters	Function
UNDP (The United Nations Development Program)	New York City, U.S.	UNDP provides many different services designed to help a country in planning and managing its own development: groundwater and mineral exploration, computer and satellite technology, seed production and agricultural extension, and research. UNDP does not itself implement projects; that is done through 29 "executing agencies," some of which are listed here.
FAO (The Food and Agricultural Organization)	Rome, Italy	FAO implements agricultural field projects that receive funding from the UNDP as well as "host governments."
WHO (The World Health Organization)	Geneva, Switzerland	WHO has four goals: developing and organizing personnel and technology for disease prevention and control; eradication of major tropical diseases; immunization of all children against major childhood diseases; and establishing primary health care services.
UNICEF (The United Nations Children's Emergency Fund)	Joint headquarters New York City and Geneva, Switzerland	UNICEF is complementary to WHO and has nearly 90 field offices in developing countries (the largest is in India). UNICEF is concerned with basic health care and social services for children. UNICEF receives about three-fourths of its funding from UN member governments and the other one-fourth from the sale of greeting cards. It is the only UN agency that receives money directly from the general public.
UNESCO (The United Nations Educational, Scientific, and Cultural Organization)	Paris, France	UNESCO is dedicated to enhancing world peace and security through education, science, and culture, as well as to promoting respect for human rights, the rule of law, and fundamental freedoms. One of UNESCO's practical concerns is to promote literacy.
UNHCR (The United Nations High Commission for Refugees)	New York City, U.S.	UNHCR is dedicated to promoting the rights and safety of refugees.
UNIFEM (The United Nations International Development Fund for Women)	New York City, U.S.	UNIFEM promotes projects directed toward raising the status of women.
UNFPA (The United Nations Fund for Population Activities)	New York City, U.S.	UNFPA supports family planning projects.

Source: Hancock 1989.

Two major units within the World Bank are the International Bank for Reconstruction and Development (IBRD) and the International Development Association (IDA). Both are administered at the World Bank headquarters in Washington, DC. They both lend for similar types of projects and often in the same country, but their conditions of lending differ. The IBRD provides loans to the poorest nations, which are generally regarded as "bad risks" on the world commercial market. Thus the IBRD is a source of interest-bearing loans to countries that otherwise would not be able to borrow. The IBRD does not allow rescheduling of debt payments. It has recorded a profit every year of its existence, so it is in the interesting position of being a profit-making aid institution. Most of its loans support large infrastructure projects and, more recently, sectoral development in health and education. The IDA is the "soft-loan" side of the World Bank because it provides interest-free loans (although there is a 0.75 percent annual "service charge") and a flexible repayment schedule averaging between 35 and 40 years (Rich 1994:77). These concessional loans are granted to the poorest countries for projects of high development priority.

The USAID has funded many development projects worldwide, such as this improved road in rural Bangladesh. Proceeds from the toll gate will help pay for maintenance of the road. The rickshaws are parked while their drivers pay their toll. The large white vehicle belongs to USAID and was being used by American researchers. ■ *What kinds of user fees have you paid in the past few months? Did you think the fees were fair?* (Source: Barbara Miller)

Critics of the multilaterals come from many directions, including politicians, scholars, students, and people whose lives have been affected negatively by their projects. Politicians in the United States who oppose foreign aid to developing countries in any form point to the overlapping and wasteful organization of these institutions and the fact that they seem to have accomplished too little in comparison to the funds required of member countries to support them. Others argue that, too often, the projects supported by these institutions have failed to help the poor but, instead, provide thousands of jobs for the people in their employ and are good business investments for first-world countries. Such critics point especially to the biased lending and aid policies that are shaped more by political factors than by economic need.

Prominent bilateral institutions include the Japan International Cooperation Agency (JICA), the United States Agency for International Development (USAID), the Canadian International Development Agency (CIDA), Britain's Department for International Development (DfID), the Swedish Agency for International Development (SIDA), and the Danish Organization for International Development (DANIDA). These agencies vary in terms of the total size of their aid programs, the types of programs they support, and the proportion of aid disbursed as loans that have to be repaid compared to aid disbursed as grants that do not require repayment. Another variation is whether the loans or grants are "tied" to supporting specific projects that also entail substantial donor country involvement in providing goods, services, and expertise versus being "untied," allowing the recipient country the freedom to decide how to use the funds. The USAID generally offers more aid in the form of loans than grants, and more in

tied than in untied aid, especially compared to aid from Sweden, the Netherlands, and Norway.

Another difference among the bilaterals is the proportion of their total aid that goes to the poorest of countries. The United Kingdom's DfID sends more than 80 percent of its aid to the poorest countries, whereas the largest chunk of U.S. foreign aid goes to Egypt and Israel. Emphasis on certain types of aid also varies from one bilateral institution to another. Cuba has long played a unique role in bilateral aid, although this fact is scarcely known in the United States. Rather than offering assistance for a wide range of development projects, Cuba has concentrated on aid for training health care providers and promoting preventive health care (Feinsilver 1993). Cuba's development assistance goes to socialist countries, including many in Africa.

Grassroots Approaches

Many countries have experimented with what are sometimes called grassroots approaches to development, or locally initiated "bottom-up" projects. This alternative to the "top-down" development pursued by the large-scale agencies described in the previous section is more likely to be culturally appropriate, supported through local participation, and successful. During the 1970s, for example, Kenya sponsored a national program whereby the government committed itself to providing teachers if local communities would build schools (Winans and Haugerud 1977). This program was part of Kenya's promotion of *harambee*, or self-help, in improving health, housing, and schooling. Local people's response to the schooling program, especially, was overwhelmingly positive. They turned out in large numbers to build schools, fulfilling their part of the bargain. Given the widespread construction of schools, the government found itself hard pressed to hold up its own end of the bargain: paying the teachers' salaries. This program shows that self-help movements can be highly successful in mobilizing local contributions, if the target—in this case, children's education—is something that is highly valued.

Many non-governmental, grassroots organizations have existed for several decades. Prominent international examples include Oxfam, CARE, and Feed the Children. Churches also sponsor grassroots development. In Bangladesh, for example, the Lutheran Relief Agency has played an important role in helping local people provide and maintain small-scale infrastructure projects such as village roads and canals.

Beginning with the Reagan administration's push toward privatization in the 1980s in the United States and a similar push in the United Kingdom, an emphasis on supporting development efforts through non-governmental organizations (NGOs) emerged. This trend prompted the formation of many NGOs in developing countries that then often became beneficiaries of foreign aid to support local projects.

At the Shan-Dany museum in Oaxaca, Mexico, indigenous people established a museum to house artifacts from their culture and to promote economic development for the village and the region by strengthening the local weaving industry. The museum also provides outreach to school children and encourages them to learn more about their culture. ■ *Use the Internet to learn about other museum or cultural heritage projects of indigenous peoples.* (Source: Jeffrey Cohen)

The Development Project

Development institutions, whether they are large multilaterals or local NGOs, rely on the concept of the development project as the specific set of activities that puts policies into action. For example, suppose a government sets a policy of increased agricultural production by a certain percent within a certain period. Development projects to achieve the policy goal might include the construction of irrigation canals that would supply water to a targeted number of farmers.

Anthropologists and the Project Cycle

The details vary between organizations, but all development projects have a basic **project cycle**, or the full process of a project from initial planning to completion (Cernea 1985). These steps include

- *Project identification:* Selecting a project to fit a particular purpose.
- *Project design:* Preparing the details of the project.
- *Project appraisal:* Assessing the project's budgetary aspects.
- *Project implementation:* Putting the project into place.
- *Project evaluation:* Assessing whether the project goals were fulfilled.

Since the 1970s, cultural anthropologists have been hired in increasing numbers to offer insights into the project cycle at different stages, and with differing impacts. In the early phase of their involvement, anthropologists were hired primarily to do project evaluations, the last step in the project cycle, to determine whether the project had achieved its goals. Unfortunately, many evaluations reported the projects to be dismal failures (Cochrane 1979). Some of the most frequent findings: (1) The target group, such as the poor or women, had not been "reached," but instead project benefits had gone to some other group. (2) The project was inappropriate for the context. (3) The intended beneficiaries were actually worse off after the project than before (as in the case of dam construction, for example). These problems are discussed further below.

One reason for these failures was that projects were typically identified and designed by Western economists located in cities far from the project site. These experts applied a universal formula, paying little or no attention to the local cultural context (Scott 1998). In other words, projects were designed by "people-distant" and culturally uninformed economists and planners but were evaluated by "people-close" and culturally informed anthropologist. By demonstrating the weaknesses in project planning that led to failed projects, the victimization of people rather than their advancement through development, and the need to take the local cultural context into account in projects, cultural anthropologists gained a reputation in development circles as troublemakers and "nay-sayers"—people to be avoided by those who favored a "move-ahead" approach to getting projects funded and implemented.

Cultural anthropologists are still considered a nuisance by many development economists and policy planners—but sometimes, at least, a necessary nuisance. On a more positive note, cultural anthropologists have worked to play a role earlier in the project cycle, especially at the project identification and design stages. Although they are still far less powerful than economists in defining development policy, many anthropologists have made notable strides in this direction, including having leadership roles in smaller-scale development organizations. Their role as watch-dogs and critics, furthermore, should not be discounted because it draws attention to important problems.

Sociocultural Fit

Through the years, anthropologists have provided many examples of projects that were culturally inappropriate, some amusing and others not. All were a waste of time and money. One glaring case of non-fit is a project intended to improve nutrition and health in the South Pacific by promoting increased milk consumption (Cochrane, class lecture 1974). The project involved the transfer of large quantities of American powdered milk to an island community. The inhabitants, however, were lactose intolerant (unable to digest raw milk) and everyone soon had diarrhea. Realizing what caused this outbreak, the people used the powdered milk to whitewash their houses. Beyond wasting resources, inappropriately designed projects can result in the exclusion of the intended beneficiaries, such as when a person's signature is required among people who cannot write or when photo identification cards are requested from Muslim women, whose faces should not be shown in public.

Conrad Kottak (1985) reviewed evaluations for sixty-eight development projects to see whether economic success of projects was related to **sociocultural fit**, or how well a project meshes with the target culture and population. Results showed a strong correlation between the two factors. One role for anthropologists is to expose areas of non-fit and provide insights about how to achieve sociocultural fit in order to enhance project success. In one such case, Gerald Murray (1987) played a positive role in redesigning a costly and unsuccessful reforestation project supported by USAID in Haiti. Since

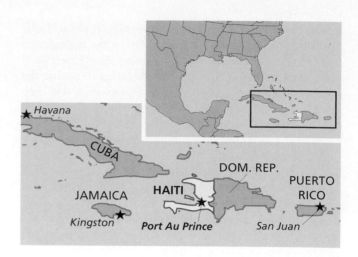

the colonial era in Haiti, deforestation has been dramatic; estimates are that around 50 million trees are cut annually. Some of the deforestation is driven by the market for wood for construction and for charcoal in the capital city of Port au Prince. Another aspect is that rural people are farmers and need cleared land for growing crops and grazing their goats. The ecological consequences of so much clearing, however, are soil erosion and declining fertility of the land.

USAID sent millions of tree seedlings to Haiti, and the Haitian government urged rural people to plant them. But the project fell flat: Farmers refused to plant the seedlings on their land and instead fed them to goats. Gerald Murray, who had done his doctoral dissertation on rural Haitian land tenure practices, was called on by USAID to suggest an alternative approach. He advised that the kind of seedling promoted be changed from fruit trees, in which the rural farmers saw little benefit because they are not to be cut, to fast-growing trees such as eucalyptus that could be cut as early as four years after planting and sold in Port au Prince. This option was quickly accepted by the farmers since it would yield profits in the foreseeable future, and they could see that losses from food production would be offset by the income. The basic incompatibility had been that USAID wanted trees planted that would stay in place for years to come, whereas the Haitian farmers viewed trees as things that were meant to be cut.

The Anthropological Critique of Development Projects

The early decades of development anthropology were dominated by what I call **traditional development anthropology (TDA)**. In TDA, the anthropologist accepts the role of helping to make development work better, a kind of "add an anthropologist and stir" approach to development. It is an option that economists and others real-

A tree nursery in Haiti established as part of a reforestation project funded by USAID. ■ *Locate the USAID web site and scan the kinds of information provided there. Is there much evidence of the involvement of anthropologists?* (Source: Birgit Pohl)

ize can help make their plans more effective. For example, an anthropologist familiar with a local culture can provide information about what kinds of consumer goods would be desired by the people or what might induce them to relocate with less resistance. This kind of participation by anthropologists can be either positive or negative for the local people, depending on the project being undertaken.

Concern exists among anthropologists that helping to make large-scale development projects work often has negative effects on local people and their environments (Bodley 1990; Horowitz and Salem-Murdock 1993; Taussig 1978). For example, a study of the welfare of local inhabitants of the middle Senegal valley (in the country of Senegal, West Africa) before and after the construction of a large dam shows that people's level of food insecurity increased (Horowitz and Salem-Murdock 1993). Formerly, the periodic flooding of the plain helped support a dense human population dependent on agriculture, fishing, forestry, and herding. Productivity of the wetlands had remained high for a long period of human occupation, with no signs of deterioration. The current practice of water control by the dam managers, however, does not provide periodic flooding. Instead, water is released less often and with disregard for the needs of the people downstream. In some years, they do not have enough water for their crops, and fishing has become a less secure source of food. At other times, a large flood

of water is released, damaging crops. As a result, many residents have been forced to leave the area. They have become development refugees, people who must leave home because of the effects of a development project.

The awareness of the negative effects of many supposedly positive development projects has led to the emergence of what I call **critical development anthropology (CDA)**. In this approach, the anthropologist does not simply accept a supportive role but rather takes on a critical-thinking role. The question is not: What can I do to make this project successful? Instead, the anthropologist asks: Is this a good project from the perspective of the target population? If the answer is yes, then that is a green light for a supportive role. If careful thinking reveals areas where revisions in the project would make it beneficial, then the anthropologist can intervene with this information. If all evidence suggests that the project will harm the target population, either in the short run or the long run, then the anthropologist should assume the role of whistle-blower and try either to stop the project completely or to change the design substantially. In the case of the Senegal Valley dam project, anthropologists working with engineers and local inhabitants devised an alternative management plan of regular and controlled amounts of released water that would reduce the harm done to people downstream and restore the area's former agricultural and fishing abundance.

Methods in Development Anthropology

Many full-scale anthropological studies of cultural change and development are based on long-term fieldwork and standard research methods as described in Chapter 2. However, often a development agency needs input from an anthropologist that requires faster turnaround than what long-term fieldwork would allow. Specialized methods have emerged to respond to the short time frame and provide answers to the specific questions at hand. Compared to standard long-term fieldwork the methods used in development anthropology are more focused with a less holistic research agenda, make more use of multidisciplinary research teams, and rely on such specialized approaches as rapid research methods and participatory research methods. These three differences are related to the need to gather dependable data in a relatively short time period.

Rapid Research Methods

Rapid research methods (RRMs) are research methods designed to provide focused cultural data in a short time period (Chambers 1983). They include strategies such as going to the field with a checklist of questions, conducting focus group interviews (talking to several people at

Patricia Delaney (center left, wearing a white shirt) facilitates a participatory research exercise with Amerindian villagers in the Rupununi Savannah of Guyana in South America. The woman (center) is participating in a village mapping exercise that was part of an assessment of village needs. ■ *How well would you be able to draw a map of your "village"?* (Source: Patricia Delaney)

the same time rather than one by one), and conducting transect observations (walking through a specific area with key informants and asking for explanations along the way) (Bernard 1995:139–140). When used correctly, RRMs can provide useful data for assessing the problems and opportunities related to development. Rapid research methods are most effective when several methods are used to complement each other and when researchers work in teams (recall Chapter 2).

An effective mix of rapid research methods was used for development project planning in rural Bali (Mitchell 1994). The research sought to identify environmental and social stresses that might be caused by economic development and then to make recommendations for the government to use in preparing its next five-year development plan. Anthropologists and graduate students at the University of Windsor in Canada and at an Indonesian university designed an eight-village study to provide data on ecological, economic, and social factors. A four-member team studied in each village, but each team spent some time in at least two villages. Teams consisted of Indonesian and Canadian researchers, both men and women. All team members could speak Bahasa Indonesian (the national language), and at least one could also speak Bahasa Bali (the local language). Researchers lived in the village for four weeks. The teams employed several methods for data collection: background data from provincial documents and village records, and interviews with key informants representing the village administration, religious figures, women, youth, school teachers, health clinic personnel, and agricultural extension workers. Household interviews were conducted with fifteen men and fifteen women from different neighborhoods in the village and with a sample of primary school children. Other observations included conditions of the village and

villagers' daily activities. For each village, the research generated a profile of relevant biophysical features, production and marketing, local government, health and welfare, and expressive culture. The findings offered a range of issues for the government's consideration, including the apparent environmental and social stresses being caused by external developments such as urbanization and tourism.

Participatory Research Methods

Building on the RRM approach, a more recent research approach called **participatory research methods (PRM)** entails more involvement of the local people. Participatory research methods respond to the growing awareness that when the target population is involved in a development project, it is more likely to be successful in the short run and sustainable over the long run. (Kabutha, Thomas-Slayter, and Ford 1993:76). Participatory research rests heavily on the anthropological assumption that local knowledge should not be bypassed but, rather, should be the foundation of development work. Participatory research proceeds by involving key community members at all stages of the research.

The best PRM work trains local people how to collect and analyze data themselves. Local people can learn how to prepare maps and charts and other forms of descriptive data. Besides sheer data gathering and analysis, a crucial feature of PRM is feedback from community members in project selection and project evaluation. Local people can be trained to continue the data collection and analysis after the team has left the village. Two important effects of PRM are fostering local autonomy in planning and boosting the odds that the projects put in place will be maintained and adjusted to changing conditions.

EMERGING ISSUES IN DEVELOPMENT

In this section we consider three major arenas in international development: indigenous people, women, and human rights. The first two are particular groups of people who have been affected by international development in various ways. They are not completely separate categories, because many indigenous people are also women, but this section reviews findings for them separately for purposes of illustration. The issue of human rights affects all social categories, including indigenous people, ethnic minorities, women, children, and others.

Indigenous Peoples' Development

This section first raises the question of who indigenous people are. We next consider findings about how indigenous peoples have been victimized by many aspects of growth-oriented development (as they were by colonialism before it) and then look at examples of how many indigenous groups are taking development into their own hands.

Who Are Indigenous Peoples?

The term indigenous people refers to groups of people who are the original inhabitants of a particular territory (recall Chapter 1). Often, indigenous peoples take the name of "First Peoples" as a way of defining themselves as original claimants to a place. This naming practice highlights one of the major problems facing most indigenous peoples today: the fact that they have lost, and are losing, claim to their ancestral lands in the face of encroachment from outsiders.

Indigenous peoples are typically a numerical minority in the states that control their territory. The United Nations distinguishes between indigenous peoples and other minority groups such as the Rom, the Tamils of Sri Lanka, and African Americans. Although this distinction is useful in some ways, it should not be taken as a hard and fast difference (Maybury-Lewis 1997b). It is most useful to think of all these groups as forming a continuum from more purely indigenous groups such as the Inuit to minority/ethnic groups, such as African Americans, that are not geographically original to a place but share many problems with indigenous peoples as a result of living within a more powerful majority culture.

Indigenous peoples differ from most national minorities by the fact that they often occupy (or occupied) remote areas and were, until the era of colonial expansion, less affected by outside interests. Now governments and international businesses have recognized that their lands often contain valuable natural resources, such as natural gas in the polar region and gold in Papua New Guinea and the Amazon. Different governments have paid varying degrees of attention to "integrating" indigenous peoples into "mainstream" culture in the interests of fostering nationalism at the expense of pluralism.

Accurate demographic statistics on indigenous peoples are difficult to obtain (Kennedy and Perz 2000). No one agrees on whom to count as indigenous. Governments may not bother to conduct a census of indigenous people, or if they do, they may report undercounts of indigenous people in order to downplay recognition of their very existence as a group (Baer 1982:12). A few island populations in India's Andaman Islands in the Bay of Bengal remain uncounted because Indian officials cannot gain access to them (Singh 1994). Given the difficulties involved in defining and counting indigenous people, therefore, it is possible to provide only estimates on their numbers. It is estimated that, globally, indigenous people make up about 5 percent of the total world population. (Bodley 1990: 365). (See Table 16.4.)

Victims of Development

Many indigenous peoples and their cultures have been exterminated as a result of contact with outsiders. Besides death and decline through contagious disease, political conflicts within indigenous people's territory often

TABLE 16.4 Population Estimates of Indigenous Peoples

Western Hemisphere
    less than 1 million in Canada
    1.75 million in the United States
    less than 13 million in Mexico and Central America
    16 million in South America
Europe
    60,000 in Greenland
    60,000 in Norway, Sweden, Finland, and Russia
    28 million within the former Soviet Union
Middle East
    5 million
Africa
    14 million
Asia
    52 million in India
    31 million in China (the government terms them *national minorities*)
    26.5 million in Southeast Asia
    50,000 in Japan and the Pacific combined
    550,000 in Australia and New Zealand
Total: About 5 percent of the world's total population.

Source: Maybury-Lewis 1997b:10–11.

A Hmong woman and child, northern Thailand. The Hmong people of highland Southeast Asia have suffered decades of war in their homeland. Many have migrated to other parts of the world, including the United States and Canada, where they were classified as refugees. ■ *What other people have come to your home country recently as refugees?* (Source: Roshani Kothari)

to expel outside intruders or use force to regulate its internal affairs; introduction of formal schooling and national court systems; appointment of state-sanctioned political leaders; the institution of compulsory military service; and enforcement of payment of taxes. These changes undermine the previous quality of life and set in motion changes that indirectly lead to the people's further impoverishment.

Anthropological analysis of government policies in Thailand for development of the highlands reveals the complex interplay between outside interests and the welfare of the "hill people" (Kesmanee 1994). The hill people include the Karen, Hmong, Mian, Lahu, Lisu, Akha, and others, totaling about half a million people, or 1 percent of the total Thai population. International pressures are for the hill people to replace opium cultivation with other cash crops. The Thai government's concerns are with political stability and national security in this area, which borders on Burma and Laos. It therefore has promoted development projects to establish more connections between the highlands and the lowlands through transportation and marketing. Thus far, efforts to find viable substitute crops (especially among the Hmong, who have traditionally been most dependent on opium as a cash crop) have been unsuccessful. Crops that have been introduced have required extensive use of fertilizers and pesticides, which have greatly increased environmental pollution. Efforts have been made to relocate upland horticulturalists to the plains, but there they have been provided plots with poor soil, and the economic status of the people has declined. In the meantime, commercial loggers have gained access to the hills and have done more damage to the forests than the traditional patterns of shifting horticulture. Increased penetration of the hill areas by lowlanders, international tourism, and communications has also promoted the increase of HIV/AIDS rates, illegal trafficking of girls and boys for sex work, and opium addiction. The effects of thirty years of development have been disastrous for the hill people, and awareness of this fact calls for a major change in how development is being pursued by international agencies and the Thai government.

The situation in Thailand is not unique. In case after case, indigenous peoples have been subjected to loss of the rights they once had, increased impoverishment, and widespread despair. Active resistance to their disenfranchisement has been mounted throughout history, but more effective and highly organized forms of protest and reclamation of rights have become prominent only since the 1980s. Many indigenous groups have acquired legal advice and expertise and have confronted power-holders in world capitals, insisting on changes. One of the most basic claims of all groups is recognition of their land rights.

threaten their survival. In the Peruvian Andes, for example, armed conflict among the Peruvian guerrillas, the Shining Path, drug traffickers, and U.S.-backed police and army units has taken a heavy toll on Native American populations.

With colonialism, indigenous peoples suffered from massive efforts to take over their land by force, to prevent them from practicing their traditional lifestyle, and to integrate them into the state. John Bodley (1988) has examined the effects of loss of autonomy for indigenous people that results from the unwillingness of the state to tolerate the presence of politically sovereign tribes within its boundaries. States intervene to prevent and quell armed resistance by indigenous people, even though such resistance may be critical to the maintenance of indigenous culture and the people's welfare. Indicators that an indigenous group has lost its autonomy include inability

From Victimization to Indigenous Peoples' Development

Much evidence attests to the value of "development from within," or efforts to increase people's welfare and livelihood promoted by indigenous organizations rather than exogenous organizations. Basic components of indigenous people's development include rights to resources, local initiatives in planning through local organizations, and local leadership. The following sections consider, first, resource issues (especially land) and indigenous organizations for change.

The many land and resource claims being made by indigenous peoples are a direct response to their earlier

A farmer walks through an oil-soaked field. About 500,000 Ogoni people live in Ogoni, a region in Nigeria. The fertility of the Niger delta has supported farming and fishing populations at high density for many years. Since Shell discovered oil there in 1958, 100 oil wells were constructed in Ogoniland and countless oil spills have occurred.
■ *Discuss the environmental and social effects of massive oil exploitation on the Ogoni people, and write a "mock memo" about the consequences for the Machiguenga people of Peru, who are being pressed to open up their unspoiled lands to oil companies.* (Source: © CORBIS. All Rights Reserved.)

losses and a major challenge to many states. Depending on how these disputes are resolved, they can be a basis for conflicts ranging from lawsuits to attempts at secession (Plant 1994).

No Latin American country government provides protection against encroachment on the land of farm families. Throughout Latin America, increasing numbers of Indians have been forced off the land and have had to seek wage labor. Those who remain live in extreme poverty. In response, a strong resurgence of activity by indigenous people and groups that support them occurred in the 1990s (Plant 1994). Some of this activity took the form of physical resistance. Violence continues to erupt between indigenous people and state-supported power structures, especially in the southern Mexican state of Chiapas.

In Canada, the law distinguishes between two different types of Native Americans and their land claims (Plant 1994). "Specific claims" concern problems arising from previous agreements or treaties, and "comprehensive claims" are those made by Native Americans who have not been displaced and have made no treaties or agreements. Most of the former claims have led to monetary compensation. In the latter category, interest in oil and mineral exploration have led governments to negotiate with indigenous people in an effort to have the latter's native claims either relinquished or redefined. So far, of the over forty comprehensive claims filed, only four have been settled. In some provinces, especially British Columbia, current claims affect most of the province.

Most Asian countries have been reluctant even to recognize the concept of special land rights of indigenous people (Plant 1994). In Bangladesh, for example, the formerly protected area of the Chittagong Hill Tracts is being massively encroached upon by settlers from the crowded plains. Nonindigenous settlers now occupy the most fertile land. A large hydroelectric dam built in 1963 displaced 100,000 hill dwellers because they could no longer practice horticulture in the flooded areas. A minority received financial aid, but most did not. Tribal opposition groups began emerging, and conflict, though suppressed in the news, has been ongoing for decades. Other sites of contestation with the state over land and resources in the Asia-Pacific region include the Moros of the southern Philippines and the people of Irian Jaya. In these cases, the indigenous peoples' fight for secession from the state that controls them is costing many lives.

In Africa, political interests of state governments in establishing and enforcing territorial boundaries have created difficulties for indigenous peoples, especially pastoralists who are, for example, accustomed to moving their herds freely. Pastoralists in the Sahel region of Africa have been particularly affected by this process. Many formerly autonomous pastoralists have been transformed into refugees living in terrible conditions. The Tuareg people, for example, have traditionally lived and herded in a territory crossing what are now five different nations: Mali, Niger, Algeria, Burkina Faso, and Libya (Childs and Chelala 1994). Because of political conflict in the region, thousands of Tuareg people now live in exile in Mauritania, and their prospects are grim. As elsewhere, resistance movements spring up, but states and local power interests move quickly to quell them. The death of Ogoni leader Ken Saro-Wiwa, in 1995, is a shocking example of the personal price of resistance (Sachs 1996). Saro-Wiwa, a Nigerian writer, Nobel Peace Prize nominee, and supporter of minority people's rights, was executed by Nigerian military rulers. He had vigorously spoken out against the Nigerian regime and the oil development being pursued in Ogoniland by Royal/Dutch Shell. As president and spokesperson of the Movement for the Survival of the Ogoni People (MOSOP), he had asked the government to respect the Ogoni people's right to self-determination. He also had asked Shell to clean up oil spills and toxic waste pits that had ruined Ogoni farming and fishing communities along the Niger River delta. His message is one that applies worldwide: States tend to impose the costs of their economic growth on the people least able to cope with it—impoverished minorities—and then apply violent means of repression if such people raise serious objections to that treatment.

Many indigenous peoples have formed their own organizations for change in order to promote "development from within." In Ethiopia, for example, many NGOs organized by local people have sprung up since the 1990s (Kassam 2002). One organization in the southern region is especially noteworthy, because it seeks to provide a model of development based on the oral traditions of the Oromo people. This new model thus combines elements of Western-defined "development" with Oromo values and laws and provides a new approach that is culturally appropriate and goes beyond external notions of development and usual Oromo lifeways. The indigenous Oromo NGO is called Hundee, which refers to "roots," or the origins of the Oromo people, and, by extension, to all Oromo people, their land, and their culture. Hundee uses a theory of development that is based in Oromo metaphors of fertility and growth and involves gradual transformation like the spirals in the horn of a ram. Hundee relies on Oromo legal and moral principles about the communal use of natural resources and the redistribution of wealth to provide a social welfare system. These are elements of "good development," as distinguished from the "bad development" that has inflicted hunger and dependency on the Oromo people.

Hundee's long-term goal is to empower Oromo communities to be self-sufficient. It takes the view the Oromo culture is a positive force for social and economic change, rather than a barrier. Hundee members use a participa-

tory approach in all their endeavors. They consult with traditional legal assemblies to identify needs and then to shape projects to address those needs. Specific activities include the establishment of a credit association and a grain bank to help combat price fluctuations and food shortages.

In many cases, indigenous peoples' development organizations have been formed that link formerly separate groups (Perry 1996:245–246), as a response to external threats. In Australia, many indigenous groups have

Nigerian author and Nobel prizewinner, Ken Saro-Wiwa founded the Movement for Survival of Ogoni People (MOSOP) in 1992 to protest Shell's actions in Ogoniland and the Nigerian government's indifference. In 1995, he was arrested, tried for murder under suspicious circumstances, and executed by hanging. His execution brought about an international outcry while Shell's response is largely denial of any problem. ■ *How many of your daily activities depend on the use of oil products?* (Source: © CORBIS)

In 2003, the Treatment Action Campaign began a program of civil disobedience to prompt the government to sign and implement a National Prevention and Treatment Plan for HIV/AIDS. TAC is using images of Hector Peterson, the first youth killed in the Soweto uprising against apartheid, and slogans such as "The Struggle Continues: Support HIV/AIDS Treatment Now." ■ *Take a position, and be prepared to defend it, on whether or not the government should take responsibility for preventing and treating HIV/AIDS in any country, rich or poor.* (Source: © Gideon Mendel/CORBIS)

formed pan-Australian organizations and regional coalitions, such as the Pitjandjatjara Land Council, that have had success in land claim cases. In Canada, the Grand Council of the Cree has collaborated with the Inuit Tapirisat and other organizations over land issues. Many indigenous groups are taking advantages of new forms of communication in order to build and maintain links with each other over large areas.

Although it is tempting to see hope in the newly emerging forms of resistance, self-determination, and organizing among indigenous peoples, such hope cannot be generalized to all indigenous peoples. Although many are making progress and their economic status is improving, others are suffering extreme political and economic repression.

Women and Development

The category of women contrasts with that of indigenous peoples per se, because women do not have a recognized territory associated with them as a group. The effects of development on women, however, share features with its effects on indigenous people: Women have often lost political power in their communities and rights to property.

Matrilineal kinship, a system that keeps property in the female line (review Chapter 8), is in decline throughout the world, often as a result of westernization and modernization. Another factor that has had a negative effect on women's status is that Western development experts have chosen to deal with men in the context of development projects.

In this section, we consider evidence that much activity in international development has been biased in favor of men to the detriment of women. We then turn to examples in which some women's groups, like some of the indigenous peoples discussed above, are taking development into their own hands and making it work to enhance their welfare.

The Male Bias in Development

In the 1970s, researchers began to notice and write about the fact that development projects were male-biased (Boserup 1970; Tinker 1976). Many projects completely bypassed women as beneficiaries, targeting men for such initiatives as growing cash crops and learning about new technology. This *male bias in development* targeting contributed to increased gender inequality by giving men greater access to new sources of income and by depriving women of their traditional economic roles. The development experts' image of a farmer, for example, was male, not female. Women's projects were focused on the domestic domain. Thus women's projects were typically concerned with infant feeding patterns, child care, and family planning. Over time, these emphases led to what has been labeled the *domestication of women* worldwide (Rogers 1979). For example, female horticulturalists were bypassed by agricultural projects and instead taught to spend more time in the house.

The male bias in development also increased the rate of project failure. In the West African country of Burkina Faso, for example, a reforestation project included men as the sole participants, whose tasks would include planting and caring for the trees. Cultural patterns there,

TABLE 16.5   An Emerging Development Issue: Violence against Girls and Women throughout the Life Cycle

Prebirth	Sex-selective abortion, battering during pregnancy, coerced pregnancy
Infancy	Infanticide, emotional and physical abuse, deprivation of food and medical care
Girlhood	Child marriage, genital mutilation, sexual abuse by family members and strangers, rape, deprivation of food and medical care, child prostitution
Adolescence	Dating and courtship violence, forced prostitution, rape, sexual abuse in the workplace, sexual harassment
Adulthood	Partner abuse and rape, partner homicide, sexual abuse in the workplace, sexual harassment, rape
Old Age	Abuse and neglect of widows, elder abuse

Source: Adapted from Heise, Pitanguy, and Germain 1994:5.

however, dictate that men do not water plants; women do. So the men planted the seedlings and left them. Because women had not been included as project participants, the young trees that were planted died.

Exclusion of women from development continues to be a problem, in spite of many years of work attempting to place and keep women's issues on the development agenda. An example of an emerging development issue related to women's welfare is gender-based violence. This issue has gained attention even among the large multilaterals, where experts now realize that women cannot participate in a credit program, for example, if they fear that their husbands will beat them for leaving the house. The United Nations Commission on the Status of Women formed a working group that drafted a declaration against violence against women; it was adopted by The General Assembly in 1993 (Heise, Pitanguy, and Germain 1994). Article 1 of the declaration states that violence against women includes "any act of gender-based violence that results in, or is likely to result in, physical, sexual or psychological harm or suffering to women, including threats of such acts, coercion or arbitrary deprivations of liberty, whether occurring in public or private life" (Economic and Social Council 1992). This definition cites "women" as the focus of concern, but it includes girls as well (see Table 16.5). A weakness of programs that target issues of violence against girls and women is that they tend to deal with their effects, not the causes, often with disastrous results. For example, they may seek to increase personal security of women and girls in refugee camps by augmenting the number of guards at the camp when, in fact, the guards are often guilty of abusing refugee women and girls.

Women's Organizations for Change

In many countries, women have made substantial gains in improving their status and welfare through forming organizations. These organizations range from "moth-

Grameen Bank, a development project begun in Bangladesh to provide small loans to poor people, is one of the most successful examples of improving human welfare through "micro-credit" or small loans. Professor Mohammed Yunnus (center) founded Grameen Bank and continues to be a source of charismatic leadership for it. ■ *How does the success of Grameen Bank cause you to question your previous image of Bangladesh?* (Source: © Robert Nickelsberg/Getty Images)

ers' clubs" that help provide for communal child care to lending and credit organizations that give women an opportunity to start their own businesses. Some are local and small-scale. Others are global in reach, such as Women's World Banking, an international organization that grew out of credit programs for poor working women in India.

One community-based credit system in Mozambique, southern Africa, helps farm women to buy seeds, fertilizers, and supplies on loan (Clark 1992). When the loan program was first started, thirty-two farm families in the village of Machel formed themselves into seven solidarity groups, each with an elected leader. The woman-headed farmer groups managed irrigation more efficiently and conferred on how to minimize the use of pesticides and chemical fertilizers. Through their efforts, the women quadrupled their harvests and were able to pay off their loans. Machel women then turned their attention to getting additional loans to improve their herds and to buy a maize mill. Overall, in the midst of poverty, military conflict, the lack of government resources, and a drought, the project and the organization it fostered allowed many women farmers to increase their economic and household security.

An informal system of social networks emerged to help support poor women vendors in San Cristobal, Mexico (Sullivan 1992). Many of the vendors around the city square are women, and most of them have been expelled from highland Chiapas because of political conflicts there. The women vendors manufacture and sell goods to tourists and thereby provide an important portion of household income. In the city, they find support in an expanded social network that compensates for the loss of support from the extensive god-parenthood system (Chapter 8) of the highlands, which has broken down because of outmigration. Instead, the vendors have established networks encompassing relatives, neighbors, and church members, as well as other vendors, regardless of religious, political, economic, or social background.

These networks first developed in response to a series of rapes and robberies that began in 1987. The perpetrators were persons of power and influence, so the women never pressed charges. Mostly single mothers and widows, they adopted a defensive strategy of self-protection: They began to group together during the slow period each afternoon. They travel in groups and carry sharpened corset bones and prongs: "If a man insults one of them, the group surrounds him and jabs him in the groin" (39–40). If a woman is robbed, the other women surround her, comfort her, and help contribute something toward compensating her for her loss. The mid-afternoon gatherings have developed into support groups that provide financial assistance, child care, medical advice, and training in job skills. These groups have also publicly, and successfully, demonstrated against city officials'

attempts to prevent them from continuing their vending. Through their organizational efforts, these women—poor, vulnerable refugees from highland Chiapas—have brought important improvements in their lives.

Human Rights

Much of the preceding discussion of indigenous peoples and women is related to the question of human rights and development. Anthropologists' cross-cultural research and their growing sense of the importance of advocacy as part of their role place them in a key position to speak about issues of global human rights (Messer 1993). In considering what cultural anthropologists have to contribute to the issue of human rights, we must first ask some basic and difficult questions:

- What are human rights?
- Is there a universal set of human rights?
- Are local cultural definitions of human rights that clash with those of other groups defensible?

Defining Human Rights

For fifty years, the United Nations has promoted human rights through its Declaration of Human Rights and other resolutions (Messer 1993). Difficulty in coming to a universal agreement on these rights is based in one sense on a split between capitalist and socialist states. The former emphasize political and civil rights such as freedom of speech as universally important. The latter emphasize socioeconomic rights such as employment and fair working conditions. Capitalist states do not acknowledge such socioeconomic rights as universal human rights, and some socialist states do not recognize political rights as valid. People living in developing countries and indigenous people throughout the world have added their voices, insisting on group rights to self-determination, locally defined paths of change, and issues such as freedom from hunger. As Ellen Messer says, "[N]o state would go on record as being opposed to human rights. . . . Yet those from different states, and from different political, cultural, and religious traditions, continue to disagree on which rights have universal force and who is protected under them" (223).

As culturally diverse groups seek to define and claim their rights around the increasingly globalized world, we are all faced with the challenge of considering contending positions. (See the Unity and Diversity box on page 388.)

Human Rights and Development

This section provides two illustrations of how development and human rights are linked. In the first, we find ties between large-scale development institutions and mili-

Unity and Diversity

HUMAN RIGHTS VERSUS ANIMAL RIGHTS: THE CASE OF THE GRAY WHALE

HUMAN RIGHTS are often understood to include the right of people, as members of a cultural group, to practice their cultural traditions. This provision extends the notion of human rights from including mainly the right to fulfilling basic physical needs such as health and personal security to including practices such as animal sacrifice, female genital cutting, hunting certain animals, and girls wearing headscarves in school—all issues that have received recent attention from European and North American governments and media because they differ from cultural practices in those countries. In the United States, as in many other countries, a debate about some cultural practices is carried out between human rights activists who support cultural rights and those who support animal rights.

In spring 1999, members of the Makah tribe, a Native American group living in Washington state, undertook a revival of their traditional practice of hunting gray whales (Winthrop 2000). Like that of many other native peoples of the Pacific Northwest, from Canada to the United States, the Makah's traditional economy depended on fish, shellfish, and marine mammals. A treaty of 1855 acknowledged the Makah's right to hunt whales and seals. The practice died out, however, in the twentieth century because of commercial overhunting and dwindling supplies. In 1982 the International Whal-

ing Commission (IWC) imposed a ban on all commercial whaling but allowed continued whale hunting for subsistence purposes. In 1994 the gray whale population had recovered, and the species was taken off the endangered list. The IWC allocated the Makah a quota of 20 whales for the period from 1998 to 2002.

When, under this new plan, the Makah killed a whale in May 1999, the Makah watching the event cheered. The animal rights activists at the scene, in contrast, protested and said this occasion should have been one of mourning, not celebration. Although the Makah see the revival of whale hunting as a sign of cultural revival, some animal rights activists say that the way the hunt is being carried out is not culturally authentic (the Makah first harpoon the whale and then use a rifle to kill it, for example) and thus the claim of whale hunting as a traditional cultural right is not legitimate. Some of the protesters are motivated by ecological concerns for preservation of the species from extinction. Others support the concept of animal (especially mammalian) rights to life.

FOOD FOR THOUGHT

What other examples of human rights versus animal rights have appeared recently in the media? What are the specific issues involved? Where do you stand in these debates and what is the basis for your position?

---

tary control in the Philippines through which violations of local people's human rights have occurred. The second example addresses the question of environmental destruction as a violation of human and cultural rights.

An in-depth study of social conditions among the Ifugao, an indigenous people of the Cordillera highland region of Northern Luzon, the Philippines, reveals the negative role of the militarization of everyday life for the Ifugao (Kwiatkowski 1998). The military presence is felt everywhere—in schools, in clinics, and especially at sites of large development projects such as dams. The military is there to ensure that people adhere to its principles and do not participate in what it would consider subversive activities. Military force has been used to suppress local resistance to dams funded by the World Bank, resulting in numerous human rights violations, including torture, killings, imprisonment, and harassment of Cordillera people for suspected subversive activities (Drucker 1988). Members of a local NGO that supports more appropri-

ate, small-scale forms of development that would benefit more people in the area have been harassed by the military. The case of the Ifugao in Northern Luzon illustrates how the powerful interests of state governments and international development institutions join together to promote their plans and projects and violate human rights along the way.

Development that leads to environmental degradation, such as pollution, deforestation, and erosion, can also be considered a form of human rights violation. Slain Ogoni leader Ken Saro-Wiwa made this point eloquently in a 1992 speech to the United Nations Working Group on Indigenous Populations:

> Environmental degradation has been a lethal weapon in the war against the indigenous Ogoni people . . . . Oil exploration has turned Ogoni into a wasteland: lands, streams, and creeks are totally and continually polluted; the atmosphere has been poisoned, charged as it is with hydrocarbon vapors, methane, carbon monoxide, car-

---

bon dioxide, and soot emitted by gas which has been flared 24 hours a day for 33 years in close proximity to human habitation . . . . All one sees and feels around is death [quoted in Sachs 1996:13–16].

Many social scientists now argue, along with Saro-Wiwa, that such forms of development violate human rights because they undermine a people's way of life and threaten its continued existence (Johnston 1994).

On to the Future

During the past few decades, cultural anthropologists have played an important role in defining and exposing a wide range of human rights abuses around the world. Although this "whistle-blowing" can promote positive change, it is also important that cultural anthropologists participate in advocacy work directed toward the prevention of human rights abuses. Determining exactly how cultural anthropologists can contribute to prevention is a challenge to a discipline whose roots lie in studying what is—rather than what might be, or, in this case, what should not be. One path is toward promoting continued dialogue on human rights and cultural diversity across groups, which should help promote greater understanding and tolerance.

Since its beginning, cultural anthropology has been a product of the knowledge gained from studying "others." In the early years, this knowledge was taken to Western centers of power. As this chapter shows, indigenous peoples, women, and other groups that have suffered from lack or loss of resources and power, often as a result of external forms of economic and political change, are beginning to reclaim their knowledge and identity and rework international ideas of development and change into models that are culturally appropriate. Local redefinitions of development, and local approaches to achieving improved human welfare, are a powerful example of how global forces can sometimes be transformed and remade to the advantage of seemingly marginalized and powerless people. We live in a time of war, but also a time of hope, in which insights and strength often come from those with the least in terms of material wealth but with cultural wealth beyond measure.

KEY CONCEPTS

assimilated, p. 369
critical development anthropology
　(CDA), p. 379
development, p. 371
development anthropology, p. 368
diachronic, p. 368
diffusion, p. 369

human development, p. 373
modernization, p. 371
participatory research methods
　(PRMs), p. 380
project cycle, p. 377
rapid research methods (RRMs),
　p. 379

social impact assessments, p. 373
sociocultural fit, p. 378
structural adjustment, p. 371
sustainable development, p. 374
synchronic, p. 368
traditional development anthropology
　(TDA), p. 378

SUGGESTED READINGS

Thomas W. Collins and John D. Wingard, eds. *Communities and Capital: Local Struggles against Corporate Power and Privatization.* Athens, GA: The University of Georgia Press, 2000. Nine case studies of local resistance against large capitalist forces follow an introductory chapter that sets the stage. Cases include clam farmers of North Carolina, a fishing community in Malaysia, and banana growers in Belize.

John J. Cove. *What the Bones Say: Tasmanian Aborigines, Science and Domination.* Ottawa; Canada: Carleton University Press, 1995. This book probes the links between science and global power and describes how their combination has affected indigenous peoples. The case of Tasmania, which is examined in depth, reveals how the control of indigenous people's bones is related to wider social relations and change.

Dolores Koenig, Tieman Diarra, Moussa Sow, and Ousmane Diarra. *Innovation and Individuality in African Development: Changing Production Strategies in Rural Mali.* Ann Arbor: University of Michigan Press, 1998. This ethnography of change looks at the history of Malian rural production, agricultural resources and crop production, and how lessons learned contribute to an improved anthropology of development.

David H. Lempert, Kim McCarthy, and Craig Mitchell. *A Model Development Plan: New Strategies and Perspectives.* Westport, CT: Praeger, 1995. A group of university students from different disciplines (including one anthropologist, Lempert) spent six weeks in Ecuador, visiting nearly every province and studying development issues there as the basis for their development plan for Ecuador. A preface explains the background of the project. The rest of the volume consists of a detailed presentation of the plan.

Mark Moberg. *Citrus, Strategy, and Class: The Politics of Development in Southern Belize.* Iowa City: University of Iowa Press, 1992. This ethnography of development considers the involvement of two villages in Belize, Central America, in the global citrus market. The author's "political economy" perspective sheds light on the formation of a rural class and on the increasing dependency of rural Belize through its participation in the global market. Profiles of five villagers show how people attempt to exercise some control over outside economic forces through cooperatives and labor unions.

Richard J. Perry. *From Time Immemorial: Indigenous Peoples and State Systems.* Austin: University of Texas Press, 1996. This book provides a comparative examination of the history and status of indigenous peoples of Mexico, the United States, Canada, and Australia. The conclusion offers findings about state policies, state violence, resistance of the indigenous people, and efforts at self-determination.

Richard Reed. *Forest Dwellers, Forest Protectors: Indigenous Models for International Development.* The Cultural Survival Series in Ethnicity and Change. Boston: Allyn and Bacon, 1997. This is a fieldwork-based study of the Guaraní, indigenous people of Paraguay and Brazil, now occupying one of the world's largest remaining subtropical rainforests. Chapters consider social organization, production patterns, and consumption patterns. The text focuses on Guaraní practices and their ideas about use of forest resources.

Kalima Rose. *Where Women Are Leaders: The SEWA Movement in India.* Atlantic Highlands, NJ: Zed Books, 1992. Although not written by an anthropologist, this in-depth case study of a pioneering credit scheme for poor women of India stands as a useful contribution to the "success story" literature. The book provides a history of SEWA (Self-Employed Women's Association) and describes different strategies of SEWA and its expansion throughout India and globally.

John van Willigen. *Anthropology in Action: A Source Book on Anthropological Practice.* Boulder, CO: Westview Press, 1991. This book first provides brief overviews of ethics, publications, and professional organizations in applied anthropology. There follows a series of case studies arranged alphabetically by topic from "Agriculture" to "Women in Development."

Robert M. VanWynsberghe. *AlterNatives: Community, Identity, and Environmental Justice on Walpole Island.* Boston: Allyn and Bacon, 2002. This study documents the environmental activism of the Walpole Island First Nation, Ontario, the southernmost reserve in Canada. During the 1990s, indigenous peoples of Walpole began to organize to protect their environment from toxic pollution caused by massive discharges of industrial waste into the St. Clair River. They successfully planned for providing clean water to the community, management of the area's wetlands, and a creation of a Heritage Centre.

HOW do cultural anthropologists study change?

Since the mid-twentieth century, cultural anthropologists have become seriously involved in the study of change. Many such cultural anthropologists have contributed to theoretical debates about how change occurs and how anthropological knowledge can contribute to culturally appropriate forms of change. Major processes of change are invention and diffusion. In contemporary times, modernization has been a powerful model of change that involves diffusion of Western technologies and values to non-Western contexts. After World War II, development became increasingly important as a form of modernization that emphasizes improved human welfare.

WHAT are various approaches to development?

Several theories or models of development exist, including modernization, growth-oriented development, distributional development, human development, and sustainable development. Institutional approaches to development, whether pursued by large-scale or grassroots organizations, tend to rely on the development project as a vehicle of local change. Cultural anthropologists have been hired as consultants on development projects, typically at the end of the project cycle to provide evaluations. Anthropologists have pushed for involvement earlier in the project so that their cultural knowledge can be used in project planning to avoid common errors. In order to provide relevant information in a short time frame, cultural anthropology has adapted its traditional methods of long-term participant observation. Rapid research methods are intended to maximize data gathering during a short period in spite of (and with awareness of) the greater limitations involved.

WHAT does cultural anthropology contribute to understanding some major issues in development?

The status of indigenous peoples, the role of women in development, and the complex issue of defining and protecting human rights are three urgent and interrelated areas in international development that have attracted anthropological research and thinking. Research on the impact of growth-oriented, large-scale development shows that many indigenous peoples and women have suffered declines in their entitlements and standard of living. Often, such losses are tied to violence and environmental degradation in their homelands. Such tragic occurrences lead directly to the question of what human rights are and how development affects them. Cultural anthropologists contribute insights from different cultures about perceptions of basic human and cultural rights and this knowledge, linked to advocacy, may be able to help prevent human rights abuses in the future.

GLOSSARY

absolute cultural relativism: a perspective that says a person from one culture should not question the rightness or wrongness of behavior or ideas in other cultures because that would be ethnocentric.

achieved position: a person's standing in society based on qualities that the person has gained through action.

adolescence: a culturally defined period of maturation from the time of puberty until adulthood.

agency: the ability of humans to make choices and exercise free will.

age set: a group of people close in age who go through certain rituals, such as circumcision, at the same time.

agriculture: a mode of production that involves growing crops with the use of plowing, irrigation, and fertilizer.

amazon: a person who is biologically female but takes on a male gender role.

ambilineal descent: a kinship system in which a person is said to be descended from both parents but that allows the individual to choose with which descent group to have more affiliation.

animatism: a belief system in which the supernatural is conceived of as an impersonal power.

animism: the belief in souls or "doubles."

anthropomorphic: a supernatural in the form of a human.

art: the application of imagination, skill, and style to matter, movement, and sound that goes beyond what is purely practical.

ascribed position: a person's standing in society based on qualities that the person has gained through birth.

assimilation: a process of culture change through which one culture becomes completely incorporated into another and no longer has a separate identity.

authority: the ability to take action based on a person's achieved or ascribed status, moral reputation, or other basis.

avunculocality: a kinship rule that defines preferred marital residence with or near the wife's brother.

balanced exchange: a form of exchange in which the goal is either immediate or eventual equality in value.

band: the political organization of foraging groups.

banditry: a form of aggressive conflict that involves taking something that belongs to someone else, sometimes practiced by a person or group of persons who are socially marginal and who may gain a mythic status.

basic needs fund: a category of a personal or household budget that includes food, beverages, shelter, clothing, and the tools needed to obtain these items.

below-replacement-level fertility: a situation in which births are fewer than deaths, leading to population decline.

berdache: a blurred gender category, usually referring to a person who is biologically male but who assumes a female gender role.

big-man or big-woman system: a form of political organization midway between tribe and chiefdom involving reliance on the leadership of key individuals who develop a political following through personal ties and redistributive feasts.

bilineal descent: a kinship system in which a child is recognized as being related by descent to both parents.

bilocality: a marital residence pattern that offers a married couple the choice of living near or with the family of either the groom or the bride.

biological determinism: a theory that explains human behavior and ideas mainly as a result of biological features such as genes, hormones, and drives.

blood sport: a form of competition that explicitly seeks to bring about a flow of blood, or even death, of human contestants, animal competitors, or in animal targets of human hunting.

bride-service: a form of marriage exchange in which the groom works for his father-in-law for a certain period of time before returning home with the bride.

brideprice: a form of marriage exchange involving a transfer of cash and goods from the groom to the bride's father.

capital: wealth used to create more wealth.

cargo cult: a form of revitalization movement that sprang up in Melanesia, the South Pacific, in response to Western and Japanese influences.

caste: a ranked group, determined by birth, often linked to a particular occupation and to South Asian cultures.

ceremonial fund: a category of a personal or household budget used for public events such as a potlatch.

chiefdom: a political unit of permanently allied tribes and villages under one recognized leader.

civil society: the collection of interest groups that function outside the government to organize economic and other aspects of life.

clan: a kinship-based group in which people claim descent from a common ancestor, although they may be unable to trace the exact relationship.

class: a way of categorizing people on the basis of their economic position in society, usually measured in terms of income or wealth.

clinical or **applied medical anthropology:** the application of anthropological knowledge to furthering the goals of health care providers.

code: a variant within a language that may include a distinct vocabulary, grammar, and intonation, associated with a particular microculture.

communication: the conveying of meaningful messages from one person, animal, or insect to another.

community healing: healing that emphasizes the social context as a key component and is likely to be carried out within the public domain.

consumerism: a mode of consumption in which people's demands are many and infinite and the means of satisfying them are insufficient and become depleted in the effort to satisfy these demands.

consumption fund: a category of a personal or household budget used to provide for consumption demands.

cooperative: an economic group whose members share surpluses and who follow the democratic decision-making principle of one person, one vote.

corporate farm: a large agricultural enterprise that produces goods solely for sale and that is owned and operated by companies that rely entirely on hired labor.

couvade: a variety of customs applying to the behavior of fathers during and shortly after the birth of their children.

creole: a language directly descended from a pidgin but possessing its own native speakers and involving linguistic expansion and elaboration.

critical cultural relativism: a perspective that prompts people in all cultures to raise questions about their own and others' cultural practices and ideas, especially regarding who ac-

cepts them and why, and whom they might be harming or helping.

critical development anthropology: an approach to international development in which the anthropologist takes on a critical-thinking role and asks why and to whose benefit particular development policies and programs are pursued.

critical legal anthropology: an approach within the cross-cultural study of law that examines how law and judicial systems serve to maintain and expand dominant power interests rather than protecting marginal and less powerful people.

critical media anthropology: an approach within the cross-cultural study of mass media that examines to what degree media messages are liberating, to what degree they are propagandizing and controlling, and whose interests the media serve.

critical medical anthropology: an approach within the cross-cultural study of health and illness involving the analysis of how economic and political structures shape people's health status, their access to health care, and the prevailing medical systems that exist in relation to them.

critical military anthropology: the study of the military as a power structure in terms of its roles and internal social dynamics.

cross cousin: the offspring of either one's father's sister or one's mother's brother.

cultural broker: a person who is familiar with the practices and beliefs of two cultures and can promote cross-cultural understanding to prevent or mediate conflicts.

cultural configuration: Ruth Benedict's theory that cultures are formed through the unconscious selection of a few cultural traits that interweave to form a cohesive pattern shared by all members of the culture.

cultural constructionism: a theory that explains human behavior and ideas as being mainly the results of learning.

cultural imperialism: a situation in which a dominant culture claims supremacy over minority cultures and makes changes in its culture and the minority culture(s) in its own interests and at the expense of the minority culture(s).

cultural materialism: a theoretical position that takes material features of life, such as the environment, natural resources, and mode of production as the bases for explaining social organization and ideology.

cultural relativism: the perspective that each culture must be understood in terms of the values and ideas of that culture and should not be judged by the standards of another.

culture: learned and shared human behaviors and ideas.

culture-bound syndrome: a collection of signs and symptoms that is restricted to a particular culture or a limited number of cultures; also called "folk illness."

culture of poverty: Oscar Lewis's theory that the personality characteristics of the poor trap them in poverty.

culture shock: persistent feelings of uneasiness, loneliness, and anxiety that often occur when a person has shifted from one culture to a different one.

dalit: the preferred name for the socially defined lowest groups in the Indian caste system, meaning "oppressed" or "ground down."

deductive research: a research method that involves posing a research question or hypothesis, gathering empirical data related to the question, and then assessing the findings in relation to the original hypothesis.

demographic transition: the change from the combined high fertility and high mortality of the agricultural mode of reproduction to the low fertility and low mortality characteristic of industrialized societies.

demography: the study of population dynamics.

development: directed change to achieve improved human welfare.

development anthropology: the study of how culture and development interact.

development-induced displacement (DID): forced migration due to development projects, such as dam building.

diachronic: the analysis of culture across time.

dialect: a way of speaking in a particular place or a variety of a language arising from local circumstances.

diaspora population: dispersed group of people living outside their original homeland.

diffusion: the spread of culture through contact.

direct entitlement: the most secure form of entitlement to providing for one's needs; in an agricultural society, owning land that produces food is a direct entitlement.

direct infanticide: the killing of an infant or child through practices such as beating, smothering, poisoning, or drowning.

discourse: people's talk, stories, and myths.

disease of development: a health problem caused or increased by economic development activities that affect the environment and people's relationship with it.

disease/illness dichotomy: the distinction between disease as an objective and universal biological pathology, and illness as the culturally specific understandings and experiences of a health problem or other form of suffering; corresponds to the etic/emic distinction.

displaced person: someone who is forced to leave his or her home and community, or country and to settle elsewhere.

displacement: a feature of human language that allows people to talk about events in the past and future.

divination: a diagnostic procedure in which a specialist uses techniques to gain supernatural insights.

doctrine: direct and formalized statements about religious beliefs.

domestication: the control and management of plants and animals by humans in terms of both their location and their reproduction.

dominant caste: one caste in a particular locale that controls most of the land and is often numerically preponderant.

dowry: a form of marriage exchange involving the transfer of cash and goods from the bride's family to the bride and groom or to the groom's family.

ecological/epidemiological approach: an approach that considers how aspects of the natural environment and social environment interact to cause illness.

emic: what insiders do and perceive about their culture, their perceptions of reality, and their explanations for why they do what they do.

endogamy: marriage within a particular group or locality.

entertainment fund: a category of a personal or household budget used to provide for leisure activities.

entitlement: a culturally defined right to life-sustaining resources.

ethnicity: a sense of group affiliation based on features such as a distinct history, language, or religion.

ethno-esthetics: cultural definitions of what is art.

ethnobotany: an area of inquiry exploring knowledge in different cultures of plants and their uses.

ethnocentrism: judging other cultures by the standards of one's own culture rather than by the standards of that particular culture.

ethnocide: destruction of a culture without physically killing its people.

ethnography: a firsthand, detailed description of a living culture, based on personal observation.

ethnology: the study of a particular topic in more than one culture using ethnographic material.

ethnomedicine: the medical system of a culture, including practices and ideas about the body, illness, and healing.

ethnomusicology: the cross-cultural study of music.

ethno-nosology: the cross-cultural study of culturally specific classifications of health problems.

ethnopsychology: the study of how various cultures define and create personality, identity, and mental health.

etic: an analytical framework used by outside analysts in studying culture. It may be based on a hypothesis or search for causal relationships.

euhemerism: the process by which a human who once lived is transformed into a deity; named after the philosopher Euhemerus of Messene.

exogamy: marriage outside a particular group or locality.

expected reciprocity: an exchange of approximately equally valued goods or services, usually between people roughly equal in social status.

expressive culture: behavior and beliefs related to the arts and leisure.

extended household: a co-resident kinship group that comprises more than one parent–child unit.

extensive strategy: a form of production involving temporary use of large areas of land and a high degree of spatial mobility.

faction: a politically oriented group that has strong ties to a leader and that vies with other factions for resources and rights.

family: a group of people who consider themselves related through a form of kinship, such as descent, marriage, or sharing.

female genital cutting: a term used for a range of genital cutting procedures, including the excision of part or all of the clitoris, excision of part or all of the labia majora, and sometimes infibulation, the stitching together of the vaginal entry.

femicide: the murder of a person based on the fact of her being female.

fertility: the rate of births in a population.

feuding: long-term, retributive violence that may be lethal between families, groups of families, or tribes.

fieldwork: research in the field, which is any place where people and culture are found.

focal vocabulary: a cluster of related words referring to important features of a particular culture.

foraging: collecting food that is available in nature, by gathering, fishing, or hunting.

formal sector: salaried or wage-based work registered in official statistics.

frontline anthropology: anthropological research carried out within zones of violent conflict and requiring specialized training and experience.

functionalism: a theory that looks at a practice or belief in terms of its contribution to cultural continuity.

gender: culturally constructed and learned behaviors and ideas attributed to males, females, or blended genders.

genealogy: a record of a person's relatives constructed beginning with the earliest ancestors.

generalized reciprocity: exchange involving the least conscious sense of interest in material gain or thought of what might be received in return.

genocide: the destruction of a culture and its people through physical extermination.

globalization: increased and intensified international ties related to the spread of Western, especially United States, capitalism that affects all world cultures.

global language: or world language, a language spoken widely throughout the world and in diverse cultural contexts often replacing indigenous languages, notably English and Spanish.

grammar: the rules by which words are organized to make sense in a string.

groomprice: a form of dowry involving transfer of large amounts of cash and goods from the bride's family to the groom's family; often called dowry.

Hawthorne effect: research bias due to informants changing their behavior to conform to expectations of the researchers.

heterotopia: the creation of an internally varied place by collecting things from diverse cultures and locations.

hijira: term used in India to refer to a blurred gender role in which a person, usually biologically male, takes on female dress and behavior.

historical linguistics: the study of language change using formal methods that compare shifts over time and across space in formal aspects of language such as phonetics, grammar, and semantics.

historical particularism: the view that individual cultures must be studied and described on their own terms and that cross-cultural comparisons and generalizations ignore cultural specificities and are invalid.

holism: the perspective in anthropology that cultures are complex systems that cannot be fully understood without paying attention to their different components, including economics, social organization, and ideology.

horticulture: a mode of production based on growing domesticated crops in gardens using simple hand tools.

household: a group of people, who may or may not be related by kinship, who share living space and budgeting.

human development: a model of change promoted by the United Nations that emphasizes improvements in human welfare such as health, education, and personal security.

humoral healing system: a medical model that emphasizes balance among natural elements within the body.

hypergyny: a marriage in which the groom is of higher status than the bride.

hypogyny: a marriage in which the bride is of higher status than the groom.

image of the limited good: George Foster's theory that in nonindustrial cultures, people have a characteristic world view of finite resources or wealth such that if someone in the group increases his or her wealth, other people will necessarily lose out.

in-kind taxation: a revenue system that involves non-cash contributions such as labor.

incest taboo: a strongly held prohibition against marrying or having sex with particular kin.

indigenous knowledge: local knowledge about the environment, including plants, animals, and resources.

indigenous people: people who have a longstanding connection with their home territory that predates colonial or outside societies that prevail in that territory.

indirect entitlement: a way of gaining one's livelihood that depends on exchanging something such as labor or goods.

indirect infanticide: the killing of an infant or child through practices such as food deprivation or failure to seek health care during illness.

inductive research: a research approach that avoids hypothesis formation in advance of the research and instead takes its lead from the culture being studied.

industrial capital agriculture: a form of agriculture that is capital-intensive, substituting machinery and purchased inputs for human and animal labor.

industrial collectivized agriculture: a form of industrialized agriculture that involves state control of land, technology, and goods produced.

industrialism: a mode of production in which goods are produced through mass employment in business and commercial operations.

infant mortality rate: the number of deaths of children under the age of one year per 1000 births.

infanticide: the killing of an infant or child.

influence: the ability to achieve a desired end by exerting social or moral pressure on someone or some group.

informal sector: work that is outside the formal sector, not officially registered, and sometimes illegal.

informed consent: an aspect of fieldwork ethics requiring that the researcher inform the research participants of the intent, scope, and possible effects of the study and seek their consent to be in the study.

infrastructure: in the framework of cultural materialism, the first and most basic level of culture, which includes the material factors of economy and reproduction.

institutional migrant: a person who moves into a social institution (such as a school or prison), voluntarily or involuntarily.

intensive strategy: a form of production that involves continuous use of the same land and resources.

intergenerational household: a residential group in which an "adult child" returns to live with his or her parents.

internally displaced person: a person forced to leave their home and community but who remain within their country.

interpretivism: the view that cultures can be understood by studying what people think about, their ideas, and the meanings that are important to them. Also called interpretive anthropology.

interview: a research technique that involves gathering of verbal data through questions or guided conversation between at least two people.

isogamy: marriage between status equals.

jajmani system: an exchange system of India in which landholding patrons (jajmans) offer food grains to service providers such as brahman priests, artisans (blacksmiths, potters), and agricultural laborers.

kinesics: the study of communication that occurs through body movements, positions, facial expressions, and spatial behavior.

kinship: a sense of being related to another person or persons through descent, sharing, or marriage.

kinship diagram: a schematic way of presenting data on kinship relationships of an individual (called "ego") depicting all of ego's relatives, as remembered by ego and reported to the anthropologist.

kinship system: the predominant form of kin relationships in a culture and the kinds of behavior involved.

language: a form of communication that is a systematic set of arbitrary symbols shared among a group and passed on from generation to generation.

language decay: condition of a language in which speakers adopt a new language for most situations, begin to use their native language only in certain contexts, and may be only semi-fluent and have limited vocabulary in their native language.

language extinction: a situation, either gradual or sudden, in which language speakers abandon their native language in favor of a new language to the extent that the native language loses functions and no longer has competent users.

law: a binding rule created through enactment or custom that defines right and reasonable behavior and is enforceable by threat of punishment.

legal pluralism: the existence, within a culture, of more than one kind of legal system.

lifeboat mentality: local resentment of an immigrant group because of perceived resource constraints.

life-cycle ritual: a ritual performed to mark a change in status from one life stage to another of an individual or group; also called *rite of passage*.

life history: a qualitative, in-depth portrait of a single life experience of a person as narrated to the anthropologist.

limited-purpose money: an item or items that can be exchanged only for specified things.

linguistic determinism: the theory that language determines consciousness of the world and behavior.

linguistic pluralism: the presence of linguistic diversity within a particular context.

linguistic relativism: the position that all languages are equally successful forms of communication.

localization: cultural change in which global or macrocultures become adapted and transformed by local microcultures.

logograph: a symbol that conveys meaning through a form or picture resembling that to which it refers.

macroculture: a distinct pattern of learned and shared behavior and thinking that crosses local boundaries, such as transnational culture and global culture.

magic: the attempt to compel supernatural forces and beings to act in certain ways.

market exchange: the buying and selling of commodities under competitive conditions in which the forces of supply and demand determine value.

marriage: a union between two people (usually), who are likely to be, but are not necessarily, co-resident, sexually involved with each other, and procreative.

material cultural heritage: monuments, buildings, sites, and movable objects considered to have outstanding value to humanity. Also called cultural heritage.

matrescence: motherhood, or the cultural process of becoming a mother.

matriarchy: a society in which women are dominant in terms of economics, politics, and ideology.

matrifocality: a household system in which a female (or females) is the central, stable figure around whom other members cluster.

matrilineal descent: a kinship system that highlights the importance of women by tracing descent through the female line, favoring marital residence with or near the bride's family, and providing for property to be inherited through the female line.

matrilocality: a kinship rule that defines preferred marital residence with or near the bride's kin.

mechanical solidarity: social bonding among groups that are similar.

medicalization: labeling a particular issue or problem as medical and requiring medical treatment when, in fact, that issue or problem is economic or political.

medical pluralism: the existence of more than one medical system in a culture, or a government policy to promote the integration of local healing systems into biomedical practice.

microculture: a distinct pattern of learned and shared behavior and thinking found within larger cultures. Examples include ethnic groups and institutional cultures.

migration: the movement of a person or people from one place to another.

minimalism: a mode of consumption that emphasizes simplicity, is characterized by few and finite (limited) consumer demands, and involves an adequate and sustainable means to achieve them.

mode of consumption: the dominant way, in a culture, of using things up or spending resources in order to satisfy demands.

mode of exchange: the dominant pattern, in a society, of transferring goods, services, and other items between and among people and groups.

mode of production: the dominant way, in a culture, of providing for people's material needs.

mode of reproduction: the predominant pattern of fertility and mortality in a culture.

modernization: a model of change based on belief in the inevitable advance of science and Western secularism and processes including industrial growth, consolidation of the state, bureaucratization, market economy, technological innovation, literacy, and options for social mobility.

money: currency or items with recognized value that can be exchanged for other kinds of things.

monogamy: marriage between two people.

mortality: deaths in a population, or rate of population decline in general or from particular causes.

multi-purpose money: a medium of exchange that can be used for all goods and services available.

multi-sited research: fieldwork conducted in more than one location in order to understand the behaviors and ideas of dispersed members of a culture or the relationships among different levels such as state policy and local culture.

myth: a narrative with a plot that involves the sacred.

nation: a group of people who share a language, culture, territorial base, political organization, and history.

national character study: a type of analysis in psychological anthropology that defined basic personality types and core values of entire countries.

neolocality: a kinship rule that defines preferred marital residence in a new location not linked to either the bride's or the groom's parents' residence.

new immigrants: international migrants who have moved since the 1960s.

norm: a generally agreed-upon standard for how people should behave, usually unwritten and learned unconsciously.

nuclear household: a domestic unit containing one adult couple (married or partners), with or without children.

observer's paradox: the logical impossibility of doing research on natural communication events without affecting the naturalness sought.

organic solidarity: social bonding among groups with different abilities and resources.

paralanguage: nonverbal communication such as body posture, voice tone, touch, smells, and eye and facial movements.

parallel cousin: offspring of either one father's brother or one's mother's sister.

participant observation: basic fieldwork method in cultural anthropology that involves living in a culture for a long period of time while gathering data.

participatory research method (PRM): a method in development anthropology that involves the local people in gathering data relevant to local development projects.

pastoralism: a mode of production based on keeping domesticated animal herds and using their products, such as meat and milk, for most of the diet.

patrescence: fatherhood, or the cultural process of becoming a father.

patrilineal descent: a kinship system that highlights the importance of men in tracing descent, determining marital residence with or near the groom's family, and providing for inheritance of property through the male line.

patrilocality: a kinship rule that defines preferred marital residence with or near the groom's kin.

personality: an individual's patterned and characteristic way of behaving, thinking, and feeling.

person-centered ethnography: anthropological research that focuses on the individual and how the individual's psychology and subjective experience both shapes and is shaped by the wider culture.

phoneme: a sound that makes a difference for meaning in a language.

phonetics: the analysis of phonemes.

pidgin: a contact language that emerges where people with different languages need to communicate; a pidgin involves linguistic simplification and reduction.

policing: the exercise of social control through processes of surveillance and the threat of punishment related to maintaining social order.

political organization: the existence of groups for purposes of public decision making and leadership, maintaining social cohesion and order, protecting group rights, and ensuring safety from external threats.

polyandry: marriage of one wife with more than one husband.

polygamy: marriage involving multiple spouses.

polygyny: marriage of one husband with more than one wife.

postmodernism: a view that questions various aspects of modernism, including the scientific method, human progress through scientific knowledge, urbanization, technological change, and mass communication.

potlatch: a grand feast in which guests are invited to eat and to receive gifts from the hosts.

power: the capacity to take action in the face of resistance, through force if necessary.

priest/priestess: male or female full-time religious specialist whose position is based mainly on abilities gained through formal training.

primary group: a social group in which members meet on a face-to-face basis.

productivity: a feature of human language that offers the ability to communicate many messages efficiently.

project cycle: the steps of a development project from initial planning to completion: project identification, project design, project appraisal, project implementation, and project evaluation.

puberty: a time in the human life cycle that occurs universally and involves a set of biological markers and sexual maturation.

public/private dichotomy: gender division in society that emerged with agriculture, whereby men are more involved with the nondomestic domain and women are more involved in activities in or near the home.

pure gift: something given with no expectation or thought of a return.

push–pull theory: a theory that attributes rural-to-urban migration to the "push" of rural areas' decreasing ability to support population growth and the "pull" of cities that offer employment and a more appealing lifestyle.

qualitative research: research that emphasizes generating description.

quantitative research: research that emphasizes gathering and analyzing numerical information and using tables and charts when presenting results.

race: a scientifically invalid way of classifying people on the basis of selected biological traits such as skin color and facial features.

rapid research method (RRM): fieldwork method designed for use in development anthropology that can yield relevant data in a short period of time.

rapport: a trusting relationship between the researcher and the study population.

recurrent costs fund: a category of a person's or household's budget used to provide for repair and maintenance of tools, shelter, and other features of one's lifestyle.

redistribution: a form of exchange that involves one person collecting goods or money from many members of a group who then, at a later time and at a public event, "returns" the pooled goods to everyone who contributed.

reflexive anthropology: anthropological research carried out and described with attention to the researcher's presence, role, and influence on the research, research informants, and research results. Also called reflexivity.

refugee: someone who is forced to leave his or her home country.

religion: beliefs and actions related to supernatural beings and forces.

religious pluralism: when one or more religions co-exist as either complementary to each other or as competitive systems.

remittance: economic transfer of money or goods by a migrant to his or her family back home.

repatriation: returning art or other objects from museums to the people with whom they originated.

replacement-level fertility: situation when births equal deaths, leading to maintenance of current population size.

revitalization movement: an organized movement, usually surrounding a prophetic leader, that seeks to construct a more satisfying culture, either by re-establishing all or parts of a religion that has been threatened by outside forces or by adopting new practices and beliefs.

revolution: a political crisis prompted by illegal and often violent actions of subordinate groups that seek to change the political institutions or social structure of a society.

right of return: United Nations guaranteed right of refugees to repatriation.

ritual: a patterned form of behavior that has to do with the supernatural realm.

ritual of inversion: a ritual in which normal social roles and order are temporarily reversed.

role: the expected behavior for someone of a particular status, with a "script" for how to behave, look, eat, and talk.

sacrifice: a ritual in which something is offered to the supernaturals.

Sapir-Whorf hypothesis: a theory that claims that language determines thought.

secondary group: people who identify with each other on some basis but may never meet with one another personally.

segmentary model: type of political organization in which smaller units unite in the face of external threats and then disunite when the external threat is absent.

sex-selective infanticide: the killing of offspring depending on their sex.

shaman/shamanka: male or female part-time religious specialist who gains his or her status through direct relationship with the supernaturals, often by being "called."

social control: processes that maintain orderly social life, including informal and formal mechanisms.

social group: a cluster of people beyond the domestic unit who are usually related on grounds other than kinship.

social impact assessment: a study conducted to gauge the potential social costs and benefits of particular innovations before change is undertaken.

social stratification: hierarchical relationships between different groups as though they were arranged in layers or "strata."

sociocultural fit: concept that refers to how well a development project meshes with the "target" culture and population.

sociolinguistics: approach that says that culture and society and a person's social position determine the content and form of language; a field of study devoted to revealing such social effects on language.

state: a centralized political unit encompassing many communities and possessing coercive power.

status: a person's position, or standing, in society.

stem household: a coresidential group that contains only two married couples related through males, commonly found in East Asian cultures.

structural adjustment: an economic policy that has been pursued by the World Bank since the 1980s requiring that countries receiving World Bank loans pursue privatization of services such as health care and schools and reduce government expenditures in these areas.

structural suffering: human health problems caused by such economic and political situations as war, famine, terrorism, forced migration, and poverty. Also called structural affliction.

structure: within the cultural materialist framework, the second level of culture, which comprises social organization, kinship, and political organization.

structurism: a theoretical position concerning human behavior and ideas that says "free choice" is an illusion since the choices themselves are determined by larger forces such as the economy, social and political organization, and ideological systems.

superstructure: within the cultural materialist framework, the third level of culture, which comprises ideology (communication, religion, and expressive culture).

sustainable development: a directed change that involves forms of development that are not environmentally destructive and are financially supportable by the host country and environmentally supportable by the earth as a whole.

symbol: something that stands for something else; symbols are arbitrary (bearing no necessary relationship with what is symbolized), unpredictable, and diverse.

synchronic: a "one-time" view of a culture that devotes little or no attention to its past.

syncretism: the blending of features of two or more cultures, especially used in discussion of religious change.

tag question: a question seeking affirmation, placed at the end of a sentence.

tax fund: a category of a person's or household's budget used as payment to a government as part of one's civic responsibilities or to a landlord for use of land or housing.

teknonymy: the practice of naming someone on the basis of his or her relationship to someone else, as in "The Mother of So and So."

theater: a form of enactment, related to other forms such as dance, music, parades, competitive games and sports, and verbal art.

trade: the formalized exchange of one thing for another according to set standards of value.

traditional development anthropology: an approach to development in which the anthropologist accepts the role of helping to make development work better by providing cultural information to planners.

transnational migrant: a person who moves back and forth regularly between two or more countries and forms a new identity that transcends association of the self with a single political unit.

trial by ordeal: a way of determining innocence or guilt in which the accused person is put to a test that may be painful, stressful, or fatal.

triangulation: research technique that involves obtaining information on a particular topic from more than one person or perspective.

tribe: a political group that comprises several bands or lineage groups, each with similar language and lifestyle and occupying a distinct territory.

unbalanced exchange: a system of transfers in which one party seeks to make a profit.

unilineal descent: a kinship system that traces descent through only one parent, either the mother or the father.

use rights: a system of property relations in which a person or group has socially recognized priority in access to particular resources such as gathering, hunting, and fishing areas and water holes.

war: organized and purposeful group action directed against another group and involving the actual or potential application of lethal force.

world religion: a term coined in the nineteenth century to refer to religions that had many followers, that crossed state borders and that exhibited other specific features such as a concern with salvation.

world view: a way of understanding how the world came to be, its design, and people's place in it with or without reference to a supernatural realm.

youth gang: a group of young people, found mainly in urban areas, who are often considered a social problem by adults and law enforcement officials.

zoomorphic: a supernatural in the shape, or partial shape, of an animal.

Abélès, Marc. 1991
Quiet Days in Burgundy: A Study of Local Politics. Trans. Annella McDermott. New York: Cambridge University Press.

Abu-Lughod, Lila.
1993 Writing Women's Worlds: Bedouin Stories. Berkeley: University of California Press.

Adams, Kathleen M.
1984 Come to Tana Toraja, "Land of the Heavenly Kings": Travel Agents as Brokers in Ethnicity. Annals of Tourism Research 11:469–485.

Adams, Vincanne. 1988
Modes of Production and Medicine: An Examination of the Theory in Light of Sherpa Traditional Medicine. Social Science and Medicine 27:505–513.

Agar, Michael. 1994
Language Shock: Understanding the Culture of Conversation. New York: William Morrow and Company, Inc.

Ahmadu, Fuambai. 2000
Rites and Wrongs: An Insider/Outside Reflects on Power and Excision. In Female "Circumcision" in Africa: Culture, Controversy, and Change. Bettina Shell-Duncan and Ylva Hernlund, eds. Pp. 283–312. Boulder, CO: Lynne Reiner Publishers.

Akinsha, Konstantin. 1992a
Russia: Whose Art Is It? ARTNews 91(5):100–105.
———. 1992b
Whose Gold? ARTNews 91(3):39–40.
———. 1992c
After the Coup: Art for Art's Sake? ARTNews 91(1): 108–113.

Allen, Susan. 1994
What Is Media Anthropology? A Personal View and a Suggested Structure. In Media Anthropology: Informing Global Citizens. Susan L. Allen, ed. Pp. 15–32. Westport, CT: Bergin & Garvey.

Allison, Anne. 1994
Nightwork: Sexuality, Pleasure, and Corporate Masculinity in a Tokyo Hostess Club. Chicago: University of Chicago Press.

Alter, Joseph S. 1992
The Sannyasi and the Indian Wrestler: Anatomy of a Relationship. American Ethnologist 19(2):317–336.

Ames, Michael, 1992
Cannibal Tours and Glass Boxes: The Anthropology of Museums. Vancouver: University of British Columbia Press.

Anderson, Benedict. 1991 [1983]
Imagined Communities: Reflections on the Origin and Spread of Nationalism. New York: Verso.

Anderson, Richard L. and Karen L. Field. 1993
Chapter Introduction. Art in Small-Scale Societies: Contemporary Readings. In Richard L. Anderson and Karen L. Fields, eds. P. 247. Englewood Cliffs, NJ: Prentice Hall.

Andriolo, Karin. 2002
Murder by Suicide: Episodes from Muslim History. American Anthropologist 104:736–742.

Appadurai, Arjun. 1986
Introduction: Commodities and the Politics of Value. In The Social Life of Things: Commodities in Cultural Perspective. Arjun Appadurai, ed. Pp. 3–63. New York: Cambridge University Press.

Applbaum, Kalman D. 1995
Marriage with the Proper Stranger: Arranged Marriage in Metropolitan Japan. Ethnology 34(1):37–51.

Ariès, Philippe. 1962
Centuries of Childhood: A Social History of Family Life. Trans. Robert Baldick. New York: Vintage Books.

Attwood, Donald W. 1992
Raising Cane: The Political Economy of Sugar in Western India. Boulder: Westview Press.

Awe, Bolanle. 1977

The Iyalode in the Traditional Yoruba Political System. In Sexual Stratification: A Cross-Cultural View. Alice Schlegel, ed. Pp. 144–160. New York: Columbia University Press.

Baer, Lars-Anders. 1982
The Sami: An Indigenous People in Their Own Land. In The Sami National Minority in Sweden. Birgitta Jahreskog, ed. Pp. 11–22. Stockholm: Almqvist & Wiksell International.

Barbash, Fred. 1996
And They'll Live Separately Ever After. The Washington Post, February 29:A1ff.

Bardhan, Pranab. 1974
On Life and Death Questions. Economic and Political Weekly, Special Number 9 (32–34):1293–1303.

Barfield, Thomas J. 1993
The Nomadic Alternative. Englewood Cliffs, NJ: Prentice-Hall.

———. 1994
Prospects for Plural Societies in Central Asia. Cultural Survival Quarterly 18 (2 & 3):48–51.

———. 2001
Pastoral Nomads or Nomadic Pastoralists. In The Dictionary of Anthropology. Thomas Barfield, ed. Pp. 348–350. Malden, MA: Blackwell Publishers.

Barkey, Nanette, Benjamin C. Campbell, and Paul W. Leslie. 2001
A Comparison of Health Complaints of Settled and Nomadic Turkana Men. Medical Anthropology Quarterly 15:391–408.

Barlett, Peggy F. 1980
Reciprocity and the San Juan Fiesta. Journal of Anthropological Research 36:116–130.

———. 1989
Industrial Agriculture. In Economic Anthropology. Stuart Plattner, ed. Pp. 253–292. Stanford: Stanford University Press.

Barnard, Alan. 2000
History and Theory in Anthropology. New York: Cambridge University Press.

Barnard, Alan and Anthony Good. 1984
Research Practices in the Study of Kinship. New York: Academic Press.

Barth, Frederik. 1993
Balinese Worlds. Chicago: University of Chicago Press.

Basch, Linda, Nina Glick Schiller, and Christina Szanton Blanc. 1994
Nations Unbound: Transnational Projects, Postcolonial Predicaments, and Deterritorialized Nation-States. Langhorne, PA: Gordon and Breach Science Publishers.

Basso, Keith. H. 1972 [1970]
"To Give Up on Words": Silence in Apache Culture. In Language and Social Context. Pier Paolo Giglioni, ed. pp. 67–86. Baltimore: Penguin Books.

Beals, Alan R. 1980
Gopalpur: A South Indian Village. Fieldwork Edition. New York: Holt, Rinehart and Winston.

Beattie, Andrew. 2002
Changing Places: Relatives and Relativism in Java. Journal of the Royal Anthropological Institute 8:469–491.

Beatty, Andrew. 1992
Society and Exchange in Nias. New York: Oxford University Press.

Beck, Lois. 1986
The Qashqa'i of Iran. New Haven: Yale University Press.

———. 1991
Nomad: A Year in the Life of a Qashqa'i Tribesman in Iran. Berkeley: University of California Press.

Beeman, William O. 1993
The Anthropology of Theater and Spectacle. Annual Review of Anthropology 22:363–393.

Belikov, Vladimir. 1994
Language Death in Siberia. UNESCO Courier 1994(2): 32–36.

Bell, Diane. 1998
Ngarrindjeri Wurruwarrin: A World That Is, Was, and Will Be. North Melbourne, Australia: Spinifex.

Benedict, Ruth. 1959 [1934]
Patterns of Culture. Boston: Houghton Mifflin Company.

———. 1969 [1946]
The Chrysanthemum and the Sword: Patterns of Japanese Culture. Rutland, VT: Charles E. Tuttle Company.

Berlin, Elois Ann and Brent Berlin. 1996
Medical Ethnobiology of the Highland Maya of Chiapas, Mexico: The Gastrointestinal Diseases. Princeton: Princeton University Press.

Bermann, Marc. 1994
Lukurmata: Household Archaeology in Prehispanic Bolivia. Princeton: Princeton University Press.

Bernal, Martin. 1987
Black Athena: The Afroasiatic Roots of Classical Civilization. New Brunswick, NJ: Rutgers University Press.

Bernard, H. Russell. 1995
Research Methods in Anthropology: Qualitative and Quantitative Approaches. Walnut Creek, CA: Altamira Press/ Sage.

Berreman, Gerald D. 1979 [1975]
Race, Caste, and Other Invidious Distinctions in Social Stratification. In Caste and Other Inequities: Essays on Inequality. Gerald D. Berreman, ed. Pp. 178–222. New Delhi: Manohar.

Best, David. 1986
Culture Consciousness: Understanding the Arts of Other Cultures. Journal of Art & Design Education 5(1&2):124–135.

Beyene, Yewoubdar. 1989
From Menarche to Menopause: Reproductive Lives of Peasant Women in Two Cultures. Albany: State University of New York Press.

Bhardwaj, Surinder M. 1973
Hindu Places of Pilgrimage in India: A Study in Cultural Geography. Berkeley: University of California Press.

Bhardwaj, Surinder M. and N. Madhusudana Rao. 1990
Asian Indians in the United States: A Geographic Ap-

praisal. In South Asians Overseas: Migration and Ethnicity. Colin Clarke, Ceri Peach, and Steven Vertovec, eds. Pp. 197–218. New York: Cambridge University Press.

Bhatt, Rakesh M. 2001
World Englishes. Annual Review of Anthropology 30:527–550.

Bigenho, Michelle. 1999
Sensing Locality in Yura: Rituals of Carnival and of the Bolivian State. American Ethnologist, 26:957–980.

Bilharz, Joy. 1995
First among Equals? The Changing Status of Seneca Women. In Women and Power in Native North America. Laura F. Klein and Lillian A. Ackerman, eds. Pp. 101–112. Norman: University of Oklahoma Press.

Billig, Michael S. 1992
The Marriage Squeeze and the Rise of Groomprice in India's Kerala State. Journal of Comparative Family Studies 23:197–216.

Bird, Sharon R. 1996
Welcome to the Men's Club: Homosociality and the Maintenance of Hegemonic Masculinity. Gender & Society 10(2):120–132.

Blackwood, Evelyn. 1995
Senior Women, Model Mothers, and Dutiful Wives: Managing Gender Contradictions in a Minangkabau Village. In Bewitching Women: Pious Men: Gender and Body Politics in Southeast Asia. Aihwa Ong and Michael Peletz, eds. Pp. 124–158. Berkeley: University of California Press.

Blaikie, Piers. 1985
The Political Economy of Soil Erosion in Developing Countries. New York: Longman.

Blanchard, Ray, Kenneth J. Zucker, Susan J. Bradley and Caitlin S. Hume. 1995
Birth Order and Sibling Sex Ratio in Homosexual Male Adolescents and Probably Prehomosexual Feminine Boys. Developmental Psychology 31(1):22–30.

Blau, Peter M. 1964
Exchange and Power in Social Life. New York: Wiley.

Bledsoe, Caroline H. 1983
Stealing Food as a Problem in Demography and Nutrition. Paper presented at the annual meeting of the American Anthropological Association.

Bledsoe, Caroline H. and Helen K. Hirschman. 1989
Case Studies of Mortality: Anthropological Contributions. Proceedings. International Union for the Scientific Study of Population, XXIst International Population Conference. Pp. 331–348. Liège: International Union for the Scientific Study of Population.

Blim, Michael. 2000
Capitalisms in Late Modernity. Annual Review of Anthropology 29:25–38.

Blok, Anton. 1972
The Peasant and the Brigand: Social Banditry Reconsidered. Comparative Studies in Society and History 14(4): 494–503.

Blood, Robert O. 1967
Love Match and Arranged Marriage. New York: Free Press.

Bodenhorn, Barbara. 2000
"He Used to Be My Relative." Exploring the Bases of Relatedness among the Inupiat of Northern Alaska. In Cultures of Relatedness: New Approaches to the Study of Kinship. Janet Carsten, ed. Pp. 128–148. New York: Cambridge University Press.

Bodley, John H. 1988
Tribal Peoples and Development Issues: A Global Overview. Mountain View, CA: Mayfield Publishing Company.

———. 1990
Victims of Progress. 3rd edition. Mountain View, CA: Mayfield Publishing Company.

Bogin, Barry. 1988
Patterns of Human Growth. New York: Cambridge University Press.

Bohannan, Paul. 1955
Some Principles of Exchange and Investment among the Tiv. American Anthropologist 57(1):60–70.

Boserup, Ester. 1970
Woman's Role in Economic Development. New York: St. Martin's Press.

Boswell, A. Ayres and Joan Z. Spade. 1996
Fraternities and Collegiate Rape Culture: Why Are Some Fraternities More Dangerous Places for Women? Gender & Society 10(2):133–147.

Bourdieu, Pierre. 1984
Distinction: A Social Critique of the Judgement of Taste. Richard Nice, trans. Cambridge: Harvard University Press.

Bourdieu, Pierre, Alain Darbet et al. 1969
The Love of Art: European Art Museums and Their Relation to Culture. Richard Nice, trans. Chicago: The University of Chicago Press.

Bourgois, Philippe I. 1995
In Search of Respect: Selling Crack in El Barrio. New York: Cambridge University Press.

Bowen, Anne M. and Robert Trotter II. 1995
HIV Risk in Intravenous Drug Users and Crack Cocaine Smokers: Predicting Stage of Change for Condom Use. Journal of Consulting and Clinical Psychology 63:238–248.

Bowen, John R. 1992
On Scriptural Essentialism and Ritual Variation: Muslim Sacrifice in Sumatra. American Ethnologist 19(4):656–671.

———. 1998
Religions in Practice: An Approach to the Anthropology of Religion. Boston: Allyn and Bacon.

Bradley, Richard. 2000
An Archaeology of Natural Places. New York: Routledge.

Brana-Shute, Rosemary. 1976
Women, Clubs, and Politics: The Case of a Lower-Class

Neighborhood in Paramaribo, Suriname. Urban Anthropology 5(2):157–185.

Brandes, Stanley H. 1985
Forty: The Age and the Symbol. Knoxville: University of Tennessee Press.

———. 2002
Staying Sober in Mexico City. Austin: University of Texas Press.

Bray, Tamara L. 1996
Repatriation, Power Relations and the Politics of the Past. Antiquity 70:440–444.

Brenneis, Donald and Laura Lein. 1977
"You Fruithead": A Sociolinguistic Approach to Children's Dispute Settlement. In Child Discourse. Susan Ervin-Tripp and Claudia Mitchell-Kernan, eds. New York: Academic Press.

Brink, Judy H. 1991
The Effect of Emigration of Husbands on the Status of Their Wives: An Egyptian Case. International Journal of Middle East Studies 23:201–211.

Brison, Karen J. and Stephen C. Leavitt. 1995
Coping with Bereavement: Long-Term Perspectives on Grief and Mourning. Ethos 23:395–400.

Brodkin, Karen. 2000
Global Capitalism: What's Race Got to Do with It? American Ethnologist 27:237–256.

Brooks, Alison S. and Patricia Draper. 1998 [1991]
Anthropological Perspectives on Aging. In Anthropology Explored: The Best of AnthroNotes. Ruth Osterweis Selig and Marilyn R. London, eds. Pp. 286–297. Washington, DC: Smithsonian Press.

Broude, Gwen J. 1988
Rethinking the Couvade: Cross-Cultural Evidence. American Anthropologist 90(4):902–911.

Brown, Carolyn Henning. 1984
Tourism and Ethnic Competition in a Ritual Form: The Firewalkers of Fiji. Oceania 54:223–244.

Brown, James. 1995
The Turkish Imbroglio: Its Kurds. Annals of the American Academy of Political and Social Science 541:116–129.

Brown, Judith K. 1970
A Note on the Division of Labor by Sex. American Anthropologist 72(5):1073–1078.

———. 1975
Iroquois Women: An Ethnohistoric Note. In Toward an Anthropology of Women. Rayna R. Reiter, ed. Pp. 235–251. New York: Monthly Review Press.

———. 1978
The Recruitment of a Female Labor Force. Anthropos 73(1/2):41–48.

———. 1982
Cross-Cultural Perspectives on Middle-Aged Women. Current Anthropology 23(2):143–156.

Brown, Nathan. 1990
Brigands and State Building: The Invention of Banditry in Modern Egypt. Comparative Studies in Society and History 32(2):258–281.

Browner, Carole H. 1986
The Politics of Reproduction in a Mexican Village. Signs: Journal of Women in Culture and Society 11(4):710–724.

Browner, Carole H. and Nancy Ann Press. 1995
The Normalization of Prenatal Diagnostic Screening. In Conceiving the New World Order: The Global Politics of Reproduction. Faye D. Ginsberg and Rayna Rapp, eds. Pp. 307–322. Berkeley: University of California Press.

———. 1996
The Production of Authoritative Knowledge in American Prenatal Care. Medical Anthropology Quarterly 10(2): 141–156.

Brownmiller, Susan. 1994
Seeing Vietnam: Encounters of the Road and Heart. New York: HarperCollins.

Brumberg, Joan Jacobs. 1988
Fasting Girls: The Emergence of Anorexia Nervosa as a Modern Disease. Cambridge: Harvard University Press.

Brumfiel, Elizabeth M. 1994
Introduction. In Factional Competition and Political Development in the New World. Elizabeth M. Brumfiel and John W. Fox, eds. Pp. 3–14. New York: Cambridge University Press.

Bruner, Edward M. 1991
The Transformation of Self in Tourism. Annals of Tourism Research 18:238–250.

Bunzel, Ruth. 1972 [1929]
The Pueblo Potter: A Study of Creative Imagination in Primitive Art. New York: Dover Publications.

Calhoun, Craig, Donald Light, and Suzanne Keller. 1994
Sociology. 6th edition. New York: McGraw Hill.

Call, Vaughn, Susan Sprecher, and Pepper Schwartz. 1995
The Incidence and Frequency of Marital Sex in a National Sample. Journal of Marriage and the Family 57: 639–652.

Cameron, Mary M. 1995
Transformations of Gender and Caste Divisions of Labor in Rural Nepal: Land, Hierarchy, and the Case of Women. Journal of Anthropological Research 51:215–246.

Camino, Linda A. and Ruth M. Krulfeld, eds. 1994
Reconstructing Lives, Recapturing Meaning: Refugee Identity, Gender and Culture Change. Basel: Gordon and Breach Publishers.

Cancian, Frank. 1989
Economic Behavior in Peasant Communities. In Economic Anthropology. Stuart Plattner, ed. Pp. 127–170. Stanford: Stanford University Press.

Caplan, Pat. 1987
Celibacy as a Solution? Mahatma Gandhi and Brahmacharya. In The Cultural Construction of Sexuality. Pat Caplan, ed. Pp. 271–295. New York: Tavistock Publications.

Carneiro, Robert L. 1994
War and Peace: Alternating Realities in Human History. In Studying War: Anthropological Perspectives. S. P.

Reyna and R. E. Downs, eds. Pp. 3–27. Langhorne, PA: Gordon and Breach Science Publishers.

Carstairs, G. Morris. 1967
The Twice Born. Bloomington: Indiana University Press.

Carsten, Janet, ed. 2000
Cultures of Relatedness: New Approaches to the Study of Kinship. New York: Cambridge University Press.

Carsten, Janet. 1995
Children in Between: Fostering and the Process of Kinship on Pulau Langkawi, Malaysia. Man (n.s.) 26:425–443.

Carter, William E., José V. Morales, and Mauricio P. Mamani. 1981
Medicinal Uses of Coca in Bolivia. In Health in the Andes. Joseph W. Bastien and John M. Donahue, eds. Pp. 119–149. Washington, DC: American Anthropological Association.

Cassell, Joan 1991
Expected Miracles: Surgeons at Work. Philadelphia: Temple University Press.

Castles, Stephen and Mark J. Miller. 1993
The Age of Migration: International Population Movements in the Modern World. New York: The Guilford Press.

Cátedra, María. 1992
This World, Other Worlds: Sickness, Suicide, Death, and the Afterlife among the Vaqueiros de Alzada of Spain. Chicago: University of Chicago Press.

Caudill, W. and David W. Plath. 1966
Who Sleeps by Whom? Parent-Child Involvement in Urban Japanese Families. Psychiatry 29:344–366.

Cernea, Michael M. 1985
Sociological Knowledge for Development Projects. In Putting People First: Sociological Variables and Rural Development. Michael M. Cernea, ed. Pp. 3–22. New York: Oxford University Press.

———. 2001
Cultural Heritage and Development: A Framework for Action in the Middle East and North Africa. Washington, DC: The World Bank.

Chagnon, Napoleon. 1992
Yanomamö. 4th edition. New York: Harcourt Brace Jovanovich.

Chambers, David L. 2000
Civilizing the Natives: Marriage in Post-Apartheid South Africa. Daedalus 129:101–124.

Chambers, Robert. 1983
Rural Development: Putting the Last First. Essex, United Kingdom: Longman.

Chanen, Jill Schachner. 1995
Reaching Out to Women of Color. ABA Journal 81 (May):105.

Chavez, Leo R. 1992
Shadowed Lives: Undocumented Immigrants in American Society. New York: Harcourt Brace Jovanovich.

Cherlin, Andrew and Frank F. Furstenberg Jr. 1992 [1983]
The American Family in the Year 2000. In One World Many Cultures. Stuart Hirschberg, ed. Pp. 2–9. New York: Macmillan Publishing Company.

Cherlin. Andrew J. 1996
Public and Private Families: An Introduction. New York: McGraw-Hill Inc.

Chernoff, John Miller. 1979
African Rhythm and African Sensibility: Aesthetics and African Musical Idioms. Chicago: University of Chicago Press.

Childs, Larry and Celina Chelala. 1994
Drought, Rebellion and Social Change in Northern Mali: The Challenges Facing Tamacheq Herders. Cultural Survival Quarterly 18(4):16–19.

Chiñas, Beverly Newbold. 1992
The Isthmus Zapotecs: A Matrifocal Culture of Mexico. New York: Harcourt, Brace, Jovanovich.

Chowdhury, Najma, Barbara J. Nelson, with Kathryn A. Carver, Nancy J. Johnson, and Paula O'Laughlin. 1994
Redefining Politics: Patterns of Women's Political Engagement from a Global Perspective. In Women and Politics Worldwide. Barbara J. Nelson and Najma Chowdhury, eds. Pp. 3–24. New Haven: Yale University Press.

Clark, Gracia. 1992
Flexibility Equals Survival. Cultural Survival Quarterly 16:21–24.

Clark, Sam, Elizabeth Colson, James Lee, and Thayer Scudder. 1995
Ten Thousand Tonga: A Longitudinal Anthropological Study from Southern Zambia, 1956–1991. Population Studies 49:91–109.

Clay, Jason W. 1990
What's a Nation: Latest Thinking. Mother Jones 15(7):28–30.

Cleveland, David A. 2000
Globalization and Anthropology: Expanding the Options. Human Organization 59:370–374.

Clifford, James, 1988
The Predicament of Culture: Twentieth Century Ethnography, Literature and Art. Cambridge: Harvard University Press.

Cochrane, D. Glynn. 1979
The Cultural Appraisal of Development Projects. New York: Praeger Publishers.

Cohen, Mark Nathan. 1989
Health and the Rise of Civilization. New Haven, CT: Yale University Press.

Cohen, Roberta. 2002
Nowhere to Run, No Place to Hide. Bulletin of the Atomic Scientists, November/December:36–45.

Cohn, Bernard S. 1971
India: The Social Anthropology of a Civilization. New York: Prentice-Hall.

Cole, Douglas. 1991
Chiefly Feasts: The Enduring Kwakiutl Potlatch. Aldona Jonaitis, ed. Seattle: University of Washington Press/New York: American Museum of Natural History.

Cole, Jeffrey. 1996
    Working-Class Reactions to the New Immigration in Palermo (Italy). Critique of Anthropology 16(2):199–220.
Colson, Elizabeth. 1995
    The Contentiousness of Disputes. In Understanding Disputes: The Politics of Argument. Pat Caplan, ed. Pp. 65–82. Providence, RI: Berg Publishers.
Comaroff, John L. 1987
    Of Totemism and Ethnicity: Consciousness, Practice and Signs of Inequality. Ethnos 1987(3–4):301–323.
Contreras, Gloria. 1995
    Teaching about Vietnamese Culture: Water Puppetry as the Soul of the Rice Fields. The Social Studies 86(1):25–28.
Corbey, Raymond. 2000
    Arts premiers in the Louvre. Anthropology Today 16:3–6.
———. 2003
    Destroying the Graven Image: Religious Iconoclasm on the Christian Frontier. Anthropology Today 19:10–14.
Cornell, Laurel L. 1989
    Gender Differences in Remarriage after Divorce in Japan and the United States. Journal of Marriage and the Family 51:45–463.
Cornia, Giovanni Andrea. 1994
    Poverty, Food Consumption, and Nutrition During the Transition to the Market Economy in Eastern Europe. American Economic Review 84(2):297–302.
Counihan, Carole M. 1985
    Transvestism and Gender in a Sardinian Carnival. Anthropology 9(1 & 2):11–24.
Coward, E. Walter, Jr. 1976
    Indigenous Organisation, Bureaucracy and Development: The Case of Irrigation. The Journal of Development Studies 13(1):92–105.
———. 1979
    Principles of Social Organization in an Indigenous Irrigation System. Human Organization 38(1):28–36.
Crapanzano, Vincent. 1980
    Tuhami: Portrait of a Moroccan. Chicago: University of Chicago Press.
Crawford, C. Joanne. 1994
    Parenting Practices in the Basque Country: Implications of Infant and Childhood Sleeping Location for Personality Development. Ethos 22(1):42–82.
Cunningham, Lawrence S. 1995
    Christianity. In The HarperCollins Dictionary of Religion. Jonathan Z. Smith, ed. Pp. 240–253. New York: HarperCollins.
Curtin, Philip D. 1989
    Death by Migration: Europe's Encounter with the Tropical World in the Nineteenth Century. New York: Cambridge University Press.
Dalby, Liza Crihfield. 1998
    Geisha. New York: Vintage Books. 2nd edition.
———. 2001
    Kimono: Fashioning Culture. Seattle: University of Washington Press.

Daly, Martin and Margo Wilson. 1984
    A Sociobiological Analysis of Human Infanticide. In Infanticide: Comparative and Evolutionary Perspectives. Glenn Hausfater and Sarah Blaffer Hrdy, eds. Pp. 487–502. New York: Aldine Publishing Company.
Dando, William A. 1980
    The Geography of Famine. New York: John Wiley and Sons.
Danforth, Loring M. 1989
    Firewalking and Religious Healing: The Anestenaria of Greece and the American Firewalking Movement. Princeton: Princeton University Press.
Dannhaeuser, Norbert. 1989
    Marketing in Developing Urban Areas. In Economic Anthropology. Stuart Plattner, ed. Pp. 222–252. Stanford: Stanford University Press.
Dasgupta, Satadal, Christine Weatherbie, and Rajat Subhra Mukhopadhyay. 1993
    Nuclear and Joint Family Households in West Bengal Villages. Ethnology 32(4):339–358.
Daugherty, Mary Lee. 1997 [1976]
    Serpent-Handling as Sacrament. In Magic, Witchcraft, and Religion. Arthur C. Lehmann and James E. Myers, eds. Pp. 347–352. Mountain View, CA: Mayfield Publishing Company.
Davis, Susan Schaefer and Douglas A. Davis. 1987
    Adolescence in a Moroccan Town: Making Social Sense. New Brunswick: Rutgers University Press.
Davis-Floyd, Robbie E. 1987
    Obstetric Training as a Rite of Passage. Medical Anthropology Quarterly 1:288–318.
———. 1992
    Birth as an American Rite of Passage. Berkeley: University of California Press.
Davison, Jean and Martin Kanyuka. 1992
    Girls' Participation in Basic Education in Southern Malawi. Comparative Education Review 36(4):446–466.
de Athayde Figueiredo, Mariza and Dando Prado. 1989
    The Women of Arembepe. UNESCO Courier 7:38–41.
de la Cadena, Marisol. 2001
    Reconstructing Race: Racism, Culture and Mestizaje in Latin America. NACLA Report on the Americas 34:16–23.
Deitrick, Lynn. 2002
    Commentary: Cultural Brokerage in the Newborn Nursery. Practicing Anthropology 24:53–54.
Delaney, Carol. 1988
    Mortal Flow: Menstruation in Turkish Village Society. In Blood Magic: The Anthropology of Menstruation. Timothy Buckley and Alma Gottlieb, eds. Pp. 75–93. Berkeley: University of California Press.
Devereaux, George. 1976
    A Typological Study of Abortion in Primitive Societies: A Typological, Distributional, and Dynamic Analysis of the Prevention of Birth in 400 Preindustrial Societies. New York: International Universities Press.
Diamond, Jared. 1994 [1987]
    The Worst Mistake in the History of the Human Race.

In Applying Cultural Anthropology: A Reader. Aaron Podolefsky and Peter J. Brown, eds. Pp. 105–108. Mountain View, CA: Mayfield Publishing Company.

Dickemann, Mildred. 1975
Demographic Consequences of Infanticide in Man. Annual Review of Ecology and Systematics 6:107–137.

Dikötter, Frank. 1998
Hairy Barbarians, Furry Primates and Wild Men: Medical Science and Cultural Representations of Hair in China. In Hair: Its Power and Meaning in Asian Cultures. Alf Hiltebeitel and Barbara D. Miller, eds. Pp. 51–74. Albany: State University of New York Press.

Divale, William T. 1974
Migration, External Warfare, and Matrilocal Residence. Behavior Science Research 9:75–133.

Divale, William T. and Marvin Harris. 1976
Population, Warfare and the Male Supremacist Complex. American Anthropologist 78:521–538.

Donlon, Jon. 1990
Fighting Cocks, Feathered Warriors, and Little Heroes. Play & Culture 3:273–285.

Dorgan, Howard. 1989
The Old Regular Baptists of Central Appalachia: Brothers and Sisters in Hope. Knoxville: The University of Tennessee Press.

Douglas, Mary. 1962
The Lele: Resistance to Change. In Economic Anthropology. Paul Bohannan and George Dalton, eds. Pp. 211–233. Evanston: Northwestern University Press.

———. 1966
Purity and Danger: An Analysis of Concepts of Pollution and Taboo. New York: Penguin Books.

Douglas, Mary and Baron Isherwood. 1979
The World of Goods: Towards an Anthropology of Consumption. New York: W. W. Norton and Company.

Drake, Susan P. 1991
Local Participation in Ecotourism Projects. In Nature Tourism: Managing for the Environment. Tensie Whelan, ed. Pp. 132–155. Washington, DC: Island Press.

Dreifus, Claudia. 2000
Saving the Orangutan, Preserving Paradise. New York Times, March 21:D3.

Drucker, Charles. 1988
Dam the Chico: Hydropower Development and Tribal Resistance. In Tribal Peoples and Development Issues: A Global Overview. John H. Bodley, ed. Pp. 151–165. Mountain View, CA: Mayfield Publishing Company.

Duany, Jorge. 2000
Nation on the Move: The Construction of Cultural Identities in Puerto Rico and the Diaspora. American Ethnologist 27:5–30.

Duranti, Alessandro. 1994
From Grammar to Politics: Linguistic Anthropology in a Western Samoan Village. Berkeley: University of California Press.

Durkheim, Emile. 1951 [1897]
Suicide: A Study in Sociology. New York: The Free Press.

———. 1965 [1915]
The Elementary Forms of the Religious Life. New York: The Free Press.

———. 1966 [1895]
On the Division of Labor in Society. Trans. G. Simpson. New York: The Free Press.

Durning, Alan Thein. 1993
Are We Happy Yet? How the Pursuit of Happiness Is Failing. The Futurist 27(1):20–24.

Durrenberger, E. Paul. 2001
Explorations of Class and Class Consciousness in the U.S. Journal of Anthropological Research 57:41–60.

Dyson, Tim. 1994
World Population and Food Supplies. International Social Science Journal 46(3):361–385.

Earle, Timothy. 1991
The Evolution of Chiefdoms. In Chiefdoms, Power, Economy, and Ideology. Timothy Earle, ed. Pp. 1–15. New York: Cambridge University Press.

Eck, Diana L. 1985
Darsán: Seeing the Divine Image in India. 2nd ed. Chambersburg, PA: Anima Books.

Eckel, Malcolm David. 1995
Buddhism. In The HarperCollins Dictionary of Religion. Jonathan Z. Smith. Pp. 135–150. New York: HarperCollins.

Economic and Social Council. 1992
Report of the Working Group on Violence against Women. Vienna: United Nations. E/CN.6/WG.2/1992/L.3.

Eickelman, Dale F. 1981
The Middle East: An Anthropological Perspective. Englewood Cliffs, NJ: Prentice-Hall.

Eisler, Kim Isaac. 2001
Revenge of the Pequots: How a Small Native American Tribe Created the World's Most Profitable Casino. New York: Simon and Schuster.

El Saadawi, Nawal. 1994 [1983]
Memoirs from the Women's Prison. Marilyn Booth, trans. Berkeley: University of California Press.

Ember, Carol R. 1983
The Relative Decline in Women's Contribution to Agriculture with Intensification. American Anthropologist 85(2):285–304.

Eriksen, Thomas Hylland. 2001
Between Universalism and Relativism: A Critique of the UNESCO Concept of Culture. In Culture and Rights: Anthropological Perspectives. Jane K. Cowan, Marie Bénédicte Dembour, and Richard A. Wilson, eds. Pp. 127–148. New York: Cambridge University Press.

Ervin, Alexander M., Antonet T. Kaye, Giselle M. Marcotte, and Randy D. Belon. 1991
Community Needs, Saskatoon—The 1990's: The Saskatoon Needs Assessment Project. Saskatoon, Canada: University of Saskatchewan, Department of Anthropology.

Escobar, Arturo. 2002
Gender, Place, and Networks: A Political Ecology of Cy-

berculture. In Development: A Cultural Studies Reader. Susan Schech and Jane Haggis, eds. Pp. 239–256. Malden, MA: Blackwell Publishers.

Esman, Milton. 1996
Ethnic Politics. In The Social Science Encyclopedia. Adam Kuper and Jessica Kuper, eds. Pp. 259–260. New York: Routledge.

Estioko-Griffin, Agnes, Madeleine J. Goodman, and Bion Griffin. 1985
The Compatibility of Hunting and Mothering among the Agta Hunter-Gatherers of the Philippines. Sex Roles 12:1199–1209.

Estioko-Griffin, Agnes. 1986
Daughters of the Forest. Natural History 95:36–43.

Estrin, Saul. 1996
Co-operatives. In The Social Science Encyclopedia. Adam Kuper and Jessica Kuper, eds. Pp. 138–139. Routledge: New York.

Etienne, Mona and Eleanor Leacock, eds. 1980
Women and Colonization: Anthropological Perspectives. New York: Praeger.

Evans, William and Julie Topoleski, 2002
The Social and Economic Impact of Native American Casinos. Cambridge, MA: NBER Working Papers, No. 9198.

Evans-Pritchard, E. E. 1951
Kinship and Marriage among the Nuer. Oxford: Clarendon.

———. 1965 [1947]
The Nuer: A Description of the Modes of Livelihood and Political Institutions of a Nilotic People. New York: Oxford University Press.

Everett, Daniel. 1995
Personal communication.

Ewing, Katherine Pratt. 2000 Legislating Religious Freedom: Muslim Challenges to the Relationship between "Church" and "State" in Germany and France. Daedalus 29:31–53.

Fabian, Johannes. 1995
Ethnographic Misunderstanding and the Perils of Context. American Anthropologist 97(1):41–50.

Fabrega, Horacio, Jr. and Barbara D. Miller. 1995
Adolescent Psychiatry as a Product of Contemporary Anglo-American Society. Social Science and Medicine 40(7):881–894.

Fabrega, Horacio, Jr. and Daniel B. Silver. 1973
Illness and Shamanistic Curing in Zinacantan: An Ethnomedical Analysis. Stanford: Stanford University Press.

Fadiman, Anne. 1997
The Spirit Catches You and You Fall Down: A Hmong Child, Her American Doctors, and the Collision of Two Cultures. New York: Farrar, Straus and Giroux.

Fasulo, Linda. 2003
An Insider's Guide to the UN. New Haven, CT: Yale University Press.

Feeley-Harnick, Gillian. 1991 [1960]
A Green Estate: Restoring Independence in Madagascar. Washington: Smithsonian Institution Press.

Feinsilver, Julie M. 1993
Healing the Masses: Cuban Health Politics at Home and Abroad. Berkeley: University of California Press.

Feldman, Gregory. 2003
Breaking Our Silence on NATO. Anthropology Today 19:1–2.

Feldman-Savelsberg, Pamela. 1995
Cooking Inside: Kinship and Gender in Bangangté Idioms of Marriage and Procreation. American Ethnologist 22(3):483–501.

Ferguson, James. 1994
The Anti-Politics Machine: "Development," Depoliticization, and Bureaucratic Power in Lesotho. Minneapolis: University of Minnesota Press.

Ferguson, R. Brian. 1990
Blood of the Leviathan: Western Contact and Amazonian Warfare. American Ethnologist 17(1):237–257.

Fischer, Edward F. 2001
Cultural Logics and Global Economies: Maya Identity in Thought and Practice. Austin: University of Texas Press.

Fiske, John. 1994
Radical Shopping in Los Angeles: Race, Media and the Sphere of Consumption. Media, Culture & Society 16:469–486.

Fitchen, Janet M. 1990
How Do You Know If You Haven't Listened First?: Using Anthropological Methods to Prepare for Survey Research. The Rural Sociologist 10(2):15–22.

Fluehr-Lobban, Carolyn. 1994
Informed Consent in Anthropological Research: We Are Not Exempt. Human Organization 53(1):1–10.

Fonseca, Isabel. 1995
Bury Me Standing: The Gypsies and Their Journey. New York: Alfred A. Knopf.

Fortune, Reo F. 1959 [1932]
Sorcerers of Dobu: The Social Anthropology of the Dobu Islanders of the Western Pacific. New York: E. P. Dutton & Co.

Foster, George M. and Barbara Gallatin Anderson. 1978
Medical Anthropology. New York: Alfred A. Knopf.

Foucault, Michel. 1970
The Order of Things: An Archaeology of the Human Sciences. New York: Random House.

———. 1977
Discipline and Punish: The Birth of the Prison. New York: Pantheon Books.

Fox, Richard G. and Andre Gingrich. 2002
Comparison and Anthropology's Public Responsibility. In Anthropology, By Comparison. Andre Gingrich and Richard G. Fox, eds. Pp. 1–24. New York: Routledge.

Fox, Robin. 1995 [1978]
The Tory Islanders: A People of the Celtic Fringe. Notre Dame: University of Notre Dame Press.

Franke, Richard W. 1993
Life is a Little Better: Redistribution as a Development Strategy in Nadur Village, Kerala. Boulder: Westview Press.

Frankel, Francine R. 1971
India's Green Revolution: Economic Gains and Political Costs. Princeton: Princeton University Press.

Fratkin, Elliot. 1998
Ariaal Pastoralists of Kenya: Surviving Drought and Development in Africa's Arid Lands. Boston: Allyn and Bacon.

Fratkin, Elliot, Kathleen Galvin, and Eric A. Roth, eds. 1994
African Pastoralist Systems: An Integrated Approach. Boulder: Westview Press.

Frazer, Sir James. 1978 [1890]
The Golden Bough: A Study in Magic and Religion. New York: Macmillan.

Freed, Stanley A. and Ruth S. Freed. 1969
Urbanization and Family Types in a North Indian Village. Southwestern Journal of Anthropology 25:342–359.

Freedman, Diane C. 1986
Wife, Widow, Woman: Roles of an Anthropologist in a Transylvanian Village. In Women in the Field: Anthropological Experiences. Peggy Golde, ed. Pp. 333–358. Berkeley: University of California Press.

Freeman, Derek. 1983
Margaret Mead and Samoa: The Making and Unmaking of an Anthropological Myth. Cambridge, MA: Harvard University Press.

Freeman, James A. 1981
A Firewalking Ceremony that Failed. In Social and Cultural Context of Medicine in India. Giri Raj Gupta, ed. Pp. 308–336. New Delhi: Vikas Publishing House.

———. 1989
Hearts of Sorrow: Vietnamese-American Lives. Stanford: Stanford University Press.

Frieze, Irene et al. 1978
Women and Sex Roles: A Social Psychological Perspective. New York: W. W. Norton.

Frisch, Rose. 1978
Population, Food Intake, and Fertility. Science 199:22–30.

Furst, Peter T. 1989
The Water of Life: Symbolism and Natural History on the Northwest Coast. Dialectical Anthropology 14:95–115.

Gable, Eric. 1995
The Decolonization of Consciousness: Local Skeptics and the "Will to Be Modern" in a West African Village. American Ethnologist 22(2):242–257.

Gage-Brandon, Anastasia J. 1992
The Polygyny-Divorce Relationship: A Case Study of Nigeria. Journal of Marriage and the Family 54:282–292.

Galdikas, Biruté. 1995
Reflections of Eden: My Years with the Orangutans of Borneo. Boston: Little, Brown.

Gale, Faye, Rebecca Bailey-Harris, and Joy Wundersitz. 1990
Aboriginal Youth and the Criminal Justice System: The Injustice of Justice? New York: Cambridge University Press.

Galuszka, Peter. 1993
BMW, Mercedes, Rolls-Royce—Could This Be Russia? Business Week [330] August 2:40.

Gardner, Katy and David Lewis. 1996
Anthropology, Development and the Post-Modern Challenge. Sterling, VA: Pluto Press.

Garland, David. 1996
Social Control. In The Social Science Encyclopedia. Adam Kuper and Jessica Kuper, eds. pp. 780–783. Routledge: New York.

Geertz, Clifford. 1966
Religion as a Cultural System. In Anthropological Approaches to the Study of Religion. Michael Banton, ed. Pp. 1–46. London: Tavistock.

———. 1983
Local Knowledge: Further Essays in Interpretive Anthropology. New York: Basic Books.

Gegiow vs. Uhl. 1915
No. 340. Supreme Court of the United States.

Gifford-Gonzalez, Diane. 1993
You Can Hide, But You Can't Run: Representation of Women's Work in Illustrations of Palaeolithic Life. Visual Anthropology Review 9(1):23–41.

Gill, Lesley. 1993
"Proper Women" and City Pleasures: Gender, Class, and Contested Meanings in La Paz. American Ethnologist 20(1):72–88.

———. 1997
Creating Citizens, Making Men: The Military and Masculinity in Bolivia. Cultural Anthropology 12:527–550.

Gilman, Antonio. 1991
Trajectories towards Social Complexity in the Later Prehistory of the Mediterranean. In Chiefdoms: Power, Economy and Ideology. Timothy Earle, ed. Pp. 146–168. New York: Cambridge University Press.

Ginsberg, Faye D. and Rayna Rapp. 1991
The Politics of Reproduction. Annual Review of Anthropology 20:311–343.

Glick Schiller, Nina and Georges E. Fouron. 1999
Terrains of Blood and Nation: Haitian Transnational Social Fields. Ethnic and Racial Studies 22:340–365.

Glínski, Piotr. 1994 Environmentalism among Polish Youth: A Maturing Social Movement? Communist and Post-Communist Studies 27(2):145–159.

Gmelch, George. 1997 [1971]
Baseball Magic. In Magic, Witchcraft, and Religion. Arthur C. Lehmann and James E. Myers, eds. Pp. 276–282. Mountain View, CA: Mayfield Publishing Company.

Godelier, Maurice. 1971
"Salt Currency" and the Circulation of Commodities among the Baruya of New Guinea. In Studies in Economic Anthropology. George Dalton, ed. Pp. 52–73. Anthropological Studies No. 7. Washington, DC: American Anthropological Association.

Gold, Stevan J. 1992
    Refugee Communities: A Comparative Field Study. New-bury Park: Sage Publications.
———. 1995
    From the Workers' State to the Golden State: Jews from the Former Soviet Union in California. Boston: Allyn and Bacon.
Goldstein, Melvyn C. and Cynthia M. Beall. 1994
    The Changing World of Mongolia's Nomads. Berkeley: University of California Press.
Goldstone, Jack. 1996
    Revolutions. In The Social Science Encyclopedia. Adam Kuper and Jessica Kuper, eds. Pp. 740–743. New York: Routledge.
González, Nancie L. 1970
    Toward a Definition of Matrifocality. In Afro-American Anthropology: Contemporary Perspectives. Norman E. Whitten, Jr. and John F. Szwed, eds. Pp. 231–244. New York: The Free Press.
Goodall, Jane. 1971
    In the Shadow of Man. Boston: Houghton Mifflin.
———. 1986
    The Chimpanzees of Gombe: Patterns of Behavior. Cambridge, MA: Harvard University Press.
Goody, Jack. 1976
    Production and Reproduction: A Comparative Study of the Domestic Domain. New York: Cambridge University Press.
———. 1977
    Cooking, Cuisine and Class: A Study of Comparative Sociology. New York: Cambridge University Press.
———. 1993
    The Culture of Flowers. New York: Cambridge University Press.
———. 1996
    Comparing Family Systems in Europe and Asia: Are There Different Sets of Rules? Population and Development Review 22:1–20.
Goody, Jack and Stanley J. Tambiah. 1973
    Bridewealth and Dowry. New York: Cambridge University Press.
Graburn, Nelson H. H., ed., 1976
    Ethnic and Tourist Arts: Cultural Expressions from the Fourth World. Berkeley: University of California Press.
Greenhalgh, Susan. 2003
    Science, Modernity, and the Making of China's One-Child Policy. Population and Development Review 29:163–196.
Greenough, Paul R. 1982
    Prosperity and Misery in Modern Bengal: The Famine of 1943–44. New York: Oxford University Press.
Gregor, Thomas. 1981
    A Content Analysis of Mehinaku Dreams. Ethos 9:353–390.
———. 1982
    No Girls Allowed. Science 82.

Gremillion, Helen. 1992
    Psychiatry as Social Ordering: Anorexia Nervosa, a Paradigm. Social Science and Medicine 35(1):57–71.
Grenier, Guillermo J., Alex Stepick, Debbie Draznin, Aileen LaBorwit, and Steve Morris. 1992
    On Machines and Bureaucracy: Controlling Ethnic Interaction in Miami's Apparel and Construction Industries. In Structuring Diversity: Ethnographic Perspectives on the New Immigration. Louise Lamphere, ed. Pp. 65–94. Chicago: University of Chicago Press.
Grieco, Elizabeth. 2003
    The Foreign Born from Mexico to the United States. www.migrationinformation.
Grinker, Roy Richard. 1994
    Houses in the Rainforest: Ethnicity and Inequality among Farmers and Foragers in Central Africa. Berkeley: University of California Press.
Gross, Daniel R. 1984
    Time Allocation: A Tool for the Study of Cultural Behavior. Annual Review of Anthropology 13:519–558.
Gross, Daniel R. and Barbara A. Underwood. 1971
    Technological Change and Caloric Costs. American Anthropologist 73:725–740.
Gross, Daniel R., George Eiten, Nancy M. Flowers, Francisca M. Leoi, Madeleine Lattman Ritter, and Dennis W. Werner. 1979
    Ecology and Acculturation among Native Peoples of Central Brazil. Science 206(30):1043–1050.
Gruenbaum, Ellen. 2001
    The Female Circumcision Controversy: An Anthropological Perspective. Philadelphia: University of Pennsylvania Press.
Guggenheim, Scott E. and Michael M. Cernea. 1993
    Anthropological Approaches to Involuntary Resettlement: Policy, Practice, and Theory. In Anthropological Approaches to Resettlement: Policy, Practice, and Theory. Michael M. Cernea and Scott E. Guggenheim, eds. Pp. 1–12. Boulder: Westview Press.
Gugler, Josef. 1988
    The Urban Character of Contemporary Revolutions. In The Urbanization of the Third World. Josef Gugler, ed. Pp. 399–412. New York: Oxford University Press.
Guidoni, Enrico. 1987
    Primitive Architecture. Robert Erich Wolf, trans. New York: Rizzoli.
Güneş-Ayara, Ayşe. 1995
    Women's Participation in Politics in Turkey. In Women in Modern Turkish Society: A Reader. Sirin Tekeli, ed. Pp. 235–249. London: Zed Books.
Hackenberg, Robert A. 2000
    Advancing Applied Anthropology: Joe Hill in Cyberspace—Steps Toward Creating "One Big Union." Human Organization 59:365–369.
Hackenberg, Robert A. et al. 1983
    Migration, Modernization and Hypertension: Blood Pressure Levels in Four Philippine Communities. Medical Anthropology 7(1):45–71.

Hacker, Andrew. 1992
Two Nations: Black and White, Separate, Hostile, Unequal. New York: Ballantine Books.

Hahn, Robert. 1995
Sickness and Healing: An Anthropological Perspective. New Haven, CT: Yale University Press.

Hakamies-Blomqvist, Liisa. 1994
Aging and Fatal Accidents in Male and Female Drivers. Journal of Gerontology [Social Sciences] 49(6):5286–5290.

Hamabata, Matthews Masayuki. 1990
Crested Kimono: Power and Love in the Japanese Business Family. Ithaca: Cornell University Press.

Hammerlsey, Martyn. 1992
What's Wrong with Ethnography: Methodological Explorations. London: Routledge.

Hammond, Peter B. 1966
Yatenga: Technology in the Culture of a West African Kingdom. New York: The Free Press.

Hancock, Graham. 1989
Lords of Poverty: The Power, Prestige, and Corruption of the International Aid Business. New York: The Atlantic Monthly Press.

Hannerz, Ulf. 1992
Cultural Complexity: Studies in the Social Organization of Meaning. New York: Columbia University Press.

Hardman, Charlotte E. 2000
Other Worlds: Notions of Self and Emotion among the Lohorung Rai. New York: Berg.

Harner, Michael. 1977
The Ecological Basis of Aztec Sacrifice. American Ethnologist 4:117–135.

Harris, Marvin. 1971
Culture, Man and Nature. New York: Thomas Y Crowell.

———. 1974
Cows, Pigs, Wars and Witches: The Riddles of Culture. New York: Random House.

———. 1975
Culture, People, Nature: An Introduction to General Anthropology. 2nd edition. New York: Thomas Y Crowell.

———. 1977
Cannibals and Kings: The Origins of Culture. New York: Random House.

———. 1984
Animal Capture and Yanomamo Warfare: Retrospect and New Evidence. Journal of Anthropological Research 40(10):183–201.

———. 1989
Our Kind: The Evolution of Human Life and Culture. New York: Harper & Row Publishers.

———. 1992
Distinguished Lecture: Anthropology and the Theoretical and Paradigmatic Significance of the Collapse of Soviet and East European Communism. American Anthropologist 94:295–305.

———. 1995
Cultural Anthropology. 4th edition. New York: HarperCollins.

Harris, Marvin and Eric B. Ross. 1987
Death, Sex and Fertility. New York: Columbia University Press.

Harrison, Simon. 1993
The Commerce of Cultures in Melanesia. Man 28:139–158.

Hart, C. W. M., Arnold R. Pilling, and Jane C. Goodale. 1988
The Tiwi of North Australia. New York: Holt, Rinehart, and Winston.

Hart, Gillian. 2002 Disabling Globalization: Places of Power in Post-Apartheid South Africa. Berkeley: University of California Press.

Hartmann, Betsy. 1987
Reproductive Rights and Wrongs: The Global Politics of Population Control and Reproductive Choice. New York: Harper & Row.

Hastrup, Kirsten. 1992 Anthropological
Visions: Some Notes on Visual and Textual Authority. In Film as Ethnography. Peter Ian Crawford and David Turton, eds. Pp. 8–25. Manchester: University of Manchester Press.

Hawn, Carleen. 2002
Please Feedback the Animals. Forbes 170(9):168–169.

Hefner, Robert W. 1998
Multiple Modernities: Christianity, Islam, and Hinduism in a Globalizing Age. Annual Review of Anthropology 27:83–104.

Heise, Lori L., Jacqueline Pitanguy and Adrienne Germain. 1994
Violence against Women: The Hidden Health Burden. World Bank Discussion Papers No. 255. Washington, DC: The World Bank.

Helweg, Arthur W. and Usha M. Helweg. 1990
An Immigrant Success Story: East Indians in America. Philadelphia: University of Pennsylvania Press.

Herdt, Gilbert. 1987
The Sambia: Ritual and Gender in New Guinea. New York: Holt, Rinehart and Winston.

Herzfeld, Michael. 1985
The Poetics of Manhood: Contest and Identity in a Cretan Mountain Village. Princeton: Princeton University Press.

Hewlett, Barry S. 1991
Intimate Fathers: The Nature and Context of Aka Pygmy Paternal Care. Ann Arbor: University of Michigan Press.

Hiatt, Betty. 1970
Woman the Gatherer. In Woman's Role in Aboriginal Society. Fay Gale, ed. Pp. 2–28. Canberra: Australian Institute of Aboriginal Studies.

Hill, Jane H. 2001
Dimensions of Attrition in Language Death. In On Biocultural Diversity: Linking Language, Knowledge, and the Environment. Luisa Maffi, ed. Pp. 175–189. Washington, DC: Smithsonian Institution Press.

Hill, Jane H. and Bruce Mannheim. 1992
    Language and World View. Annual Review of Anthropology 21:381–406.

Hiltebeitel, Alf. 1988
    The Cult of Draupadi: Mythologies from Gingee to Kuruksetra. Chicago: The University of Chicago Press.

———. 1995
    Hinduism. In The HarperCollins Dictionary of Religion. Jonathan Z. Smith, ed. Pp. 424–440. New York: HarperCollins Publishers.

Hirschon, Renee. 1989
    Heirs of the Catastrophe: The Social Life of Asia Minor Refugees in Piraeus. New York: Oxford University Press.

Hobsbawm, Eric J. 1969
    Bandits. 2nd edition. New York: Delacorte Press.

Hodge, Robert W. and Naohiro Ogawa. 1991
    Fertility Change in Contemporary Japan. Chicago: The University of Chicago Press.

Hoffman, Danny. 2003
    Frontline Anthropology: Research in a Time of War. Anthropology Today 19:9–12.

Hollan, Douglas. 2001
    Developments in Person-Centered Ethnography. In The Psychology of Cultural Experience. Carmella C. Moore and Holly F. Mathews, eds. Pp. 48–67. New York: Cambridge University Press.

Holland, Dorothy C. and Margaret A. Eisenhart. 1990
    Educated in Romance: Women, Achievement, and College Culture. Chicago: The University of Chicago Press.

Hopkins, Nicholas S. and Sohair R. Mehanna. 2000
    Social Action against Everyday Pollution in Egypt. Human Organization 59:245–254.

Hornbein, George and Marie Hornbein. 1992
    Salamanders: A Night at the Phi Delt House. Video. College Park: Documentary Resource Center.

Horowitz, Irving L. 1967
    The Rise and Fall of Project Camelot: Studies in the Relationship between Social Science and Practical Politics. Boston: MIT Press.

Horowitz, Michael M. and Muneera Salem-Murdock. 1993
    Development-Induced Food Insecurity in the Middle Senegal Valley. GeoJournal 30(2):179–184.

Hostetler, John A. and Gertrude Enders Huntington. 1992
    Amish Children: Education in the Family, School, and Community. New York: Harcourt Brace Jovanovich.

Howell, Nancy. 1979
    Demography of the Dobe !Kung. New York: Academic Press.

———. 1986
    Feedbacks and Buffers in Relation to Scarcity and Abundance: Studies of Hunter-Gatherer Populations. In The State of Population Theory: Forward from Malthus. David Coleman and Roger Schofield, eds. Pp. 156–187. New York: Basil Blackwell.

———. 1990
    Surviving Fieldwork: A Report of the Advisory Panel on Health and Safety in Fieldwork. Washington, DC: American Anthropological Association.

Howell, Signe. 1979
    The Chewong of Malaysia. Populi 6(4):48–51.

Huang, Shu-Min. 1993
    A Cross-Cultural Experience: A Chinese Anthropologist in the United States. In Distant Mirrors: America as a Foreign Culture. Philip R. DeVita and James D. Armstrong, eds. Pp. 39–45. Belmont, CA: Wadsworth Publishing Company.

Hughes, Charles C. and John M. Hunter. 1970
    Disease and "Development" in Africa. Social Science and Medicine 3:443–493.

Humphrey, Caroline. 1978
    Women, Taboo and the Suppression of Attention. In Defining Females: The Nature of Women in Society. Shirley Ardener, ed. Pp. 89–108. New York: John Wiley and Sons.

Hunte, Pamela A. 1985
    Indigenous Methods of Fertility Regulation in Afghanistan. In Women's Medicine: A Cross-Cultural Study of Indigenous Fertility Regulation. Lucile F. Newman, ed. Pp. 44–75. New Brunswick: Rutgers University Press.

Hutchinson, Sharon E. 1996
    Nuer Dilemmas: Coping with Money, War, and the State. Berkeley: University of California Press.

Hutter, Michael. 1996
    The Value of Play. In The Value of Culture: On the Relationship between Economics and the Arts. Arjo Klamer, ed. Pp. 122–137. Amsterdam: Amsterdam University Press.

Illo, Jeanne Frances I. 1985
    Who Heads the Household? Women in Households in the Philippines. Paper presented at the Women and Household Regional Conference for Asia, New Delhi.

Inhorn, Marcia C. 2003
    Global Infertility and the Globalization of New Reproductive Technologies: Illustrations from Egypt. Social Science and Medicine 56:1837–1851.

International Labour Office. 1996
    Female Asian Migrants: A Growing But Vulnerable Workforce. World of Work 15:16–17.

Jacobs-Huey, Lanita. 2002
    The Natives Are Gazing and Talking Back: Reviewing the Problematics of Positionality, Voice, and Accountability among "Native" Anthropologists. American Anthropologist 104:791–804.

Janes, Craig R. 1990
    Migration, Social Change, and Health: A Samoan Community in Urban California. Stanford: Stanford University Press.

———. 1995
    The Transformations of Tibetan Medicine. Medical Anthropology Quarterly 9(1):6–39.

Jankowski, Martín Sánchez. 1991
    Islands in the Street: Gangs and American Urban Society. Berkeley: University of California Press.

Jenkins, Gwynne L and Marcia C. Inhorn. 2003
Reproduction Gone Awry: Medical Anthropology Perspectives. Social Science and Medicine 56:1831–1836.

Jiang, David W. 1994
Shanghai Revisited: Chinese Theatre and the Forces of the Market. The Drama Review 38(2):72–80.

Jinadu, L. Adele. 1994
The Dialectics of Theory and Research on Race and Ethnicity in Nigeria. In "Race," Ethnicity and Nation: International Perspectives on Social Conflict. Peter Ratcliffe, ed. Pp. 163–178. London: University of College London Press.

Johnson, Walter R. 1994
Dismantling Apartheid: A South African Town in Transition. Ithaca: Cornell University Press.

Johnson-Hanks, Jennifer. 2002
On the Limits of Life Stages in Ethnography: Toward a Theory of Vital Conjectures. American Anthropologist 104:865–880.

Johnston, Barbara Rose. 1994
Environmental Degradation and Human Rights Abuse. In Who Pays the Price?: The Sociocultural Context of Environmental Crisis. Barbara Rose Johnston, ed. Pp. 7–16. Washington, DC: Island Press.

Jonaitis, Aldona. 1995
A Wealth of Thought: Franz Boas on Native American Art. Seattle: University of Washington Press.

Jones, Anna Laura. 1993
Exploding Canons: The Anthropology of Museums. Annual Review of Anthropology 22:201–220.

Joralemon, Donald. 1982
New World Depopulation and the Case of Disease. Journal of Anthropological Research 38:108–127.

Jordan, Brigitte. 1983
Birth in Four Cultures. 3rd edition. Montreal: Eden Press.

Jordan, Mark. 1998
Japan Takes Dim View of Fertility Treatments. New York Times, July 5:A13.

Joseph, Suad. 1994
Brother/Sister Relationships: Connectivity, Love, and Power in the Reproduction of Patriarchy in Lebanon. American Ethnologist 21:50–73.

Jourdan, Christine. 1995
Masta Liu. In Youth Cultures: A Cross-Cultural Perspective. Vered Amit-Talai and Helena Wulff, eds. Pp. 202–222. New York: Routledge.

Judd, Ellen. 2002
The Chinese Women's Movement: Between State and Market. Stanford, CA: Stanford University Press.

Kaberry, Phyllis. 1952
Women of the Grassfields: A Study of the Economic Position of Women in Bamenda, British Cameroons. London: Her Majesty's Stationery Office.

Kabutha, Charity, Barbara P. Thomas-Slaytor, and Richard Ford. 1993
Participatory Rural Appraisal: A Case Study from Kenya. In Rapid Appraisal Methods. Krishna Kumar, ed. Pp. 176–211. Washington, DC: The World Bank.

Kahn, Miriam. 1995
Heterotopic Dissonance in the Museum Representation of Pacific Island Cultures. American Anthropologist 97(2):324–338.

Kanaaneh, Rhoda. 2003
Embattled Identities: Palestinian Soldiers in the Israeli Military. Journal of Palestine Studies 127:5–20.

Kapchan, Deborah A. 1994
Moroccan Female Performers Defining the Social Body. Journal of American Folklore 107(423):82–105.

Kassam, Aneesa. 2002
Ethnodevelopment in the Oromia Regional State of Ethiopia. In Participating in Development: Approaches to Indigenous Knowledge. Paul Sillitoe, Alan Bicker, and Johan Pottier, eds. Pp. 65–81. ASA Monographs No. 39. New York: Routledge.

Katz, Nathan and Ellen S. Goldberg. 1989
Asceticism and Caste in the Passover Observances of the Cochin Jews. Journal of the American Academy of Religion 57(1):53–81.

Katz, Richard. 1982
Boiling Energy: Community Healing among the Kalahari Kung. Cambridge: Harvard University Press.

Kearney, Michael. 1986
From the Invisible Hand to Visible Feet: Anthropological Studies of Migration and Development. Annual Review of Anthropology 15:331–361.

Kehoe, Alice Beck. 1989
The Ghost Dance: History and Revitalization. Philadelphia: Holt.

Keiser, R. Lincoln. 1986
Death Enmity in Thull: Organized Vengeance and Social Change in a Kohistani Community. American Ethnologist 13(3):489–505.

Kelley, Heidi. 1991
Unwed Mothers and Household Reputation in a Spanish Galician Community. American Ethnologist 18:565–580.

Kennedy, David P. and Stephen G. Perz. 2000
Who Are Brazil's Indígenas? Contributions of Census Data Analysis to Anthropological Demography of Indigenous Populations. Human Organization 59:311–324.

Kerns, Virginia. 1992
Preventing Violence against Women: A Central American Case. In Sanctions and Sanctuary: Cultural Perspectives on the Beating of Wives. Dorothy Ayers Counts, Judith K. Brown, and Jacquelyn C. Campbell, eds. Pp. 125–138. Boulder: Westview Press.

Kesmanee, Chupinit. 1994
Dubious Development Concepts in the Thai Highlands: The Chao Khao in Transition. Law & Society Review 28:673–683.

Kideckel, David A. 1993
The Solitude of Collectivism: Romanian Villagers to the Revolution and Beyond. Ithaca: Cornell University Press.

Kirsch, Stuart. 2002
  Anthropology and Advocacy: A Case Study of the Campaign against the Ok Tedi Mine. Critique of Anthropology 22:175–200.

Kleinman, Arthur. 1995
  Writing at the Margin: Discourse between Anthropology and Medicine. Berkeley: University of California Press.

Knott, Kim. 1996
  Hindu Women, Destiny and Stridharma. Religion 26:15–35.

Kolenda, Pauline M. 1968
  Region, Caste, and Family Structure: A Comparative Study of the Indian "Joint" Family. In Structure and Change in Indian Society. Milton Singer and Bernard S. Cohn, eds. Pp. 339–396. New York: Aldine.

———. 1978
  Caste in Contemporary India: Beyond Organic Solidarity. Prospect Heights, IL: Waveland Press.

Kondo, Dorinne. 1991
  The Stakes: Feminism, Asian Americans, and the Study of Asia. CWAS Newsletter [Committee on Women in Asian Studies, Association for Asian Studies] 9(3):2–9.

———. 1992
  The Aesthetics and Politics of Japanese Identity in the Fashion Industry. In Re-Made in Japan: Everyday Life and Consumer Taste in a Changing Society. Joseph J. Tobin, ed. Pp. 176–203. New Haven: Yale University Press.

———. 1997
  About Face: Performing "Race" in Fashion and Theater. New York: Routledge.

Konner, Melvin. 1987
  Becoming a Doctor: The Journey of Initiation in Medical School. New York: Penguin Books.

———. 1989
  Homosexuality: Who and Why? New York Times Magazine. April 2:60–61.

Kottak, Conrad Phillip. 1992
  Assault on Paradise: Social Change in a Brazilian Village. New York: McGraw Hill.

———. 1985
  When People Don't Come First: Some Sociological Lessons from Completed Projects. In Putting People First: Sociological Variables and Rural Development. Michael M. Cernea, ed. Pp. 325–356. New York: Oxford University Press.

Krantzler, Nora J. 1987
  Traditional Medicine as "Medical Neglect": Dilemmas in the Case Management of a Samoan Teenager with Diabetes. In Child Survival: Cultural Perspectives on the Treatment and Maltreatment of Children. Nancy Scheper-Hughes, ed. Pp. 325–337. Boston: D. Reidel.

Kroeber, A. L. and Clyde Kluckhohn. 1952
  Culture: A Critical Review of Concepts and Definitions. New York: Vintage Books.

Kuipers, Joel C. 1990
  Power in Performance: The Creation of Textual Authority in Weyéwa Ritual Speech. Philadelphia: University of Pennsylvania Press.

———. 1991
  Matters of Taste in Weyéwa. In The Varieties of Sensory Experience: A Sourcebook in the Anthropology of the Senses. David Howes, ed. Pp. 111–127. Toronto: University of Toronto Press.

Kumar, Krishna. 1996
  Civil Society. In The Social Science Encyclopedia. Adam Kuper and Jessica Kuper, eds. Pp. 88–90. Routledge: New York.

Kumar, Sanjay. 1996
  Largest-ever World Bank Loan Mistrusted in India. The Lancet 347(April 20):1109.

Kurin, Richard. 1980
  Doctor, Lawyer, Indian Chief. Natural History 89(11):6–24.

Kwiatkowski, Lynn M. 1998
  Struggling with Development: The Politics of Hunger and Gender in the Philippines. Boulder: Westview Press.

Labov, William. 1966
  The Social Stratification of English in New York City. Washington, DC: Center for Applied Linguistics.

Lacey, Marc. 2002
  Where 9/11 News Is Late, But Aid Is Swift. New York Times, June 3:A1, A7.

Ladányi, János. 1993
  Patterns of Residential Segregation and the Gypsy Minority in Budapest. International Journal of Urbana and Regional Research 17(1):30–41.

Laderman, Carol. 1988
  A Welcoming Soil: Islamic Humoralism on the Malay Peninsula. In Paths to Asian Medical Knowledge. Charles Leslie and Allan Young, eds. Pp. 272–288. Berkeley: University of California Press.

LaFleur, William. 1992
  Liquid Life: Abortion and Buddhism in Japan. Princeton: Princeton University Press.

Lake, Amy and Steven Deller, 1996
  The Socioeconomic Impacts of a Native American Casino. Madison: Department of Agricultural and Applied Economics, University of Wisconsin.

Lakoff, Robin. 1973
  Language and Woman's Place. Language in Society 2:45–79.

———. 1990
  Talking Power: The Politics of Language in Our Lives. New York: Basic Books.

Lamphere, Louise. 1992
  Introduction: The Shaping of Diversity. In Structuring Diversity: Ethnographic Perspectives on the New Immigration. Lousie Lamphere, ed. Chicago: University of Chicago Press.

Larsen, Clark Spenser and George R. Milner. 1994
  Bioanthropological Perspectives on Postcontact Tradi-

tions. In In the Wake of Contact: Biological Responses to Conquest. Clark Spenser Larsen and George R. Milner, eds. Pp. 1–8. New York: Wiley-Liss.

Larsen, Ulla and Sharon Yan. 2000
Does Female Circumcision Affect Infertility and Fertility? A Study of the Central African Republic, Côte d'Ivoire, and Tanzania. Demography 37:313–321.

Leach, Jerry W. 1975
Trobriand Cricket: An Ingenious Response to Colonialism. Video. Berkeley: University of California Extension Media.

Leacock. Eleanor. 1993
Women in Samoan History: A Further Critique of Derek Freeman. In Sex and Gender Hierarchies. Barbara D. Miller, ed. Pp. 351–365. New York: Cambridge University Press.

Leavy, Morton L. and R. D. Weinberg. 1979
Law of Adoption. Dobbs Ferry, NY: Oceana.

Lebra, Takie. 1976
Japanese Patterns of Behavior. Honolulu: University of Hawaii Press.

Lee, Gary R. and Mindy Kezis. 1979
Family Structure and the Status of the Elderly. Journal of Comparative Family Studies 10:429–443.

Lee, Helen Morton. 2003
Tongans Overseas: Between Two Shores. Honolulu: University of Hawai'i Press.

Lee, Raymond M. and Claire M. Renzetti. 1993
Researching Sensitive Topics. Newbury Park, CA: Sage Publications.

Lee, Richard Borshay. 1979
The !Kung San: Men, Women, and Work in a Foraging Society. New York: Cambridge University Press.

Lee, Wai-Na and David K. Tse. 1994
Becoming Canadian: Understanding How Hong Kong Immigrants Change Their Consumption. Pacific Affairs 67(1):70–95.

Lein, Laura and Donald Brenneis. 1978
Children's Disputes in Three Speech Communities. Language in Society 7:299–323.

Lempert, David. 1996
Daily Life in a Crumbling Empire. 2 volumes. New York: Columbia University Press.

Lepowsky, Maria. 1990
Big Men, Big Women, and Cultural Autonomy. Ethnology 29(10):35–50.

———. 1993
Fruit of the Motherland: Gender in an Egalitarian Society. New York: Columbia University Press.

Lessinger, Johanna. 1995
From the Ganges to the Hudson: Indian Immigrants in New York City. Boston: Allyn and Bacon.

Levine, Robert, Suguru Sato, Tsukasa Hashimoto, and Jyoti Verma. 1995
Love and Marriage in Eleven Cultures. Journal of Cross-Cultural Psychology 26:554–571.

Levinson, David. 1989
Family Violence in Cross-Cultural Perspective. Newbury Park, CA: Sage Publications.

Lévi-Strauss, Claude. 1967
Structural Anthropology. New York: Anchor Books.

———. 1968
Tristes Tropiques: An Anthropological Study of Primitive Societies in Brazil. New York: Atheneum.

———. 1969 [1949]
The Elementary Structures of Kinship. Boston: Beacon Press.

Levy, Jerrold E., Eric B. Henderson, and Tracy J. Andrews. 1989
The Effects of Regional Variation and Temporal Change in Matrilineal Elements of Navajo Social Organization. Journal of Anthropological Research 45(4):351–377.

Lew, Irvina. 1994
Bathing as Science: Ancient Sea Cures Gain Support from New Research. Condé Nast Traveler 29(12):86–90.

Lewis, Oscar. 1966
The Culture of Poverty. Scientific American. 215:19–25.

Leynaud, Emile. 1961
Fraternités d'âge et sociétés de culture dans la Haute-Vallée du Niger. Cahiers d'Etudes Africaines 6:41–68.

Lincoln, Kenneth. 1993
Indi'n Humor: Bicultural Play in Native America. New York: Oxford University Press.

Lindenbaum, Shirley. 1979
Kuru Sorcery: Disease and Danger in the New Guinea Highlands. Mountain View, CA: Mayfield Publishing Company.

Linnekan, Jocelyn. 1990
Sacred Queens and Women of Consequence: Rank, Gender, and Colonialism in the Hawaiian Islands. Ann Arbor: University of Michigan Press.

Little, Kenneth. 1966
The Strange Case of Romantic Love. The Listener 7 (April).

Littman, Mark. 1993
Office of Refugee Resettlement Monthly Data Report for September 1992. Washington, DC: Office of Refugee Resettlement.

Lloyd, Cynthia B. 1995
Household Structure and Poverty: What Are the Connections? Working Papers, No. 74. New York: The Population Council.

Lock, Margaret. 1993
Encounters with Aging: Mythologies of Menopause in Japan and North America. Berkeley: University of California Press.

Lockwood, Victoria S. 1993
Tahitian Transformation: Gender and Capitalist Development in a Rural Society. Boulder: Lynne Reiner Publishers.

Loker, William. 1993
Human Ecology of Cattle-Raising in the Peruvian Ama-

zon: The View from the Farm. Human Organization 52(1):14–24.

Lorch, Donatella. 2003
Do Read This for War. Newsweek 141(11):13.

Low, Setha M. 1995
Indigenous Architecture and the Spanish American Plaza in Mesoamerica and the Caribbean. American Anthropologist 97(4):748–762.

Lu, Hanchao. 1995
Away from Nanking Road: Small Stores and Neighborhood Life in Modern Shanghai. Journal of Asian Studies 54(1):93–123.

Lubkemann, Stephen C. 2002
Refugees. In World at Risk: A Global Issues Sourcebook. Pp. 522–544. Washington, DC: CQ Press.

Luhrmann, Tanya M. 1989
Persuasions of the Witch's Craft: Ritual Magic in Contemporary England. Cambridge: Harvard University Press.

Lutz, Catherine. 2002
Making War at Home in the United States: Militarization and the Current Crisis. American Anthropologist 104:723–735.

Maclachlan, Morgan. 1983
Why They Did Not Starve: Biocultural Adaptation in a South Indian Village. Philadelphia: Institute for the Study of Human Issues.

MacLeod, Arlene Elowe. 1992
Hegemonic Relations and Gender Resistance: The New Veiling as Accommodating Protest in Cairo. Signs: The Journal of Women in Culture and Society 17(3):533–557.

Mahler, Sarah J. 1995
Salvadorans in Suburbia: Symbiosis and Conflict. Boston: Allyn and Bacon.

Major, Marc R. 1996
No Friends but the Mountains: A Simulation on Kurdistan. Social Education 60(3):C1–C8.

Makepeace, James M. 1997
Courtship Violence as Process: A Developmental Theory. In Violence between Intimate Partners: Patterns, Causes, and Effects. Albert P. Cardarelli, ed. Pp. 29–47. Boston: Allyn and Bacon.

Malinowski, Bronislaw. 1929
The Sexual Life of Savages. New York: Harcourt, Brace & World.
———. 1961 [1922]
Argonauts of the Western Pacific. New York: E. P. Dutton & Co.
———. 1962 [1926]
Crime and Custom in Savage Society. Paterson, NJ: Littlefield, Adams & Co.

Mamdani, Mahmoud. 1972
The Myth of Population Control: Family, Caste, and Class in an Indian Village. New York: Monthly Review Press.
———. 2002
Good Muslim, Bad Muslim: A Political Perspective on Culture and Terrorism. American Anthropologist 104:766–775.

Manz, Beatriz. 1988
Refugees of a Hidden War: The Aftermath of Counterinsurgency in Guatemala. Albany: State University of New York Press.

March, Kathryn S. and Rachell L. Taqqu. 1986
Women's Informal Associations in Developing Countries: Catalysts for Change? Boulder: Westview Press.

Marcoux, Alan. 2000
The Feminization of Poverty: Facts, Hypotheses, and the Art of Advocacy. http://www.undp.org.popin.fao.womnpoor.htm. 11/6/00.

Marcus, Aliza. 1996
Turkey, the Kurds, and Human Rights. Dissent (summer):104–106.

Marcus, George. 1995
Ethnography in/of the World System: The Emergence of Multi-Sited Ethnography. Annual Review of Anthropology 24:95–117.

Margolis, Maxine L. and Marigene Arnold. 1993
Turning the Tables? Male Strippers and the Gender Hierarchy in America. In Sex and Gender Hierarchies. Barbara D. Miller, ed. Pp. 334–350. New York: Cambridge University Press.

Margolis, Maxine. 1994
Little Brazil: An Ethnography of Brazilian Immigrants in New York City. Princeton: Princeton University Press.

Marshall, Robert C. 1985
Giving a Gift to the Hamlet: Rank, Solidarity and Productive Exchange in Rural Japan. Ethnology 24:167–182.

Martin, Richard C. 1995
Islam. In The HarperCollins Dictionary of Religion. Jonathan Z. Smith, ed. Pp. 498–513. New York: HarperCollins.

Martínez, Samuel. 1996
Indifference with Indignation: Anthropology, Human Rights, and the Haitian Bracero. American Anthropologist 98(1):17–25.

Massara, Emily. 1997
Que Gordita. In Food and Culture: A Reader. Carole Counihan and Penny van Esterik, eds. Pp. 251–255. New York: Routledge.

Massiah, Joycelin. 1983
Women as Heads of Households in the Caribbean: Family Structure and Feminine Status. Paris: UNESCO.

Maybury-Lewis, David. 1997a
Museums and Indigenous Cultures. Cultural Survival Quarterly 21(1):3.
———. 1997b
Indigenous Peoples, Ethnic Groups, and the State. Boston: Allyn and Bacon.
———. 2002
Genocide against Indigenous Peoples. In Annihilating Difference: The Anthropology of Genocide. Alexander Laban Hinton, ed. Pp. 43–53. Berkeley: University of California Press.

McCully, Patrick. 2003
Big Dams, Big Trouble. New Internationalist 354:14–15.

McElroy, Ann and Patricia K. Townsend. 1996
Medical Anthropology in Ecological Perspective. 3rd edition. Boulder: Westview Press.

McGrew, William C. 1998
Culture in Nonhuman Primates? Annual Review of Anthropology 27:301–328.

McMahon, April M. S. 1994
Understanding Language Change. New York: Cambridge University Press.

Mead, Margaret. 1928 [1961]
Coming of Age in Samoa: A Psychological Study of Primitive Youth for Western Civilization. New York: Dell Publishing Company.

———. 1963 [1935]
Sex and Temperament in Three Primitive Societies. New York: William Morrow.

———. 1977
Letters from the Field 1925–1975. New York: Harper & Row.

———. 1986
Field Work in the Pacific Islands, 1925–1967. In Women in the Field: Anthropological Experiences. Peggy Golde, ed. Pp. 293–331. Berkeley: University of California Press.

Meigs, Anna S. 1984
Food, Sex, and Pollution: A New Guinea Religion. New Brunswick: Rutgers University Press.

Mencher, Joan P. 1974
The Caste System Upside Down, or The Not-So-Mysterious East. Current Anthropology 15(4):469–49.

Mernissi, Fatima. 1987
Beyond the Veil: Male-Female Dynamics in Modern Muslim Society. Revised edition. Bloomington: Indiana University Press.

Merry, Sally Engle. 1992
Anthropology, Law, and Transnational Processes. Annual Review of Anthropology 21:357–379.

Messer, Ellen. 1993
Anthropology and Human Rights. Annual Review of Anthropology 22:221–249.

Meyerhoff, Miriam. 1999
Sorry in the Pacific: Defining Communities, Defining Practice. Language in Society 28:225–238.

Michaelson, Evelyn Jacobson and Walter Goldschmidt. 1971
Female Roles and Male Dominance among Peasants. Southwestern Journal of Anthropology 27:330–352.

Migration Information Source. 2003
Global Data. www.migrationinformation.org/Global Data/countrydata

Miller, Barbara D. [1997] 1981
The Endangered Sex: Neglect of Female Children in Rural North India. New Delhi: Oxford University Press.

———. 1987
Social Patterns of Food Expenditure among Low-Income Jamaicans. In Papers and Recommendations of the Workshop on Food and Nutrition Security in Jamaica in the 1980s and Beyond. Kenneth A. Leslie and Lloyd B. Rankine, eds. Pp. 13–33. Kingston, Jamaica: Caribbean Food and Nutrition Institute.

———. 1993
Surveying the Anthropology of Sex and Gender Hierarchies. In Sex and Gender Hierarchies. Barbara D. Miller, ed. Pp. 3–31. New York: Cambridge University Press

Miller, Barbara D. and Carl Stone. 1983
The Low-Income Household Expenditure Survey: Description and Analysis. Jamaica Tax Structure Examination Project, Staff Paper No. 25. Syracuse, NY: Metropolitan Studies Program, Syracuse University.

Miller, Barbara D. and Showkat Hayat Khan. 1986
Incorporating Voluntarism into Rural Development in Bangladesh. Third World Planning Review 8(2):139–152.

Miller, Bruce G. 1994
Contemporary Native Women: Role Flexibility and Politics. Anthropologica 36:57–72.

Miller, Daniel. 1993
Christmas against Materialism in Trinidad. In Unwrapping Christmas. Daniel Miller, ed. Pp. 134–153. New York: Oxford University Press.

———. 2003
Could the Internet Defetishise the Commodity? Environment and Planning D: Society and Space 21:359–372.

Mills, Mary Beth. 1995
Attack of the Widow Ghosts: Gender, Death, and Modernity in Northeast Thailand. In Bewitching Women, Pious Men: Gender and Body Politics in Southeast Asia. Aihwa Ong and Michael G. Peletz, eds. Pp. 44–273. Berkeley: University of California Press.

Milton, Katherine. 1992
Civilization and Its Discontents. Natural History 3/92:37–92.

Miner, Horace. 1965 [1956]
Body Ritual among the Nacirema. In Reader in Comparative Religion: An Anthropological Approach. William A. Lessa and Evon Z. Vogt, eds. pp. 414–418. New York: Harper & Row.

Mines, Mattison. 1994
Public Faces, Private Voices: Community and Individuality in South India. Berkeley: University of California Press.

Mitchell, Bruce. 1994
Sustainable Development at the Village Level in Bali, Indonesia. Human Ecology 22(2):189–211.

Mitter, Partha. 1977
Much Maligned Monsters: A History of European Reactions to Indian Art. Chicago: University of Chicago Press.

Miyazawa, Setsuo. 1992
Policing in Japan: A Study on Making Crime. Frank G. Bennett, Jr. with John O. Haley, trans. Albany: State University of New York Press.

Moberg, Mark. 1991
Citrus and the State: Factions and Class Formation in Rural Belize. American Ethnologist 18(20):215–233.

Modell, Judith S. 1994
> Kinship with Strangers: Adoption and Interpretations of Kinship in American Culture. Berkeley: University of California Press.

Moerman, Daniel E. 1979
> Anthropology of Symbolic Healing. Current Anthropology 20:59–80.

———. 1983
> General Medical Effectiveness and Human Biology: Placebo Effects in the Treatment of Ulcer Disease. Medical Anthropology Quarterly 14:13–16.

———. 1992
> Minding the Body: The Placebo Effect Unmasked. In Giving the Body Its Due. M. Sheets-Johnstone, ed. Pp. 69–84. Albany, NY: State University of New York Press.

Mogelonsky, Marcia. 1995
> Asian-Indian Americans. American Demographics 17(8): 32–39.

Montesquie. 1949 [1748]
> The Spirit of the Laws. T. Nugent, trans. New York: Hafner.

Montgomery, Heather. 2001
> Modern Babylon: Prostituting Children in Thailand. New York: Bergahn Books.

Moore, Carmella C. and Holly F. Mathews, 2001
> Introduction: The Psychology of Cultural Experience. In The Psychology of Cultural Experience. Carmella C. Moore and Holly F. Mathews, eds. Pp. 1–18. New York: Cambridge University Press.

Morgan, William. 1977
> Navaho Treatment of Sickness: Diagnosticians. In Culture, Disease, and Healing: Studies in Medical Anthropology. David Landy, ed. Pp. 163–168. New York: Macmillan.

Morris, Brian. 1998
> The Power of Animals: An Ethnography. New York: Berg.

Morris, Rosalind. 1994
> Three Sexes and Four Sexualities: Redressing the Discourses on Gender and Sexuality in Contemporary Thailand. Positions 2:15–43.

Mortland, Carol A. 1994
> Khmer Buddhism in the United States: Ultimate Questions. In Cambodian Culture Since 1975: Homeland and Exile. May M. Ebihara, Carol A. Mortalnd, and Judy Ledgerwood, eds. Pp. 72–90. Ithaca: Cornell University Press.

Moynihan, Elizabeth B. 1979
> Paradise as a Garden in Persia and Mughal India. New York: George Braziller.

Muecke, Marjorie A. 1987
> Resettled Refugees: Reconstruction of Identity of Lao in Seattle. Urban Anthropology 16(3–4):273–289.

Mulk, Inga-Maria. 1994
> Sacrificial Places and Their Meaning in Saami Society. In Sacred Sites, Sacred Places. David L. Carmichael, Jane Hubert, Brian Reeves and Audhild Schanche, eds. Pp. 121–131. New York: Routledge.

Mull, Dorothy S. and J. Dennis Mull. 1987
> Infanticide among the Tarahumara of the Mexican Sierra Madre. In Child Survival: Anthropological Perspectives on the Treatment and Maltreatment of Children. Nancy Scheper-Hughes, ed. Pp. 113–132. Boston: D. Reidel Publishing Company.

Murdock, George Peter. 1965 [1949]
> Social Structure. New York: The Free Press.

Murphy, Yolanda and Robert F. Murphy. 1985
> Women of the Forest. New York: Columbia University Press.

Murray, Gerald F. 1987
> The Domestication of Wood in Haiti: A Case Study of Applied Evolution. In Anthropological Praxis: Translating Knowledge into Action. Robert M. Wulff and Shirley J. Fiske, eds. Pp. 233–240. Boulder: Westview Press.

Myerhoff, Barbara. 1978
> Number Our Days. New York: Simon and Schuster.

Myers, James. 1992
> Nonmainstream Body Modification: Genital Piercing, Branding, Burning, and Cutting. Journal of Contemporary Ethnography 21(3):267–306.

Myers-Scotton, Carol. 1993
> Social Motivations for Code-Switching. New York: Oxford University Press.

Nader, Laura. 1972
> Up the Anthropologist—Perspectives Gained from Studying Up. In Reinventing Anthropology. Dell Hymes, ed. Pp. 284–311. New York: Vintage Books.

———. 1995
> Civilization and Its Negotiations. In Understanding Disputes: The Politics of Argument. Pat Caplan, ed. Pp. 39–64. Providence, RI: Berg Publishers.

———. 2001
> Harmony Coerced Is Freedom Denied. The Chronicle of Higher Education. July 13:B1.

Nag, Moni. 1972
> Sex, Culture and Human Fertility: India and the United States. Current Anthropology 13:231–238.

———. 1983
> Modernization Affects Fertility. Populi 10:56–77.

Nag, Moni, Benjamin N. F. White, and R. Creighton Peet. 1978
> An Anthropological Approach to the Study of the Economic Value of Children in Java and Nepal. Current Anthropology 19(2):293–301.

Nanda, Serena. 1990
> Neither Man Nor Woman: The Hijras of India. Belmont, CA: Wadsworth Publishing Company.

———. 1994
> Cultural Anthropology. Wadsworth, CA: Wadsworth Publishing Company.

Neale, Walter C. 1976
> Monies in Societies. San Francisco: Chandler & Sharp Publishers, Inc.

Neff, Deborah L. 1994
> The Social Construction of Infertility: The Case of the

Matrilineal Nayars in South India. Social Science and Medicine 39(4):475–485.

Neier, Aryeh. 1996
Language and Minorities. Dissent (summer):31–35.

Nelson, Sarah. 1993
Sex and Gender Hierarchies. Barbara D. Miller, ed. Pp. 297–315. New York: Cambridge University Press.

Netting, Robert Mc C. 1989
Smallholders, Householders, Freeholders: Why the Family Farm Works Well Worldwide. In The Household Economy: Reconsidering the Domestic Mode of Production. Richard R. Wilk, ed. Pp. 221–244. Boulder: Westview Press.

Neusner, Jacob. 1995
Judaism. In The HarperCollins Dictionary of Religion. Jonathan Z. Smith. Pp. 598–607. New York: Harper-Collins.

Newman Lucile, ed., 1985
Women's Medicine: A Cross-Cultural Study of Indigenous Fertility Regulation. New Brunswick: Rutgers University Pres.

Newman, Lucile. 1972
Birth Control: An Anthropological View. Module No. 27. Reading, MA: Addison-Wesley.

Ngokwey, Ndolamb. 1988
Pluralistic Etiological Systems in Their Social Context: A Brazilian Case Study. Social Science and Medicine 26:793–802.

Nichter, Mark. 1992
Of Ticks, Kings, Spirits and the Promise of Vaccines. In Paths to Asian Medical Knowledge. Charles Leslie and Allan Young, eds. pp. 224–253. Berkeley: University of California Press.

———. 1996
Vaccinations in the Third World: A Consideration of Community Demand. In Anthropology and International Health: Asian Case Studies. Mark Nichter and Mimi Nichter, eds. Pp. 329–365. Amsterdam: Gordon and Breach Publishers.

Nichter, Mimi and Nancy Vuckovic. 1994
Fat Talk: Body Image among Adolescent Girls. In Many Mirrors: Body Image and Social Relations. Nicole Sault, ed. Pp. 109–131. New Brunswick: Rutgers University Press.

Nodwell, Evelyn and Neil Guppy. 1992
The Effects of Publicly Displayed Ethnicity on Interpersonal Discrimination: Indo-Canadians in Vancouver. The Canadian Review of Sociology and Anthropology 29(1):87–99.

Norgaard, Richard B. 1994
Development Betrayed: The End of Progress and the Co-evolutionary Revisioning of the Future. New York: Routledge.

Nyambedha, Erick Otieno, Simiyu Wandibba, and Jens Aagaard-Hansen. 2003
Changing Patterns of Orphan Care Due to the HIV Epi-demic in Western Kenya. Social Science and Medicine 57:301–311.

Obeyesekere, Gananath. 1981
Medusa's Hair: An Essay on Personal Symbols and Religious Experience. Chicago: University of Chicago Press.

Ochs, Elinor. 1993
Indexing Gender. In Sex and Gender Hierarchies. Barbara D. Miller, ed. Pp. 146–169. New York: Cambridge University Press.

Oei, Tian P. S. and Farida Notowidjojo. 1990
Depression and Loneliness in Overseas Students. Journal of Social Psychiatry 14:339–364.

Ohnuki-Tierney, Emiko. 1980
Shamans and Imu: Among Two Ainu Groups. In The Culture-Bound Syndromes. Ronald C. Simons and Charles C. Hughes, eds. Pp. 91–110. Dordrecht: D. Reidel Publishing Company.

———. 1994
Brain Death and Organ Transplantation: Cultural Bases of Medical Technology. Current Anthropology 35(3):233–242.

Oinas, Felix J. 1993
Couvade in Estonia. Slavic & East European Journal 37(3):339–345.

Ong, Aihwa. 1987
Spirits of Resistance and Capitalist Discipline: Factory Women in Malaysia. Albany: State University of New York Press.

———. 1995
State versus Islam: Malay Families, Women's Bodies, and the Body Politic in Malaysia. In Bewitching Women, Pious Men: Gender and Body Politics in Southeast Asia. Aihwa Ong and Michael G. Peletz, eds. Pp. 159–194. Berkeley: University of California Press.

Ongley, Patrick. 1995
Post–1945 International Migration: New Zealand, Australia and Canada Compared. International Migration Review 29(3):765–793.

Painter, Andrew A. 1996
The Telerepresentation of Gender. In Re-Imaging Japanese Women. Anne E. Imamura, ed. Pp. 46–72. Berkeley: University of California Press.

Paley, Julia. 2002
Toward an Anthropology of Democracy. Annual Review of Anthropology 31:469–496.

Panter-Brick, Catherine and Malcolm T. Smith, eds. 2000
Abandoned Children. New York: Cambridge University Press.

Pappas, Gregory. 1989
The Magic City: Unemployment in a Working-Class Community. Ithaca: Cornell University Press.

Parrillo, Vincent N. 1997
Strangers to These Shores: Race and Ethnic Relations in the United States. Boston: Allyn and Bacon.

Parker, Richard G. 1991
Bodies, Pleasures, and Passions: Sexual Culture in Contemporary Brazil. Boston: Beacon Press.

Parry, Jonathan P. 1966
    Caste. In The Social Science Encyclopedia. Adam Kuper and Jessica Kuper, eds. Pp. 76–77. New York: Routledge.

Pasquino, Gianfranco. 1996
    Democratization. In The Social Science Encyclopedia. Adam Kuper and Jessica Kuper, eds. Pp. 173–174. Routledge: New York.

Patterson, Thomas C. 2001
    A Social History of Anthropology in the United States. New York: Berg.

Paxson, Heather. 2003
    With or Against Nature: IVF, Gender and Reproductive Agency in Athens, Greece. Social Science and Medicine 56:1853–1866.

Peacock, James L. and Dorothy C. Holland. 1993
    The Narrated Self: Life Stories in Process. Ethos 21(4):367–383.

Pechman, Joseph A. 1987
    Introduction: Recent Developments. In Comparative Tax Systems: Europe, Canada, and Japan. Joseph A. Pechman, ed. Pp. 1–32. Arlington, VA: Tax Analysts.

Pedelty, Mark. 1995
    War Stories: The Culture of Foreign Correspondents. New York: Routledge

Peletz, Michael. 1987
    The Exchange of Men in 19th-Century Negeri Sembilan (Malaya). American Ethnologist 14(3):449–469.

Pelto, Pertti. 1973
    The Snowmobile Revolution: Technology and Social Change in the Arctic. Menlo Park, CA: Cummings.

Pelto, Pertti, Maria Roman, and Nelson Liriano. 1982
    Family Structures in An Urban Puerto Rican Community. Urban Anthropology 11:39–58.

Peng Xizhe. 1991
    Demographic Transition in China: Fertility Trends Since the 1950s. New York: Oxford University Press.

Perin, Constance. 1988
    Belonging in America: Reading between the Lines. Madison: University of Wisconsin Press.

Perry, Richard J. 1996
    . . . From Time Immemorial: Indigenous Peoples and State Systems. Austin: University of Texas Press.

Pessar, Patricia R. 1995
    A Visa for a Dream: Dominicans in the United States. Boston: Allyn and Bacon.

Petras, James and Tienchai Wongchaisuwan. 1993
    Free Markets, AIDS and Child Prostitution. Economic and Political Weekly March 13:440–442.

Pillsbury, Barbara. 1990
    The Politics of Family Planning: Sterilization and Human Rights in Bangladesh. In Births and Power: Social Change and the Politics of Reproduction. W. Penn Handwerker, ed. Pp. 165–196. Boulder: Westview Press.

Plant, Roger. 1994
    Land Rights and Minorities. London: Minority Rights Group.

Plattner, Stuart. 1989
    Markets and Marketplaces. In Economic Anthropology. Stuart Plattner, ed. Pp. 171–208. Stanford: Stanford University Press.

Poirier, Sylvie. 1992
    "Nomadic" Rituals: Networks of Ritual Exchange between Women of the Australian Western Desert. Man 27:757–776.

Posey, Darrell Addison. 1990
    Intellectual Property Rights: What Is the Position of Ethnobiology? Journal of Ethnobiology 10:93–98.

Pospisil, Leopold. 1979
    Legally Induced Cultural Change in New Guinea. In The Imposition of Law. Sandra B. Bruman and Barbara E. Harrell-Bond, eds. New York: Academic Press.

Postgate, Nicholas, Tao Wang, and Toby Wilkinson. 1995
    The Evidence for Early Writing: Utilitarian or Ceremonial? Antiquity 69:459–480.

Potter, Jack M. 1976
    Thai Peasant Social Structure. Chicago: The University of Chicago Press.

Potter, Sulamith Heins. 1977
    Family Life in a Northern Thai Village: A Study in the Structural Significance of Women. Berkeley: University of California Press.

Pratt, Mary Louise. 1992
    Imperial Eyes: Travel Writing and Transculturation. London: Routledge.

Price, David H. 1995
    Water Theft in Egypt's Fayoum Oasis: Emics, Etics, and the Illegal. In Science, Materialism, and the Study of Culture. Martin F. Murphy and Maxine L. Margolis, eds. Pp. 96–110. Gainesville: University of Florida Press.

Price, David. 2003
    Personal communication, response to "Six Questions Survey," author's files, Washington, DC.

Prince, Raymond. 1985
    The Concept of Culture-Bound Syndromes: Anorexia Nervosa and Brain-Fag. Social Science and Medicine 21(2):197–203.

Purdum, Elizabeth D. and J. Anthony Paredes. 1989
    Facing the Death Penalty: Essays on Cruel and Unusual Punishment. Philadelphia: Temple University Press.

Radcliffe-Brown, A. R. 1964 [1922]
    The Andaman Islanders. New York: The Free Press.

Raheja, Gloria Goodwin. 1988
    The Poison in the Gift: Ritual, Prestation, and the Dominant Caste in a North Indian Village. Chicago: University of Chicago Press.

Rahnema, Majid. 1992
    Poverty. In The Development Dictionary: A Guide to Knowledge and Power. Wolfgang Sachs, ed. Pp. 159–176. Atlantic Highlands, NJ: Zed Press.

Ramesh, A., C. R. Srikumari, and S. Sukumar. 1989
    Parallel Cousin Marriages in Madras, Tamil Nadu: New Trends in Dravidian Kinship. Social Biology 36(3–4): 248–254.

Ramphele, Mamphela. 1996
Political Widowhood in South Africa: The Embodiment of Ambiguity. Daedalus 125(1):99–17.

Raphael, Dana. 1975
Matrescence: Becoming a Mother: A "New/Old" *Rite de Passage*. In Being Female: Reproduction, Power and Change. Dana Raphael, ed. Pp. 65–72. The Hague: Mouton Publishers.

Rapoport, Tamar, Yoni Garb, and Anat Penso. 1995
Religious Socialization and Female Subjectivity: Religious-Zionist Adolescent Girls in Israel. Sociology of Education 68:48–61.

Rapp, Rayna. 1993
Reproduction and Gender Hierarchy: Amniocentesis in America. In Sex and Gender Hierarchies. Barbara D. Miller, ed. Pp. 108–126. New York: Cambridge University Press.

Rathje, William and Cullen Murphy. 1992
Rubbish! The Archaeology of Garbage. New York: Harper & Row.

Ravaillon, Martin. 2003
The Debate on Globalization, Poverty and Inequality: Why Income Measurement Matters. International Affairs 79:739–753.

Reichel-Dolmatoff, G. 1971
Amazonian Cosmos: The Sexual and Religious Symbolism of the Tukano Indians. Chicago: University of Chicago Press.

Reid, Russell M. 1992
Cultural and Medical Perspectives on Geophagia. Medical Anthropology 13:337–351.

Reiner, R. 1996
Police. In The Social Science Encyclopedia. Adam Kuper and Jessica Kuper, eds. Pp. 619–621. New York: Routledge.

Reyna, Stephen P. 1994
A Mode of Domination Approach to Organized Violence. In Studying War: Anthropological Perspectives. S. P. Reyna and R. E. Downs, eds. Pp. 29–65. Langhorne, PA: Gordon and Breach Science Publishers.

Rhodes, Lorna A. 2001
Toward an Anthropology of Prisons. Annual Review of Anthropology 30:65–83.

Rich, Adrienne. 1980
Compulsory Heterosexuality and Lesbian Existence. Signs 5:631–660.

Rich, Bruce. 1994
Mortgaging the Earth: The World Bank, Environmental Impoverishment, and the Crisis of Development. Boston: Beacon Press.

Robertson, Carol E. 1987
Power and Gender in the Musical Experiences of Women. In Women and Music in Cross-Cultural Perspective. Ellen Koskoff, ed. Pp. 225–244. New York: Greenwood Press.

Robertson, Jennifer. 1991
Native and Newcomer: Making and Remaking a Japanese City. Berkeley: University of California Press.

Robins, Kevin. 1996
Globalization. In The Social Science Encyclopedia. 2nd edition. Adam Kuper and Jessica Kuper, eds. Pp. 345–346. New York: Routledge.

Robson, Colin. 1993
Real World Research: A Resource for Social Scientists and Practitioner-Researchers. Cambridge, MA: Blackwell Publishers.

Rogers, Barbara. 1979
The Domestication of Women: Discrimination in Developing Societies. New York: St. Martin's Press.

Rosaldo, Renato. 1980
Ilongot Headhunting 1883–1974: A Study in Society and History. Stanford: Stanford University Press.

Roscoe, Will. 1991
The Zuni Man-Woman. Albuquerque: University of New Mexico Press.

Rose, Jerome C., Thomas J. Green, and Victoria D. Green. 1996
NAGPRA is Forever: Osteology and the Repatriation of Skeletons. Annual Review of Anthropology 25:81–103.

Roseberry, William. 2001
Capitalism. In The Dictionary of Anthropology. Thomas Barfield, ed. Pp. 47–49. Malden, MA: Blackwell Publishers.

Roseman, Marina. 1987
Inversion and Conjuncture: Male and Female Performance among the Temiar of Peninsular Malaysia. In Women and Music in Cross-Cultural Perspective. Ellen Koskoff, ed. Pp. 131–149. New York: Greenwood Press.

Rosenberger, Nancy. 1992
Images of the West: Home Style in Japanese Magazines. In Re-made in Japan: Everyday Life and Consumer Taste in a Changing Society. James J. Tobin, ed. Pp. 106–125. New Haven: Yale University Press.

Rosenblatt, Paul C., Patricia R. Walsh, and Douglas A. Jackson. 1976
Grief and Mourning in Cross-Cultural Perspective. New Haven: HRAF Press.

Ross, Marc Howard. 1993
The Culture of Conflict: Interpretations and Interests in Comparative Perspective. New Haven: Yale University Press.

Rouland, Norbert. 1994
Legal Anthropology. Philippe G. Planel, trans. Stanford: Stanford University Press.

Roy, Arundhati. 1999
The Cost of Living. New York: The Modern Library.

Rubel, Arthur J., Carl W. O'Nell, and Rolando Collado-Ardon. 1984
Susto: A Folk Illness. Berkeley: University of California Press.

Rubin, Gayle. 1975
The Traffic in Women: Notes on the "Political Economy" of Sex. In Toward an Anthropology of Women. Rayna R, Rapp, ed. Pp. 157–210. New York: Monthly Review Press.

Sachs, Aaron. 1996
Dying for Oil. WorldWatch, June:10–21.

Saggers, Sherry and Dennis Gray. 1998
Dealing with Alcohol: Indigenous Usage in Australia, New Zealand and Canada. New York: Cambridge University Press.

Sahlins, Marshall. 1963
Poor Man, Rich Man, Big Man, Chief. Comparative Studies in Society and History 5:285–303.

Saitoti, Tepilit Ole. 1986
The Worlds of a Maasai Warrior. New York: Random House.

Salam, Nawaf A. 1994
Between Repatriation and Resettlement: Palestinian Refugees in Lebanon. Journal of Palestine Studies 24:18–27.

Salzman, Philip Carl. 2002
On Reflexivity. American Anthropologist 104:805–813.

Sanday, Peggy Reeves. 1973
Toward a Theory of the Status of Women. American Anthropologist 75:1682–1700.

———. 1986
Divine Hunger: Cannibalism as a Cultural System. New York: Cambridge University Press.

———. 1990
Fraternity Gang Rape: Sex, Brotherhood, and Privilege on Campus. New York: New York University Press.

———. 1996
A Woman Scorned: Date Rape on Trial. New York: Doubleday.

———. 2002
Women at the Center: Life in a Modern Matriarchy. Ithaca: Cornell University Press.

Sanders, Douglas E. 1999
Indigenous Peoples: Issues of Definition. International Journal of Cultural Property 8:4–13.

Sanders, William B. 1994
Gangbangs and Drive-Bys: Grounded Culture and Juvenile Gang Violence. New York: Aldine de Gruyter.

Sanjek, Roger. 2000
Keeping Ethnography Alive in an Urbanizing World. Human Organization 53:280–288.

———. 1990
A Vocabulary for Fieldnotes. In Fieldnotes: The Making of Anthropology. Roger Sanjek, ed. Pp. 92–138. Ithaca: Cornell University Press.

———. 1994
The Enduring Inequalities of Race. In Race. Steven Gregory and Roger Sanjek, eds. Pp. 1–17. New Brunswick: Rutgers University Press.

Sant Cassia, Paul. 1993
Banditry, Myth, and Terror in Cyprus and Other Mediterranean Societies. Comparative Studies in Society and History 35(4):773–795.

Sargent, Carolyn F. 1989
Maternity, Medicine, and Power: Reproductive Decisions in Urban Benin. Berkeley: University of California Press.

Sault, Nicole L. 1985
Baptismal Sponsorship as a Source of Power for Zapotec Women of Oaxaca, Mexico. Journal of Latin American Lore 11(2):225–243.

———. 1994
How the Body Shapes Parenthood: "Surrogate" Mothers in the United States and Godmothers in Mexico. In Many Mirrors: Body Image and Social Relations. Nicole Sault, ed. Pp. 292–318. Rutgers: Rutgers University Press.

Savishinsky, Joel S. 1974
The Trail of the Hare: Life and Stress in an Arctic Community. New York: Gordon and Breach.

———. 1990
Three Propositions for a Critically Applied Medical Anthropology. Social Science and Medicine 30(2):189–197.

———. 1991
The Ends of Time: Life and Work in a Nursing Home. New York: Bergin & Garvey.

Scheper-Hughes, Nancy. 1992
Death without Weeping: The Violence of Everyday Life in Brazil. Berkeley: University of California Press.

Schlegel, Alice. 1995
A Cross-Cultural Approach to Adolescence. Ethos 23(1):15–32.

Schlegel, Alice and Herbert Barry III. 1991
Adolescence: An Anthropological Inquiry. New York: Free Press.

Schmid, Thomas J. and Richard S. Jones. 1993
Ambivalent Actions: Prison Adaptation Strategies of First-Time, Short-term Inmates. Journal of Contemporary Ethnography 21 (4):439–463.

Schneider, David M. 1968
American Kinship: A Cultural Account. Englewood Cliffs, NJ: Prentice-Hall.

Scott, James C. 1985
Weapons of the Weak: Everyday Forms of Peasant Resistance. New Haven: Yale University Press.

———. 1998
Seeing Like a State: How Certain Schemes to Improve the Human Condition Have Failed. New Haven, CT: Yale University Press.

Scrimshaw, Susan. 1984
Infanticide in Human Populations: Societal and Individual Concerns. In Infanticide: Comparative and Evolutionary Perspectives. Glenn Hausfater and Sarah Blaffer Hrdy, eds. Pp. 463–486. New York: Aldine Publishing Company.

Scudder, Thayer. 1973
The Human Ecology of Big Dam Projects: River Basin Development and Resettlement. Annual Review of Anthropology 2:45–55.

Sen, Amartya. 1981
Poverty and Famines: An Essay on Entitlement and Deprivation. New York; Oxford University Press.

Senghas, Richard J. and Leila Monaghan. 2002
Signs of Their Times: Deaf Communities and the Culture of Language. Annual Review of Anthropology 31:69–97.

Sentumbwe, Nayinda. 1995
Sighted Lovers and Blind Husbands: Experience of Blind Women in Uganda. In Disability and Culture. Benedicte Ingstad and Susan Reynolds, eds. Pp. 159–173. Berkeley: University of California Press.

Shahrani, Nazif M. 2002
War, Factionalism, and the State in Afghanistan. American Anthropologist 104:715–722.

Sharff, Jagna Wojcicka. 1995
"We Are All Chickens for the Colonel": A Cultural Materialist View of Prisons. In Science, Materialism, and the Study of Culture. Martin F. Murphy and Maxine L. Margolis, eds. Pp. 132–158. Gainesville: University Press of Florida.

Sharp, Lesley. 1990
Possessed and Dispossessed Youth: Spirit Possession of School Children in Northwest Madagascar. Culture, Medicine and Psychiatry 14:339–364.

Shenhav-Keller, Shelly. 1993
The Israeli Souvenir: Its Text and Context. Annals of Tourism Research 20:182–196.

Sheriff, Robin E. 2000
Exposing Silence as Cultural Censorship: A Brazilian Case. American Anthropologist 102:114–132.

Shibamoto, Janet. 1987
The Womanly Woman: Manipulation of Stereotypical and Nonstereotypical Features of Japanese Female Speech. In Language, Gender, and Sex in Comparative Perspective. Susan U. Philips, Susan Steel, and Christine Tanz, eds. Pp. 26–49. New York: Cambridge University Press.

Shifflett, Peggy A. and William A. McIntosh. 1986–87
Food Habits and Future Time: An Exploratory Study of Age-Appropriate Food Habits among the Elderly. International Journal of Aging and Human Development 24 (1):2–15.

Shipton, Parker. 2001
Money. In The Dictionary of Anthropology. Thomas Barfield, ed. Pp. 327–329.

Shore, Bradd. 1998
Status Reversal: The Coming of Age in Samoa. In Welcome to Middle Age! (And Other Cultural Fictions). Richard A. Shweder, ed. Pp. 101–138. Chicago: The University of Chicago Press.

Short, James F. 1966
Gangs. In The Social Science Encyclopedia. Adam Kuper and Jessica Kuper, eds. Pp. 325–326. New York: Routledge.

Shostak, Marjorie. 1981
Nisa: The Life and Times of a !Kung Woman. Cambridge, MA: Harvard University Press.

Shweder, Richard A. 1998
Preface. In Welcome to Middle Age! (And Other Cultural Fictions). Pp. vii–viii. Chicago: The University of Chicago Press.

———. 2003
Why Do Men Barbecue? Recipes for Cultural Psychology. Cambridge: Harvard University Press.

Shweder, Richard A., Martha Minow, and Hazel Rose Markus. 2000
Introduction. Daedalus 129:v–ix.

Sidnell, Jack. 2000
Primus inter pares: Storytelling and Male Peer Groups in an Indo-Guyanese Rumshop. American Ethnologist 27:72–99.

Silver, Ira. 1993
Marketing Authenticity in Third World Countries. Annals of Tourism Research 20:302–318.

Simons, Ronald C. and Charles C. Hughes, eds. 1985
The Culture-Bound Syndromes: Folk Illnesses of Psychiatric and Anthropological Interest. Boston: D. Reidel.

Singh, K. S. 1994
The Scheduled Tribes. Anthropological Survey of India, People of India, National Series Volume III. Delhi: Oxford University Press.

Siskind, Janet. 1992
The Invention of Thanksgiving: A Ritual of American Nationality. Critique of Anthropology 12(2):167–191.

Skinner, G. William. 1964
Marketing and Social Structure in Rural China (Part 1). Journal of Asian Studies 24(1):3–43.

———. 1993
Conjugal Power in Tokugawa Japanese Families: A Matter of Life and Death. In Sex and Gender Hierarchies. Barbara D. Miller, ed. Pp. 236–270. New York: Cambridge University Press.

Skocpol, Theda. 1979
States and Social Revolutions: A Comparative Analysis of France, Russia, and China. New York: Cambridge University Press.

Slocum, Sally. 1975
Woman the Gatherer: Male Bias in Anthropology. In Toward an Anthropology of Women. Rayna R. Reiter, ed. Pp. 36–50. New York: Monthly Review Press.

Smith, Jonathan Z., ed. 1995
The HarperCollins Dictionary of Religion. New York: HarperCollins.

Sobel, Elizabeth and Gordon Bettles. 2000
Winter Hunger, Winter Myths: Subsistence Risk and Mythology among the Klamath and Modoc. Journal of Anthropological Archaeology 19:276–316.

Soh, Chunghee Sarah. 1993
Women in Korean Politics. 2nd edition. Boulder: Westview Press.

Sonenshein, Raphael J. 1996
The Battle over Liquor Stores in South Central Los Angeles: The Management of an Interminority Conflict. Urban Affairs Review 31(6):710–737.

Sperber, Dan. 1985
On Anthropological Knowledge: Three Essays. New York: Cambridge University Press.

Spiro, Melford. 1967
 Burmese Supernaturalism: A Study in the Explanation and Reduction of Suffering. Englewood Cliffs, NJ: Prentice-Hall.
———. 1990
 On the Strange and the Familiar in Recent Anthropological Thought. In Cultural Psychology: Essays on Comparative Human Development. James W. Stigler, Richard A. Shweder, and Gilbert Herdt, eds. Pp. 47–61. Chicago: University of Chicago Press.

Spitulnik, Deborah. 1993
 Anthropology and Mass Media. Annual Review of Anthropology 22:293–315.

Srinivas, M. N. 1959
 The Dominant Caste in Rampura. American Anthropologist 1:1–16.

Staats, Valerie. 1994
 Ritual, Strategy or Convention: Social Meaning in Traditional Women's Baths in Morocco. Frontiers: A Journal of Women's Studies 14(3):1–18.

Stack, Carol. 1974
 All Our Kin: Strategies for Survival in a Black Community. New York: Harper & Row Publishers.

Stambach, Amy. 2000
 Lessons from Mount Kilimajaro: Schooling, Community, and Gender in East Africa. New York: Routledge.

Stannard, David E. 1992
 American Holocaust. New York: Oxford University Press.

Stein, Gertrude. 1948
 Picasso. Boston: Beacon Press.

Stephen, Lynn. 1995
 Women's Rights Are Human Rights: The Merging of Feminine and Feminist Interests among El Salvador's Mothers of the Disappeared (CO-MADRES). American Ethnologist 22(4):807–827.

Stillman, Amy Ku'uleialoha. 1996
 Hawaiian Hula Competitions: Event, Repertoire, Performance and Tradition. Journal of American Folklore 109(434):357–380.

Stivens, Maila, Cecelia Ng, and Jomo K. S., with Jahara Bee. 1994
 Malay Peasant Women and the Land. Atlantic Highlands, NJ: Zed Books.

Stocking, George W. Jr., ed. 1985
 Objects and Others: Essays on Museums and Material Culture. History of Anthropology Series, 3. Madison: University of Wisconsin Press.

Stoler, Ann Laura. 1985
 Capitalism and Confrontation in Sumatra's Plantation Belt, 1870–1979. New Haven: Yale University Press.
———. 1989
 Rethinking Colonial Categories: European Communities and the Boundaries of Rule. Comparative Studies in Society and History 31(1):134–161.

Storper-Perez, Danielle and Harvey E. Goldberg. 1994
 The Kotel: Toward an Ethnographic Portrait. Religion 24:309–332.

Strathern, Andrew. 1971
 The Rope of Moka: Big-Men and Ceremonial Exchange in Mount Hagen, New Guinea. London: Cambridge University Press.

Stringer, Martin D. 1999
 Rethinking Animism: Thoughts from the Infancy of Our Discipline. Journal of the Royal Anthropological Institute 5:541–556.

Sullivan, Kathleen. 1992
 Protagonists of Change: Indigenous Street Vendors in San Cristobal, Mexico, Are Adapting Tradition and Customs to Fit New Life Styles. Cultural Survival Quarterly 16:38–40.

Sundar Rao, P. S. S. 1983
 Religion and Intensity of In-breeding in Tamil Nadu, South India. Social Biology 30(4):413–422.

Suttles, Wayne. 1991
 The Traditional Kwakiutl Potlatch. In Chiefly Feasts: The Enduring Kwakiutl Potlatch. Aldona Jonaitis, ed. Pp. 71–134. Washington, DC: American Museum of Natural History.

Tannenbaum, Nicola B. 1987
 Tattoos: Invulnerability and Power in Shan Cosmology. American Ethnologist 14:693–711.

Tannen, Deborah. 1990
 You Just Don't Understand: Women and Men in Conversation. New York: Morrow.

Tarlo, Emma. 2003
 Unsettling Memories: Narratives of the Emergency in Delhi. Berkeley: University of California Press.

Taussig, Michael. 1978
 Nutrition, Development, and Foreign Aid: A Case Study of U.S.-Directed Health Care in a Colombian Plantation Zone. International Journal of Health Services 8(1): 101–121.

Thompson, Julia J. 1998
 Cuts and Culture in Kathmandu. In Hair: Its Meaning and Power in Asian Cultures. In Alf Hiltebeitel and Barbara D. Miller, eds. Pp. 219–258. Albany: State University of New York Press.

Thompson, Robert Farris. 1971
 Aesthetics in Traditional Africa. In Art and Aesthetics in Primitive Societies. Carol F. Jopling, ed. Pp. 374–381. New York: E. P. Dutton.

Tice, Karin E. 1995
 Kuna Crafts, Gender, and the Global Economy. Austin: University of Texas Press.

Tierney, Patrick. 2000
 Darkness in El Dorado: How Scientists and Journalists Devastated the Amazon. New York: W. W. Norton & Company.

Tiffany, Walter W. 1979
 New Directions in Political Anthropology: The Use of Corporate Models for the Analysis of Political Organi-

zations. In Political Anthropology: The State of the Art. S. Lee Seaton and Henri J. M. Claessen, eds. Pp. 63–75. New York: Mouton.

Tinker, Irene. 1976
The Adverse Impact of Development on Women. In Women and World Development. Irene Tinker and Michele Bo Bramsen, eds. Pp. 22–34. Washington, DC: Overseas Development Council.

Tooker, Elisabeth. 1992
Lewis H. Morgan and His Contemporaries. American Anthropologist 94(2):357–375.

Toren, Christina. 1988
Making the Present, Revealing the Past: The Mutability and Continuity of Tradition as Process. Man (n.s.) 23:696–717.

Traphagan, John W. 2000
The Liminal Family: Return Migration and Intergenerational Conflict in Japan. Journal of Anthropological Research 56:365–385.

Trawick, Margaret. 1988
Death and Nurturance in Indian Systems of Healing. In Paths to Asian Medical Knowledge. Charles Leslie and Allan Young, eds. Pp. 129–159. Berkeley: University of California Press.

Trelease, Murray L. 1975
Dying among Alaskan Indians: A Matter of Choice. In Death: The Final Stage of Growth. Elisabeth Kübler-Ross, ed. Pp. 33–37. Englewood Cliffs, NJ: Prentice-Hall.

Trigger, Bruce G. 1996
State, Origins of. In The Social Science Encyclopedia. Adam Kuper and Jessica Kuper, eds. Pp. 837–838. New York: Routledge.

Trotter, Robert T. II. 1987
A Case of Lead Poisoning from Folk Remedies in Mexican American Communities. In Anthropological Praxis: Translating Knowledge into Action. Robert M. Wulff and Shirley J. Fiske, eds. Pp. 146–159. Boulder: Westview Press.

Trouillot, Michel-Rolph. 1994
Culture, Color, and Politics in Haiti. In Race. Steven Gregory and Roger Sanjek, eds. Pp. 146–174. New Brunswick: Rutgers University Press.

Turner, Victor W. 1969
The Ritual Process: Structure and Anti-Structure. Chicago: Aldine Publishing Company.

Tylor, Edward Burnett. 1871
Primitive Culture: Researches into the Development of Mythology, Philosophy, Religion, Art, and Custom. 2 volumes. London: J. Murray.

Uhl, Sarah. 1991
Forbidden Friends: Cultural Veils of Female Friendship in Andalusia. American Ethnologist 18(1):90–105.

United Nations Development Programme. 1994
Human Development Report 1994. New York: Oxford University Press.

Uphoff, Norman T. and Milton J. Esman. 1984
Local Organizations: Intermediaries in Rural Development. Ithaca: Cornell University Press.

Ury, William L. 1990
Dispute Resolution Notes from the Kalahari. Negotiation Journal 63:229–238.

Valdés, Guadalupe and Richard A. Figueroa. 1994
Bilingualism and Testing: A Special Case of Bias. Norwood, NJ: Ablex Publishing Company.

van der Geest, Sjaak, Susan Reynolds Whyte, and Anita Hardon. 1996
The Anthropology of Pharmaceuticals: A Biographical Approach. Annual Review of Anthropology 25:153–178.

Van Gennep, Arnold. 1960 [1908]
The Rites of Passage. Chicago: University of Chicago Press.

Van Maanen, John. 1988
Tales of the Field: On Writing Ethnography. Chicago: University of Chicago Press.

van Willigen, John. 1993
Applied Anthropology: An Introduction. Revised ed. Westport, CT: Bergin & Garvey.

VanWynsberghe, Robert M. 2002
AlterNatives: Community, Identity, and Environmental Justice on Walpole Island. Boston: Allyn and Bacon.

Velimirovic, Boris. 1990
Is Integration of Traditional and Western Medicine Really Possible? In Anthropology and Primary Health Care. Jeannine Coreil and J. Dennis Mull, eds. Pp. 51–778. Boulder: Westview Press.

Verdery, Katherine. 1996
What Was Socialism and What Comes Next? Princeton: Princeton University Press.

Vesperi, Maria D. 1985
City of Green Benches: Growing Old in a New Downtown. Ithaca: Cornell University Press.

Vickers, Jeanne. 1993
Women and War. Atlantic Highlands, NJ: Zed Books.

Vincent, Joan. 1996
Political Anthropology. In The Social Science Encyclopedia. Adam Kuper and Jessica Kuper, eds. P. 624. New York: Routledge.

Wallerstein, Immanuel. 1979
The Capitalist World-Economy. New York: Cambridge University Press.

Ward, Martha C. 1989
Once Upon a Time. In [eds] Nest in the Wind: Adventures in Anthropology on a Tropical Island. Martha C. Ward, ed. Pp. 1–22. Prospect Heights, IL: Waveland Press.

Warren, Carol A. B. 1988
Gender Issues in Field Research. Qualitative Research Methods, Volume 9. Newbury Park, CA: Sage Publications.

Warren, D. Michael. 2001
The Role of the Global Network of Indigenous Knowledge Resource Centers in the Conservation of Cultural and Biological Diversity. In Biocultural Diversity: Link-

ing Language, Knowledge and the Environment. Pp. 446–461. Washington, DC: Smithsonian Institution Press.

Warren, Kay B. 1998
Indigenous Movements and Their Critics: Pan-Maya Activism in Guatemala. Princeton, NJ: Princeton University Press.

Watkins, Ben and Michael L. Fleisher. 2002
Tracking Pastoralist Migration: Lessons from the Ethiopian Somali National Regional State. Human Organization 61:328–338.

Watson, Rubie S. 1986
The Named and the Nameless: Gender and Person in Chinese Society. American Ethnologist 13(4):619–631.
———. 1997
Museums and Indigenous Cultures: The Power of Local Knowledge. Cultural Survival Quarterly 21(1):24–25.

Watson, Rubie S. and James L. Watson. 1997
From Hall of Worship to Tourist Center: An Ancestral Hall in Hong Kong's New Territories. Cultural Survival Quarterly 21(1):33–35.

Weatherford, J. 1981
Tribes on the Hill. New York: Random House.

Weber, Linda R., Andrew Miracle, and Tom Skehan. 1994
Interviewing Early Adolescents: Some Methodological Considerations. Human Organization 53(1):42–47.

Websdale, Neil. 1995
An Ethnographic Assessment of the Policing of Domestic Violence in Rural Eastern Kentucky. Social Justice 22(1):102–122.

Webster, Gloria Cranmer. 1991
The Contemporary Potlatch. In Chiefly Feasts: The Enduring Kwakiutl Potlatch. Aldona Jonaitis, ed. Pp. 227–250. Washington, DC: American Museum of Natural History.

Weine, Stevan M. et al. 1995
Psychiatric Consequences of "Ethnic Cleansing": Clinical Assessments and Trauma Testimonies of Newly Resettled Bosnian Refugees. American Journal of Psychiatry 152(4):536–542.

Weiner, Annette B. 1976
Women of Value, Men of Renown: New Perspectives in Trobriand Exchange. Austin: University of Texas Press.

Weismantel, M. J. 1989
The Children Cry for Bread: Hegemony and the Transformation of Consumption. In The Social Economy of Consumption. Monographs in Economic Anthropology No. 6. Henry J. Rutz and Benjamin S. Orlove, eds. Pp. 85–99. New York: University Press of America.

Werbner, Pnina. 1988
"Sealing the Koran": Offering and Sacrifice among Pakistani Labour Migrants. Cultural Dynamics 1:77–97.

White, Douglas R. and Michael L. Burton. 1988
Causes of Polygony: Ecology, Economy, Kinship, and Warfare. American Anthropologist 90(4):871–887.

Whitehead, Tony Larry. 1986
Breakdown, Resolution, and Coherence: The Fieldwork Experience of a Big, Brown, Pretty-talking Man in a West Indian Community. In Self, Sex, and Gender in Cross-Cultural Fieldwork. Tony Larry Whitehead and Mary Ellen Conway, eds. Pp. 213–239. Chicago: University of Illinois Press.

Whiting, Beatrice B. and John W. M. Whiting. 1975
Children of Six Cultures: A Psycho-Cultural Analysis. Cambridge: Harvard University Press.

Whiting, Robert, 1979
You've Gotta Have "Wa." Sports Illustrated, September 24:60–71.

Whyte, Martin King. 1993
Wedding Behavior and Family Strategies in Chengdu. In Chinese Families in the Post-Mao Era. Deborah Davis and Stevan Harrell, eds. Pp. 89–218. Berkeley: University of California Press.

Wikan, Unni. 1977
Man Becomes Woman: Transsexualism in Oman as a Key to Gender Roles. Man 12(2):304–319.
———. 1982
Behind the Veil in Arabia: Women in Oman. Chicago: University of Chicago Press.
———. 2000
Citizenship on Trial: Nadia's Case. Daedalus 129:55–76.

Wilde, James. 1988
Starvation in a Fruitful Land. Time (December 5):43–44.

Williams, Alex. 1995
The Rituals that Still Matter to Them. The New York Times Magazine, November 19:110–113. Photographs by Larry Fink.

Williams, Brett. 1984
Why Migrant Women Feed Their Husbands Tamales: Foodways as a Basis for a Revisionist View of Tejano Family Life. In Ethnic and Regional Foodways in the United States: The Performance of Group Identity. Linda Keller Brown and Kay Mussell, eds. Pp. 113–126. Knoxville: The University of Tennessee Press.
———. 1991
Good Guys and Bad Toys: The Paradoxical World of Children's Cartoons. In The Politics of Culture. Brett Williams, ed. Pp. 109–132. Washington, DC: Smithsonian Institution Press.
———. 1994
Babies and Banks: The "Reproductive Underclass" and the Raced, Gendered Masking of Debt. In Race. Steven Gregory and Roger Sanjek, eds. Pp. 348–365. Ithaca: Cornell University Press.

Williams, Raymond. 1983 Keywords:
A Vocabulary of Culture and Society. New York: Oxford University Press.

Williams, Walter. 1992
The Spirit and the Flesh: Sexual Diversity in American Indian Cultures. 2nd edition. Boston: Beacon Press.

Williamson, Nancy. 1976
Sons or Daughters: A Cross-Cultural Study of Parental Preferences. Beverly Hills, CA: Sage Publications.

Wilson, Richard. 1995
Maya Resurgence in Guatemala: Q'eqchi' Experiences. Norman, OK: University of Oklahoma Press.

Wilson, Thomas M. 2000
The Obstacles to European Union Regional Policy in the Northern Ireland Borderlands. Human Organization 59:1–10.

Winans, Edgar V. and Angelique Haugerud. 1977
Rural Self-Help in Kenya: The Harambee Movement. Human Organization 36:334–351.

Winthrop, Rob. 2000
The Real World: Cultural Rights/Animal Rights. Practicing Anthropology 22:44–45.

Winzeler, Robert L. 1974
Sex Role Equality, Wet Rice Cultivation, and the State in Southeast Asia. American Anthropologist 76(3):563–565.

Wolf, Charlotte. 1966
Status. In The Social Science Encyclopedia. Adam Kuper and Jessica Kuper, eds. Pp. 842–843. New York: Routledge.

Wolf, Eric R. 1966
Peasants. Englewood Cliffs, NJ: Prentice-Hall.
———. 1969
Peasant Wars of the Twentieth Century. New York: Harper & Row.

Wolf, Margery. 1968
The House of Lim: A Study of a Chinese Farm Family. New York: Appleton-Century-Crofts.

Women's Health Weekly. 2003
Muslims Embrace IVF, but Sunnis Are More Restricted Than Shiites. July 24.

Woolfson, Peter, Virginia Hood, Roger Secker-Walker, and Ann C. Macaulay. 1995
Mohawk English in the Medical Interview. Medical Anthropology Quarterly 9(4):503–509.

Worldwatch Institute. 2003
Vital Signs 2003: The Trends That Are Shaping Our Future. Washington, DC: Worldwatch Institute/W.W. Norton.

Wright, Sue. 1998
The Politicization of "Culture." Anthropology Today 14:1, 7–15.

Wu, David Y. H. 1990
Chinese Minority Policy and the Meaning of Minority Culture: The Example of Bai in Yunnan, China. Human Organization 49(1):1–13.

Xenos, Peter. 1993
Extended Adolescence and the Sexuality of Asian Youth: Observations on Research and Policy. East-West Center Reprints, Population Series No. 292. Honolulu: East-West Center.

Yoon, In-Jin. 1993
The Social Origins of Korean Immigration to the United States from 1965 to the Present. Papers of the Program on Population, Number 121. Honolulu: East-West Center.

Young, Michael W. 1983
"Our Name is Women; We are Bought with Limesticks and Limepots": An Analysis of the Autobiographical Narrative of a Kalauna Woman. Man 18:478–501.

Young, Roger and Caroline Van Beers. 1991
Death of the Family Farm. Alternatives 17(4):22–23.

Zabusky, Stacia E. 1995
Launching Europe: An Ethnography of European Cooperation in Space Science. Princeton: Princeton University Press.

Zaidi, S. Akbar. 1988
Poverty and Disease: Need for Structural Change. Social Science and Medicine 27:119–127.

Zarrilli, Phillip B. 1990
Kathakali. In Indian Theatre: Traditions of Performance. Farley P. Richmond, Darius L. Swann, and Phillip B. Zarrilli, eds. Pp. 315–357. Honolulu: University of Hawaii Press.

Zureik, Elia. 1994
Palestinian Refugees and Peace. Journal of Palestine Studies 24(1):5–17.

Crime. *See also* Punishment
discriminatory treatment of, 257
policing and, 255–256
Crime and Custom in Savage Society
(Malinowski), 252
Critical cultural relativism, 19, 269
Critical development anthropology
(CDA), 379
Critical legal anthropology, 252, 257
Critical media anthropology, 287
Critical medical anthropology,
164–165, 169
Critical military anthropology, 267
CRM (cultural resource management),
6
Crop rotation, 59
Cross cousins, 187
Cross-cultural analysis, 8, 17, 36
ethnology, 17-18, 133
Cuba
development assistance from, 376
immigrants to U.S. from, 67–68, 353
revolution in, 262–263
Cuing, linguistic, 283
Cultivation
in agriculture, 61
in horticulture, 57, 59
Cultural anthropology, 2, 5–6. *See also*
Anthropology; Applied
anthropology
change and, 368
collaborations with other disciplines,
39
development and, 368, 377–380, 389
distinctive features of, 17–19
history of, 7–9, 28–29
human rights and, 389
linguistics and, 4–5. *See also*
Linguistic anthropology
methods in. *See* Fieldwork
scope of, 5–6
theoretical perspectives in, 9, 19–22.
See also specific perspectives
typologies in, 53
Cultural assessment, 372, 374
Cultural broker, 134, 224
Cultural change. *See also* Applied
anthropology; Colonialism;
Development; Globalization
anthropology and, 368
evolutionary model of, 7, 8, 216
integration of a culture and, 12
interaction of cultures and, 12–13
restudies and, 30
suicide and, 121
theories of, 370–374
two processes of, 369
Cultural configuration, 131
Cultural constructionism, 20, 21
adolescence and, 140

in critical medical anthropology, 164
gender vs. sex, 15, 136
romantic love and, 188–189
sexual orientation and, 142
Cultural diversity, 19, 63. *See also*
Pluralism
Cultural heritage, 338–339, 340
Cultural imperialism, 19, 369
Cultural Logics and Global Economics:
Maya Identity in Thought and
Practice (Fischer), 17
Cultural materialism, 9, 10, 22
adolescence and, 140–141
blood sacrifice and, 308
deductive research and, 36
food taboos and, 88–89
gender roles in music and, 330
household forms and, 193
kinship systems and, 182
myths and, 301
religion and, 298
reproduction and, 106
street gangs and, 211
warfare among Yanomami and, 264
Cultural relativism, 8, 18–19
absolute, 18
critical, 19, 269
female genital cutting and, 142, 143,
259
world peace and, 269
Cultural resource management (CRM),
6
Cultural Survival, 19
Culture(s), 9–17
definitions of, 9–10
index cultures, 13
integrated internally, 12
interactions of, 12–13
learned, 12, 21
macrocultures, 10
microcultures. *See* Microcultures
nationhood and, 243
nature and, 8, 10
in nonhuman animals, 9
personality and, 130–132
sociobiology and, 4, 140, 264
symbols and, 9, 11–12. *See also*
Symbols
UNESCO concept of, 247
universal concept of, 10
Culture and Personality School,
130–132
Culture-bound syndromes, 154–156,
170
Culture of poverty, 132
Culture shock, 35
Cunningham, Lawrence S., 314
Curtin, Philip D., 352
Customary law, 258
Cybernetworking, 226

Dalai Lama, 318
Dalby, Liza Crihfield, 34
Dalit, 220, 221, 222
Daly, Martin, 118
Dams
in Bangladesh, displacement by, 383
in Brazil, Kayapó resistance to, 235
in India, 350, 383
as indirect genocide, 124
in Philippines, militarization and,
388
population displacement by, 349,
350, 383
schistosomiasis and, 166
Senegal Valley, 39, 379
work group for rebuilding of, 212
Dance, 328, 330, 331, 339
Dando, William A., 85
Danforth, Loring M., 298
Danger, in fieldwork, 45–46
Dannhaeuser, Norbert, 93
Darwin, Charles, 7, 9
Dasgupta, Satadal, 199
Data
analysis, 36, 41–43, 275
for development project planning,
379–380
gathering techniques, 35–39
recording, 36, 39–41, 275
Daugherty, Mary Lee, 315
Davis, Douglas A., 110
Davis, Susan Schaefer, 110
Davis-Floyd, Robbie E., 135, 164
Davison, Jean, 138
Dead Sea, therapeutic use of, 160
Deaf culture, 274, 275
Death. *See also* Mortality; Widowhood
culture-bound syndromes leading to,
155, 156
definitions of, 153
experience of, 147
by human sacrifice, 256, 307, 308
humoral healing systems and, 159
potlatch on occasion of, 101
religion and, 299, 303
structural suffering and, 154
de Athayde Figueiredo, Mariza, 192
Death penalty
opposition to, in Jewish law, 313
in small-scale societies, 254, 256, 258
in state-level societies, 256
Decorative arts, 325, 331, 332–334
Deductive research, 36
Deities. *See* Supernatural forces or
beings; World religions
Deitrick, Lynn, 134
de la Cadena, Marisol, 216
Delaney, Carol, 141
Deller, Steven, 95
Demand and supply, 82, 93

Indonesia. *See also* Bali; Java; Sumatra
  child fostering in, 183–184
  Dutch colonialism in, 38, 232
  East Timor conflict, 123, 243
  Islam in, 316
  Minangkabau people of, 181, 199
  Nias people, wedding exchanges, 89
  orangutans in, 4–5
  punishment on island of Sumba, 254
  vaccination programs in, 170
  verbal arts of, 327
  Weyéwa people, flavor categories of, 10–11
Inductive research, 36
Industrial capital agriculture, 62, 64–65, 67
Industrial capitalism, 67, 75. *See also* Capitalism; Industrialism
  "the child" as category in, 137
Industrial collectivized agriculture, 62, 65–67
Industrialism, 53, 67–69
  adolescence and, 140–141
  agriculture and, 62, 64–67
  changing economies and, 70, 71, 73
  consumption and, 82, 84, 85, 86
  defined, 67
  ethnographic studies of, 17
  exchange and, 89, 93
  household structures and, 191, 192, 199–200
  illness and, 156, 164
  kinship systems and, 182, 183
  middle age and, 145–146
  modernization and, 371
  reproduction and, 107, 108–109, 110, 111
  social groups and, 206, 207
  suicide and, 121
  war-related mortality and, 123
Industrial Revolution, 216
Inequality. *See also* Redistribution; Social stratification
  in agricultural societies, 68, 73
  caste and, 222
  in consumption, 82, 84–88
  in countries of former Soviet Union, 99–100
  demographic patterns and, 109
  development and, 371, 372, 374, 385
  vs. difference, 13
  exchange patterns and, 93, 94, 95–98
  globalization and, 53, 69, 73
  in health status, 164
  in horticultural societies, 59
  institutions and, 16
  law and, 255, 257
  race and, 14, 96, 216
  structurism and, 9
Infanticide, 118–120, 127

among Yanomami, 264
  in foraging groups, 107, 119
  indirect, 118, 119, 120
  sex-selective, 4, 112–113, 116, 118, 119, 120, 264
Infant mortality rate, 119
  bonding with mother and, 135
Infants
  bonding with mother, 135
  conversation with mother, 285
  gender and, 136
  low-birthweight, in Eastern Europe, 100
  sleeping patterns, 17, 135–136
Infertility
  adoption and, 183, 184
  female genital cutting and, 143
  Nayar fertility ritual and, 310
  new technologies and, 117
Infibulation, 142, 143
Influence, 233
Informal groups, 206, 207, 216
Informal sector, 67, 68–69
Information age, 67, 76
Informed consent, 45
Infrastructure, 22, 106
Inheritance patterns, 179, 181, 184, 194
Inhorn, Marcia C., 117
Initiation rituals, 141–142, 305, 316
In-kind taxation, 239
In Search of Respect: Selling Crack in El Barrio (Bourgois), 17
Institutional migrants, 351–352
Institutions
  of civil society, 222
  development and, 374–377
  dominance maintained by, 216
  microcultures of, 13, 16–17
Integration
  within a culture, 12
  of cultures into wider spheres, 29
Intensive strategy, 61. *See also* Agriculture
Intergenerational household, 200
Interior design, 332–333
Internally displaced persons (IDPs), 349–350
Internal migration, 347
International affairs. *See also* Globalization
  anthropology of, 247
International Court of Justice, 269
International development. *See* Development
International migration, 199, 348. *See also* Migration
International Phonetic Alphabet, 274
Internet
  consumer education proposal for, 84

economic change and, 76
  gambling on, 94
  religion and, 309
  self-help groups on, 215
  shopping on, as social interaction, 94
  social movements' use of, 226
  world order and, 268
Interpersonal conflict, 259–260
Interpretivism, 9, 21–22
  inductive research and, 36
  in medical anthropology, 163
Interviews, 37, 39, 40
  medical, and Mohawk English, 283
  in rapid research, 379–380
Inuit people of North America. *See also* Circumpolar peoples
  abandonment of aged and infirm, 152
  attitudes toward death, 147
  Boas's study of, 8
  development organization, 384
  focal vocabulary, 282
  kinship system, 177
Invention, 369
Inversion, rituals of, 306–307
In vitro fertilization (IVF), 109, 117, 184
Iran
  Qashqa'i people of, 60, 236
  revolution in, 262
Iraq, U.S. military action in, 241, 352
Ireland, Tory Islanders of, 176
Iroquois people of North America
  gender roles, 58, 181, 238
  kinship system, 178, 183
  Morgan's early fieldwork, 7, 29
  political organization, 238, 239, 243
Irrigation systems
  economic development and, 371, 377
  emergence of chiefdoms and, 238
  groups for maintenance of, 212–213
  schistosomiasis and, 166
Isherwood, Baron, 97
Islam, 308, 309, 315–316
  abortion and, 116
  in Afghanistan, 266
  in Africa, 315, 316
  blessing of new baby by, 134
  Bosnian refugees, 263
  conflict with Hindus over sites, 318
  divorce under, 197
  doctrine of, 301–302
  of East Java, 184
  ethnic cleansing in Yugoslavia and, 15
  female genital cutting among, 142
  female segregation among, 242
  food taboos of, 88
  gardens of, 333

Myths, 300–301
  African, 316
  defined, 300
  exchange of, 89
  Frazer on, 28
  Freudian analysis of, 300
  Lévi-Strauss on, 9
  performance and, 331
  pilgrimages and, 305–306
  as research data, 36, 38, 41
  rituals and, 303

Nacirema, 6
Nader, Laura, 33, 247, 255, 269
Nag, Moni, 64, 111
Nagas people of India and Burma, 124
NAGPRA (Native American Graves
    Protection and Repatriation Act),
    334–335
Naiyomeh, Kimeli, 2
Naming
  in patrilineal systems, 182, 184
  timing of, 305
Nanda, Serena, 144, 324
Narrative, 330
  of myth, 300–301
National character studies, 132
National culture, 10
Nationalism
  indigenous peoples and, 381
  in Romania, 42
Nations, 243–245
  defined, 243
Nation-state, 243
  development and, 371
Native Americans of Central America.
    *See also specific countries and
    peoples*
  craft cooperatives in Panama, 214
  Kuna Indian birth ritual, 163
  genocide directed at, 123–124
Native Americans of North America.
    *See also specific countries and
    peoples*
  art of, 327
  berdache tradition of, 143–144
  Boas's collection of texts from, 38,
    274
  casinos of, 94–95
  confederacies of, 239
  gender and leadership among,
    238–239, 246
  genocide directed at, 123
  geophagia of, 161
  Ghost Dance movement of, 317
  Hare Indians of Canada, 56
  humor as resistance tactic, 268
  kinship systems, 7, 181, 199
  land claims, Canadian law on, 383
  language loss, 4, 274

Mohawk English language, 283
  myths of, 301
  personalities of, Benedict's theories,
    131
  potlatch of, 80, 96, 101, 131, 334
  puberty rites of Apache girls, 305
  repatriation of museum holdings,
    334–335
  revival of cultures, 14, 15
  sacred sites of, contested, 318
  silence among, 291
  urine as positive substance, 11
  whale hunting by Makah Tribe, 388
Native Americans of South America.
    See also Amazonian peoples;
    specific countries and peoples
  armed conflict in Peru and, 382
  encroachment on land of, 383
  Eskimo kinship terminology, 178
  gender roles in agriculture, 63–64
  geophagia of, 161
  Inuit peoples, 8, 147, 177, 152, 282,
    384
  revival of cultures, 15
Native and Newcomer (Robertson), 32
NATO, anthropological studies of, 247,
    267
Natural resources. *See* Resources
Nature. *See also* Biological determinism
  and culture, 8, 10
Navajo people of American Southwest
  adolescence in, 140
  art of, 327
  diagnosis of illness by, 157
  gender roles, 60, 61
  kinship system, 178, 199
Nayar people of southern India
  fertility ritual of, 310
  as matrilineal society, 181, 183
Ndembu people of Africa, life-cycle
    rituals, 304–305
Neale, Walter C., 91
Neff, Deborah L., 310
Neier, Aryeh, 281
Nelson, Sarah, 3
Neocolonialism, 232
Neolocality, 181, 183
Nepal
  caste system in, 220
  children's agricultural labor, 64
  cultural interactions in, 13
  healing systems in, 154, 167–168
  polyandry in, 190
  selfhood in, 132–133
Netting, Robert McC., 62
Neusner, Jacob, 311
New Guinea. *See also* Papua New
    Guinea
  Hua people of, gender segregation,
    16

kinship systems, 183
  Mead's studies in, 131, 136
  Sambia people of, male initiation,
    141
New immigrants, 352–359
Newman, Lucile, 113
New reproductive technologies (NRTs),
    109, 116–117
New social movements, 226
New Zealand
  cargo cults of, 317
  immigration to, 348
Ngokwey, Ndolamb, 157
NGOs (nongovernmental
    organizations), 224–226, 269, 362,
    377, 384, 388
Nias people of Indonesia, wedding
    exchanges, 89
Nicaragua, European extermination of
    natives, 124
Nichter, Mark, 166, 170, 286
Nichter, Mimi, 170
Niger
  cassava crop in, 58
  satellite communication in, 292
  Tuareg men's greetings in, 290
Nigeria
  esthetics of Yoruba people, 325–326
  ethnicity in, 217
  exchange system of Tiv people, 97
  oil development and Ogoni people,
    383, 384, 387, 388–389
  woman ruler in, 238
Nirvana, 310
Nisa (Shostak), 37, 38
Nodwell, Evelyn, 219
Nongovernmental organizations
    (NGOs), 224–226, 269, 362, 377,
    384, 388
Nonmarket economies
  consumption in, 81
  exchange in, 81–82, 89
Nonverbal communication, 278,
    290–292
  bowing in Japanese culture, 287
Nonviolent conflict, 267–268
Norgaard, Richard B., 371
Norms, 253
Norway
  female leader of, 246
  Saami people of, 303, 373
Nosology, 154
Note taking, 36, 39–40, 41
Notowidjojo, Farida, 352
NRTs (new reproductive technologies),
    109, 116–117
Nuclear family, 178, 181, 191
  colonialism and, 199
Nuclear household, 191, 193
  changes in, 199, 200

Nuer people of Sudan
   British colonists' legal interventions, 258
   as cattle herders, 60
   indigenous legal system, 255
   language of, 277
   marriage practices, 186, 187
Nutrition. *See also* Diet; Food
   cash cropping and, 98
   inappropriate aid project and, 378
   introduction of Western foods and, 99, 100
   malnutrition and poverty, 164
   obesity, 87
   population growth and, 107, 108
Nyambedha, Erick Otieno, 121, 122

Obesity, 87
Obeyesekere, Gananath, 38
Observation. *See* Participant observation
Observer's paradox, 275–276
Obstetric training, 164–165
Ochs, Elinor, 285
Oei, Tian P. S., 352
Ogawa, Naohiro, 109
Ogoni people of Nigeria, 383, 384, 387, 388–389
Ohnuki-Tierney, Emiko, 153, 159
Oinas, Felix J., 145
Ok Tedi people of Papua New Guinea, 224–225
Oman
   hospitality in, 90
   sexual identity in, 142
O'Nell, Carl W., 154, 155
Ong, Aihwa, 199, 302
Ongley, Patrick, 348
Oppression. *See* Discrimination; Ethnocide; Genocide; Racism; Slavery
Orang Asli people of Malaysia, 158
Orangutans, 4–5
Organic solidarity, 216, 221
Organ transplantation, Japanese resistance to, 153
Oromo people of Ethiopia, 384
Orphans
   in Chinese orphanages, 185
   in Kenya, due to AIDS, 121, 122–123
Ostracism, 253, 254, 256
Overconsumption, 87

Pacific islands. *See also specific countries and peoples*
   animatism in, 302
   big-man or -woman systems of, 236–237
   child care in, 146
   Vanuatu, 284, 318

Paine, Thomas, 222
Painter, Andrew A., 287, 290
Pakistan
   blood feuds in Thull, 261–262
   female segregation in, 242
   immigrants to U.S. from, 358
   Kurin's research in, 32–33
   patrilineal kinship system in, 197
Paleopathology, 3–4
Palestinian people, 243, 329
   in Israeli army, 267
   as refugees, 348, 362
Paley, Julia, 245
Panama
   childbirth and Kuna Indians of, 163
   craft cooperatives in, 214
Panter-Brick, Catherine, 69
Pantheons, 302–303
Pappas, Gregory, 73
Papua New Guinea. *See also* New Guinea; Trobriand Islands
   activism of anthropologist in, 224–225
   cargo cults of, 317
   consumption patterns in, 87, 88
   exchange patterns in, 89, 92, 93
   Irian Jaya conflict in, 383
   languages of, 280
   life histories in, 38
   magic in, 11
   patrilineal descent in, 180
   political organization in, 236–237
   tourism in, 337
   warfare in, 12
Paralanguage, 278, 290–292
Parallel cousins, 187
Paredes, J. Anthony, 257
Parenthood, 134, 145–146
Parker, Richard G., 44
Parrillo, Vincent N., 353
Parry, Jonathan P., 220
Participant observation, 28, 29–30, 35–38, 39–43
   of artistic traditions, 327
   of kinship systems, 179
Participatory research methods (PRM), 380
Particularism, 8, 17, 131
Pasquino, Gianfranco, 245
Pastoralism, 53, 57, 59–61
   brideprice and, 190
   changing economies of, 70, 71–72
   consumption patterns and, 82, 88
   development in Africa and, 383–384
   dwellings and, 331–332
   gender roles and, 140
   health and, 162
   household forms and, 191
   humanitarian aid and, 362, 362
   migration and, 348, 362

political organization and, 234, 235, 236
reproduction and, 107
social groups and, 206, 207
unilineal descent and, 179, 180
Patrescence, 145
Patriarch, 180
Patriarchal family relationships, 195
Patriarchal states, 242
Patrilateral parallel-cousin marriage, 187
Patrilineal descent, 179, 180–181, 182, 183
   divorce rates and, 197
   extended households and, 191–192
   in U.S. and Canada, 184
Patrilocality, 181, 182, 183
Patterns of Culture (Benedict), 131
Patterson, Thomas C., 7, 8
Paxson, Heather, 117
Peace and conflict studies, 245
Peacock, James L., 37
Peasant agriculture, 62
Pechman, Joseph A., 84
Pedelty, Mark, 287, 288–289
Peet, R. Creighton, 64
Peletz, Michael, 91
Pelto, Pertti, 194, 372, 373
Peng Xizhe, 108
Penso, Anat, 139
People, 14. *See also* Ethnicity
Performance arts, 325, 330–331, 335, 338, 339, 340
Perin, Constance, 259
Periodic market, 93
Periphery societies, 53, 69
Permanent markets, 93–94
Perry, Richard J., 384
Personality. *See also* Life cycle
   in adulthood, 144–147
   androgynous, socialization of daughters and, 233
   child rearing and, 131
   class and, 132
   Culture and Personality School, 130–132
   defined, 130
   ethnography of, 132–133
   of Japanese males, 132, 133
   kinship and, 176
   modes of production and, 137
   national character and, 131–132
   overview of, 149
Person-centered ethnography, 132–133
Peru, Shipibo Indians of, 326
Perz, Stephen G., 381
Pessar, Patricia R., 353
Petras, James, 69
Philippines
   Agta people as hunters, 55

children's personalities in, 137
household headship in, 192
Ifugao people, militarization and, 388
Ilongot people, headhunting by, 261
Macapagal-Arroyo, Gloria, president, 230
Moro people, conflict with state, 383
water distribution group in, 213
Phonemes, 276–277
Phonetics, 276–277, 279
Photography, 41
Physical anthropology, 2, 3–4
applied, 6
Pica, 161
Pidgin, 280
PIE (Proto-Indo-European), 280
Pig meat
gifts of, 89
taboo against, 88–89
Pilgrimage, 305–306
Pilling, Arnold R., 70
Pillsbury, Barbara, 115
Pinter, Harold, 340
Pitanguy, Jacqueline, 386
Placebo effect, 163
Plant, Roger, 383
Plath, David W., 136
Plato, 22
Plattner, Stuart, 93
Play, 335–337, 338
Pluralism. *See also* Diversity
defined, 167
indigenous peoples and, 381
legal, 259
linguistic, 282
in marriage practices, 198
medical, 167–169, 171
religious, 309
Pocahontas, 238, 239
Poirier, Sylvie, 89
Poland, youth environmental activism in, 225–226
Policing, 255–256
and wife abuse, 196
Political anthropology
current emphasis in, 242–243
scope of, 232, 249
theoretical approaches in, 232
Political economy, structurism and, 9
Political organization
change in, 243–247
defined, 234
features of, 234
modes of, 234–242
nationhood and, 243
overview of, 249
as structure, 22
theoretical approaches to, 232
Politics. *See also* Political organization

citizen involvement in, 241
as cultural universal, 233–234
defined, 232
globalization and, 232, 246–247
language use and, 5
local, 240–242, 245
terminology related to, 232–233
women's clubs and, in Latin America, 209
women's current roles in, 246
Pollution. *See* Environmental degradation
Polyandry, 190, 191
Polygamy, 190, 191
colonists' actions against, 258
Islam and, 302
Polygyny, 190, 191
divorce and, 197
Polytheism, 299, 309, 316
Poor people. *See* Poverty
Popular medicine, 152. *See also* Ethnomedicine
Population. *See also* Fertility; Migration; Mortality
in agricultural societies, 61
famine and, 85
focused life histories and, 179
as infrastructure, 22, 106
warfare and, 264–265
Porridge, in colonized cultures, 99
Portugal, widowhood in, 197
Posey, Darrell Addison, 160
Possession, 302
Post-colonial nations. *See also* Development
anthropologists in, 2–3
legal reform in, 259
Postgate, Nicholas, 278
Post-industrialism, 67
Postmodernism, 9
Post-partum depression, 145
Post-socialist activism, 225–226
Post-traumatic stress disorder (PTSD), 263
Potlatch, 80, 96, 101, 131, 334
Potsherds, 3
Potter, Jack M., 207, 212
Potter, Sulamith Heins, 16
Pottery, Native American, 327
Poverty. *See also* Class
abortion and, 116
adolescence and, 141
African American survival strategies, 96–97, 132, 208–209
agency vs. structurism and, 22
amniocentesis and, 116–117
child sex work and, 69
class and, 13
consumption and, 86, 100

in countries of former Soviet Union, 100
cultural heritage projects and, 340
development and, 371–373, 376, 377, 383, 384
education and, 138
in elderly population, 88
ethnographic studies of, 17
fertility and, 109
friendship and, 208–209
globalization and, 69
illness and, 164
of immigrants in U.S., 354–355, 357
infanticide and, 118, 119, 120
labor migration and, 360
mortality and, 109
of periphery nations, 53
personality and, 132
street gangs and, 211
structural suffering caused by, 154
Theory of Culture of Poverty, 132
Theory of Image of the Limited Good, 132
woman-headed households and, 194
Power. *See also* Dominance and domination; Leadership
anthropologists' critiques of, 19, 247, 252
armed forces and, 267
art forms and, 328–330
ascribed status and, 216
defined, 232–233
of elder males in African cultures, 97
globalization and, 13, 53, 97–98
health and, 164
in household, 193, 195
institutions and, 16
language use and, 275, 283, 284–286
law and, 255, 257
media institutions and, 287–290
political organization and, 232, 234, 239–242
silence and, 290–291
in state-level societies, 239–242
supernatural forces and, 302
of women in matrilineal cultures, 181
Prado, Dando, 192
Pratt, Mary Louise, 337
Pregnancy, 145. *See* Fertility; Reproduction
culture-bound illness in, 156
geophagia and, 161
teenage, 110
Prehistory. *See* Archaeology
Press, Nancy Ann, 109, 145
Price, David H., 213, 241
Priest, 308
Priestess, 308
Primary groups, 206
Primary labor market, 67

Primatology, 3
  applied, 4–5, 6
  communication and, 276
  dominance relationships and, 232
  fieldwork in, 28, 152
  group conflict and, 252
  sociobiology and, 4
Primitive Culture (Tylor), 299
"Primitive" cultures, 7
Prince, Raymond, 154
Prisons, 256
  friendships in, 208
  microcultures of, 16
Private property. *See also* Property
  relations
  in agricultural societies, 61, 66–67
  foraging and, 54
  in industrial societies, 75
  nineteenth-century anthropology and,
    7
  pastoralism and, 61, 71
  political organization and, 233
Privatization
  in Mongolia, 71–72
  in Russia and Eastern Europe,
    99–100
PRM (participatory research methods),
  380
Production. *See also* Modes of
  production
  class and, 13–14
  consumption and, 80
  defined, 52
  exchange and, 80
  regional specialization in, 93
Productivity
  economic, 371
  of human language, 276
Profit
  in global economy, 53
  in unbalanced exchange, 91, 94
Project Camelot, 43
Project cycle, 377–378
Pronatalism, 108, 109, 111, 113, 117
Property relations. *See also* Private
  property
  colonialism and, 198
  in family farming, 64
  in foraging societies, 55, 57
  in horticultural societies, 55
  household forms and, 191, 193
  overview of, 75–76
  in pastoralist societies, 60–61
Prophets, 308
Prostitution, 68–69. *See also* Sex work
  Bengal famine and, 86
Protestantism
  in Appalachia, 314–315
  colonialism and, 309
Proto-Indo-European (PIE), 280

Psychiatry, 159, 164, 167
Psychological anthropology, 130, 132,
  133, 149. *See also* Personality
PTSD (post-traumatic stress disorder),
  263
Puberty
  biological markers of, 139–140
  rituals associated with, 141–142,
    143, 305
  sexual identity and, 142
Public policy, comparative approach
  and, 17
Public/private dichotomy, 62
Pueblo Indians of North America
  myths of, 301
  personality type, 131
Puerto Ricans, 245, 353
  obesity among women, 87
Punishment
  in Amish and Mennonite
    communities, 253
  death penalty, 254, 256, 258, 313
  in small-scale societies, 254, 255, 256
  in state-level societies, 253, 254–255,
    256–257
  for violation of doctrine, 301
Purdah, 242
Purdum, Elizabeth D., 257
Pure gift, 92
  opposite of, 95
Push-pull theory, 347

Qashqa'i people of Iran, 60, 236
Qualitative research, 35, 36, 37–38,
  41–42
Quantitative research, 35, 36–37, 41,
  42
Questionnaires, 37
Qu'ran, 301–302, 303

Race. *See also* African Americans;
  Discrimination; Ethnicity
  biology and, 4, 8, 14, 217
  consumption patterns and, 87
  as cultural construct, 10, 13, 14
  of fieldworker, 33–34
  friendships and, 208
  immigration and, 348
  social stratification and, 215,
    216–219
Racism. *See also* Genocide; Slavery
  Boas's critique of, 8, 217
  denial about, 218–219
  immigrants as targets of, 360
  legal penalties and, 257
  looting after Rodney King verdict
    and, 96
  refugees from, 349
  in South Africa, 217
  in United States, 217, 218, 318

Radcliffe-Brown, A. R., 17, 42, 232
Raheja, Gloria Goodwin, 220
Rahnema, Majid, 371
Rainforest, destruction of, 4, 5, 67
Ramesh, A., 187
Ramphele, Mamphela, 197
Rao, N. Madhusudana, 358
Rape
  in Amazonian groups, 210
  by fraternity brothers in United
    States, 209–210
Raphael, Dana, 145
Rapid research methods (RRMs),
  379–380
Rap music, 330
Rapoport, Tamar, 139
Rapp, Rayna, 108, 110, 116
Rapport, 32–35, 44
Ras Tafari, 317
Rathje, William, 3
Ravaillon, Martin, 69
Raw materials, in global economy, 53,
  69, 73
Realist ethnography, 42
Reciprocity
  expected, 92–93, 97
  generalized, 91–92, 97
Recording data, 36, 39–41
  on language, 275
Recurrent costs fund, 84
Redistribution, 93
  big-man or -woman leadership and,
    236, 237, 338
  of critical resources, 372
Reductionism, in psychological
  anthropology, 132
Reflexive anthropology, 36
Reflexive ethnography, 42–43, 327
Reflexivity, 36
Reforestation projects
  in Burkina Faso, 385
  in Haiti, 378, 379
Refugees, 349
  adaptation of, 30, 350–351, 357
  Bosnian, trauma to, 263
  Cambodian, 357
  development as cause of, 379
  Hmong people from Thailand, 382
  Palestinian, 348, 362
  from Rwandan violence, 124
  Vietnamese, 38, 357
Regime change, 266
Reichel-Dolmatoff, G., 154
Reid, Russell M., 161
Reincarnation, 310
Reiner, R., 255
Relativism, cultural, 8, 18–19, 269
  female genital cutting and, 142, 143,
    259
Relativism, linguistic, 278